Preface

Designing Electrical Systems
based on the NEC® and related standards

Volume Two

Due to the size and wealth of information found within, the authors felt it was prudent this publication be published in two volumes.

Volume One: Basic National Electrical Code® (NEC®)
Chapters 1 – 13 (an overall introduction to the NEC® and its application)

Volume Two: Advanced National Electrical Code® (NEC®)
Chapters 14 – 24 (a more indepth look at the NEC® and it's purpose)

Written by James G.Stallcup, Sr.
Edited by James W. Stallcup, Jr.
Design, graphics and layout by Billy G. Stallcup

Published by GRAYBOY, Inc.
PO Box 821757
North Richland Hills, Texas 76182
Phone: 817-581-2206
Fax: 817-581-2059

Introduction

James Stallcup, Sr. has reinvented *Designing Electrical Systems* that catapulted him to the forefront of the electrical industry as a **prominent author**, **effective instructor,** and **respected authority** on the application of the ***National Electrical Code***®.

Everyone from **engineers**, **electrical contractors**, **inspectors**, **electricians,** and **instructors** of the Code have anticipated the arrival of this book. The large workbook format allows a masterful blending of valuable Design Tips, NEC Loops, Examples, Quick Calcs, and effective illustrations with authoritative Code references. Because of the abundant amount of detailed information included, it is the most comprehensive design book of its kind.

Stallcup's® *Designing Electrical Systems* explains the purpose of the *National Electrical Code* (NEC) and more particularly, its use as it applies to the design and installation of electrical wiring systems and equipment.

While the substance of design is found in the *National Electrical Code*, the art of the design is found in the applicability of that same *National Electrical Code*. With the advancement of today's technology and ever-increasing liabilities, effective electrical design must now, more than ever, consider the use of certified products, energy conservation, economy vs. quality, anticipated load growth, local codes, special applications of electrical equipment, and the use and interpretation of the National Fire Protection Association (NFPA) and the Institute of Electrical and Electronics Engineers (IEEE) standards that relate to special areas, etc. For better understanding and interpretation of these advancements, considerable effort has been made by the author to condense the more complicated rules pertaining to the design, installation, and selection of wiring methods and equipment.

For the convenience of the reader, *Designing Electrical Systems* not only contains discussions and explanations of *Code* rules, but also includes detailed illustrations and sample calculations that will help tremendously in understanding and becoming proficient in the application of the *National Electrical Code*. *Designing Electrical Systems* also points out common industry problems and shows in detail the proper procedures and techniques to use in order to ensure proper code compliance. Design Tips, Calculation Tips, and guidelines for "rule of thumb" methods for instances where a fast and approximate design answer is needed are also provided.

In order for the reader to measure his or her design skills or to prepare for a maintenance, journeyman or master electrician examination or for inspector certification, an ample number of quizzes, tests, and final examinations have been included.

With the wealth of information found in this book, it will make a valuable addition to the library of any consultant, serve as an excellent reference to the seasoned professional, and also provide valuable introductory material to the beginner.

Table of Contents

Branch Circuits

Branch circuit conductors extend between the final overcurrent protection device protecting the circuit conductors supplying power to equipment and outlets. The equipment supplied is either permanently installed and hard wired or cord-and-plug connected to properly designed and selected receptacle outlets.

Branch circuits in this chapter are designed to supply the following type of occupancies:

- Residential
- Commercial
- Industrial

RESIDENTIAL

Branch circuits utilized in residential occupancies shall be calculated differently from those in commercial and industrial locations. The general-purpose circuits are calculated at 3 VA per square foot of the dwelling unit.

For example, a dwelling unit of 2000 sq. ft has a volt-amp rating of 6000 VA (2000 sq. ft x 3 VA = 6000 VA). This VA rating shall be used to supply all the general-purpose lighting and receptacle outlets in the dwelling unit.

Another example would be the 2 - 20 amp small-appliance circuits that are used to supply countertop receptacles and other wall outlets in the kitchen, pantry, dining room, and breakfast room. Individual circuits such as a 12 kW range circuit shall be calculated as 8 kW per **Table 220.55, Column C**. Other loads in the dwelling unit shall be permitted to be reduced in VA due to their operation and use. (For more information, see Ch. 22.)

GENERAL-PURPOSE CIRCUITS
220.12 AND TABLE 220.12

The calculations for loads in various occupancies shall be based on VA (volt-amperes) per square foot. In calculating the VA per square foot, the outside dimensions of the building shall be used. They do not include the area of open porches and attached garages with dwelling unit occupancies. However, if there is an unused basement, it should be assumed that it will be finished later, so it shall be included in the calculation so that the capacity of the wiring system will be adequate to serve such loads at a later date.

The load values used in **Table 220.12** shall be considered at 100 percent power factor. If less than 100 percent power factor, equipment is installed with sufficient capacity. Such equipment shall be figured in to take care of the additional higher current values. **(See Figures 22-2 and 22-6)**

> **Design Tip:** The number of 15 or 20 amp branch circuits for a dwelling unit shall be determined by multiplying the square footage by 3 VA per sq. ft per **220.12** and **Table 220.12** and dividing by the size overcurrent protection device times the voltage of the circuit. **(See Figure 14-1)**

SMALL-APPLIANCE CIRCUITS
220.52, 210.11(C)(1), AND 210.52(B)(1)

A minimum of 2 - 20 amp, 1500 VA small-appliance circuits shall be required to supply receptacle outlets that are located in the kitchen, pantry, breakfast room, and dining room. The two small-appliance circuits shall be routed to the kitchen countertop(s), and the outlets proportioned among the two circuits as evenly as possible to prevent unbalanced loading of the circuits. Unbalanced loading may trip open the overcurrent protection device because too many portable appliances are plugged into the same small-appliance circuit. **(See Figure 14-2)**

LAUNDRY CIRCUIT
220.52(B), 210.11(C)(2), AND 210.52(F)

At least 1 - 20 amp, 1500 VA laundry circuit shall be required to supply receptacle outlets in the laundry room. All laundry equipment shall be located within 6 ft (1.8 m) of the receptacle outlet per **210.50(C)**. Sometimes a 20 amp duplex receptacle is used to cord-and-plug connect a washing machine and gas dryer. No other outlets shall be permitted to be supplied by this 20 amp, 2-wire small-appliance circuit. **(See Figure 14-3)**

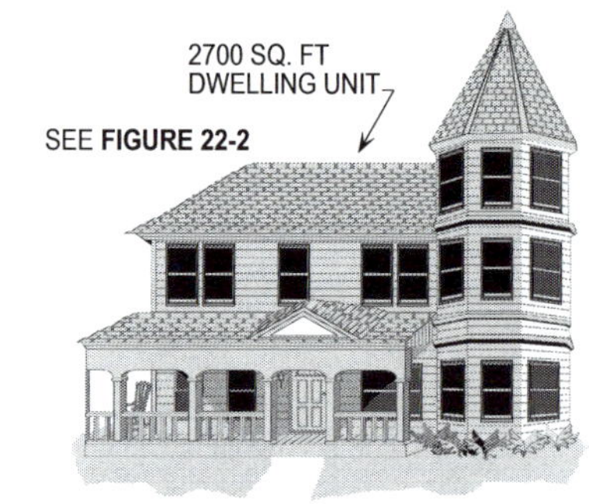

Finding Number of 15 Amp Circuits

Step 1: Finding VA per sq. ft
220.12 and Table 220.12
The VA per sq. ft is 3

Step 2: Finding total VA
Table 220.12
2700 sq. ft x 3 VA = 8100 sq. ft

Step 3: Finding the number of circuits
210.11(A)
8100 VA ÷ 1800 VA (15 A OCPD x 120 V) = 4.5
(Rounded up to 5)

Solution: The number of 15 amp, 2-wire circuits is 5.

**GENERAL-PURPOSE CIRCUITS
NEC 220.12 AND TABLE 220.12**

Figure 14-1. Determining the number of 15 amp, 2-wire circuits to supply power to the general-purpose lighting and receptacle outlets throughout the dwelling unit.

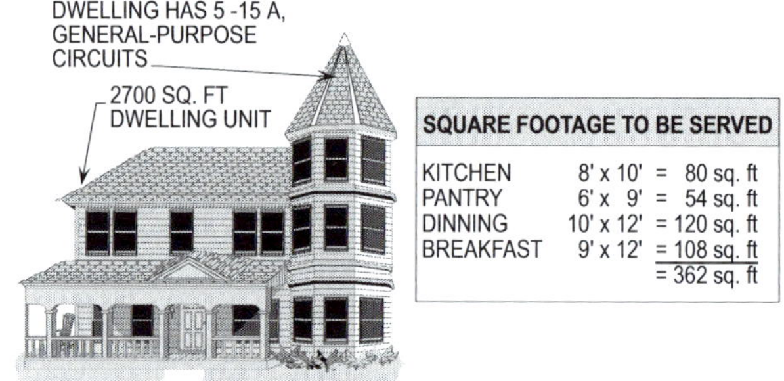

SQUARE FOOTAGE TO BE SERVED		
KITCHEN	8' x 10'	= 80 sq. ft
PANTRY	6' x 9'	= 54 sq. ft
DINNING	10' x 12'	= 120 sq. ft
BREAKFAST	9' x 12'	= 108 sq. ft
		= 362 sq. ft

FINDING NUMBER OF OUTLETS

Step 1: Finding number of 20 amp small appliance circuits
210.11(A) and Table 220.12
20 A OCPD x 120V (2400 VA ÷ 3) = 800 sq. ft

Step 2: Checking sq. ft area
210.11(A) and Table 220.12
• 2 - 20 A small-appliance circuits required
• 1 - 20 A small-appliance circuit (800 sq. ft)
• 800 sq. ft x 2 circuits = 1600 sq. ft
• 1600 sq. ft is greater than 362 sq. ft

Solution: Because the 362 sq. ft area does not exceed 1600 sq. ft, only two small-appliance circuits are required.

**SMALL-APPLIANCE CIRCUITS
NEC 220.52(A)
NEC 210.11(C)(1)
NEC 210.52(B)(1)**

Figure 14-2. Determining the number of outlets that are permitted on a 20 amp small-appliance circuit.

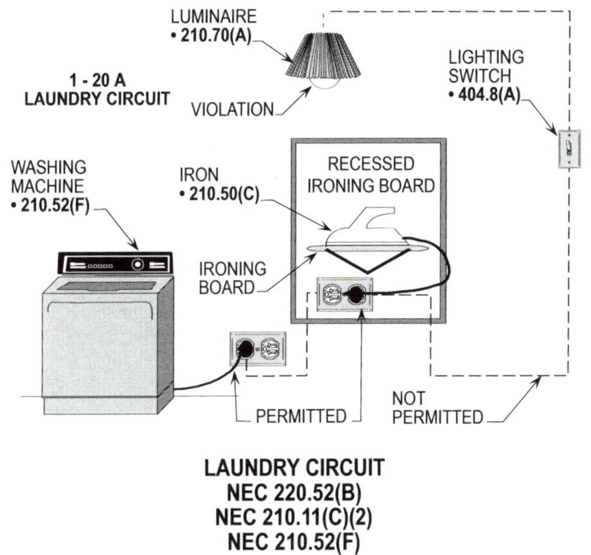

Figure 14-3. At least 1 - 20 amp, 1500 VA laundry circuit shall be required to supply receptacle outlets in the laundry room.

INDIVIDUAL CIRCUITS
210.19(A)(1)

Individual branch circuits in dwelling units shall be calculated at 100 percent or 125 percent of full-load amps of the appliance served or by applying demand factors based on the type of appliance.

RESIDENTIAL COOKING EQUIPMENT
220.55 AND TABLE 220.55

The procedure for calculating the branch-circuit loads for ranges, cooktops, and ovens shall be determined by applying the demand factors in **Table 220.55**. The demand factors listed in Columns A, B, and C are based on the size of the range, cooktop, or oven. When the kW rating exceeds 12 or there is more than one unit, one of the **Footnotes** shall be used in conjunction with **Table 220.55**.

Note, for calculating the VA for ranges, cooktops, and overs, see **Figures 22-8 through 22-13.**

COLUMN A
TABLE 220.55

Column A in **Table 220.55** shall be used for cooking equipment rated less 3.5 kW. These units vary in rating and have limited use.

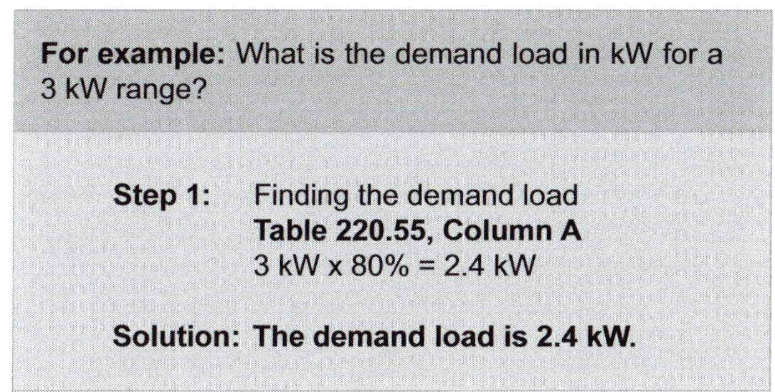

See **Figure 14-4** for calculating cooking equipment loads per **Column A** in **Table 220.55**.

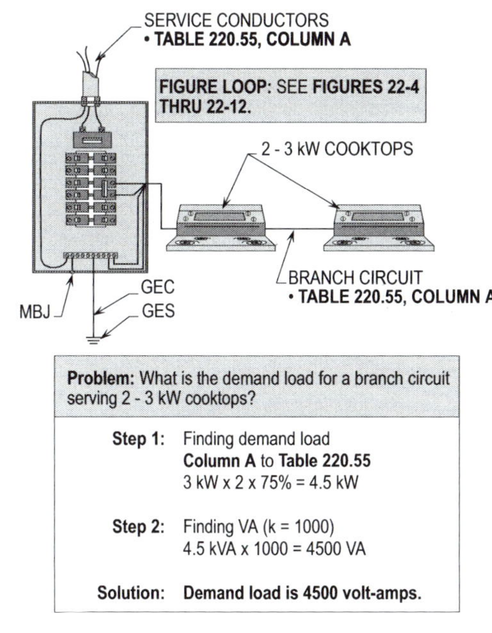

Figure 14-4. The maximum demand load shall be determined by the number of cooking units times the percentage factor applied in **Table 220.55, Column A**.

COLUMN B
TABLE 220.55

Column B in **Table 220.55** shall be used for cooking equipment rated from 3.5 kW to 8.75 kW. These size units are usually the types in use today.

For example: What is the demand load in kW for an 8.75 kW range?

    Step 1:   Finding the demand load
                Table 220.55, Column B
                8.75 kW x 80% = 7 kW

    Solution: The demand load is 7 kW.

See **Figure 14-5** for calculating cooking equipment loads per **Column B** in **Table 220.55**.

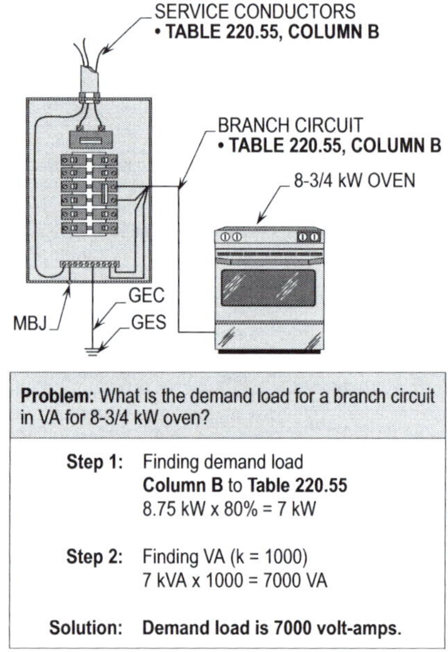

Problem: What is the demand load for a branch circuit in VA for 8-3/4 kW oven?

Step 1:   Finding demand load
           Column B to **Table 220.55**
           8.75 kW x 80% = 7 kW

Step 2:   Finding VA (k = 1000)
           7 kVA x 1000 = 7000 VA

Solution: **Demand load is 7000 volt-amps.**

TABLE 220.55, COLUMN B

Figure 14-5. The maximum demand load for a branch circuit shall be determined by the number of cooking units times the percentage factors applied in **Table 220.55, Column B**.

COLUMN C
TABLE 220.55

Column C in **Table 220.55** shall be used for cooking equipment rated from over 8.75 kW to 12 kW. These units are usually rated 9 to 12 kW, respectively.

For example: What is the demand load in kW for a 12 kW range?

    Step 1:   Finding the demand load
                Table 220.55, Column C
                12 kW range = 8 kW

    Solution: The demand load is 8 kW.

See **Figure 14-6** for calculating cooking equipment loads per **Column C** in **Table 220.55**.

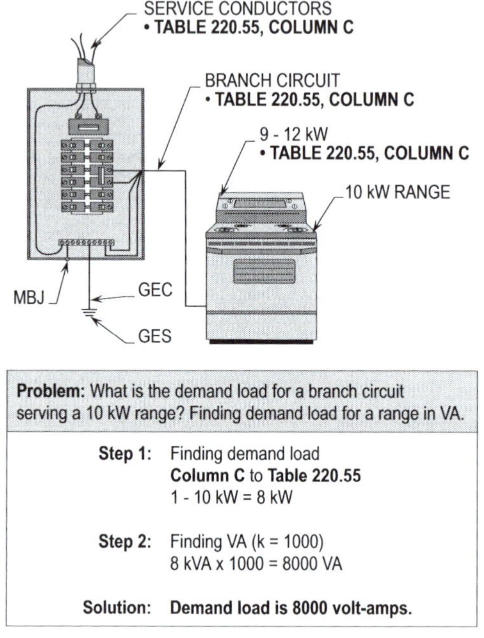

Problem: What is the demand load for a branch circuit serving a 10 kW range? Finding demand load for a range in VA.

Step 1:   Finding demand load
           Column C to **Table 220.55**
           1 - 10 kW = 8 kW

Step 2:   Finding VA (k = 1000)
           8 kVA x 1000 = 8000 VA

Solution: **Demand load is 8000 volt-amps.**

TABLE 220.55, COLUMN C

Figure 14-6. The demand load in kW for a branch circuit serving cooking equipment in **Column C** is already determined per **Table 220.55**.

NOTE 1
TABLE 220.55

Note 1 to **Table 220.55** shall be applied where the kW rating of the cooking equipment is over 12 kW but not over 27 kW. All kW ratings that exceed 12 kW shall be multiplied by 5 percent. The kW rating of one range is listed in **Column C** in **Table 220.55** and shall be multiplied by this total demand. Units of sizes larger than 12 kW are usually combination units found in kitchens with limited space.

For example: What is the demand load in kW for a 18 kW range?

Step 1: Finding percentage
Note 1 to **Table 220.55**
18 kW - 12 kW = 6 kW
6 kW x 5% = 30%

Step 2: Finding the demand load
Table 220.55, Column C
8 kW x 130% = 10.4 kW

Solution: The demand load is 10.4 kW.

See **Figure 14-7** for calculating cooking equipment loads per **Note 1** to **Table 220.55**.

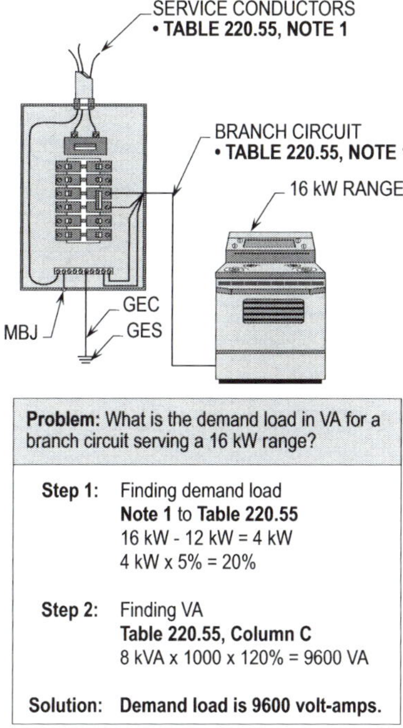

Problem: What is the demand load in VA for a branch circuit serving a 16 kW range?

Step 1: Finding demand load
Note 1 to **Table 220.55**
16 kW - 12 kW = 4 kW
4 kW x 5% = 20%

Step 2: Finding VA
Table 220.55, Column C
8 kVA x 1000 x 120% = 9600 VA

Solution: Demand load is 9600 volt-amps.

TABLE 220.55, NOTE 1

Figure 14-7. For cooking equipment rated over 12 kW to 27 kW in **Column C**, **Note 1** requires an increase of 5 percent for each kW over 12 kW. This percentage times 8 kW will determine the demand load to be used to size the elements.

NOTE 2
TABLE 220.55

For cooking equipment of unequal values rated over 12 kW to 27 kW in **Column C**, **Note 2** shall be applied and the value calculated by adding the kW ratings of all units and dividing by the number of units; all ranges below 12 kW shall be calculated at 12 kW. When an average rating is found, the number of units shall be increased by 5 percent for each kW exceeding 12 kW to derive the allowable kW.

See **Figure 14-8** for demand factors to be applied per Table **220.55, Column C, Note 2**. **Note,** the demand factor selected from **Table 220.55, Column C** shall be based on the number of units.

Design Tip: It is permissible per **Note 3** to **Table 220.55** to add all pieces of cooking equipment with ratings over 1-3/4 kW through 8-3/4 kW together and multiply by the percentage of **Columns A** or **B**; whichever produces the smaller kW rating shall be permitted to be used. This calculation shall be permitted to be applied by permission of the AHJ if it provides the smaller kW rating of all the methods available in **Table 220.55** and **Notes**.

NOTE 4
TABLE 220.55

Note 4 to **Table 220.55** shall be permitted to be applied to a counter-installed cooktop with one or two wall-mounted ovens. The total kW of each cooking unit shall be totaled, and all kW exceeding 12 kW shall be multiplied by 5 percent. The kW rating of one range, not three as listed in **Column C** in **Table 220.55**, shall be multiplied by this total. The advantage of this rule is allowing one branch circuit to be run, instead of three individual circuits, one to each unit.

For example: What is the demand load in kW for a 10 kW cooktop, an 8 kW oven, and a 6 kW oven connected to a 240 volt, single-phase, branch circuit?

Step 1: Finding percentage
Note 4 to **Table 220.55**
10 kW + 8 kW + 6 kW = 24 kW
24 kW - 12 kW = 12 kW
12 kW x 5% = 60%

Step 2: Finding the demand load
Table 220.55, Column C
8 kW x 160% = 12.8 kW

Solution: The demand load is 12.8 kW.

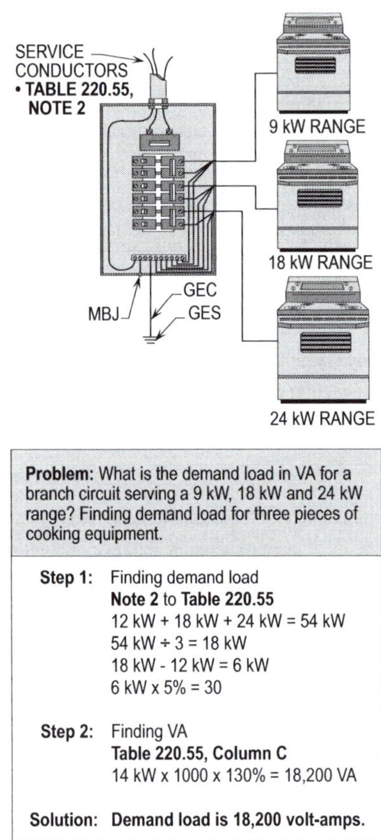

Problem: What is the demand load in VA for a branch circuit serving a 9 kW, 18 kW and 24 kW range? Finding demand load for three pieces of cooking equipment.

Step 1: Finding demand load
Note 2 to Table 220.55
12 kW + 18 kW + 24 kW = 54 kW
54 kW ÷ 3 = 18 kW
18 kW - 12 kW = 6 kW
6 kW x 5% = 30

Step 2: Finding VA
Table 220.55, Column C
14 kW x 1000 x 130% = 18,200 VA

Solution: Demand load is 18,200 volt-amps.

TABLE 220.55, NOTE 2

Figure 14-8. Cooking equipment of unequal values rated over 12 kW to 27 kW in **Column C**, **Note 2** shall be calculated by adding the kW ratings of all units and dividing by the number of units; all ranges below 12 kW shall be calculated at 12 kW. When an average rating is determined, the number of units shall be increased by 5 percent for each kW exceeding 12 kW.

See Figure 14-9 for calculating cooking equipment loads for taps per **Ex. 1** to **210.19(A)(3)**.

SIZING TAPS
210.19(A)(3), Ex. 1

A tap to connect a cooktop and ovens shall be permitted to be made from a 50 amp branch circuit when the tap conductors are sized from the kW rating of each piece of cooking equipment per **Note 4** to **Table 220.55**. Whenever taps are made from larger conductors with smaller conductors, the tap shall comply with **240.21(A)**.

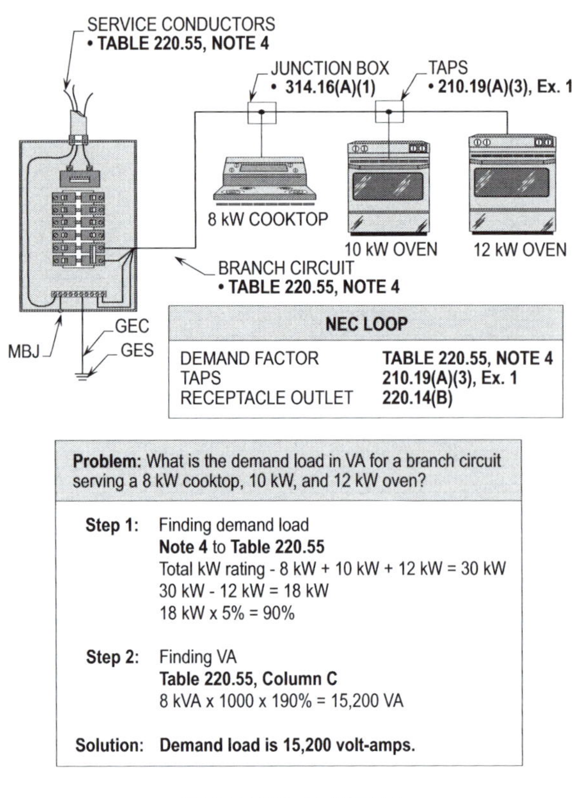

Problem: What is the demand load in VA for a branch circuit serving a 8 kW cooktop, 10 kW, and 12 kW oven?

Step 1: Finding demand load
Note 4 to Table 220.55
Total kW rating - 8 kW + 10 kW + 12 kW = 30 kW
30 kW - 12 kW = 18 kW
18 kW x 5% = 90%

Step 2: Finding VA
Table 220.55, Column C
8 kVA x 1000 x 190% = 15,200 VA

Solution: Demand load is 15,200 volt-amps.

TABLE 220.55, NOTE 4

Figure 14-9. The demand load for a cooktop and two or less wall-mounted ovens shall be determined by finding the amperage rating of each unit in kW. Each kilowatt that exceeds 12 kW shall be increased by 5 percent to obtain the multiplier. The multiplier times the demand for one unit in **Column C** in **Table 220.55** derives the demand load for the elements of the circuit.

For example, can a 14 AWG tap be made from a 12 AWG branch circuit and be downsized and used as a switch leg? Naturally, the answer is no, because the tap cannot meet the provisions of **240.21(A) through (G)** for making an approved tap. However, **240.21(A)** and **210.19(A)(3), Ex. 1** applied together permit a smaller tap to be made for cooking equipment circuits tapped from conductors of a larger sized branch circuit.

See Figure 14-10 for calculating cooking equipment loads for taps per **Ex. 1** to **210.19(A)(3)**.

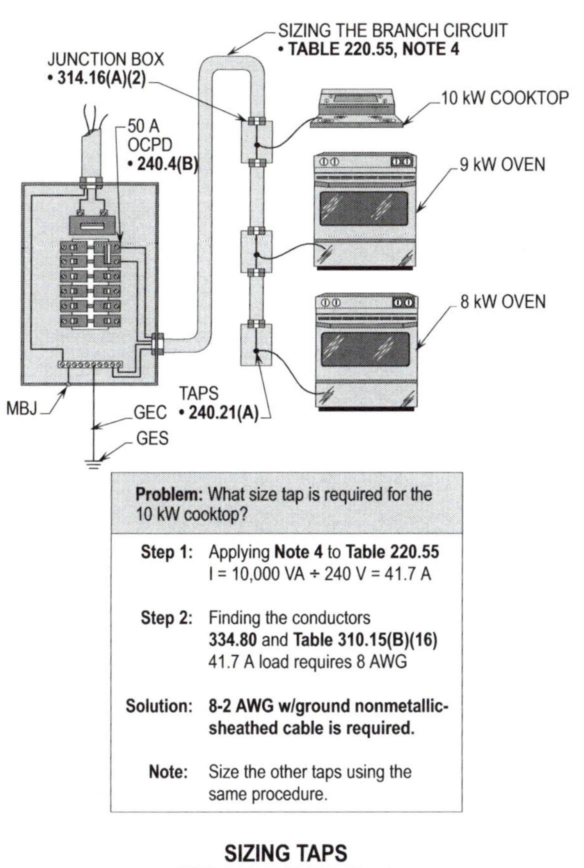

Problem: What size tap is required for the 10 kW cooktop?

Step 1: Applying Note 4 to Table 220.55
I = 10,000 VA ÷ 240 V = 41.7 A

Step 2: Finding the conductors
334.80 and Table 310.15(B)(16)
41.7 A load requires 8 AWG

Solution: 8-2 AWG w/ground nonmetallic-sheathed cable is required.

Note: Size the other taps using the same procedure.

SIZING TAPS
NEC 210.19(A)(3), Ex. 1

Figure 14-10. Determining the load in kW and amps to size the elements for a branch circuit that taps to cooking equipment.

ELECTRIC CLOTHES DRYERS
220.54

Dryer equipment loads shall be at least 5000 VA or the nameplate rating, whichever is larger. This value is used for sizing the branch-circuit load. When installing four or fewer dryers, the load shall be calculated at 100 percent. When installing five or more dryers, the load shall be calculated by the percentages listed in **Table 220.54** based on the number of dryers being installed. When calculating the load for a 4500 VA dryer, the load shall be calculated at 5000 VA for the branch circuit that is used to cord-and-plug connect the unit. Dryers installed in dwelling units shall comply with provisions of **220.14(B)** and **220.54**. Dryers shall be calculated at 100 percent for noncontinuous operation and 125 percent for continuous operation if they are installed as commercial dryers.

For example: What is the load for a 6000 W dryer when sizing the branch circuit in a dwelling unit?

Step 1: Finding VA
220.14(B) and **220.54**
6000 VA x 100% = 6000 VA

Solution: **The branch-circuit load is 6000 VA.**

See Figure 14-11 for calculating dryer equipment loads per **Table 220.54**.

Note, an existing branch circuit in a dwelling unit can be used as a wiring method to supply an electric dryer. If nonmetallic-sheathed cable is used, the grounded (neutral) conductor shall be insulated. However, the grounded (neutral) conductor shall be permitted to be uninsulated if service-entrance cable is the existing wiring method.

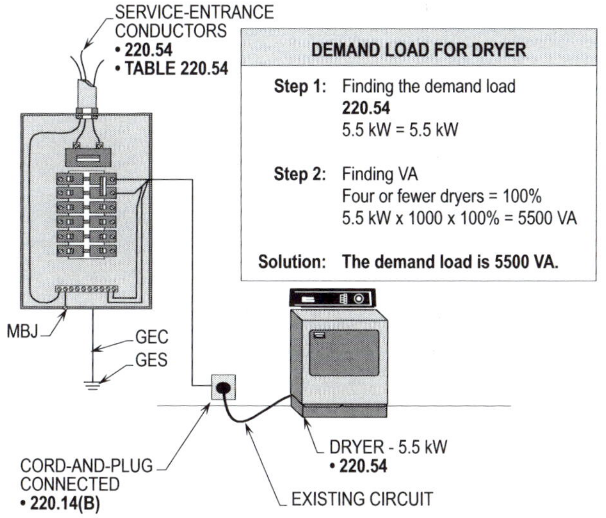

ELECTRIC CLOTHES DRYERS
NEC 220.54
TABLE 220.54

Figure 14-11. The demand load for household dryers shall be figured at 5 kVA or the nameplate rating, whichever provides the greater rating. Four or fewer dryers shall be calculated at 100 percent of the nameplate rating. Five or more dryers shall be permitted to have a percentage applied based on the number of units per **Table 220.54**. The Table is based on five dryers being used at different times and the load being limited to about 80 percent of total. **Table 220.54** is used for dwelling units in apartment complexes.

RATINGS
210.3

Branch circuits shall be classified by the rating or setting of the overcurrent protection device protecting the circuit. Two or more outlets shall be permitted to be protected by the following overcurrent protection devices based on the calculated load per **210.19(A)**:

- 15 amp
- 20 amp
- 30 amp
- 40 amp
- 50 amp

PERMISSIBLE LOADS
210.23

The rating or setting of the overcurrent protection device shall not be permitted to be exceeded by the load on an individual branch circuit. If the load is continuous, the load shall be multiplied by 125 percent. A fastened-in-place appliance shall be permitted to be connected to a general purpose circuit if its amp rating does not exceed 50 percent of the branch circuit.

15 AND 20 AMPERE BRANCH CIRCUITS
210.23(A)

A 15 or 20 amp branch circuit shall be permitted to supply luminaires and/or utilization equipment in residential, commercial, or industrial locations.

For example: What is the total VA rating for a 15 or 20 amp, 120 volt, 2-wire branch circuit supplying a noncontinuous load?

Step 1:   Finding VA
210.23(A)
VA = 15 A x 120 V
VA = 1800 VA

Solution: The total VA is 1800.

Step 1:   Finding VA
210.23(A)
VA = 20 A x 120 V
VA = 2400 VA

Solution: The total VA is 2400.

For example: What is the total VA rating for a 15 or 20 amp, 240 volt, 3-wire branch circuit supplying noncontinuous loads?

Step 1:   Finding VA
210.23(A)
VA = 15 A x 240 V
VA = 3600

Solution: The total VA is 3600.

Step 1:   Finding VA
210.23(A)
VA = 20 A x 240 V
VA = 4800

Solution: The total VA is 4800.

The rating of any one cord-and-plug connected utilization equipment shall not be permitted to exceed 80 percent of the branch circuit rating if connected to a general-purpose circuit supplying two or more outlets.

For example: What size overcurrent protection device is required to be installed for a 7 amp, 120 volt, single-phase compactor that is cord-and-plug connected per **422.16(B)(2)**?

Step 1:   Finding usable amperage of 15 or
20 amp branch circuit
210.23(A)
(If continuous)
A = 15 A x 80%
A = 12 A
A = 20 A x 80%
A = 16 A

210.23(A)
(If noncontinuous)
A = 15 A x 100%
A = 15 A
A = 20 A x 100%
A = 20 A

**Solution: The overcurrent protection device
of 15 amp shall be permitted
to be used.**

The 7 amp full-load current rating of the compactor does not exceed the (15 A x 80% = 12 A) loading range of the 15 amp overcurrent protection device. The 7 amp full-load current rating of the compactor does not exceed the (20 A x 80% = 16 A) loading range of the 20 amp overcurrent protection device. Therefore, the 20 amp overcurrent protection device shall be permitted to be used to supply the 7 amp compactor.

Note, the AHJ may require the 15 amp overcurrent protection device to be used.

Fixed appliances (fastened-in-place) shall be permitted to draw up to 50 percent of the rating of a branch circuit supplying two or more general-purpose outlets that serve lighting and receptacle loads.

For example: Can an 8 amp, 120 volt, single-phase air-conditioning window unit be connected to an existing branch circuit?

Step 1: Finding amps of branch circuit
210.23(A)
A = 50% of 20 A OCPD
A = 10 A

Step 2: Calculating amps for air-conditioning unit
210.23(A), 440.62(B); (C), and **440.32**
A = 8 A x 125%
A = 10 A

Step 3: Verifying permissive amps
210.23(A), 440.62(B); (C), and **210.3**
A = 20 A OCPD x 80%
A = 16 A

Solution: **Yes, the air-conditioning window unit rated at 8 amps shall be permitted to be connected to the 20 amp branch circuit.**

A 20 amp overcurrent protection device shall be permitted to protect a fastened-in-place appliance with a rating of 10 amps or less after applying the 50 percent rule. The remaining 50 percent of the overcurrent protection device is used to supply lighting and/or cord-and-plug connected appliances. **(See Figure 14-12)**

30 AMPERE BRANCH CIRCUITS
210.23(B)

A 30 amp branch circuit shall be permitted to be installed to supply fixed lighting units with heavy-duty lampholders in other than a dwelling unit(s) or utilization equipment in any occupancy. The rating of any individual cord-and-plug connected appliance shall not be permitted to exceed 80 percent of the branch circuit rating. The rating of any individual cord-and-plug connected appliance shall not be permitted to draw more than 24 amps (30 A x 80% = 24 A) when connected to an 30 amp overcurrent protection device. **(See Figure 14-13)**

For example: What is the load for a 23 amp dishwasher used at continuous duty?

Step 1: Finding amperage
220.18(A)
A = 23 A x 125%
A = 28.75

Step 2: Finding branch circuit
210.23(B)
28.75 A requires 30 A

Solution: **The branch circuit load is 28.75 amps.**

A 30 amp branch circuit shall be permitted to supply a single appliance that is used at continuous operation in any type occupancy.

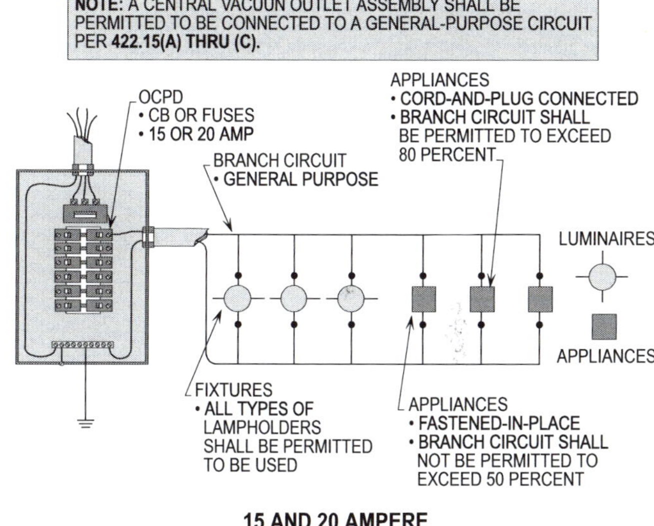

Figure 14-12. A 20 amp overcurrent protection device shall be permitted to protect a fastened-in-place appliance with a rating of 10 amps or less after applying the 50 percent rule. The remaining 50 percent of the overcurrent protection device is used to protect lighting and/or cord-and-plug connected appliances.

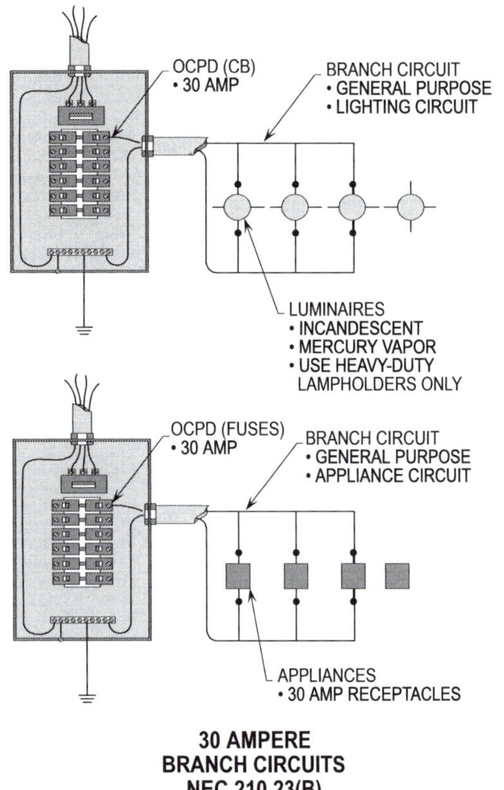

Figure 14-13. A 30 amp branch circuit shall be permitted to be installed to supply fixed lighting units with heavy-duty lampholders in other than a dwelling unit(s) or utilization equipment in any occupancy.

40 AND 50 AMPERE BRANCH CIRCUITS 210.23(C)

A 40 or 50 amp branch circuit shall be permitted to supply cooking appliances that are fastened in place in any occupancy. Fixed lighting units with heavy-duty lampholders or infrared heating units shall be permitted for such circuits except for other than dwelling units. Equipment such as a water heater, dryer, or heating unit shall be permitted to be supplied by a 40 or 50 amp branch circuit. **(See Figure 14-14)**

For example: What is the load for a 37 amp water heater used at continuous operation in a commercial building?

Step 1: Finding amperage
422.13
A = 37 A x 125%
A = 46.25

Solution: The branch-circuit load is 46.25 amps.

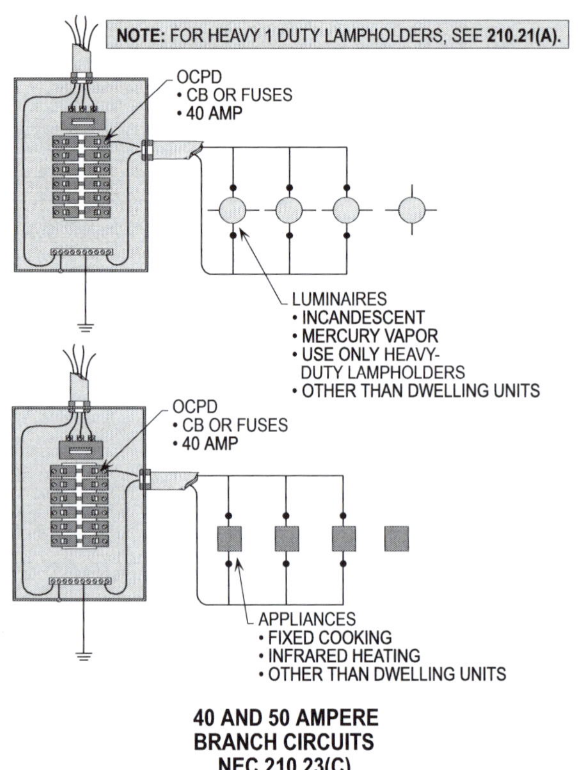

Figure 14-14. A 40 or 50 amp branch circuit shall be permitted to supply cooking appliances that are fastened in place in any occupancy.

BRANCH CIRCUITS LARGER THAN 50 AMPERES 210.23(D)

Branch circuits larger than 50 amps shall supply only nonlighting outlet loads. A maximum load of 50 amps shall be used for multioutlet branch circuits installed for lighting. A combination of loads exceeding 50 amps shall be permitted be used for multioutlet branch circuits that are not connected to lighting units, such as plugs for welders.

CONDUCTORS ARTICLE 310

Branch-circuit conductors used for general wiring shall be rated for the following insulations per **Table 310.15(B)(16)**:

- 60°C
- 75°C
- 90°C

The temperature rating of conductors and their conditions of use are listed in **Table 310.104(A)**. Not more than three current-carrying conductors in a raceway or cable run in an ambient temperature of not more than 30°C or 86°F shall be used for branch-circuit conductors based on **Table 310.15(B)(16)**. The types of insulation available are listed in **Table 310.15(B)(16)** for copper and aluminum conductors. Conductor ampacities shall be determined by condition of use and by the terminal ratings of overcurrent protection devices and equipment per **110.14(C)(1)** and **(C)(2)**. **(See Figure 8-4** of **Chapter 8)**

60°C CONDUCTORS
TABLE 310.15(B)(16), COLUMN 2 AND 110.14(C)(1)(a)

The following type of conductors shall be permitted to be installed when using **Table 310.15(B)(16), Column 2** for 60°C ampacities:

- TW
- UF

The temperature rating of the conductors are rated at 60°C per **Table 310.104(A)** and **Table 310.15(B)(16).** The conductors shall be terminated to 60°C terminals, and 60°C ampacities shall be used.

> **Design Tip:** All conductors with the "W" (60°C or 75°C) rating insulation shall be permitted to be installed in dry, damp, or wet locations per **310.10(B)** and **(C)**.

Overcurrent protection devices rated at 100 amps or less shall be permitted to be terminated with conductors 14 AWG through 1 AWG with 60°C ampacities per **110.14(C)(1)(a)**. The maximum size of 1 AWG is listed so that a 60°C conductor ampacity will match to terminals of overcurrent protection devices and equipment rated at 100 amps.

> **For example:** What size THHN copper conductor is required to supply a piece of equipment operating at 90 amps? (Load already calculated at continuous or noncontinuous operation.)
>
> | | | |
> |---|---|---|
> | Step 1: | Finding load | |
> | | **Table 310.104(A)** and | |
> | | **Table 310.15(B)(16)** | |
> | | Load = 90 A | |
> | | | |
> | Step 2: | Finding conductor amps at 60°C | |
> | | **Table 310.15(B)(16)** | |
> | | 95 A = 2 AWG THHN | |
> | | | |
> | **Solution:** | **The conductor is required to be 2 AWG THHN.** | |

The allowable ampacity for each conductor shall be rated at 60°C when installing nonmetallic-sheathed cable (Romex or rope) per **334.80**. However, these conductors have insulation rated at 90°C that permits such conductors to be used for derating purposes. **[See Figure 14-15(a)]**

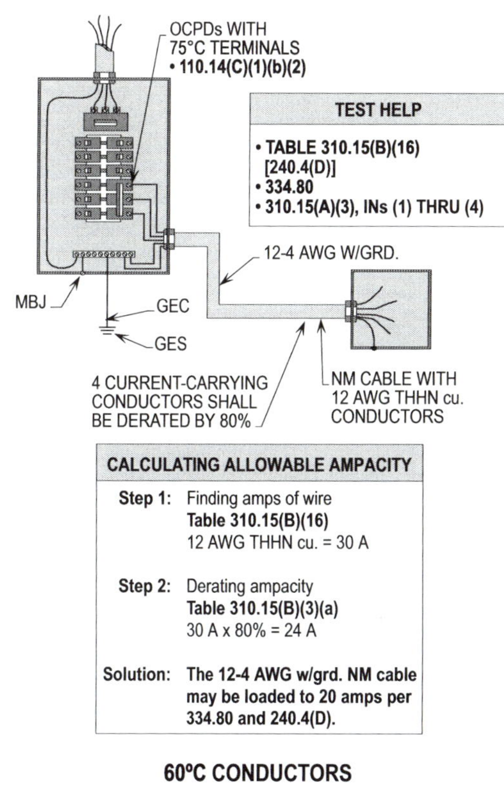

Figure 14-15(a). The allowable ampacity for each conductor is rated at 60°C, when installing nonmetallic-sheathed cable (Romex or rope) per **334.80** and **334.112**. However, these conductors have insulation rated at 90°C, which permits such conductors to be used for derating purposes.

75°C CONDUCTORS
TABLE 310.15(B)(16), COLUMN 3 AND 110.14(C)(2)(b)

The following types of conductors shall be permitted to be installed when using **Table 310.15(B)(16), Column 3** for 75°C ampacities:

- RHW
- THHW
- THW
- THWN
- XHHW
- USE
- ZW

Overcurrent protection devices rated over 100 amps shall be permitted to be terminated with conductors larger than 1 AWG with 75°C ampacities per **110.14(C)(2)(b)**. Conductors shall be permitted to be installed with higher temperature ratings if the ampacities are matched to the terminals of the overcurrent protection device and equipment. The terminals shall be marked by one of the following temperature ratings:

- 60°C
- 60°C/75°C

Note, 60°C ampacities shall only be permitted to be applied to terminals marked 60°C. 75°C ampacities shall only be permitted to be applied to terminals marked 75°C. 60°C ampacities shall only be permitted be applied using 75°C ampacities where conductors 14 AWG through 1 AWG are installed. 75°C terminals shall be permitted be used and connected with any size conductor listed in the 75°C column.

For example: What size amperage rating is allowed for a 4 AWG copper conductor using the ampacities of the 60°C column and 75°C column, respectively?

Step 1: Finding amperage
Table 310.15(B)(16), Columns 2 and **3**
60°C = 70 A
75°C = 85 A

Solution: **The allowable amperage rating is 70 amp for 60°C and 85 amps for 75°C. Note, the 60°C terminal rating reduces the 4 AWG THHN copper conductor to only 70 amps, and not 85 or 95 amps.**

90°C CONDUCTORS
TABLE 310.15(B)(16), COLUMN 4

The following types of conductors shall be permitted to be used to wire modern-day electrical systems. See **Table 310.15(B)(16), Column 4** and **Table 310.104(A)** for ampacities and conditions of use for 90°C rated conductors:

- TBS
- SA
- SIS
- FEP
- FEPB
- MI
- RHH
- RHW-2
- THHN
- THHW
- THW-2
- THWN-2
- USE-2
- XHH
- XHHW
- XHHW-2
- ZW-2

These conductors with the 90°C rated insulation shall be permitted to be connected to terminals rated at 60°C, 75°C, and 90°C. Devices and equipment with 90°C terminals shall be used for connecting higher ampacity conductors that are rated 90°C. However, such overcurrent protection devices and equipment that are mated (matched) are not available as of today.

For example: What is the allowable ampacity required for a 6 AWG THWN copper conductor connected to a 60°C overcurrent protection device installed in a panelboard?

Step 1: Finding amperage and condition of use
Table 310.15(B)(16), Column 4 and **Table 310.104(A)**
A = 75

Step 2: Finding allowable ampacity
Table 310.15(B)(16), Column 2
A = 55

Solution: **The allowable ampacity is limited to 55 amps because of the 60°C terminals.**

Design Tip: Overcurrent protection devices rated at 100 amps or less shall be terminated with conductors 14 AWG through 1 AWG with 60°C ampacities per **110.14(C)(1)(a)**, if not otherwise marked. Overcurrent protection devices rated over 100 amps shall be permitted to be terminated with conductors larger than 1 AWG with 75°C ampacities per **110.14(C)(2)(b)**.

The following ampacity values shall be used for the temperature ratings of terminals using a 1/0 AWG THHN copper conductor:

- 60°C = 125 amps
- 75°C = 150 amps
- 90°C = 170 amps

A load of 125 amps or less on 60°C terminals shall be permitted to be served by a 1/0 AWG THHN copper conductor. A load of 150 amps or less on 75°C terminals shall be permitted to be served by a 1/0 AWG THHN copper conductor. A load of 170 amps or less on 90°C terminals shall be permitted to be served by a 1/0 AWG THHN copper conductor. The ampacities shall be matched to the terminals of the overcurrent protection device and equipment. [**See Figure 14-15(b)**]

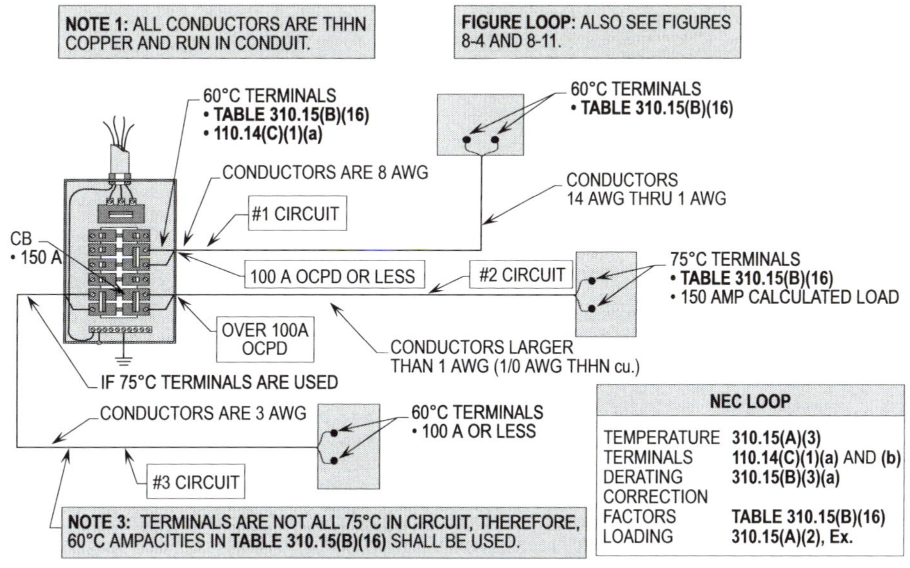

Figure 14-15(b). Determining the allowable ampacity rating of terminals and sizing conductors based on 60°C/75°C or 75°C ampacities from **Columns 2** and **3** in **Table 310.15(B)(16)**. This rule prevents terminals from being overheated.

AMBIENT TEMPERATURES
310.15(B)(3)(a)

Where there are not more than three current-carrying conductors in a raceway or cable, the allowable ampacities listed in **Table 310.15(B)(16)** shall be used. If four or more current-carrying conductors or surrounding temperature exceeding 86°F are present, derating factors shall be applied, based on their conditions of use. See the top of **Table 310.15(B)(16)** for the conditions that shall be applied before selecting the allowable ampacities of such conductors.

For example: What is the allowable ampacity for 6 - 12 AWG THHN cu. conductors that are all current-carrying? (**Note,** adjustment factors shall be applied.)

Step 1: Calculating ampacity
Table 310.15(B)(16)
12 AWG THHN cu. = 30 A

Step 2: Applying derating factors
310.15(B)(3)(a) and **310.15(A)(3), IN (4)**
30 A x 80% = 24 A

Solution: The allowable ampacity is 24 amps.

For example: What is the allowable ampacity for 4 - 12 AWG THHN copper conductors (three current-carrying) that are in an ambient temperature of 102°F? (**Note,** correction factors shall be applied.)

Step 1:	Calculating ampacity **Table 310.15(B)(16)** 12 AWG THHN cu. = 30 A
Step 2:	Applying derating factors **Table 310.15(B)(2)(a)** 30 A x 91% = 27.3 A

Solution: The allowable ampacity is 27.3 amps.

The ampacity of conductors shall be derated at least three times when applying the following rules for branch circuits and determining the allowable ampacities:

- More than three current-carrying conductors
  - Adjustment factors

- Ambient temperature exceeds 86°F
  - Correction factors

- Continuous duty loads
  - FLA x 125 percent

More than three current-carrying conductors in a raceway shall be derated by the percentages listed in **310.15(B) (3)(a)**. Conductors routed through ambient temperatures exceeding 86°F shall be derated by the percentages according to the **Ampacity Correction Factors** of **Table 310.15(B)(2)(a)**. If the load is continuous (three hours or more), the value shall be multiplied by 125 percent per **210.19(A)(1)**.

For example: What is the allowable ampacity for 4 - 12 AWG THHN cu. conductors that are all current-carrying and routed through an ambient temperature of 102°F?

Step 1:	Calculating ampacity **Table 310.15(B)(16)** 12 AWG THHN cu. = 30 A
Step 2:	Applying adjustment factors **310.15(B)(3)(a)** 30 A x 80% = 24 A
Step 3:	Applying correction factors **240.4(D)** and **Table 310.15(B)(2)(a)** 24 A x 91% = 21.8 A

Solution: The allowable ampacity is 21.8 amps.

For example: What size overcurrent protection device is required to serve a calculated continuous load of 70.5 amps using 4 AWG THHN copper conductors with an ampacity of 85 amps?

Step 1:	Finding ampacity **210.19(A)(1)** and **Table 310.15(B)(16)** 70.5 A requires 80 A OCPD 4 AWG = 85 A = 80 A OCPD

Solution: An 80 amp overcurrent protection device is required.

Design Tip: An 80 amp overcurrent protection device shall be permitted to be installed, because 56.4 amps x 125 percent is 70.5 amps and **240.4(B)** permits the next size overcurrent protection device above 70.5 amps to be used. **(See Figure 14-16)**

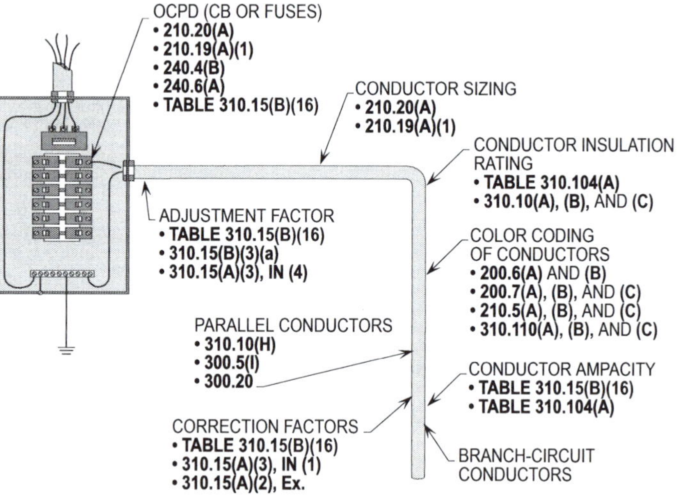

Figure 14-16. More than three current-carrying conductors in a raceway shall be derated by the percentages listed in **Table 310.15(B)(16)** and **Table 310.15(B)(3)(a)**. Conductors routed through ambient temperatures exceeding 86°F shall be derated by the percentages according to the **Ampacity Correction Factors** of **Table 310.15(B)(2)(a)**. If the load is continuous (three hours or more), the value shall be multiplied by 125 percent per **210.19(A)(1)(a)** and **Article 100** for the definition of continuous load.

BRANCH CIRCUITS NOT MORE THAN 600 VOLTS
210.19(A)(1)(a) AND (b)

Branch-circuit conductors shall have an ampacity not less than the maximum load to be served. Conductors shall be sized to carry not less than the larger of **210.19(A)(1)(a)** or **(b).**

(a) Where a branch circuit supplies continuous loads or any combination of continuous and noncontinuous loads, the minimum branch-circuit conductor size shall have an allowable ampacity not less than the noncontinuous load plus 125 percent of the continuous load.

(b) The minimum branch-circuit conductor size shall have an allowable ampacity not less than the maximum load to be served after the application of any adjustment or correction factors.

(See Figure 14-17)

BRANCH-CIRCUIT VOLTAGE LIMITATIONS
210.6

The following voltage limitations are divided into three categories, and each category of voltage ratings is designed to supply certain loads:

- 120 volts between conductors
- 277 volts-to-ground
- 600 volts between conductors

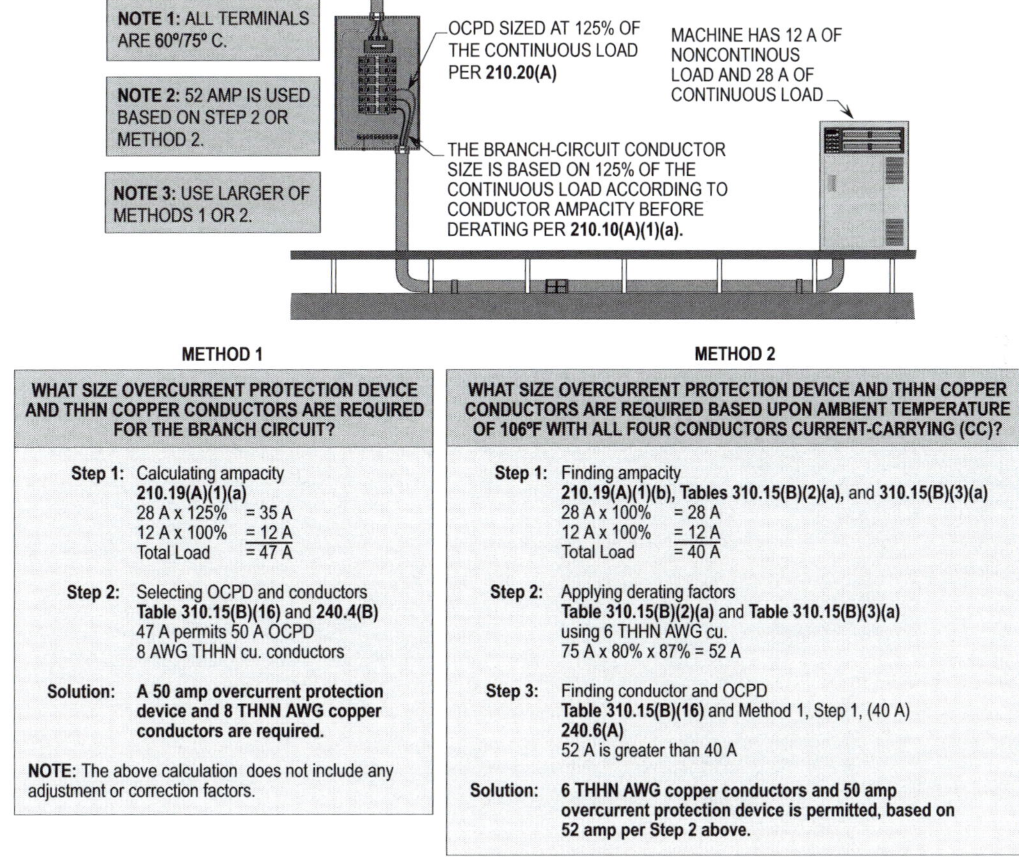

Figure 14-17. This illustration clarifies that two separate calculations shall be made and the larger size branch circuit conductor is then selected per the 2014 NEC.

120 VOLTS BETWEEN CONDUCTORS
210.6(B)

120 volts between conductors is not a restricted voltage and shall be permitted to be used to supply the following loads in any type of occupancy:

- Terminals of lampholders applied within their voltage ratings
- Ballasts for fluorescent or high-intensity discharge (HID) luminaires
- Cord-and-plug connected or permanently connected appliances

Cord-and-plug connected or permanently (hard wired) connected appliances rated over 1440 VA are usually supplied by individual circuits. These appliances are generally connected to general-purpose circuits that supply more than one outlet, etc. Such appliances shall be permitted to be any one of the following types of equipment:

- Heating units
- Air-conditioning units
- Welders
- Water heaters
- Processing machine
- Etc.

See Figure 14-18 for a detailed illustration pertaining to cord-and-plug connected or permanently (hard wired) connected appliances over 1440 VA.

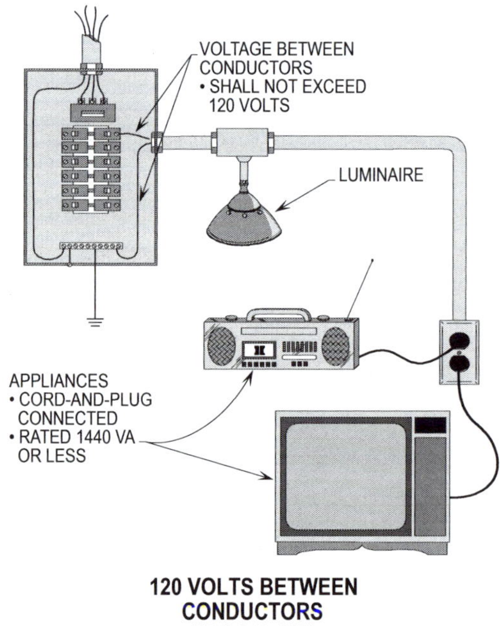

Figure 14-18. Cord-and-plug connected or permanently (hard wired) connected appliances rated over 1440 VA are usually supplied by individual circuits.

277 VOLTS-TO-GROUND
210.6(C) AND 225.7(C)

Circuits exceeding 120 volts between conductors and not exceeding 277 volts-to-ground shall be permitted to supply any one of the following types of electrical apparatus:

- Listed electric-discharge or listed light-emitting diode-type luminaires
- Listed incandescent luminaires
- Mogul-base screw-shell lampholders
- Other than screw-shell type lampholders applied within their voltage ratings
- Ballasts for fluorescent or high-intensity discharge (HID) luminaires
- Cord-and-plug connected or permanently connected appliances or other utilization equipment

See Figures 14-19(a) through (d) for detailed illustrations showing circuits exceeding 120 volts between conductors and not exceeding 277 volts-to-ground.

> **Design Tip:** Listed electric-discharge or incandescent luminaires are no longer required to be installed at a minimum height of 8 ft (2.5 m) above finished grade when supplied by 480/277 volt, three-phase, four-wire system.

Luminaires for illumination shall be permitted to be installed for outdoor areas of industrial establishments, office buildings, schools, stores, and other commercial or public buildings where the luminaires are supplied by 480/277 volt circuits per **225.7(C)**. However, luminaires shall not be permitted to be located within 3 ft (900 mm) from windows, platforms, fire escapes, etc.

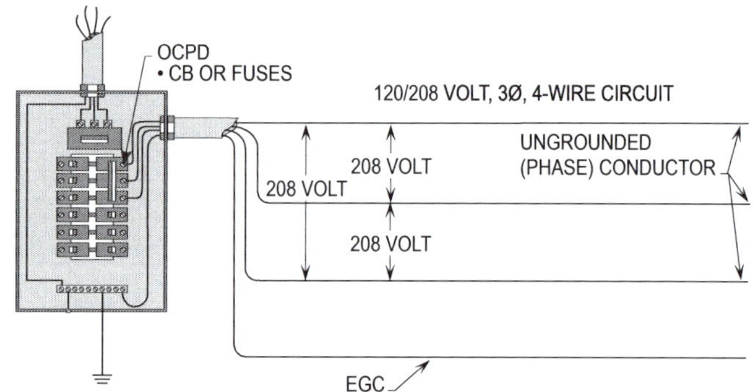

Figure 14-19(a). This illustration shows a diagram of a 120/208 volt, three-phase, four-wire circuit.

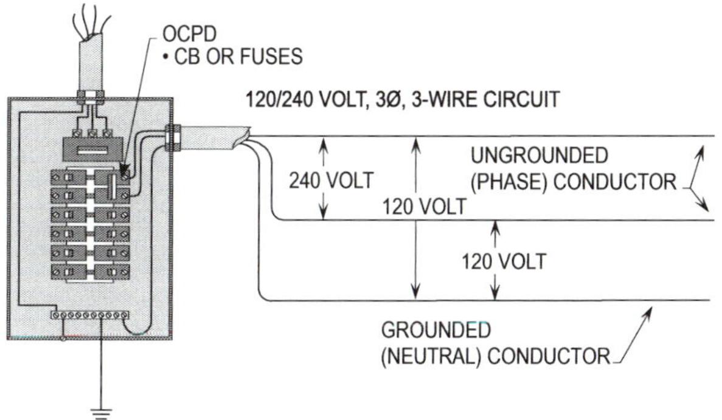

Figure 14-19(b). This illustration shows a diagram of a 120/240 volt, single-phase, three-wire circuit.

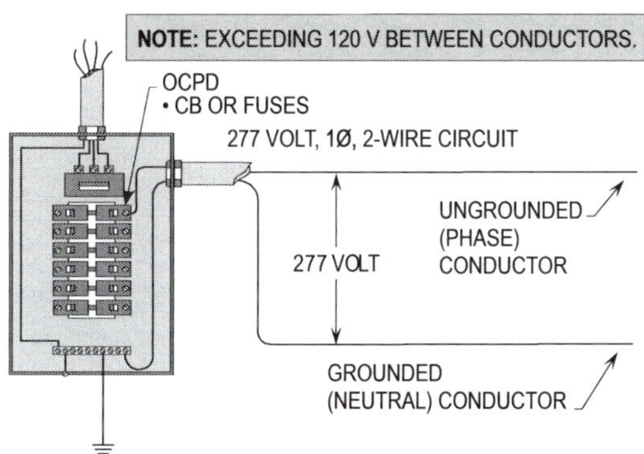

Figure 14-19(c). This illustration shows a diagram of a 277 volt, single-phase, two-wire circuit.

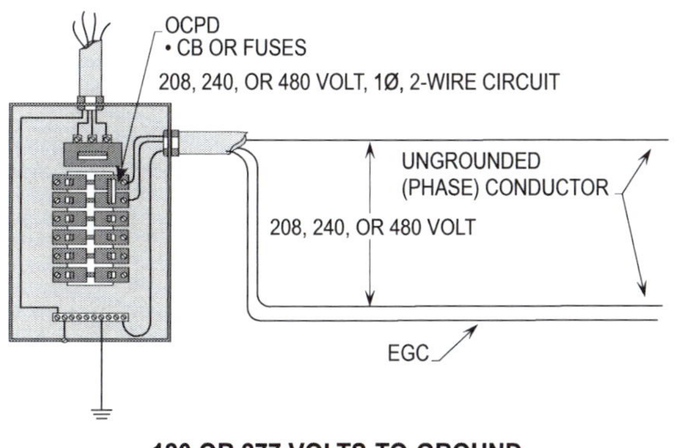

Figure 14-19(d). This illustration shows a diagram of a 208, 240, or 480 volt, single-phase, two-wire circuit.

600 VOLTS BETWEEN CONDUCTORS 210.6(D) AND 225.7(D)

Circuits exceeding 277 volts-to-ground and not exceeding 600 volts between conductors shall be permitted to supply the following types of electrical apparatus:

- Ballasts for electric-discharge luminaires where mounted by one of the following methods:

    (a) At a height not less than 22 ft (6.7 m) on poles or similar structures for the illumination of outdoor areas such as highways, roads, bridges, athletic fields, or parking lots

    (b) At a height not less than 18 ft (5.5 m) on other structures, such as tunnels

- Utilization equipment that is cord-and-plug connected or permanently connected

- Luminaires powered from direct-current systems

These circuits are usually derived by the following types of electrical systems:

- Ungrounded 480 volt, three-wire systems
- Corner grounded 480 volt, three-wire systems

Ungrounded 480 volt, three-wire systems will have 480 volts-to-ground; if one of the legs is accidentally grounded, the power is not lost. Corner grounded 480 volt, three-wire systems will have 480 volts-to-ground because one leg is intentionally grounded. Circuits exceeding 277 volts and not exceeding 600 volts between conductors shall be permitted to supply the auxiliary equipment of electric-discharge lamps as permitted in **225.7(D)**.

DETERMINING AMPERAGE

The amperage for single-phase branch circuits shall be determined by dividing the VA by the supply voltage (I = VA ÷ V). The amperage for three-phase branch circuits shall be determined by dividing the VA by the supply voltage times the square root of three (I = VA ÷ V x 1.732). The 1.732 is determined by taking the $\sqrt{3}$. These amperage ratings shall be used to select the conductors and overcurrent protection devices and other elements of branch circuits.

FINDING AMPERAGE SINGLE-PHASE CIRCUITS

The amperage for single-phase branch circuits shall be determined by dividing the VA rating of electrical equipment by the supply voltage of the circuit. (See **page 4-2** of **Chapter 4**)

For example: What is the amperage rating of a 2400 VA calculated load connected to a 120 volt, single-phase branch circuit?

> **Step 1:** Finding amperage
> $I = VA \div V$
> $I = 2400\ VA \div 120\ V$
> $I = 20\ A$
>
> **Solution: The branch circuit amperage is 20 amps.**

FINDING AMPERAGE
THREE-PHASE CIRCUITS

The amperage for three-phase branch circuits shall be determined by dividing the VA rating for the electrical equipment by the supply voltage times 1.732. The amperage is evenly (as possible) distributed on legs 1, 2, and 3 when dividing the VA by the voltage times 1.732. (See **page 4-3** of **Chapter 4**)

In some cases, the values shown on the three-phase chart are used when determining the three-phase amperage instead of multiplying the supply voltage by 1.732. However, other calculations with the full square root of 3 times the voltage will be used. (See **page 4-4** of **Chapter 4**)

For example: What is the amperage rating of an 8960 VA calculated load connected to a 208 volt, three-phase branch circuit?

> **Step 1:** Finding amperage
> $I = VA \div V \times 1.732$
> $I = 8960\ VA \div 360\ V\ (208 \times 1.732)$
> $I = 25\ A$
>
> **Solution: The branch-circuit amperage is 25 amps.**

COMMERCIAL AND INDUSTRIAL

Branch circuits used in commercial and industrial locations shall be calculated differently from those in residential dwelling units. Most loads in commercial and industrial locations are used continuously for three hours or more without being interrupted. Therefore, such branch circuits supplying these loads shall be calculated at 125 percent of their rating. However, there are loads that operate at noncontinuous operation; some are thermostatically controlled, and these do not fall under such rules.

LIGHTING LOADS
ARTICLE 220, PART III

Incandescent or electric-discharge luminaires shall be permitted to be installed in or on a premise. Such loads shall be calculated at noncontinuous operation (100 percent) or continuous operation (125 percent). Noncontinuously operated loads shall be calculated at 100 percent when used for less than three hours at any given time. Continuously operated loads shall be calculated at 125 percent when used for more than three hours without employing an OFF or cycle period.

NONCONTINUOUS OPERATION
210.19(A)(1)(a) AND 210.20(A)

Noncontinuous lighting shall be calculated at 100 percent of the total VA or amperage rating of the branch circuit. Luminaires and cord-and-plug connected table lamps or floor lamps used for various periods of time shall be permitted to be installed or connected to these circuits. The branch circuit will never be overloaded during their time of use if proper calculations are made and the correct size elements selected.

For example: How many outlets (1.5 A per outlet) are permitted to be connected to a 20 amp branch circuit used at noncontinuous operation?

> **Step 1:** Finding amperage of outlets
> **210.11(A), 210.19(A)(1)(a),** and **210.20(A)**
> $A = 180\ VA \times 100\% \div 120\ V$
> $A = 1.5$
>
> **Step 2:** Finding number of outlets
> **210.11(A)**
> $No. = 20\ A\ OCPD \div 1.5\ A$
> $No. = 13$
>
> **Solution: The number of noncontinuous outlets permitted on a 20 amp branch circuit is 13.**

Design Tip: Applying the same procedure (15 A OCPD ÷ 1.5 A = 10), 10 outlets shall be permitted on a 15 amp branch circuit. The limitation of outlets on a branch circuit alleviates the nuisance tripping of the overcurrent protection device.

CONTINUOUS OPERATION
210.19(A)(1)(a) AND 210.20(A)

Continuous lighting loads shall be calculated at 125 percent of the total VA or amperage rating of the branch circuit. Incandescent or electric-discharge luminaires shall be permitted to be installed in or on commercial or industrial buildings for continuously operated lighting loads.

For example: How many lighting outlets are permitted to be installed on a 20 amp branch circuit used at continuous operation?

Step 1: Finding amperage of outlets
210.11(A), 210.19(A)(1)(a), and 210.20(A)
A = 225 VA (180 VA x 125%) ÷ 120 V
A = 1.875

Step 2: Finding number of outlets
210.11(A)
No. = 20 A OCPD ÷ 1.875 A
No. = 10

Solution: **The number of continuously operated lighting outlets permitted on a 20 amp branch circuit is 10.**

Design Tip: Applying the same procedure (15 A OCPD ÷ 1.875 A = 8), eight outlets shall be permitted on a 15 amp branch circuit. The limitation of outlets on branch circuit alleviates the nuisance tripping of the overcurrent protection device.

For example: What is the maximum continuous operated load that can be connected to a 20 amp branch circuit?

Step 1: Finding amperage
210.19(A)(1)(a) and **210.20(A)**
A = 20 A x 80%
A = 16 A
A = 16 A x 125%
A = 20

Solution: **The branch-circuit load is limited to 16 amps.**

For example: What size overcurrent protection device is permitted to serve a continuously operated load of 14 amps and a noncontinuous load of 2.5 amps?

Step 1: Finding amperage
210.20(A) and **210.19(A)(1)(a)**
14 A x 125% = 17.5 A
2.5 A x 100% = 2.5 A
Total   = 20   A

Solution: **A 20 amp overcurrent protection device is required.**

Design Tip: The grounded (neutral) conductor shall not be required to be considered a current-carrying conductor if it is designed to carry only the unbalanced load from resistive loads connected to the ungrounded (phase) conductors.

OTHER LOADS
210.20(A)

The rating of the branch-circuit overcurrent device serving continuous loads, such as store lighting and similar loads, shall not be less than the noncontinuous load plus 125 percent of the continuous load.

Design Tip: The minimum branch-circuit conductor size, without the application of any adjustment or correction factors, shall have an allowable ampacity equal to or greater than the noncontinuous load plus 125 percent of the continuous load. **(See Figure 14-20)**

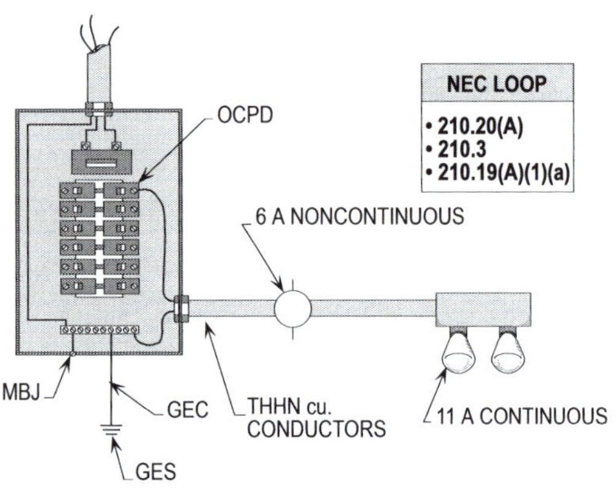

What size OCPD and THHN cu. conductors are required
based on an ambient temperature of 155°F?

Step 1: Finding load
210.19(A)(1)(a) AND 210.20(A)
Conductors	OCPD
11 A x 125% = 13.75 A	
6 A x 100% = 6.00 A	
17 A	19.75 A

Step 2: Finding percentage
Table 310.15(B)(2)(a)
using 12 AWG THHN cu.
30 A x 58% = 17.4 A

Step 3: Finding conductor and OCPD
Table 310.15(B)(16), 240.4, and 240.6(A)
17.4 A supplies 17 A load
19.75 A requires 20 A OCPD
20 A is the next size above 17.4 A

Solution: **12 AWG THHN cu. conductors and 20 amp
overcurrent protection device are required.**

**OTHER LOADS
NEC 210.20(A)**

Figure 14-20. Both the overcurrent protection device and
conductors are calculated at 100 percent for noncontinuous
loads and 125 percent for continuous loads. These values
are added together to obtain the total load.

ELECTRIC DISCHARGE LOADS
220.14, 210.20(A), AND 310.15(A)(3), IN (2)

Branch-circuit overcurrent protection devices shall be sized
at 125 percent of the VA or amperage rating of each ballast
installed to supply the ballast of electric discharge lighting
units. Such electric discharge lighting units and loads are
as follows:

- Fluorescent
- Mercury vapor
- High-pressure sodium
- Low-pressure sodium
- Metal halide

The total wattage of each bulb or lamp shall not be permitted
to be calculated at 125 percent to determine the total lighting
load. This type of calculation does not comply with the NEC
and usually requires a larger lighting load than the VA rating
of each ballast times the number times 125 percent.

Design Tip: The grounded (neutral) conductor shall be
considered a current-carrying conductor if it is installed
for electric-discharge lighting loads unless the loading
does not comply with **310.15(B)(5)(c)**.

For example: What is the lighting load for a branch
circuit supplying 12 - 1.5 amp ballasts that serve 24 -
F25 CW lamps used at continuous operation?

Step 1: Finding amperage
220.18(B)
I = ballast A x No. of outlets
I = 1.5 A x 12
I = 18 A

Step 2: Applying percentage
210.19(A)(1)(a) and **210.20(A)**
I = 18 A x 125%
I = 22.5 A

Solution: **The branch-circuit load is 22.5
amps.**

OUTLETS
220.14(D), (E), AND (L)

Branch circuits of 120 volts shall be calculated at 180 VA
(1.5 A) per outlet where the VA rating of ballasts or the
wattage of incandescent bulbs is unknown. Heavy-duty
lampholders of 120 volts shall be calculated at 600 VA
(5 A). Lampholders connected to a branch circuit having a
rating in excess of 20 amps shall have a rating of not less
than 660 watts (5.5 A) if of the admedium type and not less
than 750 watts (6.25 A) if of any other type per **210.21(A)**.
Outlets shall be calculated at noncontinuous operation (100
percent) and continuous operation (125 percent) times their
VA rating to determine the branch-circuit load. Overcurrent
protection devices shall be calculated at 125 percent. **(See
Figure 14-21)**

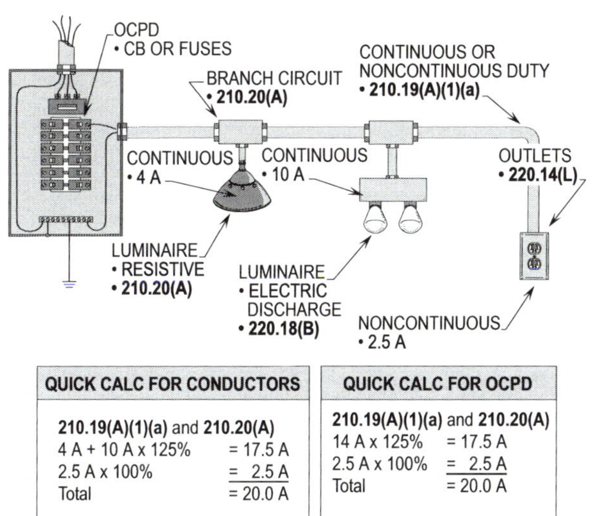

Figure 14-21. Outlets shall be calculated at noncontinuous operation (100 percent) and continuous operation (125 percent) times their VA rating to determine the branch-circuit load. Overcurrent protection devices shall be calculated at 125 percent.

For example: What size overcurrent protection device and THHN copper conductors (branch circuits) are required for 11 outlets used at noncontinuous operation to supply luminaires?

Step 1: Finding VA
210.19(A)(1)(a) and **210.20(A)**
VA = No. of outlets x VA x 100%
VA = 1980 VA (11 x 180 VA) x 100%
VA = 1980

Step 2: Finding amperage
210.11(A)
I = VA ÷ V
I = 1980 VA ÷ 120 V
I = 16.5

Step 3: Finding conductor and OCPD
Table 310.15(B)(16) and **Asterisk, 240.4(B), 240.6(A)**, and **240.4(D)**
12 AWG THHN cu. = 30 A
Protected by 20 A OCPD

Solution: **The branch-circuit conductors are sized 12 AWG, and the overcurrent protection is selected at 20 amps.**

For example: What size overcurrent protection device and THHN copper conductors (branch circuit) are required for nine outlets used at continuous operation to supply luminaires?

Step 1: Finding VA
210.19(A)(1)(a) and **210.20(A)**
VA = No. of outlets x VA x 125%
VA = 1620 VA (9 x 180 VA) x 125%
VA = 2025

Step 2: Finding amperage
210.11(A)
I = VA ÷ V
I = 2025 VA ÷ 120 V
I = 16.9

Step 3: Finding conductor and OCPD
Table 310.15(B)(16) and **Asterisk, 240.4(B), 240.6(A)**, and **240.4(D)**
12 AWG cu. = 30 A

Solution: **The branch-circuit conductors are sized 12 AWG, and the overcurrent protection device is 20 amps per Asterisk to Table 310.15(B)(16).**

SHOW WINDOWS
220.14(G) AND 220.43(A)

Show window lighting loads shall be calculated at a minimum of 180 VA per outlet for branch circuits if the VA is unknown. The total VA rating for show window lighting loads shall be multiplied by 125 percent for each branch circuit. Show window lighting loads shall be multiplied by 125 percent because they can operate for a period of three hours or more to provide illumination for advertisement of goods.

For example: What is the number of outlets permitted to be installed on a 20 amp branch circuit supplying lighting loads in a show window?

Step 1: Finding No. of outlets
220.14(G), 210.19(A)(1)(a), and **210.20(A)**
No. of outlets =
device x 120 V ÷ VA x 125%
No. of outlets =
(20 A x 120 V) ÷ 180 VA x 125%
(2400 VA ÷ 180 VA) x 125%
13.30 x 125%
No. of outlets = 10.7

Solution: The number of outlets permitted to be installed on a 20 amp branch circuit is 10.7. Note, inspectors usually permit 180 VA to be used if the load for such units is unknown.

See Figure 14-22 for calculating the load for show windows based on either linear foot or individual outlets.

TRACK LIGHTING
220.43(B)

Lighting track loads shall be calculated at 150 VA for each 2 ft (600 mm) of track to determine the load of branch circuits. To properly balance the load, the VA rating is divided between the number of circuits supplying the length of lighting track.

For example: What is the VA rating for 30 ft of lighting track?

Step 1: Finding VA
220.43(B)
VA = Track length ÷ 2' x 150 VA
VA = (30' ÷ 2') x 150 VA
VA = 2250

Solution: The total VA rating to be used for calculating the service or feeder load is 2250 VA.

The load on multicircuit lighting tracks shall be balanced as adequately as possible using one of the following methods:

Calculating 2 circuits
2 branch circuits
150 VA for each 2 ft
VA = 150 VA ÷ 2
VA = 75

Calculating 3 circuits
3 branch circuits
150 VA for each 2 ft
VA = 150 VA ÷ 3
VA = 50

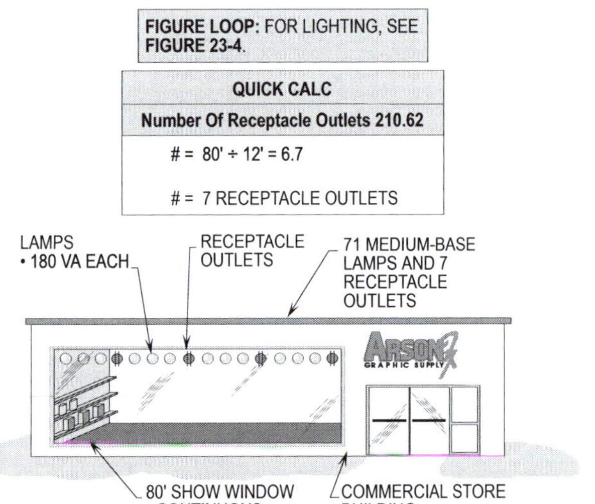

What is the lighting load for the show window based on the number of lamp outlets and linear feet?

	Finding load	Finding number of outlets
Step 1:	Calculating the load **220.43(A)** 80 ft x 200 VA = 16,000 VA	Number of outlets **220.14(G)** 71 x 180 VA = 12,780 VA
Step 2:	Calculating the load for the OCPD **230.42(A)(1)** 16,000 VA x 125% = 20,000 VA	Calculating the load for the OCPD **230.42(A)(1)** 12,780 VA x 125% = 15,975 VA
Solution:	**The lighting load is 20,000 volt-amps.**	**The lighting load is 15,975 VA**
Note:	The 20,000 VA calculation is used because it is greater than 15,975 VA.	

SHOW WINDOWS
NEC 220.14(G)
NEC 220.43(A)

Figure 14-22. Calculating the load for a show window using largest load. Either the number of outlets or the linear feet shall be used, whichever is greater.

Design Tip: Use the actual load on the track if possible.

The 150 VA multicircuit track lighting shall not apply to dwelling units per **220.43(B)**. The load for track lighting would be included in the 3 VA per sq. ft listed in **Table 220.12**. **(See Figure 14-23)**

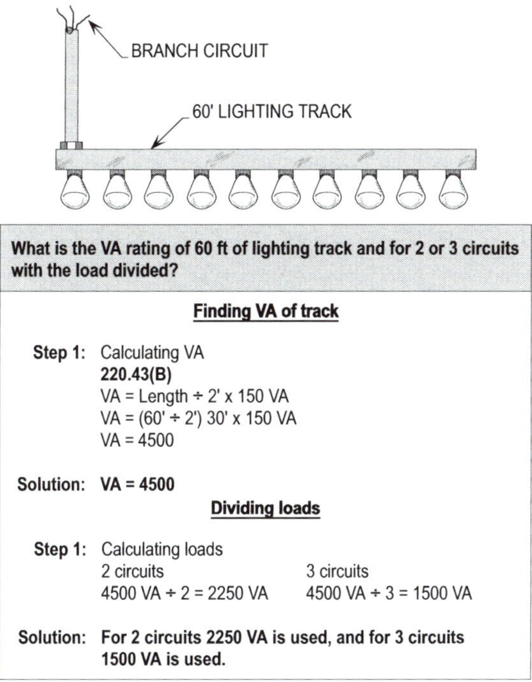

Figure 14-23. The 150 VA for each 2 ft (600 mm) of lighting track shall be used to calculate the load for service or feeder loads. The load of the track shall be divided as evenly as possible on each circuit supplying the track.

SIGN LOADS
ARTICLE 600, PART I

Each commercial building and each commercial occupancy accessible to pedestrians shall be provided with a sign circuit that is accessible at each entrance for pedestrians from a sidewalk, street, etc. Signs shall be considered to be in continuous operation (three hours or more) if installed and used in commercial occupancies.

REQUIRED BRANCH CIRCUIT
600.5(A)

Each commercial building and each commercial occupancy shall be required to be installed with at least one 20 amp branch circuit to supply an outlet for a sign or outline lighting that is located in an accessible location. This 20 amp branch circuit shall not be permitted to have any other loads connected to the overcurrent protection device protecting such circuits.

RATING
600.5(B)(1) AND (B)(2)

Branch circuits that supply signs and outline lighting systems containing incandescent and fluorescent forms of illumination shall be limited to 20 amps or less. Branch circuits that supply transformers for neon tubing installations shall be limited to 30 amps or less.

For example, transformers installed for channel letters and ballasts for electric discharge lamps shall be rated 20 amps or less for branch circuits. Transformers installed only to connect branch circuits for neon or channel letters shall be rated 30 amps or less.

CALCULATED LOAD
220.14(F)

When sizing the service or feeder calculation for a sign calculated at a minimum of 1200 VA, the load shall be multiplied by 125 percent for continuous operation if the sign burns for three hours or more. When sizing the load for the overcurrent protection device, the load shall be multiplied by 125 percent to obtain the load that is based on continuous operation.

For example: What is the total load allowed for a 16 amp wall sign supplied by a 20 amp, 120 volt branch circuit?

Step 1: Finding amperage
600.5(A)
OCPD = 20 A

Step 2: Calculating amperage
220.14(F) and **210.20(A)**
20 A x 80% = 16 A
16 A x 125% = 20 A

Step 3: Selecting OCPD
220.14(F) and **210.20(A)**
16 A load is permitted

Solution: **The size overcurrent protection device required is 20 amps for a sign that burns three hours or more at 16 amps or less.**

See Figure 14-24 for calculating the load for a sign.

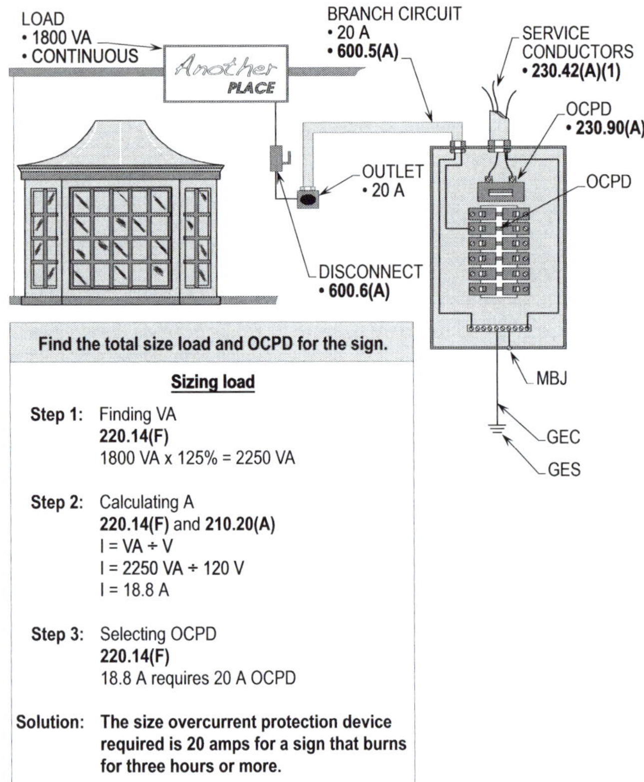

Figure 14-24. Sign loads that operate for three hours or more shall be calculated at 125 percent, and elements selected from this value.

RECEPTACLE LOADS
ARTICLE 220, PART III

Receptacle outlets shall be permitted to be installed for cord-and-plug connected appliances, utilization equipment, and table or floor lamps in dwelling units, apartments, condominiums, townhouses, and commercial or industrial locations. Cord-and-plug connected loads shall be connected in an arrangement not to load up the branch circuit. Cord-and-plug connected loads are general purpose, serving more than one outlet or individually serving one outlet from a branch circuit. Cord-and-plug connected items shall be installed and located in a manner to prevent the use of extension cords except for temporary use.

RECEPTACLE OUTLETS
220.14(I)

A general-purpose branch circuit shall be calculated at 180 VA for each outlet where supplying more than one outlet utilizing cord-and-plug connected items. The number of outlets shall be calculated at 180 VA times noncontinuous operation at 100 percent and continuous operation at 125 percent.

Note, overcurrent protection devices and conductors shall be sized at 125 percent. **(See Figure 14-25)**

For example: What is the load for 8 receptacle outlets that are supplying cord-and-plug connected loads used at noncontinuous operation?

Step 1:   Finding VA
          Load = No. of outlets x 180 VA x 100%
          Load = 8 x 180 VA x 100%
          Load = 1440 VA

Solution: **The load is 1440 VA.**

For example: How many noncontinuous duty receptacle outlets can be connected to a 20 amp general-purpose branch circuit?

Step 1:   Finding amperage of outlets
          220.14(I)
          180 VA ÷ 120 V = 1.5 A

Step 2:   Finding number of outlets
          220.14(I) and **210.11(A)**
          20 A OCPD ÷ 1.5 A x 100% = 13

Solution: **The number of outlets permitted on a 20 amp overcurrent protection device is 13.**

For example: How many continuous-duty receptacle outlets can be connected to a 20 amp general-purpose branch circuit?

Step 1:   Finding amperage of outlets
          220.14(I)
          180 VA ÷ 120 V = 1.5 A

Step 2:   Finding number of outlets
          220.14(I) and **210.11(A)**
          20 A OCPD ÷ 1.5 A x 125% = 10

Solution: **The number of outlets permitted on a 20 amp overcurrent protection device is 10.**

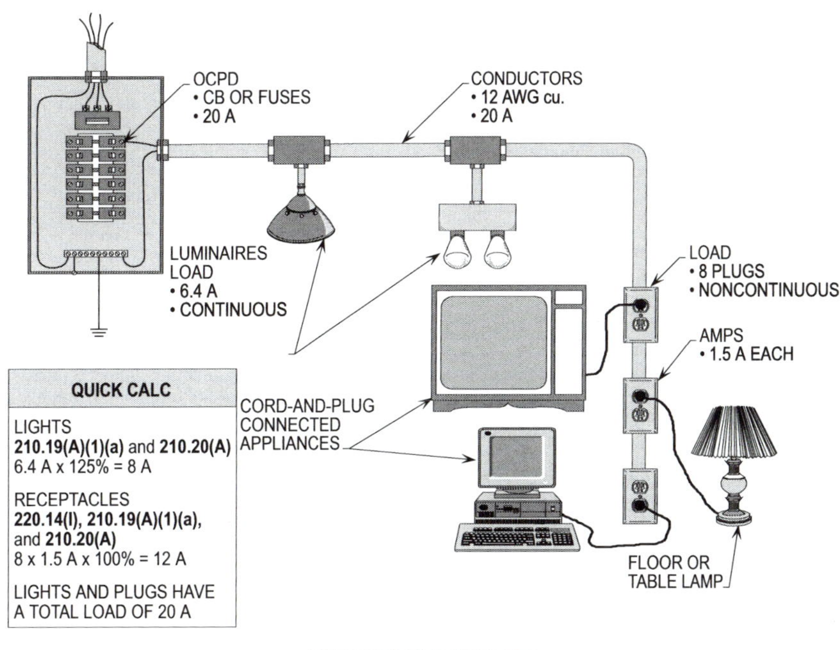

Figure 14-25. Receptacle outlets shall be calculated at 180 VA times noncontinuous operation at 100 percent and continuous operation at 125 percent.

INDIVIDUAL LOADS
210.19(A)(1)(a)

Individual cord-and-plug connected loads for branch circuits shall be determined by multiplying the noncontinuously operated load by 100 percent and the continuously operated load by 125 percent. The amount of amperage for each cord-and-plug connected load shall be found by applying the power formula. The following shall apply when using the power formula:

I = amps	I = VA ÷ V
P = volt-amps	VA = I x V
E = voltage	V = VA ÷ I

Design Tip: When applying calculations in this book, the variation of the power formula is used, since the NEC recognizes volt-amps (VA) for load calculations per the **Examples** in **Annex D**.

When calculating voltage drop (VD) for branch circuits, see the requirements for feeders on page 15-9 of this book.

For example: What size THWN copper conductors and overcurrent protection device are required for an individual branch circuit to a hot tub having a nameplate current rating of 42 amps?

Step 1: Finding amperage
680.9
42 A is the circuit current rating

Step 2: Calculating load
680.9
42 A x 125% = 52.5 A

Step 3: Selecting conductors
Table 310.15(B)(16)
52.5 A requires 6 AWG THWN cu.

Step 4: Selecting OCPD
240.4(B) and **680.9**
52.5 A load requires 60 A OCPD
65 A conductor allows 70 A OCPD

Solution: A 60 amp overcurrent protection device and a 6 AWG THWN copper conductor are permitted.

See Figure 14-26 for calculating the load to an individual cord-and-plug connected load.

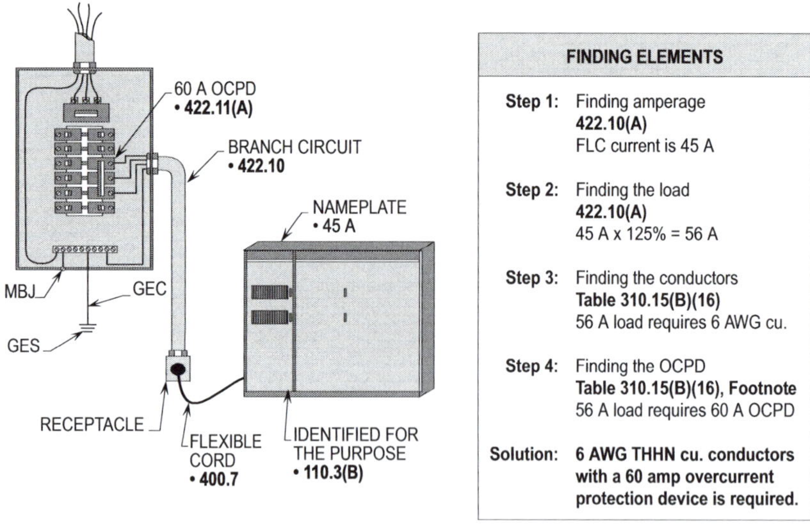

Figure 14-26. Individual loads shall be calculated at 100 percent for noncontinuous and 125 percent of continuous, times the nameplate FLA of the appliance.

MULTIWIRE BRANCH CIRCUITS
210.4

Multiwire branch circuits are used to supply power to line-to-neutral loads only when more than one ungrounded (phase) conductor is sharing the grounded (neutral) conductor. All conductors of a multiwire branch circuit shall originate from the same panelboard or similar distribution equipment and shall be switched by individual circuit breakers. Multiwire branch circuits shall be supplied by double-pole circuit breakers or individual circuit breakers with handle ties to provide safety from electrical shock while serving the circuits or equipment.

Section **300.13(B)** makes it mandatory that grounded (neutral) conductors be pigtailed to prevent different voltage levels between the ungrounded (phase) conductors should the grounded (neutral) conductor become loose due to bad connections, etc.

Multiwire branch circuits shall be permitted to serve power to one outlet for an individual piece of equipment with the other circuit(s) supplying power to a number of outlets that are used for receptacles, lights, and other cord-and-plugged equipment. **(See Figure 14-27)**

All ungrounded (phase) conductors shall be simultaneously disconnected at the point where each multiwire branch circuit originates.

The ungrounded (phase) and grounded (neutral) conductors of each multiwire branch circuit shall be grouped by wire or similar means in at least one location within the panelboard or other point of origination.

COMMERCIAL COOKING EQUIPMENT
210.19(A)(1)(a) AND 210.20(A)

Commercial cooking equipment shall be calculated at noncontinuous operation (100 percent) or continuous operation (125 percent) to determine the branch circuit load. When installing more than one piece of cooking equipment, the demand factors shall be selected from **Table 220.56**.

For example: What is the load for a 10 kW cooking unit that is supplied by a 240 volt, single-phase branch circuit used at continuous operation?

Step 1:   Finding kW for OCPD
             210.20(A)
             10 kW x 125% = 12.5 kW

Step 2:   Finding kW for conductor
             210.19(A)(1)(a)
             10 kW x 125% = 12.5 kW

Solution: **The continuous operated load is 12.5 kW.**

Design Tip: The overcurrent protection device shall be calculated at 125 percent, and the conductors shall be calculated at 125 percent. The overcurrent protection device shall be permitted to be increased and decreased in size per **240.4** or **240.4(E)**.

See Figure 14-28 for calculating the load for a commercial cooking unit.

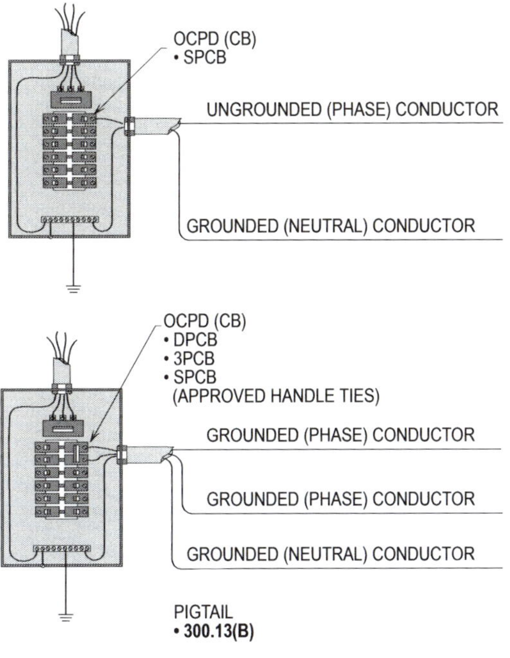

Figure 14-27. Multiwire branch circuits are used to supply power to line-to-neutral loads only when more than one ungrounded (phase) conductor is sharing the grounded (neutral) conductor.

WATER HEATER LOADS
ARTICLE 422, PART II

Water heaters are designed with elements to heat water at different stages of use. For larger amounts of hot water, more of the elements shall be connected into the circuit to heat the water to replace that which was used. When smaller amounts of hot water are needed, fewer elements are used in the circuit to heat the water.

CONDUCTORS
422.13 AND 422.10(A)

Storage-type water heaters having a capacity of 120 gallons (450 L) or less shall have a rating not less than 125 percent of the nameplate rating to size the branch-circuit conductors.

For example: What size conductors are required to supply power to a 240 volt, single-phase water heater pulling 5000 VA?

Step 1: Finding amperage
5000 VA ÷ 240 V = 21 A

Step 2: Finding the loads
422.13 and **422.10(A)**
21 A x 125% = 26 A

Step 3: Finding the conductors
334.80 and **Table 310.15(B)(16)**
26 A load requires 10 AWG cu.

Solution: The size conductors required are 10 AWG.

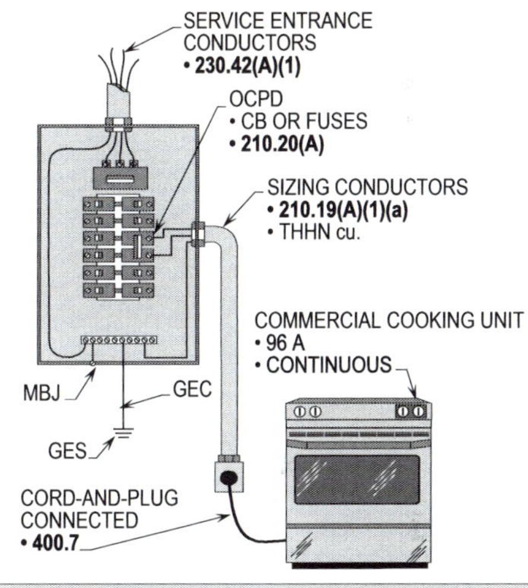

What size conductor and OCPD is required, based on load calculations?

Step 1: Finding the load
210.19(A)(1)(a), 422.10(A), and **422.11(A)**
96 A x 125% = 120 A

Step 2: Finding conductor and OCPD
Table 310.15(B)(16) and **240.6(A)**
Conductors = 1 AWG THHN cu.
OCPD = 125 A

Solution: **The conductors are 1 AWG THHN copper and the size overcurrent protection device is 125 amp based on calculated load.**

COMMERCIAL COOKING EQUIPMENT
NEC 210.19(A)(1)(a)
NEC 210.20(A)

Figure 14-28. Commercial cooking equipment shall be calculated at noncontinuous operation (100 percent) or continuous operation (125 percent) to determine the branch-circuit load.

OVERCURRENT PROTECTION
422.13 AND 422.11(A)

Overcurrent protection devices shall be sized not less than 125 percent of the heating load to prevent tripping open the overcurrent protection device and disconnecting all the elements connected into the circuit. Approximately 100 percent of the water heater's connected load is pulled from resistance heating elements.

For example: What size overcurrent protection device is required to supply power to a 240 volt, single-phase water heater pulling 5000 VA (21 A) at continuous operation?

Step 1:   Finding load for OCPD
422.13 and **422.11(A)**
21 A x 125% = 26 A

Step 2:   Finding the OCPD
422.13 and **240.4(B)**
26 A load requires a 30 A OCPD

Solution: The overcurrent protection device is 30 amps.

DISCONNECTING MEANS
422.31(B)

A disconnecting means shall not be required to be installed at the water heater when the overcurrent protection device is readily accessible. The overcurrent protection device shall be permitted to be installed as the disconnect where installed in a service panel that is readily accessible and is located outside or inside the building. An accessible cord-and-plug shall be permitted to serve as the disconnecting means for cord-and-plug connected water heaters where readily accessible per **422.33(A)**. However, such units shall be listed for cord-and-plug connection. **(See Figure 14-29)**

HEATING LOADS
ARTICLE 424, PART I

Heating elements in heating units are rated at 5 kW each. The elements are stacked in the heating unit to provide the rated kW for a particular size occupancy. Two stacked elements provide a 10 kW heating unit. Three stacked elements provide a 15 kW heating unit and so forth. Branch-circuit conductors and overcurrent protection devices shall be sized and selected based on the kW rating of each heating unit plus the blower motor per **424.3(B)**.

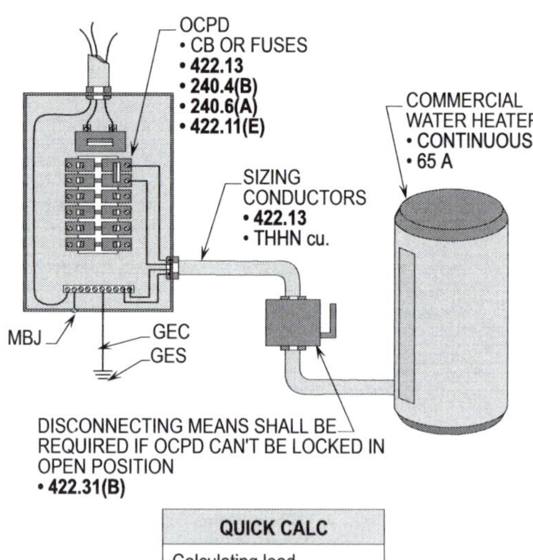

Figure 14-29. A disconnecting means shall not be required to be installed at the water heater when the overcurrent protection device is readily accessible.

Heating units with a number of elements shall be subdivided so that they may be more easily supplied from a local panelboard or from the service equipment. Individual branch circuits or a feeder shall be utilized in routing power to the heating unit.

CONDUCTORS
424.3(B)

Heating units shall be calculated at 125 percent of the heating element load plus 125 percent of the blower motor load when present for sizing the branch-circuit conductors. The heating elements and blower motor load shall be at least 125 percent when sizing the ampacity of conductors.

Note, the branch circuit from the panelboard to the heating unit shall not be considered a feeder as outlined in **430.24, Ex. 2.**

> **For example:** What size THWN copper conductors are required for a 25 kW, 240 volt, single-phase heating unit with a 4 amp blower motor?
>
> **Step 1:** Finding amperage
> 25 kVA x 1000 ÷ 240 V = 104 A
>
> **Step 2:** Finding the load
> **424.3(B)**
> 104 A + 4 A x 125% = 135 A
>
> **Step 3:** Finding the conductors
> **Table 310.15(B)(16)**
> 150 A load requires 1/0 AWG THWN cu.
>
> **Solution: 1/0 AWG THWN copper conductors are required.**

OVERCURRENT PROTECTION
424.3(B)

Heating units shall be calculated at 125 percent of the heating element load plus 125 percent of the blower motor load when present for sizing the overcurrent protection device. The next higher size rating overcurrent protection device shall be permitted to be installed if it does not correspond to this rating per **240.4(B)**. The next higher size overcurrent protection device prevents tripping open when the heating unit requires all the 5 kW rated elements to satisfy the heating load called for by the thermostat.

> **For example:** What size overcurrent protection device is required for a 25 kW, 240 volt, single-phase heating unit with a 4 amp blower motor?
>
> **Step 1:** Finding load for OCPD
> **424.3(B)**
> 104 A + 4 A x 125% = 135 A
>
> **Step 2:** Finding OCPD
> **240.6(A)** and **240.4(B)**
> 150 A is the next higher standard size
>
> **Solution: The size overcurrent protection device is 150 amps.**

DISCONNECTING MEANS
424.19

A disconnecting means shall be installed for a self-contained heating unit with a controller that energizes the circuits to the heating elements and blower motor. A fused or nonfused disconnect, an automatic breaker, or a nonautomatic circuit breaker used as the disconnecting means for a heating unit shall be located within sight and within 50 ft (15 m) of the heating unit per **Article 100, 424.19(A)**, and **430.102**. **(See Figure 14-30)**

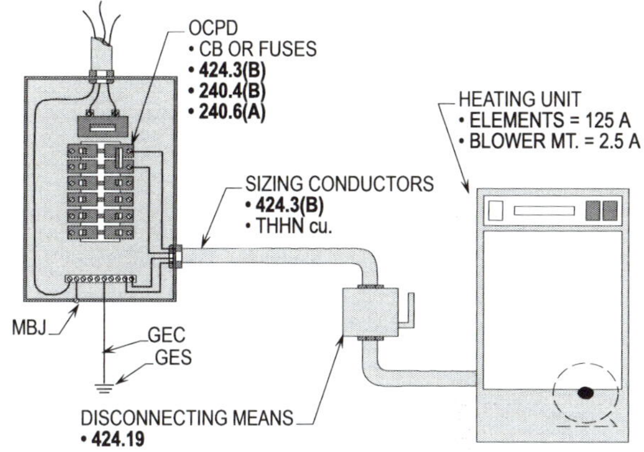

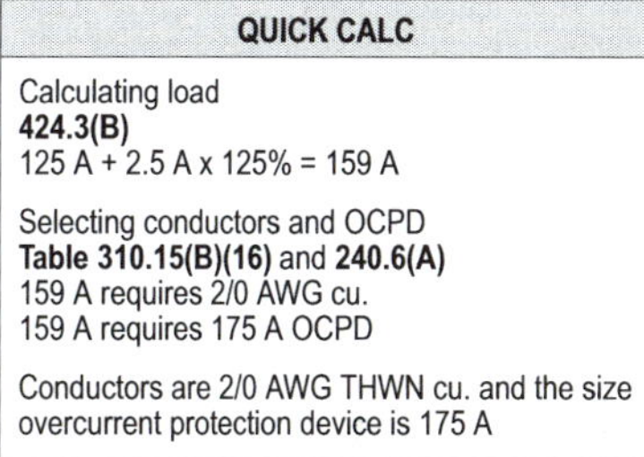

DISCONNECTING MEANS
NEC 424.19

Figure 14-30. A disconnecting means shall be installed for a self-contained heating unit with a controller that energizes the circuits to the heating elements and blower motor.

AIR-CONDITIONING LOADS
ARTICLE 440, PART III

Air-conditioning units are rated in Btu or tons. One ton contains 12,000 Btu. A 5 ton compressor in a central air-conditioner unit has 60,000 Btu (5 x 12,000 Btu = 60,000 Btu). The air-conditioner load shall be calculated by the square footage and construction of the premises. The size air-conditioner rated in Btu shall be selected from this calculation. The conductors shall be sized large enough to carry the load of the compressor, and the overcurrent protection device shall be selected to allow the compressor to start without tripping open, due to inrush current from high head pressures.

CONDUCTORS
440.32

Branch circuit conductors supplying a single motor-compressor shall have an ampacity not less than 125 percent of either the motor-compressor rated load current or the branch-circuit selection current, whichever is greater.

The branch-circuit conductors shall be sized large enough to prevent damage to the insulation of the conductor caused by an overload. Overload relays are installed and are usually adjusted to trip open on an overload exceeding 140 percent of full-load current rating of the compressor. This type of condition shall be compensated for by sizing and selecting the conductors at 125 percent of the compressor's full-load current rating. The condenser motor load shall be added at 100 percent when present.

For example: What size conductors are required to supply power to a 240 volt, single-phase air-conditioning unit with a compressor rating of 6000 VA plus a 3 amp condenser motor? (Use THHN copper conductors terminated to 60°C terminals.)

Step 1:	Finding amperage of compressor 6000 VA ÷ 240 V = 25 A
Step 2:	Finding the total load **440.32** 25 A x 125% + 3 A = 34 A
Step 3:	Finding the conductors **Table 310.15(B)(16)** 34 A load requires 8 AWG cu.
Solution:	**8 AWG THHN copper conductors are required.**

OVERCURRENT PROTECTION
440.22(A)

To allow the compressor to start and run, the overcurrent protection device shall be sized properly. The overcurrent protection device shall have a rating or setting not exceeding 175 percent of the motor-compressor rated full-load current or the branch-circuit selection current, whichever is greater to determine the minimum rating. The overcurrent protection device shall be permitted to be increased up to 225 percent of the full-load current if an air-conditioner unit will not start using 175 percent. Condenser motors shall be calculated at 100 percent and added to this total, and the overcurrent protection device selected accordingly.

When air-conditioning units are installed on the roof or on the outside of the premises where the sun goes down, the air-conditioning unit may have trouble starting and operating during hot summer months. Overcurrent protection devices shall be sized by the listing on the nameplate of the unit. Fuses and circuit breakers (HACR) shall be installed where listed on the nameplate of the unit. For further information, see Underwriters Laboratories book, *Electrical Appliance and Utilization Equipment Directory*.

Note, overcurrent protection devices for air-conditioning units installed on the roofs are already calculated and sized at the maximum value of 225 percent per **110.3(B)** and **440.22(A)**.

Conductors supplying air-conditioning units on roofs are calculated already per **440.4(C)** and **440.32**, and the nameplate will list the size conductors or circuit needed.

For example: What minimum and maximum size overcurrent protection devices are required to supply power to a 240 volt, single-phase air-conditioning unit with a compressor rating of 6000 VA plus a 3 amp condenser motor?

Step 1:	Finding load for OCPD **440.22(A)** 25 A x 175% + 3 A = 46.7 A
Step 2:	Finding OCPD **240.4(G)** and **240.6(A)** 45 A is the next lower size permitted
Solution:	**The lower size overcurrent protection device is 45 amps.**
Step 1:	Finding load for OCPD **440.22(A)** 25 A x 225% + 3 = 59.25 A
Step 2:	Finding OCPD **240.4(G)** and **240.6(A)** 50 A is the next higher size permitted
Solution:	**The higher size overcurrent protection device is 50 amps.**

DISCONNECTING MEANS
440.14

The disconnecting means shall be located within 50 ft (15 m) and within sight from the air-conditioning unit per **Article 100**. The disconnecting means shall be permitted to be installed on or within the air-conditioning unit. The disconnecting means shall be permitted to be installed where capable of being locked in the open position where conditions of maintenance and supervision ensure that only qualified personnel will service the equipment.

Note, **Ex. 1** to **440.14** applies only to industrial compressors and not to air-conditioning units. A disconnecting means shall not be required where within sight of such equipment. **(See Figure 14-31)**

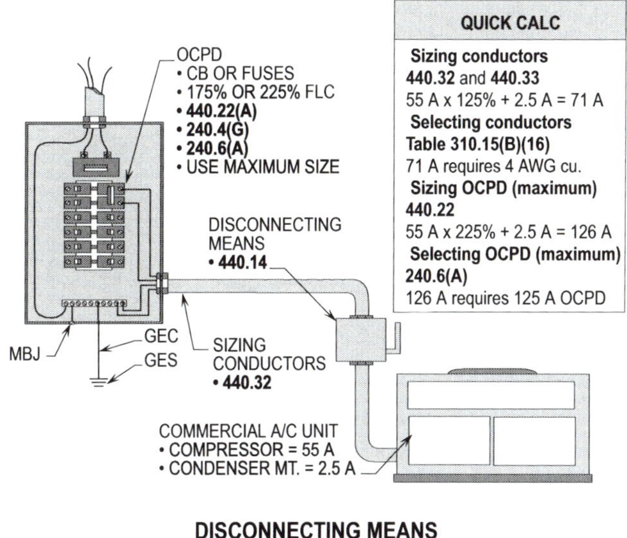

Figure 14-31. The disconnecting means shall be located within 50 ft (15 m) and within sight from the air-conditioning unit per **Article 100**. Also, see **Figures 19-9** and **19-16**.

MOTOR LOADS
ARTICLE 430, PARTS II AND IV

Motors are rated in horsepower (HP). The amount of work that a motor can perform depends upon its HP rating class, code letter, or design letter. A motor with a high horsepower rating may do more work than a motor with a low horsepower rating. The overcurrent protection devices and conductors used to supply power to motors shall be sized and based on the horsepower, voltage, and number of phases. The starting current of a motor shall be based on its code letter per **Table 430.7(B)** or design letter per **Tables 430.251(A)** and **(B)**.

CONDUCTORS
430.22

Branch circuit conductors supplying a single motor shall have an ampacity not less than 125 percent of the motor full-load current rating. Single-phase motors shall have their full-load current ratings selected from **Table 430.248** per **430.6(A)(1)**. Three-phase motors shall have their full-load current rating selected from **Table 430.250** per **430.6(A)(1)**.

For example: What size conductors are required to supply power to a 10 HP, 208 volt, single-phase motor? (Using THWN copper conductors)

Step 1:   Finding amperage
430.6(A)(1) and **Table 430.248**
10 HP = 55 A

Step 2:   Finding the load
430.22
55 A x 125% = 68.75 A

Step 3:   Finding the conductors
Table 310.15(B)(16)
68.75 A load requires 4 AWG cu.

Solution: **The branch-circuit conductors required are 4 AWG copper.**

For example: What size conductors are required to supply power to a 10 HP, 208 volt, three-phase motor? (Using THWN copper conductors)

Step 1:   Finding amperage
430.6(A)(1) and **Table 430.250**
10 HP = 30.8 A

Step 2:   Finding the load
430.22
30.8 A x 125% = 38.5 A

Step 3:   Finding the conductors
Table 310.15(B)(16)
38.5 A load requires 8 AWG cu.

Solution: **The branch-circuit conductors required are 8 AWG copper.**

OVERCURRENT PROTECTION
430.52 AND TABLE 430.52

When power is applied to the windings of a motor and it starts, the motor has high inrush currents. The amount of current required to drive a load is called running current. Inrush currents of the motor shall be held by an overcurrent protection device sized large to allow the motor to accelerate the driven load. The inrush current of most motors is four to six times the running current of the motor, based on its code letter per **Table 430.7(B)** or design letter per **Table 430.52**.

Note, Design E motors can have 8-1/2 to 15 times FLA.

Overcurrent protection devices shall not be permitted to exceed the percentages listed in **Table 430.52**. Section **430.52(C)(1)** requires the overcurrent protection device to based on the percentages for the type of device used in the columns of **Table 430.52**. If the percentage does not correspond to a standard device listed in **240.6(A)**, the higher standard size rating shall be permitted to be used per **430.52(C)(1), Ex. 1**. If the motor will not start and run, the percentage shall be permitted to be increased per **430.52(C)(1), Ex. 2(a) through (c)**. These percentages for the overcurrent protection device are as follows:

- Nontime-delay fuses shall not be permitted to exceed 400 percent of the full-load current for fuses rated 600 amps or less per **430.52(C)(1), Ex. 2(a)**.

- Time-delay fuses shall not be permitted to exceed 225 percent of the full-load current per **430.52(C)(1), Ex. 2(b)**.

- Circuit breakers shall not be permitted to exceed 400 percent of the full-load current for ratings of 100 amps or less, or shall not be permitted to exceed 300 percent of the full-load current for ratings over 100 amps per **430.52(C)(1), Ex. 2(c)**.

- Instantaneous trip circuit breakers shall not be permitted to exceed 1300 or 1700 percent of the full-load current per **430.52(C)(3), Ex. 1**.

For example: What size nontime-delay fuse, time-delay fuse, circuit breaker, and instantaneous circuit breaker are required for a 20 HP, 230 volt, three-phase motor with a full-load current rating of 54 amps per **Table 430.250**? (Nameplate amps is 49 amps)

Nontime-delay fuses

Step 1: Finding percentage
430.52(C)(1) and **Table 430.52**
300%

Step 2: Finding amperage
430.52(C)(1)
54 A x 300% = 162 A

Step 3: Finding NTDF (round down size)
430.52(C)(1), 240.4(G), and **240.6(A)**
162 A requires 150 A OCPD

Step 4: Finding NTDF (round up size)
430.52(C)(1), Ex. 1, 240.4(G), and **240.6(A)**
The next higher standard size above 162 A is 175 A OCPD

Step 5: Finding NTDF (max. size)
430.52(C)(1), Ex. 2(a)
52 A x 400% = 208 A
The largest size below 208 is 200 A OCPD

Solution: The next higher size nontime-delay fuses required are 175 amps.

Note: Smaller nontime-delay fuses can be used, other than what is shown in the calculation above, to start and run a motor.

Time-delay fuses

Step 1: Finding percentage
430.52(C)(1) and **Table 430.52**
175%

Step 2: Finding amperage
430.52(C)(1)
54 A x 175% = 94.5 A

Step 3: Finding TDF (round down size)
430.52(C)(1), 240.4(G), and **240.6(A)**
94.5 A requires 90 A OCPD

Step 4: Finding TDF (round up size)
430.52(C)(1), Ex. 1, 240.4(G), and
240.6(A)
The next standard size above 94.5 A
is 100 A OCPD

Step 5: Finding TDF (max. size)
430.52(C)(1), Ex. 2(b)
54 A x 225% = 121.5 A
The largest size below 121.5 A is
110 A OCPD

**Solution: The next higher size time-delay
fuse required is 100 amps.**

Note: Smaller time-delay fuses and circuit breakers can be used, other than what is shown in the calculation above, to start and run a motor.

Circuit breaker

Step 1: Finding percentage
430.52(C)(1) and **Table 430.52**
250%

Step 2: Finding amperage
430.52(C)(1)
54 A x 250% = 135 A

Step 3: Finding CB (round down size)
430.52(C)(1), 240.4(G), and **240.6(A)**
135 A requires 125 A OCPD
The next size below 135 A is 125 A
OCPD

Step 4: Finding CB (round up size)
430.52(C)(1), Ex. 1, 240.4(G), and
240.6(A)
The next standard size above 135 A
is 150 A OCPD

Step 5: Finding CB (max. size)
430.52(C)(1), Ex. 2(c)
54 A x 400% = 216 A
The largest size below 216 A is 200 A
OCPD

**Solution: The next higher size circuit breaker
required is 150 amps.**

Instantaneous circuit breaker

Step 1: Finding percentage
430.52(C)(3) and **Table 430.52**
800%

Step 2: Finding amperage
430.52(C)(3)
54 A x 800% = 432 A

Step 3: Finding CB
430.52(C)(1), 240.4(G), and **240.6(A)**
The minimum setting is 432 A

Step 4: Finding CB
430.52(C)(3), Ex. 1
54 A x 1300% = 702 A
The maximum setting is 702 A

**Solution: The maximum size instantaneous
circuit breaker setting is 702 amps.**

DISCONNECTING MEANS
430.102 AND 430.107

A disconnecting means shall be located within sight from the controller and shall disconnect the controller to allow personnel to service the motor without the danger of the branch circuit accidentally being energized. The disconnecting means shall be permitted to be installed by one of the following methods to disconnect a motor circuit:

- The disconnecting means shall be located adjacent to the controller within sight and located within 50 ft (15 m). The same rule shall be applied for the motor.

- The disconnecting means shall be capable of being locked in the open position if located adjacent to the controller. Under this rule, the motor shall not be required to be located within sight.

- An additional disconnecting means shall be provided within 50 ft (15 m) of the motor and within sight if the disconnecting means by the controller cannot be locked in the open position and the motor is located out of sight. **(See Figure 14-32)**

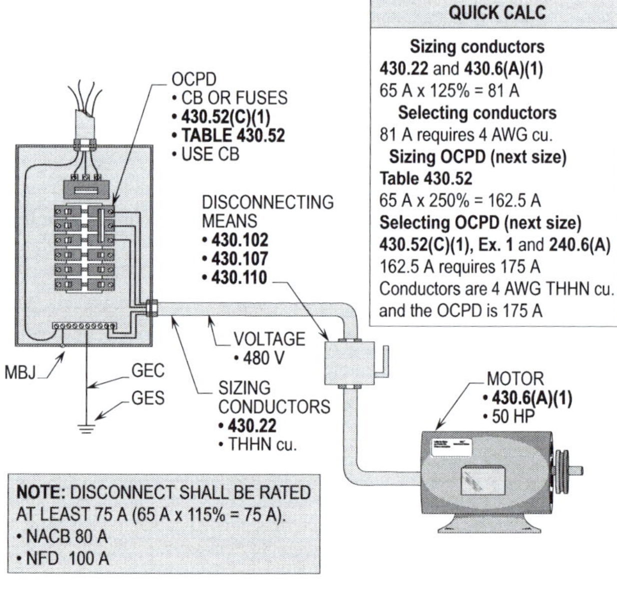

DISCONNECTING MEANS
NEC 430.102
NEC 430.107

Figure 14-32. A disconnecting means shall be located within sight from the controller and shall disconnect the controller (controller not sown) to allow personnel to service the motor without the danger of the branch circuit accidentally being energized. Also, see **Figures 18-1, 18-2,** and **18-24(a) through (d)**.

WELDER LOADS
ARTICLE 630, PARTS II AND III

There are three types of welders used in modern-day welding shops. The type used determines how the circuit elements shall be designed.

The procedure for calculating the full-load amps for welders is to obtain the duty-cycle factor and select the multiplier. The primary amps of the welder shall be multiplied by the multiplier to derive full-load amps to size the elements of the branch circuit. The following are the three types of welders that shall be permitted to be used:

- AC/DC arc welders
- Motor-generator arc welders
- Resistance welders

AC/DC ARC WELDERS
ARTICLE 630, PART III

Arc welders are used to perform welding operations through the medium of an arc drawn between the weld and a metal rod. The metal from the rod (electrode) is added to the weld, making the weld substantially strong.

CONDUCTORS
630.11(A)

When sizing the branch-circuit conductors for AC/DC arc welders, the current-carrying capacity shall not be permitted to be less than the primary current of the welder times a duty cycle factor listed in **Table 630.11(A)**.

For example: What size THWN copper conductors are required to supply an AC transformer and DC rectifier arc welder rated at 68 amps with a 50 percent duty cycle?

Step 1: Finding FLC
630.11(A)
Welder = 68 A

Step 2: Finding multiplier
630.11(A)
50% = .71

Step 3: Calculating amps
630.11(A)
68 A x 71% = 48.28 A

Step 4: Selecting conductors
Table 310.15(B)(16)
48.28 A requires 8 AWG cu.

Solution: The size THWN copper conductors are 8 AWG.

OVERCURRENT PROTECTION
630.12(A)

The welder's primary full-load current rating listed on the nameplate shall be selected at not more than 200 percent for sizing the overcurrent protection device. Branch circuit conductors shall be protected at a rating not exceeding 200 percent of their allowable ampacities per **630.12(B)**. **(See Figure 14-33)**

For example: What size overcurrent protection device is required for the conductors supplying an AC transformer and DC rectifier arc welder rated at 68 amps with a 50 percent duty cycle?

Step 1:	Finding FLC **630.12(A), 630.12(B),** and **Table 310.15(B)(16)** Welder = 68 A x 71% = 48 A Conductors = 50 A
Step 2:	Finding multiplier **630.12(A)** and **630.12(B)** Multiplier = 200%
Step 3:	Calculating amps **630.12(A)** and **630.12(B)** 68 A x 200% = 136 A
Step 4:	Selecting OCPD **240.4(G), 240.6(A),** and **630.12** 136 A requires 125 A
Step 5:	Protecting conductors **630.12(B)** 8 AWG THWN cu. = 50 A 50 A x 200% = 100 A 100 A requires 100 A

Solution: The size overcurrent protection device required is 100 amps based on the amps of conductors times 200 percent. The overcurrent protection device at the welder is 125 amps.

MOTOR-GENERATOR ARC WELDERS
ARTICLE 630, PART II

The arc welding principles are used to perform work for motor-generator arc welders. Two metal parts are welded together by a main electrode used to strike an arc that melts the electrode and supplies the metal necessary to join the metal parts together.

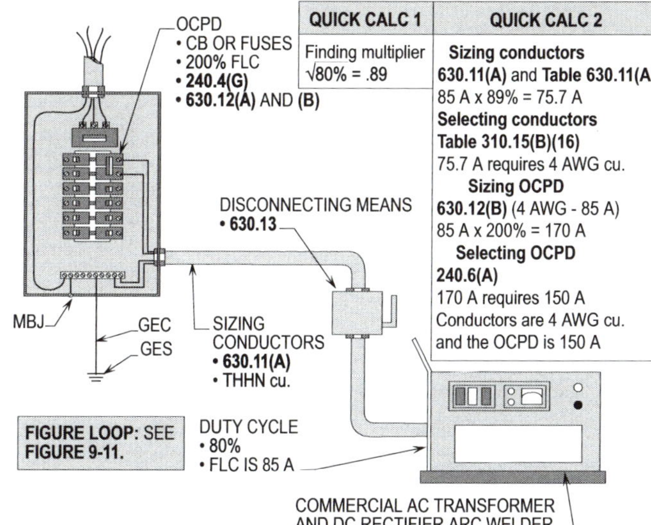

Figure 14-33. The welder's primary full-load current rating listed on the nameplate shall be selected at not more than 200 percent for the overcurrent protection device to be installed. Branch-circuit conductors shall be protected at a rating not exceeding 200 percent of their allowable ampacities.

CONDUCTORS
630.11(A)

When sizing the branch-circuit conductors for motor-generator arc welders, the current-carrying capacity shall not be permitted to be less than the rated primary current of the welder times a duty cycle factor listed in **Table 630.11(A)**.

For example: What size THWN copper conductors are required to supply a motor-generator arc welder rated at 76 amps having a 90 percent duty cycle?

Step 1:	Finding FLC **630.11(A)** Welder = 76 A
Step 2:	Finding multiplier **630.11(A)** 90% = .96
Step 3:	Calculating amps **630.11(A)** 76 A x 96% = 72.96 A
Step 4:	Selecting conductors **Table 310.15(B)(16)** 72.96 A requires 4 AWG cu.

Solution: The size THWN copper conductors are 4 AWG.

OVERCURRENT PROTECTION
630.12(A)

The welder's primary full-load current rating listed on the nameplate shall be selected at not more than 200 percent for sizing the overcurrent protection device. Branch circuit conductors shall be protected at a rating not exceeding 200 percent of their allowable ampacities per **630.12(B)**. **(See Figure 14-34)**

For example: What size overcurrent protection device is required for the conductors to supply a motor-generator arc welder rated at 76 amps having a 90 percent duty cycle?

Step 1: Finding FLC
630.12(A), 630.12(B), and
Table 310.15(B)(16)
Welder = 76 A x 96% = 73 A
Conductors = 85 A (4 AWG cu.)

Step 2: Finding multiplier
630.12(A) and **630.12(B)**
Multiplier = 200%

Step 3: Calculating amps
630.12(A) and **630.12(B)**
76 A x 200% = 152 A

Step 4: Selecting OCPD for welder
240.4(G), 240.6(A), and **630.12(A)**
152 A requires 150 A

Step 5: Selecting OCPD for conductors
630.12(B)
85 A x 200% = 170 A

Solution: The size overcurrent protection device required for the conductors is 150 amps.

RESISTANCE WELDERS
ARTICLE 630, PART III

Resistance welders use a heavy current that flows through the small area of material in contact with such material at a particular time. This type of welding is accomplished by pressing two metal parts together as they reach the molten state. Resistance welders do not add metal to the weld. Resistance welders may have high inrush current while welding together certain materials.

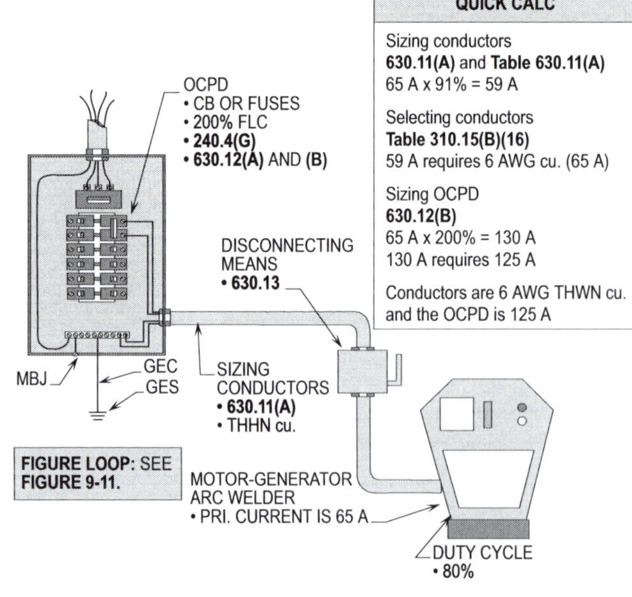

Figure 14-34. The welder's primary full-load current rating listed on the nameplate shall be selected at not more than 200 percent for the overcurrent protection device. Branch-circuit conductors shall be protected at a rating not exceeding 200 percent of their allowable ampacities.

CONDUCTORS
630.31(A)

When sizing the branch-circuit conductors for resistance welders, the current-carrying capacity shall not be permitted to be less than the primary current of the welder times a duty cycle factor listed in **Table 630.31(A)(2)**.

For example: What size THWN copper conductors are required to supply a resistance welder rated at 91 amps having a 40 percent duty cycle?

Step 1: Finding FLC
630.31(A)
Welder = 91 A

Step 2: Finding multiplier
630.31(A)
40% = .63

Step 3: Calculating amps
630.31(A)
91 A x 63% = 57.33 A

Step 4: Selecting conductors
Table 310.15(B)(16)
57.33 A requires 6 AWG cu.

Solution: The size THWN copper conductors are 6 AWG.

OVERCURRENT PROTECTION
630.32(A)

The welder's primary full-load current rating listed on the nameplate shall be selected at not more than 300 percent for sizing the overcurrent protection device. Branch-circuit conductors protected at a rating not exceeding this value shall be considered protected from overloading per **630.32(B)**. **(See Figure 14-35)**

> **For example:** What size overcurrent protection device is required for the conductors supplying power to a resistance welder rated at 91 amps having a 40 percent duty cycle?

Step 1:	Finding FLC **630.32(A)** Welder = 91 A
Step 2:	Finding multiplier **630.32(A)** Multiplier = 300%
Step 3:	Calculating amps **630.32(A)** 91 A x 300% = 273 A
Step 4:	Selecting OCPD **240.4(G), 240.6(A),** and **630.12** 273 A requires 250 A
Step 5:	Protecting conductors **630.32(B)** 6 AWG THWN cu. = 65 A 65 A x 300% = 195 A 195 A requires 175 A
Solution:	**The size overcurrent protection device required to protect the conductors is 175 amps. The size overcurrent protection device for the welder is 250 amps.**

or larger shall be identified by polarity at all termination, connection, and splice points by marking tape, tagging, or other approved means; each ungrounded conductor of 6 AWG or smaller shall be identified by polarity at all termination, connection, and splice points in compliance with **210.5(C)(2)(a)** and **(b)**.

The identification methods utilized for conductors originating within each branch-circuit panelboard or similar branch-circuit distribution equipment shall be documented in a manner that is readily available or shall be permanently posted at each branch-circuit panelboard or similar branch-circuit distribution equipment. **(See Figure 14-36)**

Note, for feeders, see **Figures 16-15 thru 16-17** in Ch.16 of this book.

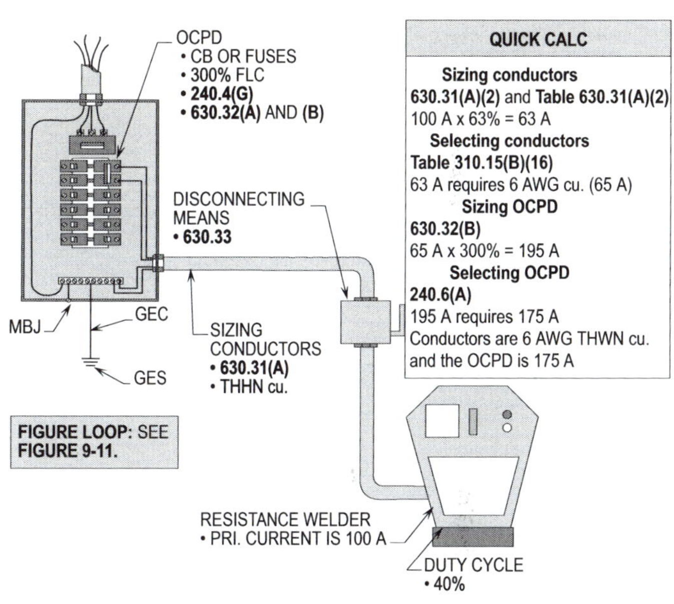

Figure 14-35. The welder's primary full-load current rating listed on the nameplate shall be selected at not more than 300 percent for sizing the overcurrent protection device. Branch-circuit conductors protected at a rating not exceeding this value shall be considered protected from overloading.

BRANCH CIRCUITS SUPPLIED FROM DIRECT CURRENT SYSTEMS
210.5(C)(2)

Ungrounded conductors shall be identified in accordance with **210.5(C)(1)** or **(2)** as applicable.

Where a branch circuit is supplied from a dc system operating at more than 50 volts, each ungrounded conductor of 4 AWG

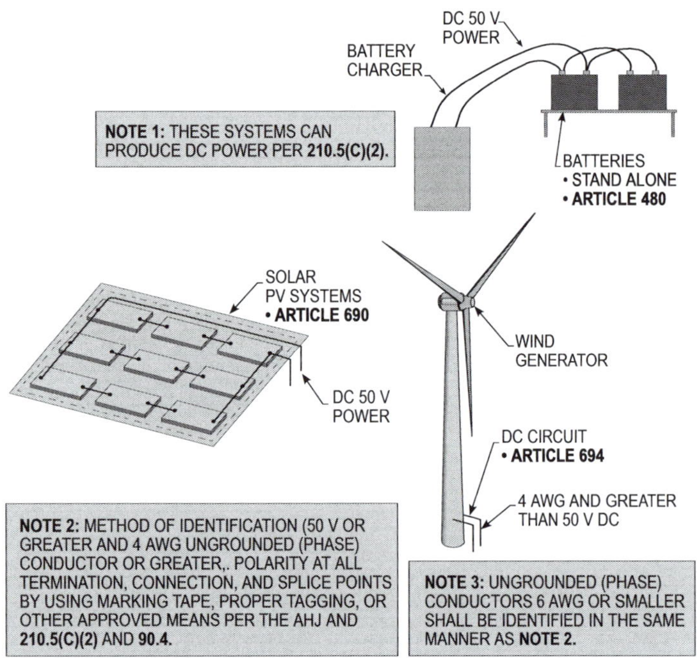

Figure 14-36. This illustration shows the requirements for branch circuits supplied from direct current systems.

POSITIVE POLARITY, SIZES 6 AWG OR SMALLER
210.5(C)(2)(a)

Where the positive polarity of a dc system does not serve as the connection point for the grounded conductor, each positive ungrounded conductor shall be identified by one of the following means:
(1) A continuous red outer finish.

(2) A continuous red stripe durably marked along the conductor's entire length on insulation of a color other than green, white, gray, or black.

(3) Imprinted plus signs (+) or the word POSITIVE or POS durably marked on insulation of a color other than green, white, gray, or black, and repeated at intervals not exceeding 610 mm (24 in.) in accordance with **310.120(B)**.
(See Figure 14-37)

NEGATIVE POLARITY, SIZES 6 AWG OR SMALLER
210.5(C)(2)(b)

Where the negative polarity of a dc system does not serve as the connection point for the grounded conductor, each negative ungrounded conductor shall be identified by one of the following means:

(1) A continuous black outer finish.

(2) A continuous black stripe durably marked along the conductor's entire length on insulation of a color other than green, white, gray, or red.

(3) Imprinted minus signs (–) or the word NEGATIVE or NEG durably marked on insulation of a color other than green, white, gray, or red, and repeated at intervals not exceeding 610 mm (24 in.) in accordance with **310.120(B).**
(See Figure 14-38)

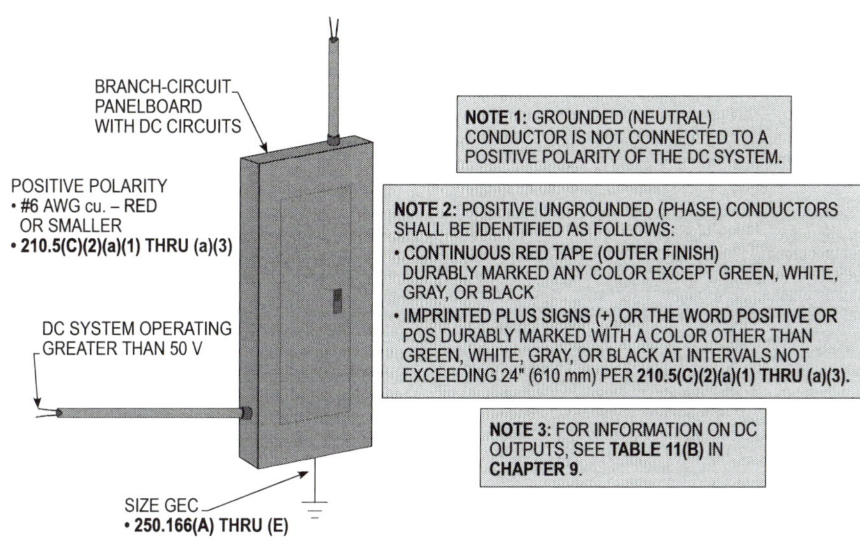

Figure 14-37. This illustration shows the requirements for branch circuits from direct current systems with positive polarity of conductors 6 AWG or smaller.

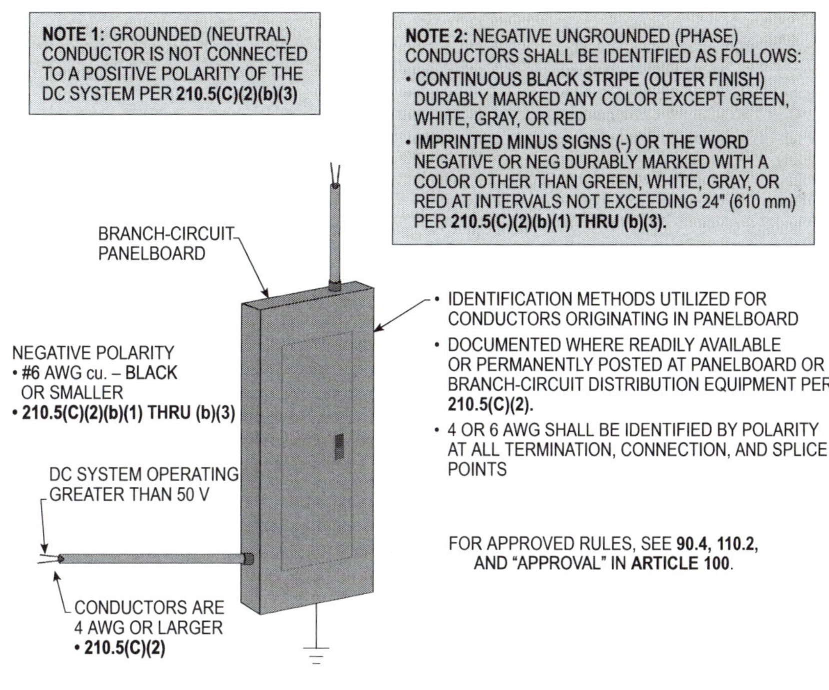

Figure 14-38. This illustration shows the requirements for branch circuits from direct current systems with negative polarity of conductors 6 AWG or smaller.

Chapter 14. Branch Circuits

Section   Answer

1. A minimum of 2-20 amp, _______ VA small appliance circuits are required to supply receptacle outlets that are located in the kitchen, pantry, breakfast room, and dining room.
   (a) 1000
   (b) 1200
   (c) 1500
   (d) 1800

2. At least 1-20 amp, _______ VA laundry circuit is required to supply receptacle outlets in the laundry room.
   (a) 1000
   (b) 1500
   (c) 1800
   (d) 2400

3. A tap to connect a cooktop and ovens can be made from a _______ amp branch circuit when the tap conductors are sized from the kW rating of each piece of cooking equipment per **Note 4** to **Table 220.55**.
   (a) 30
   (b) 40
   (c) 50
   (d) 60

4. Dryer equipment loads shall be at least _______ VA or the nameplate rating, whichever is larger, when selecting a VA for the branch circuit load.
   (a) 1500
   (b) 3000
   (c) 4500
   (d) 5000

5. A _______ amp branch circuit shall be permitted to be installed to supply fixed lighting units with heavy-duty lampholders in other than a dwelling unit(s) or utilization equipment in any occupancy.
   (a) 30
   (b) 40
   (c) 50
   (d) 60

6. Continuous lighting loads in commercial buildings shall be calculated at _______ percent of the total VA or amperage rating of the branch circuit.
   (a) 80
   (b) 100
   (c) 110
   (d) 125

7. Show window lighting loads shall be calculated at a minimum of _______ VA per outlet for branch circuits if the VA is unknown.
   (a) 180
   (b) 200
   (c) 250
   (d) 300

8. When installing four or fewer dryers, the load shall be calculated at _______ percent.
   (a) 100
   (b) 110
   (c) 115
   (d) 125

9. A fastened-in-place appliance shall be permitted to be connected to a general purpose circuit if its amp rating does not exceed _______ percent of the branch circuit.
   (a) 50
   (b) 60
   (c) 75
   (d) 80

Section   **Answer**

10. Overcurrent protection devices rated over _______ amps are allowed to be terminated with conductors larger than 1 AWG with 75°C ampacities.

(a) 50   (b) 60
(c) 75   (d) 100

11. General purpose circuits shall be calculated at _______ VA per sq. ft based on the square footage of the dwelling unit.

(a) 2   (b) 3
(c) 3.5   (d) 4

12. The rating of any one cord-and-plug connected utilization equipment shall not exceed _______ percent of the branch circuit rating if connected to a general purpose circuit supplying two or more outlets.

(a) 50   (b) 75
(c) 80   (d) 100

13. Branch circuits larger than _______ amps shall supply only nonlighting outlet loads.

(a) 20   (b) 30
(c) 40   (d) 50

14. Cord-and-plug connected or permanently (hard-wired) connected receptacles rated over _______ VA are usually supplied by individual circuits.

(a) 1440   (b) 1660
(c) 2250   (d) 2440

15. Lighting track loads, other than dwelling units, shall be calculated at _______ VA for each 2 ft of track to determine the load for branch circuits.

(a) 150   (b) 180
(c) 200   (d) 220

16. How many 15 amp circuits are allowed to supply power to the general purpose lighting and receptacle outlets in a 3000 sq. ft dwelling unit?

17. What is the demand load in VA for a branch circuit serving a 9 kW range?

18. What is the demand load in VA for a branch circuit serving 2-3 kW cooktops?

19. What is the demand load in VA for a branch circuit serving a 8.5 kW oven?

20. What is the demand load in VA for a branch circuit serving a 18 kW range?

21. What is the demand load in VA for a service or feeder serving a 10 kW, 18 kW, and 20 kW range?

22. What is the demand load in VA for a branch circuit serving a 9 kW cooktop, 8 kW, and 14 kW oven?

23. What size nonmetallic-sheathed cable tap is required for a 12 kW cooktop?

Section   **Answer**

24. What is the demand load in VA for a branch circuit serving a 4500 VA dryer?

25. What is the demand load in VA for a branch circuit serving a 6500 VA dryer?

26. What is the total VA rating for a 15 amp, 120 volt, two-wire branch circuit supplying a continuous load?

27. What is the total VA rating for a 15 amp, 240 volt, two-wire branch circuit supplying a continuous load?

28. What is the load in amps for a 24 amp dishwasher used at continuous duty?

29. What is the load in amps for a 32 amp water heater used at continuous operation in a commercial building?

30. What size amperage rating is allowed for a 2 AWG copper conductor using the ampacities of the 60°C column and 75°C column?

31. What is the allowable ampacity for 8-10 AWG THHN copper conductors that are all current-carrying?

32. What is the allowable ampacity for 3-10 AWG THHN copper conductors that are in an ambient temperature of 105°F?

33. What is the allowable ampacity for 6-10 AWG THHN copper conductors that are all current-carrying in an ambient temperature of 105°F?

34. What is the amperage rating of an 2800 VA calculated load connected to a 120 volt, single-phase branch circuit?

35. What is the amperage rating of an 9250 VA calculated load connected to a 208 volt, three-phase branch circuit?

36. How many outlets are permitted to be connected to a 20 amp branch circuit used at noncontinuous operation?

37. How many outlets are permitted to be connected to a 20 amp branch circuit used at continuous operation?

38. What size overcurrent protection device is allowed to serve a continuous operated load of 13.5 amps and noncontinuous load of 3 amps in an ambient temperature of 155°F?

39. What is the lighting load in amps for a branch circuit supplying 10-1.5 amp ballasts that serve 24-F25, CW lamps used at continuous operation?

40. What size overcurrent protection device and THHN copper conductors are required for 12 outlets used at noncontinuous operation to supply luminaires used at 120 volts?

41. What size overcurrent protection device and THHN copper conductors are required for 10 outlets used at continuous operation to supply luminaires?

Section   **Answer**

42. How many outlets are permitted to be installed on a 20 amp branch circuit supplying lighting loads in a show window?

43. What is the lighting load in VA for 70 ft of show window? (Lighting is used at continuous duty but not required by manufacturer.)

44. What is the show window lighting load in VA for 70 medium-base lamps? (Lamps are used at continuous duty per the manufacturer.)

45. What is the VA rating for 25 ft of lighting track? (Lighting is used at noncontinuous duty.)

46. The positive polarity for a DC system can be identified as ______ in color.
(a) black   (b) white
(c) green   (d) none of the above

47. The negative polarity for a DC system can be identified as ______ in color.
(a) white   (b) gray
(c) black   (d) red

48. Solar (PV) systems can be utilized as ______ or ______ systems.
(a) AC   (b) DC
(c) all of the above   (d) none of the above

49. DC systems can be marked and identified by using ______.
(a) marking tape   (b) proper tagging
(c) all of the above   (d) none of the above

50. Table ______ covers requirements in VA per ft. when an occupancy is considered a listed occupancy.
(a) 250.66   (b) 250.122
(c) 250.102(C)(1)   (d) 220.12

15

Feeders

Feeders are all circuit conductors between the service equipment, the source of a separately derived system or other power supply source, and the final overcurrent protection devices protecting the branch-circuit conductors and equipment. Feeders may be installed to supply subpanels in dwelling units, apartments, and commercial and industrial occupancies. Feeders may also be installed in commercial and industrial occupancies and routed through the plant, where taps are sometimes made to these conductors and connected to supply panelboards, disconnect switches, control centers, and other types of electrical equipment.

LOADS
ARTICLE 220, PART III

The rules and regulations of **Article 220, Part III** shall be used to size and select the feeder conductors, overcurrent protection devices, and other pertinent elements. Demand factors shall be permitted to be applied to loads that are grouped, and percentages shall be permitted to be applied that will reduce the load. These percentages shall be based on how the equipment is used in the electrical system.

VOLTAGES
220.5(A)

The ampacity of electrical components for feeders shall be determined by the voltage ratings listed in **220.5(A)**. Unless another voltage is specified, the following voltage ratings shall be used to calculate feeder loads:

- 120 volt
- 120/240 volt
- 208 Y/120 volt
- 240 volt
- 347 volt
- 480 Y/277 volt
- 480 volt
- 600 Y/347 volt
- 600 volt

UNGROUNDED (PHASE) CONDUCTORS
215.2(A)(1)(a) AND (b) AND 215.3

Ungrounded (phase) conductors that are used in feeders shall be sized and selected based on the total amps or the total VA divided by the voltage of the circuit. The total amps or VA of the feeder loads shall be calculated at continuous or noncontinuous operation or a combination of both. Also, loads with demand factors shall be calculated at percentages less than those used for continuous or noncontinuous loads, and such percentages shall be derived for how the loads are used on the feeder. The smallest size feeder shall not be less than 30 amps per **215.2(A)(3)**. To comply with this minimum rating, 10 AWG copper or 8 AWG aluminum conductors shall be used, per asterisk below **Table 310.15(B)(16)** and **240.4(D)**.

Ungrounded (phase) conductors shall be considered current-carrying conductors for derating purposes when applying adjustment or correction factors per **310.15(B)(3) (a)** and **Table 310.15(B)(16)**.

CALCULATING AMPS

If the VA is known, amps may be found by dividing the VA by the configuration of voltage for the feeder.

For example: What is the ampacity for a feeder load of 18,400 VA that is supplied by a 120/240 volt, single-phase system?

Step 1: Finding amperage
$I = VA \div A$
$I = 18,400 \text{ VA} \div 240 \text{ V}$
$I = 77 \text{ A}$

Solution: **The feeder ampacity is 77 amps.**

For example: What is the ampacity for a feeder load of 18,400 VA supplied by a 120/208 volt, three-phase, four-wire system?

Step 1: Finding amperage
$I = VA \div (V \times 1.732)$
$I = 18,400 \text{ VA} \div 360 \text{ V}$
$I = 51.1 \text{ A}$

Solution: **The feeder ampacity is 51 amps. Note, the .1 amp is dropped per 220.5(B).**

The feeder components shall be selected from the 51 amps per phase. The 51 amps per phase shall be connected to Phase A, Phase B, and Phase C. This calculation shall be verified by dividing the VA by the voltage per phase and dividing the total by 3.

For example: What is the ampacity for a feeder load of 18,400 VA supplied by a 120/208 volt, three-phase system?

Step 1: Finding amperage
$I = VA \div V$
$I = 18,400 \text{ VA} \div 120 \text{ V}$
$I = 153.3$
$I = 153.3 \text{ A} \div 3$
$I = 51 \text{ A}$

Solution: **The feeder ampacity is 51 amps.**

See Figure 15-1 for calculating amps based on volt-amps and voltage.

POWER FACTOR

Power factor (PF) is the ratio of actual power used in a circuit to the apparent power drawn from the line. Actual power is the true power used to produce heat or work. Actual power is also known in the industry as real, true, or useful power.

Terms:
- Power factor   = PF
- Watts   = W
- Volts   = V
- Amps   = I

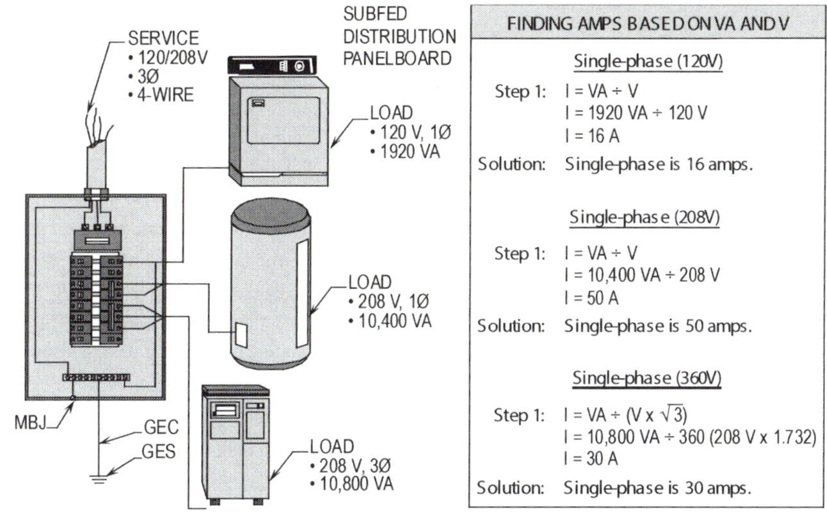

Figure 15-1. Finding the amps of a feeder based on volt-amps and voltage.

ACTUAL POWER – SINGLE-PHASE

The actual power in watts in a pure resistance circuit shall be found by multiplying volts times amps.

> **For example:** A 240 volt, single-phase feeder with a 51 amp load has a load of 12,240 watts.
>
> **Step 1:** $W = V \times I$
> $W = 240\ V \times 51\ A$
> $W = 12{,}240$
>
> **Solution: Actual power equals 12,240 watts.**

If the circuit above has a poor power factor of 75 percent because of inductive loads, the load in amps shall be calculated as follows:

> **For example:** A 240 volt, single-phase feeder of 51 amps having a power factor of 75 percent has a load of 9180 watts.
>
> **Step 1:** $W = V \times I \times PF$
> $W = 240\ V \times 51\ A \times 75\%$
> $W = 9180$
>
> **Solution: Actual power equals 9180 watts.**

ACTUAL POWER – THREE-PHASE

The actual power in watts in a three-phase circuit with inductive loads shall be found by multiplying $V \times \sqrt{3} \times I \times PF$.

> **For example:** The actual power in watts for a three-phase circuit with a load of 51 amps that is supplied by a 208 volt circuit with a power factor of 75 percent is 13,770 watts. (Using 360 V)
>
> **Step 1:** $W = (V \times \sqrt{3}) \times I \times PF$
> $W = (208\ V \times 1.732) \times 51\ A \times 75\%$
> $W = 13{,}770$
>
> **Solution: Actual power equals 13,770 watts.**

Note, the actual power is 18,360 watts (208 V x 1.732 x 51 A = 18,360 W) if the power factor is 100 percent instead of 75 percent.

See Figure 15-2 for calculating amps for a feeder having poor power factor.

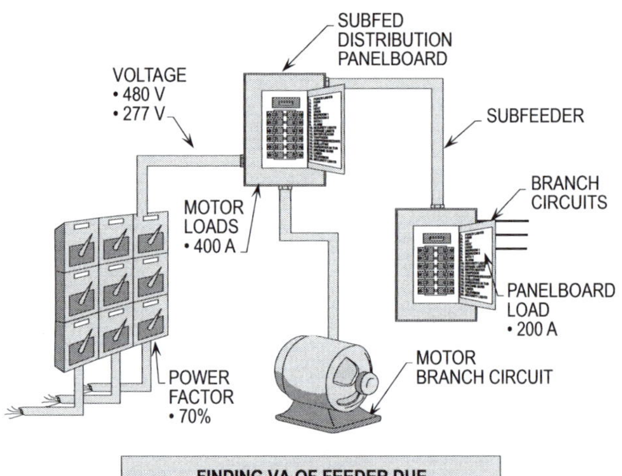

Figure 15-2. Calculating amps for a feeder based on poor power factor.

NONCONTINUOUSLY OPERATED LOADS
215.2(A)(1)(a) AND 215.3

Noncontinuously operated loads shall be calculated at 100 percent or where appropriate demand factors shall be permitted to be applied to specific loads. Based on their condition of use, the total VA rating for such loads may be derived. Noncontinuous loads are classified as loads that operate for a period of time less than three hours per **Article 100**. Portable or fixed cord-and-plug connected or permanently connected loads may be classified as noncontinuous loads.

For example: What is the VA rating for a connected load of 34,500 VA to size the elements of the feeder at noncontinuous operation?

Step 1:   Finding VA
             215.2(A)(1)(a) and **215.3**
             VA = VA x 100%
             VA = 34,500 VA x 100%
             VA = 34,500

Solution: The total VA for the feeder is 34,500 VA.

CONTINUOUSLY OPERATED LOADS
215.2(A)(1)(a) AND 215.3

Continuously operated loads are classified as loads that are operate for a period of three hours or more. Continuous loads do not operate at varying or intermittent operation. A continuously operated load shall be supplied continuously for a period of three hours or more without the circuit being interrupted. An industrial processing machine used in a facility to perform a work task for a work day of eight hours falls under such use and classification.

The total VA rating for sizing conductors to such a machine shall be obtained by multiplying the continuous load by 125 percent. Feeder conductors shall be increased in size due to voltage drop, ambient temperature, or too many current-carrying conductors in a raceway or cable.

For example: What is the VA rating for a continuously operated processing machine with a connected load of 34,500 VA ?

Step 1:   Finding VA
             215.2(A)(1)(a) and **215.3**
             VA = VA x 125%
             VA = 34,500 VA x 125%
             VA = 43,125 VA

Solution: The total VA for the feeder is 43,125 VA.

See Figure 15-3 for calculating the load in amps based upon continuous or noncontinuous operation.

DEMAND FACTORS
ARTICLE 220, PART II

Demand factors shall be permitted to be applied to the VA rating for specific loads, depending on their conditions of use. The percentages for which demand factors shall be permitted to be applied are listed in the NEC. Feeders supplying loads under a specific condition of use shall be permitted to be reduced by applying demand factors to obtain the total rating. Loads that shall be permitted to be reduced by applying a demand factor are as follows:

Types of loads having demand factor per the NEC:

- Lighting — **Table 220.42**
- Receptacles — **Table 220.44** and **220.14(I)**

- Dryers   **- Table 220.54**
- Ranges   **- Table 220.55**
- Kitchen equipment   **- Table 220.56**
- Dwelling units   **- 220.82(B)** and **(C)**
- Existing dwelling units   **- 220.83**
- Multifamily dwelling units   **- Table 220.84**
- Schools   **- Table 220.86**
- Existing loads   **- 220.87**
- Restaurants   **- Table 220.88**
- Farms   **- Table 220.102** and **Table 220.103**

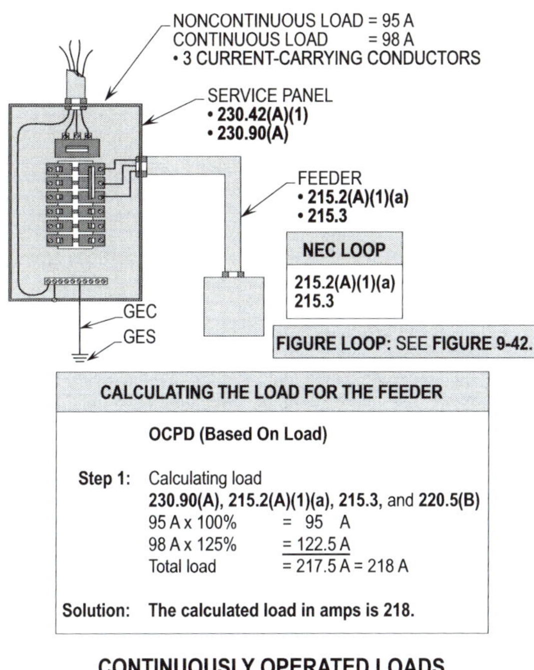

Figure 15-3. Calculating the load in amps for a feeder based on continuous and noncontinuous operation.

APPLYING DEMAND FACTORS FOR RECEPTACLE LOADS
220.44, TABLE 220.44, AND TABLE 220.42

The VA rating for receptacle loads shall be calculated at 100 percent for the first 10,000 VA, and the remaining VA shall be calculated at 50 percent per **Table 220.44**. **Table 220.44** shall only be permitted to be applied to receptacles that are used at noncontinuous operation. The demand factors of **Table 220.42** shall be permitted to be used to determine the load for receptacle outlets that are figured at 180 VA and then added to the lighting load.

For example: What is the load for a number of general-purpose receptacles used at noncontinuous operation that are utilized to supply a connected load of 24,800 VA?

Step 1:	Finding VA
	Table 220.44
	First 10,000 VA at 100%
	10,000 VA x 100% = 10,000 VA
	Remaining VA at 50%
	14,800 x 50% = 7,400 VA
	Total load = 17,400 VA

Solution: The total VA load is 17,400 VA.

See Figure 15-4 for calculating the load in amps for a feeder with loads having demand factors.

GROUNDED (NEUTRAL) CONDUCTOR ARTICLE 220, PART III AND ARTICLE 310

The grounded (neutral) conductor shall be intentionally grounded at the service equipment. The grounded (neutral) conductor shall be sized to carry the maximum unbalanced current. The largest load between the grounded (neutral) conductor and any one ungrounded (phase) conductor is the maximum unbalanced current that shall be carried. A demand factor shall be permitted to be applied to the grounded (neutral) conductor, under specific conditions of use.

SIZING
220.61(A) THRU (C)

The feeder grounded (neutral) conductor load shall be the maximum unbalanced load connected between the grounded (neutral) conductor and any one ungrounded (phase) conductor. The first 200 amps of neutral current shall be calculated at 100 percent. All resistive loads on the grounded (neutral) conductor exceeding 200 amps shall be permitted to have a demand factor of 70 percent applied, and this value added to the first 200 amps taken at 100 percent. All inductive neutral current shall be calculated at 100 percent with no demand factor applied. The feeder grounded (neutral) conductor load shall be 70 percent of the demand load for cooking equipment or dryer loads that, for example, are installed in dwelling units. **(See Figure 15-5)**

The neutral current in amps for a three-wire, two-phase or five-wire, two-phase system shall be multiplied by 140 percent, which is derived by taking the square root of 2.

By multiplying the grounded (neutral) conductor amps by 140 percent ($\sqrt{2}$ = 141%), the unbalanced current in the grounded (neutral) conductor will be collected from all ungrounded (phase) conductors. The grounded (neutral) conductor shall be multiplied by 140 percent instead of 141 percent (rounded down), based on the ungrounded (phase) conductor with the highest ampacity per **220.61(A), Ex**. Basically, if calculated using this procedure, the grounded (neutral) conductors are not overloaded because 120 volt loads are switched in and out on the circuits at different intervals of time.

For example: What is the grounded (neutral) conductor load for a five-wire, two-phase feeder with each phase rated at 150 amps?

Step 1: Finding amperage
220.61(A), Ex.
150 A x 140% = 210 A

Solution: The grounded (neutral) conductor load is 210 amps.

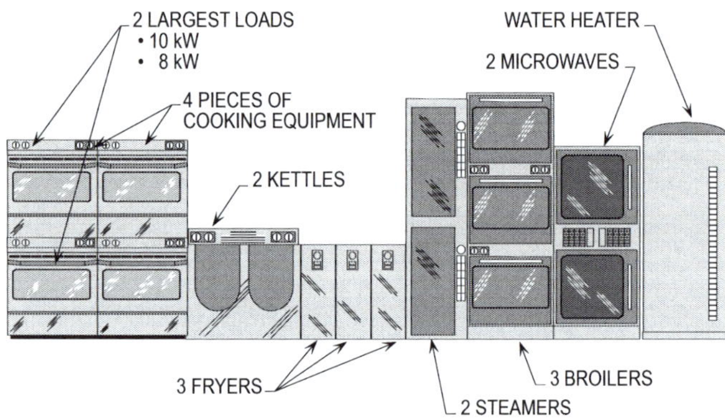

What is the demand load for the 82 kW cooking equipment load?

Finding demand load

Step 1: Calculating percentage
Table 220.56
17 pieces allows 65%

Step 2: Applying demand factors
Table 220.56 and 220.56
82 kW x 65% = 53.3 kW

Solution: The demand load is 53.3 kV.

Note: 53.3 kW is greater than the two largest loads of 18 kVA.

APPLYING DEMAND FACTORS FOR RECEPTACLE LOADS
NEC 220.56 AND TABLE 220.56

Figure 15-4. Calculating the load in amps for a feeder with 17 pieces of commercial cooking equipment.

For example: What is the neutral load for a feeder with an inductive load of 400 amps?

Step 1: Calculating neutral load
220.61(C) and 310.15(B)(5)(c)
First 200 A x 100%   = 200 A
Remaining 200 A x 100%   = 200 A
Total load   = 400 A

Solution: The total inductive neutral load is 400 amps.

For example: What is the neutral load for a feeder with a resistive load of 400 amps?

Step 1: Calculating neutral load
220.61(B) and 310.15(B)(5)(c)
First 200 A x 100%   = 200 A
Remaining 200 A x 70%   = 140 A
Total load   = 340 A

Solution: The total resistive neutral load is 340 amps.

For example: What is the neutral load for a 9 kW range?

Step 1: Finding demand
Table 220.55, Column C
9 kW = 8 kW

Step 2: Calculating neutral load
220.61(B)
8 kW x 70% = 5.6 kW

Solution: The total neutral range load is 5.6 kW

SIZING
NEC 220.61(A) THRU (C)

Figure 15-5. Calculating the feeder grounded (neutral) conductor load for an inductive, resistive, and range load.

UTILIZING THE GROUNDED (NEUTRAL) CONDUCTOR 310.15(B)(5)

Section **310.15(B)(5)** is divided into three main subdivisions to explain the loading conditions and use of the grounded (neutral) conductors. The following are three subdivisions to be used to derive loading conditions based on use as follows:

• Subdivision (a) – unbalanced current

• Subdivision (b) – common conductor carries

• Subdivision (c) – to determine if current-carrying

Note, when sizing the neutral, see **Sections 220.61; 215.2(A)(1)(a); (A)(1)(b), Ex. 2; 230.42(A)(1), Ex.; 310.15(B)(5)(c);** and **Annex D, Example D3(a).**

SUBDIVISION (a)
310.15(B)(5)(a)

The grounded (neutral) conductor shall not be considered a current-carrying conductor when carrying only the unbalanced current from other ungrounded (phase) conductors. When circuits are properly balanced, the grounded (neutral) conductor carries very little current.

When sizing the load for a two-wire circuit, the grounded (neutral) conductor carries the same amount of current as the ungrounded (phase) conductor. This type of installation has no unbalanced load, therefore the grounded (neutral) conductor carries full current.

For example: What is the grounded (neutral) conductor load for a single-phase, 120 volt, two-wire circuit supplying a load of 14 amps?

Step 1: Finding amperage
220.61 and **310.15(B)(5)(a)**
Ungrounded (phase) conductor = 14 A
Grounded (neutral) conductor = 14 A

Solution: The grounded (neutral) conductor carries a load of 14 amps.

When sizing the load for a three-wire circuit, the grounded (neutral) conductor carries the unbalanced load of the two ungrounded (phase) conductors. This type of installation has an unbalanced load unless both ungrounded (phase) conductors pull the same amount of current on each ungrounded (phase) conductor.

For example: What is the unbalanced grounded (neutral) conductor load for a three-wire circuit carrying 64 amps and 52 amps on the ungrounded (phase) conductors?

Unbalanced condition

Step 1: Finding amperage
220.61 and **310.15(B)(5)(a)**
Ungrounded (phase) conductor
Phase A   =   64 A
Ungrounded (phase) conductor
Phase B   = - 52 A
Total   =   12 A

Balanced condition

Step 1: Finding amperage
220.61 and **310.15(B)(5)(a)**
Ungrounded (phase) conductor
Phase A   =   64 A
Ungrounded (phase) conductor
Phase B   = - 64 A
Total   =   0 A

Solution: The grounded (neutral) conductor load is 12 amps for the unbalanced condition and 0 amps for the balanced condition.

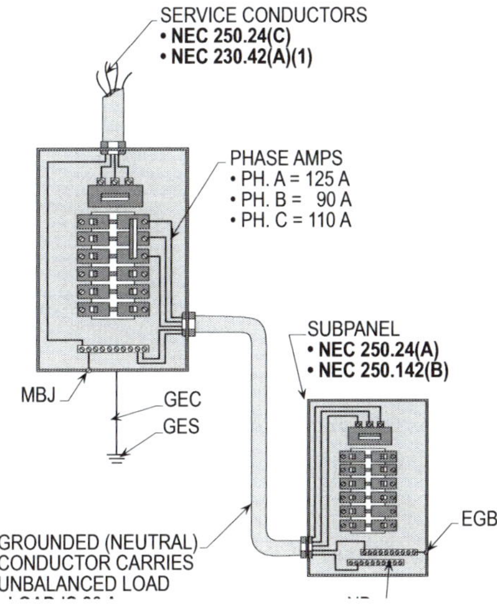

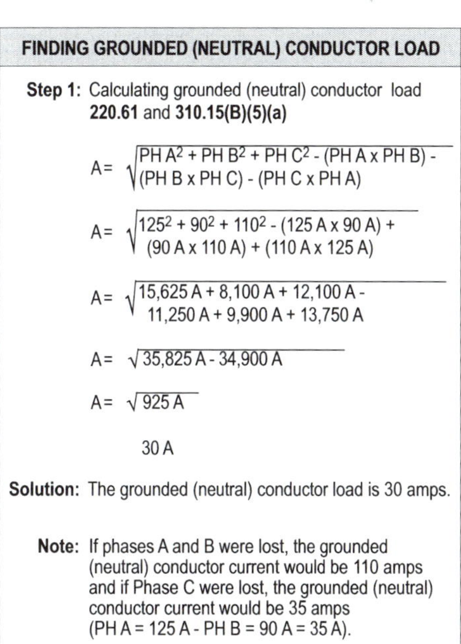

FINDING GROUNDED (NEUTRAL) CONDUCTOR LOAD

Step 1: Calculating grounded (neutral) conductor load
220.61 and **310.15(B)(5)(a)**

$$A = \sqrt{\begin{array}{l} PH\,A^2 + PH\,B^2 + PH\,C^2 - (PH\,A \times PH\,B) - \\ (PH\,B \times PH\,C) - (PH\,C \times PH\,A) \end{array}}$$

$$A = \sqrt{\begin{array}{l} 125^2 + 90^2 + 110^2 - (125\,A \times 90\,A) + \\ (90\,A \times 110\,A) + (110\,A \times 125\,A) \end{array}}$$

$$A = \sqrt{\begin{array}{l} 15{,}625\,A + 8{,}100\,A + 12{,}100\,A - \\ 11{,}250\,A + 9{,}900\,A + 13{,}750\,A \end{array}}$$

$$A = \sqrt{35{,}825\,A - 34{,}900\,A}$$

$$A = \sqrt{925\,A}$$

30 A

Solution: The grounded (neutral) conductor load is 30 amps.

Note: If phases A and B were lost, the grounded (neutral) conductor current would be 110 amps and if Phase C were lost, the grounded (neutral) conductor current would be 35 amps (PH A = 125 A - PH B = 90 A = 35 A).

CALCULATING NEUTRAL CURRENT
FOR THREE-PHASE CIRCUITS

Figure 15-6. Calculating grounded (neutral) conductor current for three-phase circuits.

CALCULATING NEUTRAL CURRENT FOR THREE-PHASE CIRCUITS

A specific formula shall be used to calculate the grounded (neutral) conductor current for three-phase feeders. Where currents on Phases A, B, and C are of different values, the grounded (neutral) conductor current shall be calculated as shown in **Figure 15-6.**

SUBDIVISION (b)
310.15(B)(5)(b)

The grounded (neutral) conductor of a three-wire, 120/208 volt feeder shall be the same size as the ungrounded (phase) conductors for a feeder derived from a four-wire, 120/208 volt system. The reason for this is the grounded (neutral) conductor of a three-wire circuit consisting of two-phase conductors. A three-wire system carries approximately the same amount of current as the ungrounded (phase) conductor. Therefore, a reduction in ampacity is not permitted.

For example: What is the grounded (neutral) conductor load for a 120/208 volt, single-phase circuit taken from a four-wire wye, three-phase system with 190 amps on phase A, 170 amps on phase B, and 90 amps for the neutral?

Step 1: Finding ampacity of neutral
220.61 and **310.15(B)(5)(b)**
Ungrounded (phase) conductor
A = 190 A
Ungrounded (phase) conductor
B = 170 A
Grounded (neutral) conductor
N = 190 A

Solution: The grounded (neutral) conductor load is 190 amps based on the largest ungrounded (phase) conductor.

SUBDIVISION (c)
310.15(B)(5)(c)

The grounded (neutral) conductor for a four-wire, three-phase system supplying nonlinear loads shall be the same size as the ungrounded (phase) conductors. The grounded (neutral) conductor shall be considered a current-carrying conductor due to the harmonic currents generated by these loads.

For example, harmonic loads generated by ballasts are approximately 25 percent per phase in a four-wire wye, three-phase system. Such harmonic currents are collected by the grounded (neutral) conductor from the ungrounded (phase) conductors in a four-wire system because they are all in phase. Because these loads produce third harmonics, harmonic currents present in the grounded (neutral) conductor add up to 75 percent that is derived from 25 percent of such current on each ungrounded (phase) conductor. Under this condition of use, the grounded (neutral) conductor shall not be permitted to be reduced by 70 percent for current from 120 volt loads exceeding 200 amps per **220.61(C)**.

HARMONIC CURRENT
310.15(A)(3), IN (2)

Harmonic currents usually appear in power distribution equipment that supplies nonlinear loads. There are two basic types of nonlinear loads – single-phase and three-phase. Single-phase nonlinear loads are found in offices, while three-phase nonlinear loads are dominant in industrial plants. However, there are other nonlinear loads that present problems to the electrical system because of their harmonic content.

EFFECTS ON NEUTRAL
220.61(C)(2), IN 2

In electrical systems with many single-phase nonlinear loads, the grounded (neutral) conductor current may actually exceed the ungrounded (phase) current. Excessive overheating may occur because there is no overcurrent protection device in the grounded (neutral) conductor to limit the current to a safe value.

In a four-wire system with single-phase nonlinear loads, there are certain odd-numbered harmonics called triplens. These odd multiples of harmonic current are known as the 3rd, 9th, 15th, etc., and they do not cancel but add together in the grounded (neutral) conductor of a wye-connected circuit.

Design Tip: Under normal conditions of use for a balanced linear load, the fundamental 60 Hz portion of the ungrounded (phase) conductor currents will cancel in the grounded (neutral) conductor. Therefore, there is not an excessive heating problem in the grounded (neutral) conductor.

SIZING GROUNDED (NEUTRAL) CONDUCTOR ELEMENTS

Grounded (neutral) conductors, busbars, and connecting lugs shall be sized to carry the full rating of ungrounded (phase) conductor currents. Such elements easily become overloaded due to grounded (neutral) conductors being overloaded with the triplen harmonics.

Design Tip: Triplen harmonics are in addition to the normal grounded (neutral) conductor current.
[See **IN 2** to **220.61(C)(2)**]

DEMAND FACTORS
220.61(B)

A demand factor of 70 percent shall be applied to all grounded (neutral) conductor loads exceeding 200 amps for nonlinear loads. Nonlinear related loads shall be calculated at 100 percent.

For example: What is the load for the grounded (neutral) conductor if it exceeds 200 amps and has more than 50 percent of its load harmonically related? The ungrounded (phase) conductors are carrying a total grounded (neutral) conductor load of 275 amps.

Step 1:   Finding amperage
310.15(B)(5)(c)
Ungrounded (phase) conductors
• 275 amps

Step 2:   Calculating amperage
220.61(C)
First 200 A x 100%   = 200 A
Next 75 A x 100%   = 75 A
Total   = 275 A

Solution: **The grounded (neutral) conductor load is 275 amps.**

The grounded (neutral) conductor shall be considered a current-carrying conductor because of the harmonic currents generated by these loads, and **310.15(B)(3)(a)** shall be applied for four or more current-carrying conductors in a conduit, cable, etc.

For example: What is the grounded (neutral) conductor load for 120 volt loads having harmonic currents of 400 amps per phase?

Step 1:   Finding amperage
310.15(B)(5)(c)
Ungrounded (phase) conductors
• 400 A

Step 2:   Calculating amperage
220.61(C)
400 A x 100% = 400 A

Solution: **The grounded (neutral) conductor load is 400 amps. Note, no reduction of ampacity shall be permitted due to harmonic currents.**

VOLTAGE DROP
ARTICLE 215

Conductors are sometimes increased in size to prevent excessive voltage drop (VD) due to long runs between the overcurrent protection devices and the load served. Due to the long runs of feeder conductors, they shall be increased in size to compensate for poor voltage drop. The voltage drop on the feeder and branch circuit conductors should not exceed 2 to 3 percent at the farthest outlet supplying power to the loads. The voltage drop on the feeder conductors should not exceed 5 percent overall. (For neutrals, see **Figure 9-35.**)

SINGLE-PHASE CIRCUITS
215.2(A)(4), IN 2

The following formula shall be applied when calculating the voltage drop in a two-wire or three-wire, single-phase or three-phase feeder:

Resistive method

• VD = 2 x R x L x I ÷ 1000

Circular-mil method

• VD = 2 x R x L x I ÷ CM

The following values shall be used when calculating the voltage drop:

VD=   voltage drop

R=   resistivity for conductor material
Use **Chapter 9, Table 8, Columns 6** or **8** (uncoated, ohm/MFT), or use 12.9 for copper and 21.2 for aluminum

L =   one-way length of circuit conductor in feet

For example: Using the resistivity method to determine the voltage drop and size elements of a single-phase feeder having the following characteristics:

- VD is held to 3%
- Voltage is 240
- Length is 300 ft
- Load is 180 amps
- OCPD is 200 amps
- Conductors are 3/0 AWG THWN copper

Finding the VD using the resistivity method

Step 1: Selecting percentage
215.2(A)(4), IN 2
Feeder = 3%

Step 2: Calculating VD
215.2(A)(4), IN 2 and **Table 8, Ch. 9**
VD = 2 x R x L x I ÷ 1000
VD = 2 x .0766 x 300 x 180 ÷ 1000
VD = 8.2728

Step 3: Calculating allowable VD
VD = supply V x 3%
VD = 240 V x 3%
VD = 7.2 V

Step 4: Checking percentage
215.2(A)(4), IN 2
% = VD ÷ V
% = 8.2728 ÷ 240
% = .03447 or 3.447

Solution: The voltage drop rating of 8.2728 is greater than 7.2 V and a larger conductor shall be used to reduce the 3.447% to 3% or less.

Lowering VD using larger 4/0 AWG conductor

Step 1: Selecting percentage
215.2(A)(4), IN 2
Feeder = 3%

Step 2: Calculating VD
215.2(A)(4), IN 2 and **Table 8, Ch. 9**
VD = 2 x R x L x I ÷ 1000
VD = 2 x .0608 x 300 x 180 ÷ 1000
VD = 6.5664

Step 3: Checking percentage
215.2(A)(4), IN 2
% = 6.5664 V ÷ 240 V
% = .02736 or 2.736

Solution: The voltage drop rating of 6.5664 volts is less than 7.2 volts, which is well below the 3% limit. The 4/0 AWG conductors are large enough to reduce the voltage drop to 3% or less.

FIGURE LOOP: FOR SIZING GROUNDED (NEUTRAL) CONDUCTOR AND EGC TO CORRECT VD, SEE FIGURES 9-35 AND 15-9.

SINGLE-PHASE CIRCUITS
NEC 215.2(A)(4), IN 2

Figure 15-7(a). Calculating the VD using the resistivity method and using the larger conductor.

For example: Using the CM method to determine the voltage drop and size elements of a single-phase feeder having the following characteristics:

- VD is held to 3%
- Voltage is 240
- Length is 300 ft
- Load is 180 amps
- OCPD is 200 amps
- Conductors are 3/0 AWG THWN copper

Finding the VD using the CM method

Step 1: Selecting percentage
215.2(A)(4), IN 2
Feeder = 3%

Step 2: Calculating VD
215.2(A)(4), IN 2 and **Table 8, Ch. 9**
VD = 2 x R x L x I ÷ CM
VD = 2 x 12.9 x 300 x 180 ÷ 167,800
VD = 8.3027

Step 3: Calculating allowable VD
VD = supply V x 3%
VD = 240 V x 3%
VD = 7.2 V

Step 4: Checking percentage
215.2(A)(4), IN 2
% = VD ÷ V
% = 8.3027 ÷ 240
% = .0345 or 3.45

Solution: The voltage drop rating of 8.3027 is greater than 7.2 V and a larger conductor shall be used to reduce the 3.45% to 3% or less.

Lowering VD using larger 4/0 AWG conductor

Step 1: Selecting percentage
215.2(A)(4), IN 2
Feeder = 3%

Step 2: Calculating VD
215.2(A)(4), IN 2 and **Table 8, Ch. 9**
VD = 2 x R x L x I ÷ 211,600
VD = 2 x 12.9 x 300 x 180 ÷ 211,600
VD = 6.584

Step 3: Checking percentage
215.2(A)(4), IN 2
% = 6.584 V ÷ 240 V
% = .0274 or 2.74

Solution: The voltage drop rating of 6.584 volts is less than 7.2 volts, which is well below the 3% limit. The 4/0 AWG conductors are large enough to reduce the voltage drop to 3% or less.

FIGURE LOOP: FOR SIZING GROUNDED (NEUTRAL) CONDUCTOR AND EGC TO CORRECT VD, SEE FIGURES 9-35 AND 15-9. FOR CALCULATING VD IN 3Ø CIRCUITS, SEE FIGURE 15-8.

SINGLE-PHASE CIRCUITS
NEC 215.2(A)(4), IN 2

Figure 15-7(b). Calculating the VD using the CM method and using the larger conductor.

I   = current in conductor in amperage
CM   = conductor area in circular mils
       See **Chapter 9, Table 8**
1000 = length of conductors based on **Table 8,**
       Chapter 9

Conductors routed at greater lengths will have the resistance of each conductor increased that will oppose the flow of current. By running larger conductors, the diameter of each conductor is increased in size, creating a greater path for the flow of current and less opposition to the movement of electrons that keeps the voltage high at the conductor end.

As listed above, there are two methods that are used by designers and installers to calculate voltage drop in a feeder. One is the resistivity concept, considered the most accurate. The second is the circular mil (CM) method, which has been used for many years. The resistivity method is utilized by selecting the resistivity of the conductors. The CM method consists of selecting the CM rating of the conductors from **Table 8, Ch. 9**. These values, whichever chosen, are inserted into the formula with other data, and the voltage drop is calculated. **[See Figures 15-7(a) and (b)]**

THREE-PHASE CIRCUITS
215.2(A)(4), IN 2

The voltage drop for three-phase circuits shall be calculated by multiplying the voltage drop by .866. The same formula for finding voltage drop in single-phase circuits shall be used to determine the voltage drop in three-phase circuits. Voltage drop multiplied by .866 is found by dividing $\sqrt{3}$ by 2 (1.732 ÷ 2 = .866). The .866 is basically produced from the additional conductor (third conductor), which is derived from a three-phase system instead of a two-phase system. **(See Figure 15-8)**

FINDING THE SIZE EQUIPMENT GROUNDING CONDUCTOR
250.122(B)

Where current-carrying conductors have to be larger to compensate for voltage drop, the equipment grounding conductors shall be adjusted proportionally to the circular-mil area.

> **Design Tip:** If a single equipment grounding conductor is run with multiple circuits in the same raceway, it shall be sized for the largest overcurrent device protecting the conductors in the raceway or cable.

See Figure 15-9 for a detailed procedure for calculating and selecting the size equipment grounding conductor to be installed.

For example: Using the resistivity method to determine the voltage drop and size elements of a three-phase feeder having the following characteristics:

- VD is held to 3%
- Voltage is 480/277
- Length is 700 ft.
- Load is 180 amps
- OCPD is 200 amps
- Conductors are 4/0 AWG THWN copper

Finding the VD using the resistivity method

Step 1: Selecting percentage
215.2(A)(4), IN 2
Feeder = 3%

Step 2: Calculating VD
215.2(A)(4), IN 2 and **Table 8, Ch. 9**
VD = 2 x R x L x I ÷ 1000
VD = 2 x .0608 x 700 x 180 ÷ 1000
VD = 15.3216

Step 3: Applying .866 for three-phase
VD = VD x .866
VD = 15.3216 x .866
VD = 13.269

Step 4: Calculating allowable VD
VD = supply V x 3%
VD = 480 V x 3%
VD = 14.4 V

Step 5: Checking percentage
215.2(A)(4), IN 2
% = VD ÷ V
% = 13.269 ÷ 480
% = .0276 or 2.76

Solution: The voltage drop rating of 13.269 is less than 14.4 V; therefore the 4/0 AWG THWN copper shall be used.

**THREE-PHASE CIRCUITS
NEC 215.2(A)(4), IN 2**

Figure 15-8. Calculating the VD using the resistivity method for a three-phase feeder.

FINDING THE SIZE GROUNDED (NEUTRAL) CONDUCTOR
240.23

Where a change in the size of the ungrounded (phase) conductors occurs due to voltage drop, a similar change may have to be made in the size of the grounded (neutral) conductor.

For example, if the ungrounded (phase) conductor supplying a 120 volt load of 175 amps were increased from 2/0 AWG THWN copper to 3/0 AWG THWN copper due to voltage drop problems, the grounded (neutral) conductor would have to be increased from 2/0 AWG copper to 3/0 AWG copper also.

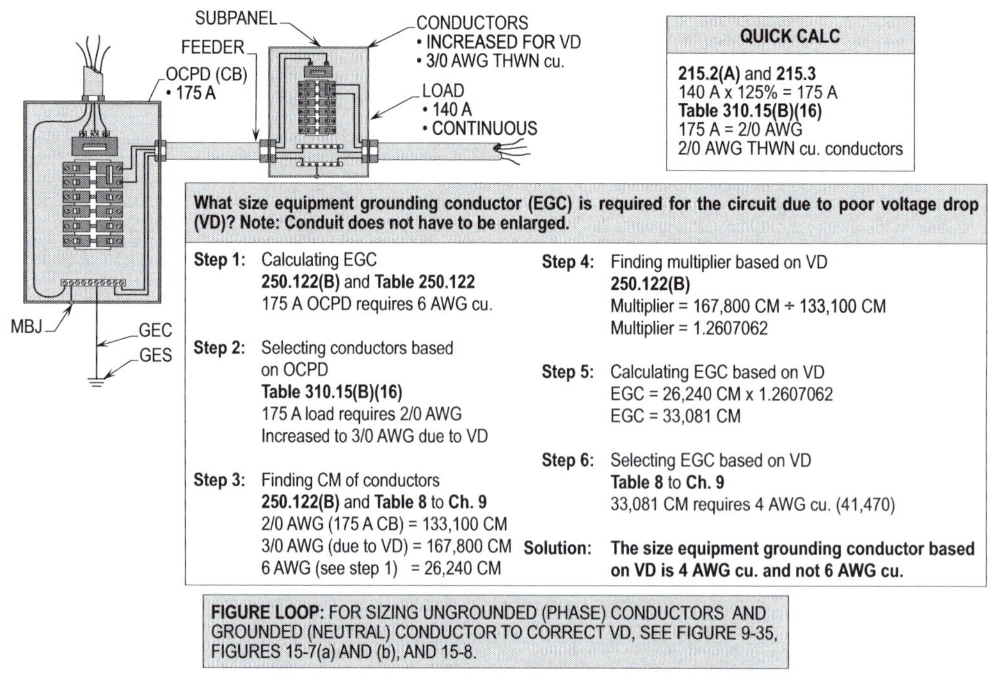

Figure 15-9. Calculating the size equipment grounding conductor based on poor VD in the feeder due to excessive length of conductors.

SIZING CONDUCTORS BASED ON VD
215.2(A)(4), IN 2

Sometimes, it is desirable to size and select the conductors based on the percentage of VD needed for the circuit to operate properly. Such conductors may be found by dividing R (12.9 for copper and 21.2 for aluminum) x L (length) x I (amps) by VD percent.

These rules and examples are also used for branch circuits to determine the amount of voltage drop where there are excessive long runs of conductors between the protection devices and load served. (**See Figure 15-10**)

CALCULATION OF A FEEDER
215.2(A)(1)(a) AND 215.3

A feeder may consist of loads such as lighting, receptacles, appliances, heating, air conditioning, and motors. Each load shall be evaluated and calculated at continuous or noncontinuous operation.

If loads with demand factors are present, they shall be separated into individual loads and demand factors shall be applied based on their condition of use in the electrical system.

See Figure 15-11 for calculation procedures pertaining to a feeder with combination loads.

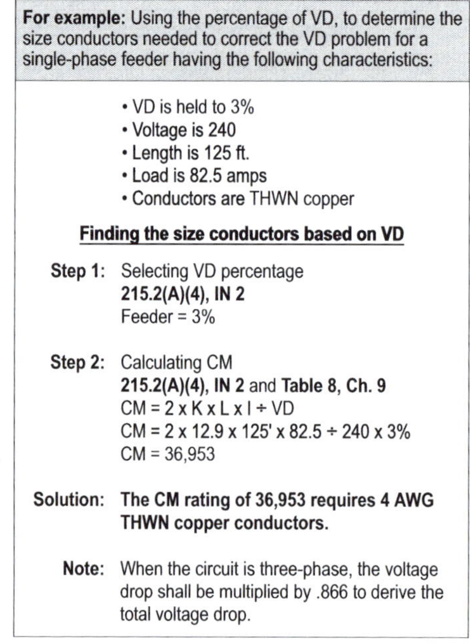

Figure 15-10. Calculating the size conductors based on VD to size conductors needed to correct the VD problem for a feeder.

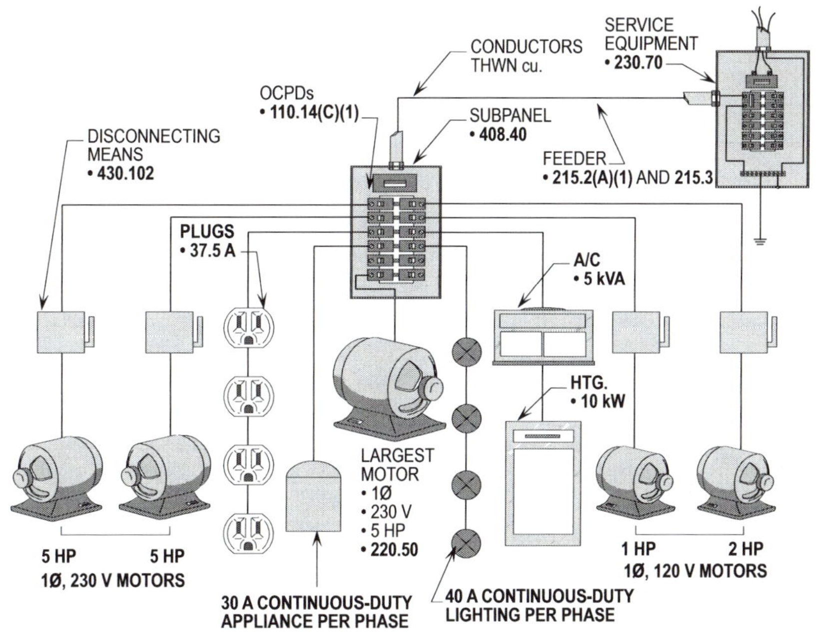

Note: For simplicity, a one line diagram is shown.

SIZING FEEDER OCPD BASED ON AMPACITY OF CONDUCTORS	SIZING FEEDER OCPD BASED ON LARGEST OCPD FOR ANY MOTOR OF THE GROUP

Step 1: Calculating loads
215.2(A)(1)(a), Table 430.248, 220.50, and 430.63
• Lighting load
  40 A x 125%   = 50 A
• Receptacle load
  37.5 A x 100% = 37.5A
• Appliance load
  30 A x 125%   = 37.5A
• Heat or A/C load
  10 kW x 1000 x
  100% ÷ 240 V   = 42 A
• Motor load; **Table 430.248**
    5 HP = 28 A x 100% = 28 A
    5 HP = 28 A x 100% = 28 A
    1 HP = 16 A x 100% = 16 A
    2 HP = 24 A x 100% = 24 A
• Largest motor load
  28 A x 25%   =   7 A
Total load   =270 A
 	
Step 2: Selecting conductors
310.15(A)(3), IN (2) and **Table 310.15(B)(16)**
270 A requires 300 AWG KCMIL THWN cu.
 	
Step 3: Selecting OCPD based on conductors
215.3; 240.4(B), 430.63, and **240.6(A)**
300 KCMIL THWN cu. = 285 A
285 A = 300 A OCPD
 	
Solution: The size overcurrent protection device is permitted to be a 300 amp circuit breaker, based on amps of conductors.
 	
Note: If the largest overcurrent protection device for any motor of the group is calculated and added to the remaining loads, the same overcurrent protection device is produced as in Step 3 above.
	Step 1: Calculating loads
	215.3 and **Table 430.248**
	• Lighting load
	  40 A x 125% = 50 A
	• Receptacle load
	  37.5 A x 100% = 37.5A
	• Appliance load
	  30 A x 125% = 37.5A
	• Heat or A/C load
	  10 kW x 1000 x
	  100% ÷ 240 V = 42 A
	• Motor load
	430.62(A), 430.52(C)(1), and **Table 430.52**
	    5 HP = 28 A x 250% = 70 A
	    5 HP = 28 A x 100% = 28 A
	    1 HP = 16 A x 100% = 16 A
	    2 HP = 24 A x 100% = 24 A
	Total load =305 A
	
	Step 2: Selecting overcurrent protection device
	430.62(A) and **240.6(A)**
	300 A is the next standard size below 305 A
	
	Solution: The size overcurrent protection device is a 300 amp.
	
	Note: The overcurrent protection device for the feeder is the same size (300 A) whether sized from the ampacity of the conductors or largest overcurrent protection device for any one motor of the group.
	
	**CALCULATION OF A FEEDER
	NEC 215.2(A)(1)(a)
	NEC 215.3**

Figure 15-11. Calculating a feeder with loads such as lighting, receptacle, appliances, heating, air-conditioning, and motors with continuous and noncontinuous loads.

Design Tip: For more detailed rules on sizing taps, sizing conductors, and overcurrent protection schemes, see the appropriate chapter in this book pertaining to such subjects. Also, see the calculation chapters for a variety of calculations pertaining to various types of buildings and loads.

FEEDERS NOT MORE THAN 600 VOLTS 215.2(A)(1)(a) AND (b)

(1) General. Feeder conductors shall have an ampacity not less than required to supply the load as calculated in **Parts III, IV,** and **V** of **Article 220**. Conductors shall be sized to carry not less than the larger of **215.2(A)(1)(a)** or **(b)**.

(a) Where a feeder supplies continuous loads or any combination of continuous and noncontinuous loads, the minimum feeder conductor size shall have an allowable ampacity not less than the noncontinuous load plus 125 percent of the continuous load.

(b) The minimum feeder conductor size shall have an allowable ampacity not less than the maximum load to be served after the application of any adjustment or correction factors.

(See Figure 15-12

OPTIONAL CALCULATION FOR A FEEDER 220.87, Ex.

If the maximum demand data for a one-year period is not available, the calculated load shall be permitted to be based on the maximum demand (measure of average power demand over a 15-minute period) continuously recorded over a minimum 30-day period using a recording ammeter or power meter connected to the highest loaded ungrounded (phase) conductor of the feeder or service, based on the initial loading at the start of the recording. The recording shall reflect the maximum demand of the feeder or service being taken when the building or space is occupied and shall include, by measurement or calculation, the larger of the heating or cooling equipment load and other loads that may be periodic in nature due to seasonal or similar conditions.

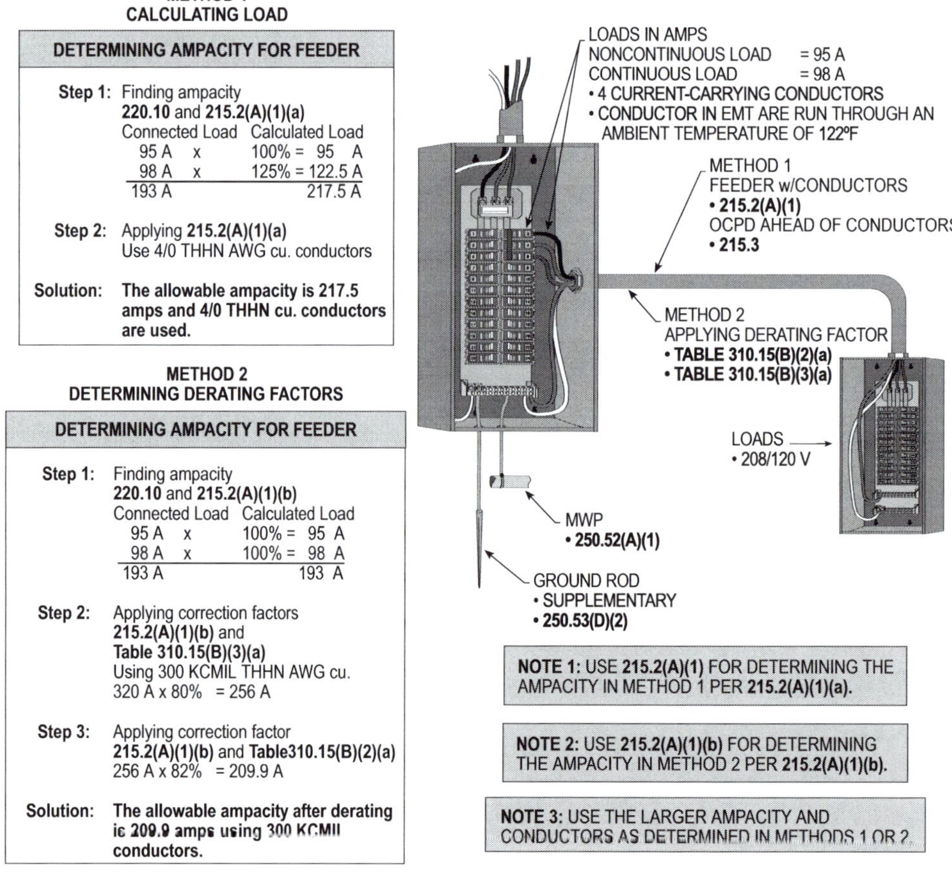

Figure 15-12. This illustration clarifies that two separate calculations shall be made and the large size ampacity and feeder conductor size is then selected per the 2014 NEC.

Design Tip: The existing demand at 125 percent plus the new load calculated at continuous and noncontinuous operation shall not be permitted to exceed the ampacity of the feeder rating. The feeder shall have overcurrent protection provided as required by **240.4** and **230.90**. **(See Figure 15-13)**

See **Figure 15-14** for a detailed illustration for applying such a procedure.

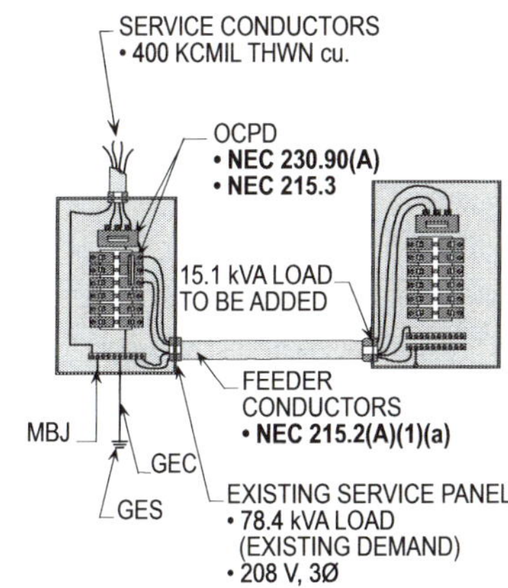

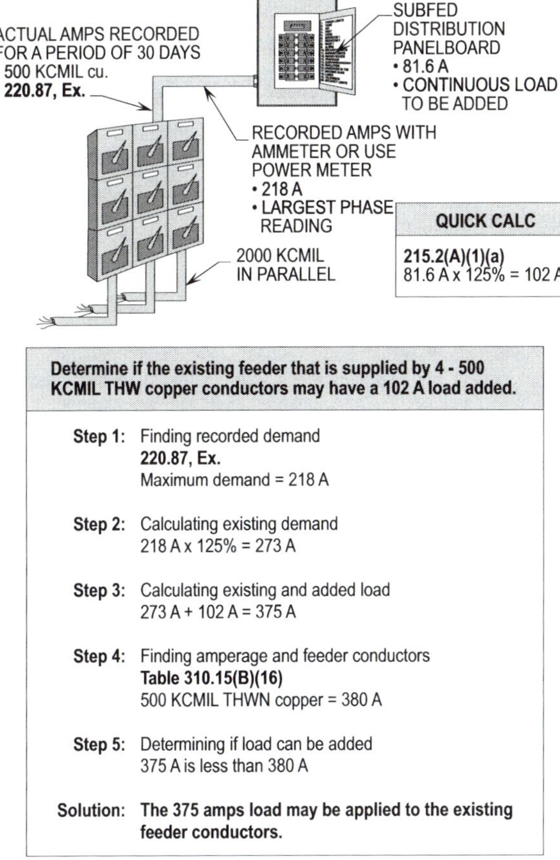

Determine if the existing feeder that is supplied by 4 - 500 KCMIL THW copper conductors may have a 102 A load added.

Step 1: Finding recorded demand
220.87, Ex.
Maximum demand = 218 A

Step 2: Calculating existing demand
218 A x 125% = 273 A

Step 3: Calculating existing and added load
273 A + 102 A = 375 A

Step 4: Finding amperage and feeder conductors
Table 310.15(B)(16)
500 KCMIL THWN copper = 380 A

Step 5: Determining if load can be added
375 A is less than 380 A

Solution: **The 375 amps load may be applied to the existing feeder conductors.**

OPTIONAL CALCULATION FOR A FEEDER
NEC 220.87, Ex.

Figure 15-13. Calculating the load in amps for a feeder using the optional calculation.

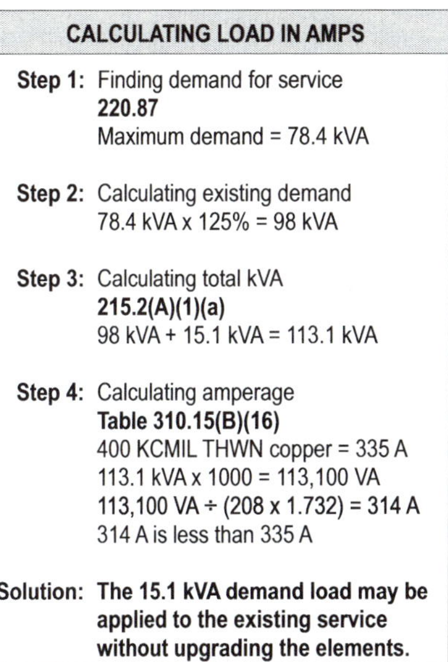

CALCULATING LOAD IN AMPS

Step 1: Finding demand for service
220.87
Maximum demand = 78.4 kVA

Step 2: Calculating existing demand
78.4 kVA x 125% = 98 kVA

Step 3: Calculating total kVA
215.2(A)(1)(a)
98 kVA + 15.1 kVA = 113.1 kVA

Step 4: Calculating amperage
Table 310.15(B)(16)
400 KCMIL THWN copper = 335 A
113.1 kVA x 1000 = 113,100 VA
113,100 VA ÷ (208 x 1.732) = 314 A
314 A is less than 335 A

Solution: **The 15.1 kVA demand load may be applied to the existing service without upgrading the elements.**

OPTIONAL CALCULATION
FOR A SERVICE
NEC 220.87

Figure 15-14. This illustration is a calculation for a service to verify if a load may be added.

OPTIONAL CALCULATION FOR A SERVICE
220.87

The optional calculation shall be permitted to be used to determine if additional loads may be added to existing feeder or service conductors. This rule permits the actual maximum demand figures to be utilized when the following conditions are complied with:

- The maximum demand data is available for one year.

- The existing demand at 125 percent plus the new load does not exceed the ampacity of such service.

- Overcurrent protection devices comply with **240.4** and **230.90**.

IDENTIFICATION OF UNGROUNDED CONDUCTORS
215.12(C)

Ungrounded conductors shall be identified in accordance with **215.12(C)(1)** or **(C)(2)**, as applicable.

FEEDER SUPPLIED FROM DIRECT-CURRENT SYSTEMS
215.12(C)(2)

Where a feeder is supplied from a dc system operating at more than 50 volts, each ungrounded conductor of 4 AWG or larger shall be identified by polarity at all termination, connection, and splice points by marking tape, tagging, or other approved means; each ungrounded conductor of 6 AWG or smaller shall be identified by polarity at all termination, connection, and splice points in compliance with **215.12(C)(2)(a)** and **(b)**. The identification methods utilized for conductors originating within each feeder panelboard or similar feeder distribution equipment shall be documented in a manner that is readily available or shall be permanently posted at each feeder panelboard or similar feeder distribution equipment. **(See Figure 15-15)**

POSITIVE POLARITY, SIZES 6 AWG OR SMALLER
215.12(C)(2)(a)

Where the positive polarity of a dc system does not serve as the connection for the grounded conductor, each positive ungrounded conductor shall be identified by one of the following means:

(1) A continuous red outer finish.

(2) A continuous red stripe durably marked along the conductor's entire length on insulation of a color other than green, white, gray, or black.

(3) Imprinted plus signs (+) or the word POSITIVE or POS durably marked on insulation of a color other than green, white, gray, or black, and repeated at intervals not exceeding 610 mm (24 in.) in accordance with **310.120(B)**.
(See Figure 15-16)

NEGATIVE POLARITY, SIZES 6 AWG OR SMALLER
215.12(C)(2)(b)

Where the negative polarity of a dc system does not serve as the connection for the grounded conductor, each negative ungrounded conductor shall be identified by one of the following means:

(1) A continuous black outer finish.

(2) A continuous black stripe durably marked along the conductor's entire length on insulation of a color other than green, white, gray, or red.

(3) Imprinted minus signs (–) or the word NEGATIVE or NEG durably marked on insulation of a color other than green, white, gray, or red, and repeated at intervals not exceeding 610 mm (24 in.) in accordance with **310.120(B)**.
(See Figure 15-16)

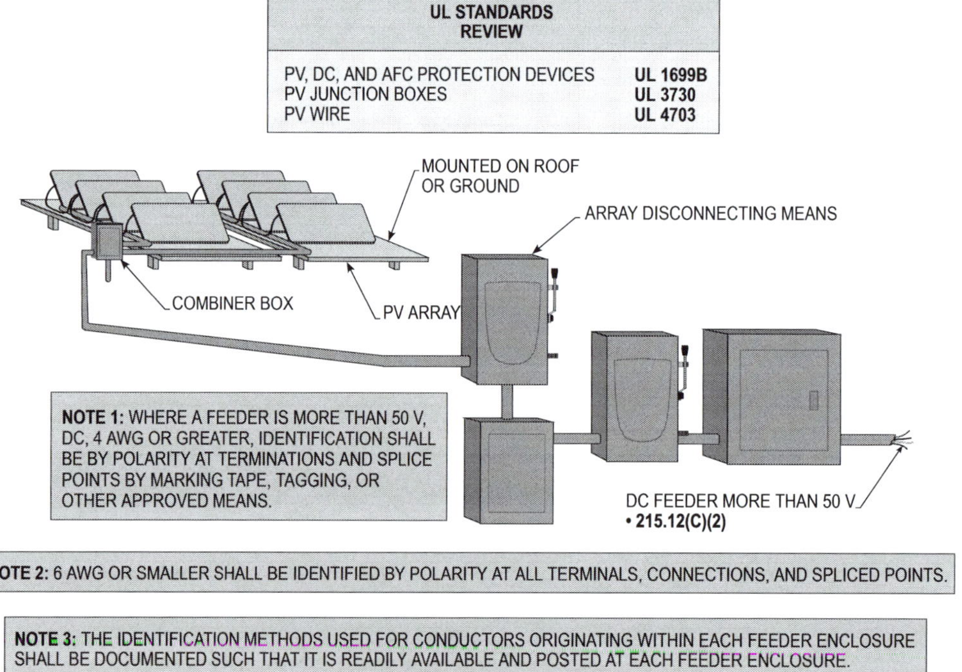

Figure 15-15. This illustration shows feeder requirements supplied from direct current systems.

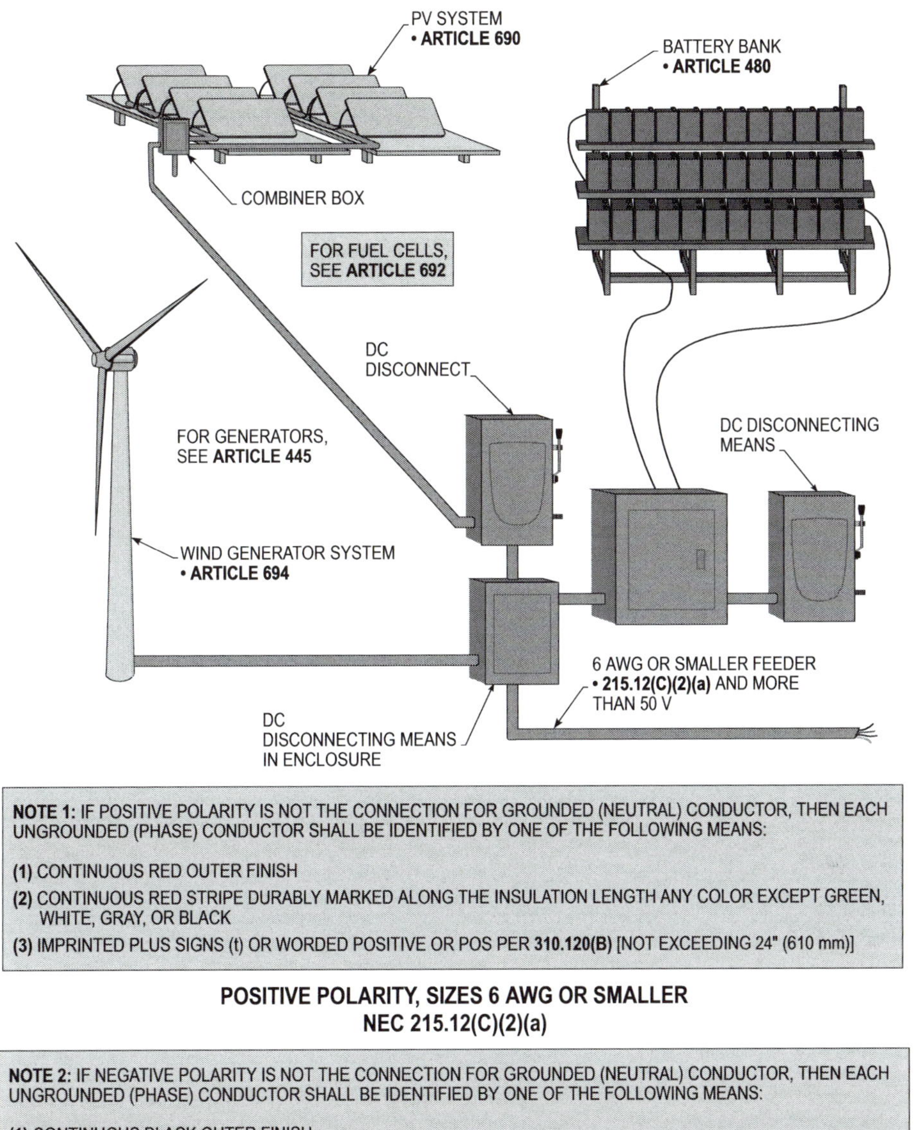

NOTE 1: IF POSITIVE POLARITY IS NOT THE CONNECTION FOR GROUNDED (NEUTRAL) CONDUCTOR, THEN EACH UNGROUNDED (PHASE) CONDUCTOR SHALL BE IDENTIFIED BY ONE OF THE FOLLOWING MEANS:

(1) CONTINUOUS RED OUTER FINISH

(2) CONTINUOUS RED STRIPE DURABLY MARKED ALONG THE INSULATION LENGTH ANY COLOR EXCEPT GREEN, WHITE, GRAY, OR BLACK

(3) IMPRINTED PLUS SIGNS (t) OR WORDED POSITIVE OR POS PER **310.120(B)** [NOT EXCEEDING 24" (610 mm)]

POSITIVE POLARITY, SIZES 6 AWG OR SMALLER
NEC 215.12(C)(2)(a)

NOTE 2: IF NEGATIVE POLARITY IS NOT THE CONNECTION FOR GROUNDED (NEUTRAL) CONDUCTOR, THEN EACH UNGROUNDED (PHASE) CONDUCTOR SHALL BE IDENTIFIED BY ONE OF THE FOLLOWING MEANS:

(1) CONTINUOUS BLACK OUTER FINISH

(2) CONTINUOUS BLACK STRIPE DURABLY MARKED ALONG THE INSULATION LENGTH ANY COLOR EXCEPT GREEN, WHITE, GRAY, OR RED

(3) IMPRINTED MINUS SIGNS (–) OR WORDED NEGATIVE OR NEG PER **310.120(B)** [NOT EXCEEDING 24" (610 mm)]

NEGATIVE POLARITY, SIZES 6 AWG OR SMALLER
NEC 215.12(C)(2)(b)

Figure 15-16. This illustration shows feeder requirements supplied from direct current systems.

Chapter 15. Feeders

Section Answer

1. Continuous loads for feeders are classified as loads that operate for a period of _____ hours or more.

  (a) 1   (b) 2
  (c) 3   (d) 5

2. All inductive neutral current, even if noncontinuous, shall be calculated at _____ percent with no demand factor applied.

  (a) 80   (b) 100
  (c) 125   (d) 150

3. The voltage drop on the feeder conductors should not exceed _____ percent overall, if the VD on the branch circuit does not exceed 2 percent.

  (a) 2   (b) 3
  (c) 4   (d) 5

4. Noncontinuous operated loads shall be calculated at _____ percent, or demand factors can be applied to specific loads under certain conditions.

  (a) 75   (b) 80
  (c) 100   (d) 125

5. The VA rating for receptacle loads shall be calculated at 100 percent for the first 10,000 VA, and the remaining VA shall be calculated at _____ percent per **Table 220.44**.

  (a) 25   (b) 50
  (c) 60   (d) 75

6. The feeder resistive neutral load shall be calculated at 100 percent for the first 200 amps, and the remaining load shall have a demand factor of _____ percent applied.

  (a) 50   (b) 60
  (c) 70   (d) 75

7. The voltage drop on feeder conductors should not exceed 2 percent to _____ percent at the farthest outlet supplying power to the loads.

  (a) 2   (b) 3
  (c) 4   (d) 5

Section   **Answer**

____________ __________ **8.** If the maximum demand data for a one year period is not available, the calculated load shall be permitted to be based on the maximum demand (measure of average power demand over a 15 minute period) continuously recorded over a minimum ______ day period using a recording ammeter or power meter connected to the highest loaded phase of the feeder or service, based on the initial loading at the start of the recording .

(a) 7   (b) 10
(c) 24   (d) 30

____________ __________ **9.** The neutral current in amps for a three-wire, two-phase or five-wire, two-phase system shall be multiplied by ______ percent.

(a) 140   (b) 150
(c) 175   (d) 200

____________ __________ **10.** The feeder grounded (neutral) conductor load shall be ______ percent of the demand load for cooking equipment.

(a) 50   (b) 65
(c) 70   (d) 75

____________ __________ **11.** What is the ampacity for a feeder load of 20,800 VA supplied by a 120/240 volt, single-phase system?

____________ __________ **12.** What is the ampacity for a feeder load of 20,800 VA supplied by a 120/208 volt, three-phase system?

____________ __________ **13.** What is the actual power for a 240 volt, single-phase feeder with a 58 amp load?

____________ __________ **14.** What is the actual power for a 240 volt, single-phase feeder with a 58 amp load with a power factor of 75 percent?

____________ __________ **15.** What is the ampacity for a 208 volt, three-phase feeder with a 58 amp load with a power factor of 75 percent?

____________ __________ **16.** What is the VA rating for a connected load of 32,800 VA to size the elements of the feeder at noncontinuous operation?

____________ __________ **17.** What is the VA rating for a for a continuously operated processing machine with a connected load of 32,800 VA?

____________ __________ **18.** What is the load in VA for a number of general purpose receptacles used at noncontinuous operation that are utilized to supply a connected load of 28,400 VA?

____________ __________ **19.** What is the neutral load for a feeder with a inductive load of 300 amps?

____________ __________ **20.** What is the neutral load for a feeder with a resistive load of 300 amps?

____________ __________ **21.** What is the neutral load in kW for a 10 kW range?

Section   **Answer**

22. What is the voltage drop using the resistivity method with the following characteristics? (Use larger conductor if necessary)

    • VD is held to 3%
    • Voltage is 240
    • Length is 300 ft
    • Load is 180 amps
    • OCPD is 200 amps
    • Conductors are 3/0 AWG THWN copper

23. What is the voltage drop using the CM method with the following characteristics? (Use larger conductor if necessary)

    • VD is held to 3%
    • Voltage is 240
    • Length is 300 ft
    • Load is 180 amps
    • OCPD is 200 amps
    • Conductors are 3/0 AWG THWN copper

24. What size feeder overcurrent protection device is required for the following loads based on the ampacity of conductors?

    • Lighting load = 30 A (continuous operation)
    • Receptacle load = 35 A
    • Appliance load = 30 A (continuous operation)
    • Heating load = 10 kW
    • A/C load = 6 kVA

    Motor loads
    • 5 HP, 230 V, single-phase
    • 5 HP, 230 V, single-phase
    • 2 HP, 120 V, single-phase
    • 1 HP, 120 V, single-phase

25. Determine whether an existing service supplied by 4 - 400 KCMIL THWN copper conductors can have an 86 amp load (already calculated at continuous duty) added to a service with a 198 amp recorded amperage rating for a period of 30 days.

16

Receptacle Outlets

The rules for installing receptacle outlets in one- and two-family dwelling units are more stringent than for commercial or industrial occupancies. If the required number of receptacles are not installed in a dwelling unit, the power needed to serve the number of appliances in use today will not be available. Therefore, in dwelling units only, a specific number shall be installed. However, this rule does not apply to commercial and industrial locations. Receptacles are installed as needed for cord-and-plug electrical items. Extension cords used improperly create a fire hazard. For this reason, the *National Electrical Code* requires outlets in all types of occupancies to be installed in such a manner as to cord-and-plug connect appliance loads without the use of extension cords.

GFCI and AFCI protection of 15 or 20 amp, 125 volt receptacle outlets shall be required in specified areas, some of which are located indoors and outdoors to protect personnel and property from electric shock and arcing faults while using cord-and-plug connected electric hand tools, radios, televisions, stereos, etc. GFCI protection applies to certain areas in dwelling units, commercial locations, and industrial locations.

Note, for information on ADA Standards for accessible design, see **Annex J** in the NEC.

GROUNDING RECEPTACLES 406.4(A)

Receptacles installed on 15 or 20 amp general-purpose branch circuits shall be the grounding type. They are required to be the three-wire type with a brass terminal for the ungrounded (phase) conductor, a silver terminal for the grounded (neutral) conductor, and a green terminal for the equipment grounding conductor. The brass terminal is for the short slot and represents the connection for the ungrounded (phase) conductor. The U slot is for the equipment grounding conductor terminal on the receptacle, while the long slot represents the grounded (neutral) conductor terminal. Any color conductor but white, gray, green, green with a yellow stripe, or bare shall be permitted to be connected to the ungrounded (phase) brass terminal per **210.5(C)** and **310.110(C)**. Only white or gray shall be connected to the grounded (neutral) silver terminal per **200.6(A), 210.5(A),** and **310.110(A)**. A conductor with a green or green with yellow stripe shall be the only color permitted to be connected to the green equipment grounding conductor terminal per **250.134(B), 210.5(B), 250.119(A),** and **310.110(B)**. The insulation of the equipment grounding conductor for 4 AWG or larger shall be permitted to be stripped per **250.119(A). (See Figure 16-1)**

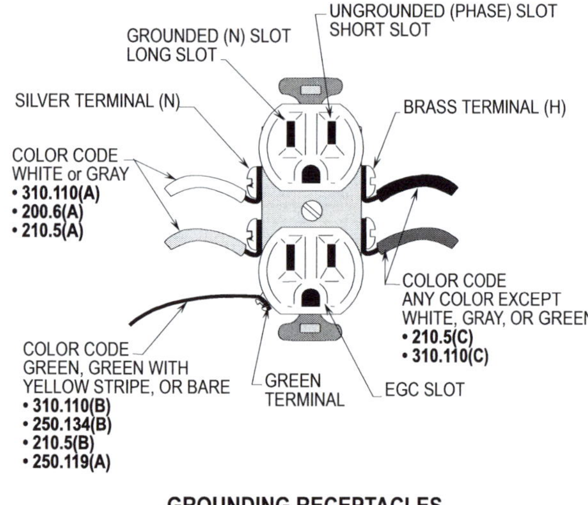

Figure 16-1. Identifying the components and correct color coding for receptacles.

Receptacles shall be rated for the voltage and current based upon the size of the general-purpose branch circuit to which they are connected.

Receptacles shall be permitted to be connected to an individual branch circuit, a general-purpose branch circuit, a general-purpose branch circuit with two or more receptacles, or a combination of lighting and receptacle outlets.

A receptacle shall be permitted to be connected to an individual branch circuit, but to do so, it shall be rated not less than the ampacity of the branch circuit. The size of the overcurrent protection device shall be utilized in determining the rating of the branch circuit.

For example, a 20 amp overcurrent protection device (circuit breaker or fuse) classifies the branch circuit as 20 amp even if the conductors of the circuit are 10 AWG per **210.19(A)(1), 210.20(A),** and **210.23**. Sometimes conductors are increased for voltage drop correction, adjustment, or correction factors that create a larger conductor than normally required per **250.122(B). (See Figure 16-2)**

An individual branch circuit supplies power to a single load that is cord-and-plug connected to a single receptacle. To determine the size of the load permitted to be connected to the receptacle, refer to **Table 210.21(B)(2)**, which lists the maximum cord-and-plug connected load that shall be permitted to be plugged into a receptacle.

For example: What is the maximum size load that may be cord-and-plug connected to a receptacle supplied by a general-purpose branch circuit?

Step 1: Maximum load permitted
Table 210.21(B)(2)
Column 1 Branch circuit   = 15 or 20 A
Column 2 Receptacle   = 15 A
Column 3 Maximum load = 12 A

Solution: Maximum load is 12 amps.

Table 210.21(B)(3) lists the amperage rating of a receptacle that shall be permitted be connected to a branch circuit based on the rating of the overcurrent protection device and conductors.

For example: What is the minimum and maximum size receptacle in amps that may be connected to a 20 amp general-purpose branch circuit?

Step 1: Maximum size receptacle permitted
Table 210.21(B)(3)
Column 1 Branch circuit   = 20 A
Column 2 Receptacle   = 15 or 20 A

Solution: Maximum size receptacle is 15 or 20 amps.

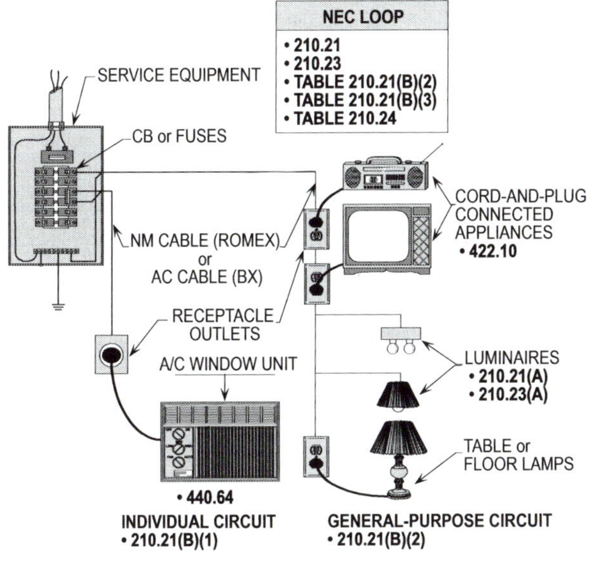

Figure 16-2. An individual branch circuit has only one outlet and a single load whereas a general-purpose branch circuit has more than one outlet and load that may be cord-and-plug connected or hard wired.

NONGROUNDING RECEPTACLES 406.4(A)(D)(2), (D)(3), AND Ex.

The general rule requires receptacles of the grounding type to be installed in existing dwelling units. Conductors of copper should be used to connect the terminals of the receptacle to the branch-circuit conductors. Otherwise, copper and aluminum type receptacles shall be installed listed for such use.

Aluminum conductors of a branch circuit should be pigtailed to a 6 in. (150 mm) copper jumper and connected to the terminals of the receptacle. This is suggested because the existing terminals of receptacles are not usually rated for aluminum connections. Unless certain techniques are applied, nongrounding receptacles shall be connected to branch circuits not having an equipment grounding conductor.

If an existing branch circuit is wired with an AC cable and the existing receptacle outlet is the nongrounding type, a grounding receptacle shall be used to replace the existing nongrounding receptacle, since an AC listed cable may be used as an equipment grounding means per **320.108** and

250.118(8). Only one conductor shall be placed under the bonding screw on the terminal of the receptacle unless it is approved for more than one conductor per **110.3(B)** and **110.14(A)**. **(See Figure 16-3)**

REPLACEMENT OF RECEPTACLES 250.130(C)

The basic rule for replacement of receptacles is that grounding-type receptacles shall be used to replace existing receptacles. There is no problem in applying this requirement as long as the branch circuit is equipped with an equipment grounding conductor or grounding means that complies with **250.118**. A nongrounding-type receptacle shall be used with a branch circuit that has no equipment grounding conductor or grounding means. There are two conditions in the NEC that permit a GFCI receptacle to be used. Either a GFCI receptacle shall be permitted to be used to replace and protect a single receptacle outlet, or a GFCI feed-through receptacle shall be permitted to be used to protect additional outlets downstream. The receptacle outlets downstream shall be permitted to be of the grounding type but shall be identified as being protected by a GFCI circuit with no ground. **Section 250.130(C)** permits an equipment grounding conductor sized from the overcurrent protection device of the branch circuit per **Table 250.122** to be utilized. The equipment grounding conductor shall connect the green grounding terminal of the receptacle to the closest metal water pipe as required by **250.104(A), 250.52(A)(1)**, and **250.53(D)**. The equipment grounding conductor shall not be permitted to be connected to a driven rod. [Also, see **250.50** per **250.130(C)(1)**.]

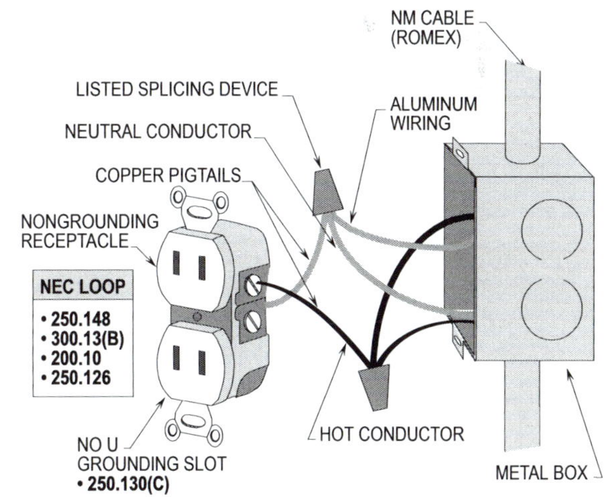

Figure 16-3. Nongrounding receptacles are used where the branch circuit is not provided with an equipment grounding conductor. If the branch-circuit wiring method is aluminum, a copper pigtail should be used to terminate the aluminum conductor to the terminals of the receptacle. **Note,** the splicing device shall be listed.

Design Tip: Check with the inspector for his or her interpretation of the point of connection to the metal water pipe. The AHJ may require the connection of the equipment grounding conductor to be made within 5 ft (1.52 m) of where the metal water pipe enters the dwelling unit per **250.68(C)(1)**. However, with the metal water pipe in the earth and entering the premises from more than one point, the AHJ may permit connection to any one of such entries.

The NEC permits five methods by which a nongrounding receptacle shall be permitted to be replaced, and they are as follows:

- A nongrounding receptacle
- A GFCI receptacle protecting a single outlet
- A GFCI receptacle protecting a single outlet and additional outlets downstream
- An equipment grounding conductor routed from the receptacle to a metal water pipe or an EGC from an existing outlet
- A GFCI circuit breaker protecting all outlets

See Figure 16-4 for a detailed illustration on methods used for replacing nongrounding receptacles on branch circuits without an equipment grounding conductor.

NUMBER ON A CIRCUIT
210.11(A)

Section **210.11** is used to determine the number of outlets permitted on a branch circuit. Section **220.10** refers to **220.12** and **Table 220.12**, which requires 3 VA per sq. ft for a dwelling unit to determine the total VA to select the number of branch circuits.

For example, a 3000 sq. ft dwelling unit has a total of 9000 VA (3000 sq. ft x 3 VA = 9000 VA) to supply general-purpose receptacle outlets. Using this concept, there are 4 - 120 volt, 20 amp branch circuits provided to supply general-purpose receptacle outlets. (See below)

To determine the number of outlets permitted on a branch circuit, the overcurrent protection device shall be multiplied by 120 volts per **210.11(B)** and divided by 3 VA per **Table 220.12**. This number may be verified as follows:

No. = (3000 sq. ft x 3 VA) ÷ (20 A OCPD x 120 V)
No. = 3.75
3.75 requires 4 - 20 amp branch circuits

For example: How many receptacle outlets in a dwelling unit may be connected to a 20 amp general-purpose branch circuit?

Step 1:   Finding VA
210.11(B)
20 A OCPD x 120 V = 2400 VA

Step 2:   Finding sq. ft
Table 220.12
2400 VA ÷ 3 VA = 800 sq. ft

Step 3:   Finding number of outlets permitted
220.14(J), 220.12, and **210.11(B)**
Permits any number to be installed

Solution: **There is no limit to the number of outlets permitted in the 800 sq. ft area. Note, local codes may limit the number of outlets that can be connected to a branch circuit.**

In commercial and industrial locations, the number of receptacle outlets permitted on a general-purpose branch circuit are calculated differently from the number in dwelling units.

For example: In a commercial or industrial area, the limited number of 13 outlets on a general-purpose branch circuit is based on the following procedure.

Step 1:   Finding amperage of outlets
220.14(J) AND **(I)**
180 VA ÷ 120 V = 1.5 A

Step 2:   Finding number of outlets
220.14(J) AND **(I)**
20 A OCPD ÷ 1.5 A = 13
A 20 A circuit is limited to 13

Solution: **The number of outlets permitted on a 20 amp branch circuit is 13.**

Design Tip: Using the same procedure, 10 outlets shall be permitted on a 15 amp overcurrent protection device. The limitation of outlets presents nuisance tripping of the overcurrent protection device.

Municipal electrical boards may amend the NEC and permit different numbers of outlets on a 15 or 20 amp branch circuit. The two methods listed in determining the number of receptacle outlets on a branch circuit in dwellings, commercial locations, and industrial locations are the most common methods used. **(See Figure 16-5)**

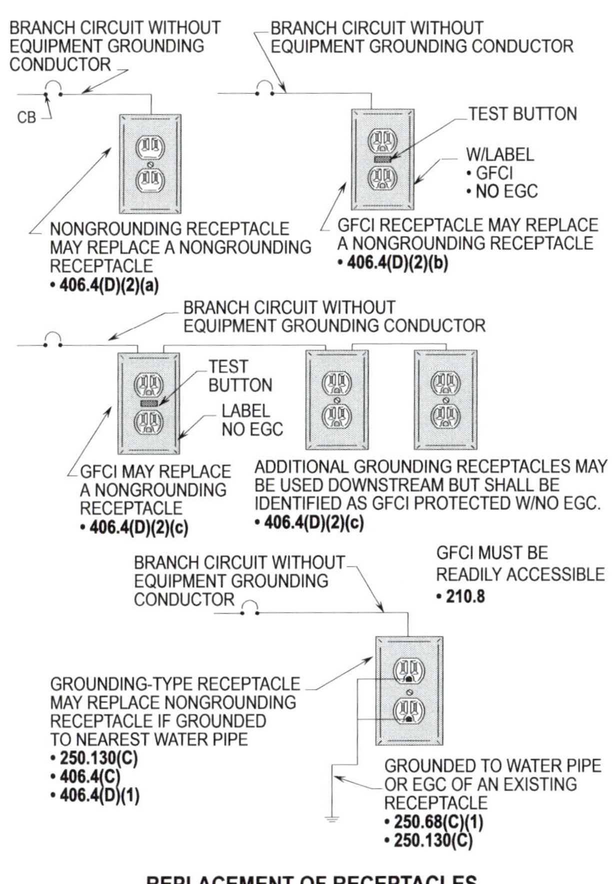

Figure 16-4. Methods for replacing nongrounding receptacles on branch circuits without an equipment grounding conductor.

DWELLING UNIT LOCATIONS
210.52(A) THRU (I)

The provisions for installing the required number of receptacle outlets in dwelling units are listed in **210.52(A) through (I)**. The basic rule requires receptacle outlets to be installed where flexible cords are used to connect electrical appliances and equipment. This Section, with **Subdivisions (A) through (I)**, lists the exact location and number to be installed. The number of receptacle outlets required differs according to whether installation is inside or outside the dwelling unit.

Design Tip: Commercial and industrial installations of receptacle outlets shall be permitted to be either inside or outside and located where needed. **Note,** a specific number of outlets is not required.

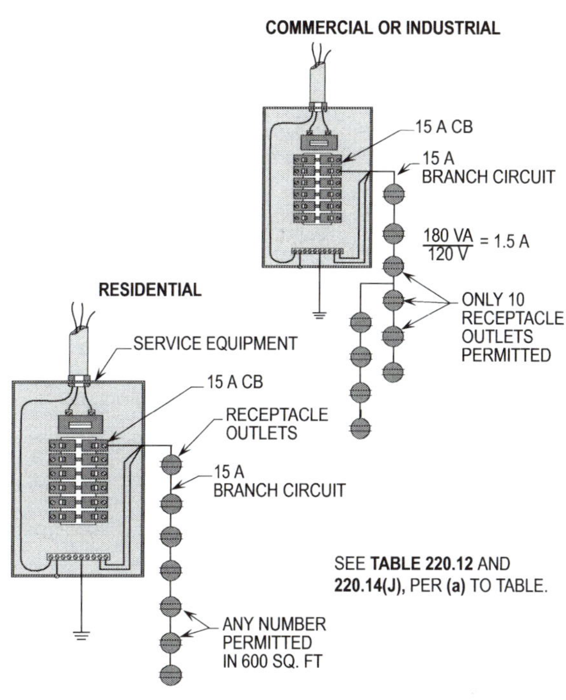

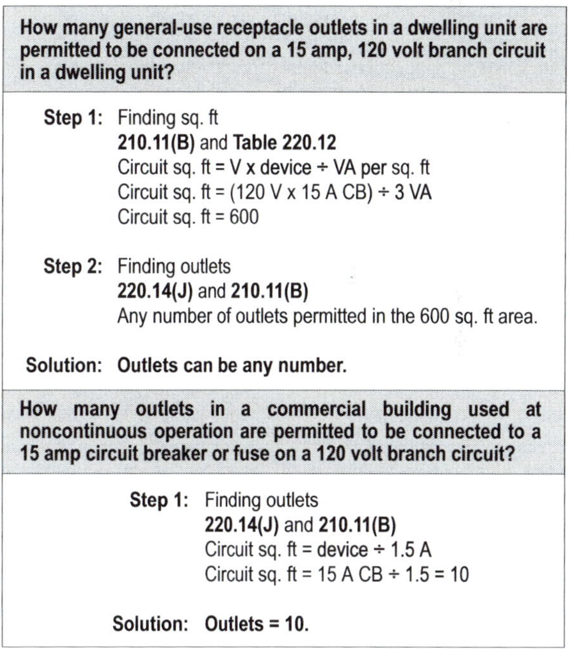

How many general-use receptacle outlets in a dwelling unit are permitted to be connected on a 15 amp, 120 volt branch circuit in a dwelling unit?

Step 1:	Finding sq. ft	
	210.11(B) and **Table 220.12**	
	Circuit sq. ft = V x device ÷ VA per sq. ft	
	Circuit sq. ft = (120 V x 15 A CB) ÷ 3 VA	
	Circuit sq. ft = 600	
Step 2:	Finding outlets	
	220.14(J) and **210.11(B)**	
	Any number of outlets permitted in the 600 sq. ft area.	
Solution:	**Outlets can be any number.**	

How many outlets in a commercial building used at noncontinuous operation are permitted to be connected to a 15 amp circuit breaker or fuse on a 120 volt branch circuit?

Step 1:	Finding outlets	
	220.14(J) and **210.11(B)**	
	Circuit sq. ft = device ÷ 1.5 A	
	Circuit sq. ft = 15 A CB ÷ 1.5 = 10	
Solution:	**Outlets = 10.**	

NUMBER ON A CIRCUIT
NEC 210.11(A)

Figure 16-5. For determining the number of receptacle outlets on a 15 amp branch circuit using the "any number permitted" method or the limited method is at the discretion of the AHJ. **Note,** the number per circuit may vary from city to city or from state to state based upon the electrical ordinances of each area. [Also, see **210.11(C)(1) thru (C)(3)**]

WALL RECEPTACLE OUTLETS
210.52(A)(1) THRU (A)(4)

Section **210.52(A)** lists the requirements for installing receptacle outlets in dwelling units, including single-family dwellings, duplexes, single-family dwellings in apartment complexes, townhouses, and condominiums. Per **Article 100**, a dwelling unit is defined as a single unit, providing complete and independent living facilities for one or more persons, including permanent provisions for:

- Living
- Sleeping
- Sanitation
- Cooking

See Figure 16-6 for a detailed illustration of a dwelling unit.

Receptacles that are an integral part of a luminaire, appliance, or cabinet shall not be counted as one of the required receptacle outlets. Those outlets installed more than 5 ft 6 in. (1.7 m) above the finished floor are not permitted to be counted per **210.52(4)**. In other words, they shall not be counted as one of the required outlets for normal use. In these cases, additional outlets shall be installed to comply with the number of outlets required per **210.52(A)(1)**. **(See Figure 16-7)**

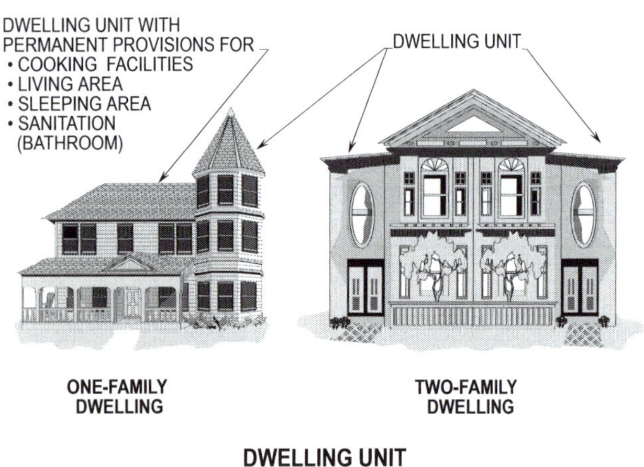

DWELLING UNIT
ARTICLE 100

Figure 16-6. A dwelling unit in a one-family house or duplex contains provisions for permanent cooking and sanitation as well as facilities for living and sleeping. These provisions shall be permitted to be located in one or more rooms to be classified as a dwelling unit per **Article 100**.

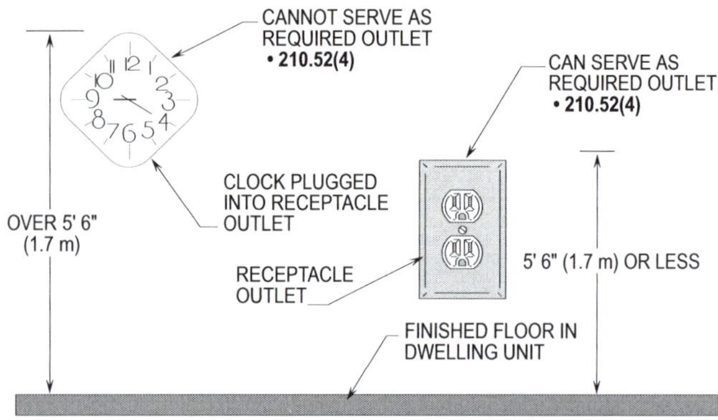

WALL RECEPTACLE OUTLETS
NEC 210.52

Figure 16-7. Receptacle outlets located more than 5 ft 6 in. (1.7 m) from the floor in a dwelling unit shall not serve as one of the required outlets listed in **210.52**.

Section **210.52** gives permission for a receptacle to be installed in a listed factory-assembled baseboard heater, so as to prevent extension cords from being plugged into the receptacle outlet above the baseboard heater. Heat from the electric heater elements may overheat the insulation of the cord and cause a fire hazard from the arcing and sparking that can occur. The **IN** recommends that baseboard heaters be installed according to the instructions accompanying the heater unit per **90.7** and **110.3(B)**.

> **Design Tip:** This rule applies strictly to electric baseboard heater with heating elements. **(See Figure 16-8)**

Receptacle outlets shall be installed on walls in every inhabitable room, including the hallway, of every dwelling unit, except the bathroom. The procedure for properly spacing the receptacles along the floor line of an unbroken wall is to provide an outlet within 6 ft (1.8 m) of the cord-and-plug connected equipment per **210.52(A)(1)**.

The first outlet shall be installed 6 ft (1.8 m) from the door entering the room. The measurement for installing this outlet shall be permitted to be made on either side of the door. From the outlet measured at 6 ft (1.8 m), additional outlets measured at 12 ft (3.7 m) intervals along the unbroken wall shall be installed. Outlets installed in this manner allow electrical appliances with 6 ft (1.8 m) cords to be cord-and-plug connected without the use of an extension cord. Installing the first outlet at 6 ft (1.8 m) and each additional outlet every 12 ft (3.7 m) thereafter complies with this requirement and makes it possible to cord-and-plug connect appliances without creating a fire hazard. Any wall space of 2 ft (600 mm) or more requires an outlet for a receptacle to be installed.

> **Design Tip:** The wall space of 2 ft (600 mm) is based on trimmed-out walls, etc. and not from a 2 ft (600 mm) rough-in measurement of framing members.

A wall space is a wall unbroken along the floor line by a door or similar opening, bookcase, fireplace, fixed cabinets, or window that extends all the way to the floor line. A floor receptacle outlet located close to the wall shall be permitted to be counted as one of the outlets required by **210.52(A)(3)**. **(See Figure 16-9)**

Railings used for room dividers, where furniture with floor or table lamps is backed up to the railing, shall have receptacle outlets installed for cord-and-plug connections such as table or floor lamps. This rule is to prevent the use of extension cords, which are usually run through walls, doors, under carpets, etc. per **400.8(1) through (7)**. **[See Figure 16-10(a)]**

The sliding portion of an exterior door shall not be considered wall space. Fixed panels, including the fixed portion of a sliding glass door unit in an exterior wall, shall be considered wall space for the purpose of spacing the required number of receptacle outlets per **210.52(A)(2)(2)**. The NEC permits a floor receptacle to be used to provide the required number of receptacle outlets per **210.52(A)(3)**. **[See Figure 16-10(b)]**

Receptacles installed for countertop surfaces shall not be considered as the receptacles required per **210.52(A)**.

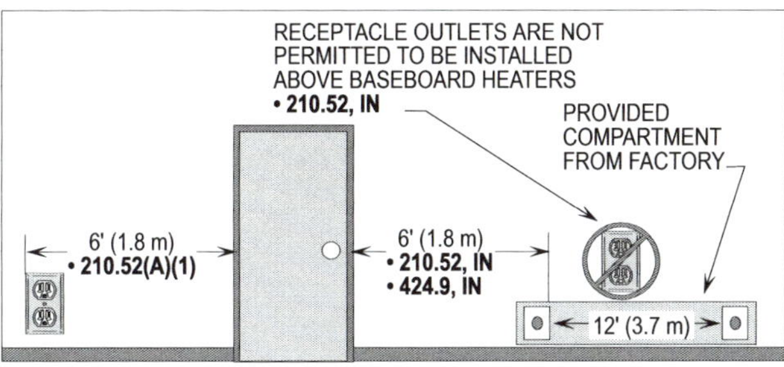

Figure 16-8. Electric baseboard heaters shall not be located below a receptacle outlet. Partitions from the factory meant for installing receptacles shall be permitted to be put in the baseboard heater to comply with the 12 ft (3.7 m) requirement of **210.52(A)(1)**.

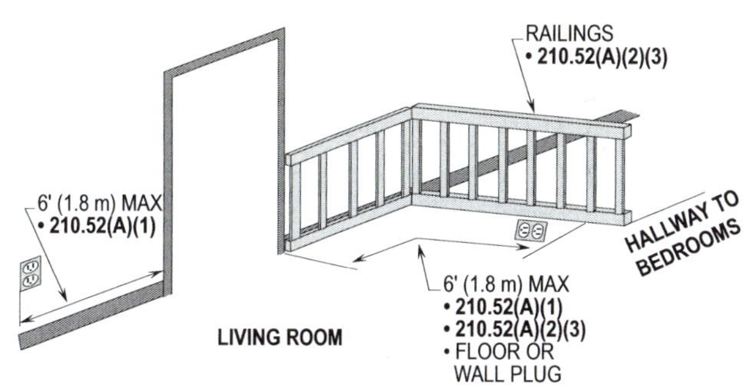

Figure 16-10(a). Railings used as room dividers shall have receptacle outlets installed per **210.52(A)(2)(3)** to cord-and-plug connect floor lamps, table lamps, etc.

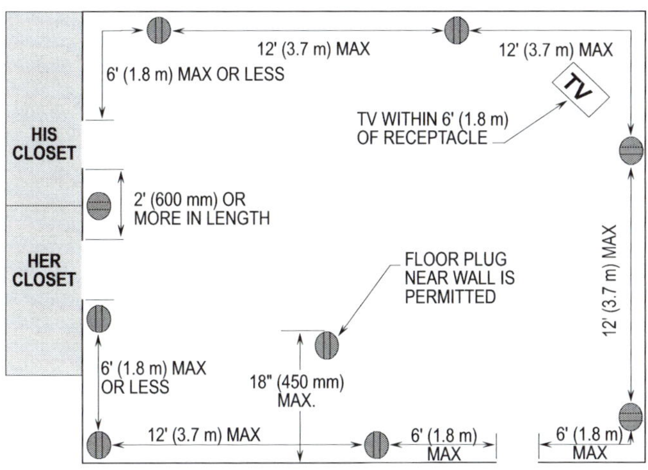

Figure 16-9. Receptacle outlets shall be installed so that there is no point on the wall greater than 6 ft (1.8 m) from a receptacle outlet.

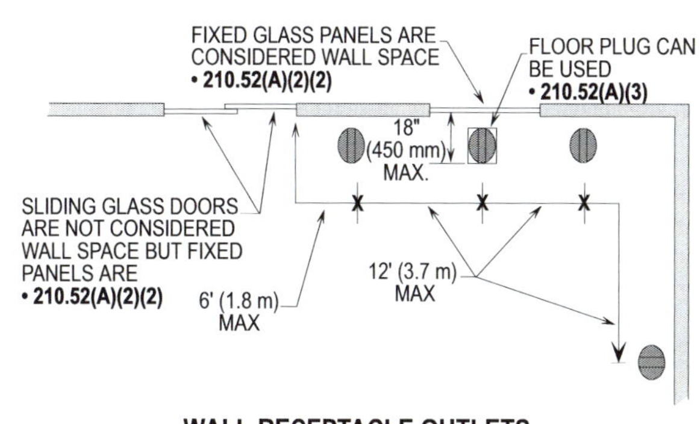

Figure 16-10(b). Sliding glass doors or panels shall not be considered wall space when spacing receptacles to comply with **210.52(A)**. However, fixed panels shall be considered wall space.

RECEPTACLE OUTLETS FOR SMALL-APPLIANCE CIRCUITS 210.52(B), 210.52(C), 210.11(C)(1), AND 220.52(A)

A minimum of 2 - 20 amp, 120 volt, 1500 VA small-appliance circuits shall be required to supply receptacle outlets that are located in the kitchen, pantry, breakfast room, and dining room. The two small-appliance circuits shall be routed to the kitchen countertop(s), and the outlets proportioned among the two circuits as evenly as possible to prevent unbalanced loading of the circuits. Unbalanced loading may trip open the overcurrent protection device if too many portable appliances are plugged into the same small-appliance circuit. **(See Figure 16-11)**

The 2 - 20 amp small-appliance circuits wired with 12-2 AWG w/ground, nonmetallic-sheathed cable (Romex or rope) shall only supply receptacle outlets located in the kitchen, pantry, breakfast room, and dining room. All other receptacle outlets shall be served by the general-purpose branch circuits or individual branch circuits per **Table 220.12** and **210.23(A),** or **210.19(A)(1)**. Switched receptacle outlets connected to the general-purpose branch circuits per **210.52(B)(1), Ex. 1** and **210.70(A)(1), Ex. 1** to serve swag lights, table lamps, floor lamps, etc. shall also be permitted. These are in addition to those required in **210.52(B)**. All receptacle outlets shall be installed so that no point along the floor line of an unbroken wall is farther than 6 ft (1.8 m) from an outlet per **210.52(A)(1)**.

Exception 2 to **210.52(B)(1)** permits a receptacle outlet to be installed from an individual branch circuit to supply a compressor motor for refrigeration equipment.

Exception 2 to **210.52(B)(2)** permits receptacle outlets to be installed on the small-appliance circuits to supply loads such as timers, clocks, burner ignition systems on gas ovens, cooktops, and ranges.

> **Design Tip:** This rule makes it clear that such mentioned motor loads shall be permitted to be supplied by an individual 15 amp branch circuit per **210.19(A)(1)**, a general-purpose motor branch circuit per **430.53(A)**.

There is an **Ex.** to **210.52(B)(2)**, which permits another outlet to be supplied by the small-appliance circuits. The **Ex. 1** permits a clock outlet to be served by any one of the small-appliance circuits. To apply this exception, the clock outlet shall be located in the kitchen, pantry, dining room, or breakfast room. **(See Figure 16-12)**

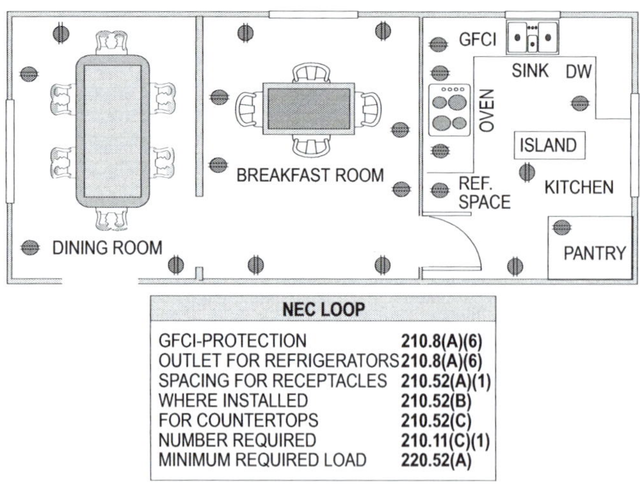

Figure 16-11. A minimum of 2 - 20 amp small-appliance circuits shall be provided to serve the receptacle outlets located in the kitchen, pantry, breakfast room, and dining room.

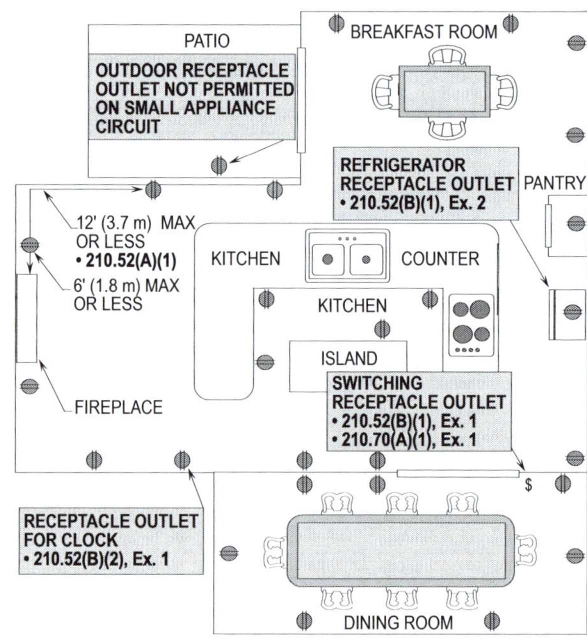

Figure 16-12. A clock outlet shall be permitted to be installed on the small-appliance circuits. In addition, a switched receptacle outlet shall be permitted to be installed on the general-purpose branch circuit.

RECEPTACLE OUTLETS OVER COUNTERTOPS
210.52(C)

There are five types of countertops that may be present in dwelling units, and they are as follows:

- Countertop with a wall behind it per **210.52(C)(1)**
- Island countertops per **210.52(C)(2)**
- Countertop with no wall behind it (peninsular) per **210.52(C)(3)**
- Separate spaces per **210.52(C)(4)**
- Receptacle outlet location per **210.52(C)(5)**

WALL COUNTERTOP SPACES
210.52(C)(1)

A receptacle outlet shall be provided at each countertop space 12 in. (300 mm) or wider in the kitchen and dining room areas. No point along the wall shall be permitted to be more than 24 in. (600 mm) from a receptacle outlet. Each countertop shall be treated separately in providing the number and spacing of outlets. Countertops divided by a sink, a range, a cooktop, an oven, or a refrigerator shall have receptacle outlets installed on each side where there is 12 in. (300 mm) or more of countertop space along the wall.

The procedure for laying out the location of these outlets is to measure 24 in. (600 mm) and then at 4 ft (1.2 m) intervals until the last receptacle outlet is no farther than 24 in. (600 mm) in any direction from an outlet. Receptacle outlets will be accurately provided for each countertop space by applying these measurements. Any receptacle outlets rendered inaccessible by the position of installed appliances such as a refrigerator shall not be considered as one of the required outlets. **(See Figure 16-13)**

ISLAND COUNTERTOP SPACES
210.52(C)(2)

An island countertop stands alone with no wall behind or beside it. Island countertops with a short dimension of 12 in. (300 mm) or greater or a long dimension of 24 in. (600 mm) or greater shall have at least one receptacle installed. **(See Figure 16-14)**

> **Design Tip:** See **210.52(B)(2)**, which lists the requirements for installing the small-appliance circuits for countertops in the kitchen and dining room areas. Refer to **210.8(A)(6)** for countertop receptacle outlets requiring GFCI protection.

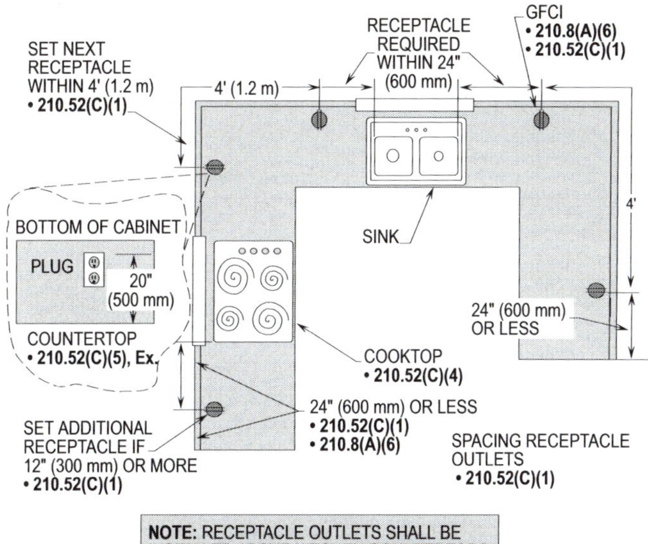

Figure 16-13. Receptacle outlets installed at kitchen countertops shall be located so no point along the countertop space is more than 24 in. (600 mm), measured horizontally, from a receptacle outlet. (Also, see **210.52(C)(4)** and **(C)(5)**.]

PENINSULAR COUNTERTOP SPACES
210.52(C)(3)

At least one receptacle outlet shall be installed at each peninsular countertop. A peninsular is a countertop without a wall on either side. Receptacle outlet(s) shall be installed for each peninsular with a long dimension of 24 in. (600 mm) or greater and a short dimension of 12 in. (300 mm) or greater. A peninsular countertop shall be measured from the connecting edge, and receptacle outlet(s) installed accordingly. The receptacle outlet(s) shall be installed above or within 12 in. (300 mm) below the countertop or a tombstone type receptacle shall be permitted to be installed on the countertop.

> **Design Tip:** If the countertop has an overhang of more than 6 in. (150 mm), a receptacle outlet shall not be permitted to be installed below the countertop per **210.52(C)(5), Ex. (See Figure 16-14)**

RECEPTACLE OUTLETS IN BATHROOMS
210.52(D)

A bathroom is not just a room but is an area including a basin(s) with a toilet, a urinal, a tub, a shower, a bidet, or similar plumbing fixtures per **Article 100**.

A utility sink or wet bar sink shall not be considered a bathroom, because no other fixtures mentioned are present.

> **Design Tip:** The key to defining a bathroom is that a basin and at least one or more of the other fixtures shall be present per **Article 100**.

Section **210.52(D)** requires at least one receptacle outlet to be installed in bathrooms within 3 ft (900 mm) of the outside edge of each basin in a dwelling unit. The receptacle outlet shall be located on a wall or partition that is adjacent to the basin or basin countertop, located on the countertop, or installed on the side or face of the basin cabinet not more than 12 in. (300 mm) below the countertop. Receptacle outlet assemblies listed for the application shall be permitted to be installed in the countertop. Section **210.8(A)(1)** requires all 15 or 20 amp, 125 volt receptacles to be GFCI protected for the safety of personnel using electric grooming tools. **(See Figure 16-15)**

> **Design Tip:** Each basin is required to have a receptacle outlet installed within 3 ft (900 mm) and located in such a manner so as to serve the sink area safely, without the use of extension cords.

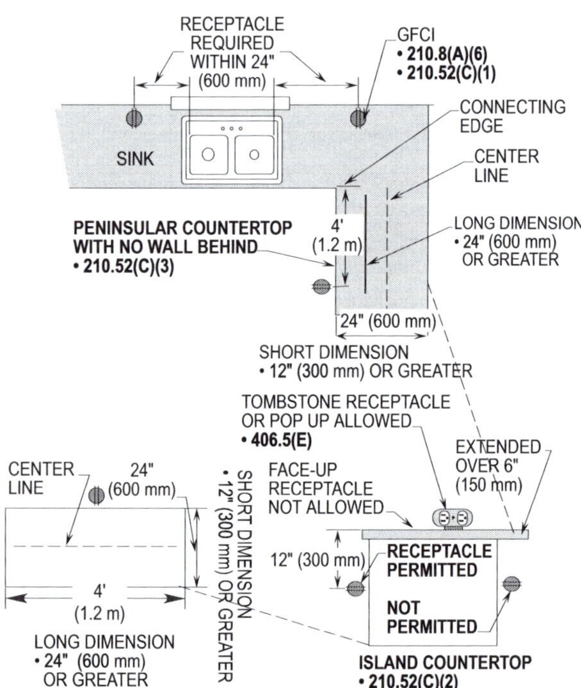

ISLAND AND PENINSULAR COUNTERTOP SPACES NEC 210.52(C)(2) AND (C)(3)

Figure 16-14. Installation requirements for receptacle outlet(s) on island or peninsular countertops.

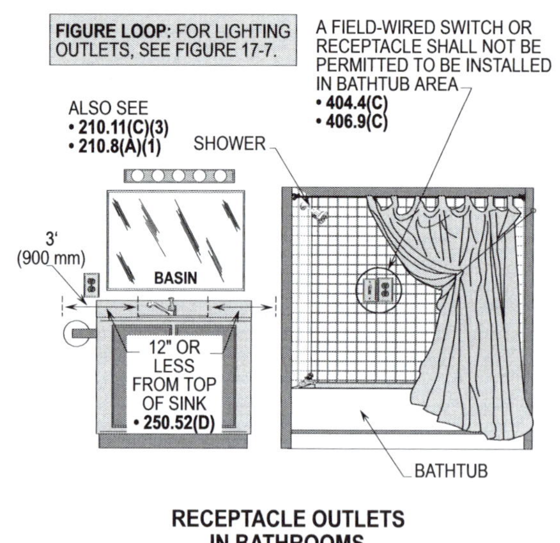

Figure 16-15. At least one receptacle outlet to serve the bathroom area shall be installed within 3 ft (900 mm) of the outside edge of each basin in a dwelling unit.

RECEPTACLE OUTLETS OUTDOORS 210.52(E)

At least two receptacle outlets shall be installed outdoors for one- and two-family dwellings. There shall be at least one receptacle outlet installed in the front and the back of such units. Section **210.8(A)(3)** requires such outdoor receptacle outlets to be GFCI protected to protect personnel from electrical shock when using such tools as drill motors, lawn mowers, hedge clippers, etc.

All outdoor receptacles with direct grade-level access shall be GFCI protected. *Direct grade-level* access is defined as a location 6 ft 6 in. (2 m) or less while standing from grade level and readily accessible to the user. Outdoor receptacle outlets shall be located on outside walls or open porches. Receptacle outlets located in the eaves of dwellings to connect Christmas lights or on balconies to cord-and-plug connect radios, VCRs, stereos, or TVs shall be GFCI protected even if they are located over 6 ft 6 in. (2 m) from direct grade level.

At least one receptacle outlet shall be installed within the perimeter for balconies, decks, and porches that are accessible from inside the dwelling unit. The receptacle shall be installed not more than 6-1/2 ft (2 m) above the balcony, deck, or porch surface.

Section **406.9(B)(1)** requires unattended receptacle outlets to be listed weather-resistant type with raintight covers to protect the components. Unattended outlets are those serving items such as outdoor Christmas lights, water pumps, etc. For receptacle outlets located outdoors for townhouses and condominiums with zero lot lines, see **210.8(A)(3)** and **210.52(E)**. **(See Figure 16-16)**

For example, a 20 amp small-appliance laundry circuit (20 A OCPD x 80% = 16 A) should be loaded with no more than 16 amps if used for long periods of time, such as three hours or longer. **(See Figure 16-17)**

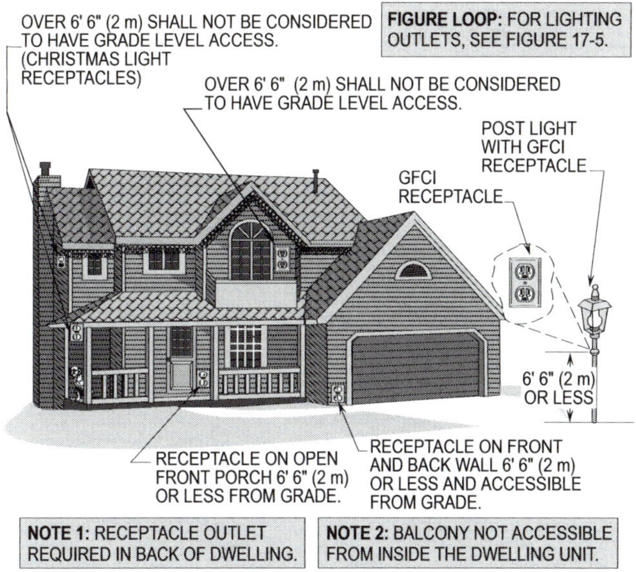

Figure 16-16. Receptacle outlets mounted on a wall or located on an open front porch or stoop of a dwelling unit shall be GFCI protected. **Note,** all the receptacles above shall be GFCI protected.

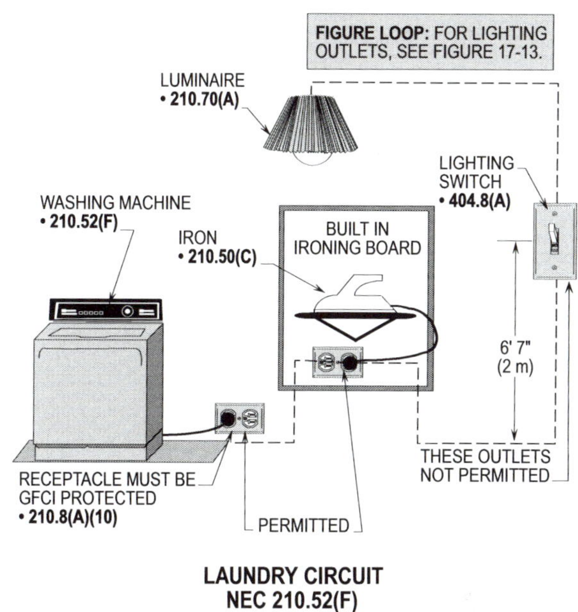

Figure 16-17. At least one 20 amp laundry circuit shall be required to serve laundry equipment in a one or two family dwelling. The laundry circuit shall be permitted to be routed to the garage, basement, utility room, or wherever the laundry room is located.

LAUNDRY CIRCUIT
210.52(F)

All laundry receptacle outlets shall be supplied by a 20 amp circuit utilizing a 12-2 AWG nonmetallic-sheathed cable with ground. This cable is usually nonmetallic-sheathed cable or armored cable. These outlets shall be AFCI protected per **210.8(A)(10).**

> **Design Tip:** A conduit system shall be permitted to be used with individual conductors pulled in after the conduit is installed. For the installer to use this wiring method, a local code usually requires it.

At least one receptacle outlet shall be installed for the laundry area. All laundry equipment shall be located within 6 ft (1.8 m) of the receptacle outlet per **210.50(C)**. Sometimes a 20 amp duplex receptacle is used to cord-and-plug connect a washing machine and a gas dryer. No other outlets shall be supplied by this 20 amp, 2-wire small-appliance circuit.

RECEPTACLE OUTLETS IN BASEMENTS AND GARAGES
210.52(G)

At least one receptacle outlet shall be installed in the basement and garage, attached or detached, with electric power. GFCI-protected receptacles shall be installed in basements and garages to protect people from electric shock when using electric hand tools.

RECEPTACLES IN BASEMENTS
210.52(G)

At least one GFCI-protected receptacle outlet per **210.8(A)(5)** shall be installed in the basement, when it is left unfinished. An unfinished basement means that the basement is used for storage or a workshop. If more than one receptacle outlet is installed, then all of the receptacle outlets shall be GFCI protected. These outlets are to protect people from electric shock when using electrical hand tools such as electric drills, saws, sanders, etc. If the basement is finished into one or more habitable rooms, each separate unfinished portion of the basement shall have a receptacle outlet installed.

The **Exception** to **210.8(A)(5)** does not require GFCI protection where a receptacle supplies only a permanently installed fire alarm or burglar alarm system.

At least one GFCI-protected receptacle per **210.8(A)(4)** shall be installed in a crawl space at or below grade level. This receptacle shall be permitted to be used for serving HVAC equipment or be used for a drop light, hand tool, etc.

See Figure 16-18 and **210.70(A)(3)** for the requirements of lighting outlets.

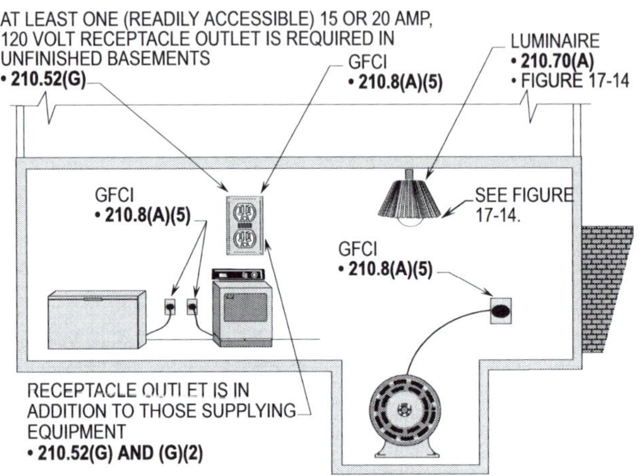

RECEPTACLES IN BASEMENTS
NEC 210.52(G)

Figure 16-18. At least one 15 or 20 amp, 125 volt receptacle shall be installed in an unfinished basement.

RECEPTACLES IN GARAGES
210.52(G)

At least one GFCI receptacle per **210.52(G)** and **210.8(A)(2)** shall be installed for each car space in an attached or unattached garage.

A GFCI receptacle outlet shall not be required in a detached garage unless electric power is routed to the garage. Refer to **210.70(A)(2)(a)** for luminaire requirements. **(See 210.52(G), Ex.'s 1 and 2 and Figure 16-19)**

RECEPTACLES IN HALLWAYS
210.52(H)

Hallways in dwelling units that are 10 ft (3 m) or more in length without passing through a doorway shall have a receptacle outlet installed. This receptacle outlet may be

used for the connection of plugged-in appliances such as table lamps, floor lamps, vacuum cleaners, etc. The length of the hallway shall be measured along its center line to determine whether a receptacle outlet is required. The receptacle outlet should be located so it serves the hallway in the most convenient manner. **(See Figure 16-20)**

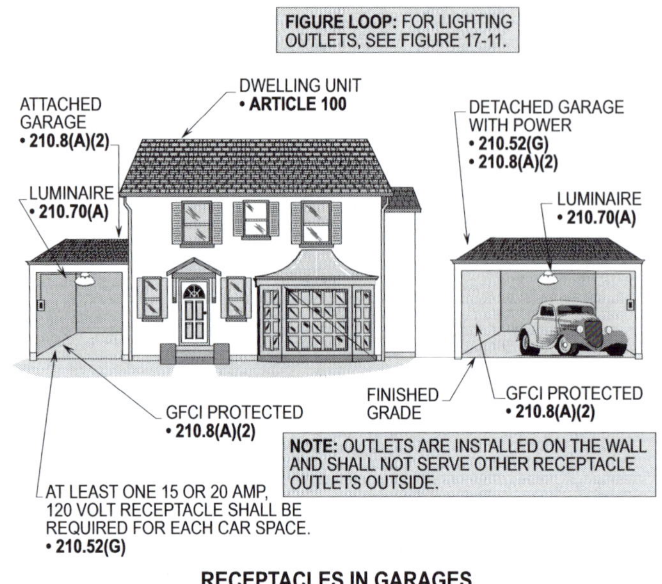

RECEPTACLES IN GARAGES
NEC 210.52(G) AND Ex. 1 AND 2

Figure 16-19. At least one 15 or 20 amp receptacle outlet shall be installed for each car space in the garage at 5 ft 6 in. (1.7 m) or less from the finished floor to be considered a required outlet.

Note, the receptacle outlet installed per **210.52(G)** is in addition to outlets supplying equipment.

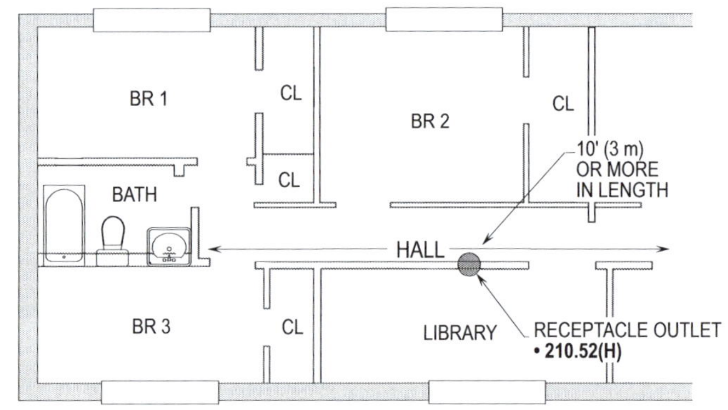

RECEPTACLES IN HALLWAYS
NEC 210.52(H)

Figure 16-20. At least one receptacle outlet shall be installed in dwelling unit hallways that are 10 ft (3 m) or more in length without passing through a doorway.

FOYERS
210.52(I)

Foyers that are not part of a hallway and have an area greater than 60 ft² (5.6 m²) shall have a receptacle(s) located in each wall space 3 ft (900 mm) or more in width and unbroken by doorways, floor-to-ceiling windows, and similar openings. **(See Figure 16-21)**

GFCI PROTECTION OF RECEPTACLES
210.8(A)(1) THRU (A)(10)

A GFCI circuit breaker or receptacle detects any imbalance current in the circuit such as current leaking to ground through the body of a person using an electric hand tool. This imbalance of current trips open the GFCI unit at about 4 to 6 milliamps plus or minus 1 milliamp. The action of the GFCI prevents any harm to the person using the receptacle under adverse conditions of use.

It only takes a relatively small amount of current flowing through the body to be fatal. Electrocution may occur at about 380 milliamps. GFCI protection protects people from such hazards while working with electrical hand tools.

Design Tip: GFCI protection of receptacles shall be required in bathrooms, garages, outdoors, basements, crawl spaces, kitchens, wet bars, and boathouses. **(See Figure 16-22)**

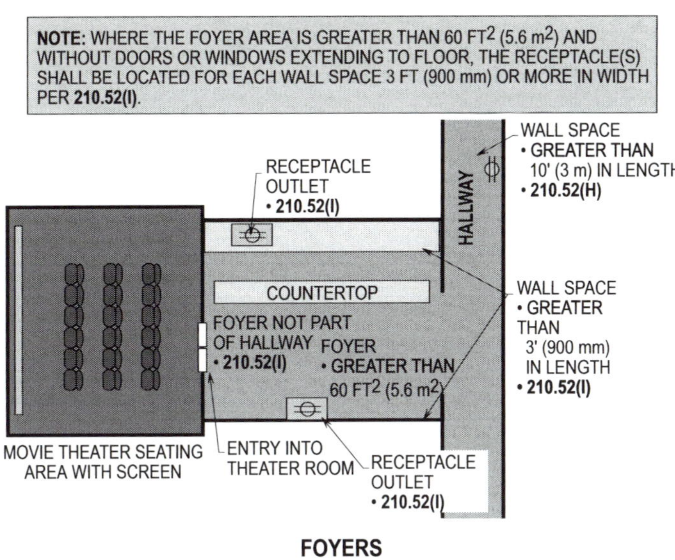

Figure 16-21. This illustration shows the spacing requirements for receptacles installed in foyers.

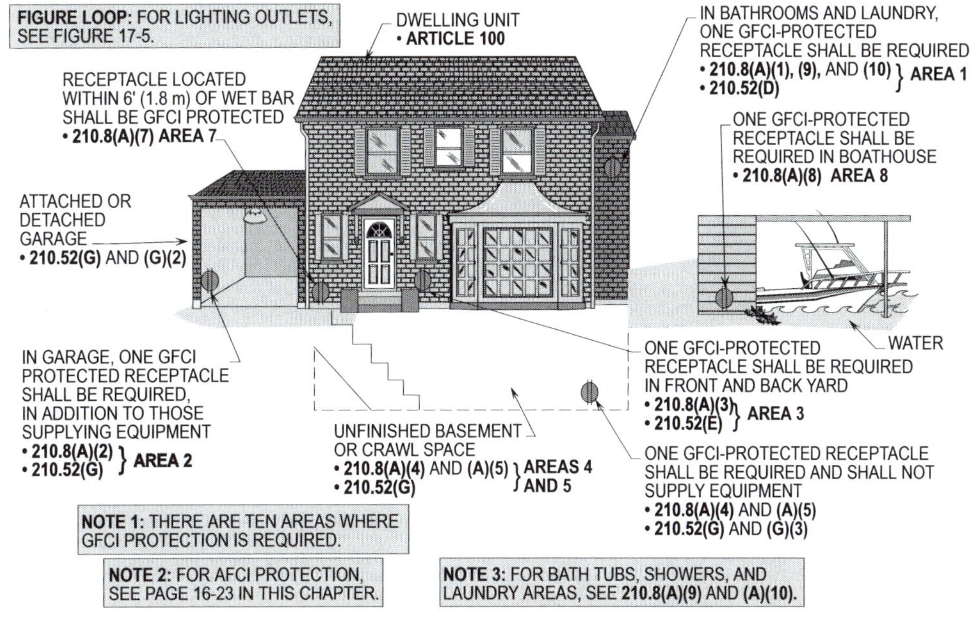

Figure 16-22. One or more GFCI-protected receptacles shall be required for the bathroom, kitchen, garage, crawl space, unfinished basement, and the outdoors (front and back) of a dwelling unit. GFCI-protected receptacles are also required within 6 ft (1.8 m) of the wet bar or similar sink. At least one GFCI-protected receptacle outlet shall be required for a boathouse.

PROTECTION IN BATHROOMS
210.8(A)(1)

All 15 or 20 amp, 125 volt receptacles shall be provided with GFCI protection if located in the bathroom. (For the definition of bathroom, see **Article 100**.) The receptacles shall be supplied by a circuit protected by a GFCI circuit breaker or by a GFCI receptacle, or be served by a fed-through GFCI-protected receptacle.

At least one receptacle outlet shall be installed within 3 ft (900 mm) of the outside edge of each sink per **210.52(D)** and **210.8(A)(1)** and also requires this receptacle and all others, if present, to be GFCI protected. Sections **404.4** and **406.9(C)** do not permit a switch outlet to be installed in the bathtub area, where the elements of such devices may be sprayed with water.

Design Tip: If a 20 amp, 120 volt laundry receptacle is installed in the bathroom, it is required to be GFCI protected per **210.8(A)(1)**. **(See Figure 16-23)**

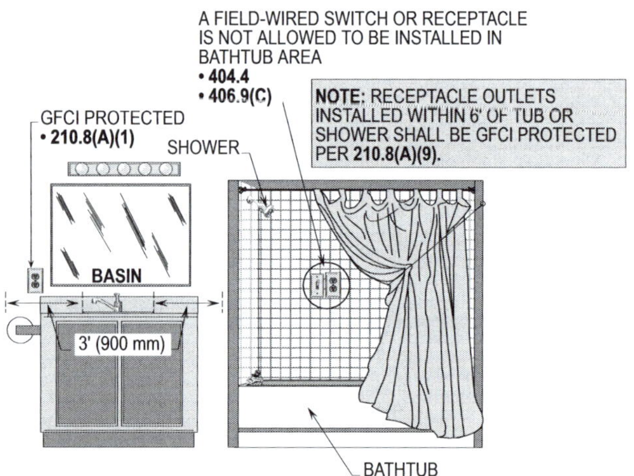

PROTECTION IN BATHROOMS
NEC 210.8(A)(1)

Figure 16-23. At least one GFCI receptacle outlet shall be installed within 3 ft (900 mm) of each basin in a bathroom.

PROTECTION IN GARAGES
210.8(A)(2)

All 15 or 20 amp, 125 volt receptacles installed in garages shall have GFCI protection for the safety of personnel. Since the concrete slab is in direct contact with the earth, the garage shall be considered a hazardous area for people using electric hand tools. Leakage current from a faulty electric hand tool may flow through the human body, through the concrete slab, and through the earth to complete the circuit.

The NEC requires only one 15 or 20 amp, 125 volt receptacle outlet to be installed for each car space. If there are more installed, such as over a workbench, they shall be GFCI protected.

See Figure 16-24 for a detailed illustration pertaining to receptacles installed in garages.

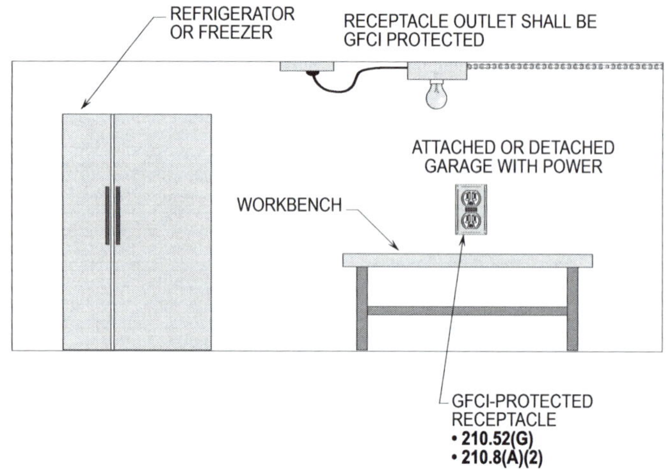

PROTECTION IN GARAGES
NEC 210.8(A)(2)

Figure 16-24. All 15 or 20 amp, 125 volt receptacles installed in garages shall be GFCI protected. **Note,** at least one shall be installed for each car space.

PROTECTION IN ACCESSORY BUILDINGS
210.8(A)(2)

Accessory buildings (unfinished or finished) for a dwelling unit not intended to be used as a habitable room and limited to storage areas, work areas, or similar purposes, shall have GFCI protection for all 125 volt, single-phase, 15 and 20 amp receptacles. **(See Figure 16-25)**

PROTECTION OUTDOORS
210.8(A)(3)

All 15 or 20 amp, 125 volt receptacle outlets located outdoors that are installed 6 ft 6 in. (2 m) or less from direct grade level shall be GFCI protected. Direct grade level is defined as being readily accessible and located 6 ft 6 in. (2 m) or less from grade level, while standing.

Receptacles at 6 ft 6 in. (2 m) or less from grade and located in the front and back yard of houses shall be GFCI protected. Receptacles located in post lights at 6 ft 6 in. (2 m) or less shall be GFCI protected. Receptacle outlets located above 6 ft 6 in. (2 m), such as in eaves for the connection of Christmas lights or on balconies, shall also be GFCI protected per **426.28** and **427.22**. **(See Figure 16-26)**

At least one receptacle outlet shall be installed within the perimeter of the balcony, deck, or porch area if accessible from inside the dwelling unit. The receptacle shall not be located more than 6 ft 6 in. (2 m) above the balcony, deck, or porch surface.

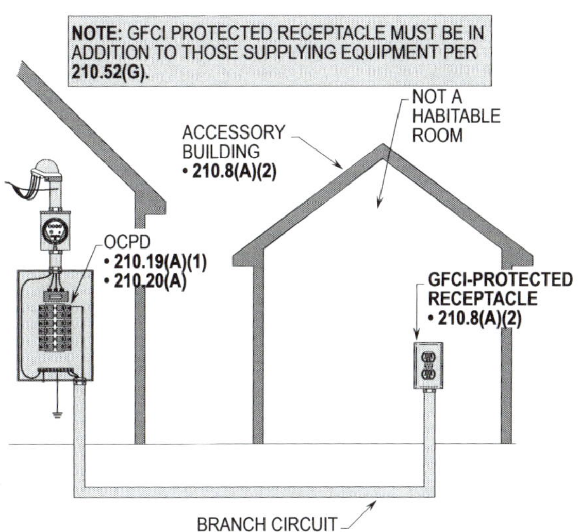

Figure 16-25. GFCI protection shall be provided for all 125 volt, single-phase, 15 and 20 amp receptacles for accessory buildings (unfinished or finished) for a dwelling unit.

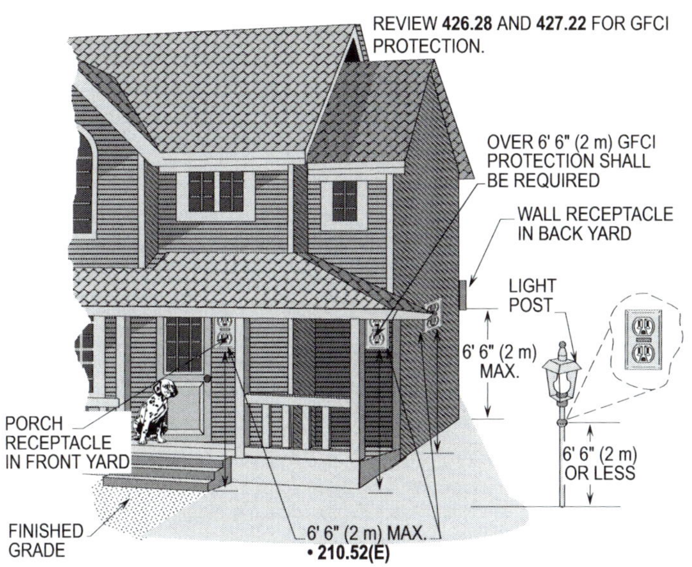

Figure 16-26. At least one receptacle outlet located outdoors in the front and back shall be installed 6 ft 6 in. (2 m) or less from finished grade and be readily accessible to the user. These outlets shall be GFCI protected.

PROTECTION IN BASEMENTS AND CRAWL SPACES
210.8(A)(4) AND 210.8(A)(5)

All 15 or 20 amp, 125 volt receptacle outlets installed in crawl spaces at or below grade level to serve electrical equipment shall be GFCI protected per **210.8(A)(4)**. Most mechanical codes require a receptacle outlet to be installed for the servicing of mechanical and related equipment.

See Figure 16-27 for rules pertaining to the installation and protection of receptacles in crawl spaces and basements.

At least one 15 or 20 amp, 125 volt receptacle outlet shall be installed in unfinished basements of dwelling units. These basements are unfinished and are not habitable. If they were habitable, they would be finished as a bedroom, den, game room, etc. and occupied by people. An unfinished basement is not trimmed out and may be utilized as a workshop area or storage area.

The **Exception** to **210.8(A)(5)** and **760.41(B),** as well as **760.121(B)** does not require a permanently installed fire alarm or burglar alarm system receptacle to be GFCI protected.

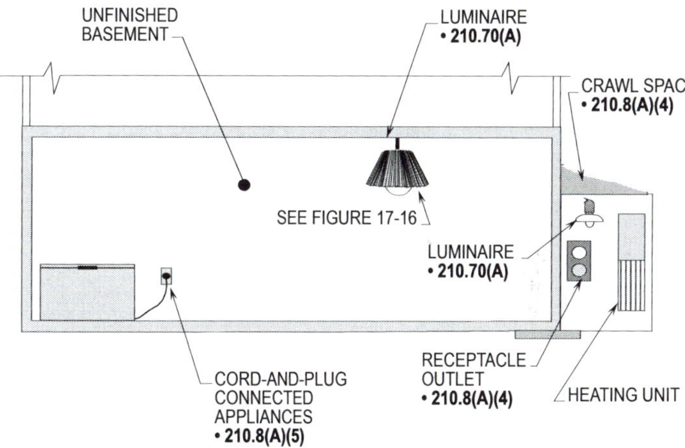

Figure 16-27. All 15 or 20 amp, 125 volt receptacle outlets installed in crawl spaces at or below grade level to serve electrical equipment shall be GFCI protected.

PROTECTION OVER COUNTERTOPS
210.8(A)(6) AND (A)(7)

All 15 or 20 amp, 125 volt receptacle outlets installed over kitchen countertops shall be GFCI protected. Receptacle outlets included are those located over or below the countertop and on islands or peninsulas that are supplied by the small-appliance circuits per **210.11(C)(1), 210.52(B),** and **210.52(C). (See Figure 16-28)**

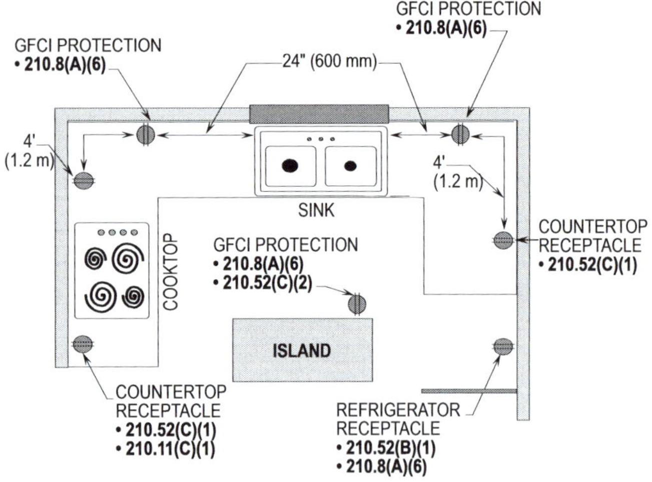

PROTECTION OVER COUNTERTOPS
NEC 210.8(A)(6)

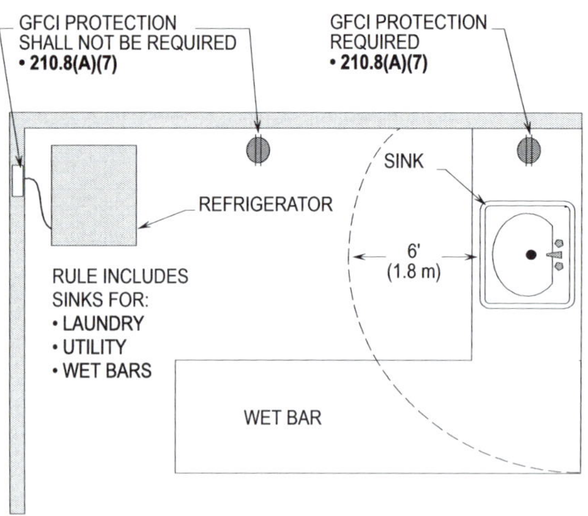

PROTECTION OVER COUNTERTOPS WITH SINKS
NEC 210.8(A)(7)

Figure 16-28. All 15 or 20 amp, 125 volt receptacles serving kitchen countertop surfaces located above or below shall be GFCI protected. This rule is to protect the user.

> **Design Tip:** If a pull chain luminaire with a receptacle outlet is installed over the kitchen sink, it shall be GFCI protected per **210.8(A)(6)**.

Receptacle outlets located over utility sinks shall not be required to be GFCI protected, because the sink does not have an additional fixture such as a toilet, a tub, or shower per **Article 100**. Receptacle outlets installed within 6 ft (1.8 m) of laundry, utility, and wet bar sinks shall be GFCI protected to protect personnel using blenders and other drink-related appliances per **210.8(A)(7)**.

Utility sinks are usually used to clean mops, etc., while wet bar sinks are utilized to entertain guests at parties and other social functions in the home.

> **Design Tip:** A receptacle used to cord-and-plug connect a refrigerator shall not be required to be GFCI protected per **210.8(A)(6)**. **(See Figure 16-29)**

PROTECTION FOR BOATHOUSES
210.8(A)(8) AND 210.8(C)

All receptacle outlets rated at 15 or 20 amps, 125 volts that are installed in boathouses to provide power for electric hand tools to work on boats shall be GFCI protected. Personnel using electric hand tools are exposed to wet locations due to the presence of water. GFCI-protected circuits protect personnel from electrical shock while using electricity around such hazardous conditions. See **555.19(B)(1)** for such protection pertaining to marinas and boat yards. **(See Figure 16-30)**

Figure 16-29. All 15 or 20 amp, 125 volt receptacle outlets located within 6 ft (1.8 m) of a wet bar sink shall be GFCI protected except for a properly located refrigerator plug.

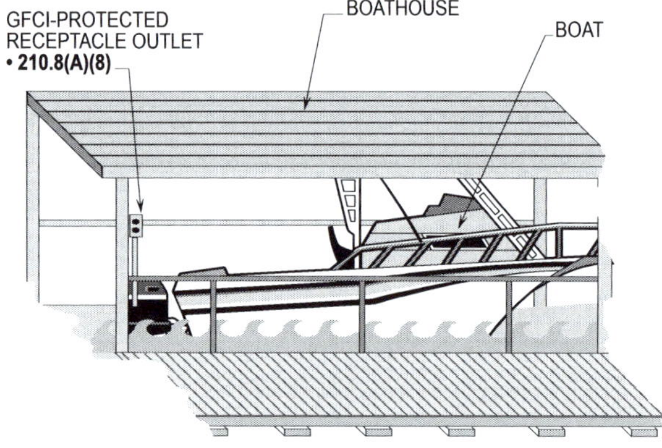

PROTECTION FOR BOATHOUSES
NEC 210.8(A)(8)

Figure 16-30. All 15 or 20 amp, 125 volt receptacle outlets shall be GFCI protected when installed in boathouses.

PROTECTION FOR DWELLING UNITS
210.8(A)(9) AND (A)(10)

Ground-fault circuit-interruption for personnel shall be provided as required in **210.8(A) through (C)**. The ground-fault circuit-interrupter shall be installed in a readily accessible location.

In dwelling units all 125-volt, single-phase, 15- and 20-ampere receptacles installed in the locations specified in **210.8(A)(1) through (10)** shall have ground-fault circuit-interrupter protection for personnel. (**See Figure 16-31(a)** for bathtubs and shower stalls and **Figure 16-31(b)** for laundry areas.)

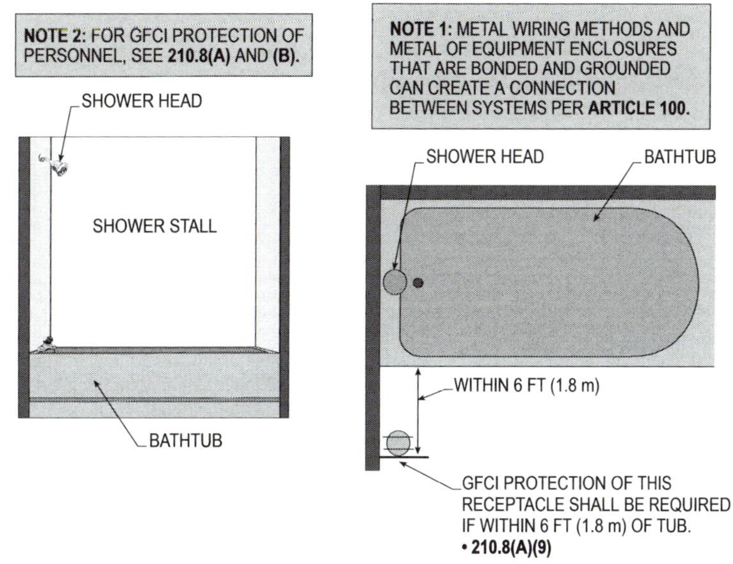

Figure 16-31(a) shows receptacles that are installed within 6 ft (1.8 m) of the outside edge of the bathtub or shower are required to be GFCI protected.

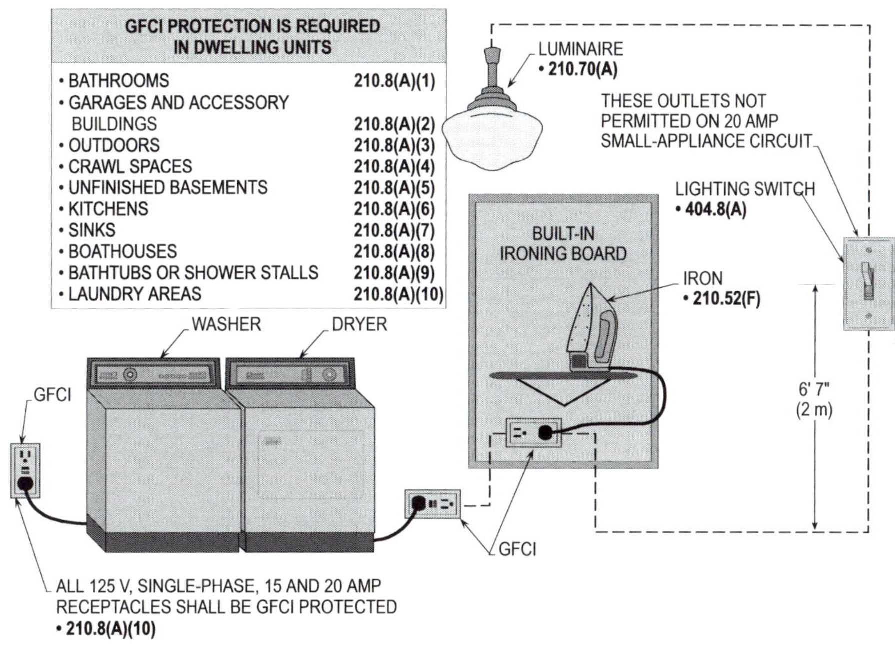

Figure 16-31(b) shows receptacles that are installed in laundry areas are required to be GFCI protected

PROTECTION AROUND SWIMMING POOLS 680.22(A)(1) THRU (A)(5)

The following requirements for protection around swimming pools apply to residential, commercial, and industrial locations.

Receptacle outlets installed near swimming pools and fountains shall be properly located to minimize the threat of shock hazards to personnel in or around the pool. Receptacles shall not be permitted to be located within 6 ft (1.83 m) of the inside walls of the pool per **680.22(A)(2)** and **(A)(3)**.

At least one 15 or 20 amp, 125 volt receptacle outlet shall be installed at a minimum of 6 ft (1.83 m) from and not more than 20 ft (6 m) from the inside walls of the pool or fountain per **680.22(A)(2), (A)(3),** and **(A)(5)**. Receptacle outlets that are installed behind enclosed rooms with hinged or sliding doors, windows, or other barriers shall be permitted within the 6 ft (1.83 m) limitation of a swimming pool per **680.22(A)(5)**. The receptacle outlet located within the 20 ft (6 m) boundary of the swimming pool shall be GFCI protected per **680.22(A)(4)**. **[See Figures 16-32(a)** and **(b)]**

Design Tip: See **680.22(A)(1)** that permits a single locking receptacle outlet to be located not less than 6 ft (1.83 m) from the inside walls of the pool. This receptacle outlet shall be GFCI protected per **680.22(A)(1)**. A cord-and-plug connected recirculating pool pump can easily be removed in winter. **(See Figure 16-33)**

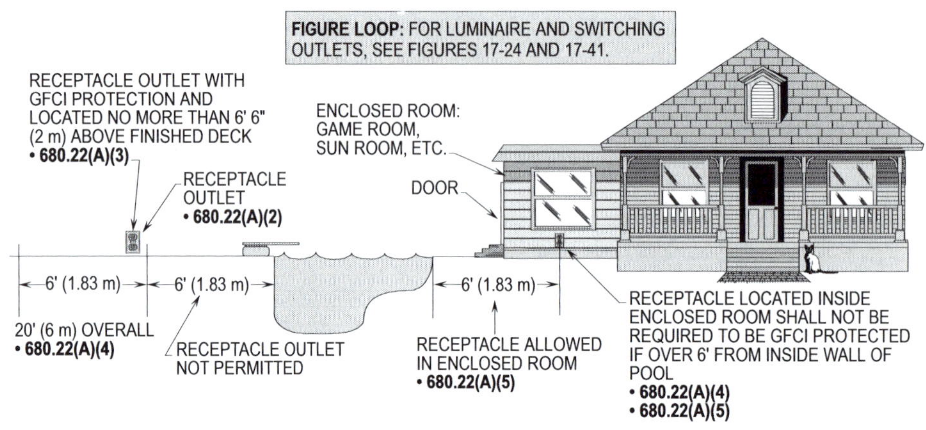

Figure 16-32(a). At least one GFCI protected receptacle shall be located in an area within 6 ft (1.83 m) to 20 ft (6 m) from the inside wall of the pool. Receptacles located inside enclosed rooms and within 6 ft (1.83 m) of the inside walls of the pool shall be required to be GFCI protected. Personnel inside the enclosed room are not exposed to the pool area.

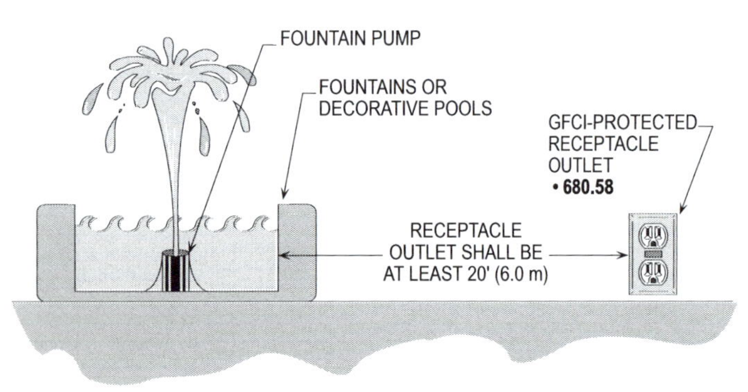

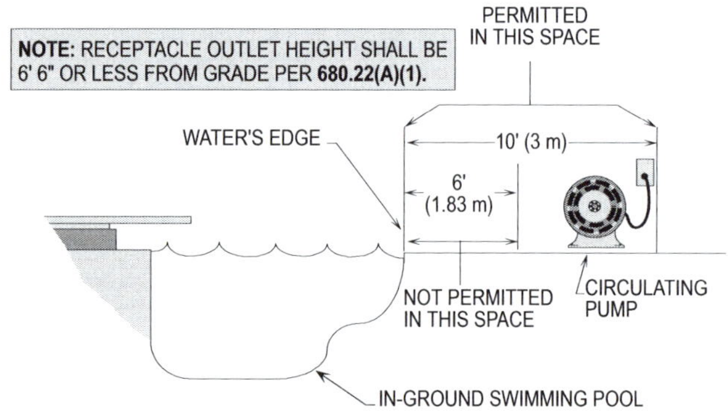

Figure 16-32(b). Receptacle outlets for fountains or decorative pools shall be located at least 20 ft (6.0 m) from the receptacle to the inside walls. **Note,** this receptacle is not required, but if installed it shall be GFCI protected.

Figure 16-33. A single locking type GFCI-protected receptacle outlet shall be permitted to be installed between 6 ft (1.83 m) and 10 ft (3 m) from the inside walls of a swimming pool or fountain to supply power to a water pump motor.

PROTECTION FOR STORABLE POOLS
680.32

Storable pools shall be installed at least 6 ft (1.83 m) from any receptacle outlet per **680.34**. Electrical equipment associated with storage pools shall be provided with GFCI protection for the safety of personnel using the pool. See **90.7** and **110.3(B)**.

Design Tip: The cord supplying power from the receptacle outlet to the pool equipment shall also have GFCI protection. The supply cord may be longer than 3 ft (900 mm) per **680.7(A)**. There are UL-listed supply cords of 25 ft (7.5 m) in length and approved to be used to cord-and-plug connect filter pumps to storable pools. The 3 ft (900 mm) limitation does not apply to cords used to connect filter pumps to storable pools. The GFCI protection shall be permitted to be provided by a GFCI-protected receptacle or a remote GFCI-protected receptacle or circuit breaker per **680.32**. **(See Figure 16-34) Note,** All receptacle outlets within 6 ft of storable pools shall be GFCI protected.

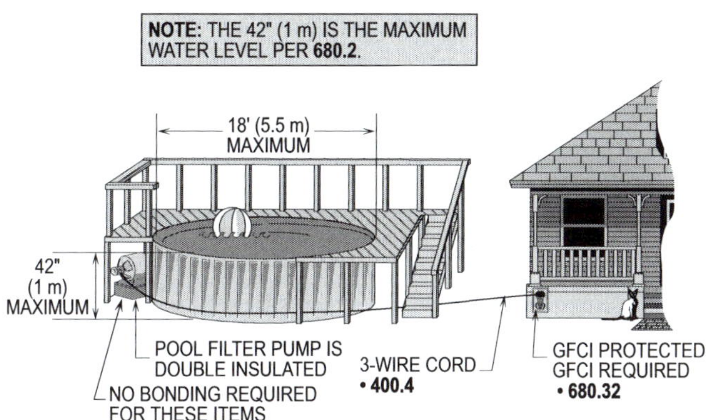

PROTECTION FOR STORABLE POOLS
NEC 680.32

Figure 16-34. Electrical equipment that is cord-and-plug connected shall be served by a GFCI-protected receptacle outlet or circuit.

PROTECTION FOR SPAS OR HOT TUBS
680.43(A)(1) AND (A)(2)

Receptacle outlets shall be located at least 6 ft (1.83 m) from the inside walls of a spa or hot tub to ensure the safety of the user. Receptacle outlets installed 6 ft (1.83 m) to 10 ft (3 m) from the inside walls of the spa or hot tub shall be GFCI protected by a GFCI-protected receptacle or circuit breaker.

At least one receptacle outlet shall be provided in this area for the protection of personnel using cord-and-plug connected radios, TVs, stereos, etc. Receptacle outlets supplying power to a spa or hot tub shall be GFCI protected per **680.43(A)(3)**. **(See Figure 16-35)**

Design Tip: See **680.42** for the installation requirements of spas or hot tubs that are located outdoors and apply **Parts I** and **II** of **Article 680** that pertain to swimming pools.

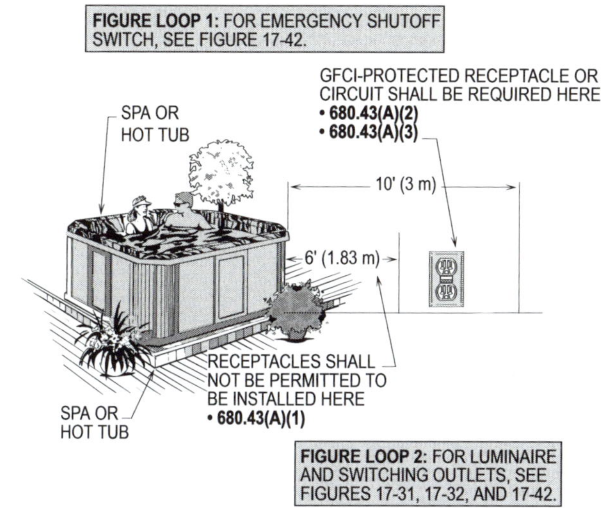

PROTECTION FOR SPAS OR HOT TUBS
NEC 680.43(A)(1) AND (A)(2)

Figure 16-35. Receptacle outlets installed around a spa or hot tub that are located inside the dwelling unit. For spa or hot tubs located outside, see **680.40**.

PROTECTION FOR HYDROMASSAGE TUBS
680.71 THRU 680.74

Receptacle outlets installed near hydromassage tubs shall be provided with GFCI protection per **210.8(A)(1)**. Hydromassage tubs are treated just like regular bathtubs per **680.72**. All electrical elements for hydromassage tubs shall be supplied by GFCI circuits per **680.71**. The wiring methods shall comply with the provisions of **Chapters 1 through 4,** which are to be applied generally. Circulating motors shall comply with the requirements of **430.14(A)** and **680.73** for accessibility, so that proper maintenance and adequate ventilation may be provided. **(See Figure 16-36)**

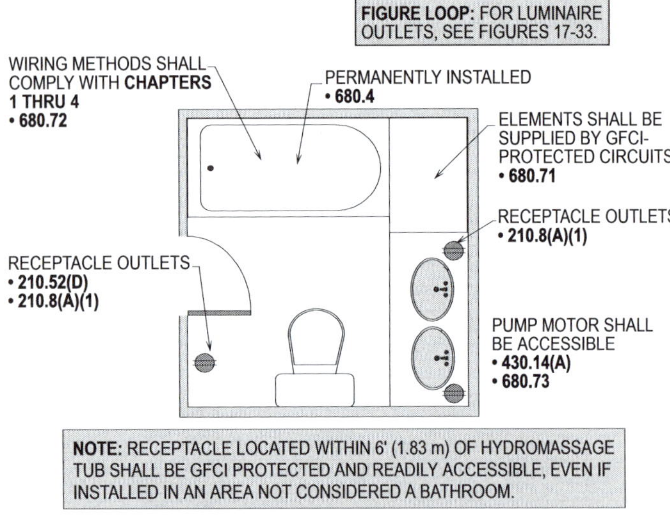

Figure 16-36. Hydromassage bathtubs are treated as regular bathtubs and shall comply with **680.70, 680.71, 680.72, 680.73,** and **680.74** and other pertinent Sections of the NEC.

RECEPTACLES ON CONSTRUCTION SITES 590.6(A) AND (B)

All 15, 20, and 30 amp, 125 volt receptacles used by personnel during construction, remodeling, maintenance, repair, or demolition of buildings, structures, equipment, or similar activities shall have GFCI protection per **590.6(A)(1)**. **(See Figure 16-37)**

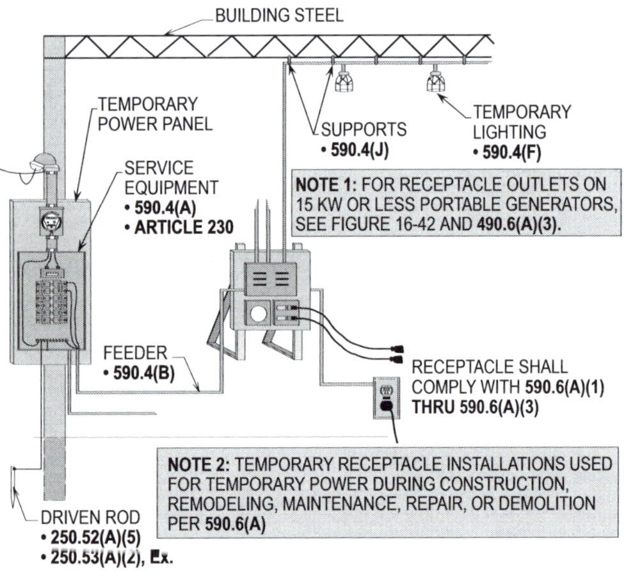

Figure 16-37. This illustration shows the requirements for temporary receptacle installations supplying power for temporary use.

GFCI protection shall be provided for all 15, 20, and 30 amp, 125 volt receptacles that are not a part of the permanent wiring of the building or structure. **(See Figure 16-38)**

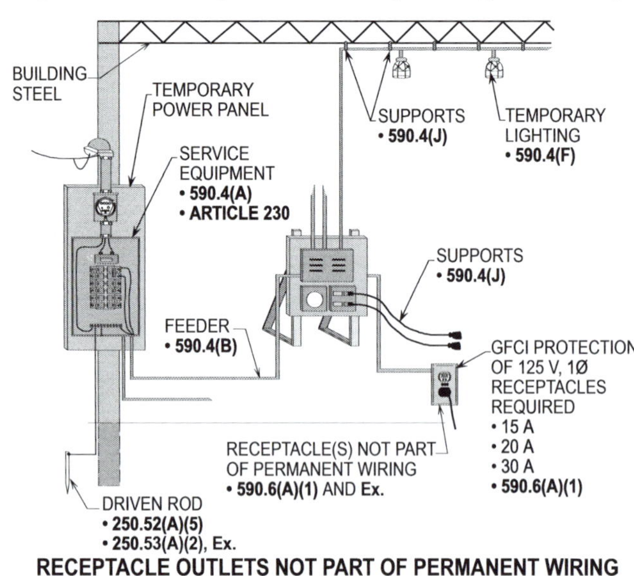

Figure 16-38. This illustration shows the requirements for receptacle outlets not part of permanent wiring to be GFCI protected.

All 15, 20, and 30 amp, 125 volt receptacles shall have GFCI protection where installed or existing as part of the permanent wiring of the building or structure and used for temporary electric power. Listed cord sets or devices incorporating listed GFCI protection for personnel identified for portable use shall be permitted. **(See Figure 16-39)**

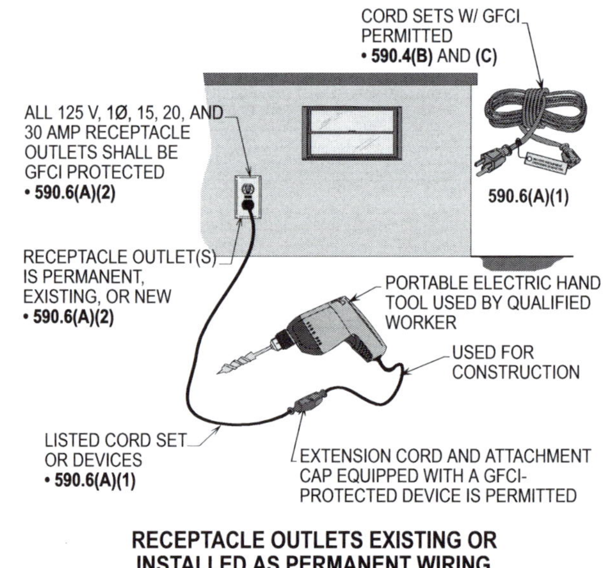

Figure 16-39. This illustration shows the requirements for receptacle outlets existing or installed as permanent wiring to be GFCI protected.

GFCI protection shall be provided for all 15, 20, and 30 amp, 125 volt receptacles that are a part of a 15 kW or smaller portable generator. All 15 and 20 amp, 125 and 250 volt receptacles, including those that are part of a portable generator, used in a damp or wet location shall comply with **406.9(A)** and **(B). (See Figure 16-40)**

Note, listed cord sets or devices incorporating listed GFCI protection for personnel identified for portable use shall be permitted for use with 15 kW or less portable generators manufactured or remanufactured prior to January 1, 2011.

The AHJ has the authority to approve a written procedure that requires three-wire extension cords with equipment grounding conductors. Personnel shall be designated to enforce the program utilizing the following procedures:

- All equipment grounding conductors shall be tested for continuity and shall be electrically continuous.

- Each receptacle and attachment plug shall be tested for correct attachment of the equipment grounding conductor.

- All required tests shall be performed as follows:

  (a) Before first use on site

  (b) When there is evidence of damage

  (c) Before equipment is returned to service following any repairs

  (d) At intervals not exceeding 3 months

Note, the assured equipment grounding conductor program only applies to industrial sites where conditions of maintenance and supervision ensure that only qualified personnel are involved per **590.6(B)(2)** and **590.6(A), Ex.**

Receptacle outlets shall not be connected to any branch circuits supplying power to lighting outlets per **590.4(D).** The reason for this rule is to prevent a ground fault on an electric hand tool from opening the overcurrent protection device on the circuit and putting the worker in the dark, which could be dangerous.

> **Design Tip:** Section **590.6(B)(2)(a)(1)** and **OSHA 1926, Subpart K** must be studied carefully and applied properly to protect the users of such cords and provide a safe workplace for employees building or remodeling dwelling units.

RECEPTACLES INSTALLED IN BATHROOMS OF COMMERCIAL AND INDUSTRIAL LOCATIONS
210.8(B)(1)

In the bathrooms of commercial and industrial locations, GFCIs shall be installed for the protection of personnel. This will include all 125 volt, 15 and 20 ampere circuits in the bathroom.

Note, such receptacle outlets shall not be required to be installed, but if they are, they shall be GFCI protected. By definition, a bathroom is an area including a basin and at least one of the following: a toilet, a urinal, a tub, a shower, a bidet, or similar plumbing fixtures. **(See Figure 16-41)**

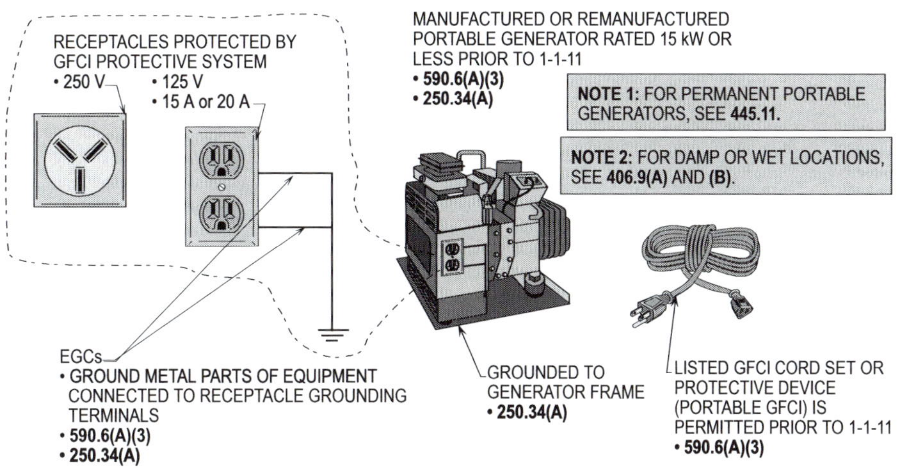

Figure 16-40. This illustration shows the GFCI requirements for temporarily used receptacle outlets on 15 kW or smaller portable generators.

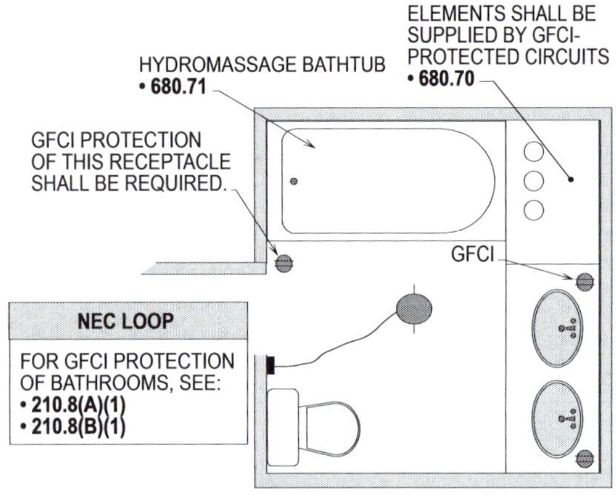

**RECEPTACLES INSTALLED IN BATHROOMS OF
COMMERCIAL AND INDUSTRIAL LOCATIONS
NEC 210.8(B)(1)**

Figure 16-41. In the bathrooms of commercial and industrial locations, GFCIs shall be installed for the protection of personnel.

RECEPTACLES INSTALLED IN KITCHENS OF COMMERCIAL AND INDUSTRIAL BUILDINGS
210.8(B)(2)

All 125, 15 or 20 amp receptacles installed in kitchens of commercial and industrial buildings shall have ground-fault protection for personnel. **(See Figure 16-42)**

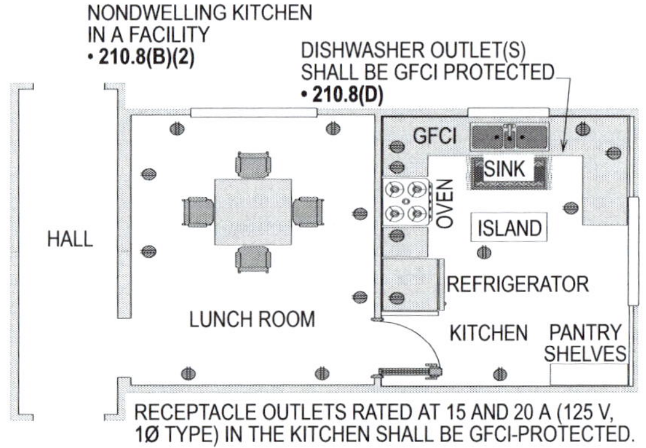

**RECEPTACLES INSTALLED IN KITCHENS OF
COMMERCIAL AND INDUSTRIAL BUILDINGS
NEC 210.8(B)(2)**

Figure 16-42. All 125 volt, 15 or 20 amp receptacles installed on roofs shall have ground-fault protection for personnel. **Note,** dishwasher outlet(s) shall be GFCI protected per **210.8(D)**

RECEPTACLES INSTALLED ON ROOFTOPS OF COMMERCIAL AND INDUSTRIAL BUILDINGS
210.8(B)(3)

All 125 volt, 15 or 20 amp receptacles installed on roofs shall have ground-fault protection for personnel.

Note, this does not apply to receptacles installed on the roofs of dwelling units. **(See Figure 16-43)**

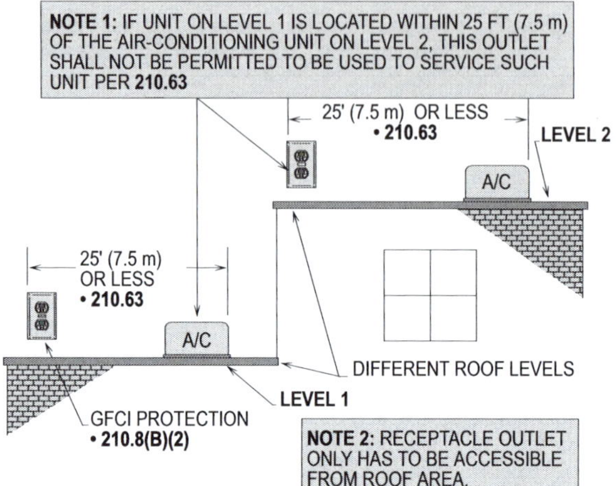

**RECEPTACLES INSTALLED ON ROOFTOPS OF
COMMERCIAL AND INDUSTRIAL BUILDINGS
NEC 210.8(B)(3) AND Ex. 1 to (3)**

Figure 16-43. All 125, 15 or 20 amp receptacles installed in kitchens of commercial and industrial buildings shall have ground-fault protection for personnel. (Review the **Ex.** to **210.63**)

RECEPTACLES INSTALLED OUTDOORS
210.8(B)(4)

All 125 volt, 15 and 20 amp receptacles installed outdoors shall have GFCI protection. **(See Figure 16-44)**

RECEPTACLE OUTLETS INSTALLED IN INDOOR WET LOCATIONS
210.8(B)(6)

All 125 volt, 15, 20 and 30 amp receptacles installed in indoor wet locations shall have GFCI protection. **(See Figure 16-45)**

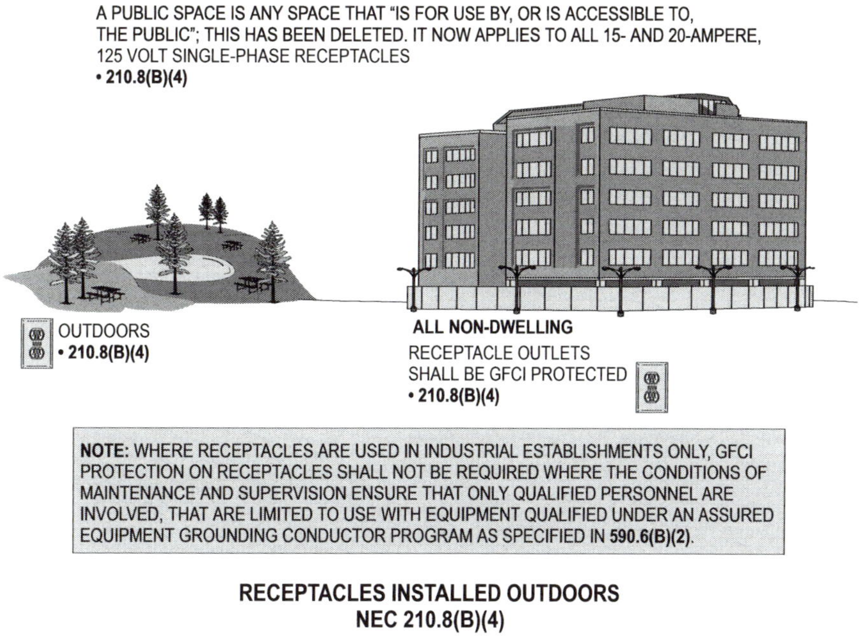

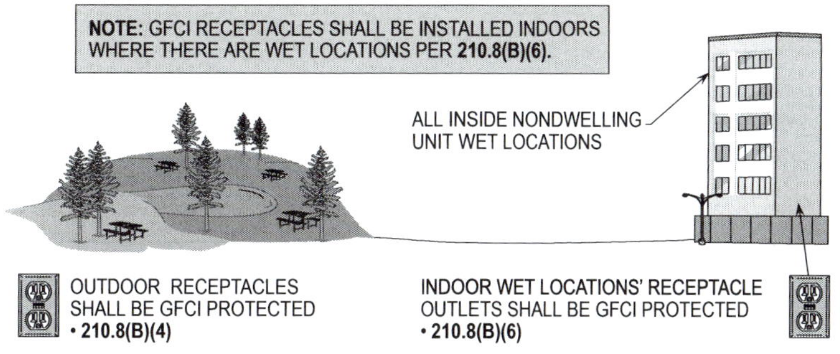

Figure 16-44. GFCI protection shall be required for all 125 volt, 15 and 20 amp receptacles installed outdoors.

Figure 16-45. This illustration shows that inside receptacles of nondwelling units installed in wet locations shall be GFCI protected. (Wet locations are defined in **Article 100** under "Location, wet".

LOCKER ROOMS WITH SHOWERS
210.8(B)(7)

All 125 volt, 15 and 20 amp receptacles installed in locker rooms with associated showering facilities shall be GFCI protected. **(See Figure 16-46)**

GARAGES, SERVICE BAYS, AND SIMILAR AREAS
210.8(B)(8)

All 125 volt, 15 and 20 amp receptacles installed in garages, service bays, and similar areas(vehicle exhibition halls and show rooms) where electrical diagnostic equipment, electrical hand tools, or portable lighting equipment are to be used shall be GFCI protected. **(See Figure 16-47)**

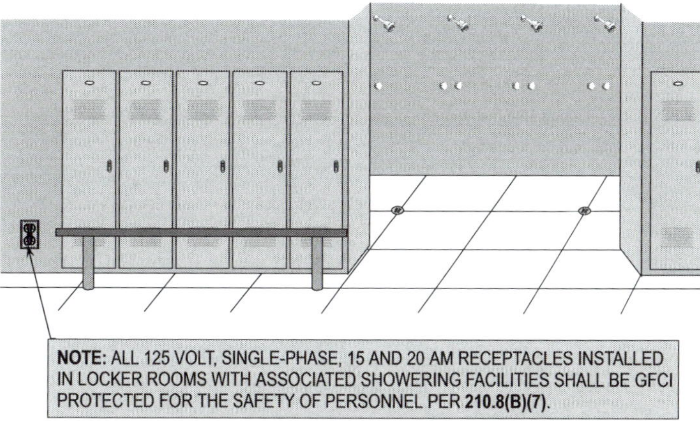

Figure 16-46. This illustration shows that GFCI protection shall be provided for locker rooms with associated showering facilities.

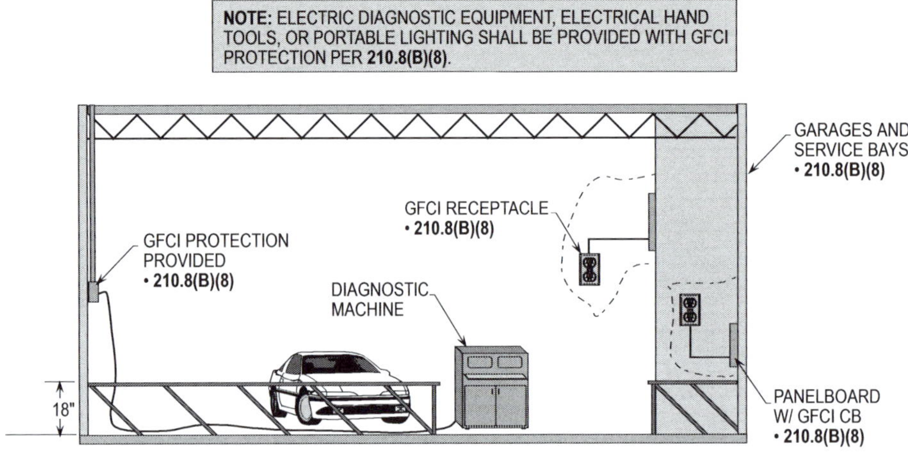

Figure 16-47. This illustration shows the procedures for providing GFCI protection for receptacles in garages, service bays, and similar areas.

RECEPTACLE MOUNTING
406.5

Receptacles shall be mounted in identified boxes or assemblies. The boxes or assemblies shall be securely fastened in place unless otherwise permitted elsewhere in the *Code*. Screws used for the purpose of attaching receptacles to a box shall be of the type provided with a listed receptacle, or shall be machine screws having 32 threads per inch or part of listed assemblies or systems, in accordance with the manufacturer's instructions.

RECEPTACLES IN SEATING AREAS AND OTHER SIMILAR SURFACES
406.5(F)(1) THRU (F)(4)

In seating areas or similar surfaces, receptacles shall not be installed in a face-up position, unless the receptacle is any of the following:

(1) Part of an assembly listed as a furniture power distribution unit, if cord- and plug-connected

(2) Part of an assembly listed either as household furnishings or as commercial furnishings

(3) Listed either as a receptacle assembly for countertop applications or as a GFCI receptacle assembly for countertop applications

(4) Installed in a listed floor box

(See Figure 16-48)

Note, in Figure 16-47, electric diagnostic equipment or portable lighting units shall be provided with GFCI protection per **210.8(B)(8).**

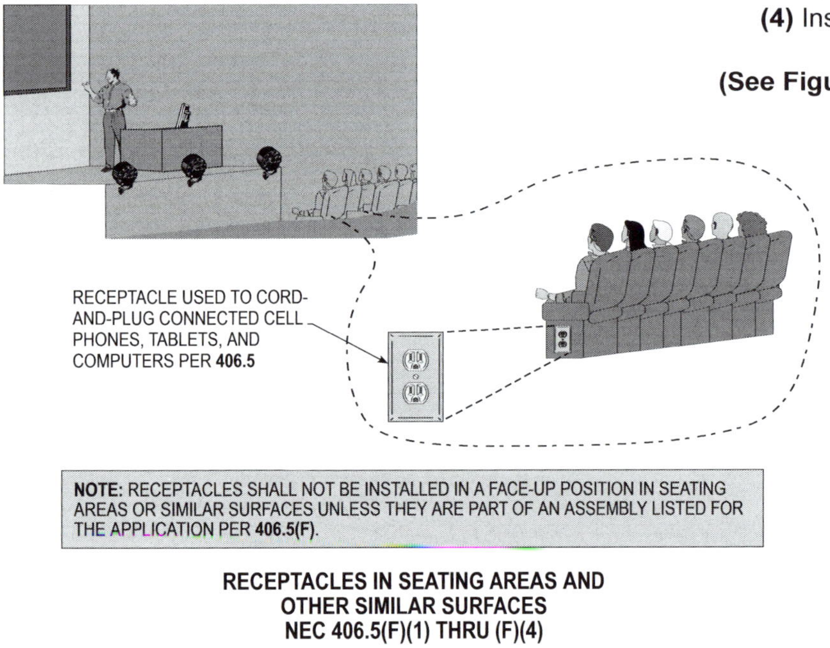

Figure 16-48. This illustration shows receptacles in seating areas and other similar surfaces are not to be installed in the face up position.

RECEPTACLES USED FOR MAINTENANCE ACTIVITIES 590.6(A)

All 125 volt, 15, 20, and 30 amp receptacles used for electric hand tools, etc. to pull maintenance on electrical apparatus and equipment shall be GFCI protected. **(See Figure 16-49)**

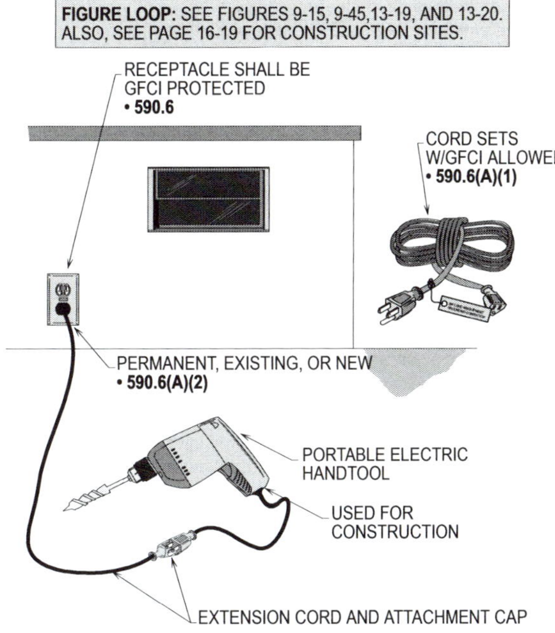

**RECEPTACLES USED FOR MAINTENANCE ACTIVITIES
NEC 590.6 AND 6(A)**

Figure 16-49. Employees using electric hand tools to pull maintenance on electrical equipment shall be fully protected by GFCI protection of power circuit and elements.

AFCI-PROTECTED OUTLETS 210.12(A) AND (B)

All 120 volt, single-phase, 15- and 20-ampere branch circuits supplying outlets in the following rooms of a dwelling unit shall be protected by a listed arc-fault circuit interrupter, combination type, installed to provide protection of the branch circuit:

- Family rooms,
- Dining rooms,
- Living rooms,
- Parlors,
- Libraries,
- Dens,
- Bedrooms,
- Sun rooms,
- Recreation rooms,
- Closets,
- Hallways, or
- Similar rooms or areas
- Laundry rooms or areas
- Kitchens

See Figure 16-50 for a detailed illustration pertaining to AFCI protection in dwelling units.

Where the branch-circuit wiring is modified, replaced, or extended in any of the areas per **210.12(A)**, the branch circuit shall be protected by one of the following:

- A listed combination-type AFCI located at the origin of the branch circuit
- A listed outlet branch-circuit type AFCI located at the first receptacle outlet of the existing branch circuit.

See Figure 16-51 and 16-52 for a detailed illustration pertaining to branch-circuit extensions or modifications of dwelling units.

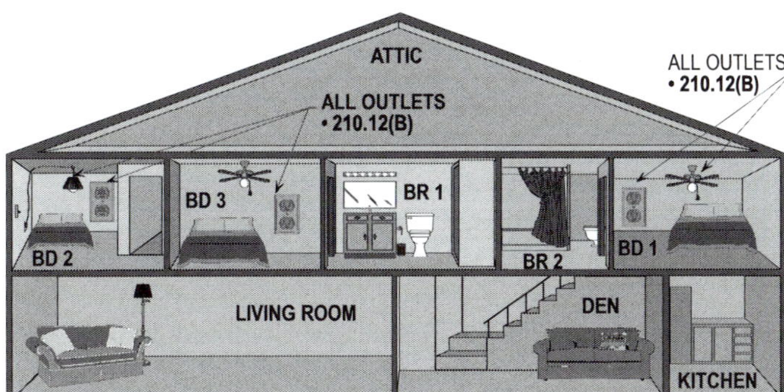

**AFCI-PROTECTED OUTLETS
NEC 210.12(A)**

Figure 16-50. Certain outlets in bedrooms of dwelling units shall be AFCI protected.

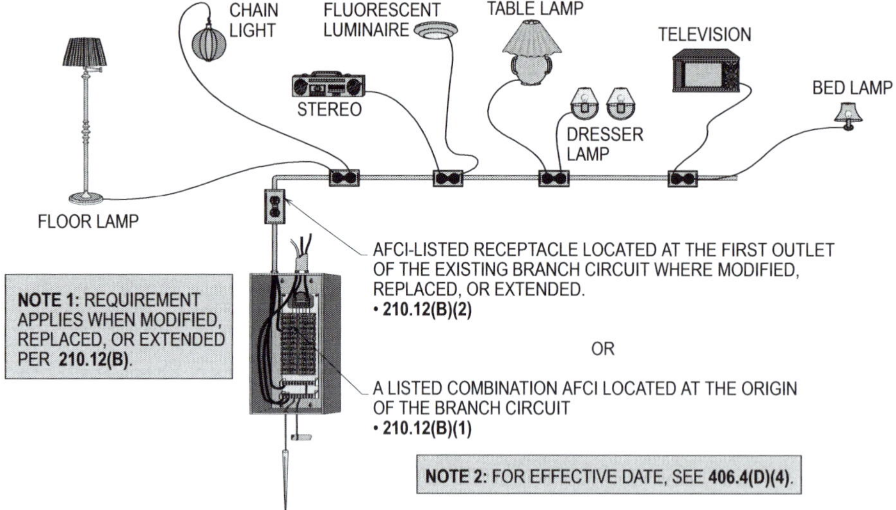

Figure 16-51. This illustration shows the requirements for providing AFCI protection for receptacles in dwelling units.

ARC-FAULT CIRCUIT-INTERRUPTER PROTECTION
210.12

Arc-fault circuit-interrupter protection shall be provided as required in 210.12(A), (B), and (C). The arc-fault circuit interrupter shall be installed in a readily accessible location.

DWELLING UNITS
210.12(B)

All 120-volt, single phase, 15- and 20-ampere branch circuits supplying outlets or devices installed in dwelling unit kitchens, family rooms, dining rooms, living rooms, parlors, libraries, dens, bedrooms, sunrooms, recreation rooms, closets, hallways, laundry areas, or similar rooms or areas shall be protected by any of the means described in **210.12(A)(1) through (6)**:

(1) A listed combination-type arc-fault circuit inter-rupter, installed to provide protection of the entire branch circuit.

(2) A listed branch/feeder-type AFCI installed at the origin of the branch-circuit in combination with a listed outlet branch-circuit type arc-fault circuit interrupter in-stalled at the first outlet box on the branch circuit. The first outlet box in the branch circuit shall be marked to indicate that it is the first outlet of the circuit.

(3) A listed supplemental arc protection circuit breaker installed at the origin of the branch circuit in combina-tion with a listed outlet branch circuit type arc-fault circuit interrupter installed at the first outlet box on

the branch circuit where all of the following conditions are met:

a. The branch circuit wiring shall be continuous from the branch circuit overcurrent device to the outlet branch circuit arc-fault circuit interrupter.

b. The maximum length of the branch-circuit wiring from the branch circuit overcurrent device to the first outlet shall not exceed 15.2 m (50 ft) for a 14 AWG conductor or 21.3 m (70 ft) for a 12 AWG conductor.

c. The first outlet box in the branch circuit shall be marked to indicate that it is the first outlet of the circuit.

(4) A listed outlet branch-circuit type arc-fault circuit interrupter installed at the first outlet on the branch circuit in combination with a listed branch-circuit over-current protective device where all of the following conditions are met:

a. The branch-circuit wiring shall be continuous from the branch-circuit overcurrent device to the outlet branch-circuit arc-fault circuit interrupter.

b. The maximum length of the branch-circuit wiring from the branch-circuit overcurrent device to the first outlet shall not exceed 15.2 m (50 ft) for a 14 AWG conductor or 21.3 m (70 ft) for a 12 AWG conductor.

c. The first outlet box in the branch circuit shall be marked to indicate that it is the first outlet of the circuit.

d. The combination of the branch-circuit overcur-rent device and outlet branch-circuit AFCI shall be identified as meeting the requirements for a system combination-type AFCI and shall be listed as such.

(5) If RMC, IMC, EMT, Type MC, or steel-armored Type AC cables meeting the requirements of 250.118, metal wireways, metal auxiliary gutters, and metal outlet and junction boxes are installed for the portion of the branch circuit between the branch-circuit over-current device and the first outlet, it shall be permitted to install a listed outlet branch-circuit type AFCI at the first outlet to provide protection for the remaining portion of the branch circuit.

(6) Where a listed metal or nonmetallic conduit or tubing or Type MC cable is encased in not less than 50 mm (2 in.) of concrete for the portion of the branch circuit between the branch-circuit overcurrent device and the first outlet, it shall be permitted to install a listed outlet branch-circuit type AFCI at the first outlet to provide protection for the remaining portion of the branch circuit. **(See Figure 16-52)**

BRANCH CIRCUIT EXTENSION OR MODIFICATIONS – DWELLING UNITS 210.12(B)

In any of the areas specified in **210.12(A)**, where branch-circuit wiring is modified, replaced, or extended, the branch circuit shall be protected by one of the following:

(1) A listed combination-type AFCI located at the origin of the branch circuit

(2) A listed outlet branch-circuit type AFCI located at the first receptacle outlet of the existing branch circuit

Exception: AFCI protection shall not be required where the extension of the existing conductors is not more than 1.8 m (6 ft) and does not include any additional outlets or devices. **(See Figure 16-53)**

> **Design Tip:** Code users, by now, know that the 1999 NEC in **210.12**, talked about this new type of protection for the first time.

AFCI devices must be used for all circuits supplying outlets, for both receptacles and otherwise, in dwelling units per **210.52**. The devices have electronic circuitry capable of recognizing the low levels of electrical arcing. AFCIs are calibrated to cause a trip action to take place, based on the likely ignition energy being released in an arc. This type of low-level arcing causes many fires because it is often well below the point that would cause an ordinary overcurrent protection device to trip.

Note, circuit breakers, along with AFCI receptacles listed for the purpose can be used to protect the entire branch circuit if installed at the first outlet on the circuit. Because most arcing faults are series events, with an electrical load being drawn across a bad section of wiring such as a frayed extension cord of some type. Interrupting the series load stops the failure even if it occurs on the line side of the device and prevents a fire from occurring.

Although these devices have a "push to test" button on them that looks like a GFCI, they are not GFCIs and they have an entirely different protective scheme. However, some do have GFCI sensing capability within that same unit.

Note 1: For a detailed illustration on providing AFCI protection, see **Figure 16-52.**

Note 2: For a detailed summary of AFCI installation methods and procedures, see **Figures 16-50 through 16-53.**

Note 3: Figure 16-53 includes requirements and detailed methods for AFCI installations.

ALL 120-VOLT, SINGLE PHASE, 15- AND 20-AMPERE BRANCH CIRCUITS SERVING OUTLETS OR DEVICES INSTALLED IN CERTAIN AREAS OF DWELLING UNITS SHALL BE PROTECTED BY ONE OF THE METHODS IN (1) THROUGH (6):

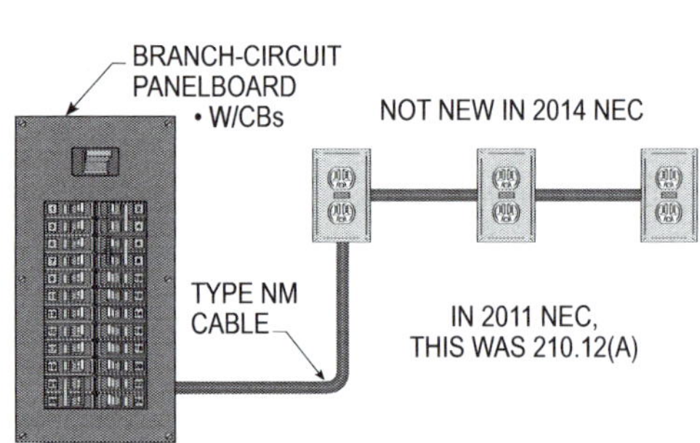

COMBINATION AFCI CIRCUIT BREAKER

METHOD (1) A LISTED COMBINATION TYPE ARC-FAULT CIRCUIT INTERRUPTER, INSTALLED TO PROVIDE PROTECTION OF THE ENTIRE BRANCH CIRCUIT.

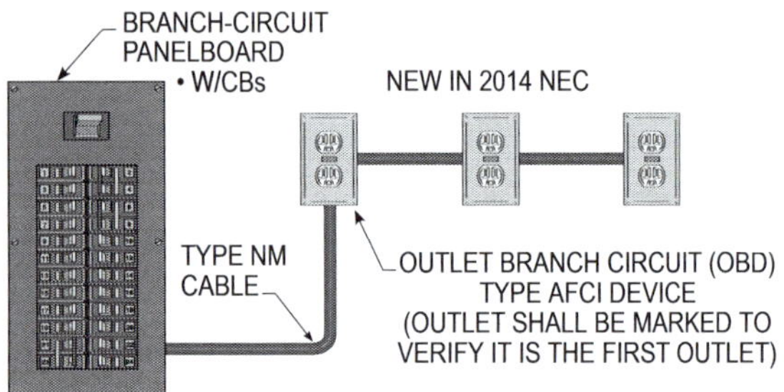

BRANCH/FEEDER AFCI CIRCUIT BREAKER

METHOD (2) A LISTED BRANCH/FEEDER TYPE AFCI INSTALLED AT THE ORIGIN OF THE BRANCH CIRCUIT IN COMBINATION WITH A LISTED OUTLET BRANCH CIRCUIT TYPE AFCI IN STALLED AT THE FIRST OUTLET BOX ON THE BRANCH CIRCUIT (FIRST OUTLET MARKED TO VERIFY THAT IT IS THE FIRST OUTLET)

ARC-FAULT CIRCUIT-INTERRUPTER PROTECTION
210.12(A)(1) AND (A)(2)

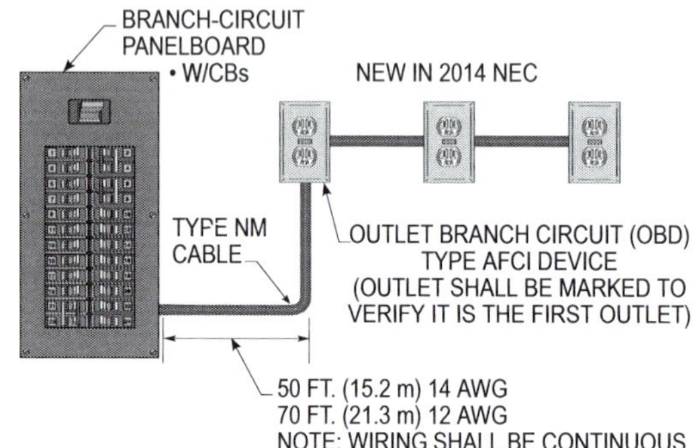

SUPPLEMENTAL ARC PROTECTION CIRCUIT BREAKER IN PANELBOARD

METHOD (3) A LISTED SUPPLEMENTAL ARC PROTECTION CIRCUIT BREAKER INSTALLED AT THE ORIGIN OF THE BRANCH CIRCUIT IN COMBINATION WITH A LISTED OUTLET BRANCH CIRCUIT TYPE AFCI IN STALLED AT THE FIRST OUTLET BOX ON THE BRANCH CIRCUIT.

LISTED BRANCH CIRCUIT OCPD (CIRCUIT BREAKER OR FUSE) IN PANELBOARD

METHOD (4) A LISTED OUTLET BRANCH CIRCUIT TYPE AFCI INSTALLED AT THE FIRST OUTLET IN COMBINATION WITH A LISTED BRANCH CIRCUIT OVERCURRENT PROTECTIVE DEVICE.

ARC-FAULT CIRCUIT-INTERRUPTER PROTECTION
210.12(A)(3) AND (A)(4)

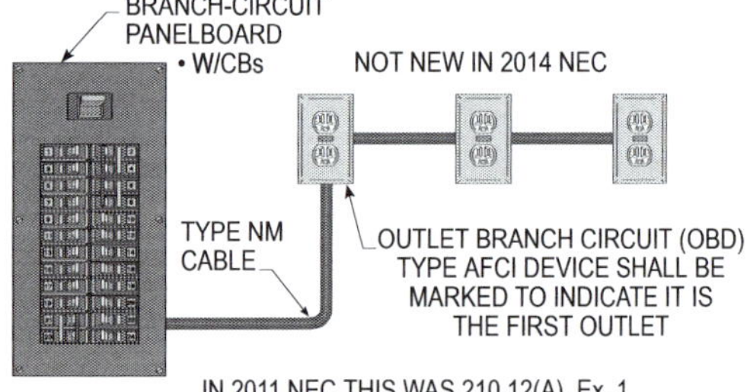

LISTED BRANCH CIRCUIT OCPD CAN BE CIRCUIT BREAKER OR FUSE IN PANELBOARD

METHOD (5) A LISTED OUTLET BRANCH-CIRCUIT TYPE AFCI DEVICE AT FIRST OUTLET IS PERMITTED WITH RMC, IMC, EMT, TYPE MC, STEEL ARMORED TYPE AC CABLES, METAL WIREWAYS, OR METAL AUXILIARY GUTTERS AND METAL OUTLET AND JUNCTION BOXES INSTALLED FOR THE PORTION OF THE BRANCH CIRCUIT BETWEEN THE OCPD AND THE FIRST OUTLET.

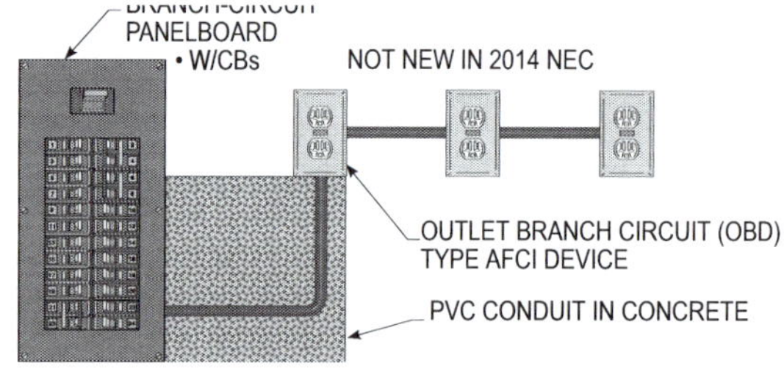

LISTED BRANCH CIRCUIT OCPD CAN BE CIRCUIT BREAKER OR FUSE IN PANELBOARD

METHOD (6) WHERE A LISTED METAL OR NON METALLIC CONDUIT OR TUBING OR TYPE MC IS ENCASED IN NOT LESS THAN 2 IN. (50MM) OF CONCRETE FOR THE PORTION OF THE BRANCH CIRCUIT BETWEEN THE OCPD AND THE FIRST OUTLET, IT SHALL BE PERMITTED TO INSTALL AN A LISTED BRANCH CIRCUIT TYPE AFCI AT THE OUTLET.

ARC-FAULT CIRCUIT-INTERRUPTER PROTECTION
210.12(A)(5) AND (A)(6)

Figure 16-52. This illustration shows that all 120 volt, 15- and 20- ampere branch circuits supplying outlets installed in dwelling unit family rooms, dining rooms, living rooms, parlors, libraries, dens, bedrooms, sun rooms, recreation rooms, closets, or similar rooms or areas per 210.12(A) shall be permitted to be protected by a listed combination type arc-fault circuit interrupter (AFCI) that is installed to provide protection for the entire branch circuit.

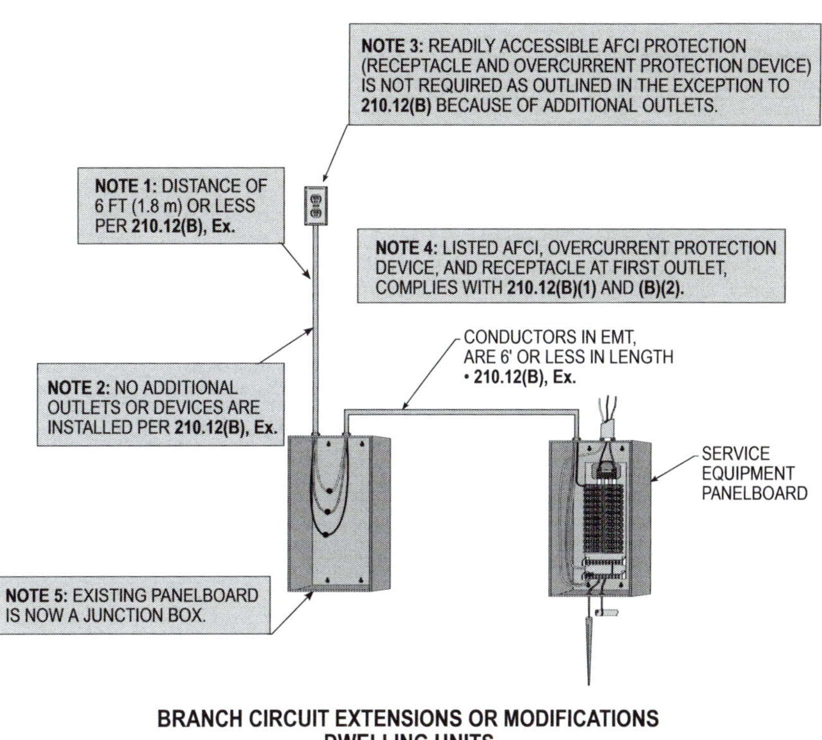

Figure 16-53. This illustration shows that arc-fault circuit-interrupter (AFCI) protection shall not be required where the extension of the existing conductors is not more than 6 ft (1.8 m) and does not include any additional outlets or devices.

Chapter 16. Receptacle Outlets

Section   Answer

1. A minimum of 2 - 20 amp, ______ VA small appliance circuits are required to supply receptacle outlets in dwelling units that are located in the kitchen, pantry, breakfast room, and dining room.

   (a) 1000   (b) 1200
   (c) 1500   (d) 1800

2. Receptacle outlets shall be installed so that there is no point on the wall greater than ______ ft from a receptacle outlet.

   (a) 2   (b) 4
   (c) 5   (d) 6

3. An island countertop with a short dimension of ______ in. or greater shall have a receptacle outlet for each 4 ft in a dwelling unit.

   (a) 10   (b) 12
   (c) 18   (d) 24

4. A bathroom is an area including a basin(s), with a ______.

   (a) toilet   (b) tub
   (c) shower   (d) all of the above

5. A receptacle outlet shall be installed, at a minimum of ______ ft from and not more than 20 ft from the inside walls of a pool. (General Rule)

   (a) 5   (b) 6
   (c) 10   (d) 12

6. Receptacle outlets installed by a hydromassage tub shall be provided with GFCI protection if they are located within ______ ft.

   (a) 6   (b) 8
   (c) 10   (d) 12

7. Receptacle outlets shall be installed for each peninsular countertop with a long dimension of ______ in. or greater and a short dimension of   12 in. or greater.

   (a) 12   (b) 18
   (c) 24   (d) 30

8. Grade level access, while standing, shall be considered ______ or less from finished grade.

   (a) 5 ft 6 in.   (b) 6 ft 6 in.
   (c) 7 ft 6 in.   (d) 8 ft

Section   **Answer**

9. At least _______ GFCI protected receptacle shall be installed in a basement.

(a) 1   (b) 2
(c) 3   (d) 4

10. Receptacles located inside enclosed rooms and within _______ ft of the inside walls of the pool shall not be required to be GFCI protected.

(a) 4   (b) 5
(c) 6   (d) 10

11. Receptacle outlets shall be installed so that there is no point on the wall is greater than _______ from a receptacle.

(a) 4 ft   (b) 5 ft
(c) 6 ft   (d) 10 ft

12. Receptacle outlets in a dwelling unit shall not serve as one of the required outlets if located more than _______ from the floor.

(a) 4 ft 6 in.   (b) 5 ft 6 in.
(c) 6 ft 6 in.   (d) 7 ft 6 in.

13. What is considered wall space when spacing receptacles?

(a) sliding glass doors   (b) sliding panels
(c) fixed panels   (d) none of the above

14. Which of the following countertops are present in a dwelling unit?

(a) wall type   (b) peninsular
(c) island   (d) all of the above

15. All receptacle outlets in a dwelling unit installed in kitchens shall be GFCI protected if located within:

(a) 4 ft 0 in. of the sink   (b) 5 ft 6 in. of the sink
(c) 6 ft 6 in. of the sink   (d) all of the above

16. What is the minimum wall space for receptacle outlets to be installed in a dwelling unit?

(a) 1 ft   (b) 2 ft
(c) 6 ft   (d) 12 ft

17. When installing receptacles in a dwelling unit for hallways, at least one receptacle outlet shall be installed at a minimum of _______ ft or more in length.
(a) 2   (b) 6
(c) 10   (d) 12

18. Receptacle outlets shall be GFCI protected if they are located from the inside walls of an indoor spa or hot tub at _______.

(a) 2 ft to 10 ft   (b) 6 ft to 10 ft
(c) 10 ft to 20 ft   (d) 10 ft to 25 ft

Section   **Answer**

19. All laundry equipment shall be located with ______ ft of the receptacle outlet.

    (a) 6   (b) 8
    (c) 10   (d) 12

20. At least one receptacle outlet shall be installed in bathrooms within ______ ft of the outside edge of each basin in a dwelling unit.

    (a) 2   (b) 3
    (c) 5   (d) 6

17

Lighting and Switching Outlets

Lighting outlets can be installed in specified locations to ensure the proper illumination for residential, commercial, and industrial locations. Lighting shall be provided by luminaires, or be controlled by a wall switch or by table lamps, floor lamps, swag lamps, etc., that are cord-and-plug connected into wall switch-controlled receptacles. Pull-chain luminaires may be installed without wall switches in some locations and under certain conditions of use.

Luminaires supported by metallic or nonmetallic boxes are either ceiling mounted or wall mounted. For the convenience of the user, wall-switched receptacle outlets can be mounted to boxes installed in the wall, baseboard, or floor and may be used to cord-and-plug connect table or floor lamps.

Switches may be installed to operate luminaires and receptacles from more than one location in a residential, commercial, or industrial location. Switching outlets are mounted on the wall at convenient locations and heights to switch the lighting outlets or receptacle outlets on and off. Only in residential occupancies are lighting outlets and switches mandated by the *National Electrical Code* to be installed in specific locations to switch on and illuminate certain areas. **Note,** a dimmer switch can only be used to dim a floor or table lamp that is cord and plug connected to a receptacle that is listed as a combination assembly. (See **NEC 406.15**)

Note: Lighting outlets in dwelling units shall be AFCI protected per **210.2(A)** in the NEC.

GROUNDING LUMINAIRES
410.42 AND 410.44

In residential, commercial, and industrial locations, the exposed metal parts of luminaires shall be connected to an equipment grounding conductor if the branch circuit is provided with an equipment grounding conductor. The equipment grounding conductor shall be selected from any of the wiring methods listed in **250.118** and sized per **Table 250.122**, based on the size of the overcurrent protection device. Section **410-92** of the 1971 NEC and earlier editions required luminaires with metal parts to be used with metallic wiring systems such as metal conduit or metal-clad cables.

The metal-clad AC cables (BX) and metal-clad cables (MC) were used to ground the exposed metal parts. The metal of metal conduits such as rigid metal conduit and electrical metallic tubing was mostly used as a grounding means. Copper or aluminum conductors were also pulled in conduits and utilized as an additional grounding means. Because nonmetallic wiring systems were not always equipped with an equipment grounding conductor, the 1975 NEC in **410-18(a)** required the exposed metal parts of luminaires to be grounded with an approved grounding means per **250-91(b)**. Section **250-114(a)** required the metal of boxes supporting luminaires to be grounded with the metal of the conduit or cable or with an equipment grounding conductor. Since the 1975 NEC, luminaires with exposed metal parts have been required to be grounded in new or existing installations. **(See Figure 17-1)**

UNGROUNDED LUMINAIRES
410.44, Ex. 1

The branch-circuit wiring in older sites of residential, commercial, and industrial locations does not have an equipment grounding conductor in the nonmetallic-sheathed cable (Romex) or in knob-and-tube wiring systems to ground the exposed metal parts of luminaires. Luminaires in older facilities were not required by the NEC to be grounded with an equipment grounding conductor until the 1975 edition.

Part R and **410-91 through 410-93** in the 1971 NEC (grounding lighting fixtures) were deleted and relocated to **Part E** and **410-18(a)** and **(b)** of the 1975 NEC.

The **Ex.** to **410-93** in the 1971 NEC permitted luminaires with metal parts to be wired with nonmetallic raceways and nonmetallic-sheathed cables. If a metal cable was used as a wiring method, it had to have a listed grounding means. To accomplish this rule, the cable had to be AC (BX) or metal clad (MC) of the grounding type.

In those days, nonmetallic wiring systems were systems that did not have an equipment grounding means. Such wiring systems were knob-and-tube, nonmetallic raceways, or nonmetallic-sheathed cable (Romex).

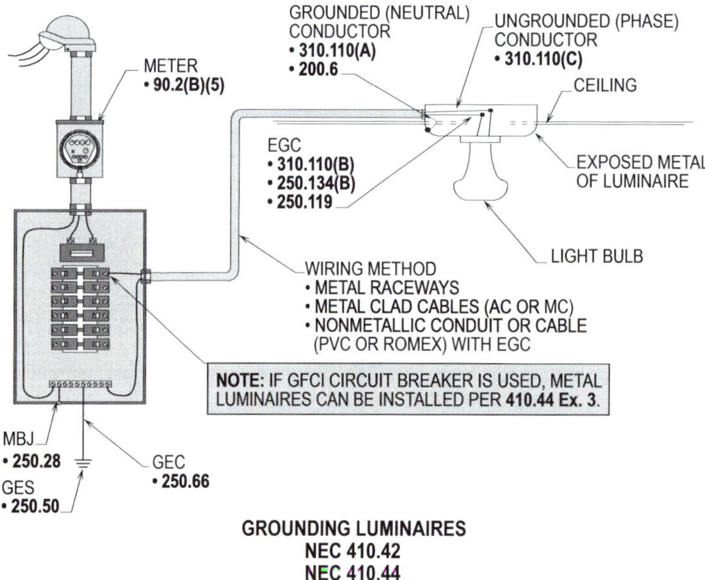

Figure 17-1. The metal parts of luminaires have been required to be grounded in new or existing work since the 1975 NEC. For exceptions to the rule, see **Ex.** to **410-18** in the 1975 NEC.

The **Ex.** to Sec. **410-93** in the 1971 NEC permitted metal luminaires and boxes that were mounted on nonconducting ceilings or walls and located not less than 8 ft (2.5 m) vertically or 5 ft (1.5 m) horizontally from grounded surfaces to be installed without grounding the metal of the luminaires and boxes. **(See Figure 17-2)**

> **Design Tip:** The 1971 NEC and earlier editions required metal boxes that were not grounded to be located 5 ft (1.5 m) from a bathtub or shower. It was the metal box and not the snap switch that required either grounding or being located over 5 ft (1.5 m) from the bathtub or shower. (See **404.4** of the 2002 NEC.)

The 1975 NEC required the metal boxes to be grounded with an equipment grounding conductor that had to be installed in nonmetallic cables from the factory, or the use of metal conduits, or the metal cladding of cables had to provide such grounding. Therefore, the 5 ft (1.5 m) requirement was deleted and a grounding means was no longer required to be provided in the wiring method. See **404.4(C)** and **406.9(C)** for rules pertaining to field wiring switches and receptacle outlets in the bathtub area.

> **Design Tip:** Boxes were not required for the mounting of luminaires until the 1928 edition of the NEC. Because of this requirement, older existing occupancies may not have boxes installed for the mounting and supporting of luminaires and switches.

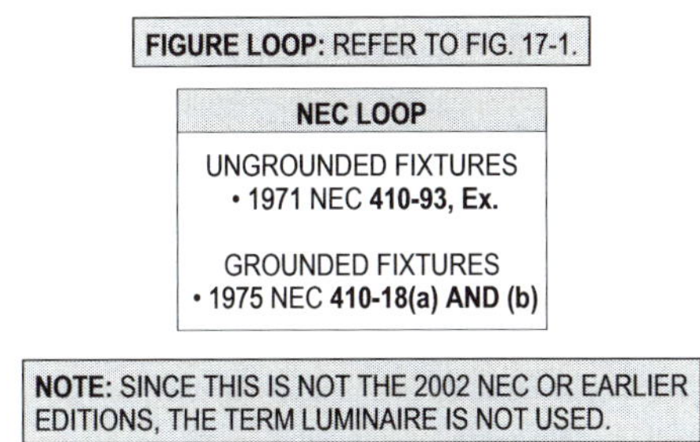

UNGROUNDED LUMINAIRES
NEC 410.42(B)

Figure 17-2. The metal exposed parts of luminaires were not required to be grounded by the 1971 NEC and earlier editions. The 1975 NEC and later editions do require exposed metal parts of luminaires to be grounded.

REPLACEMENT LUMINAIRES
410.44, Ex. 2

Luminaires with exposed metal parts shall not be used to replace luminaires on existing wiring systems that are not equipped with an equipment grounding means. Section **410-18(b)** in the 1975 NEC as well as recent editions require a luminaire with an insulated material to be used to replace an existing metal luminaire in an existing wiring system. If luminaires with exposed metal parts are used for replacements, a branch circuit with an equipment grounding conductor shall be provided per **410.44**. **(See Figure 17-3)**

Care shall be taken when replacing an existing luminaire with a new one. If a luminaire with exposed metal parts is installed as a replacement, an insulating nonmetallic type or any insulating type that isolates the metal of the luminaire should be used. The branch circuit shall have a wiring method that has an equipment grounding conductor or shall be installed as permitted by the one of the exceptions to **410.44**. See **250.118**, **250.122**, and **250.134(B)** for the selection, routing, and termination of the equipment grounding conductor.

Note, the above rules and regulations apply to residential, commercial, and industrial locations.

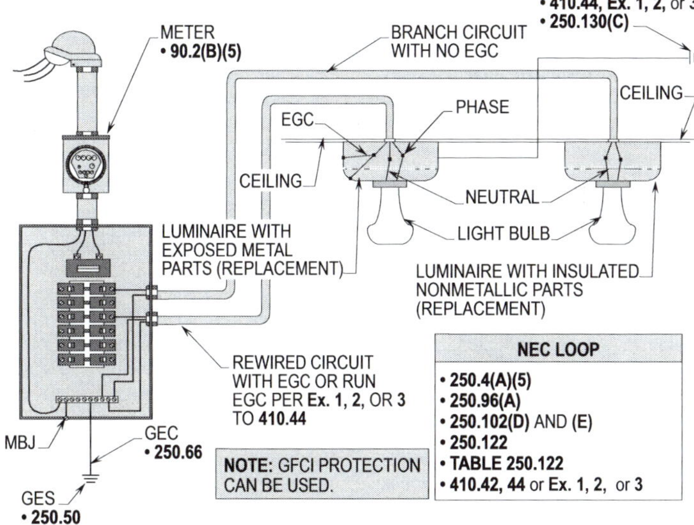

REPLACEMENT LUMINAIRES
NEC 410.44, Ex. 2

Figure 17-3. Since the publication of the 1975 NEC, replacement luminaires installed on branch circuits without an equipment grounding conductor must be of the insulated or nonmetallic type. The parts of luminaires that are not insulated to isolate the exposed metal parts of the luminaires shall be wired with a branch circuit having an equipment grounding conductor to ground all metal parts or an equipment grounding conductor can be installed, as permitted by **410.44, Ex. 1, 2,** or **3.**

NUMBER ON A CIRCUIT
210.11(A)

In residential dwelling units, the number of lighting outlets that may be connected to a 15 or 20 amp general-purpose branch circuit can be determined by multiplying the rating of the branch circuit by 120 volts and dividing by 3 VA per square foot. (Also, see **210.18.**)

> **For example:** The number of lighting outlets permitted on a 15 amp branch circuit in a dwelling unit is determined by the following procedure.
>
> **Step 1:** Finding VA
> **210.11(A)** AND **(B)**
> VA = V x OCPD
> VA = 120 V x 15 A
> VA = 1800
>
> **Step 2:** Finding number of outlets
> Table 220.12
> No. = VA ÷ 3 VA sq. ft
> No. = 1800 ÷ 3
> No. = 600 sq. ft
>
> **Solution: In a residential dwelling unit, there is no limit to the number of lighting outlets permitted in the 600 sq. ft area.**

The concept of the number of outlets permitted on a 15 or 20 amp general-purpose branch circuit is more easily understood by referencing **220.12**, **Table 220.12**, and **210.11(A)** and **(B)**. **Table 220.12** requires 3 VA per sq. ft times the sq. ft area of a dwelling unit to determine the VA rating to supply the number of outlets for general-purpose lighting and receptacle outlets. Notice that the reference [a], by "dwelling units," **Table 220.12**, refers to the footnote and verifies this procedure for determining the number of outlets on a branch circuit.

Inspection authorities who disagree with this concept and want to limit the number usually apply the 1.5 amp (180 VA ÷ 120 V = 1.5) method per **220.14(I)**. The rating of the overcurrent protection device of 15 amps is divided by 1.5 amp to determine the number of lighting outlets permitted on a 15 or 20 amp branch circuit. A 15 amp overcurrent protection device divided by 1.5 amps (15 A OCPD ÷ 1.5 A = 10) permits 10 lighting outlets to be connected to a 15 amp general-purpose branch circuit.

The AHJ may permit any number of lighting outlets (high or low) by the local electrical ordinance to be connected to a

15 or 20 amp general-purpose branch circuit.

For example, by applying such local codes, a 15 amp general-purpose branch circuit is permitted to have 10 outlets installed for lighting and a 20 amp circuit is permitted to have only 13 outlets for lighting. **[See Figure 17-4(a)]**

> **For example:** Finding the number of lighting outlets on a 20 amp general-purpose branch circuit.
>
> **Step 1:** Finding VA
> **210.11(A)** AND **(B)**
> VA = V x OCPD
> VA = 120 x 20
> VA = 2400
>
> **Step 2:** Finding number of outlets
> **Table 220.12**
> No. = VA ÷ 3 VA per sq. ft
> No. = 2400 ÷ 3 VA
> No. = 800 sq. ft
>
> **Solution: In a residential dwelling unit, there is not a limit to the number of lighting outlets permitted in the 800 sq. ft area.**

> **Design Tip:** There are cases where the AHJ wishes to limit the number of outlets on a circuit; see text for methods used to determine the number of lighting outlets permitted on a general-purpose branch circuit.

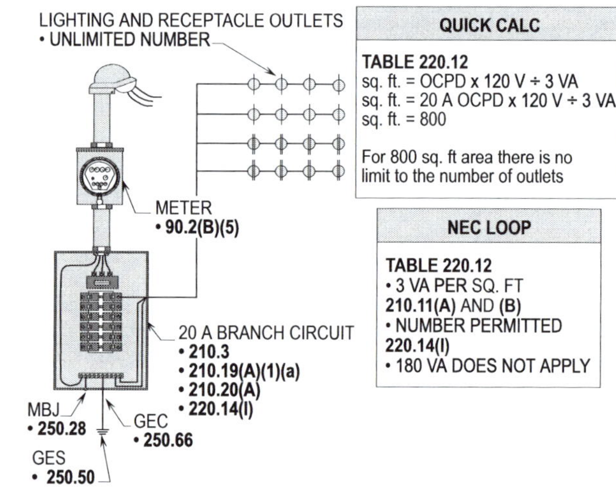

Figure 17-4(a). Section **210.11(A)** and **(B)** can be used to determine the number of lighting outlets permitted on a general-purpose branch circuit for a dwelling unit.

NUMBER ON A CIRCUIT
210.11(A)

In commercial and industrial locations, the outlets on a general-purpose branch circuit shall be calculated at 180 VA each or the load rating, whichever is greater. The number of outlets times 180 VA, times 100 percent, or with demand factors is used to calculate the load of a branch circuit supplying outlets of noncontinuous operation. The number of outlets times 180 VA times 125 percent is used to calculate the load of a branch circuit supplying outlets of continuous operation. Overcurrent protection devices and conductors shall be calculated at 125 percent and selected per **240.4** and **240.6(A)** for overcurrent protection devices and per **Table 310.15(B)(16)** for conductors.

For example: What is the VA rating for 13 receptacle outlets supplying cord-and-plug connected loads used at noncontinuous operation?

Noncontinuous operation

Step 1: Finding VA
220.14(I) and **210.19(A)(1)(a)**
VA = No. of outlets x 180 VA x 100%
VA = 13 x 180 VA x 100%
VA = 2340

Solution: The VA is 2340 and the number of outlets at noncontinuous operation is limited to 13 as calculated.

For example: What is the VA rating for 10 receptacle outlets supplying cord-and-plug connected loads used at continuous operation?

Continuous operation

Step 1: Finding VA
220.14(I) and **210.19(A)(1)(a)**
VA = No. of outlets x 180 VA x 125%
VA = 10 x 180 VA x 125%
VA = 2250

Solution: The VA is 2250 for 10 outlets used at continuous operation.

See **Figure 17-4(b)** for calculating the number of outlets permitted on a branch circuit for commercial and industrial locations. (To define "continuous load", see **Article 100** of the NEC.)

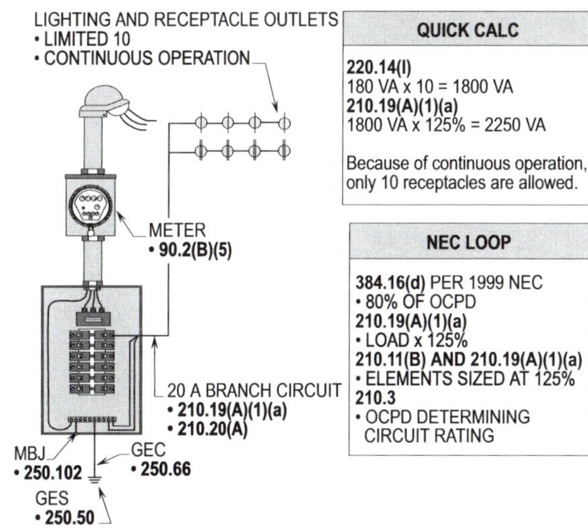

COMMERCIAL AND INDUSTRIAL RECEPTACLES
NEC 210.11(B) AND 210.19(A)(1)(a)

Figure 17-4(b). Receptacles in commercial and industrial locations shall be calculated at continuous or noncontinuous operation based on each outlet at a minimum of 180 VA.

LIGHTING OUTLETS IN DWELLING UNITS
210.70(A)

At least one wall switch-controlled lighting outlet is required in all habitable rooms, halls, stairways, attached garages or detached garages with electric power, bathrooms, and outdoor exits and entrances to the dwelling unit. Kitchens and bathrooms shall have a lighting outlet on the ceiling or wall that is controlled by a wall switch. In addition, a luminaire shall be installed in an unfinished or finished basement, attic, or crawl space used for storage or for air handling equipment, etc.

Note, in some cases, these rules pertaining to lighting outlets may be applied to commercial and industrial locations as well as residential. Such will be noted in the text when appropriate. **(See Figure 17-5)**

LIGHTING OUTLETS IN HABITABLE ROOMS
210.70(A)(1)

At least one lighting outlet shall be installed to provide lighting for the illumination of habitable rooms. Habitable rooms are rooms in the dwelling unit such as the bedroom, living room, den, dining room, breakfast room, etc. The lighting outlets may be installed in the ceiling or on the wall if the location in which they are mounted provides proper lighting. Section **210.70(A)(1), Ex. 1** permits wall-switched receptacle outlets to be mounted on the wall at a height such that floor lamps or table lamps may be cord-and-plug connected to provide proper lighting. The only rooms in a dwelling unit not permitted to have a wall-switched receptacle outlet to provide lighting are the kitchen and bathroom(s). The kitchen is required to have at least one lighting outlet mounted to the ceiling or wall that is switched by a wall switch. A pull-chain lighting outlet installed over the sink or a lighting outlet in the vent-a-hood is in addition to, and shall not be counted as, the lighting outlet required per **210.70(A)(1)**. **(See Figure 17-6)**

Design Tip: Ex. 2 to **210.70(A)(1)** permits lighting outlets to be controlled by occupancy sensors listed for such use. This rule permits an occupancy sensor to control lighting outlets in habitable rooms of dwelling units, which includes bathrooms, hallways, stairways, and garages and at each outdoor entrance and exit. However, a manual override that will allow the sensor to function as a wall switch shall be provided.

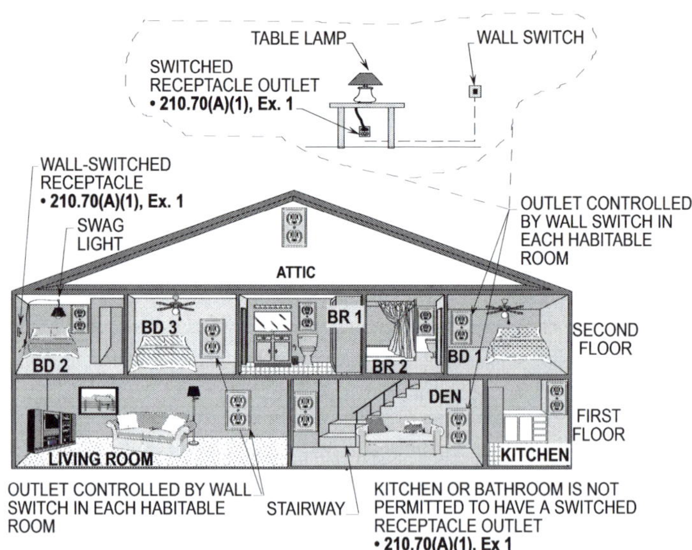

Figure 17-6. Habitable rooms in a dwelling unit shall be provided with a wall or ceiling lighting outlet switched by a wall switch. Rooms, except the kitchen and bathroom(s), shall be permitted to have a switched receptacle outlet with cord-and-plug connected table lamps or floor lamps to provide the necessary lighting.

LIGHTING OUTLETS IN BATHROOMS 210.70(A)(1)

Lighting outlets are required in bathrooms to provide lighting for bathing and personal care. The lighting outlets may be installed in the ceiling or on the wall above the mirror. Lighting outlets are sometimes installed over bathtubs or in showers to prevent shadows due to the location of the required lighting outlets per **210.70(A)(1)**. Luminaires installed over bathtubs or in showers are usually surface gasket or recessed type. At least one lighting outlet shall be provided in the bathroom, and it shall be wall-switched. Check with the inspector for the type that is permitted. **(See Figure 17-7)**

Design Tip: The lighting outlet could be a combination vent/fan/heater/luminaire that complies with **210.70(A) (1)**.

WALL-SWITCHED RECEPTACLE LIGHTING OUTLETS 210.70(A)(1), Ex. 1

A wall-switched receptacle outlet may be used in lieu of a wall-switched lighting outlet in habitable rooms other than kitchens and bathrooms. A wall-switched receptacle with

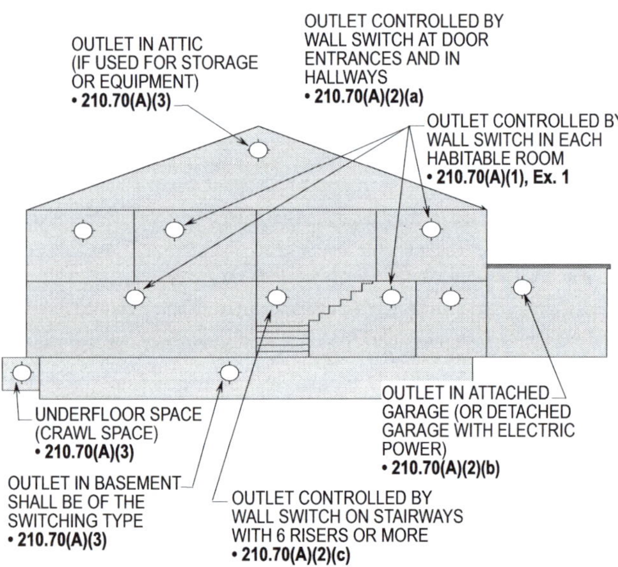

Figure 17-5. At least one lighting outlet shall be installed in these locations to provide proper lighting for safety, pleasure, etc. For receptacle outlets, see **Figure 16-9**.

Note, a dimmer switch can be used to dim a receptacle outlet, when a plug/receptacle is combination listed per **406.15** in the NEC.

cord-and-plug connected table lamps or floor lamps that are used to provide lighting per **210.70(A)(1), Ex. 1** shall be permitted to be used. **(See Figure 17-8)** Regular dimmer type switches shall not be used to dim receptacle outlets per **406.3(E)** and **Ex.**

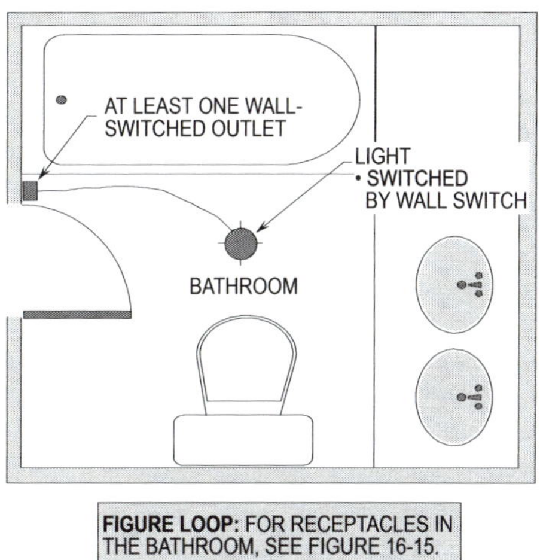

LIGHTING OUTLETS IN BATHROOMS
NEC 210.70(A)(1)

Figure 17-7. Bathrooms are required to have a wall-switched lighting outlet. Other outlets are in addition to this switch.

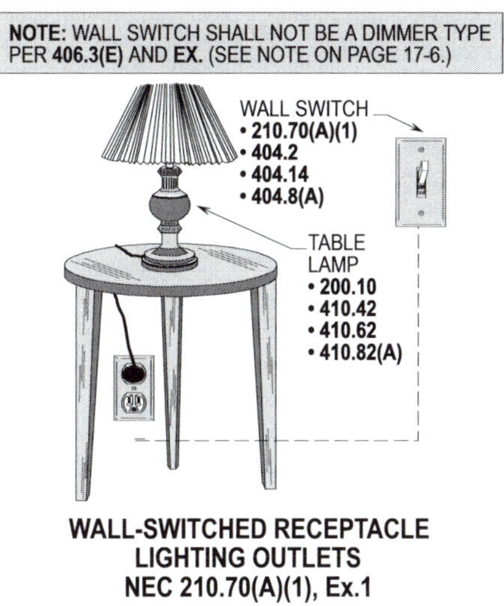

WALL-SWITCHED RECEPTACLE
LIGHTING OUTLETS
NEC 210.70(A)(1), Ex.1

Figure 17-8. Wall-switched receptacles with table lamps or floor lamps plugged into an outlet shall be permitted to be used instead of a wall switch outlet in certain rooms.

LIGHTING OUTLETS IN HALLWAYS
210.70(A)(2)(a)

The hallways in dwelling units shall have a wall-switched ceiling or wall-mounted lighting outlet to provide proper lighting. Section **210.70(A)(2), Ex.** permits remote, central,

or automatic control of lighting outlets installed in hallways. The control method used to switch lighting outlets in hallways shall turn the lighting outlets on and off as needed to provide the necessary lighting. **(See Figure 17-9)**

LIGHTING OUTLETS IN STAIRWAYS
210.70(A)(2)(a)

Lighting outlets shall be installed in interior stairways for illumination, and a wall switch shall be provided at each level to control the lighting outlets. Where there is a difference between floor levels of six risers or more, a wall switch to control the lighting outlet or outlets shall be provided at each level. A lighting outlet at a door on a landing in a stairway that provides the proper lighting and switching complying with **210.70(A)(2)** is also required. **(See Figure 17-10)**

For remote, central, or automatic control of lighting for hallways and stairways in multifamily dwellings, it may be desirable to locate switches or use time clocks where they may not be intentionally or inadvertently turned to the OFF position.

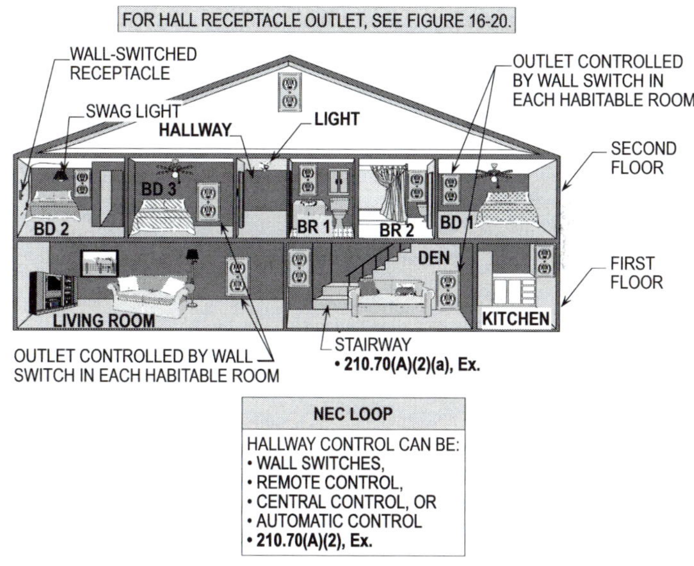

LIGHTING OUTLETS IN HALLWAYS
NEC 210.70(A)(2)(a)

Figure 17-9. Hallways in dwelling units shall have a lighting outlet installed that is switched by a wall switch.

Note: For AFCI protection of lighting outlets, see **210.12(A)** in the NEC.

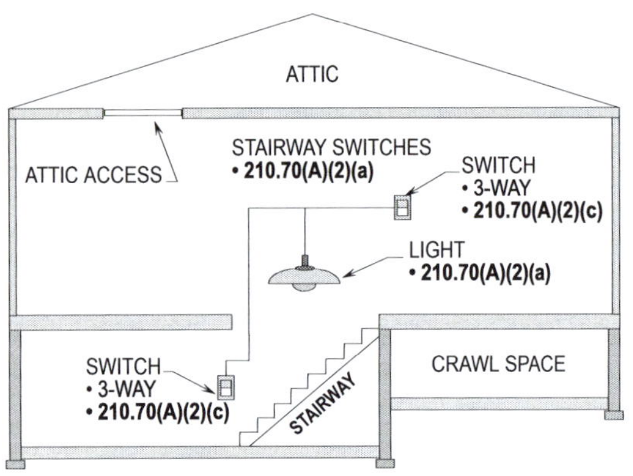

LIGHTING OUTLETS IN STAIRWAYS
NEC 210.70(A)(2)(a)

Figure 17-10. Stairways in dwelling units shall have wall-switched lighting outlets installed to provide proper illumination. Floor levels with six or more risers between them are considered different levels.

LIGHTING OUTLETS IN GARAGES
210.70(A)(2)(a) AND (A)(2)(b)

One lighting outlet shall be installed in the garage to provide lighting for parking vehicles. If a utility room is in the garage, there shall be lighting for washing and drying clothes. One or more of the lighting outlets shall be controlled by a wall-mounted switch.

A lighting outlet is not required at a vehicle door in an attached or unattached garage because it is not considered an outdoor entrance per **210.70(A)(2)**.

A detached garage with power routed to it requires a lighting outlet. If the detached garage has a walkway between the dwelling unit and garage, a lighting outlet is usually installed with a set of three-way switches **[404.2(A)]** to control the lighting outlet at either the dwelling or garage. **(See Figure 17-11)**

LIGHTING OUTLETS AT
OUTSIDE DOORS
210.70(A)(2)(b)

A lighting outlet is required at each outside door that is classified as an entrance or exit. This lighting outlet must be installed in a location that provides lighting at the door and steps, to prevent people from accidentally falling due to darkness. The lighting outlet may be mounted on the ceiling or wall and shall be wall-switched. The wall switch should

be located by the door in a location so that the control of the lighting outlet and luminaire can easily be found. **(See Figure 17-12)** For 3- and 4-way switches, see **404.2(A).**

> **Design Tip:** The switch should not be located behind a closing door because of safety as well as easy access for switching purposes by the user. If supporting over 50 lbs, box must be identified with maximum support capability.

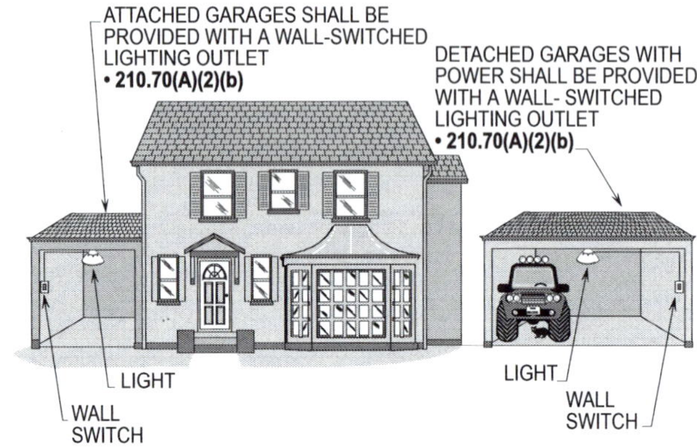

LIGHTING OUTLETS IN GARAGES
NEC 210.70(A)(2)(a) AND (A)(2)(b)

Figure 17-11. Attached garages shall be provided with a wall-switched lighting outlet. Detached garages with power are also required to have lighting outlets controlled by a wall switch. These switches are usually the three-way type per **404.2(A)**. (For receptacle outlets, see **Figure 16-19.**)

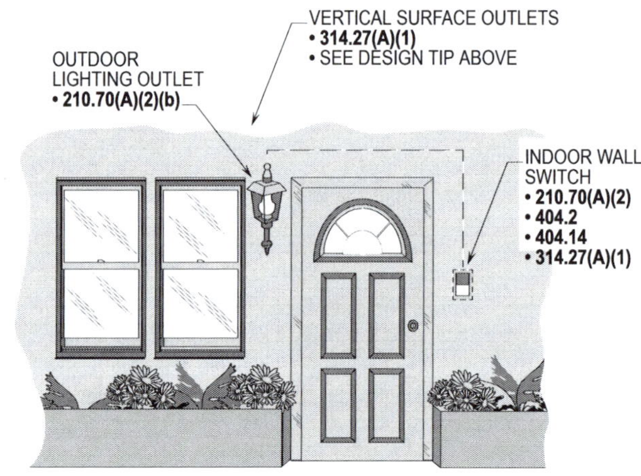

LIGHTING OUTLETS AT OUTSIDE DOORS
NEC 210.70(A)(2)(b)

Figure 17-12. Wall switches installed in the dwelling unit shall control a lighting outlet that is located at each door used as an entrance or exit.

LIGHTING OUTLETS IN UTILITY ROOMS
210.70(A)(3)

One wall-switched lighting outlet shall be required in utility rooms. The wall switch shall be located at the entry of the utility room. At least one lighting outlet is required if the utility room is used for storage or equipment that needs to be serviced. If the washing machine and clothes dryer are located in the utility room, lighting outlets are required for washing and drying clothes and servicing the machines. **(See Figure 17-13)**

Design Tip: The lighting outlet located in a utility room does not necessarily require a wall switch to switch the lighting unit on or off. In other words, a properly located pull chain could serve as such a lighting outlet.

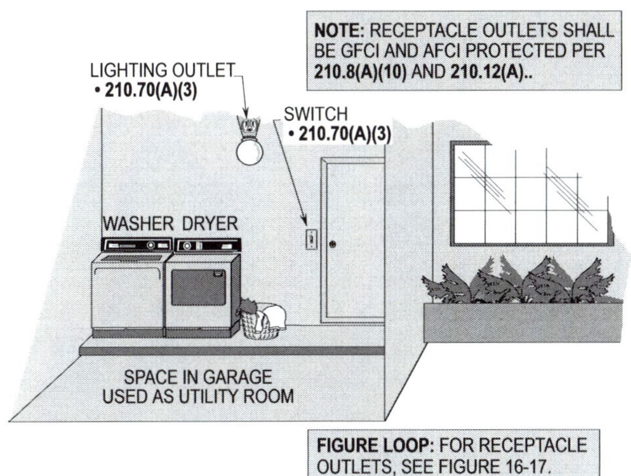

LIGHTING OUTLETS IN UTILITY ROOMS
NEC 210.70(A)(3)

Figure 17-13. A lighting outlet controlled by a pull chain or wall switch shall be installed in a utility room. The utility room may be located in the dwelling unit or garage.

The lighting outlet installed in the utility room may be surface or recess mounted. It could be cove lighting or any other wall-switched type lighting. The type of luminaire may be incandescent or fluorescent, whichever type the designer wants to install. The type really depends on the number of footcandles needed to illuminate the area.

LIGHTING OUTLETS IN BASEMENTS
210.70(A)(3)

At least one lighting outlet shall be required for the illumination of basements where there is storage or equipment installed that requires servicing. Such equipment can be air-handling equipment, refrigeration equipment, air- conditioning equipment, etc. Table saws, routers,

sanders, etc. may be located in the basement for the purpose of a workshop. More than one lighting outlet may be required, in this case, to provide the proper lighting. Lighting for servicing the sump pump should be provided. The sump pump, with its equipment, is usually considered equipment requiring servicing, because it is located in a pit. **(See Figure 17-14)**

Section **210.70(A)(3)** requires the lighting outlet to be switched. However, it does not specifically state that it must be a wall-switched lighting outlet. If **210.70(A)(3)** required this lighting outlet to be wall-switched, it would not comply with the various mechanical codes that permit it to be a pull-chain type under certain conditions of use.

Design Tip: The *Uniform Mechanical Code* requires a wall switch, while the *Standard Mechanical Code* requires only a switched lighting outlet that could be a pull-chain type luminaire.

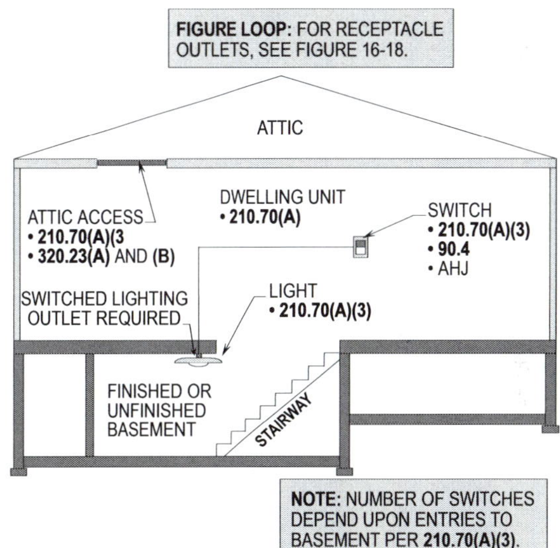

LIGHTING OUTLETS IN BASEMENTS
NEC 210.70(A)(3)

Figure 17-14. A switched lighting outlet shall be required in the basement of a dwelling unit to provide lighting for safe entrance, exiting, and servicing of equipment. This lighting outlet may be controlled by a pull chain or wall switch.

LIGHTING OUTLETS IN ATTICS
210.70(A)(3)

At least one lighting outlet shall be required in attics that are floored and used for storage or for electric equipment that requires servicing. A switch is required to turn the lighting outlet on and off. The switch may be incorporated into the luminaire or be controlled by a wall switch at the point of entry into the attic. Some inspectors permit a wall switch only, while others allow a pull chain at the point of entry. Either complies, depending on which mechanical code is used. The pull chain is usually controlled by an extended string from the luminaire at the point of entry. Also see **320.23(A)** and **(B). (See Figure 17-15)**

Design Tip: See *Uniform Mechanical Code, Southern Mechanical Code* or other appropriate codes for requirements concerning the switching rules for lighting outlets installed in attics to service the HVAC.

Note, 210.70(C) requires a wall-switched lighting outlet for such use in commercial and industrial locations.

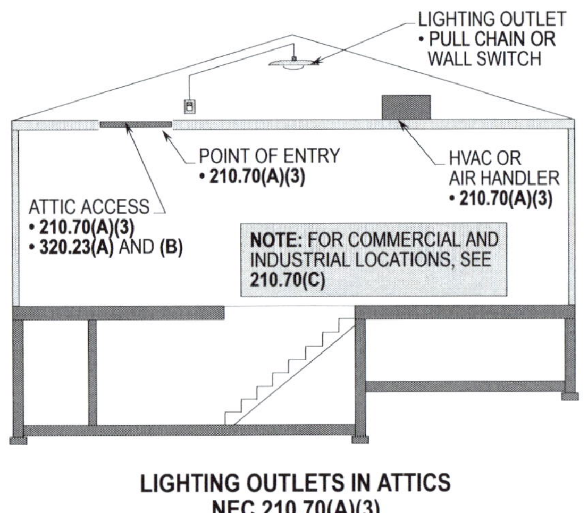

LIGHTING OUTLETS IN ATTICS
NEC 210.70(A)(3)

Figure 17-15. Attic space used for storage or equipment shall have a pull chain or wall-switched lighting outlet.

Note, see local mechanical code for the type required and receptacle outlet requirements.

LIGHTING OUTLETS IN UNDERFLOOR SPACES
210.70(A)(3) AND (C)

A switched lighting outlet shall be required at underfloor spaces or crawl spaces where the space is used for storage or for equipment that requires servicing. Crawl spaces are located at or below grade level. Underfloor spaces are usually located under pier-and-beam type dwelling units or those constructed on the side of a hill. Lighting outlets shall not be required where there is no storage or equipment needing service. **(See Figure 17-16)**

Note, 210.70(C) requires a wall-switched lighting outlet for such use in commercial and industrial locations.

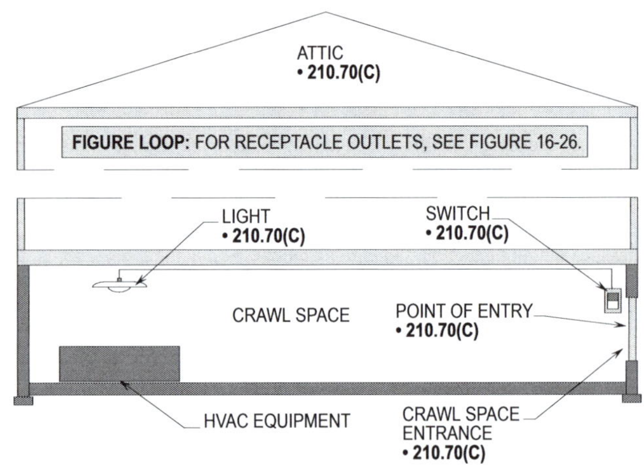

LIGHTING OUTLETS IN UNDERFLOOR SPACES
NEC 210.70(A)(3) AND (C)

Figure 17-16. Underfloor spaces such as crawl spaces shall be provided with a lighting outlet that is controlled by a pull chain or wall switch. The lighting outlet shall not be required if the space is not used for storage or HVAC.

LIGHTING OUTLETS OVER BATHTUBS
410.10(D)

Hanging luminaires, track lighting, and ceiling-suspended (paddle) fans shall not be permitted to be hung over bathtubs. There is the hazard of electrical shock when changing lightbulbs and the danger of electrocution due to grabbing the hanging luminaire for support if the bather should slip when stepping from the tub. Due to these hazardous conditions, hanging units shall be installed at least 8 ft (2.5 m) vertically and shall be located at least 3 ft (900 mm) horizontally from the tub or shower threshold in all directions.

Luminaires that are marked for damp locations or for wet locations where subject to shower spray, shall be permitted to be located within the actual outside dimensions of the bathtub or shower to a height of 8 ft (2.5 m) vertically from the top of the bathtub or shower threshold.

The AHJ usually requires luminaires to be surface mounted with a gasket or to be recessed if the bathtub is used for bathing and showering. Bathtubs used just for bathing are usually permitted to have regular surface-mounted luminaires installed. (Check with the AHJ.)
(See Figure 17-17)

Design Tip: The bathroom is not classified as a wet location, and these rules apply to hydromassage tubs and bathtubs where luminaires are concerned.

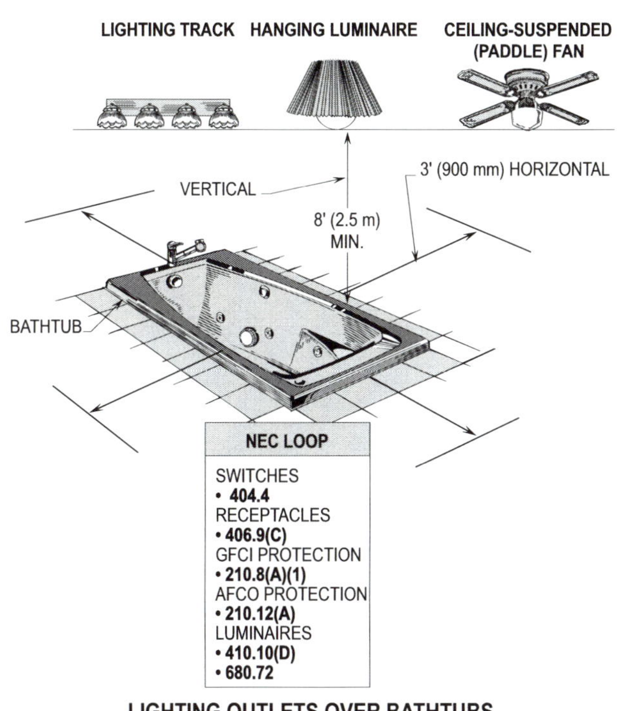

Figure 17-17. Hanging luminaires, ceiling-suspended (paddle) fans, and track lighting shall be permitted to be hung over bathtubs if installed at least 8 ft (2.5 m) over the tub or shower threshold and located at least 3 ft (900 mm) from the tub or shower threshold in all directions.

LUMINAIRES IN CLOTHES CLOSETS
410.16(A) THRU (C)

In residential, commercial, and industrial locations, **210.70(A)** does not require a lighting outlet to be installed in clothes closets. If a lighting outlet is installed in a clothes closet, **410.16** lists the requirements for locating and installing the lighting outlets. Section **410.16** is divided into three subdivisions. Subdivision **(A)** lists the types of luminaires that are permitted to be used. Subdivision **(B)** lists the types of luminaires that are not permitted. Subdivision **(C)** deals with the location in the closet where the luminaire can be mounted.

TYPES PERMITTED
410.16(A)(1), (A)(2), AND (A)(3)

Section **410.16(A)** lists the types of luminaires that are permitted in clothes closets. Surface-mounted, recessed incandescent, or LED luminaires with completely enclosed light sources are permitted. Surface-mounted or recessed fluorescent luminaires are permitted. Incandescent lamps, depending on wattage rating, get very hot, and

the elements, if accidentally broken, can fall into stored combustible materials and cause fires. The NEC requires incandescent luminaires to be provided with a lens that covers the luminaire completely to prevent such accidents.

Fluorescent lamps operate much cooler than incandescent bulbs and therefore can be mounted closer to the storage area than the incandescent type.

Surface-mounted fluorescent or LED luminaires identified as suitable for installation are permitted.

LUMINAIRE TYPES NOT PERMITTED
410.16(B)

Section **410.16(B)** does not permit incandescent luminaires with open or partially enclosed light bulbs (pull chain or keyless) to be installed. Pendant luminaires or lampholders such as rosettes or the hanging type are not permitted.

LOCATION
410.16(C)(1) THRU (C)(5)

Section **410.16(C)** lists the dimensions at which luminaires shall be positioned from the storage area. The luminaires permitted are grouped into three types: the surface-mounted, recessed, or LED type. Surface-mounted luminaires are mounted to a ceiling box and recessed luminaires are recessed in the ceiling with an approved can (hat) listed for the purpose. Surface-mounted or LED luminaires of the incandescent type shall be mounted at least 12 in. (300 mm) from the storage space (area). The incandescent luminaire may be mounted on the wall above the door or ceiling per **410.16(C)(1)**.

Surface-mounted fluorescent luminaires shall have a clearance of at least 6 in. (150 mm) from the storage area. The luminaire may be mounted on the wall above the door or on the ceiling in the same way as the incandescent luminaire per **410.16(C)(1)**.

Recessed luminaires are available as an incandescent, LED, or fluorescent type. The minimum clearance of 6 in. (150 mm) or less shall be maintained from the storage area whether incandescent, LED, or fluorescent recessed luminaires are installed per **410.16(C)(3)** and **(C)(4)**. **(See Figure 17-18)**

Surface-mounted fluorescent or LED luminaires shall be permitted to be installed within the storage space where identified for this use.

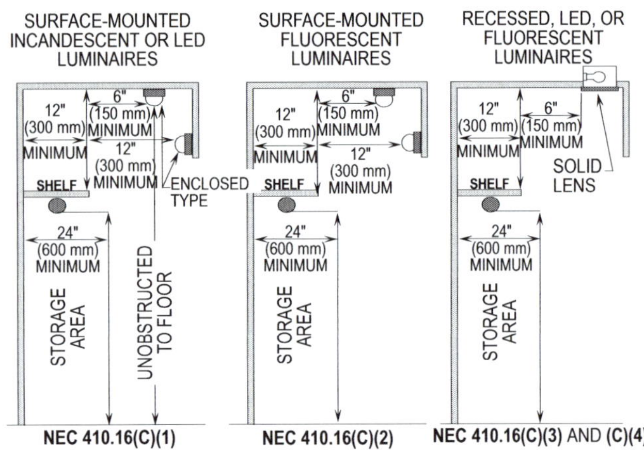

Figure 17-18. Installation requirements for luminaires located in clothes closets.

GUEST ROOMS OR GUEST SUITES IN HOTELS AND MOTELS
210.70(B)

At least one wall-switched controlled lighting outlet or receptacle for a table, floor, or hanging lamp shall be installed in the guest rooms or guest suites of hotels, motels, etc. **(See Figure 17-19)**

COMMERCIAL AND INDUSTRIAL ATTICS AND UNDERFLOOR SPACES
210.70(C)

One or more switch-controlled lighting outlets shall be installed near equipment requiring service, such as heating or air-conditioning equipment installed in attics or underfloor spaces. The switch shall be installed at the entry point to the attic or underfloor space. This rule provides a wall-switched outlet at the point of entry so the user or maintenance person does not have to search for the switch, which could cause a safety problem. **(See Figure 17-20)**

ILLUMINATION FOR ELECTRICAL EQUIPMENT IN COMMERCIAL AND INDUSTRIAL LOCATIONS
110.26(D)

Illumination shall be provided for all working spaces about service equipment, switchboards, panelboards, or motor control centers installed indoors. Additional luminaires shall not be required where the workspace is illuminated by an adjacent light source. In electrical equipment rooms, the illumination shall not be controlled by automatic means only. **(See Figure 17-21)**

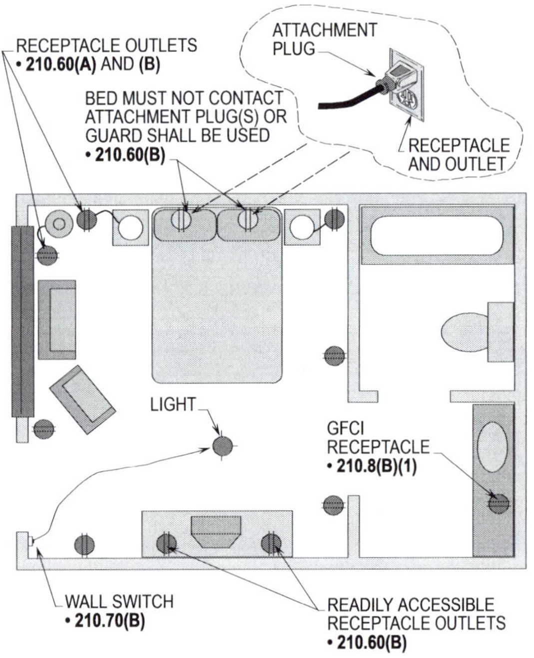

Figure 17-19. At least one wall-switched outlet shall be provided to switch on a lamp in the guest rooms of hotels and motels.

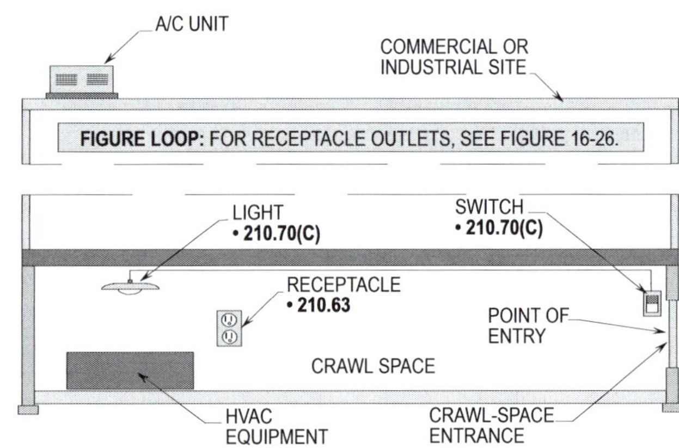

Figure 17-20. At least one wall-switched outlet shall be provided at the crawl space entry to switch light for storage and equipment service area.

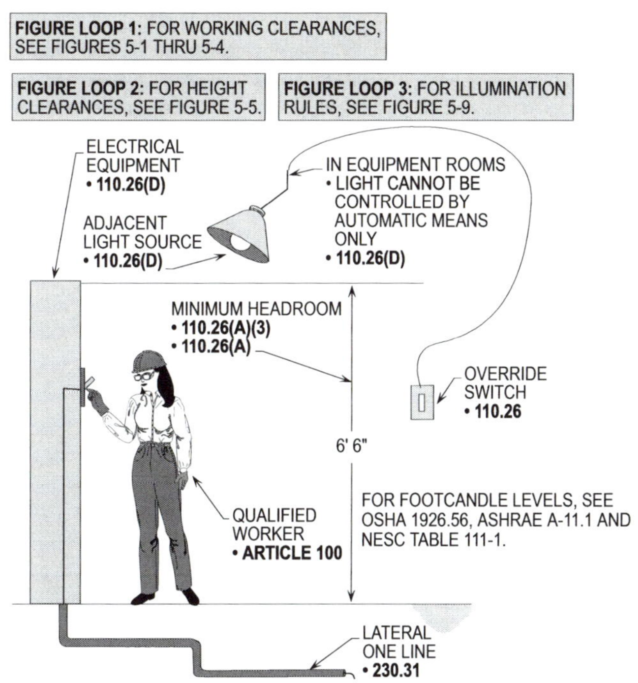

ILLUMINATION FOR ELECTRICAL EQUIPMENT IN COMMERCIAL AND INDUSTRIAL LOCATIONS
NEC 110.26(D)

Figure 17-21. Lighting outlets providing illumination over electrical equipment may be controlled automatically. However, a regular switch for overriding purposes shall be provided.

RECESSED LUMINAIRES
410.115(C) AND Ex.'s 1 AND 2

In residential, commercial, and industrial locations, recessed luminaires are found in new or existing installations. In such premises, per the 1987 NEC, all recessed luminaires were required to be equipped with a thermal protector to prevent overheating. There have been two types permitted since the 1987 NEC, and they are thermal protected (TP) and insulation covered (IC) with thermal protection. The thermal-protected type shall be clear of all insulation by 3 in. (75 mm) on the top and sides per **410.116(B)**.

The luminaire can (hat) shall have a clearance of at least 1/2 in. (13 mm) from combustible materials such as wooden rafters per **410.116(A)(1)**. The IC recessed listed luminaire may be covered with insulation and set against the wooden rafter for support per **410.116(A)(2)**.

In existing facilities with hung (suspended) ceilings, a suspended recessed luminaire may be used per the 1984 NEC. All other types of recessed incandescent luminaires shall have a clearance of at least 3 in. (75 mm) from the top to the sides and be located at 1/2 in. (13 mm) from combustible material. Fluorescent recessed luminaires are also permitted to be installed. **(See Figure 17-22)**

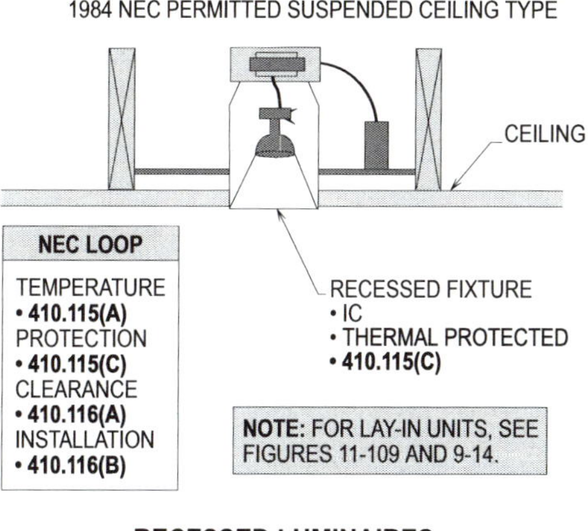

RECESSED LUMINAIRES
NEC 410.115(C) AND Ex. 1 AND 2

Figure 17-22. Recessed luminaires may be utilized with certain installation requirements being applied.

DISCHARGE LIGHTING
410.140(B)

Discharge lighting systems requiring open secondary voltage of more than 1000 volts shall not be permitted to be installed inside or outside dwelling units. Open secondary voltage is the secondary output side of a ballast or transformer that supplies power to the electric discharge lighting unit. The primary is the input side and is supplied by a 120 volt branch circuit that is protected by an overcurrent protection device per **210.20(A)**. **(See Figure 17-23)**

Design Tip: This rule has been interpreted to apply only to discharge lighting units installed inside. It clearly permits them to be installed both inside or outside of such premises.

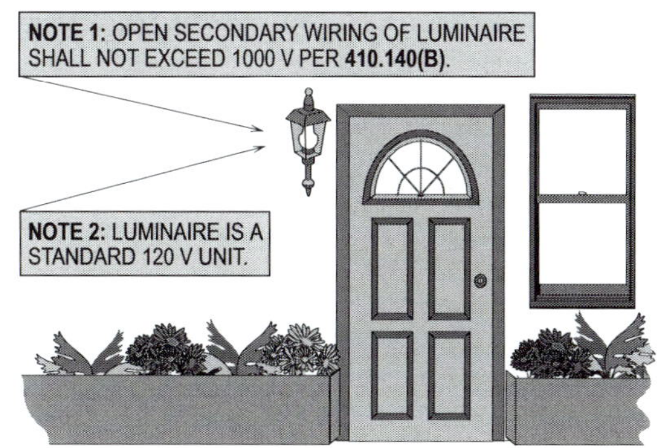

DISCHARGE LIGHTING
NEC 410.140(B)

Figure 17-23. The open-circuit voltage of ballast and transformers supplying electric discharge lighting units shall not exceed 1000 volts when installed outside or inside dwelling units.

LIGHTING OUTLETS AT SWIMMING POOLS
680.22(B)

In residential, commercial, and industrial locations, lighting outlets used to support luminaires and ceiling-suspended (paddle) fans shall be located at specific locations over or around swimming pools. The positioning and location of the lighting outlets are measured from the inside walls of the pool. This basic rule prohibits lighting outlets from being installed 5 ft (1.5 m) horizontally or 5 ft (1.5 m) vertically from the inside walls of the pool per **680.22(B)(3)**.

Lighting outlets with luminaires or ceiling-suspended (paddle) fans shall be located at least 12 ft (3.7 m) above the maximum water level of the pool per **680.22(B)(1)**. A swimming pool built at an existing premise may have luminaires located in the area above the 5 ft (1.5 m) horizontal boundary per **680.22(B)(3)**. The luminaire shall be existing (not new) and rigidly attached to the structure. Luminaires may be installed between 5 ft (1.5 m) and 10 ft (3 m) horizontally with GFCI-protected circuits per **680.22(B)(4)**.

Luminaires located at safe heights over and around the pool protect personnel while they are servicing or changing lamps. Persons swimming in or playing near the pool will be protected from contacting live parts in a luminaire if it is located at these required heights. **(See Figure 17-24)**

Lighting outlets and ceiling-suspended (paddle) fans shall be installed over swimming pools located inside such structures. The lighting outlets supporting the luminaires or ceiling-suspeneded (paddle) fans shall be located at least 7 ft 6 in. (2.3 m) above the maximum water level of the swimming pool. The branch circuit supplying power to these luminaires shall be GFCI protected per **680.22(B)(2)**. **(See Figure 17-25)**

UNDERWATER LUMINAIRES
680.23(A)(1) THRU (A)(8)

In residential, commercial, and industrial locations, underwater luminaires shall be installed in such a manner so as to prevent electrical shock to persons swimming in the pool. Luminaires installed underwater shall be located at least 18 in. (450 mm) below the normal water level per **680.23(A)(5)**. Section **680.23(A)(5)** permits specially designed underwater luminaires to be installed not less than 4 in. (100 mm) below the normal water level per **90.7** and **110.3(B)**.

Underwater luminaires shall be inherently equipped with thermal protection to protect against overheating when the luminaire relies on submersion in water for safe operation.

The luminaire shall be supplied by a branch circuit with 150 volts or less between conductors. The branch circuit shall include a grounded (neutral) conductor. There are three types and they are as follows:

- Wet-niche
- Dry-niche
- No-niche

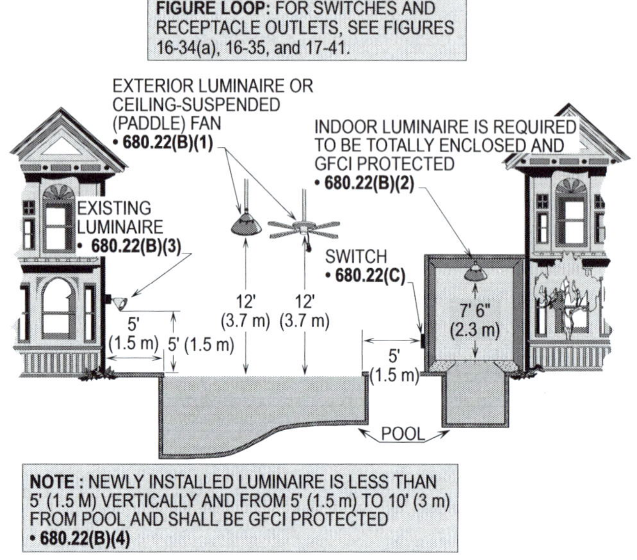

Figure 17-24. Location of luminaires around a swimming pool shall be a certain height and distance from the inside walls of the pool. This rule protects personnel from electrical hazards and shock.

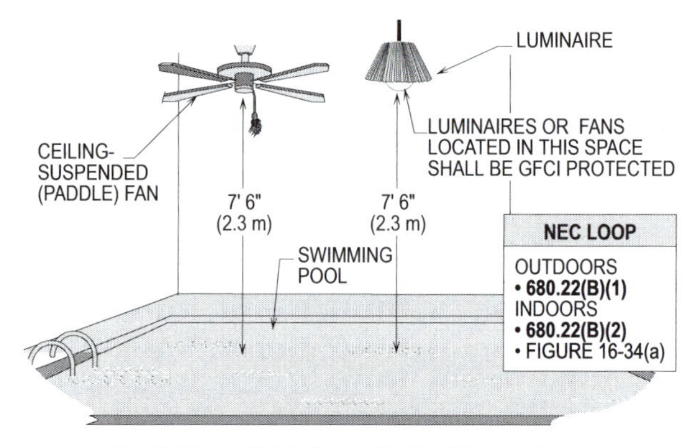

Figure 17-25. Installation requirements for installing luminaires and ceiling-suspended (paddle) fans over swimming pools located inside.

WET-NICHE LUMINAIRES
680.23(B)(1) THRU (B)(6)

Where used in residential, commercial, and industrial locations, wet-niche luminaires shall be equipped with a metal or plastic forming shell that is approved for installation in swimming pool walls. The forming shell should be equipped with threaded entries to connect rigid metal conduit, intermediate metal conduit, liquidtight flexible nonmetallic conduit, RTRC, or rigid nonmetallic conduit, and be made with metallic or nonmetallic material. The conduit shall extend from the shell to a junction box on the deck or yard area. The deck box shall be located under the diving board or in another protected area used for this purpose. The deck box shall be located at least 4 ft (1.2 m) from the inside walls of the pool and be at least 4 in. (100 mm) from the deck to the inside bottom of the deck box per **680.24(A)(2)(a)** and not less than 8 in. (200 mm) from the maximum water level. The measurement that produces the greater elevation is naturally chosen.

For example, if 4 in. (100 mm), measured from the deck to the inside bottom of the box, is greater than 8 in. (200 mm) from the maximum water level, the deck box shall be installed using the 4 in. (100 mm) measurement. **(See Figure 17-26)**

Design Tip: The deck box may be located in a flower bed at the side of the facility where an approved conduit is routed all the way between the forming shell and deck box. If rigid metal brass conduit is used, it shall be routed as a complete system. In the same manner, if polyvinyl chloride conduit is used, the 8 AWG solid or stranded copper conductor shall be pulled unbroken from the shell to the deck box, wherever it is located.

The 4 ft (1.2 m) minimum distance of the deck box shall be permitted to be reduced with an effective barrier between the deck box and inside walls of the pool.

For example, a solid fence may be located 2 ft (600 mm) from the pool with the deck box located on the opposite side of such barrier and pool. **(See Figure 17-27)**

Where polyvinyl chloride conduit is used to connect the shell to the junction box (deck box), an 8 AWG solid or stranded insulated copper conductor shall be run through the polyvinyl chloride conduit and connected to the forming shell. The termination of the 8 AWG conductor shall be potted (listed) to prevent corrosion. The cord end and terminals within the wet-niche luminaire shall be sealed to prevent the entry of water per **680.23(B)(4)**. The equipment grounding conductor in the cord is used to ground the wet-niche luminaire when it is removed from the shell to be serviced. **(See Figure 17-28)**

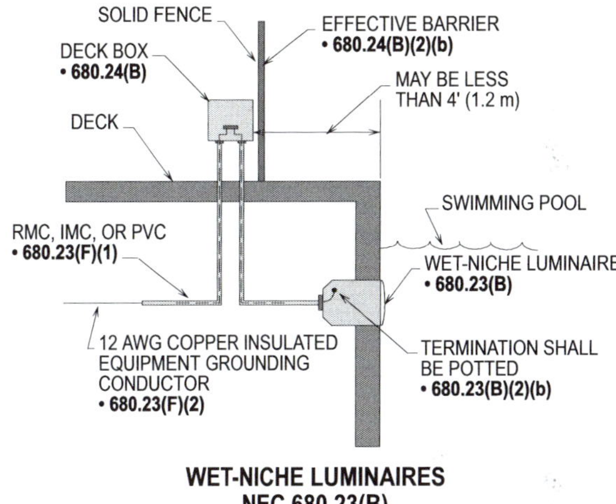

Figure 17-27. The deck box located behind a solid permanent barrier may be located less than 4 ft (1.2 m) from the inside walls of the pool. The barrier prevents easy access if properly designed and isolates personnel between box and pool.

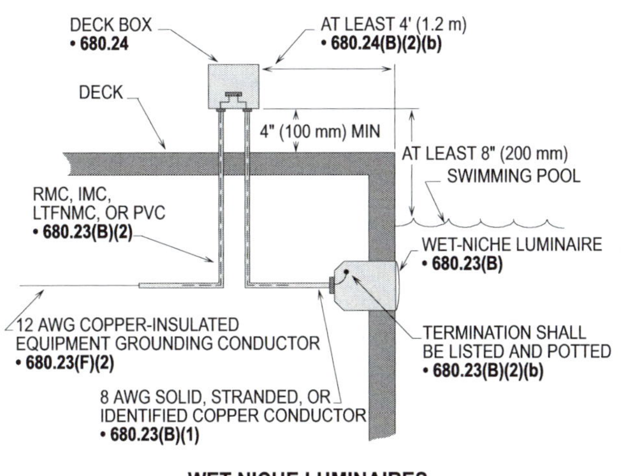

Figure 17-26. The deck box shall be located at least 4 ft (1.2 m) from the inside wall of the pool and have a height of 4 in. (100 mm) measured from the deck or 8 in. (200 mm) measured from the water, whichever is greater.

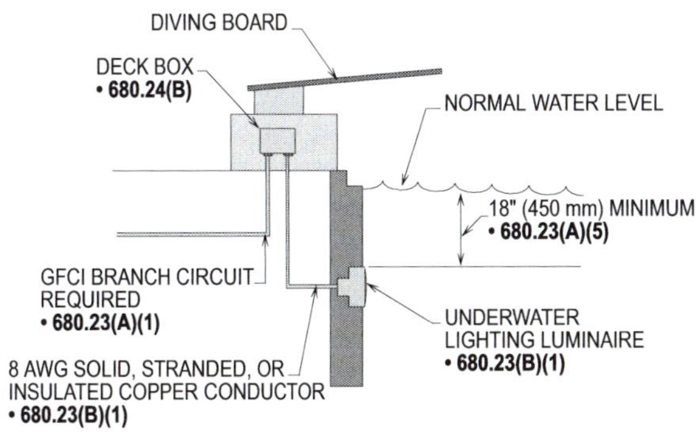

Figure 17-28. An 8 AWG insulated copper conductor shall be routed in polyvinyl chloride conduit to ground to the metal forming shell.

DRY-NICHE LUMINAIRES
680.23(C)

In the walls of pools installed in residential, commercial, and industrial locations, dry-niche luminaires may be installed instead of wet-niche luminaires. This type of luminaire is installed outside the walls of the pool in closed recesses that provide for drainage of water that might accumulate. Dry-niche luminaires shall be wired with approved rigid metal conduit, intermediate metal conduit, RTRC, or polyvinyl chloride conduit with an equipment grounding conductor for each conduit entry. The luminaire shall have adequate provisions for drainage of water per **680.23(C)(1)**. **(See Figure 17-29)**

NO-NICHE LUMINAIRES
680.23(D)

No-niche luminaires may be installed instead of wet- or dry-niche luminaires. No-niche luminaires have no exposed metal parts, and they contain impact-resistant polymeric lenses. If installed in residential, commercial, and industrial pools, they shall be required to be of the listed type per **680.23(D), 90.7**, and **110.3(B)**. **(See Figure 17-30)**

LUMINAIRES OVER
SPAS OR HOT TUBS
680.43(B)

Lighting outlets with luminaires and ceiling-suspended (paddle) fans located over spas or hot tubs shall have a clearance of 7 ft 6 in. (2.3 m) above the maximum water level. This clearance is required within 5 ft (1.5 m) in all directions. The supplying branch circuit shall be GFCI protected per **680.43(B)(1)(b)**. If luminaires and ceiling-suspended (paddle) fans are located 12 ft (3.7 m) above spas or hot tubs, the supplying branch circuit is not required to be GFCI protected per **680.43(B)(1)(a)**. **(See Figure 17-31)**

Recessed and surface-mounted luminaires may be hung over a spa or hot tub, under certain conditions. Recessed luminaires with glass or plastic lenses and nonmetallic trim suitable for wet locations are permitted to be hung less than 7 ft 6 in. (12.3 m) per **680.43(B)(1)(b)** and **(B)(1)(c)**. Luminaires installed in this manner will protect users of spas and hot tubs from serious electrical shock. Surface-mounted luminaires with glass or plastic globes and nonmetallic bodies suitable for wet locations per **680.43(B)(c)(1)** and **(B)(c)(2)** may also be used.

Note, the above rules apply to residential, commercial, and industrial installed spas and hot tubs. **(See Figure 17-32)**

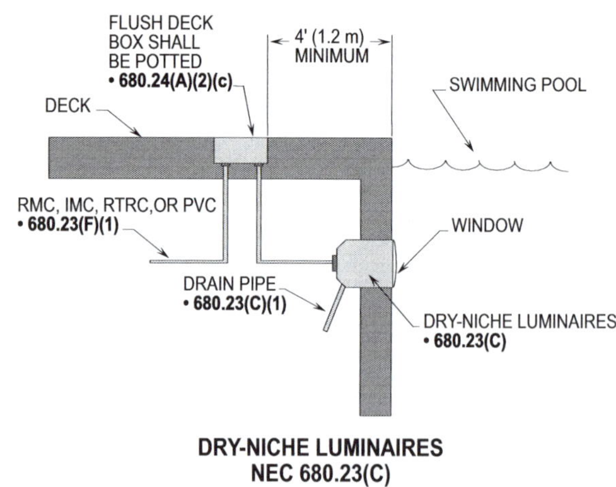

Figure 17-29. Installation requirements for dry-niche luminaires in swimming pool walls shall be carefully designed.

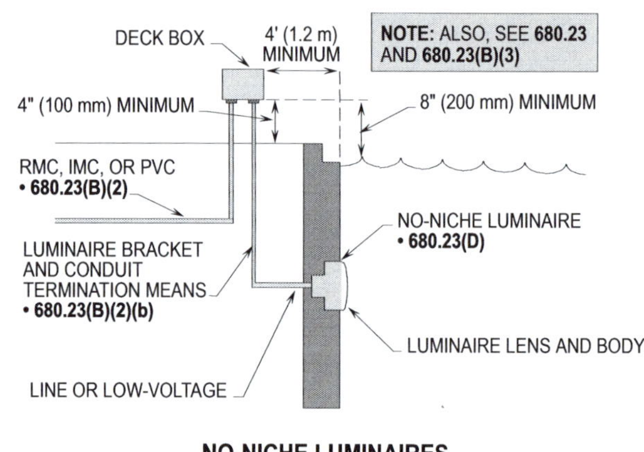

Figure 17-30. No-niche luminaires are now available in both line and low-voltage type.

Note, all grounding connections are to be made to the mounting bracket to ensure grounding.

LUMINAIRES OVER
HYDROMASSAGE BATHTUBS
680.72 THRU 680.74

In residential, commercial, and industrial locations, hydromassage bathtubs are treated as conventional bathtubs.

Lighting outlets and luminaires shall be installed per **410.10(D)**. All the elements for hydromassage bathtubs shall be wired with GFCI-protected circuits whether they are cord-and-plug connected or permanently hard wired per **680.72**. Receptacle outlets shall be GFCI protected per **210.8(A)(1)**. Motors used to circulate the water shall be accessible for maintenance and service by a removable cover or trap door per **430.14(A)** and **680.73**. **(See Figure 17-33)**

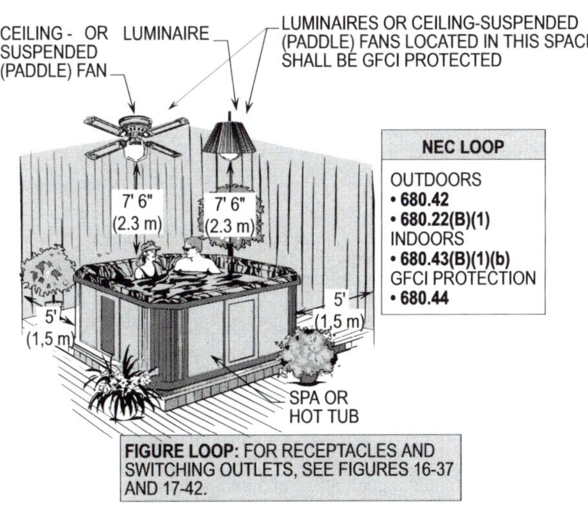

LUMINAIRES OVER SPAS OR HOT TUBS
NEC 680.43(B)

Figure 17-31. GFCI-protected lighting outlets with luminaires or ceiling-suspended (paddle) fans shall be located at least 7 ft 6 in. (2.3 m) from the maximum water level of the spa or hot tub.

Note, luminaires or ceiling-suspended (paddle) fans located over 12 ft (3.7 m) above the maximum water level are not required to be GFCI protected.

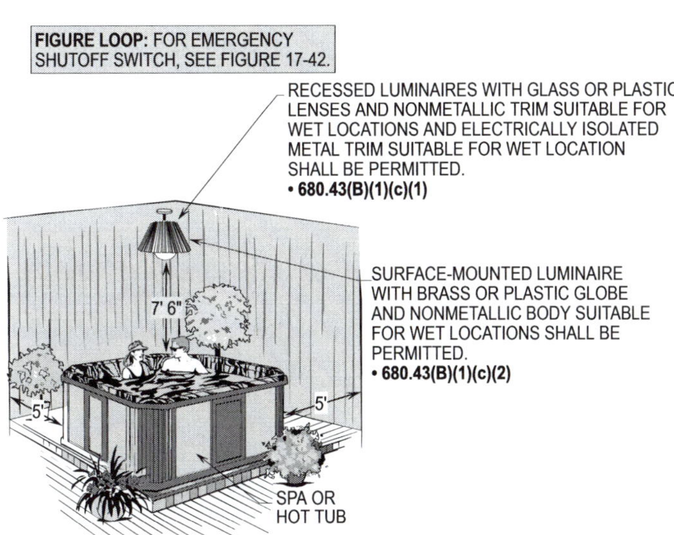

LUMINAIRES OVER SPAS OR HOT TUBS
NEC 680.43(B)(1)(c)(1)
NEC 680.43(B)(1)(c)(2)

Figure 17-32. Location and installation requirements for recessed surface-mounted luminaires over hot tubs or spas.

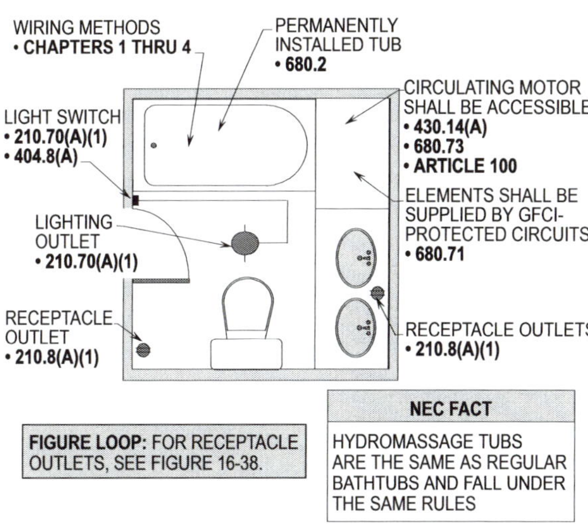

LUMINAIRES OVER HYDROMASSAGE BATHTUBS
NEC 680.70 THRU 680.74

Figure 17-33. Installation requirements for luminaires over a hydromassage bathtub. **Note,** luminaires shall not be installed and hung over this type of tub.

SWITCHING OUTLETS
404.2(A) AND (B)

In residential, commercial, and industrial locations, switches are used to control wiring systems, providing easy access to complete circuits for energizing and deenergizing electrical equipment. A variety of types and styles is available to meet the various requirements and locations. Switches are designed so that they are ON when they are in the up position and OFF in the down position. This position indicates, in a precise manner, whether they are ON or OFF.

Switches shall disconnect only the ungrounded (phase) conductors to an electrical load. They shall not disconnect the grounded (neutral) conductor unless the phase and neutral conductors are disconnected simultaneously. Switches shall disconnect all ungrounded (phase) conductors from the terminals of a screw shell type lampholder. Switches shall be located and mounted at specific heights that are acceptable to the user per **404.8(A)**.

TYPES OF SWITCHES
404.2(A)

Single-pole switches have two terminals and are designed to switch only one ungrounded (phase) and return conductor. A single conductor must not be routed between the switch and the luminaire. Where nonmetallic-sheathed cable (Romex) or armored cable (BX) is used as the wiring method, the white or natural gray conductor in the cable may be used as a switch leg, while the black conductor in the cable may be used as the return leg (switch leg) per **200.7(C)(2)**. The switch leg supplies power to the line side of the switch and the return line from the load side of the switch, connects power to the luminaire or other type of load. The conductor of the other side (return) of the circuit shall be run with the switched (leg) conductor to prevent induced currents. Induced currents are only a problem where metal conduits or metal-clad cables are used as the wiring method. Since current in one conductor is equal to and opposite in direction to current in the other conductor, the inductive effect is canceled. **(See Figure 17-34)**

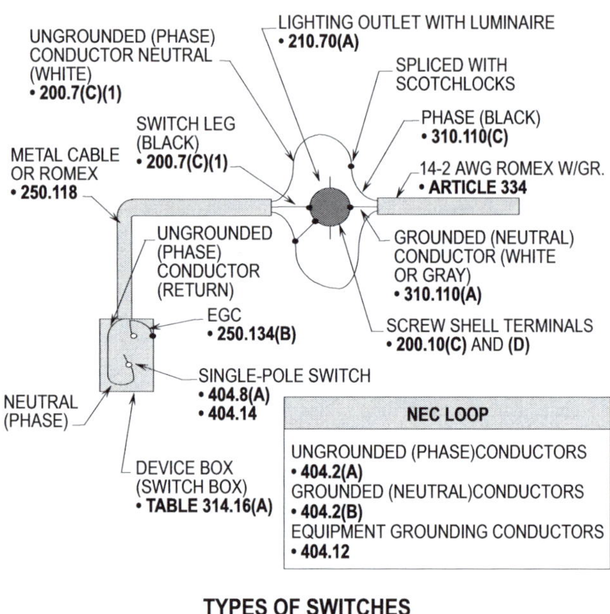

Figure 17-34. The white or gray conductor in a nonmetallic-sheathed cable (Romex) can be used to run the phase conductor to a switch and return as a black conductor (switch leg) to the luminaire.

Design Tip: Always run the switch leg and return leg in the same conduit or cable. See **300.3(B)** and **300.20** for more information on methods used to prevent inductive heating.

Three-way switches have three terminals to connect conductors. The odd-color terminal can be used for the connection of the phase supply or switch leg conductor. The other two of the same color can be used for the traveler conductors. Four-way switches have the same color terminals identified for the travelers. Travelers for three-way and four-way switches may be routed alone in metal conduits or metal-clad cables, where used as wiring methods in residential, commercial, and industrial locations.

The grounded (neutral) conductor does not have to be run with the travelers. A set of three-ways (two switches) may be used to switch one or more luminaires from two locations. A set of three-ways and a four-way may control one or more luminaires from three locations.

For example, a set of three-ways with three four-ways will switch ON and OFF one or more luminaires in five different locations.

Design Tip: With each four-way switch added, the luminaire(s) may be controlled at additional locations. **(See Figure 17-35)**

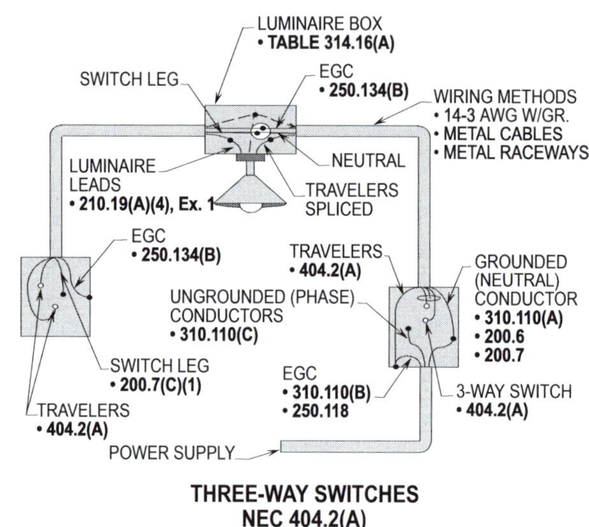

Figure 17-35. Three-way switches may be used to switch a luminaire from two different locations by using a set of travelers.

SWITCHES CONTROLLING LIGHTING LOADS 404.2(C)

The grounded circuit conductor for the controlled lighting circuit shall be provided at the switch location where switches control lighting loads supplied by a grounded general-purpose branch circuit. **(See Figure 17-36)**

The grounded circuit conductor shall be permitted to be omitted from the switch enclosure where one of the following conditions applies, as well as five others:

- Conductors for switches controlling lighting loads enter the box through a raceway.

- Cable assemblies for switches controlling lighting loads enter the box through a framing cavity that is open at the top or bottom on the same floor level, or through a wall, floor, or ceiling that is finished on one side.

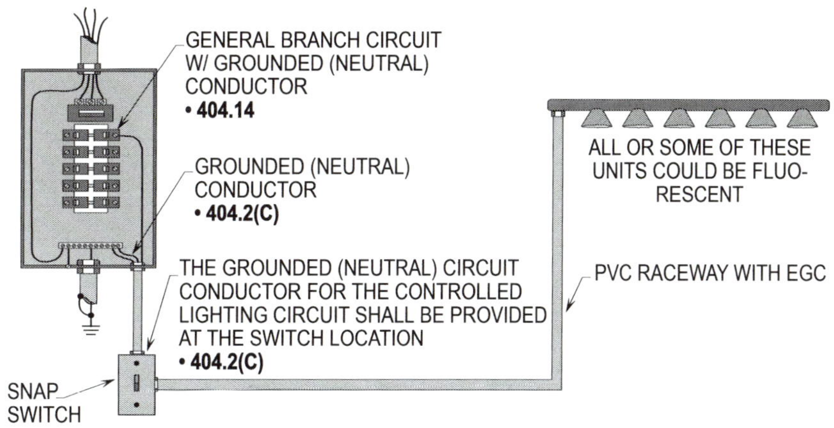

SWITCHES CONTROLLING LIGHTING LOADS
NEC 404.2(C)

Figure 17-36. This illustration shows the requirements for the grounded circuit conductor (may be a neutral) when controlling lighting units.

See Figure 17-37 for a detailed illustration pertaining to the requirements for using the grounded (neutral) conductor in installations pertaining to switching of lighting units.

SWITCHING OUTLET HEIGHTS
404.8(A)

In residential, commercial, and industrial locations, switches shall be located at a height accessible to the user. To comply with this requirement, switches should be located at 6 ft 7 in. (2 m) or less from the toggle of the switch in the ON position. (Most inspectors apply this rule.) Switching outlet boxes are usually installed at 56 in. (1.4 m) to the center of the box to provide a height accessible to users. Lesser heights may be used where needed. **(See Figure 17-38)**

Design Tip: Switches may be located at any height below the 6 ft 7 in. (2 m) to the toggle in the ON position as long as they comply with **404.8(A)**. This rule is usually applied by electrical inspectors to ensure a maximum height.

LOADING SWITCHES
404.14

General-use switches are basically divided into two types for energizing and deenergizing loads. AC general-use switches may be used to control resistive loads (incandescent lights) or electric discharge lighting (fluorescent lights). The switch rating shall be at least equal to the load it controls.

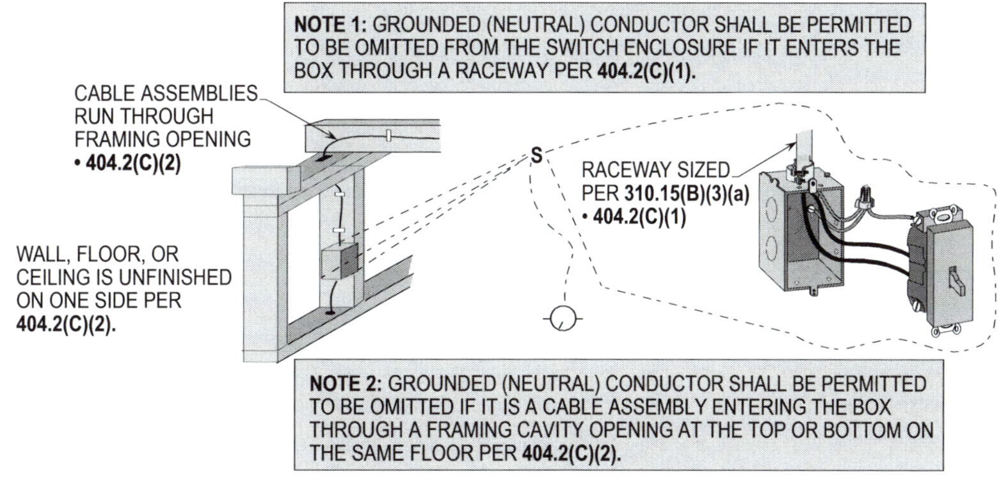

SWITCHES CONTROLLING LIGHTING LOADS
NEC 404.2(C)(1) AND (C)(2)

Figure 17-37. This illustration shows the requirements for using the grounded (neutral) conductor in installations pertaining to switching of lighting units.

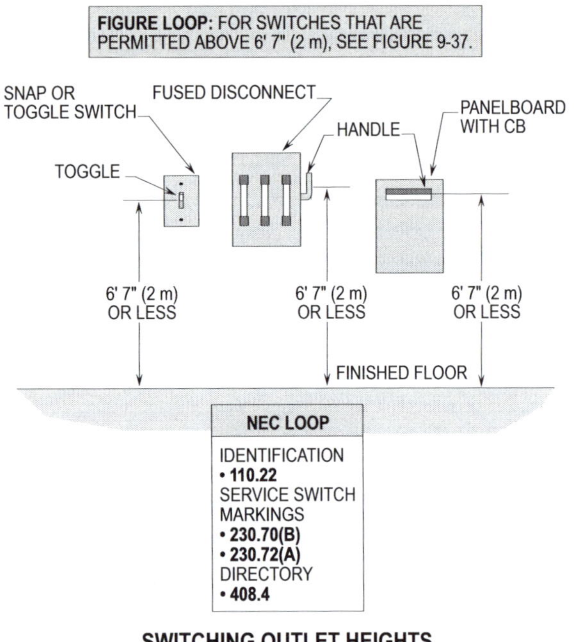

SWITCHING OUTLET HEIGHTS
NEC 404.8(A)

Figure 17-38. Enclosure with switching devices such as (toggle) snap switches, disconnects with fuses, or panelboards with circuit breakers may be located to a maximum height of 6 ft 7 in. (2 m) from the finished grade to the center of the toggle, disconnect handle, or circuit breaker handle in the ON position.

For example, a load for luminaires of 15 amps may be connected to a 15 amp AC rated switch. A load of 20 amps may be connected to a 20 amp AC rated switch.

AC general-use switches controlling motor loads shall be calculated at 125 percent of the full load current of the motor or be limited to not more than 80 percent of the switch rating.

For example, a motor load of 12 amps requires a 15 amp AC toggle switch (12 A x 125% = 15 A).

Note, 80 percent of a 15 amp AC toggle switch (15 A x 80% = 12 A) permits a 12 amp load to be switched. **(See Figure 17-39)**

AC-DC general-use switches may be used to turn ON and OFF incandescent or inductive lighting loads. The rating of an AC-DC switch shall be twice the amperage rating of the inductive load at 50 percent of the amperage rating of the switch at the applied voltage.

For example, a 15 amp AC-DC toggle switch is required to supply a lighting load of 7.5 amps (7.5 A x 2 = 15 A).

Note, 50 percent of a 15 amp AC-DC toggle switch (15 A x 50% = 7.5 A) permits a load of 7.5 amp to be switched.

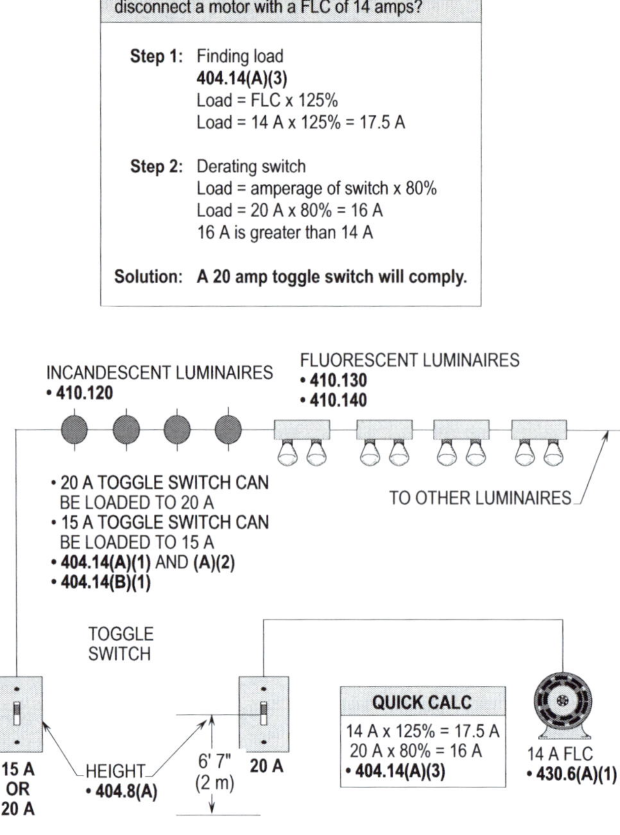

LOADING SWITCHES
NEC 404.14

Figure 17-39. The size load that a toggle switch will supply and disconnect is determined by the load served. Switches supplying lighting loads can be loaded to 100 percent of their rating. Switches supplying motors are sized at 125 percent of the FLC.

The above rules for switches apply to residential, commercial, and industrial locations where switches are used for such use. **(See Figure 17-40)**

SWITCHING OUTLETS BY SWIMMING POOLS 680.22(C)

Switching devices installed in residential, commercial, and industrial locations shall be located at least 5 ft (1.5 m) from the inside walls of swimming pools. If the swimming pool and switching devices are separated by a permanent barrier, this rule does not apply. Switching devices such as toggle switches, safety switches, meters, overcurrent protection devices in panelboards, etc. shall not be permitted within 5 ft (1.5 m) of the inside walls of the pool. A distance of 5 ft (1.5 m) or less shall be permitted with proper barriers between switches and pool. **(See Figure 17-41)**

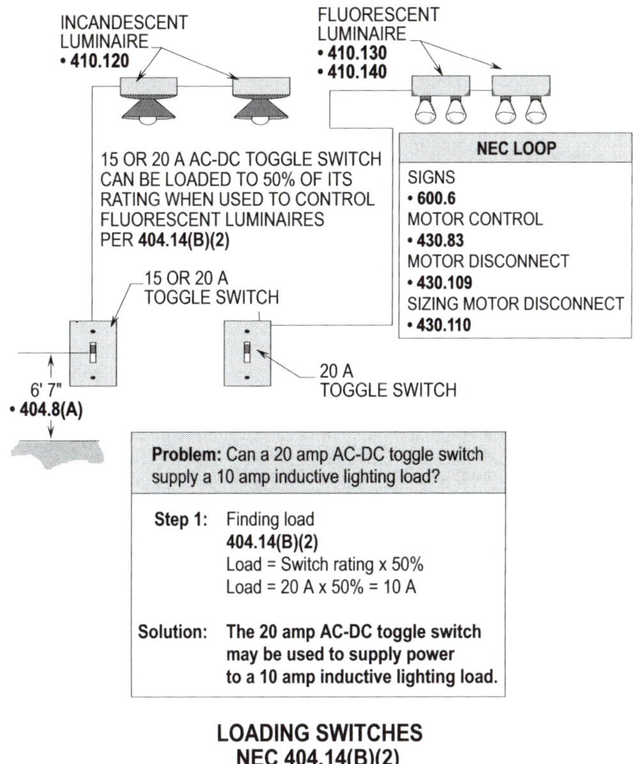

Figure 17-40. A 20 amp AC-DC toggle switch may be used at 100 percent of its rating to control incandescent lighting loads. It is limited to only 50 percent of its amp rating to control inductive lighting loads.

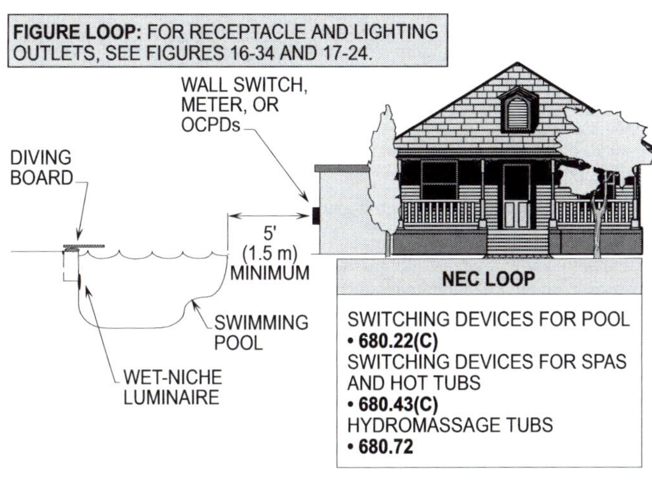

Figure 17-41. As a general rule, switching devices shall not be permitted to be installed within 5 ft (1.5 m) of the inside walls of swimming pools. Switching devices include electrical apparatus such as wall switches, meter bases with meters, and panelboards with overcurrent protection devices, etc.

EMERGENCY SWITCH FOR SPAS AND HOT TUBS
680.41

A clearly labeled emergency shutoff switch for control of the recirculation system and jet system shall be installed at least 5 ft (1.5 m) away, adjacent to and within sight of the spa or hot tub.

Note, this requirement does not apply to single-family dwellings. For a maintenance disconnect, see **680.12**. **(See Figure 17-42)**

SWITCHING OUTLETS BY SPAS OR HOT TUBS
680.43(C)

Switching outlets with toggle switches installed in residential, commercial, and industrial locations shall be located at least 5 ft (1.5 m) from the inside walls of spas or hot tubs. This is to prevent someone from receiving an electrical shock from a faulty switch while turning a lighting load ON or OFF. Switches and controls associated with a spa or hot tub may be closer than 5 ft (1.5 m), where used as an approved (listed) assembly. **(See Figure 17-43)**

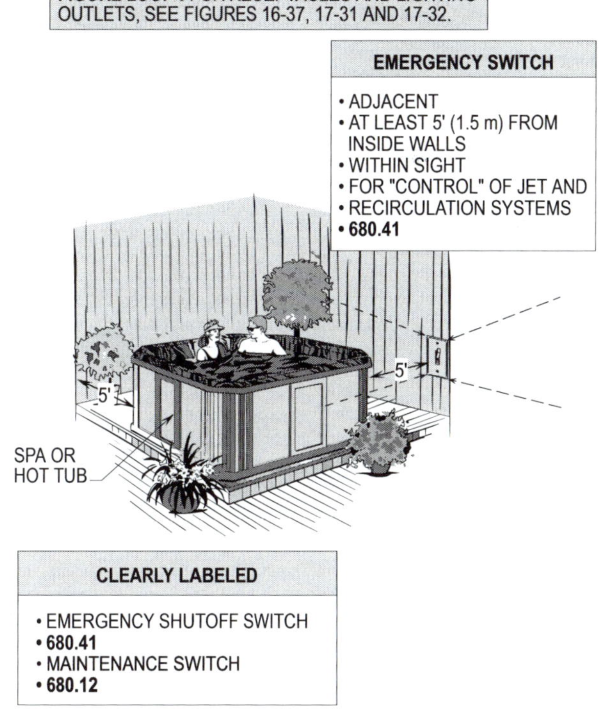

Figure 17-42. A clearly labeled emergency shutoff switch for control of the recirculation system and jet system shall be installed at least 5 ft (1.5 m) away, adjacent to and within sight of the spa or hot tub.

GROUNDED OR UNGROUNDED
404.12

Switching outlets and boxes that are used to support switches shall be connected to an equipment grounding conductor if they are metal per **250.148(A)**. Outlets that are nonmetallic shall not be required to be grounded per **250.148(B)**. A means shall be provided to ensure grounding continuity of the branch circuit. The equipment grounding conductor may be used for this purpose. Toggle switches, without metal plates and used to control one or more luminaires, are not required to be grounded per **110.3(B)** and **404.12**. **(See Figure 17-44)**

> **Design Tip:** See **410.42** for the grounding of metal boxes if they are used. Nonmetallic boxes are not required to be grounded per **410.44, Ex. 1** for lighting outlets. See **250.96, 404.9(B), Ex. 1,** and **404.12** for the grounding of device yokes and metal switch plates.

Note, the rules above shall be required for switching outlets and boxes used to support switches that are installed in residential, commercial, and industrial locations.

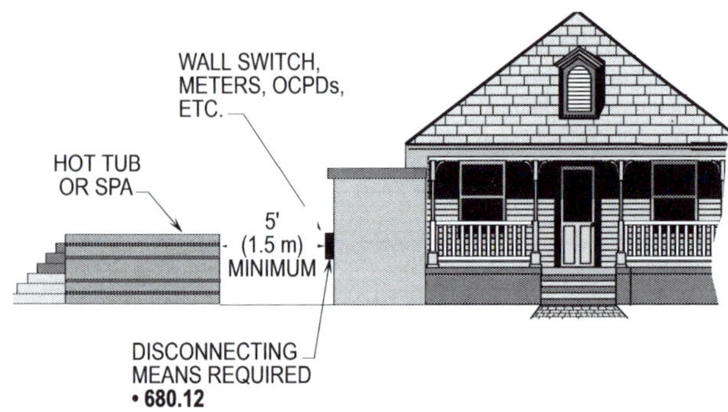

SWITCHING OUTLETS BY SPAS OR HOT TUBS
NEC 680.43(C)

Figure 17-43. Switching devices shall not be permitted to be installed within 5 ft (1.5 m) of hot tubs or spas. Switching devices include electrical apparatus such as wall switches, meter bases with meters per utility, panelboards with overcurrent protection devices, etc. Check with local utility for requirements.

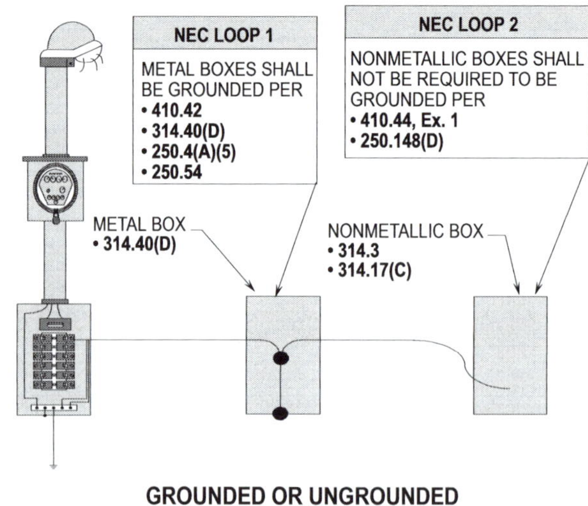

GROUNDED OR UNGROUNDED
NEC 404.12

Figure 17-44. Metal boxes are required to be connected to an equipment grounding conductor. Nonmetallic boxes shall not be required to be grounded with a grounded means. See **250.4(A)(5)** and **250.54** for further explanation.

CONNECTION OF SWITCHES
404.6(C), Ex.

Single-throw knife switches and switches with butt contacts shall be connected such that their blades are de-energized when the switch is in the open position. Bolted pressure contact switches shall have barriers that prevent inadvertent contact with energized blades. Single-throw knife switches, bolted pressure contact switches, molded case switches, switches with butt contacts, and circuit breakers used as switches shall be connected so that the terminals supplying the load are de-energized when the switch is in the open position.

An exception to this rule is where the blades and terminals supplying the load of a switch shall be permitted to be energized when the switch is in the open position and where the switch is connected to circuits or equipment inherently capable of providing a backfeed source of power. For such installations, a permanent sign shall be installed on the switch enclosure or immediately adjacent to open switches with the following words or equivalent: WARNING – LOAD SIDE TERMINALS MAY BE ENERGIZED BY BACKFEED. The warning sign or label shall comply with **110.21(B)**. **(See Figure 17-45)**

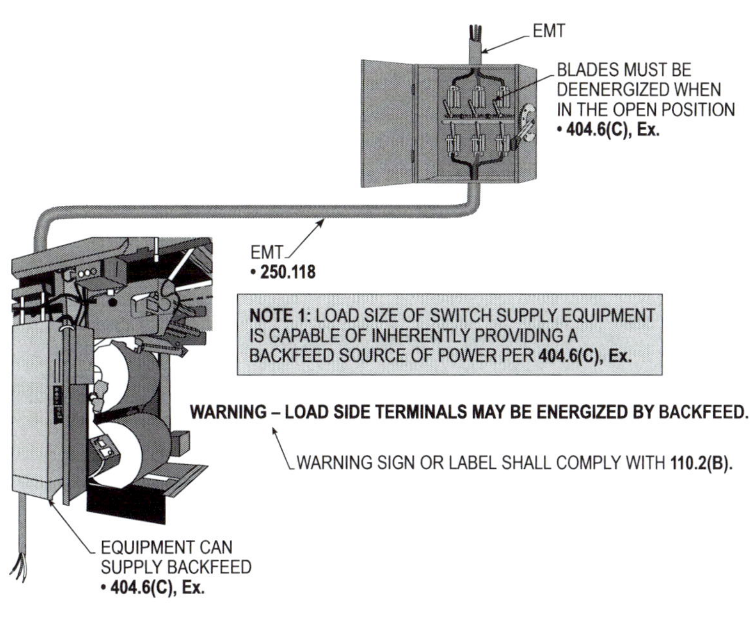

Figure 17-45. This illustration shows that warning labels must be placed on the switch for the switchgear where a backfeed could be supplied by equipment to the disconnect switch.

Chapter 17. Lighting and Switching Outlets

Section   Answer

1 Lighting outlets with luminaires or ceiling (paddle) fans located _____ ft above spas or hot tubs shall not be required to be GFCI protected.

(a) 8　　　　　　　　　　　　　(b) 10
(c) 12　　　　　　　　　　　　　(d) 16

2. AC general-use switches controlling motor loads shall be calculated at _____ percent of the full-load current (in amps) of the motor or not more than _____ percent of the switch rating.

(a) 100; 75　　　　　　　　　　(b) 125; 75
(c) 100; 80　　　　　　　　　　(d) 125; 80

3. Toggle switches supplying motors shall be sized at _____ percent of the FLC (in amps).

(a) 100　　　　　　　　　　　　(b) 125
(c) 150　　　　　　　　　　　　(d) 200

4. A distance of less than _____ ft shall be permitted, with proper barriers between switches and pool.

(a) 5　　　　　　　　　　　　　(b) 6
(c) 10　　　　　　　　　　　　　(d) 12

5. Hanging luminaires shall be installed at least _____ ft over the tub and shall be located at least _____ ft from the tub in all directions in dwelling units.

(a) 6; 3　　　　　　　　　　　　(b) 6; 5
(c) 8; 3　　　　　　　　　　　　(d) 8; 5

6. The lighting outlets supporting luminaires or ceiling fans shall be located at least _____ ft _____ in. above the maximum water level of the swimming pool, if installed indoors.

(a) 5; 6　　　　　　　　　　　　(b) 7; 6
(c) 5; 8　　　　　　　　　　　　(d) 7; 8

7. Specially designed underwater lighting luminaires shall be installed not less than _____ in. below the normal water level.

(a) 1　　　　　　　　　　　　　(b) 2
(c) 3　　　　　　　　　　　　　(d) 4

8. An _____ AWG insulated copper conductor shall be routed in PVC conduit to ground to the metal forming shell.

(a) 8　　　　　　　　　　　　　(b) 6
(c) 4　　　　　　　　　　　　　(d) 2

Section   **Answer**

9. Habitable rooms are such rooms in the dwelling units as:

(a) bedroom   (b) living room
(c) dining room   (d) all of the above

10. Surface-mounted luminaires of the incandescent type shall be mounted in dwelling units from the storage space (area) at least ______ in.

(a) 6   (b) 10
(c) 12   (d) 24

11. Surface-mounted luminaires of the fluorescent type shall be mounted in dwelling units from the storage space (area) at least ______ in.

(a) 6   (b) 12
(c) 18   (d) 24

12. Underwater lighting luminaires shall be located below the normal water level at least ______.

(a) 6   (b) 12
(c) 18   (d) 24

13. A wall switch to control the lighting outlets in dwelling units shall be provided at each level, where there is a difference between floor levels of ______ risers or more.

(a) 4   (b) 5
(c) 6   (d) 10

14. In a commercial location, the outlets on a general purpose branch circuit shall be calculated at ______ VA or the load rating, whichever is greater.

(a) 100   (b) 120
(c) 180   (d) 200

15. Surface-mounted LED luminaires of the incandescent type shall be mounted at least ______ in. from the storage space (area).

(a) 6   (b) 12
(c) 18   (d) 24

16. Recessed luminaires that are thermal protected (tp) shall be clear of all insulation by ______ in. on the top and sides.

(a) 3   (b) 4
(c) 6   (d) 12

17. A recessed luminaire can (hat) shall have a clearance of at least ______ in. from combustible materials such as wooden rafters.

(a) 1/16   (b) 1/8
(c) 1/4   (d) 1/2

Section   **Answer**

18. Discharge lighting systems requiring open secondary voltage of more than _____
volts are not permitted to be installed inside or outside dwelling units.

        (a) 1000   (b) 1200
        (c) 1500   (d) 1800

19. The deck box for a swimming pool shall be located at least _____ ft from the inside
walls of the pool.

        (a) 2   (b) 3
        (c) 4   (d) 5

20. The deck box for a swimming pool shall be 4 in. from the deck to the inside bottom
of the deck box and not less than _____ in. from the maximum water level.

        (a) 6   (b) 8
        (c) 10   (d) 12

18

Motors

There are three currents that must be determined before designing and selecting the elements to make up circuits supplying power to motors. The first current that must be found is the full-load amps (FLA) from **Table 430.248** for single-phase motors and **Table 430.250** for three-phase motors. This current rating in amps, per **430.6(A)(1)**, is used to size all the elements of the circuit except the overload protection. The second current to be determined is the nameplate amps on the motor per **430.6(A)(2)**. This current rating in amps is used to size the overloads (OLs) to protect the motor windings and conductors. The third current, per **430.7(A)(9)**, is the locked-rotor current (LRC), in amps, from **Tables 430.251(A)** and **(B)**. The overcurrent protection device shall be sized large enough to hold this current rating (LRC) in amps and permit the motor to start and run. When using the code letter to determine the locked-rotor current (starting current), see **Table 430.7(B)**.

Electrical systems containing AC and DC motors must have their circuits and elements designed per **Article 430**. AC and DC motors are available in various types and sizes. To protect such motors and circuits and still allow them to operate, the conductors, controllers, starters, protection devices, and disconnecting means must be designed and installed properly.

BRANCH-CIRCUIT AND FEEDER CONDUCTORS
430.1

The following branch-circuit and feeder elements of a motor system are designed and installed based on the characteristics of the motor involved:

- Motor branch-circuit and feeder conductors
- Motor branch-circuit and feeder overcurrent protection devices
- Motor overload protection
- Motor control circuits
- Motor controllers and motor control centers
- Motor disconnecting means and location

SIZING CONDUCTORS FOR SINGLE MOTORS
430.6(A)(1) AND 430.22

Branch-circuit conductors supplying a single motor shall have an ampacity not less than 125 percent of the motor full-load current rating, in amps, per **Tables 430.247, 430.248, 430.249,** and **430.250,** respectively.

For example, a 20 HP, 208 volt, three-phase motor per **Table 430.250** has a full-load current of 59.4 amps. The full-load amps (FLA) for sizing the conductors is determined by multiplying 59.4 amps x 125 percent, which equals 74.25 amps.

A motor will normally have a starting current of 4 to 6 times the full-load current of the motor's FLA for motors marked with code letters A through G, and 8-1/2 to 15 times for NEMA B, high-efficiency motors. Design B, C, and D motors have a starting current of about 4 to 6 times their full-load amps when starting and driving a motor load.

There are heating effects on the conductors that develop when motors are starting and accelerating the driven load. To eliminate such effects, the conductor's current-carrying capacity is increased by taking 125 percent of the motor's full-load current rating in amps.

For example, a motor with an FLC rating of 42 amps shall have conductors with a current-carrying capacity of at least 52.5 amps (42 A x 125% = 52.5 A) to safely carry the load when starting and also protect insulation due to overload conditions.

SIZING CONDUCTORS FOR SINGLE-PHASE MOTORS
430.22

Section **430.6(A)(1)** requires the full-load current in amps for single-phase motors to be obtained from **Table 430.248**. This FLC rating in amps is then multiplied by 125 percent per **Table 220.3** and **430.22** to derive the total amps to select the conductors from **Table 310.15(B)(16)** to supply power to the motor windings. **(See Figure 18-1)**

SIZING CONDUCTORS FOR THREE-PHASE MOTORS
430.22

Section **430.6(A)(1)** requires the full-load current in amps for three-phase motors to be obtained from **Table 430.250**. This FLC rating in amps is multiplied by 125 percent per **Table 220.3** and **430.22** to derive the total amps to select the conductors for the motor windings. **(See Figure 18-2)**

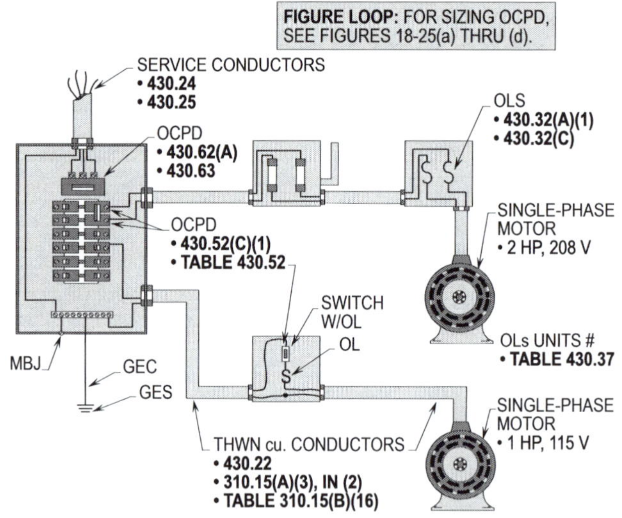

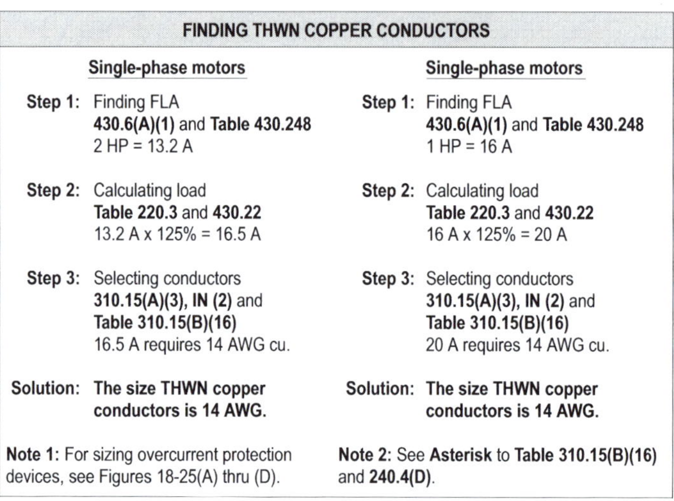

FINDING THWN COPPER CONDUCTORS

Single-phase motors	Single-phase motors
Step 1: Finding FLA **430.6(A)(1)** and **Table 430.248** 2 HP = 13.2 A	**Step 1:** Finding FLA **430.6(A)(1)** and **Table 430.248** 1 HP = 16 A
Step 2: Calculating load **Table 220.3** and **430.22** 13.2 A x 125% = 16.5 A	**Step 2:** Calculating load **Table 220.3** and **430.22** 16 A x 125% = 20 A
Step 3: Selecting conductors **310.15(A)(3), IN (2)** and **Table 310.15(B)(16)** 16.5 A requires 14 AWG cu.	**Step 3:** Selecting conductors **310.15(A)(3), IN (2)** and **Table 310.15(B)(16)** 20 A requires 14 AWG cu.
Solution: The size THWN copper conductors is 14 AWG.	**Solution:** The size THWN copper conductors is 14 AWG.
Note 1: For sizing overcurrent protection devices, see Figures 18-25(A) thru (D).	**Note 2:** See **Asterisk** to **Table 310.15(B)(16)** and **240.4(D)**.

SIZING CONDUCTORS FOR SINGLE-PHASE MOTORS
NEC 430.22

Figure 18-1. Determining the size branch-circuit conductors to supply single-phase motors.

DIRECT-CURRENT MOTOR-RECTIFIER SUPPLIED
430.22(A)

The conductor ampacity on the input of the rectifier shall not be less than 125 percent of the rated input current to the rectifier for DC motors operating from a rectified power supply. Where DC motors operate from a rectified single-phase power supply, the conductors between the field wiring output terminals of the rectifier and the motor shall have an ampacity of not less than the following percentages of the motor full load current rating:

- 190 percent, where a rectifier bridge of the single-phase, half-wave type is used
- 150 percent, where a rectifier bridge of the single-phase, full-wave type is used

See Figure 18-3 for a detailed illustration pertaining to DC motors of direct-current motor-rectifier design.

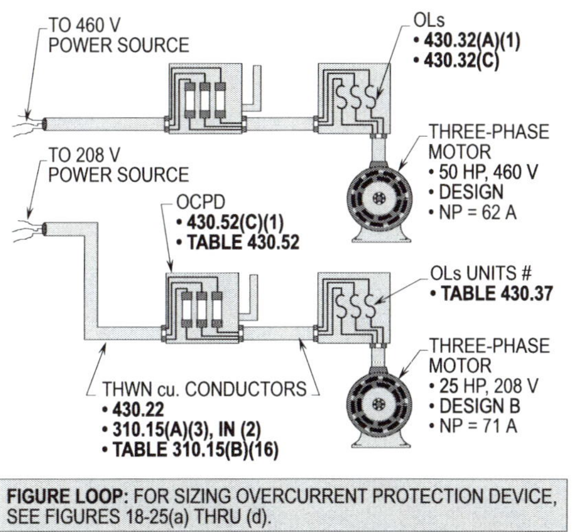

FINDING THWN COPPER CONDUCTORS

Three-phase motors	Three-phase motors
Step 1: Finding FLA **430.6(A)(1)** and **Table 430.250** 50 HP = 65 A	**Step 1:** Finding FLA **430.6(A)(1)** and **Table 430.250** 25 HP = 74.8 A
Step 2: Calculating load **Table 220.3** and **430.22** 65 A x 125% = 81.25 A	**Step 2:** Calculating load **Table 220.3** and **430.22** 74.8 A x 125% = 93.5 A
Step 3: Selecting conductors **310.15(A)(3), IN (2)** and **Table 310.15(B)(16)** 81.25 A requires 4 AWG cu.	**Step 3:** Selecting conductors **310.15(A)(3), IN (2)** and **Table 310.15(B)(16)** 93.5 A requires 3 AWG cu.
Solution: **The size THWN copper conductors is 4 AWG.**	**Solution:** **The size THWN copper conductors is 3 AWG.**

**SIZING CONDUCTORS FOR THREE-PHASE MOTORS
NEC 430.22**

Figure 18-2. Determining the size branch-circuit conductors to supply three-phase motors.

SIZING CONDUCTORS FOR MULTISPEED MOTORS 430.22(B)

The circuit conductors for multispeed motors shall be sized large enough, to the controller, to supply the highest nameplate full-load current rating of the multispeed motor winding involved. A single overcurrent protection device is permitted to serve each speed for a multispeed motor per **430.22(B)**. The speed with the greater amps is used to size the overcurrent protection device and conductors. Overload protection shall be provided for each speed to protect each winding from excessive current during an overload condition. **(See Figure 18-4)**

SIZING CONDUCTORS FOR WYE-START AND DELTA-RUN MOTORS 430.22(C)

The branch-circuit conductors for wye-start and delta-run connected motors shall be selected based on the full-load current on the line side of the controller and shall not be less than 125 percent of the motor full-load current. The ampacity of the conductors between the controller and the motor shall not be less than 72 percent of the motor full-load current rating.

Note, the selection of conductors between the controller and the motor shall be based on 58 percent (1 ÷ 1.732 = .58) of the motor's full-load current, in amps, times 125 percent for continuous use. **(See Figure 18-5)**

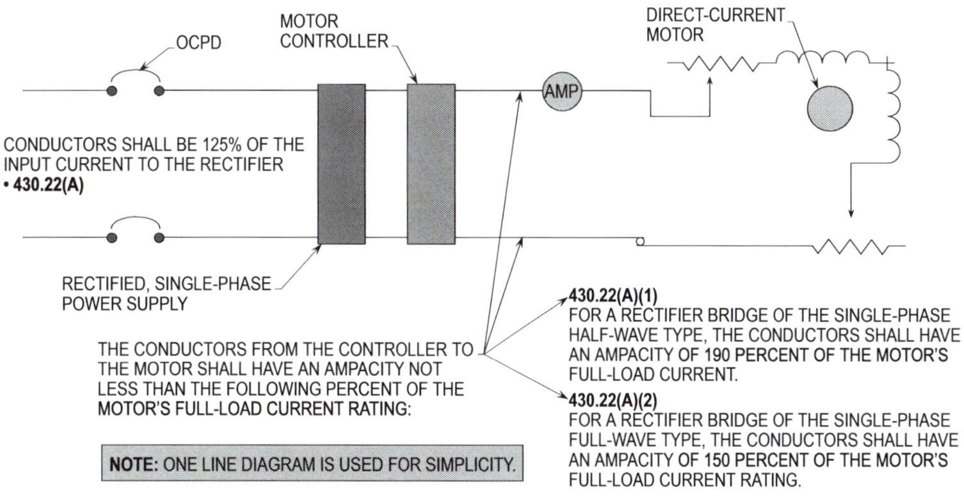

**DIRECT-CURRENT MOTOR-RECTIFIER SUPPLIED
NEC 430.22(A)**

Figure 18-3. This illustration shows the requirements for DC motors of direct-current motor-rectifier design.

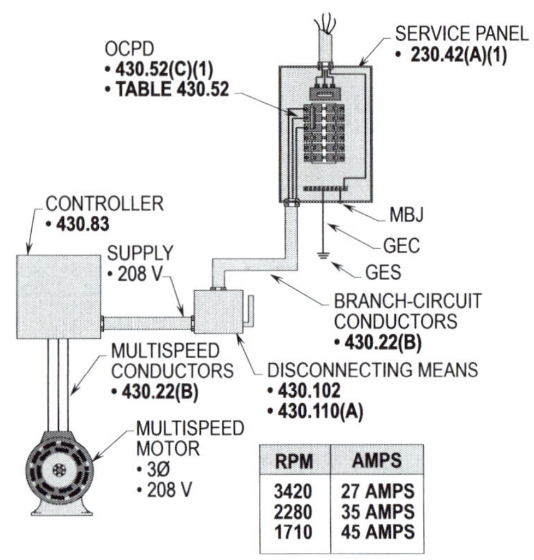

RPM	AMPS
3420	27 AMPS
2280	35 AMPS
1710	45 AMPS

FINDING THWN COPPER CONDUCTORS

Sizing branch-circuit conductors

Step 1: Finding FLA
430.22(B)
45 A largest amperage

Step 2: Calculating load
430.22(B)
45 A x 125% = 56.25

Step 3: Selecting conductors
310.15(A)(3), IN (2) and
Table 310.15(B)(16)
56.25 A requires 6 AWG cu.

Solution: **The size THWN copper conductors are 6 AWG.**

Figure Loop: For sizing circuit breaker to start and run the motor, see Figure 18-25(d).

Sizing multispeed conductors

Step 1: Finding FLA
430.22
3,420 RPM = 27 A
2,280 RPM = 35 A
1,710 RPM = 45 A

Step 2: Calculating load
430.22
27 A x 125% = 33.75 A
35 A x 125% = 43.75 A
45 A x 125% = 56.25 A

Step 3: Selecting conductors
310.15(A)(3), IN (2) and
Table 310.15(B)(16)
33.75 A requires 10 AWG cu.
43.75 A requires 8 AWG cu.
56.25 A requires 6 AWG cu.

Solution: **The size THWN copper conductors are 10 AWG cu., 8 AWG cu., and 6 AWG cu. size for each speed.**

SIZING CONDUCTORS FOR MULTISPEED MOTORS
NEC 430.22(B)

Figure 18-4. Determining the size branch-circuit conductors to supply multispeed motors.

SIZING CONDUCTORS FOR PART-WINDING MOTORS 430.22(D)

Induction or synchronous motors that have a part-winding start are designed so that at starting they energize the primary armature winding first. After starting, the remainder of the winding is energized in one or more steps. The purpose of this arrangement is to reduce the initial inrush current until the motor accelerates to its running speed.

The inrush current at start is locked-rotor current and at times can be quite high. A standard part-winding-start induction motor is designed so that only half of its winding is energized at start; then, as it comes up to speed, the other

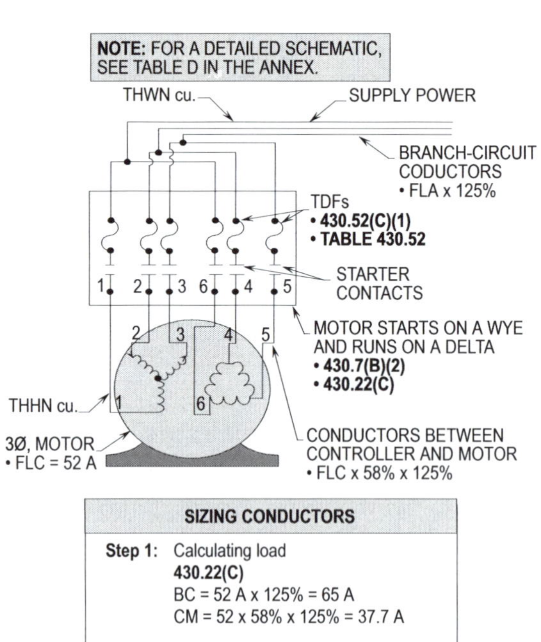

SIZING CONDUCTORS

Step 1: Calculating load
430.22(C)
BC = 52 A x 125% = 65 A
CM = 52 x 58% x 125% = 37.7 A

Step 2: Selecting conductors
Table 310.15(B)(16)
65 A = 6 AWG cu.
37.7 A = 8 AWG cu.

Solution: **Branch circuit requires 6 AWG and conductors between the controller and motor require 8 AWG THHN copper conductors.**

SIZING CONDUCTORS FOR WYE-START AND DELTA-RUN MOTORS
NEC 430.22(C)

Figure 18-5. Determining the size conductors to supply motors starting on a wye and running on delta.

half is energized, so both halves are energized and carry equal current to drive the load.

Separate overload devices shall be used on a standard part-winding-start induction motor to protect the windings from excessive, damaging currents. This means that each half of the motor winding has to be individually provided with overload protection. These requirements are covered in **430.32** and **430.37**. Each half of the windings has a trip current value that is one half of the specified running current. As required by **430.52(C)(1)**, each of the two motor windings shall have branch-circuit, short-circuit, and ground-fault protection that is to be selected at not more than one half the percentages listed in **430.52(C)(1)** and **Table 430.52**. **(See Figure 18-6)**

Design Tip: Section **430.4, Ex.** permits a single device with this one half rating, for both windings, provided that it will permit the motor to start and run. If a time-delay (dual element) fuse is used as a single device for both windings, its rating shall be permitted if it does not exceed 150 percent of the motor's full-load current.

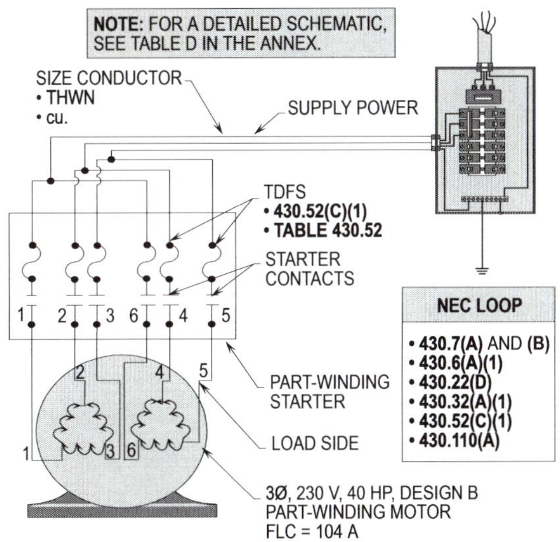

SIZING CONDUCTORS

SIZING CONDUCTORS

Step 1: Selecting FLC
430.6(A)(1) and **Table 430.250**
40 HP = 104 A

Step 2: Sizing conductors
430.22(D)
104 A x 125% = 130 A

Step 3: Selecting conductors
Table 310.15(B)(16)
130 A requires 1 AWG cu.

Solution: **The size conductors are 1 AWG THWN copper.**

SIZING CONDUCTORS FOR
PART-WINDING MOTORS
NEC 430.22(D)

Figure 18-6. Determining the size conductors to supply part-winding motors.

SIZING CONDUCTORS FOR DUTY CYCLE MOTORS
430.22(E)

Conductors for a motor used for short-time, intermittent, periodic, or varying duty do not require conductors to be sized with a current-carrying capacity of 125 percent of the motor's full-load current, in amps. **Table 430.22(E)** permits the conductors to be sized with a percentage times the nameplate current rating, in amps, based on the duty cycle classification of the motor.

When sizing conductors to supply individual motors that are used for short time, intermittent, periodic, or varying duty, the requirements of **Table 430.22(E)** shall apply. Varying heat loads are produced on the conductors by the starting and stopping duration of operation cycles, which permits conductor sizing changes. In other words, such conductors are never subjected to continuous operation due to ON and OFF periods, and therefore conductors are never fully

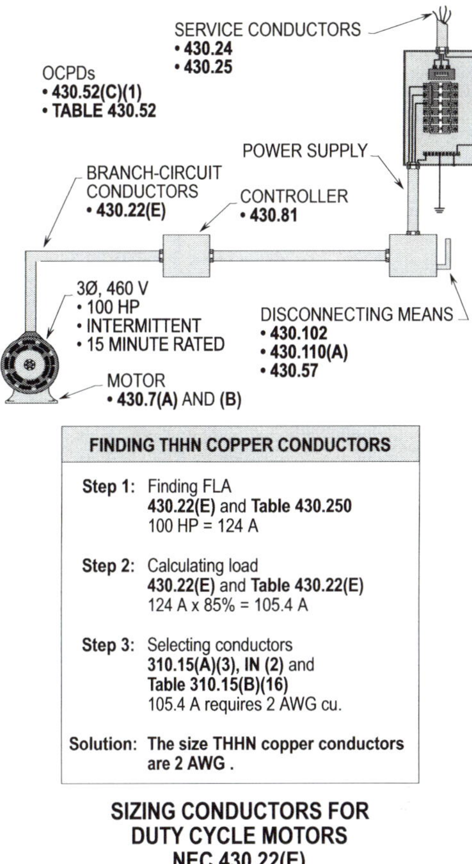

FINDING THHN COPPER CONDUCTORS

Step 1: Finding FLA
430.22(E) and **Table 430.250**
100 HP = 124 A

Step 2: Calculating load
430.22(E) and **Table 430.22(E)**
124 A x 85% = 105.4 A

Step 3: Selecting conductors
310.15(A)(3), IN (2) and
Table 310.15(B)(16)
105.4 A requires 2 AWG cu.

Solution: **The size THHN copper conductors are 2 AWG .**

SIZING CONDUCTORS FOR
DUTY CYCLE MOTORS
NEC 430.22(E)

Figure 18-7. Determining the size conductors to supply duty cycle related motors. (Duty cycle defined per **Article 100.**)

loaded for long intervals of time. For this reason, conductors can be downsized. **(See Figure 18-7)**

SIZING CONDUCTORS FOR ADJUSTABLE SPEED DRIVE SYSTEMS
430.122(A) AND 430.2

Power conversion equipment, when supplied from a branch circuit, includes all elements of the adjustable speed drive system. The rating in amps is used to size the conductors, which are based upon the power required by the conversion equipment. When the power conversion equipment provides overcurrent protection for the motor, no additional overload protection is required.

The disconnecting means can be installed in the line supplying the conversion equipment, and the rating of the disconnect shall not be less than 115 percent of the input current rating of the conversion unit.

Power conversion equipment requires the conductors to be sized at 125 percent of the rated input of such equipment.

Note, for more information on adjustable speed drives, see **430.122(A) through 430.128** at the end of this chapter.

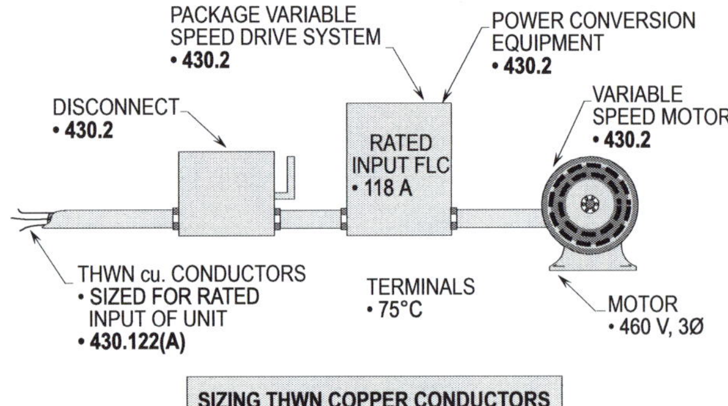

Figure 18-8. Determining the size conductors to supply power conversion equipment. **(See Figure 18-63)**

WOUND-ROTOR SECONDARY
430.23

Wound-rotor motors are three-phase motors that are installed with two sets of leads. The main leads to the motor windings (field poles) are one set, and the secondary leads to the rotor are the other set. The secondary leads on one end connect to the rotor through slip rings, and the other end of the leads connects through a controller and a bank of resistors. The speed of the motor varies when the amount of resistance in the motor circuit is varied. The rotor will turn slower when the resistance is greater in the rotor, and faster when such resistance is lowered.

SIZING CONDUCTORS FOR
CONTINUOUS DUTY
430.23(A)

The motor shall have an ampacity not less than 125 percent of the full-load secondary current of the motor where secondary leads are installed between the controller and the motor. The secondary full-load current rating, in amps, is obtained from the manufacturer or found on the nameplate of the motor.

SIZING CONDUCTORS FOR OTHER
THAN CONTINUOUS DUTY
430.23(B)

When installing a motor to be used for short-time, intermittent, periodic, or varying duty, the secondary conductors shall be sized not less than 125 percent of the secondary current per **Table 430.22(E)**. The classification of service determines the correct percentages to select and apply, when sizing the conductors, based on the cycles of the motor.

SIZING CONDUCTORS FOR RESISTORS,
SEPARATED FROM CONTROLLER
430.23(C)

Where the secondary resistor is separate from the controller, the ampacity of the conductors between the controller and resistor shall not be less than the resistor duty classification percentages listed in **Table 430.23(C)**. **(See Figure 18-9)**

SIZING CONDUCTORS FOR SEVERAL
MOTORS
430.24

The full-load current rating of the largest motor shall be multiplied by 125 percent to select the size of conductors for a feeder supplying a group of two or more motors. The remaining motors of the group shall have their full-load current ratings added to this value, and this total amperage is then used to size the conductors. Noncontinuous nonmotor loads shall be sized at 100 percent. Continuous nonmotor loads shall be sized at 125 percent. **(See Figure 18-10)**

SIZING CONDUCTORS FOR DUTY
CYCLE MOTORS
430.24, Ex. 1

Table 430.22(E) shall be used for sizing the amperage rating for a motor that is classified as either short-time, intermittent, periodic, or varying duty. The amperage rating shall be based on 100 percent of the full-load current rating on the motor's nameplate if rated for continuous operation.

The full-load current rating, in amps, of the largest motor shall be multiplied by 125 percent to select the size conductors for a feeder supplying a group of two or more motors. The remaining motors of the group shall have their total full-load current ratings added to the calculated amps of the duty cycle motor or to the amps of the 125 percent motor, whichever is greater. The feeder conductors shall be sized by this total full-load current, in amperes. **(See Figures 18-7** and **18-11)**

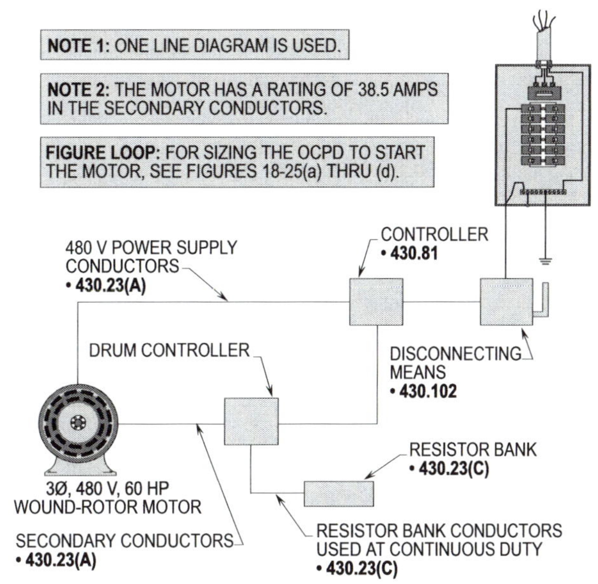

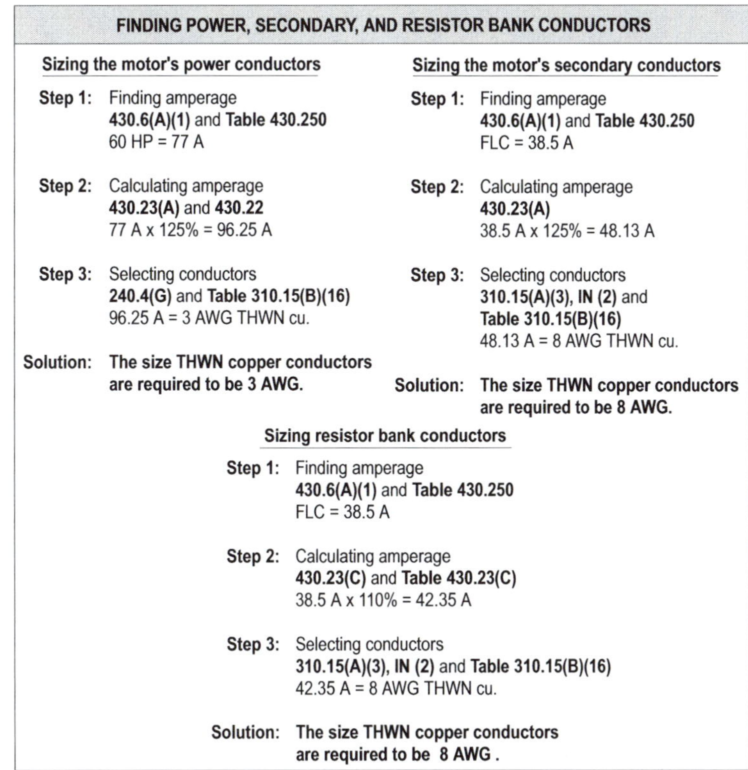

FINDING POWER, SECONDARY, AND RESISTOR BANK CONDUCTORS

Sizing the motor's power conductors

Step 1: Finding amperage
430.6(A)(1) and **Table 430.250**
60 HP = 77 A

Step 2: Calculating amperage
430.23(A) and **430.22**
77 A x 125% = 96.25 A

Step 3: Selecting conductors
240.4(G) and **Table 310.15(B)(16)**
96.25 A = 3 AWG THWN cu.

Solution: The size THWN copper conductors are required to be 3 AWG.

Sizing the motor's secondary conductors

Step 1: Finding amperage
430.6(A)(1) and **Table 430.250**
FLC = 38.5 A

Step 2: Calculating amperage
430.23(A)
38.5 A x 125% = 48.13 A

Step 3: Selecting conductors
310.15(A)(3), IN (2) and
Table 310.15(B)(16)
48.13 A = 8 AWG THWN cu.

Solution: The size THWN copper conductors are required to be 8 AWG.

Sizing resistor bank conductors

Step 1: Finding amperage
430.6(A)(1) and **Table 430.250**
FLC = 38.5 A

Step 2: Calculating amperage
430.23(C) and **Table 430.23(C)**
38.5 A x 110% = 42.35 A

Step 3: Selecting conductors
310.15(A)(3), IN (2) and **Table 310.15(B)(16)**
42.35 A = 8 AWG THWN cu.

Solution: The size THWN copper conductors are required to be 8 AWG .

SIZING CONDUCTORS FOR RESISTORS,
SEPARATED FROM CONTROLLER
NEC 430.23(A), (B), AND (C)

Figure 18-9. Determining the size conductors to supply wound-rotor motors.

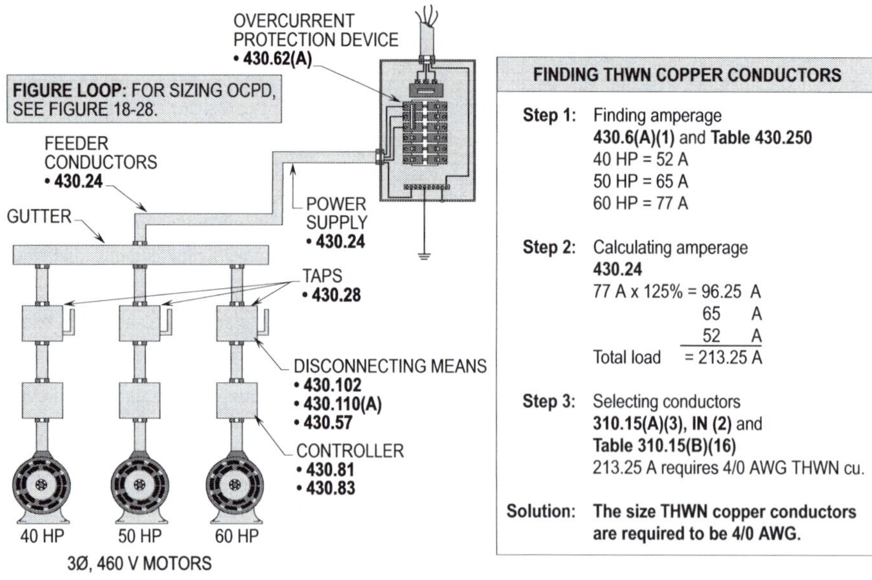

Figure 18-10. Determining the size conductors for a feeder to supply several motors.

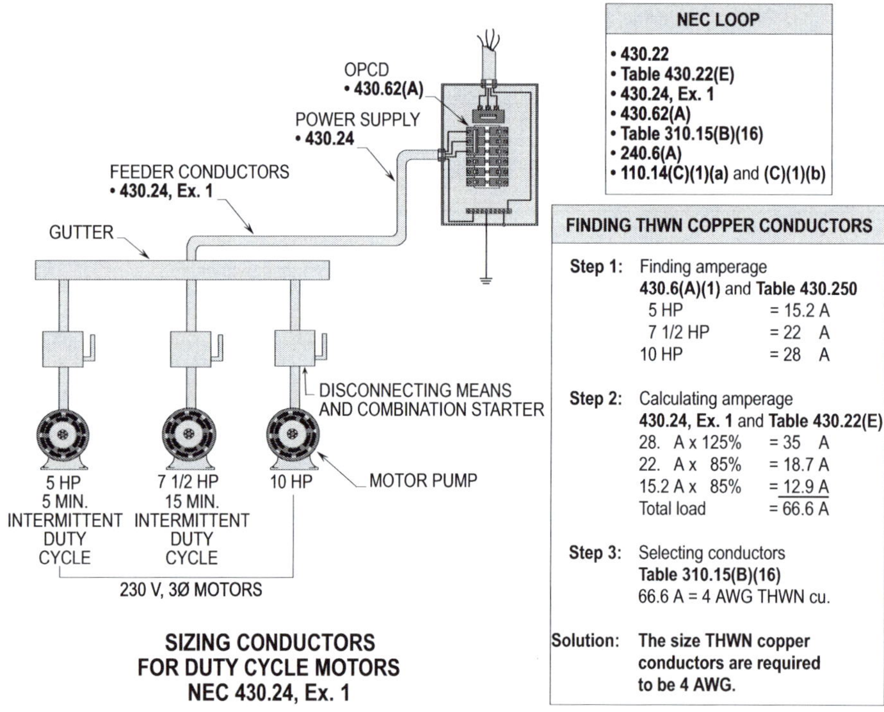

Figure 18-11. Determining the size conductors for a feeder to supply duty cycle-related motors.

SIZING CONDUCTORS SUPPLYING MOTORS AND OTHER LOADS 430.25

The motor load shall be calculated per **430.22** or **430.24** when designing combination loads that consist of one or more motor loads on the same circuit with lights, receptacles, appliances, or any combination of such loads. For other than motor loads, **Article 220** and other applicable articles shall be used to calculate such loads. The ampacity required for the feeder conductors shall be equal to all the total loads involved. The overcurrent protection devices used to protect conductors and elements from short circuits and ground faults shall be sized per **430.62(A)** and **430.63**. **(See Figure 18-12)**

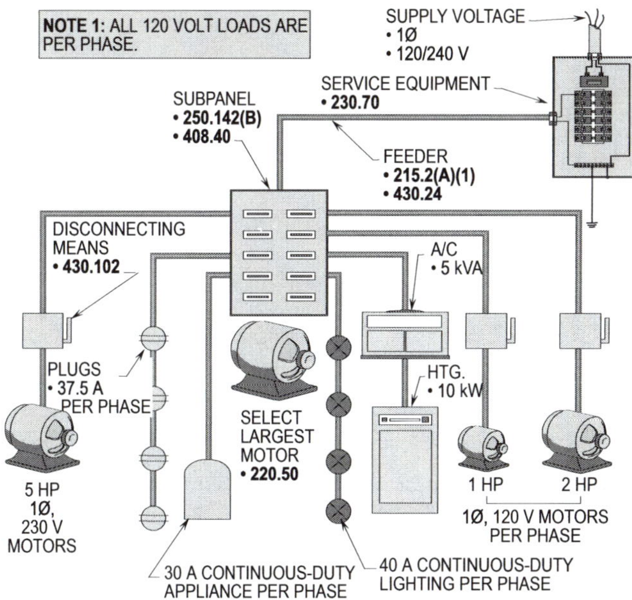

NOTE 2: WHEN CALCULATING LOADS FOR BRANCH CIRCUITS, FEEDERS, AND SERVICES, SEE **220.14(A) THROUGH 14(L), 220.50, 210.19(A)(1), 215.2(A)(1), AND 230.42(A)(1).**

SIZING OCPD AND THWN COPPER CONDUCTORS

Sizing OCPD based on loads

Step 1: Calculating loads
215.3, 215.2(A)(1)(a), Table 430.248, and **220.50**
- Lighting load
  40 A x 125% = 50 A
- Receptacle load
  37.5 A x 100% = 37.5 A
- Appliance load
  30 A x 125% = 37.5 A
- Heat or A/C load
  10 kVA x 1,000 x 100% / 240 V = 42 A
- Motor load
  5 HP = 28 A x 100% = 28 A
  1 HP = 16 A x 100% = 16 A
  2 HP = 24 A x 100% = 24 A
- Largest motor load
  28 A x 25% = 7 A
  Total load = 242 A

Step 2: Selecting OCPD based on load
215.3, 240.4(G), and **430.63**
242 A permits 250 A OCPD

Solution: The size overcurrent protection device based on calculated load is 250 amps.

Sizing OCPD based on motor load

Step 1: Calculating OCPD
430.52(A)(1), 430.62(A), 240.4(G), and **Table 430.52**
Motor loads
- 5 HP = 28 A x 250% = 70 A
- 1 HP = 16 A x 100% = 16 A
- 2 HP = 24 A x 100% = 24 A

Step 2: Other loads
- Lighting load = 50 A
- Receptacle load = 37.5 A
- Appliance load = 37.5 A
- Heating load = 42 A
  Total load = 277 A

Step 3: Selecting OCPD
430.62(A) and **240.6(A)**
250 A is the next size below 277 A

Solution: The size overcurrent protection device based on motor loads is 250 amps.

Note: In most cases, the calculated load produces the largest or same size overcurrent protection device, unless there is an unusually large motor involved.

Sizing conductors

Step 1: Calculating loads
215.2(A)(1)(a)
- Lighting load
  40 A x 125% = 50 A
- Receptacle load
  37.5 A x 100% = 37.5 A
- Appliance load
  30 A x 125% = 37.5 A
- Heat or A/C load
  10 kVA x 1,000 x 100% ÷ 240 V = 42 A
- Motor load
  5 HP = 28 A x 100% = 28 A
  1 HP = 16 A x 100% = 16 A
  2 HP = 24 A x 100% = 24 A
- Largest motor load
  28 A x 25% = 7 A
  Total load = 242 A

Step 2: Selecting conductors
310.15(A)(3), IN (2) and **Table 310.15(B)(16)**
242 A requires 250 KCMIL

Solution: The size conductors are 250 KCMIL THWN cu.

Sizing neutral

Step 1: Calculating load
430.24 and **220.61**
- Lighting load
  40 A x 100% = 40 A
- Receptacle load
  37.5 A x 100% = 37.5 A
- Appliance load
  30 A x 100% = 30 A
- Motor load
  1 HP = 16 A x 100% = 16 A
  2 HP = 24 A x 100% = 24 A
- Largest motor load
  24 A x 25% = 6 A
  Total load = 153.5 A

Step 2: Selecting conductors
310.15(A)(3), IN (2) and **Table 310.15(B)(16)**
153.5 A requires 2/0 AWG cu.

Solution: The size of the conductors based on 100 percent are 2/0 AWG THWN copper.

Note: The AHJ may require the continuous loads to be multiplied by 125 percent when calculating the neutral load.

SIZING CONDUCTORS SUPPLYING MOTORS AND OTHER LOADS
NEC 430.25

Figure 18-12. Determining the size conductors for motors and other loads supplied by a feeder.

SIZING THE BRANCH-CIRCUIT PROTECTIVE DEVICE
TABLE 430.52, 430.52(C)(1), AND (C)(3)

The motor branch-circuit overcurrent device shall be capable of carrying the starting current of the motor. Short-circuit and ground-fault current is considered to be properly taken care of when the overcurrent protection device does not exceed the values in **Table 430.52,** as permitted by the provisions of **430.52(C)(1)** with exceptions.

Different percentages are selected for particular devices based on one of the four columns listed in **Table 430.52**. The percentages are used to size and select the proper size overcurrent protection device to allow a certain type of motor to start and run. The motor has a momentary starting current that is necessary for the motor to have power to start and drive the connected load at the driven equipment.

Note, the overcurrent protection device sized per **430.52(C)(1)** provides protection from short circuits and ground faults. Overload protection shall be provided for conductors and motor windings per **430.32(A)(1)** and **430.32(C)**. **(See Figure 18-13)**

> **Design Tip:** In cases where the values for branch-circuit protective devices determined by **Table 430.52** do not correspond to the standard sizes or ratings of fuses, nonadjustable circuit breakers, or thermal devices, or possible settings of adjustable circuit breakers adequate to carry the starting currents of the motor, the next higher size rating or setting shall be permitted to be used.

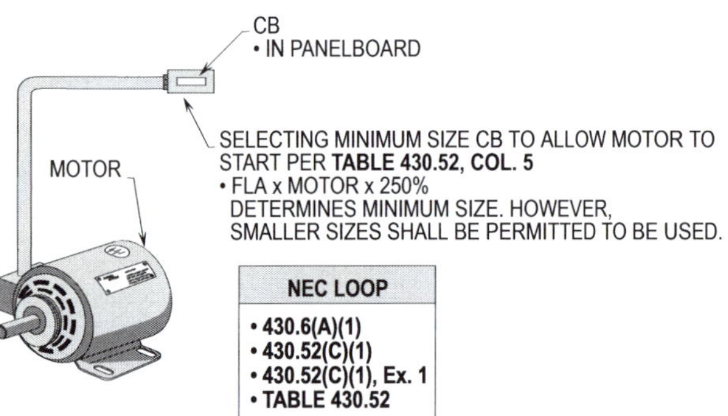

SIZING THE BRANCH-CIRCUIT PROTECTIVE DEVICE
NEC TABLE 430.52
NEC 430.52(C)(1) AND (C)(3)

Figure 18-13. Selecting the percentages to determine the minimum size (rounding down), next size (rounding up), and maximum size circuit breaker to allow a motor to start and run. **[See Figure 18-14 through 18-15(b)]**

APPLYING THE EXCEPTIONS
430.52(C)(1), Ex. 1 AND Ex. 2

There are Exceptions that permit larger overcurrent protection devices to be used where the overcurrent protection device, as specified in **Table 430.52,** will not permit the starting current of the motor to start and run. Where the motor fails to start and run because of excessive inrush starting currents, one of the following exceptions can be applied.

APPLYING Ex. 1

If the values of the branch-circuit, short circuit, and ground-fault protection devices determined from **Table 430.52** do not conform to standard sizes or ratings of fuses, nonadjustable circuit breakers, or possible settings on adjustable circuit breakers, it does not matter if they are capable or not capable of adequately carrying the load involved; the next higher setting or rating shall be permitted. In other words, you can round up or round down the size of the overcurrent protection device automatically by choice. **(See Figure 18-14)**

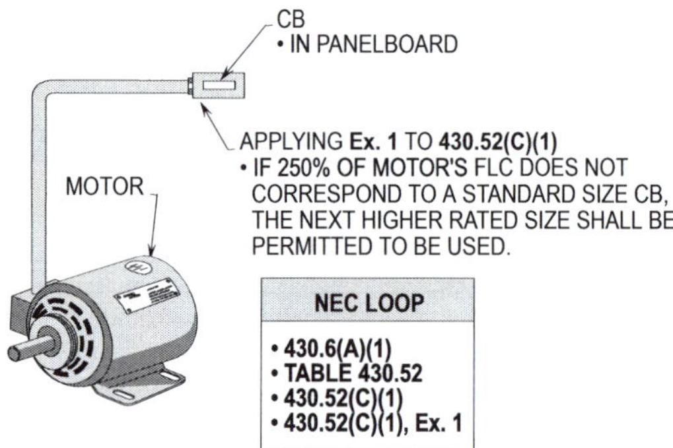

SIZING THE BRANCH-CIRCUIT PROTECTIVE DEVICE
NEC TABLE 430.52
NEC 430.52(C)(1), Ex. 1

Figure 18-14. Where the percentages of **Table 430.52** times the full-load current of motor in amps does not correspond to a standard size overcurrent protection device, the next higher size rating above this percentage shall be permitted to be used.

APPLYING Ex. 2

If the ratings listed in **Table 430.52** and **Ex. 1** to **430.52(C)(1)** are not sufficient for the starting current of the motor, the following overcurrent protection devices with percentages shown can be used to start and run motors having high inrush starting currents. **[See Figure 18-15(a)]**

When nontime-delay fuses are used and they do not exceed 600 amperes in rating, it shall be permitted to increase the fuse size up to 400 percent of the full-load current, but never over 400 percent.

Time-element fuses (dual-element) shall not exceed 225 percent of the full-load current in amps, but they may be increased to up this percentage.

Inverse time-element breakers shall be permitted to be increased in rating. However:

- They shall not exceed 400 percent of full-load current of the motor for 100 amperes or less, or
- They may be increased to 300 percent where a full-load current is greater than 100 amperes.

See Figure 18-15(b) for a detailed illustration on selecting percentage for sizing overcurrent protection devices.

USING INSTANTANEOUS TRIP CIRCUIT BREAKERS
430.52(C)(3), Ex. 1

An instantaneous trip circuit breaker shall be used only if it is adjustable, and it is a part of a combination controller that has overcurrent protection in each controller. Such combination, when used, has to be approved. An instantaneous trip circuit breaker is allowed to have a damping device, to limit the inrush current when the motor is started.

If the specified setting in **Table 430.52** is not sufficient for the starting current of the motor, the setting on an instantaneous trip circuit current may be increased, provided that in no instance it exceeds 1300 percent of the motor's full-load current rating, in amps, for motors marked as Class B, C, or D.

> **Design Tip:** For Design E and Class B NEMA motors (energy efficient), the setting on the instantaneous trip circuit breakers shall be permitted to be adjusted up to 1700 percent to allow the motor to start and run.

See Figure 18-16 for adjusting the maximum trip settings on instantaneous trip circuit breakers to allow motors to start and accelerate their driven load.

TYPES OF MOTORS
TABLE 430.52

The following are five types of motors to be considered when sizing overcurrent protection devices to allow motors to start and run:

- Single-phase AC squirrel-cage
- Three-phase AC squirrel-cage
- Wound-rotor
- Synchronous
- DC

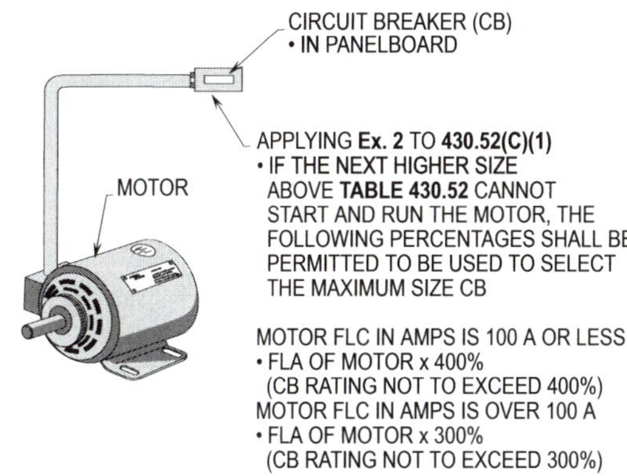

SIZING THE BRANCH-CIRCUIT PROTECTIVE DEVICE
NEC TABLE 430.52
NEC 430.52(C)(1), Ex. 2

Figure 18-15(a). When the percentages of **Table 430.52** and **430.52(C)(1), Ex. 1** will not allow the motor to start and run the driven load, the maximum size circuit breaker of **430.52(C)(1), Ex. 2(c)** shall be permitted to be used.

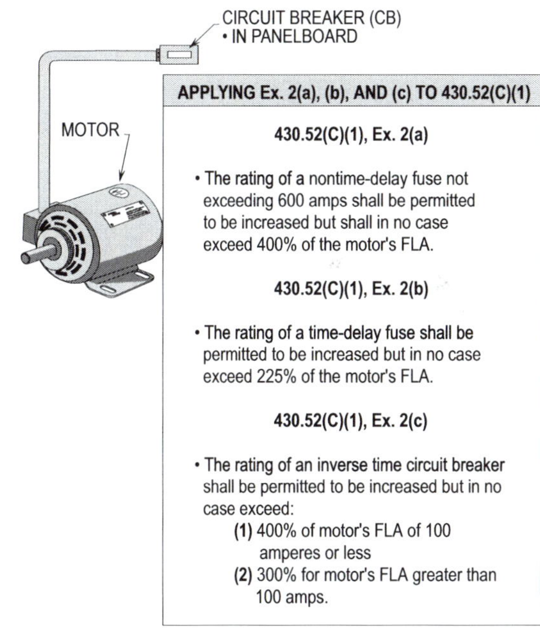

SIZING THE BRANCH-CIRCUIT PROTECTIVE DEVICE
NEC 430.52(C)(1), Ex. 2(a), (b) AND (c)

Figure 18-15(b). When the percentages of **Table 430.52** and **430.52(C)(1), Ex. 1** will not allow the motor to start and run, the maximum percentages of **430.52(C)(1), Ex. 2(a), (b),** and **(c)** shall be permitted to be applied.

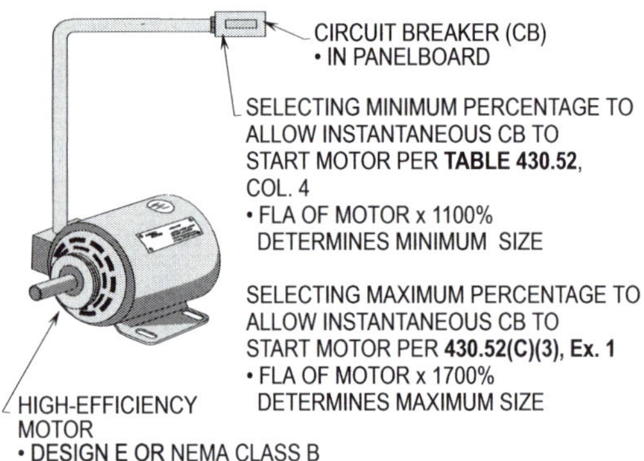

USING INSTANTANEOUS TRIP CIRCUIT BREAKERS
NEC TABLE 430.52
NEC 430.52(C)(3), Ex. 1

Figure 18-16. Determining the minimum and maximum size setting on an instantaneous trip circuit breaker to allow a motor to start and run a driven load. **Note,** after the minimum size overcurrent protection device has been determined, a smaller size shall be permitted to be selected.

SINGLE-PHASE AC SQUIRREL-CAGE MOTORS

Squirrel-cage motors are known in the electrical industry as induction motors. An induction motor operates on the same principles as the primary and secondary windings of a transformer. When power energizes the field windings, they serve as the primary by inducing voltage into the rotor that serves as the secondary windings. Squirrel-cage motors have two windings on the stator: one winding is the run winding, and the other is the starting winding. This additional starting winding on the stator is required for split-phase, single-phase, induction motors to have the capacity to start and run. The starting winding has a higher resistance to ground than the running winding, which creates a phase displacement between the two windings. It is this phase displacement between the two windings that gives split-phase motors the power to start.

The phase displacement is about 18 degrees to 30 degrees in angular phase displacement, which provides enough starting torque (twist or force) to start the motor. The motor operates on the running winding when the rotor starts turning and has established a running speed at about 75 percent to 80 percent of the motor's synchronous speed. The starting winding is disconnected by a centrifugal switch that is installed in the circuit of the starting winding. **(See Figure 18-17)**

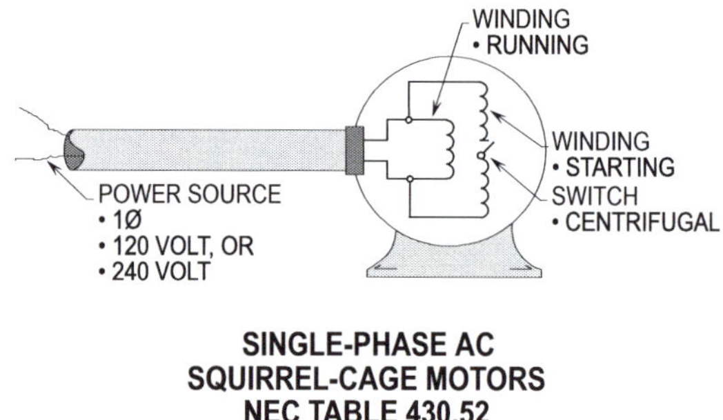

SINGLE-PHASE AC SQUIRREL-CAGE MOTORS
NEC TABLE 430.52

Figure 18-17. This illustration is an example of a single-phase squirrel-cage induction motor that is listed in **Table 430.52** and **Table 430.248**.

THREE-PHASE SQUIRREL-CAGE MOTORS

Three-phase induction motors have three separate windings per pole on the stator that generate magnetic fields that are 120 degrees out of phase with each other. An additional starting winding is not required for three-phase motors to start and run. An induction motor will always have a peak phase of current. This is due to alternating current reversing its direction of flow. In other words, when alternating current of one phase reverses its direction of flow, a peak current will be developed on one phase and, as current reverses direction again, a second phase will peak, etc. Three-phase motors provide a smooth and continuous source of power once they are started and driving their load. **(See Figure 18-18)**

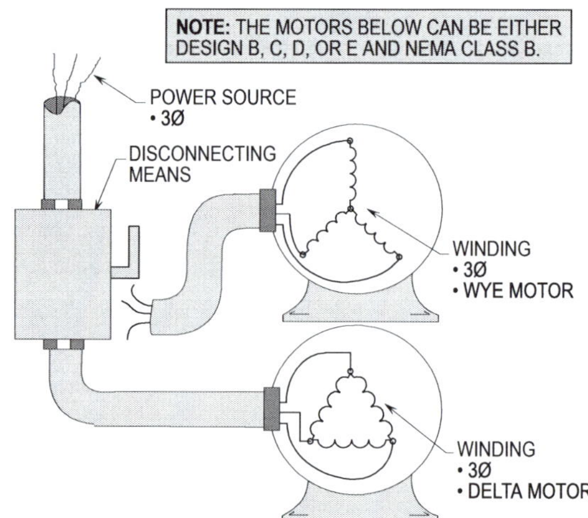

THREE-PHASE SQUIRREL-CAGE MOTORS
NEC TABLE 430.52

Figure 18-18. This illustration is an example of a three-phase squirrel-cage induction motor that is listed in **Table 430.52** and **Table 430.250**.

WOUND-ROTOR MOTORS

Wound-rotor motors are classified as three-phase induction motors. They are similar in design to squirrel-cage induction motors. Wound-rotor motors are three-phase motors having two sets of leads. One set is the main leads to the motor windings (field poles) and the other set is the secondary leads to the rotor. The secondary leads are connected to the rotor through the slip rings, while the other ends of the leads are connected through a controller and a bank of resistors. The speed of the motor varies with the amount of resistance added in the motor circuit. The rotor will turn slower when the resistance is greater in the rotor, and vice versa. The resistance may be incorporated in the controller, or the resistor banks may be separate from the motor. **(See Figure 18-19)**

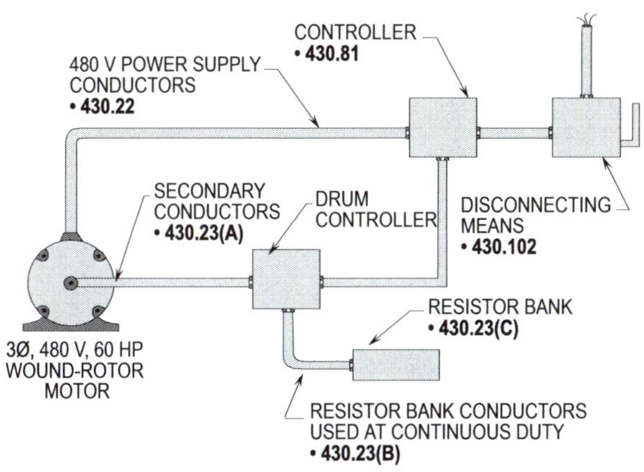

Figure 18-19. This illustration is an example of a three-phase wound-rotor motor listed in **Table 430.52** and **Table 430.250**.

SYNCHRONOUS MOTORS

The following are two types of synchronous motors that are available:

- Nonexcited
- Direct-current excited

Synchronous motors are available in a wide range of sizes and types that are designed to run at designed speeds. A DC source is required to excite a direct-current excited synchronous motor. The torque required to turn the rotor of a synchronous motor is produced when the DC current of the rotor field locks in with the magnetic field of the stator AC current. **(See Figure 18-20)**

DC MOTORS

Direct current only is used to operate DC-related motors. A DC motor is designed with the following two main parts:

- The stator
- The rotor

The stationary frame of the motor is called the stator. The armature mounted on the drive shaft is known as the rotor. By applying direct current to the rotor, the speed may be adjusted for a DC motor that drives the driven load at a specific speed. **(See Figure 18-21)**

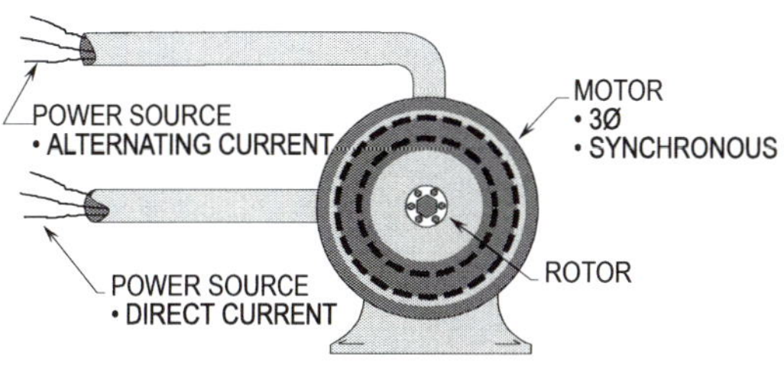

Figure 18-20. This illustration is an example of a three-phase synchronous motor that is listed in **Table 430.52** and **Table 430.250**.

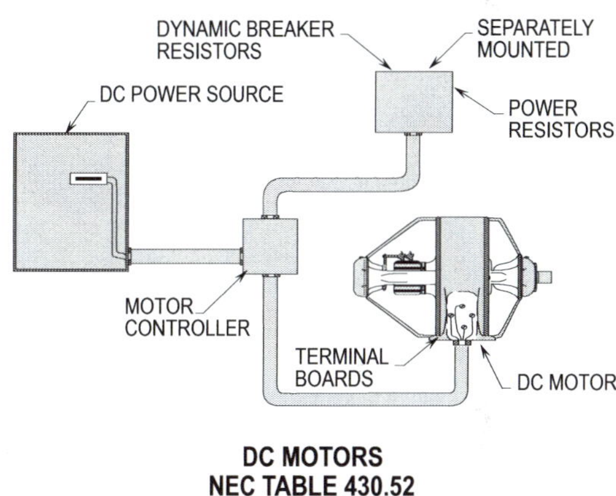

Figure 18-21. This illustration is an example of a DC motor that is listed in **Table 430.52** and **Table 430.247**.

CODE LETTERS
430.7(B) AND TABLE 430.7(B)

Code letters are installed on motors by manufacturers for calculating the locked-rotor current (LRC) in amps based on the kVA per horsepower that is selected from the motor's code letter. Overcurrent protection devices shall be set above the locked-rotor current of the motor to prevent the overcurrent protection device from opening when the rotor of the motor is starting. The following two methods can be used to calculate and select the locked-rotor current of motors:

- Utilizing code letters to determine LRC
- Utilizing horsepower to determine LRC

UTILIZING CODE LETTERS TO FIND LRC 430.7(B) AND TABLE 430.7(B)

Code letters shall be marked on the nameplate, and such letters are used for designing locked-rotor current. Locked-rotor current (LRC) for code letters is listed in **Table 430.7(B)** in kVA (kilovolt-amps) per horsepower, based on a particular code letter.

For example: What is the locked-current rating for a three-phase, 208 volt, 20 horsepower motor with a code letter B marked on the nameplate of the motor?

Step 1: Finding LRC amps
Table 430.7(B)
A = (kVA per HP) x (1000 ÷ V x 1.732)
A = (3.54 x 20 x 1000) ÷ (208 V x 1.732)
A = 70,800 ÷ 360
A = 197

Solution: The locked-rotor current is 197 amps.
Note, Table 430.7(B) must be used to find LRCs of the motor, based on their code letters per the 1996 NEC and earlier editions.

LOCKED-ROTOR CURRENT UTILIZING HORSEPOWER TABLES 430.251(A) AND (B)

The locked-rotor current of a motor may be found in **Tables 430.251(A)** and **(B)**. The locked-rotor current for single-phase and three-phase motors are selected from one of these Tables, based upon the phases, voltage, and horsepower rating of the motor. For motors with code letters A through G, round the nameplate current in amps up to an even number (unit of 10) and multiply by 6 to obtain the LRC of the motor. (Rule of Thumb)

Note, code letters are not found in **Tables 430.251(A)** and **(B)**; they are listed on the motor's nameplate. Motors will be marked either as Design B, C, or D letter to indicate which locked-rotor currents are to be selected from **Tables 430.251(A)** and **(B)** based on horsepower, phases, and voltages.   **Note, Table 430.7(B)** is used when code letters are placed on the motor.

For example: What is the locked-rotor current rating for a three-phase, 460 volts, 50 horsepower, Design B motor?

Table method using Design letter

Step 1: Finding LRC amps
Table 430.251(B)
50 HP requires 363 A

Solution: The locked-rotor current is 363 amps.

For example: What is the locked-rotor current of a motor with a nameplate current of 63 amps, based on code letter A through G?

Rule-of-thumb method using code letter

Step 1: Finding even number (unit of 10)
Table 430.7(B)
Round up 63 A to 70 A

Step 2: Calculating LRC
Table 430.7(B)
70 A x 6 = 420 A

Solution: The locked-rotor current is 420 amps. Note, this method can be used only for code letters A thru G.

See Figures 8-22(a) and (b) for calculating and selecting the locked-rotor current of a motor.

Design Tip: Engineers and electricians shall select the locked-rotor current rating from **Tables 430.251(A)** and **(B)** when using Design B, C, or D motors. The overcurrent protection device shall be set above the locked-rotor current of the motor so the motor can start and run.

SIZING AND SELECTING OVERCURRENT PROTECTION DEVICES TABLE 430.52, COLUMNS 2, 3, 4, AND 5

The overcurrent protection device shall be sized for the starting current of the motor and selected to allow the motor to start and run. The overcurrent protection device per **Table**

430.52 shall protect the branch-circuit conductors from short circuits and ground faults. The following four overcurrent protection devices selected from **Table 430.52** will start most motors under normal starting conditions:

- Nontime-delay fuses per Column 2
- Time-delay fuses per Column 3
- Instantaneous trip circuit breakers per Column 4
- Inverse-time circuit breakers per Column 5

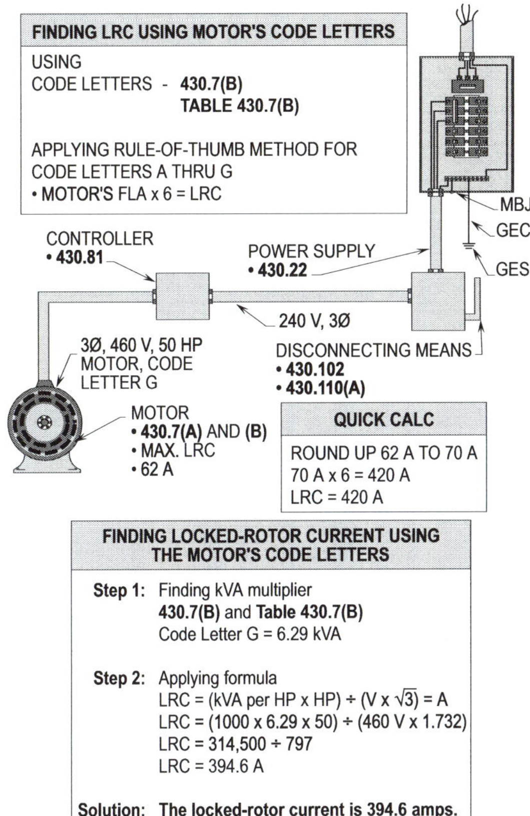

Figure 18-22(a). For motors using code letters instead of Design letters, the LRC shall be calculated per **Table 430.7(B)** using the code letter of the motor.

NONTIME-DELAY FUSES
TABLE 430.52, COLUMN 2

Nontime-delay fuses are installed with instantaneous trip features to detect short circuits and thermal characteristics to sense slow heat buildup in the circuit. A nontime-delay fuse will hold five times (500 percent) its rating for approximately 1/4 to 2 seconds based upon the type used.

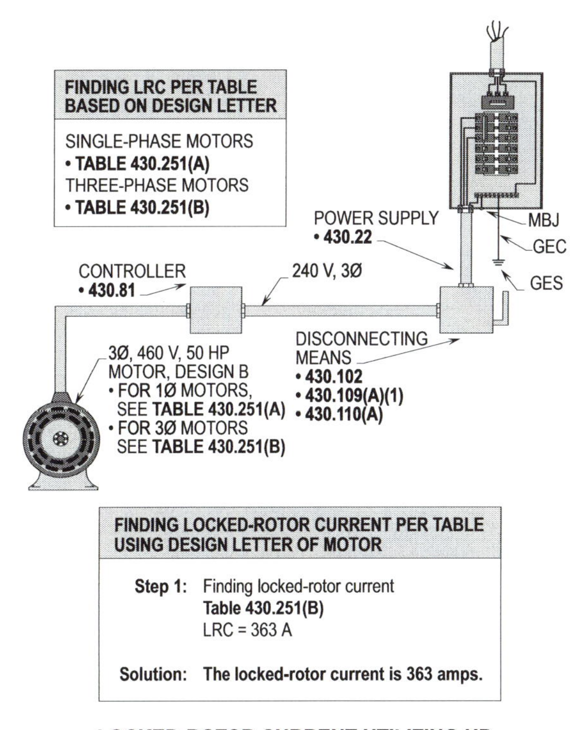

Figure 18-22(b). Tables **430.251(A)** and **(B)** shall be permitted to be used to determine the LRC in amps for motors with Design letters (DLs).

For example: What is the holding time in amps for a nontime-delay fuse of 150 amps?

Step 1: Finding holding amps
A = fuse rating x 500%
A = 150 A x 500%
A = 750

Solution: The holding time in amps of a nontime-delay fuse is 750 amps. Note, this fuse will blow in 1/4 to 2 seconds so the motor will have to start and accelerate the load quickly.

See Figure 18-23(a) for a detailed illustration of sizing nontime-delay fuses to allow motors to start and run.

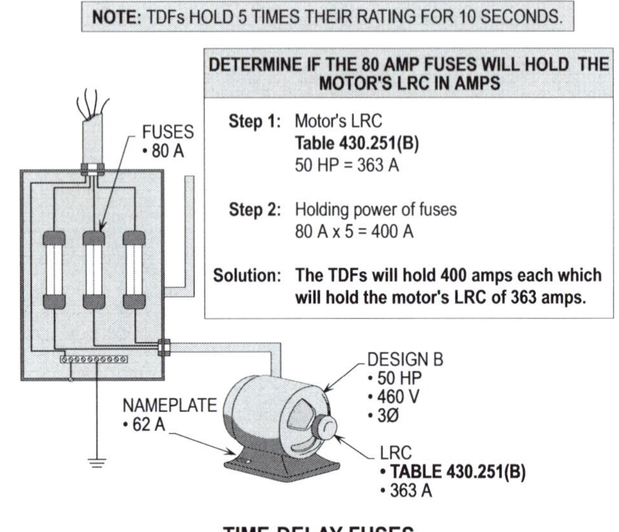

Figure 18-23(a). Nontime-delay fuses will hold five times their rating, and when this rating is above the locked-rotor current it should allow the motor to start and run based on the LRC. **Note,** they can be sized larger.

TIME-DELAY FUSES
USING MAXIMUM SIZE
TABLE 430.52, COLUMN 3

Time-delay fuses are also equipped with instantaneous trip features to detect short circuits and thermal characteristics to sense slow heat buildup in the circuit. Time-delay fuses are used because of their time-delay action to allow a motor to start. Time-delay fuses will hold 5 times (500 percent) of their rating, which will permit most motors to start and accelerate the driven load.

Note, time-delay fuses that are sized at 125 percent or less of the motor's FLC rating can provide overload protection for the motor.

A time-delay fuse will hold five times its rating for 10 seconds, and this delayed action provides more acceleration time to allow the motor to start without tripping the overcurrent protection device.

For example: What is the holding power in amps for a time-delay fuse of 150 amps?

Step 1: Finding holding amps
A = fuse x 500%
A = 150 A x 500%
A = 750

Solution: The rating of a time-delay fuse is 750 amps. Note, this fuse holds five times its rating for ten seconds without blowing and opening the circuit.

See Figure 18-23(b) for sizing time-delay fuses to hold the motors locked-rotor current, in amps.

Figure 18-23(b). Time-delay fuses will hold five times their rating, and when this rating is above the locked-rotor current, in amps, it should allow the motor to start and run based on the LRC.

INSTANTANEOUS TRIP
CIRCUIT BREAKERS
TABLE 430.52, COLUMN 4

Instantaneous trip circuit breakers are installed with instantaneous values of current to respond to short circuits only. Thermal protection is not provided for instantaneous trip circuit breakers. Instantaneous trip circuit breakers will hold about three times their rating on the low setting and five times their next setting, seven times their next setting, and approximately ten times their rating on the high setting. Certain types allow such settings to be adjusted from 0 to 1700 percent. **[See Figure 18-24(a)]**

INVERSE-TIME CIRCUIT BREAKERS
TABLE 430.52, COLUMN 5

Inverse-time circuit breakers are designed with instantaneous trip features to detect short circuits and thermal characteristics to sense slow heat buildup in the circuit. If heat should occur in the windings of the motor, the instantaneous values of current will be detected by the thermal action of the circuit breaker and the current will trip open the circuit if it is sized properly. The magnetic action of the circuit breaker will clear the circuit if short circuits or ground faults should occur on the circuit elements or equipment served.

> **Design Tip:** Inverse-time circuit breakers will hold about three times their rating for different periods of time based on their frame size.
>
> **For example,** a motor with a full-load current of 585 amps can usually be started with a 200 amp circuit breaker.

This can be verified by multiplying the 200 amp circuit breaker by 3, which is equal to 600 amps; 585 amps divided by 3 is equal to 195 amps. By rounding up to the next size circuit breaker per **430.52(C)(1), Ex. 1**, the size circuit breaker is 200 amps, per **240.6(A)**. This size circuit breaker allows the motor to start and run. **[See Figure 18-24(b)]**

SIZING MAXIMUM OVERCURRENT PROTECTION DEVICE
430.52(C)(1), Ex. 2(a) THRU (c)

Where the rating specified in **Table 430.52** is not sufficient for the starting current of the motor, the following ratings (percentages) shall be applied:

- Nontime-delay fuses (400 percent)

- Time-delay fuses (225 percent)

- Inverse-time circuit breakers (400 and 300 percent)

- Instantaneous-trip circuit breakers (0 - 1700 percent based on Design letter or code letter)

SIZING OVERCURRENT PROTECTION DEVICES TO ALLOW MOTORS TO START AND RUN
430.52(C)(1) AND TABLE 430.52

The branch-circuit protection for a motor may be a fuse or circuit breaker located in the line at the point where the branch circuit originates. The fuse or circuit breaker is located either at a service cabinet or distribution panel or in the motor control center. When there is only one motor on a branch circuit, the fuse or circuit breaker is sized according to **Table 430.52** and **430.52(C)(1)**. **Note,** a motor is listed in Table 240.4(G) and therefore the overcurrent protection device can be increased above a 125%, if necessary.

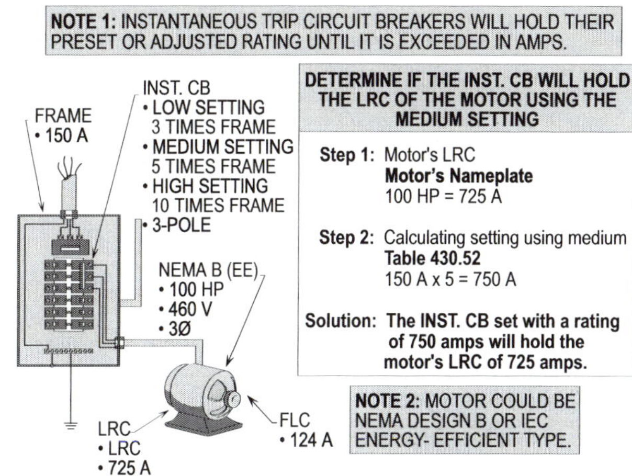

Figure 18-24(a). An instantaneous circuit breaker with its rating set above the locked-rotor current, in amps, of a motor will allow the motor to start and run.

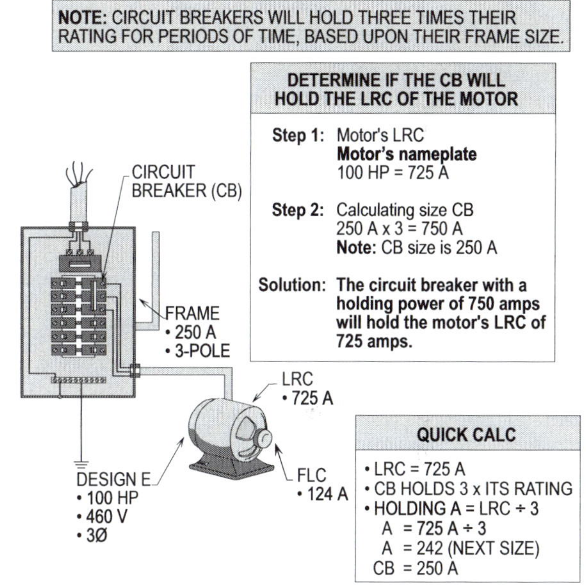

Figure 18-24(b). Circuit breakers sized at least three times their rating provide an amp rating above the locked-rotor current of the motor and will hold such LRC.

To use the table properly will require explanation. There is the matter of "Design letters." A Design letter indicates certain electrical characteristics of a particular motor that are needed to size the overcurrent protection device to permit the motor to start and accelerate its load. To apply **Table 430.52**, it is necessary to take the following steps:

- Select the phase of the motor
  (a) Single-phase
  (b) Three-phase (poly-phase)

- Select type of motor
  - (a) Squirrel-cage induction
  - (b) Wound-rotor
  - (c) DC
  - (d) Synchronous

Note, motors can be single-phase or three-phase types.

- Select the Design letter of the motor
  - (a) Design B
  - (b) Design C
  - (c) Design D

- Select the type overcurrent protection device
  - (a) Column 2 is for NTDFs
  - (b) Column 3 is for TDFs
  - (c) Column 4 is for circuit breakers with instantaneous trip settings or adjustments
  - (d) Column 5 is for circuit breakers with both instantaneous trip settings and thermal trip characteristics

See Figures 18-25(a) through (d) for sizing and selecting the size overcurrent protection devices per **Table 430.52** to allow motors to start and run their driven loads. Note that the minimum (rounded down) and next size overcurrent protection device will be sized for a particular size (rounded up) motor. **Note,** smaller sizes are permitted.

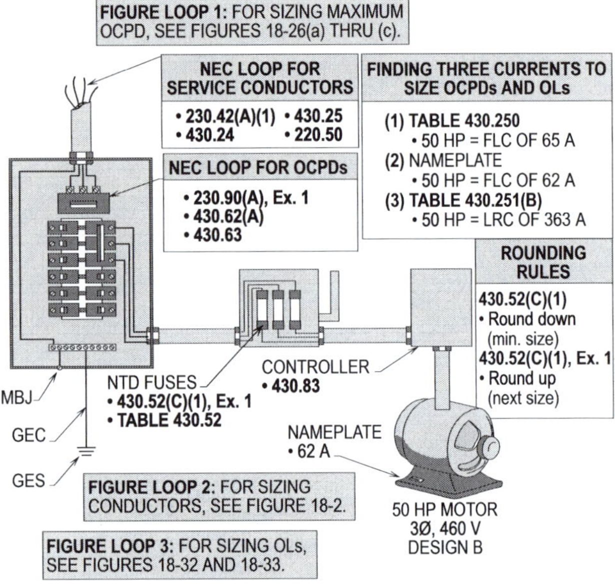

Figure 18-25(a). Determining the minimum and next-size nontime-delay fuses per **Table 430.52** and **430.52(C)(1)** and **Ex. 1** to start and run a motor. **Note,** a smaller overcurrent protection device than the minimum size (rounded down) shall be permitted to be used, if it will start the motor.

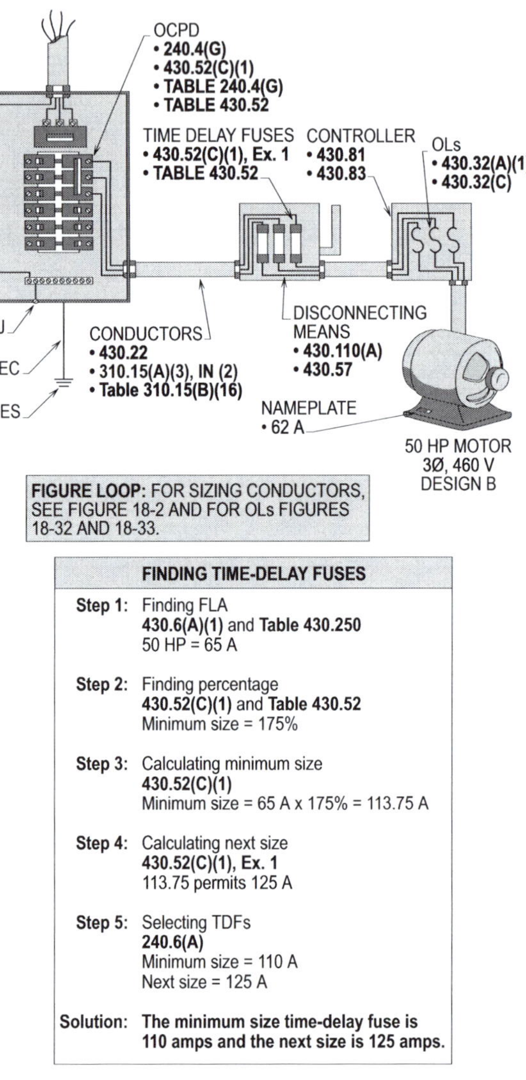

Figure 18-25(b). Determining the minimum and next-size time-delay fuses to start and run a motor. **Note,** a smaller time-delay fuse than the minimum size (rounded down) shall be permitted to be used, if it will start the motor.

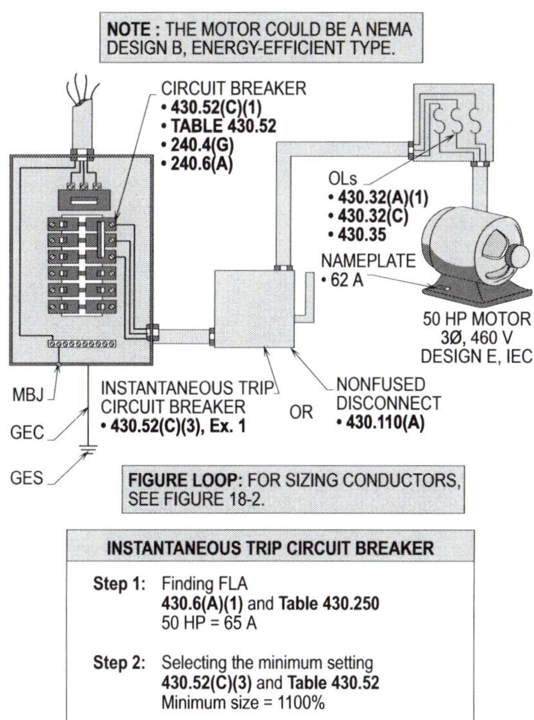

INSTANTANEOUS TRIP CIRCUIT BREAKER

Step 1: Finding FLA
430.6(A)(1) and Table 430.250
50 HP = 65 A

Step 2: Selecting the minimum setting
430.52(C)(3) and Table 430.52
Minimum size = 1100%

Step 3: Calculating minimum setting
430.52(C)(3)
Minimum size = 65 A x 1100% = 715 A

Step 4: Calculating maximum setting
430.52(C)(3), Ex. 1
65 A x 1700% = 1105 A

Step 5: Selecting instaneous trip circuit breaker
Minimum setting = 715 A
Maximum setting = 1105 A

Solution: **The minimum setting is 715 amps and the maximum setting is 1105 amps. However, a smaller setting shall be permitted to be used.**

SIZING OVERCURRENT PROTECTION DEVICES
TO ALLOW MOTORS TO START AND RUN
NEC 430.52(C)(3) AND Ex. 1

Figure 18-25(c). Determining the minimum and maximum setting for an instantaneous trip circuit breaker to start and run a motor per **Table 430.52**. **Note,** a smaller minimum setting shall be permitted to be used, if it will start the motor.

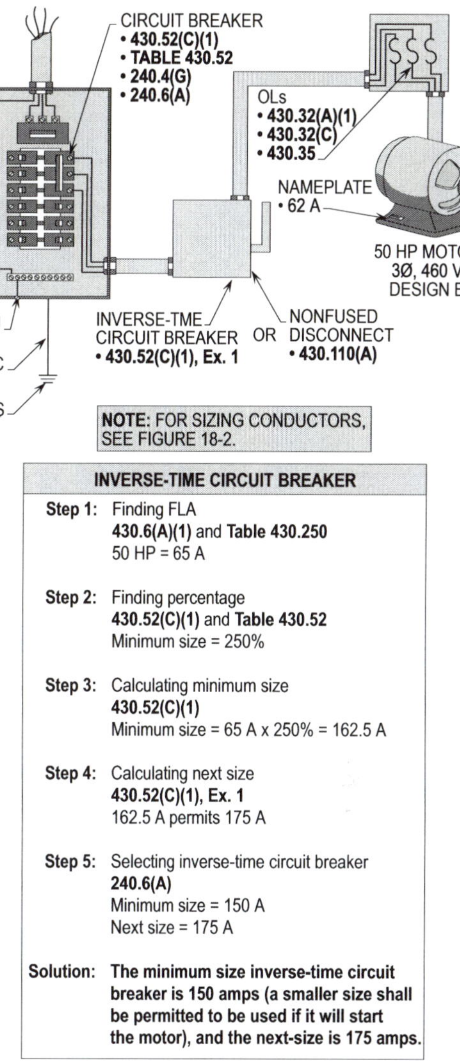

INVERSE-TIME CIRCUIT BREAKER

Step 1: Finding FLA
430.6(A)(1) and Table 430.250
50 HP = 65 A

Step 2: Finding percentage
430.52(C)(1) and Table 430.52
Minimum size = 250%

Step 3: Calculating minimum size
430.52(C)(1)
Minimum size = 65 A x 250% = 162.5 A

Step 4: Calculating next size
430.52(C)(1), Ex. 1
162.5 A permits 175 A

Step 5: Selecting inverse-time circuit breaker
240.6(A)
Minimum size = 150 A
Next size = 175 A

Solution: **The minimum size inverse-time circuit breaker is 150 amps (a smaller size shall be permitted to be used if it will start the motor), and the next-size is 175 amps.**

SIZING OVERCURRENT PROTECTION DEVICES
TO ALLOW MOTORS TO START AND RUN
NEC 430.52(C)(1) and Ex. 1

Figure 18-25(d). Determining the minimum and next-size inverse-time circuit breaker per **Table 430.52** to start and run a motor. **Note,** a smaller minimum setting shall be permitted to be used, if it will start the motor.

NONTIME-DELAY FUSES USING THE MAXIMUM SIZE 430.52(C)(1), Ex. 2(a)

If the minimum or next-size overcurrent protection device does not allow the motor to start and run, the maximum size rating of a nontime-delay fuse not exceeding 600 amps shall be permitted to be increased but shall in no case exceed 400 percent of the FLA of the motor. **[See Figure 18-26(a)]**

TIME-DELAY FUSES USING MAXIMUM SIZE 430.52(C)(1), Ex. 2(b)

To allow a motor to start and run, the rating of a time-delay fuse shall be permitted to be increased but shall in no case exceed 225 percent of the full-load current, in amps, of the motor. **[See Figure 18-26(b)]**

INVERSE-TIME CIRCUIT BREAKERS
430.52(C)(1), Ex. 2(c)

The rating for inverse-time circuit breakers shall be permitted to be increased but shall in no case exceed 400 percent for a full-load current of 100 amps or less. Full-load current greater than 100 amps shall be permitted to be increased 300 percent. **[See Figure 18-26(c)]**

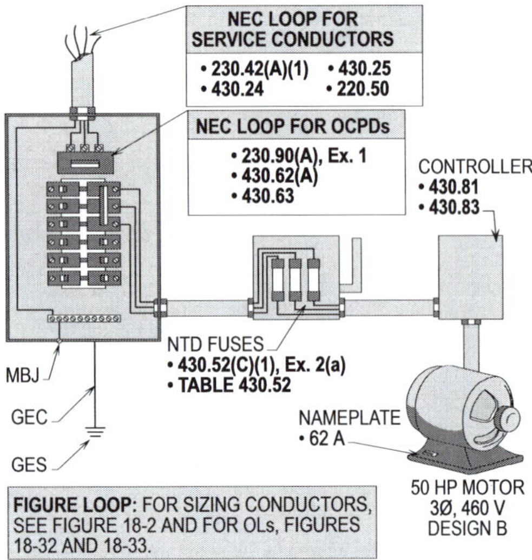

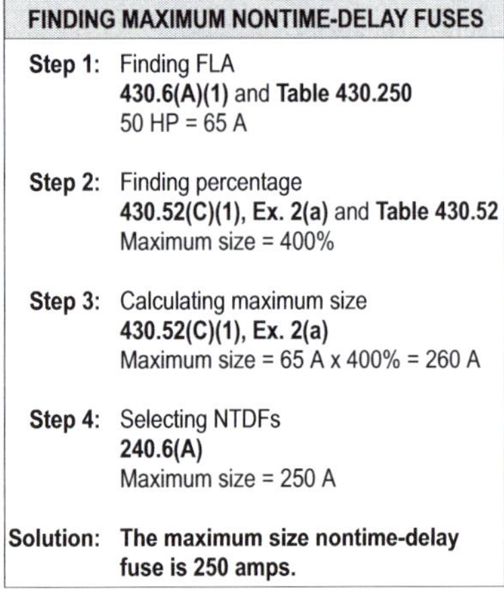

Figure 18-26(a). Nontime-delay fuses shall be permitted to be increased to a maximum size of 400 percent of the

SIZING OVERCURRENT PROTECTION DEVICE FOR TWO OR MORE MOTORS
430.62(A)

To determine the size overcurrent protection device (OCPD) to be installed for a feeder supplying two or more motors,

the following procedures shall be applied:

- Apply Table **430.52** to select largest motor
- Size largest overcurrent protection device for any one motor of group
- Add FLA of remaining motors
- Do not exceed this value with overcurrent protection device rating

See Figure 18-27 for a detailed procedure of sizing overcurrent protection device for a feeder motor circuit.

The largest overcurrent protection device shall be selected based on the motor's full-load current rating times the percentages selected from **Table 430.52**. The next higher standard size rating shall be permitted to be applied per **430.52(C)(1), Ex. 1**. The next higher standard size shall be used for the largest motor in the group. The full-load

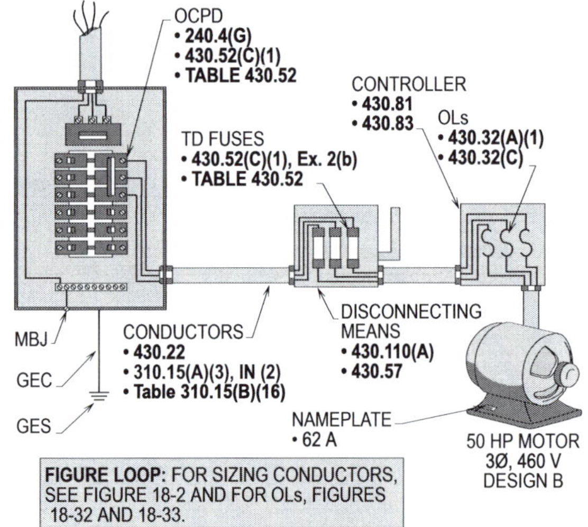

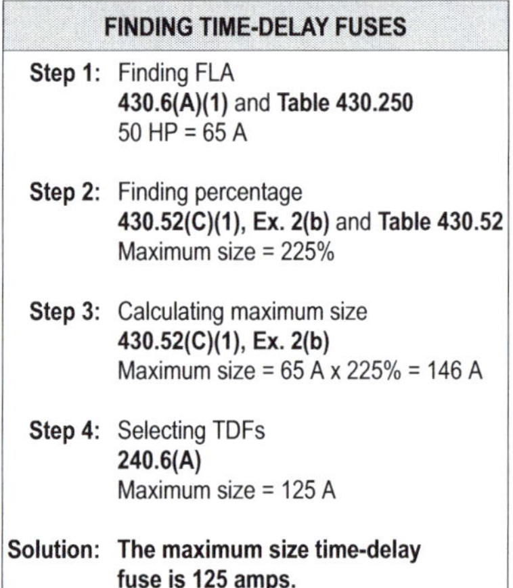

Figure 18-26(b). Determining the maximum size time-delay fuse to start and run a motor (smaller size permitted).

current ratings, in amps, of the remaining motors are added to the rating of the largest overcurrent protection device. The next lower standard size overcurrent protection device (round down) shall be selected from this total per **240.6(A)**, if this value does not correspond to a standard overcurrent protection device.

A larger overcurrent protection device shall not be permitted to be installed because there is no exception to **430.62(A)** to permit the next size above this rating to be selected.

Note, 430.62(A) only permits a smaller overcurrent protection device to be installed ahead of such feeder conductors, which is the next size below the calculation. **(See Figure 18-28)**

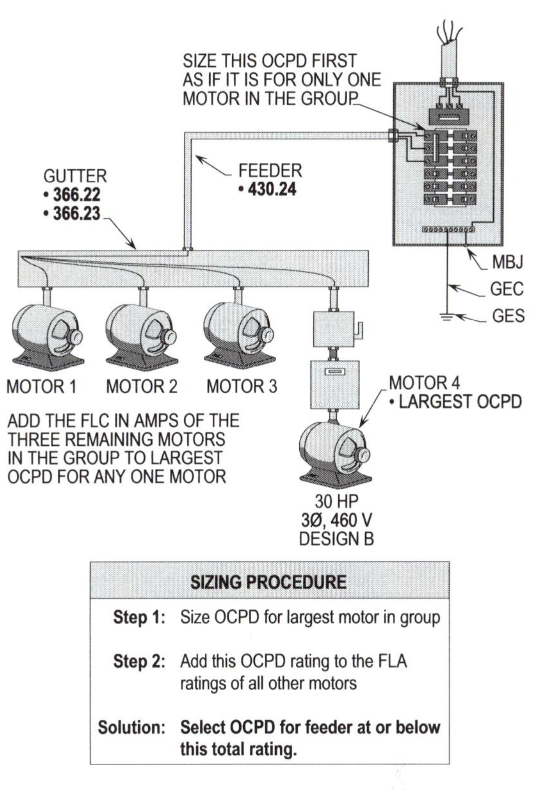

Figure 18-27. Determining overcurrent protection device for a feeder with several motors being protected from short-circuit and ground-fault conditions.

SIZING BRANCH CIRCUIT TO SUPPLY TWO OR MORE MOTORS 430.52 AND 430.53

Section **430.53** outlines the rules where two or more motors, or one or more motors, and other loads are installed and connected to one branch circuit protected by an individual overcurrent protection device.

MOTOR NOT OVER 1 HP 430.53(A)

Two or more motors may be installed without individual overcurrent protection devices if rated less than 1 horsepower each and the full-load current rating of each motor does not exceed 6 amps. Motors not rated over 1 horsepower shall be within sight of the motor, manually started, and portable per **430.53(A)**. Sections **430.32** and **430.42** shall be applied for running overload protection for each motor if these conditions are not met.

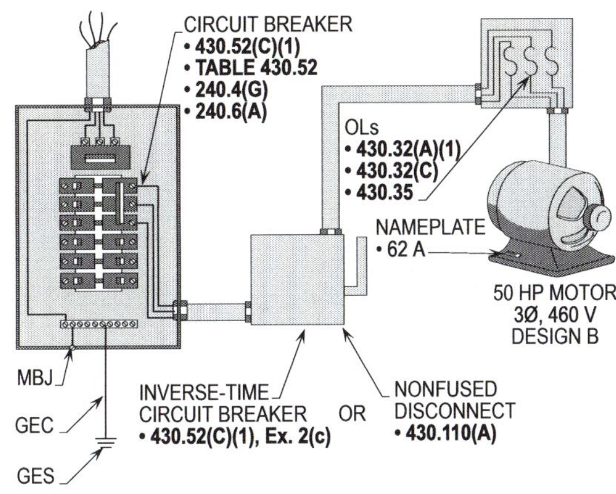

Figure 18-26(c). An inverse-time circuit breaker shall be permitted to be a maximum size of 400 percent of the motor's full-load current rating in amps because the motor's FLA rating is 100 amps or less. **Note,** a smaller circuit breaker shall be permitted to be used.

The overcurrent protection device rated at 20 amps or less can protect a 120 volt or less branch circuit supplying these motors. Branch circuits of 600 volts or less can be protected by a 15 amp or less overcurrent protection device. **(See Figure 18-29)**

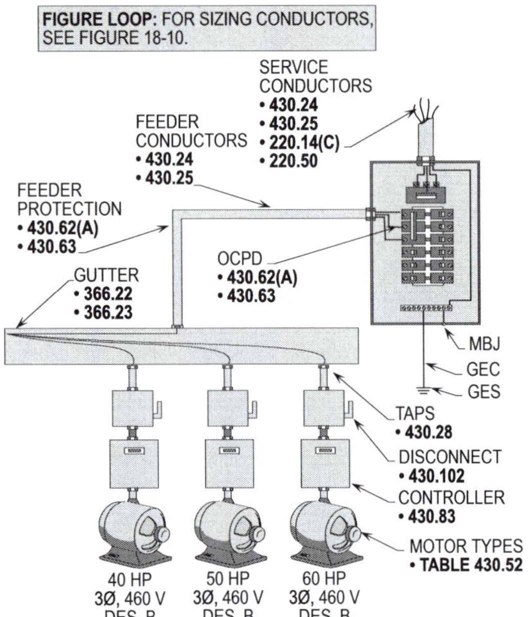

FINDING OCPD FOR FEEDER LOADS

Step 1: Finding FLA of motors
430.6(A)(1) and **Table 430.250**
40 HP = 52 A
50 HP = 65 A
60 HP = 77 A

Step 2: Calculating feeder OCPD
430.52(C)(1), **Table 430.52**, and **430.62(A)**
77 A x 250% = 192.5 A
192.5 A   = 200   A
                52   A
                65   A
Total load = 317   A

Step 3: Selecting OCPD
430.62(A), 240.4(G), and 240.6(A)
300 A is a standard OCPD

Solution: **The size OCPD required for the feeder is 300 amp circuit breaker.**

SIZING OVERCURRENT PROTECTION DEVICE FOR TWO OR MORE MOTORS
NEC 430.62(A)

Figure 18-28. Sizing an overcurrent protection device for a feeder.

Note: For a service tap, see **230.82**
For a feeder tap, see **240.21(B)** and **Table 240.92(B)**
For a transformer tap, see **240.21(C)** and **240.92(C)** and **(E)**
For motor taps, see **430.28**

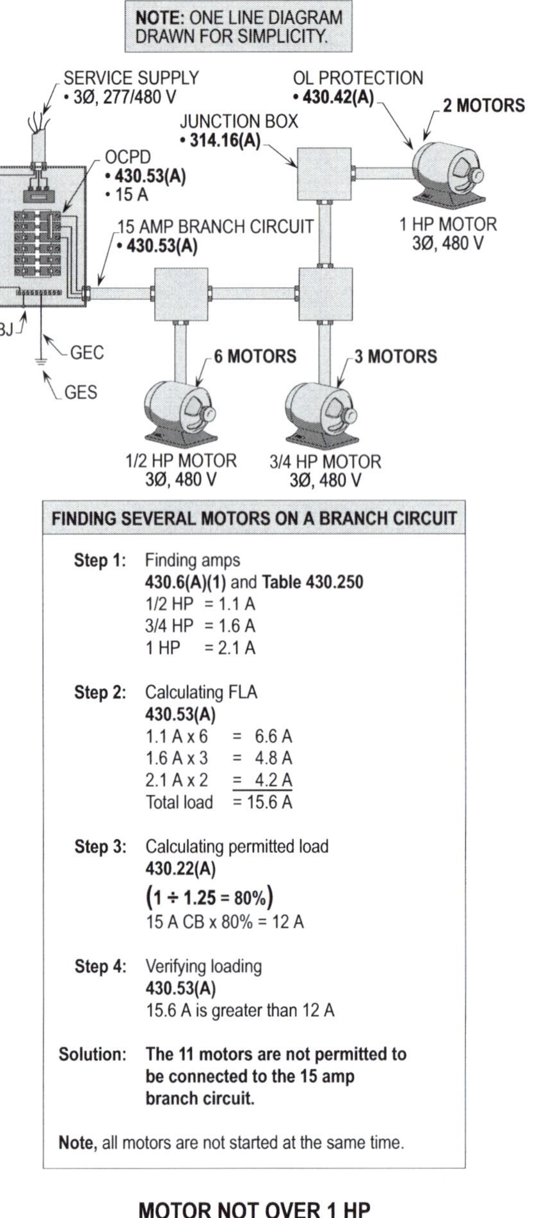

FINDING SEVERAL MOTORS ON A BRANCH CIRCUIT

Step 1: Finding amps
430.6(A)(1) and **Table 430.250**
1/2 HP = 1.1 A
3/4 HP = 1.6 A
1 HP   = 2.1 A

Step 2: Calculating FLA
430.53(A)
1.1 A x 6 = 6.6 A
1.6 A x 3 = 4.8 A
2.1 A x 2 = 4.2 A
Total load = 15.6 A

Step 3: Calculating permitted load
430.22(A)
$(1 \div 1.25 = 80\%)$
15 A CB x 80% = 12 A

Step 4: Verifying loading
430.53(A)
15.6 A is greater than 12 A

Solution: **The 11 motors are not permitted to be connected to the 15 amp branch circuit.**

Note, all motors are not started at the same time.

MOTOR NOT OVER 1 HP
NEC 430.53(A)

Figure 18-29. Determining the number of motors permitted on a 15 amp branch circuit.

SMALLEST RATED MOTOR PROTECTED 430.53(B)

The branch-circuit overcurrent protection device shall be permitted to protect the smallest rated motor of the group for two or more motors of different ratings if the largest motor is permitted to start. The smallest rated motor of the group shall have its overcurrent protection device set at no higher value than permitted per **Table 430.52**. The smallest rated motor and other motors of the group shall be provided with overload protection if necessary per **430.32**. **(See Figure 18-30)**

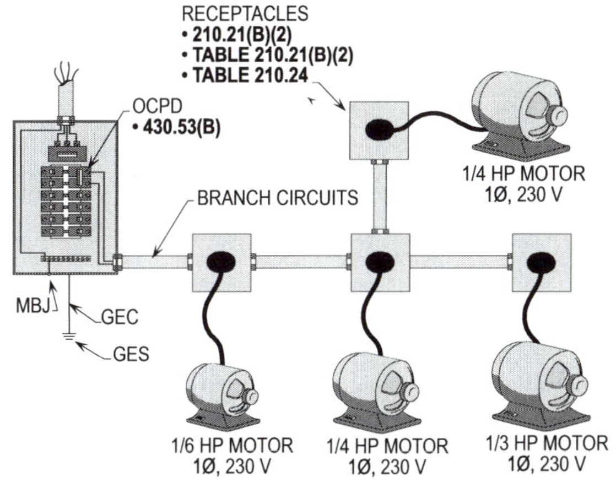

FINDING SEVERAL MOTORS ON A BRANCH CIRCUIT

Step 1: Finding amps
430.6(A)(1) and **Table 430.248**
1/6 HP = 2.2 A
1/4 HP = 2.9 A
1/4 HP = 2.9 A
1/3 HP = 3.6 A

Step 2: Calculating FLA
430.53(B)
2.2 A x 1 = 2.2 A
2.9 A x 1 = 2.9 A
2.9 A x 1 = 2.9 A
3.6 A x 1 = 3.6 A
Total load = 11.6 A

Step 3: Calculating permitted load
Table 210.21(B)(2)
1 ÷ 1.25 = 80%
15 A OCPD x 80% = 12 A

Step 4: Verifying loading
430.53(B) and **Table 210.21(B)(2)**
11.6 A is less than 12 A

Step 5: Protecting smaller motor
430.53(B) and **Table 430.52**
2.2 A x 250% = 5.5 A

Step 6: Selecting OCPD
430.53(B), 240.4(B), and **240.6(A)**
5.5 A allows 15 A CB

Solution: **Section 430.53(B) permits the next-size circuit breaker, which is 15 amps.**

Note, most inspectors allow this concept since the next size circuit breaker is 15 amps per **240.6(A)**.

SMALLEST RATED MOTOR PROTECTED
NEC 430.53(B)

Figure 18-30. Determining the number of motors allowed on a 15 amp branch circuit.

For reference:
Service tap – **230.82**,
Feeder tap – **240.21(B)**,
Transformer tap – **240.21(C), 240.92(C)** and **(E)**,
Motor tap – **430.28**.

OTHER GROUP INSTALLATIONS
430.53(C)

Two or more motors of any size shall be permitted to be installed and connected to an individual branch circuit. However, the largest motor of the group shall be protected by the percentages listed in **Table 430.52** for sizing and selecting fuses and circuit breakers. Each motor controller and component installed in the group shall be approved for such use. The following are elements that shall be sized and selected properly:

- Overcurrent protection devices
- Controllers
- Running overload protection devices

The elements shall be permitted to be installed as a listed factory assembly or field installed as separate assemblies listed for such conditions of use.

Design Tip: Any number of motor taps shall be permitted to be installed where a fuse or circuit breaker is installed at the point where each motor is tapped to the line. This type of installation made with a branch circuit from a feeder per **430.28** and **430.53(D)** is often utilized. **(See Figure 18-31)**

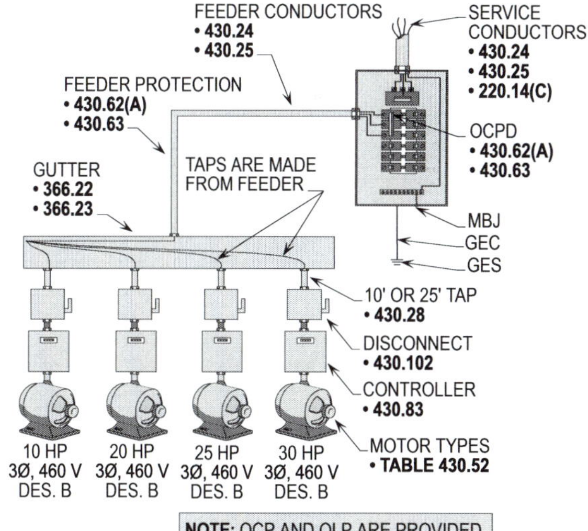

SINGLE MOTOR TAPS
NEC 430.53(D)

Figure 18-31. Taps can be made from a feeder with the proper conductor size and overcurrent protection device with each tap.

SIZING THE RUNNING OVERLOAD PROTECTION FOR MOTORS 430.32(A)

Devices such as thermal protectors, thermal relays, or fusetrons may be installed to provide running overload protection for motors rated more than 1 horsepower. The service factor or temperature rise of the motor shall be used when sizing and installing the running overload protection for motors. The running overload protection is set to open at 115 percent or 125 percent of the motor's full-load current. Under certain conditions of use, the running overload protection shall be set at 115 percent when the motor is not marked with a service factor or temperature rise. Time-delay fuses selected and sized at these percentages provide overload or backup overload protection.

MINIMUM SIZE OVERLOAD PROTECTION DEVICE 430.32(A)(1)

The amperage for full-load current ratings listed in **Tables 430.247 through 430.250** shall not be used when sizing the running overload protection. The full-load current listed with the motor's nameplate shall be used to size the setting of the separate running overload protection.

The running overload protection shall be selected and rated no larger than the following minimum percentages based on the full-load current rating, in amps, listed on the motor's nameplate:

- Motors, with a marked service factor not less than 1.15, use 125 percent x FLA
- Motors, with a marked temperature rise not over 40°C, use 125 percent x FLA
- All other motors, 115% x FLA

See Figure 18-32 for a detailed illustration pertaining to determining the minimum size overloads based on service factor and temperature rise.

MAXIMUM SIZE OVERLOAD PROTECTION DEVICE 430.32(C)

The selection of the running overload protection (overload relay) shall be permitted to be selected at higher percentages if the percentages of **430.32(A)(1)** are not sufficient. The running overload protection device shall be selected to trip or shall be rated no larger than the following percentages of the motor's (nameplate) full-load current rating:

- Motors, with marked service factor not less than 1.15, use 140% x FLA

- Motors, with a marked temperature rise not over 40°C, use 140% x FLA

- All other motors, use 130% x FLA

See Figure 18-33 for a detailed illustration pertaining to determining the maximum size overloads based on service factor and temperature rise.

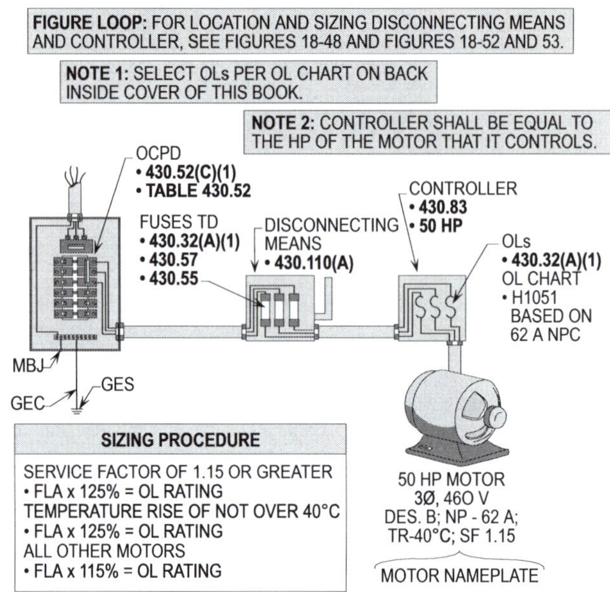

FINDING MOTOR OVERLOAD PROTECTION

Sizing OLs using fuses

Step 1: Finding FLA
430.6(A)(2)
Nameplate = 62 A

Step 2: Finding percentage
430.32(A)(1)
SF = 125%
TR = 125%

Step 3: Calculating FLA
430.32(A)(1)
62 A x 125% = 77.5 A

Step 4: Selecting TD fuses
430.32(A)(1) and 240.6(A)
77.5 A requires 70 A

Solution: The size of the time delay fuses is 70 amps.

Note, 80 amp TDFs provide backup OL protection.

Sizing OLs in controller

Step 1: Finding FLA
430.6(A)(2) and 430.32(A)(1)
62 A x 125% = 77.5 A

Solution: The size overloads are selected from a manufacturer's chart based on 62 amps. (See back inside cover.)

Note, the OL units are already calculated at 77.5 amps when selected from the chart.

MINIMUM SIZE OVERLOAD PROTECTION DEVICE
NEC 430.32(A)(1)

Figure 18-32. Determining the minimum size overloads based on service factor and temperature rise.

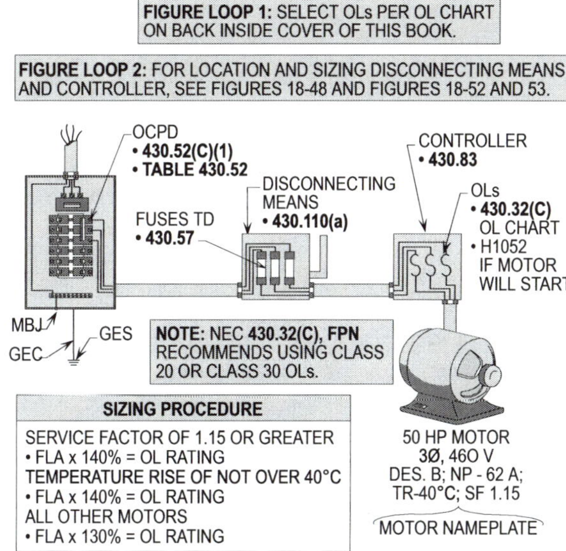

Figure 18-33. Determining the maximum size overloads based on service factor and temperature rise.

SIZING THE CONTROLLER TO START AND STOP THE MOTOR 430.81 AND 430.83

The sizes and types of motor controllers shall be installed with a horsepower rating at least equal to the motor to be controlled. However, there is an Exception to this rule for motors rated at and below a certain horsepower rating.

STATIONARY MOTOR OF 1/8 HORSEPOWER OR LESS 430.81(A)

The branch-circuit protective device shall be permitted to serve as the controller where the motor is rated 1/8 horsepower or less. **(See Figure 18-34)**

For example, for motors less than 1/8 horsepower, where they are mounted stationary or permanent and the construction is such that one or more might fail during operation, the branch-circuit elements plus the motor(s) will not be damaged. In other words, the components of the circuit will not be burned out, etc.

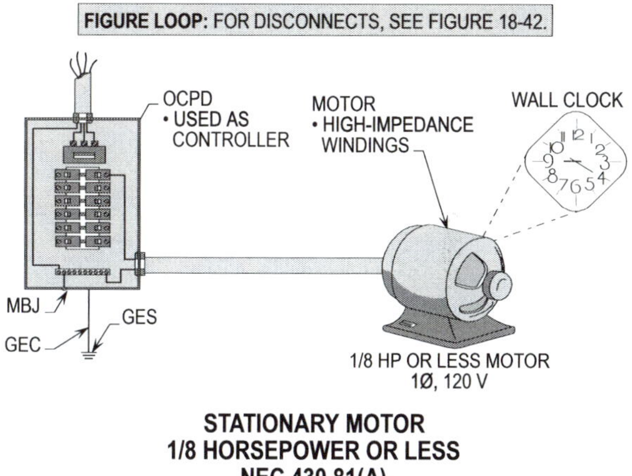

Figure 18-34. The branch-circuit overcurrent protection device shall be permitted to serve as a controller for 1/8 HP or less motor.

PORTABLE MOTOR OF 1/3 HORSEPOWER OR LESS 430.81(B)

The controller shall be permitted to be an attachment plug and receptacle or cord connector that is acceptable for use with portable motors rated 1/3 horsepower or less. **(See Figure 18-35)**

GENERAL REQUIREMENTS 430.83

The controller shall have a rating as specified in **430.83(A)**, unless otherwise permitted in **430.83(B)** or **(C)**, or as outlined in **(D)**, under the conditions specified in these sections.

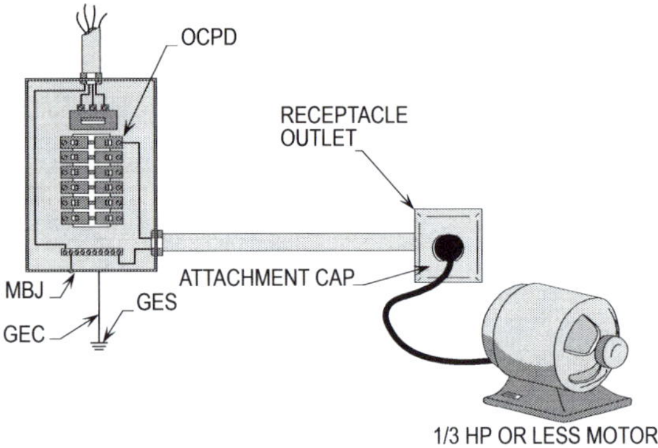

Figure 18-35. The controller for a motor of 1/3 HP motor or less shall be permitted to be an attachment cap and receptacle or cord connector.

HORSEPOWER RATINGS
430.83(A)(1)

Controllers, other than inverse-time circuit breakers and molded case switches, shall have horsepower ratings at the application voltage not lower than the horsepower rating of the motor. **(See Figure 18-36)**

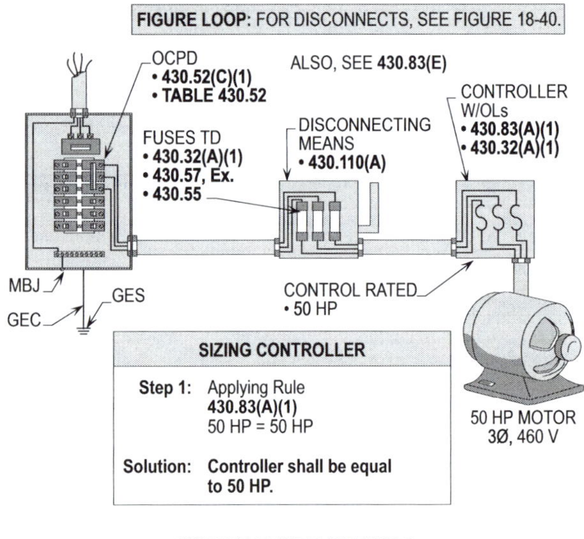

Figure 18-36. Controllers shall have a horsepower rating at least equal to the horsepower of the motor.

CIRCUIT BREAKERS
430.83(A)(2)

Inverse-time circuit breakers shall only be permitted to be installed as a controller where rated in amps. If such a circuit breaker is also used for motor overload protection, it shall be

sized at 125 percent or less of the motor's nameplate current rating per **430.6(A)(2)** and **430.32(A)(1)**. **(See Figure 18-37)**

When used as a disconnecting means for a motor, it shall be sized with an interrupting rating of at least 115 percent of the motor's FLC rating (in amps) per **430.110(A)**.

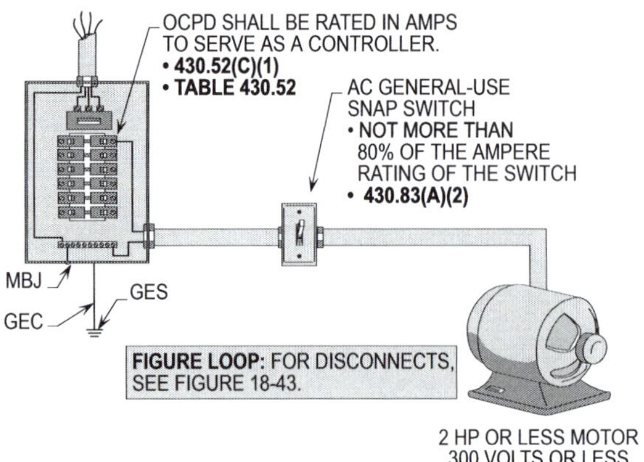

Figure 18-37. A circuit breaker rated at 125 percent of the motor's FLA can be used as a controller for the motor and also to provide overload protection.

SMALL MOTORS
430.83(B)

Stationary motors rated 1/8 horsepower or less and portable motors rated 1/3 horsepower or less shall be permitted to serve as controllers and shall not be required to be horsepower rated. These horsepower-rated motors, because of their smaller locked-rotor currents, can be disconnected by cord-and-plug connections.

STATIONARY MOTORS OF
2 HORSEPOWER OR LESS
430.83(C)

For a stationary motor rated 2 horsepower or less, the controller shall be permitted to be a general-use switch rated for at least twice the motor's full-load current. An AC general-use snap switch shall be permitted to be installed as the controller where the full-load current rating of the switch does not exceed 80 percent (1÷1.25 = 80%) of the branch-circuit rating. **(See Figure 18-38) Note,** review **430.83(E)**.

TORQUE MOTORS
430.83(D)

The motor controller for a torque motor shall have a continuous duty, full-load current rating not less than the nameplate current rating of the motor. **(See Figure 18-39)**

Design Tip: If the motor controller is rated in horsepower and not marked or rated as above, to determine the amperage or horsepower rating, use **Tables 430.247 through 430.250**.

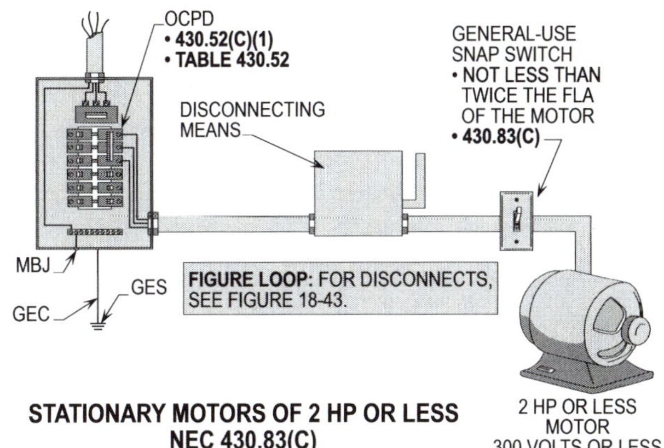

STATIONARY MOTORS OF 2 HP OR LESS
NEC 430.83(C)

Figure 18-38. For stationary motors rated 2 HP or less, a general-use snap switch shall be permitted to be used if sized not less than twice the motor's full-load current in amps.

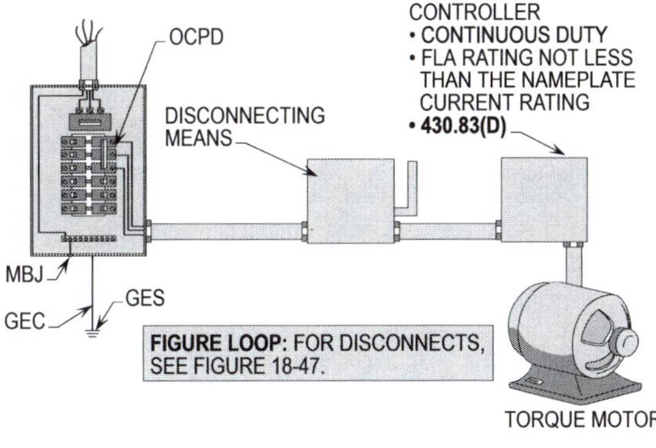

TORQUE MOTORS
NEC 430.83(D)

Figure 18-39. The controller for a torque motor shall be capable of holding the amps indefinitely.

SIZING THE DISCONNECTING MEANS TO DISCONNECT BOTH THE CONTROLLER AND MOTOR 430.109(A) AND 430.110(A)

The disconnecting means for motor circuits shall have an ampere rating of at least 115 percent of the full-load current rating of the motor per **430.110(A)**. The disconnecting means shall be horsepower rated and capable of deenergizing locked-rotor currents per **Tables 430.251(A)** and **(B)**.

Figure Loop: For sizing controller, see **Figure 18-36**. For sizing control circuits, see **Figures 18-52** and **18-53**.

OTHER THAN HORSEPOWER RATED 430.109(B) THRU (G)

Sections **430.109(B) through (G)** permit other than a horsepower rated disconnecting means to be used to deenergize the power circuit to certain types of motors:

- Stationary motors rated 1/8 horsepower or less
- Stationary motors rated 2 horsepower or less (300 volts or less)
- Autotransformer-type controlled motors
- Torque motors

GENERAL REQUIREMENTS 430.109(A)

The disconnecting means shall be permitted to be one of the following, as specified in this section:

- A listed motor-circuit switch rated horsepower,
- A listed molded case circuit breaker,
- A listed molded case switch,
- An instantaneous trip circuit breaker that is part of a listed combination motor controller, or
- Listed self-protected combination controller.

See **Figure 18-40** and **Figure 18-41** for permitted disconnecting means to deenergize the power circuit.

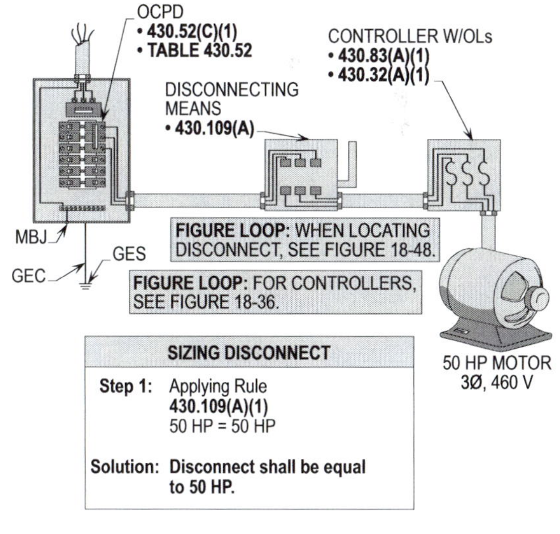

GENERAL RULE
NEC 430.109(A)(1)

Figure 18-40. Disconnecting means shall be at least equal to the horsepower of the motor.

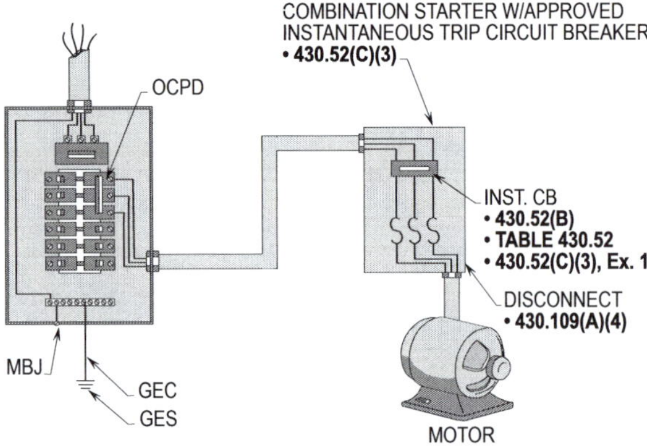

INSTANTANEOUS TRIP CIRCUIT BREAKER
NEC 430.109(A)(4)

Figure 18-41. The disconnecting means for a motor shall be permitted to be an approved instantaneous trip circuit breaker.

STATIONARY MOTORS OF 1/8 HORSEPOWER OR LESS 430.109(B)

For a stationary motor rated 1/8 horsepower or less, the branch-circuit overcurrent protective device shall be permitted to serve as the disconnecting means. This rule is permitted because the windings of such motors do not produce locked-rotor currents high enough to damage such motors, circuit conductors, or elements. **(See Figure 18-42)**

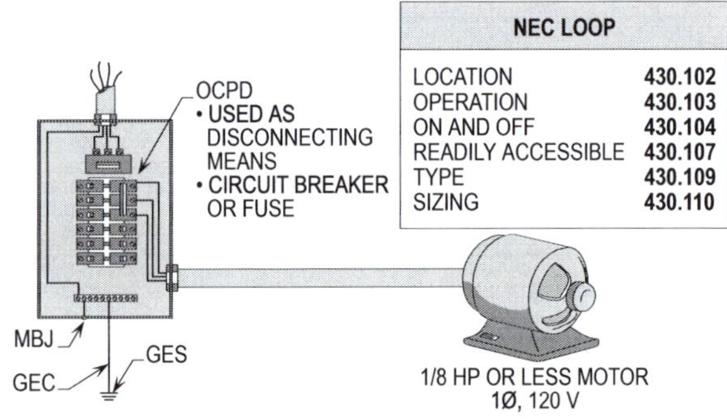

NEC LOOP	
LOCATION	430.102
OPERATION	430.103
ON AND OFF	430.104
READILY ACCESSIBLE	430.107
TYPE	430.109
SIZING	430.110

STATIONARY MOTORS OF 1/8 HORSEPOWER OR LESS
NEC 430.109(B)

Figure 18-42. Motors rated 1/8 horsepower or less shall be permitted to be disconnected by the overcurrent protection device located in the panelboard that is used to supply the circuit.

STATIONARY MOTORS OF 2 HORSEPOWER OR LESS 430.109(C)

For a stationary motor rated 2 horsepower or less, the controller shall be permitted to be a general-use switch rated for at least twice the motor's full-load current. An AC general-use snap switch may be installed as the controller,

where the full-load current rating, in amps, of the switch, does not exceed 80 percent (1÷1.25 = 80%) of the branch-circuit rating. **(See Figure 18-43)**

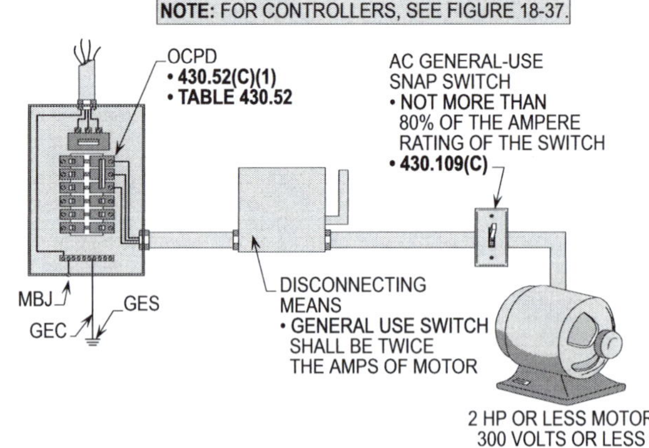

STATIONARY MOTORS OF 2 HORSEPOWER OR LESS
NEC 430.109(C)

Figure 18-43. This illustration shows lists the rules pertaining to the disconnecting means for motors rated 2 horsepower or less.

AUTOTRANSFORMER-TYPE CONTROLLED MOTORS 430.109(D)

Motors rated over 2 horsepower through 100 horsepower shall be permitted to be installed with a separate disconnecting means (general-use switch) if the motor is equipped with an autotransformer-type controller and complies with all the following conditions:

- The motor drives a generator that is provided with overload protection.

- The controller is capable of interrupting the locked-rotor current of the motor.

- The controller is provided with a no-voltage release.

- The controller is provided with running overload protection not exceeding 125 percent of the motor's full-load current rating, in amps.

- Separate fuses or an inverse-time circuit breaker is rated at 150 percent or more of the motor's full-load current, in amps. **(See Figure 18-44)**

ISOLATING SWITCHES 430.109(E)

The disconnecting means shall be permitted to be a general-use or isolating switch for DC stationary motors rated at 40 horsepower or greater and AC motors rated 100 horsepower or greater. However, such disconnects shall be plainly marked, "Do not operate under load." **(See Figure 18-45)**

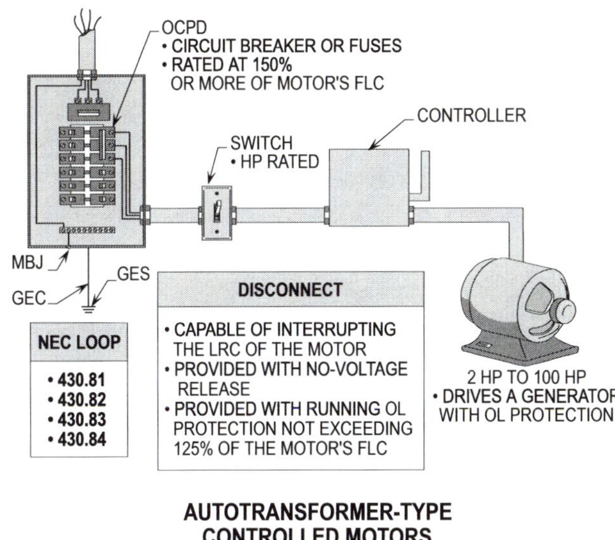

Figure 18-44. This illustration shows lists the rules for a disconnecting means and controller used to disconnect and control motors rated 2 horsepower to 100 horsepower.

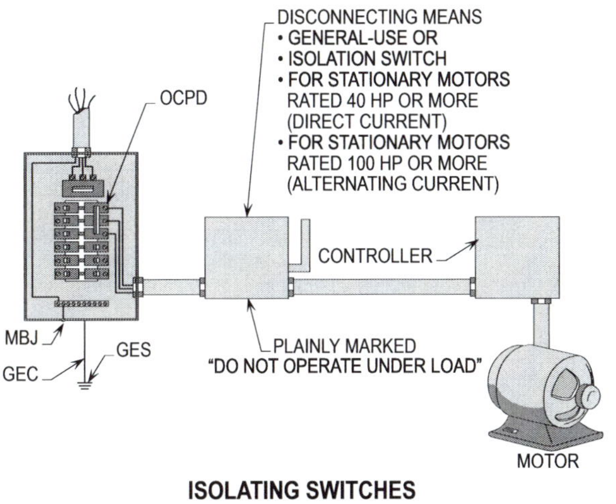

Figure 18-45. This illustration shows lists the rules for disconnecting means used to disconnect motors rated at 40(DC) or 100 (AC) horsepower or more.

CORD-AND-PLUG CONNECTED MOTORS
430.109(F)

For a cord-and-plug connected motor, a horsepower-rated attachment plug and receptacle, flanged surface inlet and cord connector having ratings no less than the motor ratings shall be permitted to serve as the disconnecting means. A horsepower-rated attachment plug, flanged surface inlets, receptacles, or cord connectors shall not be required for a cord-and-plug connected appliance in accordance with **422.33**, a room air conditioner in accordance with **440.63**, or a portable motor rated 1/3 horsepower or less. **(See Figure 18-46)**

TORQUE MOTORS
430.109(G)

The disconnecting means for a torque motor shall be permitted to be installed as a general-use switch. Such switch shall be capable of handling the locked-rotor current, in amps, of the motor indefinitely. **(See Figure 18-47)**

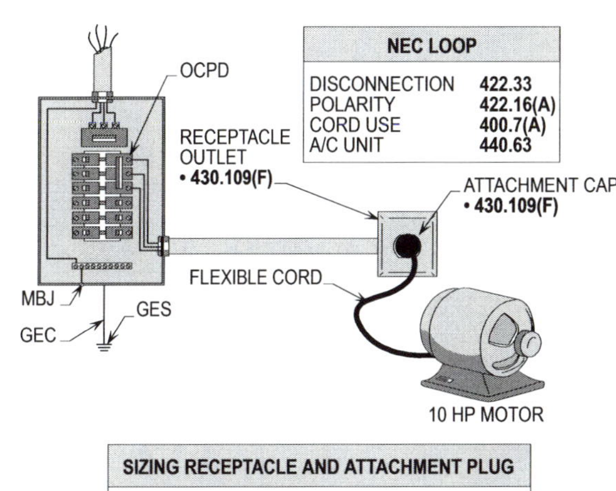

Figure 18-46. A receptacle and attachment cap used as a disconnecting means for motors shall be at least equal to the motor's horsepower rating.

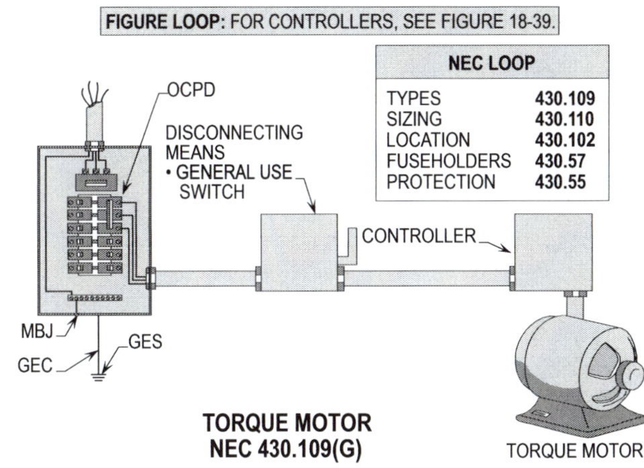

Figure 18-47. The disconnecting means for a torque motor shall be permitted to be a general-use switch.

LOCATION OF THE DISCONNECTING MEANS FOR THE CONTROLLER AND MOTOR
430.102 AND 430.107

A motor and its driven machinery or load shall be installed within sight of the controller for the motor. This rule provides safety for electricians and maintenance personnel while servicing such machinery and circuit elements.

WITHIN SIGHT
ARTICLE 100, 430.102(A), AND 430.102(B)(2)

The disconnecting means shall be installed within sight of the motor controller. All of the ungrounded (phase) conductors shall be disconnected from both the motor and controller supplying the motor circuit. The disconnecting means shall be installed within sight of the motor and not more than 50 ft (15 m) from the motor. If such disconnecting means is not installed within 50 ft (15 m) of the controller, motor, and driven equipment, other provisions for disconnecting the motor shall be made. The controller has a direct relationship to the disconnecting means and shall be installed within sight and within 50 ft (15 m) of the disconnecting means. The motor does not have a direct relationship with the controller. **(See Figure 18-48)**

Note, a disconnecting means shall always be required to be located in sight from the controller location. A single disconnecting means shall be permitted to be located adjacent to a group of coordinated controllers mounted adjacent one to another, such as on a multi motor continuous process machine. For further information pertaining to sizing, selecting, and locating such controllers and disconnecting means, review **430.83, 430.102, 430.103, 430.107,** and **430.109** very carefully.

LOCKED IN THE OPEN POSITION
430.102(A) AND (B)

Section **430.102(A)** and **(B)** permits the disconnect on the line side of the controller, if within sight and within 50 ft (15 m), and capable of being individually locked open, to serve as the disconnecting means for both the controller and motor. In this case, note that the motor shall be installed within sight and within 50 ft (15 m) of the disconnecting means of the controller. **[See Figures 18-49(a) and (b)]**

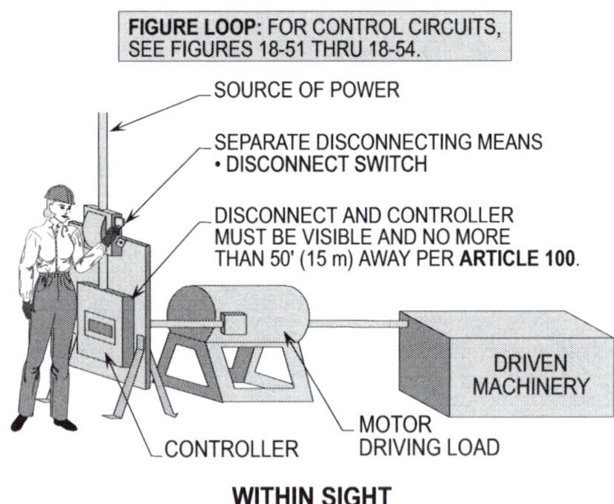

Figure 18-48. The disconnecting means shall be within sight and within 50 ft (15 m) of the controller, motor, and driven machinery.

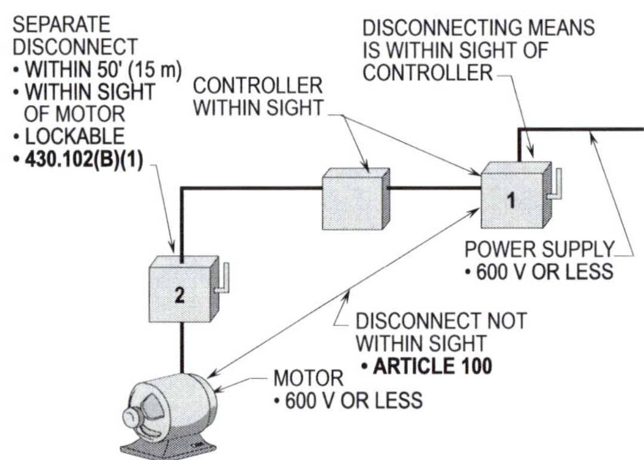

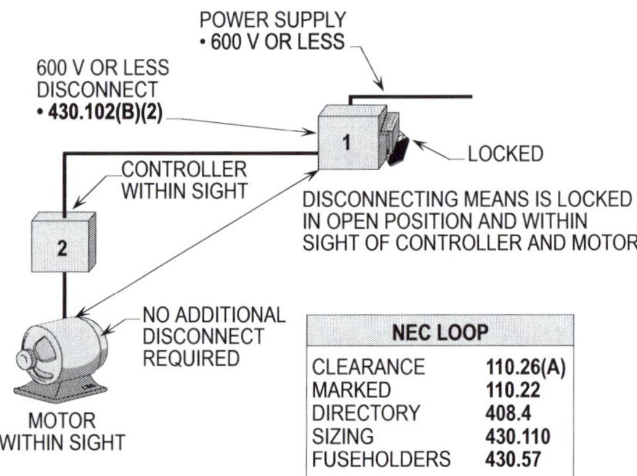

NEC LOOP	
CLEARANCE	110.26(A)
MARKED	110.22
DIRECTORY	408.4
SIZING	430.110
FUSEHOLDERS	430.57

Figure 18-49(a). Locating the disconnecting means to disconnect power conductors to motors rated 600 volts or less.

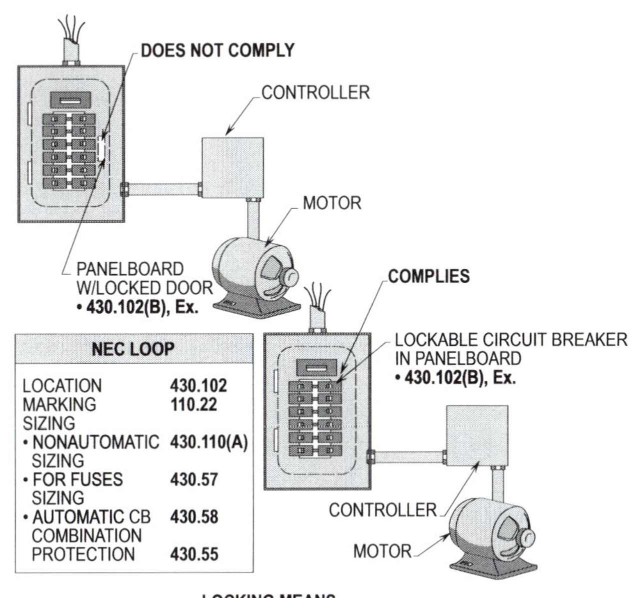

NEC LOOP	
LOCATION	430.102
MARKING	110.22
SIZING	
• NONAUTOMATIC	430.110(A)
SIZING	
• FOR FUSES	430.57
SIZING	
• AUTOMATIC CB	430.58
COMBINATION	
PROTECTION	430.55

**LOCKED IN THE OPEN POSTION
NEC 430.102(B), Ex.**

Figure 18-49(b). The locked door of a panelboard shall not be permitted to serve as the required disconnecting means for a motor. However, an individual locked circuit breaker shall be permitted to serve as the disconnecting means.

CANNOT BE LOCKED IN THE OPEN POSITION 430.102(A) AND 430.102(B)

For motors rated 600 volts or less, an additional disconnecting means shall be mounted by the motor and within sight where the disconnecting means installed by the controller cannot be locked in the open position. **[See Figure 18-50(a)]** The controller disconnecting means for a motor branch circuit over 600 volts shall be permitted to be located out of sight of the motor branch-circuit controller and motor. However, the controller shall have a warning label that marks and lists the location and identification of the disconnecting means. To completely satisfy this rule, such disconnecting means shall be capable of being locked in the open position. **[See Figure 18-49(a)]**

APPLYING EXCEPTION 430.102(B)

Ex. (a) and **(b)** to **430.102(B)** do not require an additional disconnect to be installed within sight of the motor where the disconnecting means would be impractical or increase hazards. An additional disconnecting means is not required where it is located in an industrial installation that has written safety procedures and only qualified employees are permitted to work on the equipment involved. **[See Figure 18-50(b)]**

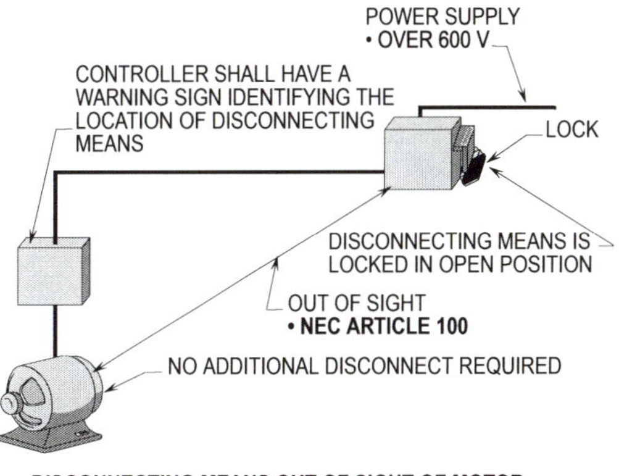

**DISCONNECTING MEANS OUT OF SIGHT OF MOTOR
AND LOCKED IN THE OPEN POSITION**

**CANNOT BE LOCKED IN THE OPEN POSITION
NEC 430.102(A), Ex. 1**

Figure 18-50(a). If the disconnecting means is within sight and 50 ft (15 m) of controller and can not be locked in the open position, an additional disconnecting means shall be installed by the motor.

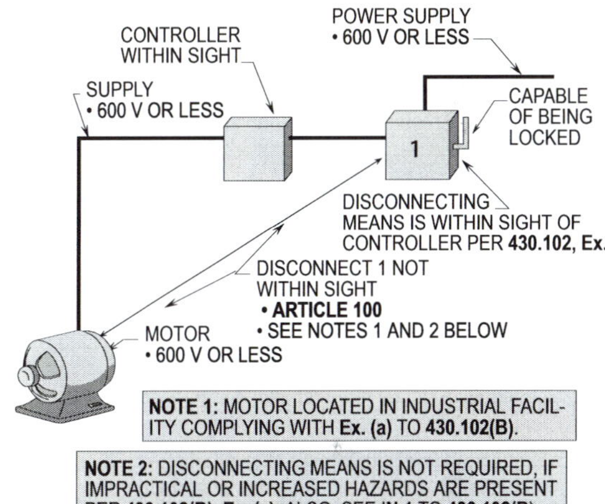

**APPLYING EXCEPTION
NEC 430.102(B), Ex. (a) AND (b)**

Figure 18-50(b). Under certain conditions of use, an additional disconnecting means is not required to be installed within sight of the motor. When disconnecting valve actuator motors (vams), see **430.102(A), Ex. 3**.

SIZING CONDUCTORS FOR CONTROL CIRCUIT 430.72 AND 725.43

A motor control circuit tapped on the load side of fuses and circuit breakers utilized for motor branch circuits shall protect such conductors, or supplementary protection devices shall be provided.

The size of the control circuit conductors and the rating of the motor's branch-circuit device will be determined by this method of protection. Motor control circuits are classified as remote-control circuits where such circuits derive their power from other than the motor's branch-circuit conductors. Various situations permit fuses or circuit breakers to be utilized to protect remote motor control circuits. For further information, see **725.43** and **725.45**.

> **Design Tip:** Remote-control circuits shall have their disconnecting means located immediately adjacent to the disconnecting means used to disconnect the branch-circuit conductors supplying the controller and motor. Sometimes an interlock in the disconnect for the motor controller is used for this purpose that allows the controller, motor, and remote-control circuit to be disconnected simultaneously. **(See 430.113)**

CONDUCTOR PROTECTION
430.72(B)

Conductors larger than 10 AWG are selected from **Tables 310.15(B)(16) through 310.15(B)(19)** for motor-control circuit conductors that are tapped from a motor power circuit. Overcurrent protection for conductors smaller than 14 AWG shall not exceed the values listed in **Table 430.72(B), Column A**. Conductors 18 AWG and 16 AWG shall be protected at the following amperage ratings:

- 18 AWG shall be protected at 7 amps when used for remote-control circuits.

- 16 AWG shall be protected at 10 amps when used for remote-control circuits.

Fuses selected at either 1 amp, 3 amps, 6 amps, or 10 amps are normally used to protect these conductors from short circuits, ground faults, and overloads. See **240.6(A)** for selection of such fuse sizes as well as other sizes.

PROTECTION OF CONDUCTORS
430.72(B), Ex. 2

The secondary conductors of the control transformer circuit shall be permitted to be protected by the primary side of the transformer. The transformer shall be protected per **450.3(B)** and **Table 450.3(B)**. A two-wire secondary for a transformer installed outside or within the control starter enclosure shall be permitted to be protected per **240.4(F)** and **240.21(C)(1)**.

The secondary conductor ampacity shall be multiplied by the secondary-to-primary voltage ratio to provide protection in accordance with **450.3(B)** and **Table 450.3(B)**. Where the rated primary current is 9 amps or greater and 125 percent of this current does not correspond to a standard rating of a fuse or circuit breaker, the next higher standard size

shall be permitted to be selected. Where the rated primary current is less than 9 amps, but is 2 amps or greater, an overcurrent protection device rated or set at not more than 167 percent of the primary current shall be permitted to be used. Where the rated primary current is less than 2 amps, an overcurrent protection device rated or set not greater than 300 percent to 500 percent shall be permitted to be used. **(See Figure 18-51)**

For example, if the primary full-load current of a motor control transformer is less than 2 amps, the overcurrent protection device shall be permitted to be calculated and sized at 500 percent times such full-load current in amps per **430.72(C)(4)**.

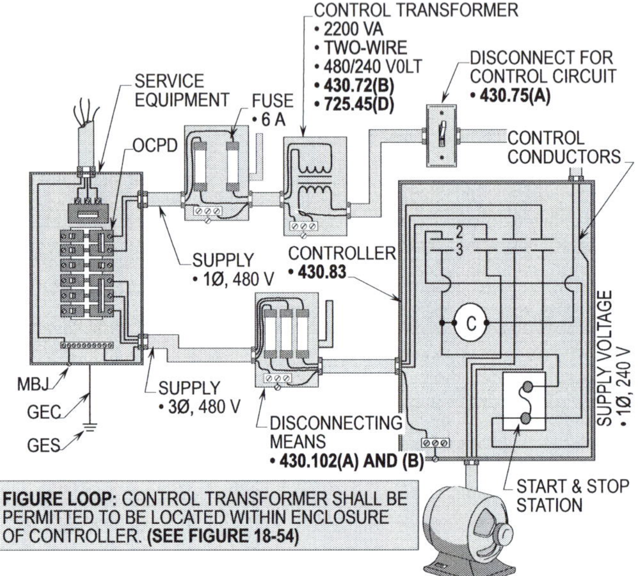

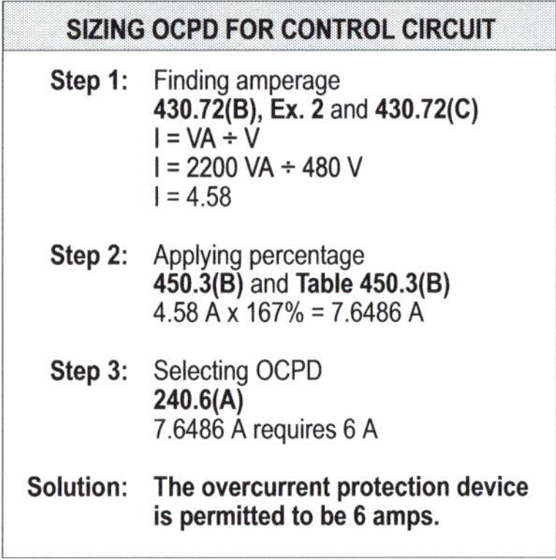

PROTECTION OF CONDUCTORS
NEC 430.72(B), Ex. 2

Figure 18-51. Control circuit conductors are supplied by a control transformer and protected by fuses in the primary side.

Note, for explanation of the transformer's three levels of current, see **Figures 20-11(a) thru 11(c)** in Chapter 20.

PROTECTION OF CONDUCTORS
430.72(B)(2)

Motor-control circuit conductors that do not extend beyond the control equipment enclosure shall be permitted to be protected by the motor's branch-circuit fuses or circuit breakers. **Table 430.72(B), Column B** permits this type of installation where the devices do not exceed 400 percent of the ampacity rating of sizes 14 AWG and larger conductors. Overcurrent protection for conductors smaller than 14 AWG shall not exceed the values listed in **Table 430.72(B), Column B**. Conductors rated 18 AWG through 10 AWG shall be permitted to be protected with the following sized overcurrent protection devices:

- 18 AWG = 25 amps (7 A x 400% = 28 A and requires 25 A OCPD)
- 16 AWG = 40 amps (10 A x 400% = 40 A and requires 40 A OCPD)
- 14 AWG = 100 amps (25 A x 400% = 100 A and requires 100 A OCPD)
- 12 AWG = 120 amps (30 A x 400% = 120 A and requires 110 A OCPD)
- 10 AWG = 160 amps (40 A x 400% = 160 A and requires 150 A OCPD)
- 8 AWG and larger = 400 percent

> **Design Tip:** The free air ampacities of **Table 310.15(B)(17)** for 60°C wire are used to determine the ampacity ratings for the control circuit conductors. This type of installation has more free space to dissipate the heat where control conductors are installed in the open air space of enclosures instead of enclosed raceways.

See **Figure 18-52** for selecting such conductors based on the overcurrent protection device rating.

PROTECTION OF CONDUCTORS
430.72(B)(2)

Motor-control circuit conductors that extend beyond the control equipment enclosure shall be permitted to be protected by the motor's branch-circuit fuse or circuit breaker. **Table 430.72(B), Column C** permits this type of installation where the devices do not exceed 300 percent of the ampacity rating of sizes 14 AWG and larger conductors. Overcurrent protection for conductors smaller than 14 AWG shall not exceed the values listed in **Table 430.72(B), Column C**. Conductors rated 18 AWG through 10 AWG shall be permitted to be protected with the following sized overcurrent protection devices:

- 18 AWG = 7 amps and requires 7 A OCPD
- 16 AWG = 10 amps and requires 10 A OCPD

- 14 AWG = 45 amps (15 A OCPD x 300% = 45 A and requires 45 A OCPD)
- 12 AWG = 60 amps (20 A OCPD x 300% = 60 A and requires 60 A OCPD)
- 10 AWG = 90 amps (30 A OCPD x 300% = 90 A and requires 90 A OCPD)
- 8 AWG and larger = 300 percent

Note, the above protection shall be required anytime the control circuit is used for the remote control of a coil in the motor controller enclosure.

See **Figure 18-53** for selecting such conductors based on the overcurrent protection device rating.

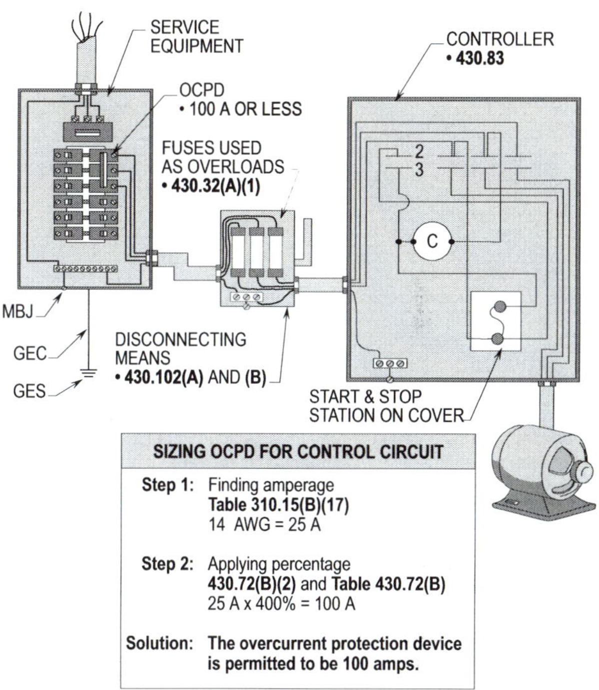

Figure 18-52. Control circuit conductors located in controller and protected by the branch-circuit overcurrent protection device.

CONTROL CIRCUIT TRANSFORMER
430.72(C)(1) THRU (C)(5)

When a motor-control circuit transformer is provided, the transformer shall be protected by the rules and regulations of **Article 450**. A fuse or circuit breaker shall be permitted to be installed in the secondary circuit of the transformer per **430.72(C)(1) through (C)(5)**. The primary overcurrent protection device shall be permitted to be used to provide protection for the conductors tapped from the secondary side of a control transformer, if its rating does not exceed the secondary-to-primary ratio of the transformer. **(See Figure 18-54)**

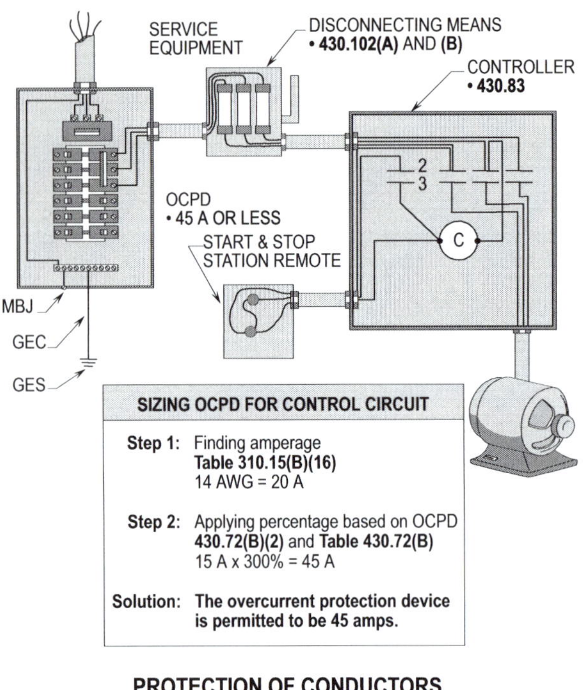

**PROTECTION OF CONDUCTORS
NEC 430.72(B)(2)**

Figure 18-53. Control circuit conductors are run remote and protected by the branch circuit's overcurrent protection device in the panelboard. (Also, see **Figure 9-12**)

MOTOR CONTROL AND MOTOR POWER CIRCUIT CONDUCTORS
430.75

Motor control circuits shall be disconnected from all sources of supply when the disconnecting means is in the open position. The disconnecting means for the starter may be installed to serve as the disconnecting means for the motor circuit conductors if the control circuit conductors are tapped from the line terminal of the magnetic starter. An auxiliary contact shall be installed in the disconnecting means of the controller, or an additional disconnecting means shall be mounted adjacent to the controller, to disconnect the motor control circuit conductors if they are fed from another source and not tapped from the starter conductors. **(See Figure 18-55)**

CAPACITOR
460.8(A)

The ampacity of capacitor circuit conductors shall not be less than 135 percent of the rated current of the capacitor. The leads for a capacitor that supplies a motor shall not be less than one-third the ampacity of the motor circuit conductors. The larger of the above conductors shall be used for the capacitor supply conductors. **(See Figure 18-56)**

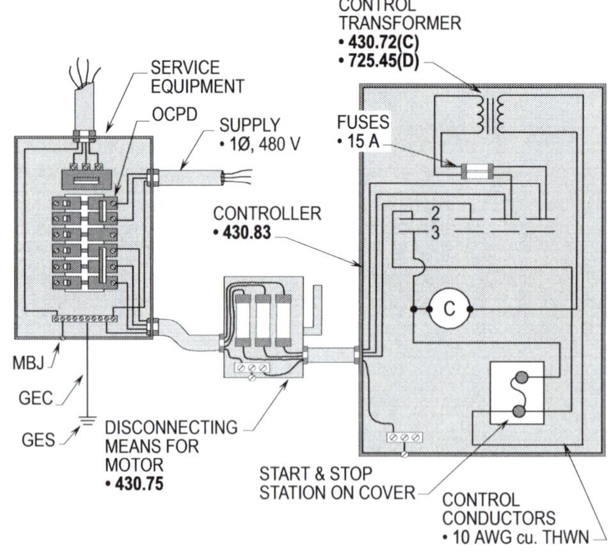

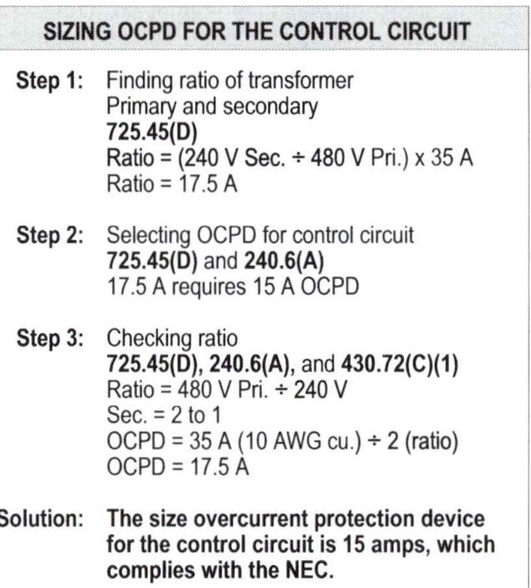

SIZING OCPD FOR THE CONTROL CIRCUIT

Step 1: Finding ratio of transformer
Primary and secondary
725.45(D)
Ratio = (240 V Sec. ÷ 480 V Pri.) x 35 A
Ratio = 17.5 A

Step 2: Selecting OCPD for control circuit
725.45(D) and 240.6(A)
17.5 A requires 15 A OCPD

Step 3: Checking ratio
725.45(D), 240.6(A), and 430.72(C)(1)
Ratio = 480 V Pri. ÷ 240 V
Sec. = 2 to 1
OCPD = 35 A (10 AWG cu.) ÷ 2 (ratio)
OCPD = 17.5 A

Solution: The size overcurrent protection device
for the control circuit is 15 amps, which
complies with the NEC.

**CONTROL CIRCUIT TRANSFORMER
NEC 430.72(C)(1) THRU (C)(5)**

Figure 18-54. The primary overcurrent protection device shall be permitted to be used to provide the protection for the conductors tapped from the secondary side of a control transformer, if its rating does not exceed the secondary-to-primary voltage ratio of the transformer.

ROUTING CONTROL CIRCUIT CONDUCTORS
300.3(C)(1) AND 725.48(B)(1)

Conductors of different systems shall be permitted to occupy the same raceway without regard to the use of AC or DC per **300.3(C)(1)**. Conductors shall be insulated for the maximum voltage of any one conductor when occupying the same raceway. These conductors shall not exceed 1000 volts. Class 1 conductors shall be permitted to occupy the same raceway when installed with the power conductors supplying the magnetic starter and motor per **725.48(B)(1)**. For control circuit conductors to occupy the same raceway as the motor circuit conductors, they shall be functionally associated with the motor system. **(See Figure 18-57)**

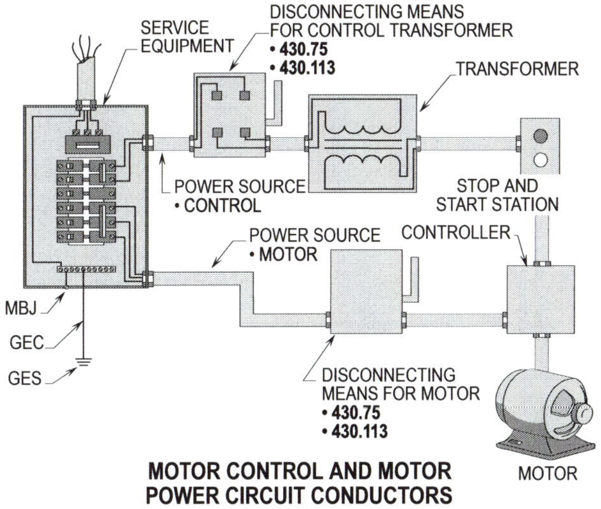

OCCUPYING THE SAME ENCLOSURE 300.3(C)(2)(d) AND 300.32

Motor excitation, magnetic starter, control relay, or ammeter conductors shall be permitted to occupy the same enclosure if rated at 1000 volts and less or over 1000 volts. These conductors shall not be permitted to occupy the same raceway where installed as a combination of conductors of 1000 volts or less with conductors of over 1000 volts. The motor enclosure and the starter enclosure can contain motor excitation, control, relay, and ammeter conductors of 1000 volts or less, together with power conductors of over 1000 volts. **(See Figure 18-58)**

Figure 18-55. One disconnecting means or a number of disconnects may be required to disconnect a control circuit and power supply to a motor.

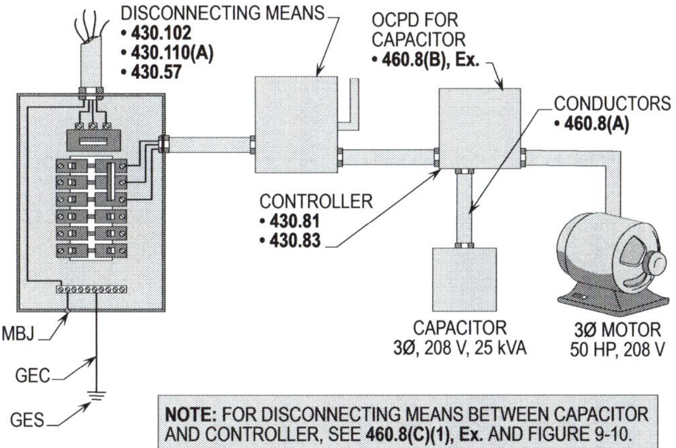

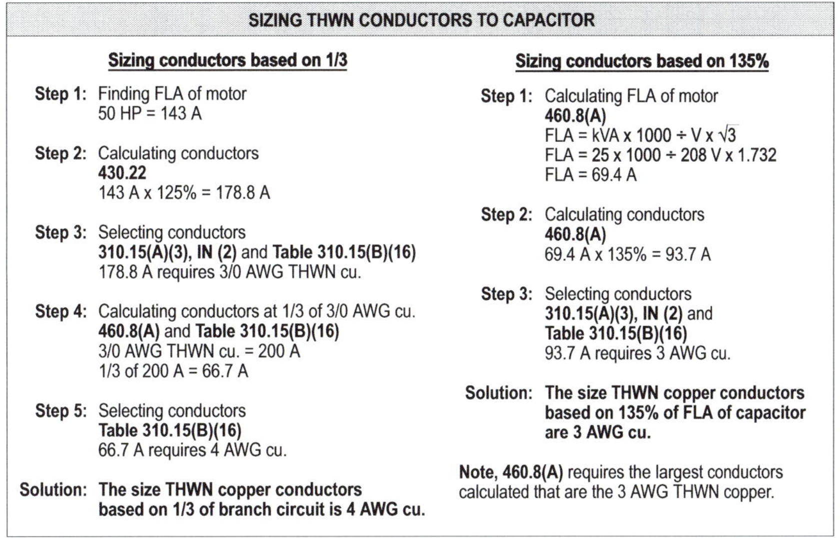

SIZING THWN CONDUCTORS TO CAPACITOR

Sizing conductors based on 1/3	Sizing conductors based on 135%
Step 1: Finding FLA of motor 50 HP = 143 A	**Step 1:** Calculating FLA of motor **460.8(A)** FLA = kVA x 1000 ÷ V x $\sqrt{3}$ FLA = 25 x 1000 ÷ 208 V x 1.732 FLA = 69.4 A
Step 2: Calculating conductors **430.22** 143 A x 125% = 178.8 A	**Step 2:** Calculating conductors **460.8(A)** 69.4 A x 135% = 93.7 A
Step 3: Selecting conductors **310.15(A)(3), IN (2)** and **Table 310.15(B)(16)** 178.8 A requires 3/0 AWG THWN cu.	**Step 3:** Selecting conductors **310.15(A)(3), IN (2)** and **Table 310.15(B)(16)** 93.7 A requires 3 AWG cu.
Step 4: Calculating conductors at 1/3 of 3/0 AWG cu. **460.8(A)** and **Table 310.15(B)(16)** 3/0 AWG THWN cu. = 200 A 1/3 of 200 A = 66.7 A	**Solution:** **The size THWN copper conductors based on 135% of FLA of capacitor are 3 AWG cu.**
Step 5: Selecting conductors **Table 310.15(B)(16)** 66.7 A requires 4 AWG cu.	Note, **460.8(A)** requires the largest conductors calculated that are the 3 AWG THWN copper.
Solution: **The size THWN copper conductors based on 1/3 of branch circuit is 4 AWG cu.**	

CAPACITOR
NEC 460.8(A)

Figure 18-56. There are two calculations to be performed, and one of them shall be selected to size the capacitor circuit conductors. **Note,** the greater of the 1/3 calculation or 135 percent calculation shall be used.

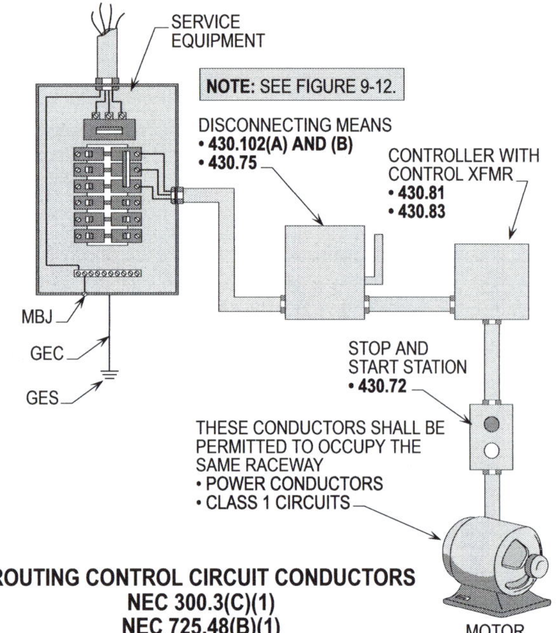

Figure 18-57. When functionally associated with motor operation, a Class 1 control circuit shall be permitted to occupy the same raceway as the motor's power circuit conductors.

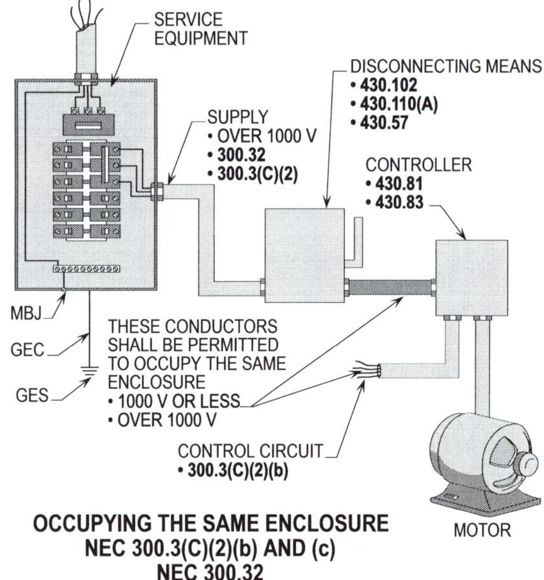

Figure 18-58. Conductors over 1000 volts and those 1000 volts or less shall be permitted to occupy the same enclosure under certain conditions of use.

MAGNETIC STARTER CONTACTOR AND ENCLOSURE 725.51(A) AND (B)

When installing four or more current-carrying conductors that are continuously operated in a raceway and used for Class 1 remote-control, signal, and power-limited circuit conductors, they may have to be derated by the derating factors of **310.15(B)(3)(a)** per **725.51(B)(1)** or **(B)(2)**. Conductors that are noncontinuously operated shall not be required to be derated by the derating factors of **310.15(B)(3)(a)**. When installing power and control conductors in the same raceway, **310.15(B)(3)(a)** shall be applied to all current-carrying conductors operating for three hours or more. **(See Figure 18-59)**

Design Tip: Control circuit conductors operating for three hours or more shall not be required to be derated per **310.15(B)(2)(a)** if their ampacity does not exceed 10 percent of the control conductor's ampacity rating.

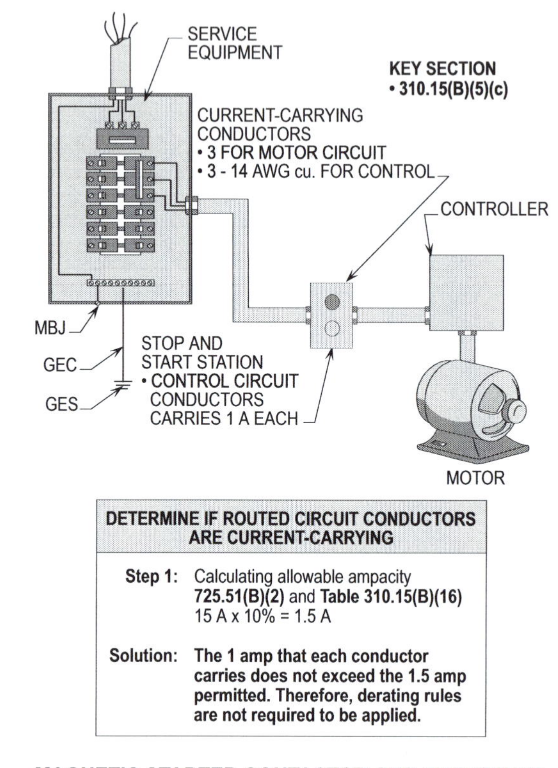

Figure 18-59. Circuit conductors that do not carry more than 10 percent of their ampacity shall not be considered current-carrying conductors.

TABLE CURRENT IN AMPS TABLES 430.247 THRU 430.250

The following methods can be used to determine the full-load current rating in amps for motors that are not listed in **Tables 430.247 through 430.250**:

- The horsepower rating of a listed motor shall be selected to be below that of the unlisted motor.

- The motor's full-load current rating shall be divided by its horsepower rating to obtain the multiplier.

- The multiplier times the horsepower of the unlisted motor derives FLC in amps for the unlisted motor.

Design Tip: The full-load current rating of the motor is determined by multiplying these values by the horsepower rating of the unlisted motor. **(See Figure 18-60)**

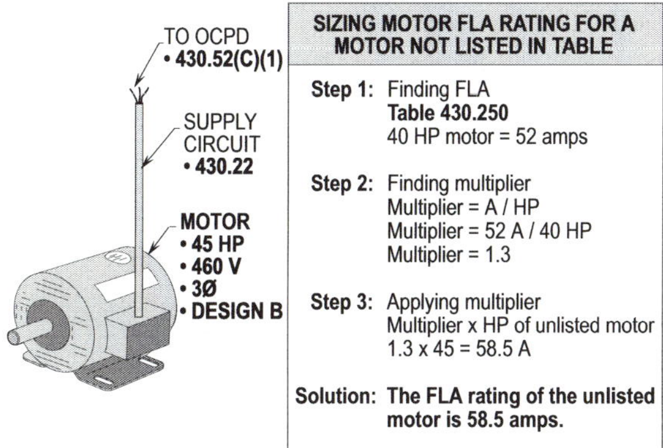

Figure 18-60. This illustration shows the procedure for calculating the FLA of a motor not listed in **Tables 430.247 through 430.250**. (Also, see **Figure 18-61**.)

RULE-OF-THUMB – AMPS

The full-load current of a motor may be found by using the rule-of-thumb method in **Table 430.248** for single-phase and **Table 430.250** for three-phase. The Table current will not always be exactly the same as the rule-of-thumb amps.

Overcurrent protection devices, conductors, and other elements can be sized with the full-load current ratings obtained by the rule-of-thumb method. The full-load current ratings are within a usable range when applying the rule-of-thumb method to determine the full-load current rating in amps. These amperage ratings will provide values to calculate elements for a complete and safe operation of an electrical motor system.

The following percentages can be applied when using a rule-of-thumb method to derive full-load amps for a particular size motor:

- When installing 550, 575, or 600 volt, three-phase motors, the horsepower rating of the motor shall be multiplied by 1.00 to obtain full-load current in amps.

- When installing 440, 460, or 480 volt, three-phase motors, the horsepower rating of the motor shall be multiplied by 1.25 to obtain full-load current in amps.

- When installing 220, 230, or 240 volt, three-phase motors, the horsepower rating of the motor shall be multiplied by 2.50 to obtain full-load current in amps.

- When installing 220, 230, or 240 volt, single-phase motors, the horsepower rating of the motor shall be multiplied by 5.00 to obtain full-load current in amps.

- When installing 110, 115, or 120 volt, single-phase motors, the horsepower rating of the motor shall be multiplied by 10.00 to obtain full-load current in amps.

See **Figure 18-61** for a detailed illustration of calculating full-load currents in amps for motors using the rule-of-thumb method.

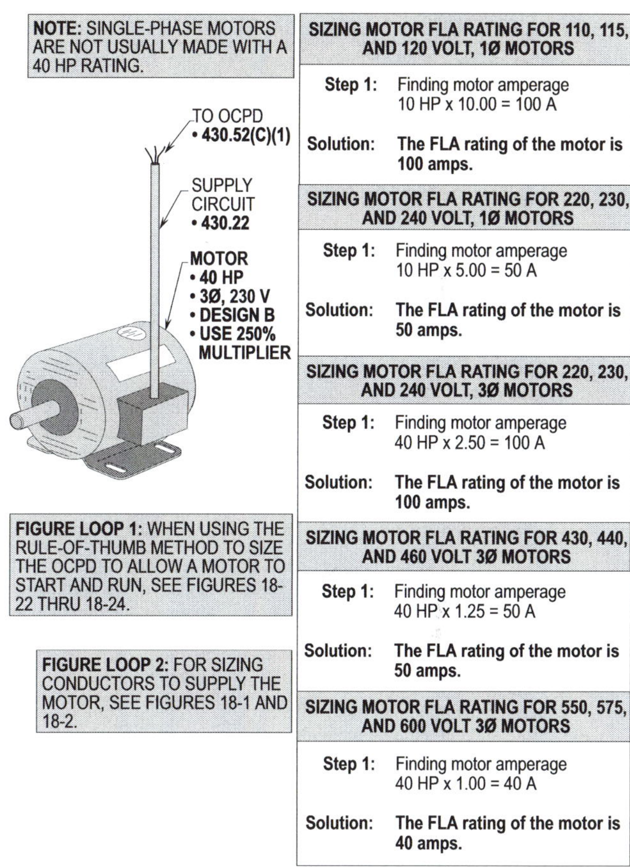

Figure 18-61. This illustration shows a rule-of-thumb method used by the electrical industry to determine the FLA of motors whether found or not found in **Tables 430.248 through 430.250**. **Note,** this method is used in the field or office when a code book is not available. Also, see **Figure 18-60.**

NUMBER OF MOTORS SERVED BY EACH DISCONNECT AND CONTROLLER
430.87, Ex. 1 AND 430.112, Ex.

Each controller shall be installed with a disconnecting means located within sight and within 50 ft (15 m). Unauthorized energizing of the electrical power circuit shall be prevented during maintenance procedures. A single disconnect and controller shall be permitted to be installed to control and disconnect any number of motors of 1000 volts or less per **430.87, Ex. 1** and **430.112, Ex.** Motors used to drive different parts of the same machine is an example of a number of motors that can be protected by a single disconnect and controller. **(See Figure 18-62)**

A single overcurrent protection device shall be permitted to be installed to protect a group of motors only if they are rated in the fractional-horsepower range and installed on a general-purpose circuit of 20 amps or less per **430.87, Ex. 2** and **430.53(A)**.

Motors installed to be served by the same disconnect and controller shall be within sight and located within one room. Unauthorized energizing of the electrical power circuit can be prevented during maintenance procedures if the above rules are complied with. For lockout and tagout procedures, see **OSHA 1910, Subpart S** and **NFPA 70E, Chapter 1**.

Note, for defining sight from (within sight), see **Article 100** in the NEC.

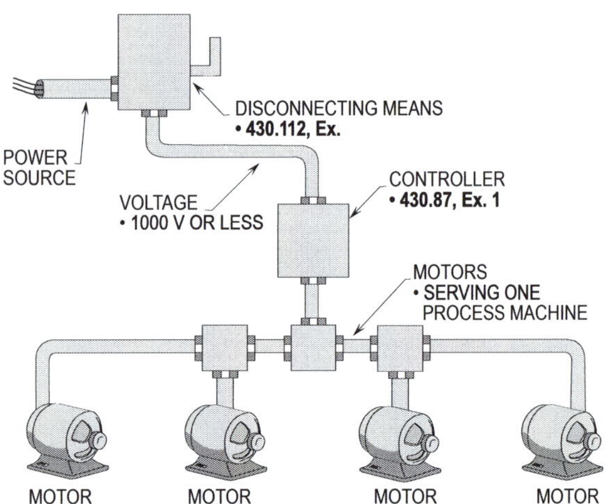

Figure 18-62. Under certain conditions of use, one disconnect and controller shall be permitted to be used for several motors serving a machine.

REDUCED STARTING METHODS

As to methods of starting a motor, there are seven methods used in the electrical industry, and they are as follows:

- Full voltage (not reduced at starting)
- Resistor starting
- Reactor starting
- Autotransformer starting
- Solid-state starting
- Part winding
- Start wye and run delta
- Adjusted-speed drive

AC motors up to about 10 or 15 horsepower are usually started on full voltage. For larger motors, a resistance or reactance is inserted in the motor circuit at starting to reduce the starting current. The voltage at starting can be reduced by the use of an autotransformer. A solid-state starter can also be used to reduce starting currents.

ADJUSTABLE-SPEED DRIVE SYSTEMS PART X TO ARTICLE 430

When designing and installing electrical systems for adjustable-speed drives, the installation provisions of **Part I through Part IX** are applicable unless modified or supplemented by **Part X** in the NEC.

BRANCH/FEEDER CONDUCTORS
430.122(A)

Circuit conductors supplying power conversion equipment included as part of an adjustable-speed drive system shall have an ampacity not less than 125 percent of the rated input to the power conversion equipment. **(See Figure 18-63)**

Note, electrical resonance can result from the interaction of the nonsinusoidal currents from this type of load with power factor correction capacitors.

BYPASS DEVICE
430.122(B)

For an adjustable speed drive system that utilizes a bypass device, the conductor ampacity shall not be less than required by **430.6**. The ampacity of circuit conductors supplying power conversion equipment included as part of an adjustable speed drive system that utilizes a bypass device shall be the larger of either of the following:

(1) 125 percent of the rated input to the power conversion equipment

(2) 125 percent of the motor full-load current rating as determined by **430.6**

For an illustrated description, see **Figure 18-64**.

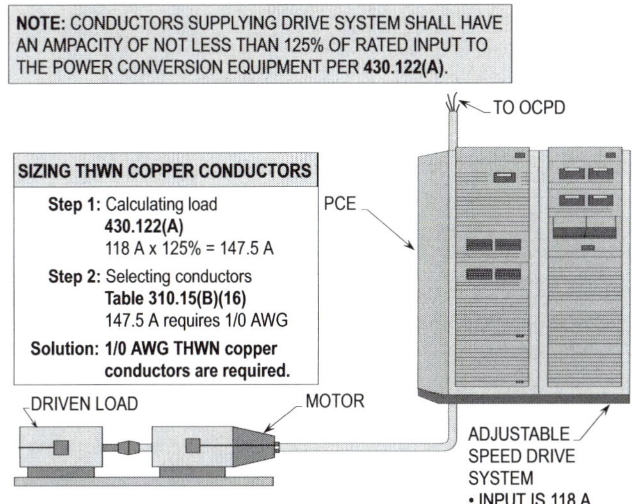

BRANCH/FEEDER CONDUCTORS
NEC 430.122(A)

Figure 18-63. This illustration shows the procedure for calculating the load in amps to size the conductors supplying the power conversion equipment.

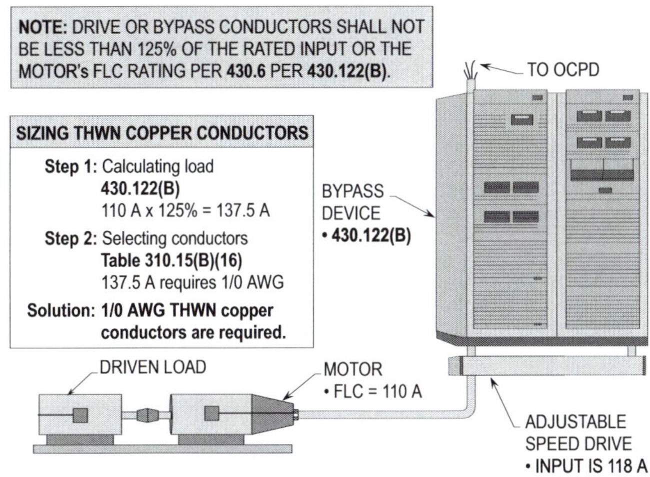

BYPASS DEVICE
NEC 430.122(B)

Figure 18-64. This illustration shows the procedures for calculating the load in amps to size the conductors for a bypass drive system.

OVERLOAD PROTECTION
430.124

Overload protection of the motor shall be provided.

INCLUDED IN POWER CONVERSION EQUIPMENT
430.124(A)

Where the power conversion equipment is marked to indicate that motor overload protection is included, additional overload protection shall not be required.

BYPASS CIRCUITS
430.124(B)

For adjustable speed drive systems that utilize a bypass device to allow motor operation at rated full load speed, motor overload protection as described in **Article 430, Part III**, shall be provided in the bypass circuit.

MULTIPLE MOTOR APPLICATIONS
430.124(C)

For multiple motor application, individual motor overload protection shall be provided in accordance with **Article 430, Part III**. **(See Figure 18-65)**

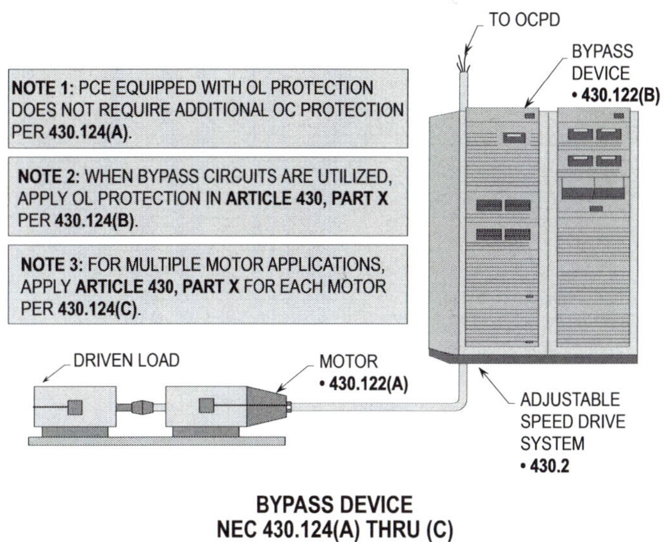

BYPASS DEVICE
NEC 430.124(A) THRU (C)

Figure 18-65. This illustration shows the procedure for protecting the motor from overload when using a bypass device.

MOTOR OVERTEMPERATURE PROTECTION – GENERAL
430.126(A)

Adjustable speed drive systems shall protect against motor overtemperature conditions where the motor is not rated to operate at the nameplate rated current over the speed range required by the application. This protection shall be provided in addition to the conductor protection required in **430.32**. Protection shall be provided by one of the following means:

(1) Motor thermal protector in accordance with **430.32**

(2) Adjustable speed drive system with load- and speed-sensitive overload protection and thermal memory retention upon shutdown or power loss

Thermal memory retention upon shutdown or power loss is not required for continuous duty loads per **430.126(A) (2), Ex**.

(3) Overtemperature protection relay utilizing thermal sensors embedded in the motor and meeting the requirements of **430.32(A)(2)** or **(B)(2)**

(4) Thermal sensor embedded in the motor whose communications are received and acted upon by an adjustable speed drive system

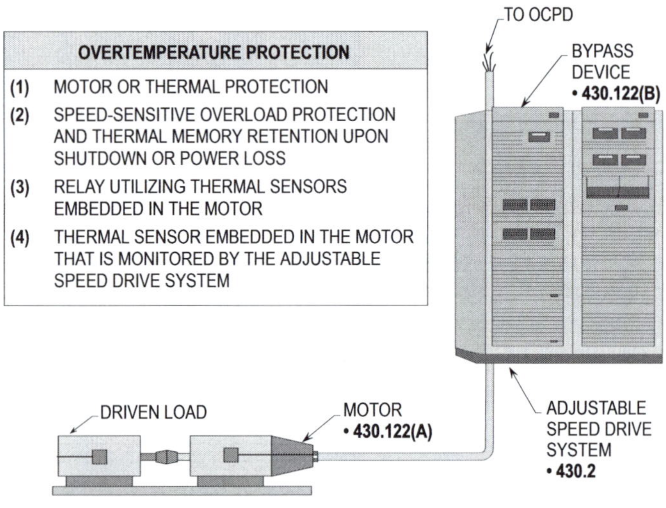

MOTOR OVERTEMPERATURE PROTECTION – GENERAL NEC 430.126(A)(1) THRU (A)(4)

Figure 18-66. This illustration shows the procedure for determining protection for motor overtemperature problems.

For a detailed description of these requirements, see **Figure 18-66** and **IN** to **430.126(A)**.

MULTIPLE MOTOR APPLICATIONS
430.126(B)

For multiple motor application, individual motor overtemperature protection shall be provided per **430.126(A)**.

Note, the relationship between motor current and motor temperature changes when the motor is operated by an adjustable speed drive. When operated at reduced speed, overheating of motors may occur at current levels less than or equal to a motor's rated full-load current. This is the result of reduced motor cooling when its shaft-mounted fan is operating at less than rated nameplate RPM.

AUTOMATIC RESTARTING AND ORDERLY SHUTDOWN
430.126(C)

The provisions of **430.43** and **430.44** shall apply to the motor overtemperature protection means.

DISCONNECTING MEANS
430.128

The disconnecting means shall be permitted to be in the incoming line to the conversion equipment and shall have a rating not less than 115 percent of the rated input current of the conversion unit.

For example, if the rated input current of the conversion unit is 118 amps, the disconnecting means shall be rated at least 200 amps (118 A x 115% = 135.7 A) per **430.128**.

INDUSTRIAL CONTROL PANELS
ARTICLE 409

Article 409 covers the installation of industrial control panels intended for general use and operating procedures at 1000 volts or less. UL 508A governs the procedures for safety when installing components in industrial control panels.

CONDUCTOR – MINIMUM SIZE AND AMPACITY
409.20

The size of the industrial control panel supply conductor shall have an ampacity not less than 125 percent of the full-load current rating of all resistance heating loads, plus 125 percent of the full-load current rating of the highest rated motor plus the sum of the full-load current ratings of all other connected motors and apparatus based on their duty cycle that may be in operation at the same time. **(See Figure 18-67)**

OVERCURRENT PROTECTION – GENERAL
409.21(A)

Industrial control panels shall be provided with overcurrent protection in accordance with **Parts I, II,** and **IX** of **Article 240**.

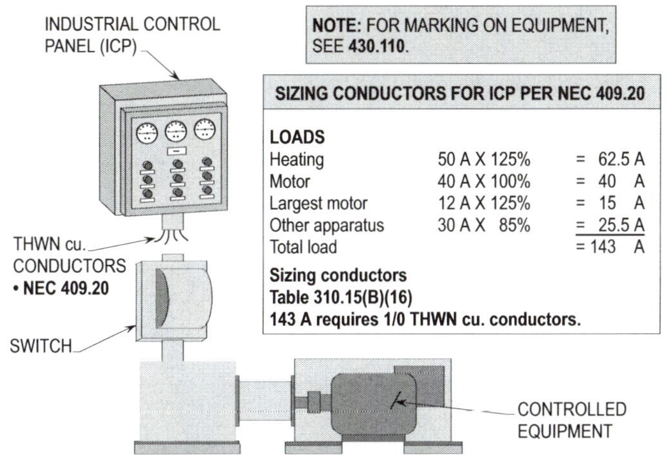

Figure 18-67. This illustration shows the procedure for calculating the load in amps to size the conductors supplying the industrial control panel.

LOCATION
409.21(B)(1) AND (B)(2)

Overcurrent protection for each incoming supply circuit shall be provided by either of the following:

(1) An overcurrent protective device located ahead of the industrial control panel

(2) A single main overcurrent protective device located within the industrial control

Where overcurrent protection is provided as part of the industrial control panel, the supply conductors shall be considered as either feeders or taps as covered by **240.21**.

RATING
409.21(C) AND Ex.

The rating or setting of the overcurrent protective device for the circuit supplying the industrial control panel shall not be greater than the sum of the largest rating or setting of the branch-circuit short circuit, and ground fault protective device provided with the industrial control panel, plus 125 percent of the full-load current rating of all resistance heating loads, plus the sum of the full-load currents of all other motors and apparatus that could be in operation at the same time. **(See Figure 18-68)**

Applying **Exception** to **409.21(C)**: Where one or more instantaneous trip circuit breakers or motor short-circuit protectors are used for motor branch-circuit, short-circuit, and ground fault protection as permitted by **430.52(C)**, the procedure specified above for determining the maximum rating of the protective device for the circuit supplying the industrial control panel shall apply, with the following provision:

- For the purpose of the calculation, each instantaneous trip circuit breaker or motor short circuit shall be assumed to have a rating not exceeding the maximum percentage of motor full-load current permitted by **Table 430.52** for the type of control panel supply circuit protective device employed.

Where no branch-circuit, short-circuit, and ground-fault protective device is provided with the industrial control panel for motor or combination of motor and nonmotor loads, the rating or setting of the overcurrent protective device shall be based on **430.52** and **430.53**, as applicable.

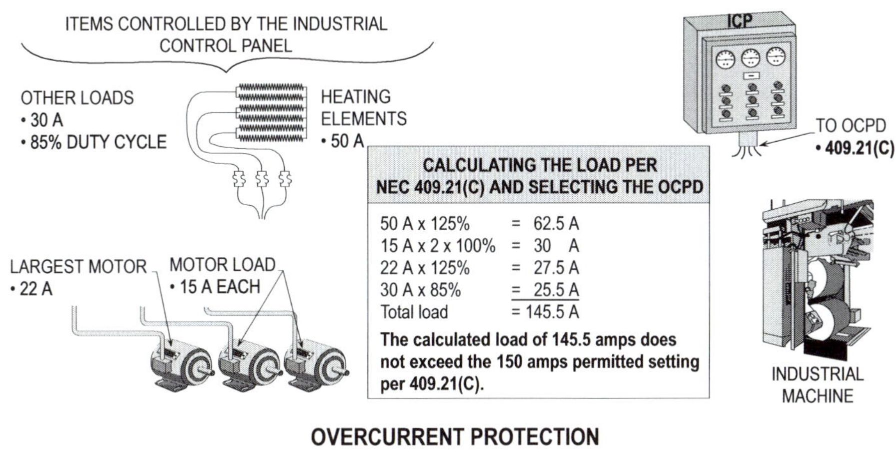

Figure 18-68. This illustration shows the procedure for calculating the load in amps to size the overcurrent protection device protecting the industrial control panel.

DISCONNECTING MEANS
409.30

Disconnecting means that supply motor loads shall comply with **Part IX** of **Article 430**.

> **For example,** if the motor loads on an industrial process add up to 173 amps, the size disconnecting would be 200 amps (173 A x 115% = 198.95 A) per **430.110(A). (See Figure 18-69)**

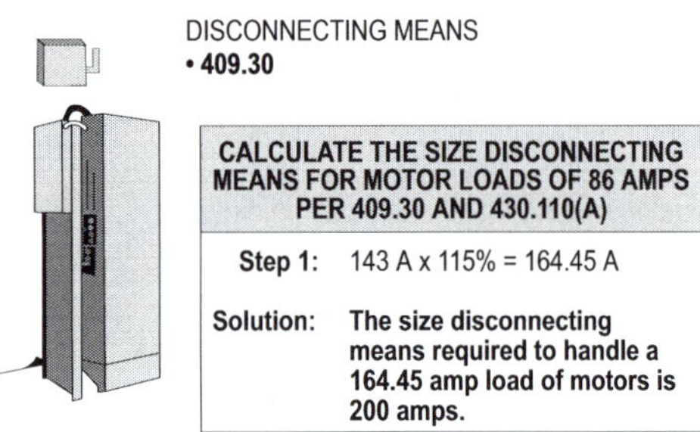

DISCONNECTING MEANS
NEC 409.30

Figure 18-69. This illustration shows the procedure for calculating motor loads in amps to size the disconnecting means.

WIRING SPACE IN INDUSTRIAL CONTROL PANELS – GENERAL
409.104(A)

Industrial control panel enclosures shall not be used as junction boxes, auxiliary gutters, or raceways for conductors feeding through or tapping off to other switches, overcurrent devices, or other equipment, unless adequate for this purpose. The conductors shall not fill the wiring space at any cross section to more than 40 percent of the cross-sectional area of the space, and the conductors, splices, and taps shall not fill the wiring space at any cross section to more than 75 percent of the cross-sectional area of that space. **[See Figure 18-70 and 110.21(B) in the NEC.]**

PHASE CONVERTERS
455.6(A) AND 455.7(A)

Phase converters are used to convert single-phase power to three-phase power. The disconnecting means shall be located within 50 ft (15 m) and within sight per **455.8(A)**. Where the voltage is not the same, the output-to-input ratio shall be applied per **455.6(A)(1)** and **(A)(2)**.

Branch-circuit conductors shall be sized at 125 percent times the phase converter's nameplate single-phase input full-load current rating, in amps. The overcurrent protection device shall be sized at 125 percent times the phase converter's nameplate single-phase input full-load amps. The overcurrent protection device shall not exceed the 125 percent but shall be equal to or lower than 125 percent. **(See Figure 18-71)**

Branch-circuit elements such as overcurrent protection devices and conductors supplying specific loads shall be calculated at 250 percent of the equipment's full-load amp rating. **(See Figure 18-72)**

Feeder conductors that convert single-phase power to three-phase power to supply power to two or more phase converters shall be sized at 250 percent times the three-phase amperage of all motors and other loads served. The overcurrent protection device shall be sized at 250 percent times the full-load three-phase amps of all motors and other loads. If the percentage does not correspond to a standard size, the next size overcurrent protection device above this percentage shall be permitted to be selected per **455.7**. **(See Figure 18-73)**

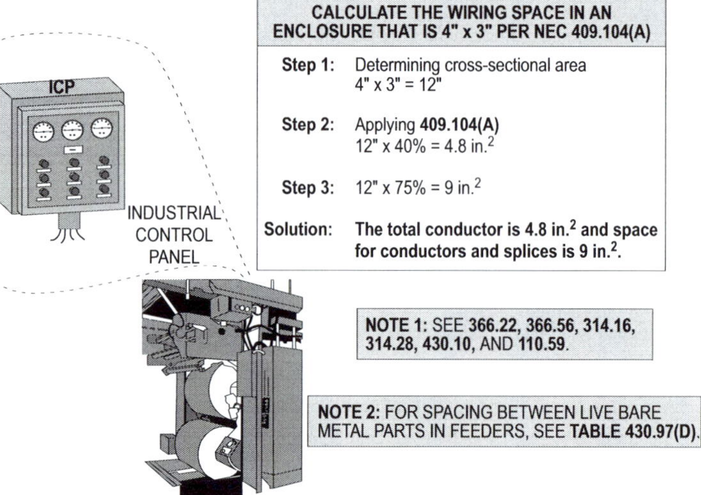

WIRING SPACE IN INDUSTRIAL CONTROL PANELS – GENERAL
NEC 409.104(A)

Figure 18-70. This illustration shows the procedure for calculating the wiring space necessary for accommodating conductors and splices in an industrial control panel.

FIRE PUMPS
ARTICLE 695

Article 695 covers the installation of electric power sources, interconnecting circuits, and switching and control equipment dedicated to fire pumps.

Note, for more information on fire pump installations, see **NFPA 20, NFPA 37,** and for maintenance checks, **NFPA 110**.

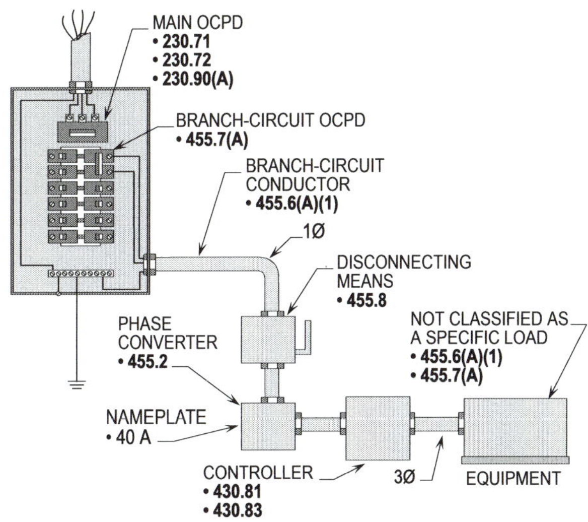

FINDING THWN CONDUCTORS AND OCPD FOR PHASE CONVERTER

Sizing conductors

Step 1: Finding amperage
455.4
Nameplate = 40 A

Step 2: Calculating amperage
240.4(G) and **455.6(A)(1)**
40 A x 125% = 50 A

Step 3: Selecting conductors
Table 310.15(B)(16)
50 A = 8 AWG THWN cu.

Solution: The size THWN copper conductors are required to be 8 AWG.

Sizing OCPD

Step 1: Finding amperage
455.4
Nameplate = 40 A

Step 2: Calculating amperage
455.7(A)
40 A x 125% = 50 A

Step 3: Selecting OCPD
455.7(A) and **240.6(A)**
50 A = 50 A OCPD

Solution: A 50 amp overcurrent protection device is required.

PHASE CONVERTERS
NEC 455.6(A)
NEC 455.7(A)

Figure 18-71. Branch-circuit conductors shall be sized at 125 percent times the phase converter's nameplate single-phase input full-load amperage. The overcurrent protection device shall be sized at 125 percent times the phase converter's nameplate single-phase input full-load current, in amps.

POWER SOURCES
695.3(A)

Section **695.3(A)** covers power sources that are permitted to supply power to fire pump installations.

Power sources such as a reliable service, an on-site generator, a separately derived system, or a tap ahead of the service disconnecting means are considered dependable power supply systems when serving fire pumps and other related equipment. **(See Figure 18-74)**

Note, for what is considered reliable power, see NFPA 20 – A.9.2.3.1(4).

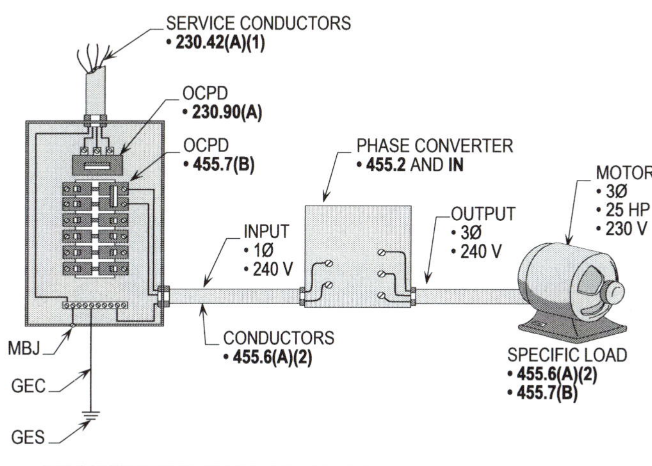

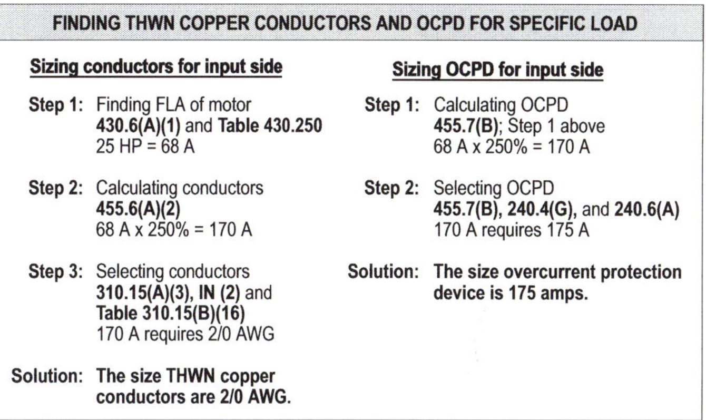

FINDING THWN COPPER CONDUCTORS AND OCPD FOR SPECIFIC LOAD

Sizing conductors for input side

Step 1: Finding FLA of motor
430.6(A)(1) and **Table 430.250**
25 HP = 68 A

Step 2: Calculating conductors
455.6(A)(2)
68 A x 250% = 170 A

Step 3: Selecting conductors
310.15(A)(3), IN (2) and **Table 310.15(B)(16)**
170 A requires 2/0 AWG

Solution: The size THWN copper conductors are 2/0 AWG.

Sizing OCPD for input side

Step 1: Calculating OCPD
455.7(B); Step 1 above
68 A x 250% = 170 A

Step 2: Selecting OCPD
455.7(B), 240.4(G), and **240.6(A)**
170 A requires 175 A

Solution: The size overcurrent protection device is 175 amps.

PHASE CONVERTERS
NEC 455.6(A)(2)
NEC 455.7(B)

Figure 18-72. Branch-circuit elements such as overcurrent protection devices and conductors supplying specific loads shall be calculated at 250 percent of the equipment's full-load current rating, in amps.

SIZING CONDUCTORS
695.6(B)(1) AND 430.22

Conductors shall be sized with enough capacity so that they are protected against short-circuit currents. By sizing the conductors to the fire pump motors at 125 percent of the motor's FLA, this should be accomplished. For sizing the conductors to one motor, see **430.22,** and for more than one motor, plus other loads, see **430.24** . **(See Figure 18-75)**

SIZING OVERCURRENT
PROTECTION DEVICE
695.5(B), (C)(2), AND 230.90(A), Ex. 4

The overcurrent protection device shall protect the conductors and fire pump motor and accessories from short circuits. **(See Figure 18-76)**

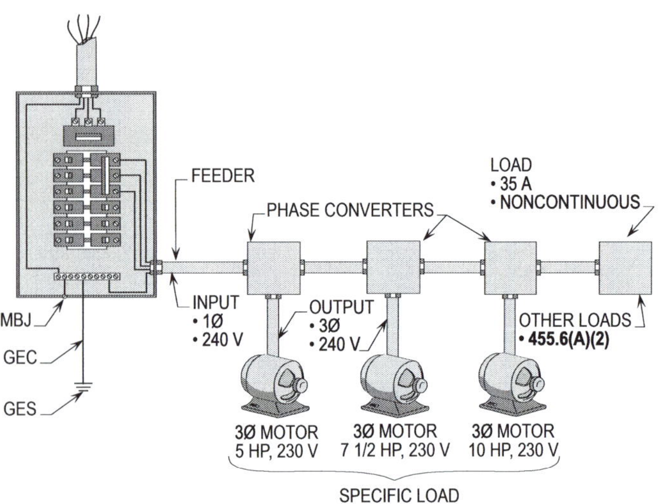

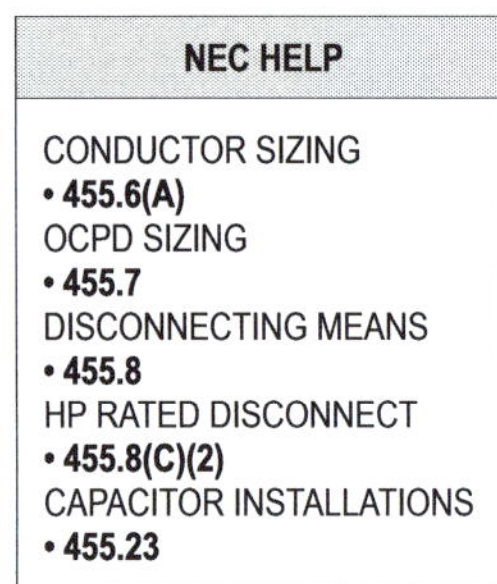

NEC HELP

CONDUCTOR SIZING
• **455.6(A)**
OCPD SIZING
• **455.7**
DISCONNECTING MEANS
• **455.8**
HP RATED DISCONNECT
• **455.8(C)(2)**
CAPACITOR INSTALLATIONS
• **455.23**

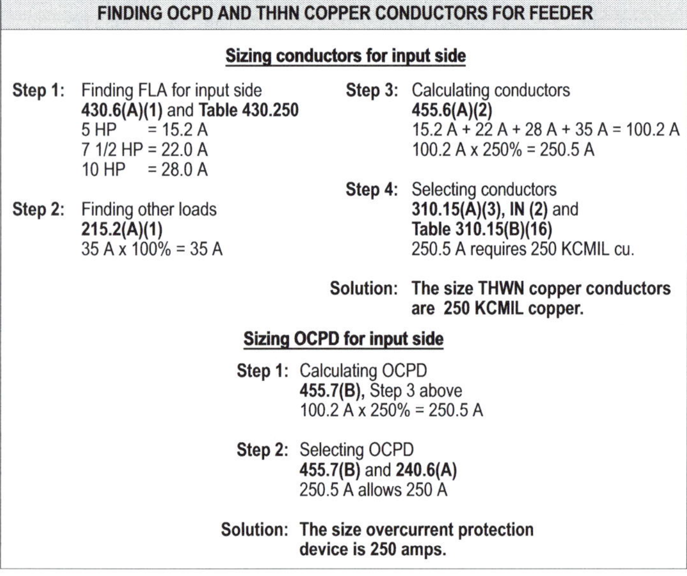

FINDING OCPD AND THHN COPPER CONDUCTORS FOR FEEDER

Sizing conductors for input side

Step 1: Finding FLA for input side
430.6(A)(1) and **Table 430.250**
5 HP = 15.2 A
7 1/2 HP = 22.0 A
10 HP = 28.0 A

Step 2: Finding other loads
215.2(A)(1)
35 A x 100% = 35 A

Step 3: Calculating conductors
455.6(A)(2)
15.2 A + 22 + 28 A + 35 A = 100.2 A
100.2 A x 250% = 250.5 A

Step 4: Selecting conductors
310.15(A)(3), IN (2) and
Table 310.15(B)(16)
250.5 A requires 250 KCMIL cu.

Solution: The size THWN copper conductors
are 250 KCMIL copper.

Sizing OCPD for input side

Step 1: Calculating OCPD
455.7(B), Step 3 above
100.2 A x 250% = 250.5 A

Step 2: Selecting OCPD
455.7(B) and **240.6(A)**
250.5 A allows 250 A

Solution: The size overcurrent protection
device is 250 amps.

PHASE CONVERTERS
NEC 455.6(A)(2)
NEC 455.7
NEC 455.7(B)

Figure 18-73. Feeder conductors that convert single-phase power to three-phase power for supplying power to two or more phase converters shall be sized at 250 percent times the three-phase amperage of all motors and other loads served. The overcurrent protection device shall be sized at 250 times the full-load three-phase amps of all motors and other loads.

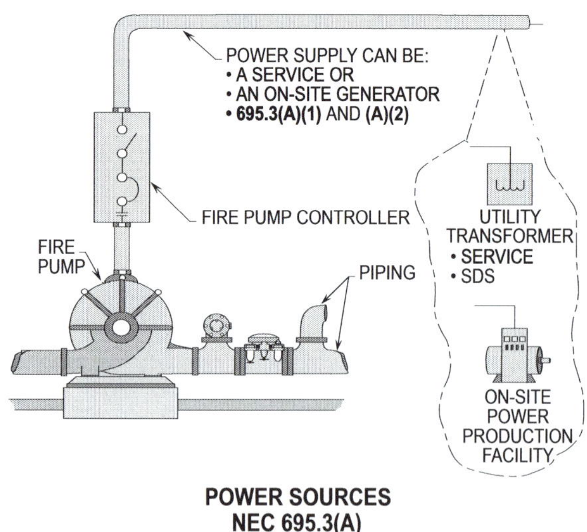

POWER SOURCES
NEC 695.3(A)

Figure 18-74. This illustration shows the power sources that are permitted to supply fire pump installations.

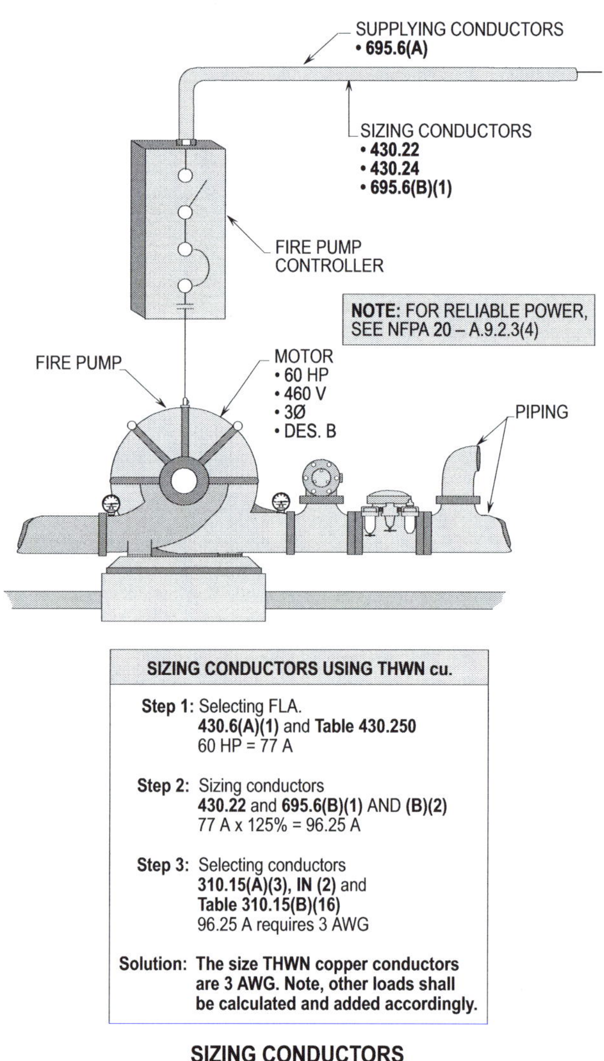

SIZING CONDUCTORS USING THWN cu.

Step 1: Selecting FLA.
430.6(A)(1) and **Table 430.250**
60 HP = 77 A

Step 2: Sizing conductors
430.22 and **695.6(B)(1)** AND **(B)(2)**
77 A x 125% = 96.25 A

Step 3: Selecting conductors
310.15(A)(3), IN (2) and
Table 310.15(B)(16)
96.25 A requires 3 AWG

Solution: The size THWN copper conductors
are 3 AWG. Note, other loads shall
be calculated and added accordingly.

SIZING CONDUCTORS
NEC 695.6(B)(2)
NEC 430.22

Figure 18-75. The procedure for sizing the conductors to supply a fire pump.

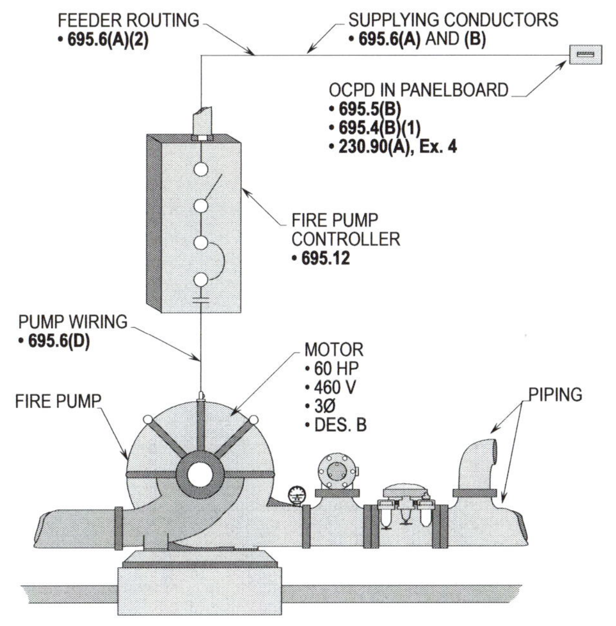

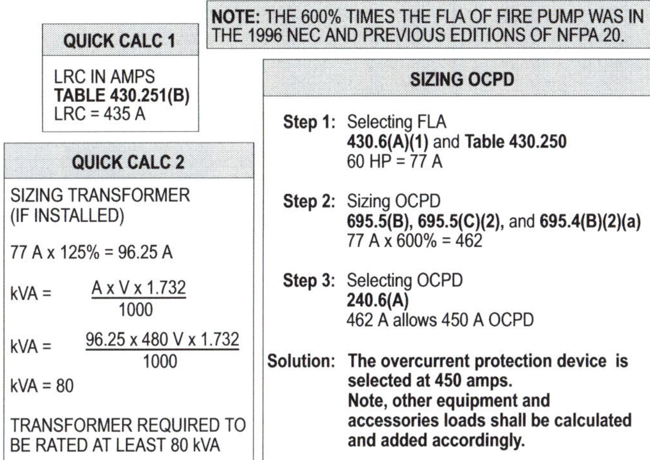

FEEDER ROUTING
• 695.6(A)(2)
SUPPLYING CONDUCTORS
• 695.6(A) AND (B)
OCPD IN PANELBOARD
• 695.5(B)
• 695.4(B)(1)
• 230.90(A), Ex. 4
FIRE PUMP
CONTROLLER
• 695.12
PUMP WIRING
• 695.6(D)
MOTOR
• 60 HP
• 460 V
• 3Ø
• DES. B
FIRE PUMP
PIPING
NOTE: THE 600% TIMES THE FLA OF FIRE PUMP WAS IN THE 1996 NEC AND PREVIOUS EDITIONS OF NFPA 20.
QUICK CALC 1
LRC IN AMPS
TABLE 430.251(B)
LRC = 435 A
QUICK CALC 2
SIZING TRANSFORMER
(IF INSTALLED)
77 A x 125% = 96.25 A
kVA = A x V x 1.732 / 1000
kVA = 96.25 x 480 V x 1.732 / 1000
kVA = 80
TRANSFORMER REQUIRED TO BE RATED AT LEAST 80 kVA
SIZING OCPD
Step 1: Selecting FLA
430.6(A)(1) and Table 430.250
60 HP = 77 A
Step 2: Sizing OCPD
695.5(B), 695.5(C)(2), and 695.4(B)(2)(a)
77 A x 600% = 462
Step 3: Selecting OCPD
240.6(A)
462 A allows 450 A OCPD
Solution: The overcurrent protection device is selected at 450 amps.
Note, other equipment and accessories loads shall be calculated and added accordingly.

SIZING OVERCURRENT PROTECTION DEVICE
NEC 695.5(B)
NEC 695.5(C)(2)
NEC 230.90(A), Ex. 4

Figure 18-76. This illustration shows the procedure for sizing the overcurrent protection device to protect a fire pump.

SIZING TRANSFORMER USED AS A SEPARATELY DERIVED SYSTEM 695.5(A)

Section **695.5(A)** permits a transformer dedicated to supplying a fire pump to be rated at a minimum of 125 percent of the sum of the rated full load of the fire pump motor(s), the rated full loads of pressure maintenance pump motor(s), and the full-load amps of any associated fire pump accessory equipment connected to the transformer.

Secondary overcurrent protection for the transformer shall not be permitted, and the primary overcurrent protection device shall not be set above 600 percent of the transformer's full-load current rating, in amps.

SIZING TRANSFORMER ELEMENTS

Section **695.5(A)** covers the requirements for sizing a separately derived system, **695.5(B)** deals with sizing the overcurrent protection device, and **695.5(C)(2)** outlines the rules that require the overcurrent protection device to carry the locked-rotor current of the transformer indefinitely. **(See Figure 18-76** and **18-77)**

SIZING OVERCURRENT PROTECTION DEVICE FOR A SEPARATELY DERIVED SYSTEM 695.5(B)

Section **696.5(B)** requires the overcurrent protection device on the primary side of a separately derived system, supplying power to a fire pump installation, to carry the secondary circuit indefinitely.

Note, such secondary currents include both normal full-load operating current, in amps, as well as the locked-rotor current, in amps, of the motor. **(See Figure 18-77)**

When separately derived systems are used to supply power to fire pumps and accessories, they are usually installed in the fire pump room with the fire pump controller.

Note, the transformer shall supply power until pump motor failure. This requirement allows the motor to pump water to fight the fire for as long as possible.

PUMP WIRING 695.6(D)

Wiring from the controllers to the pump motor shall be routed in any one of the following wiring methods:

- RMC
- IMC
- EMT
- LFMC
- LFNC
- LFNC – B
- MC Cable
- MI Cable

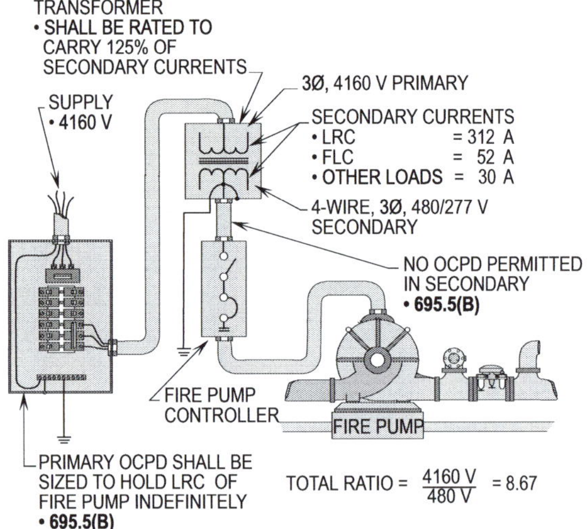

SIZING PRIMARY OCPD

Step 1: Sizing sec. conductors
695.6(C)(1) and **695.5(A)**
52 A x 125% = 65 A
30 A x 100% = 30 A
Total load = 95 A

Step 2: Selecting conductors using
TWHN copper
310.15(A)(3), IN (2) and
Table 310.15(B)(16)
95 A Requires 3 AWG cu.

Step 3: Calculating OCPD
OCPD = Total A ÷ Ratio
OCPD = 342 A ÷ 8.67
OCPD = 39.5

Step 4: Selecting OCPD
450.3(A) and **240.6(A)**
39.5 A Requires 40 A

Solution: The size overcurrent
protection device in the
primary side is 40 amps.

Note: 52 A x 125% + 30 A = 95 A
• Transformer shall carry a normal current rating of 95 A per **695.5(A)**

**SIZING OVERCURRENT PROTECTION DEVICE FOR
A SEPARATELY DERIVED SYSTEM
NEC 695.5(B)**

Figure 18-77. This illustration shows the procedure for sizing the transformer and primary overcurrent protection device for a fire pump installation.

SIZING PRIMARY OCPD FOR TRANSFORMER (XFMR) QUICK CALC 2 IN FIGURE 18-76

Step 1: XFMR FLC = kVA x 1000 ÷ V x 1.732

Step 2: XFMR FLC = 80 x 1000 ÷ 480 x 1.732

Step 3: XFMR FLC = 96 A

Step 4: Table 450.3(B) [Select 125%]

Step 5: 96 A x 125% = 120 A

Solution: 125 A CB or fuses selected for primary protection.

NEC REVIEW SECTIONS

Electric Utility Service Connections
• NEC **695.3(A)(1)**
• NFPA 20 – 9.2.2(1)

On-Site Power Production Facility
• NEC **695.3(A)(2)**
• NFPA 20 – 9.2.2(3)

Dedicated Feeders
• NEC **695,3(A)(3)**
• NFPA 20 – 9.2.2.(3)

Multiple Sources
• NEC **695.3(B)**
• NFPA 20 – 9.3.2

Individual Source and On-Site Standby Generator
• NEC **695.3(B)(2)** and **Ex.**
• NFPA 20 – 9.3.3 and 9.3.4

On-Site Standby Generator As Alternate
• NEC 695.3(D)
• NFPA 20 – 9.6.2.1

For Capacity
• NEC **695.3(D)(1)**
• NFPA 20 – 9.6.1.1

For Connection
• NEC **695.3(D)(2)**
• NFPA 20 – 9.6.1.2

For Arrangement
• NEC **695.3(E)**
• NFPA 20 – 9.1.4

For Transfer Of Power
• NEC **695.3(F)**
• NFPA 20 – 9.6.4

For Power Source Selection
• NEC **695.3(I)**
• NFPA 20 – 10.8.1.3.1

For Phase Converters
• NEC **695.3(G)**
• NFPA 20 – 9.1.7

For OCPD Selection
• NEC **695.4(B)(2)(a)** and **(b)**
• NFPA 20 – 9.2.3.4

Chapter 18. Motors

Section   Answer

1. Conductors for a motor used for periodic duty and rated for 5 minutes shall be sized with a current-carrying capacity of _______ percent of the motor's full-load amps.

   (a) 85   (b) 100
   (c) 110   (d) 125

2. Wound-rotor motors are three-phase motors that are installed with _______ sets of leads.

   (a) 1   (b) 2
   (c) 3   (d) 4

3. Time-delay fuses that are sized at _______ percent or less of a motor's FLA rating can provide overload protection for the motor.

   (a) 100   (b) 110
   (c) 115   (d) 125

4. The maximum percentage that shall be permitted to be applied to a time-delay fuse is _______ percent of a motor's FLA.

   (a) 175   (b) 200
   (c) 225   (d) 300

5. Two or motors shall be permitted to be installed without individual overcurrent protection devices if rated less than _______ horsepower each and if the full-load current rating, in amps, of each motor does not exceed 6 amps.

   (a) 1   (b) 2
   (c) 3   (d) 5

6. Thermal protectors and thermal relays shall be permitted to be installed to provide running overload protection for motors rated more than _______ horsepower.

   (a) 1   (b) 2
   (c) 3   (d) 4

7. The controller shall be permitted to be an attachment plug and receptacle that is acceptable for use with portable motors rated _______ horsepower or less.

   (a) 1/8   (b) 1/4
   (c) 1/3   (d) 1/2

8. The controller shall be permitted to be a general-use switch rated for at least twice the motor's full-load current, in amps, for stationary motors rated _______ horsepower or less.

   (a) 1/8   (b) 1/2
   (c) 1   (d) 2

Section   **Answer**

9. For a stationary motor rated ______ horsepower or less, the branch-circuit overcurrent protection device shall be permitted to serve as the disconnecting means.

    (a) 1/16   (b) 1/8
    (c) 1/4   (d) 1/2

10. The general rule requires the disconnecting means for a motor to be installed within sight of the motor and not more than ______ ft from the motor.

    (a) 20   (b) 25
    (c) 50   (d) 75

11. Branch-circuit conductors shall be sized at ______ percent times the phase converter's (variable loads) nameplate single-phase input FLA rating.

    (a) 125   (b) 175
    (c) 200   (d) 250

12. Feeder conductors supplying power to two or more phase converters shall be sized at ______ percent times the three-phase amperage of all motors and other loads served.

    (a) 125   (b) 175
    (c) 200   (d) 250

13. Branch-circuit conductors supply a single motor shall have an ampacity not less than ______ percent of the motor's FLC, in amps.

    (a) 100   (b) 125
    (c) 135   (d) 150

14. The selection of conductors for wye start and delta run motors between the controller and motor shall be based on ______ percent of the motor's full load current, in amps, times 125 percent for continuous use.

    (a) 58   (b) 67
    (c) 75   (d) 80

15. The disconnecting means for power conversion equipment shall not be less than ______ percent of the input FLA rating of the conversion unit.

    (a) 100   (b) 110
    (c) 115   (d) 125

16. The full-load current rating, in amps, of the largest motor shall be multiplied by ______ percent to select the size of conductors for a feeder supplying a group of two or more motors.

    (a) 100   (b) 110
    (c) 115   (d) 125

Section   Answer

17. The motor branch-circuit overcurrent device shall be capable of carrying the _______ current, in amps, of the motor.

    (a) starting   (b) varying
    (c) torque   (d) continuous

18. When a motor won't start and run, a nontime-delay fuse not exceeding 600 amperes in rating shall be permitted to be increased up to _______ percent of the full-load current, in amps, of the motor.

    (a) 250   (b) 300
    (c) 400   (d) 600

19. When a motor won't start and run, a inverse-time circuit breaker greater than 100 amps shall be permitted to be increased up to _______ percent of the motor's full-load current, in amps.

    (a) 250   (b) 300
    (c) 400   (d) 600

20. Three-phase squirrel-cage induction motors have three separate windings per pole on the stator that generate magnetic fields that are _______ degrees out of phase with each other.

    (a) 120   (b) 125
    (c) 150   (d) 180

21. Time-delay fuses will hold _______ times their rating, which will permit most induction motors to start and accelerate their driven loads.

    (a) 1   (b) 2
    (c) 3   (d) 5

22. Inverse-time circuit breakers will hold about _______ times their rating for different periods of time based upon their frame size.

    (a) 1   (b) 2
    (c) 3   (d) 5

23. An overcurrent protection device rated at _______ amps or less can protect a 120 volt or less branch circuit supplying motors rated less than 1 horsepower.

    (a) 10   (b) 15
    (c) 20   (d) 30

24. The branch-circuit protective device shall be permitted to serve as the controller for stationary motors where the motor is rated _______ horsepower or less.

    (a) 1/16   (b) 1/8
    (c) 1/4   (d) 1/2

Section   **Answer**

25. A branch-circuit inverse-time circuit breaker rated in amperes shall be permitted as a _______ disconnecting means.

    (a) motor   (b) horsepower
    (c) controller   (d) stationary

26. The motor controller for a torque motor shall have a continuous duty, FLC rating, in amps, of not less than the _______ current rating of the motor.

    (a) labeling   (b) nameplate
    (c) listing   (d) table

27. A listed motor circuit switch rated in _______ shall be permitted as a disconnecting means.

    (a) horsepower   (b) amperage
    (c) voltage   (d) resistance

28. The disconnecting means shall be permitted to be a general-use or isolating switch for AC motors rated _______ horsepower or greater.

    (a) 40   (b) 60
    (c) 75   (d) 100

29. A motor and its driven machinery or load shall be installed within sight and within _______ of the controller for the motor.

    (a) 25   (b) 50
    (c) 75   (d) 100

30. The ampacity of capacitor circuit conductors shall not be less than _______ percent of the rated current, in amps, of the capacitor.

    (a) 100   (b) 125
    (c) 135   (d) 150

31. When applying the rule-of-thumb method, the horsepower rating of the motor shall be multiplied by _______ to obtain full-load current in amps for 440, 460, and 480 volt, three-phase motors.

    (a) 1.00   (b) 1.10
    (c) 1.25   (d) 5.0

32. When applying the rule-of-thumb method, the horsepower rating of the motor shall be multiplied by _______ to obtain full-load current in amps for 220, 230, and 240 volt, single-phase motors.

    (a) 1.00   (b) 1.10
    (c) 1.25   (d) 5.0

33. Power conversion equipment requires the conductors to be sized at _______ percent of the rated input, in amps, of such equipment.

    (a) 100   (b) 115
    (c) 125   (d) 150

Section   Answer

34. For Design B high efficient motors, the setting of an instantaneous circuit breaker shall be permitted to be adjusted up to _______ percent to allow the motor to start and run.

     (a) 1000   (b) 1200
     (c) 1300   (d) 1700

35. A nontime-delay fuse will hold _______ times its rating for approximately 1/4 to 2 seconds based upon type used.

     (a) 2   (b) 3
     (c) 5   (d) 10

36. Motors with a marked service factor not less than 1.15 shall have the minimum running overload protection sized at _______ percent.

     (a) 115   (b) 125
     (c) 130   (d) 140

37. Motors with a marked temperature rise not over 40°C shall have the minimum running overload protection sized at _______ percent.

     (a) 115   (b) 125
     (c) 130   (d) 140

38. Motors with a marked service factor not less than 1.15 shall have the maximum running overload protection sized at _______ percent.

     (a) 115   (b) 125
     (c) 130   (d) 140

39. Motors with a marked temperature rise not over 40°C shall have the maximum running overload protection sized at _______ percent.

     (a) 115   (b) 125
     (c) 130   (d) 140

40. An AC general-use snap switch shall be permitted to be installed as the controller for a stationary motor where the full-load current of the switch does not exceed _______ percent of the branch-circuit rating.

     (a) 50   (b) 75
     (c) 80   (d) 90

41. When applying the rule-of-thumb method, the horsepower rating of the motor shall be multiplied by _______ to obtain full-load current in amps for 220, 230, and 240 volt, three-phase motors.

     (a) 100   (b) 125
     (c) 250   (d) 500

42. The overcurrent protection device (variable loads) shall be sized at _______ percent times the phase converter's nameplate single-phase input FLA rating.

     (a) 100   (b) 125
     (c) 250   (d) 500

Section   **Answer**

43. Circuit conductors supplying power conversion equipment included as part of an adjustable-speed drive system shall have an ampacity not less than _______ percent of the rated input to the power conversion equipment.

(a) 100   (b) 125
(c) 150   (d) 250

44. The disconnecting means shall be permitted to be in the incoming line to the conversion equipment and shall have a rating not less than _______ percent of the rated input current of the conversion unit.

(a) 115   (b) 125
(c) 135   (d) 150

45. The conductors in industrial control panels shall not fill the wiring space at any cross section to more than _______ percent of the cross-sectional area of the space.

(a) 20   (b) 30
(c) 40   (d) 75

46. The conductors, splices, and taps in industrial control panels shall not fill the wiring space at any cross section to more than _______ percent of the cross-sectional area of that space.

(a) 20   (b) 30
(c) 40   (d) 75

47. Motors rated over 2 horsepower through _______ horsepower shall be permitted to be installed with a separate disconnecting means (general-use switch) if the motor is equipped with an autotransformer-type controller and certain conditions are complied with.

(a) 50   (b) 60
(c) 100   (d) 150

48. The disconnecting means shall be permitted to be an isolating switch for DC stationary motors rated at _______ horsepower or greater.

(a) 40   (b) 50
(c) 100   (d) 150

49. Conductors supplying a fire pump motor(s), pressure maintenance pumps, and associated fire pump accessory equipment shall have a rating not less than _______ percent of the sum of the fire pump motor(s) and pressure maintenance motor(s) full load currents.

(a) 100   (b) 125
(c) 150   (d) 250

50. Conductors that are 16 AWG in size shall be protected at _______ amps when used for remote-control circuits.

(a) 3   (b) 6
(c) 7   (d) 10

Section   **Answer**

51. What size THWN branch-circuit copper conductors are required for a 3 HP, 208 volt, single-phase, Design B motor?

52. What size THWN branch-circuit copper conductors are required for a 20 HP, 230 volt, three-phase, Design B motor?

53. What size THWN branch-circuit copper conductors are required for a 75 HP, 460 volt, three-phase, 15 minute-rated intermittent duty cycle motor?

54. What size THWN copper conductors are required to supply power conversion equipment with a rated input of 112 amps?

55. What size THWN branch-circuit copper conductors are required to supply a 50 HP, 208 volt, three-phase, Design B part-winding motor?

56. What size THWN branch-circuit copper conductors are required to supply a 30 HP, 40 HP, and 50 HP, 460 volt, three-phase, Design B motor?

57. What size THWN branch-circuit copper conductors are required to supply an 10 HP, 208 volt, three-phase, 5-minute rated intermittent duty cycle, an 15 HP, 208 volt, three-phase, 15-minute rated intermittent duty cycle motor, and a 20 HP, 208 volt, three-phase motor?

58. Based on the code letter, what is the LRC (maximum) for a 40 HP, 230 volt, three-phase, code letter G motor?

59. What is the LRC for a 40 HP, 230 volt, three-phase, Design letter B motor?

60. What is the rounded-down and rounded-up size nontime-delay fuse for a 50 HP, 230 volt, three-phase, Design letter B motor?

61. What is the rounded-down and rounded-up size time-delay fuse for a 50 HP, 230 volt, three-phase, Design letter B motor?

62. What is the minimum and maximum setting for an instantaneous trip circuit breaker for a 50 HP, 230 volt, three-phase, high efficiency motor?

63. What is the rounded-down and rounded-up size inverse time circuit breaker for a 50 HP, 230 volt, three-phase, Design letter B motor?

64. What is the maximum size nontime-delay fuse for a 50 HP, 230 volt, three-phase, Design letter B motor?

65. What is the maximum size time-delay fuse for a 50 HP, 230 volt, three-phase, Design letter B motor?

66. What is the maximum size inverse time circuit breaker for a 50 HP, 230 volt, three-phase, Design letter B motor?

67. What size overcurrent protection device (CB) is required for a feeder that supplies a 10 HP, 15 HP, 20 HP, and 25 HP, 460 volt, three-phase, Design letter B group of motors?

Section   **Answer**

68. What size overload protection (minimum per Table) is required for a 20 HP, 460 volt, three-phase, Design letter B motor with a nameplate rating of 48 amps, temperature rise of 40°C, and a service factor of 1.15?

69. What size overload protection (maximum per Table) is required for a 20 HP, 460 volt, three-phase, Design letter B motor with a nameplate rating of 48 amps, temperature rise of 40°C, and a service factor of 1.15?

70. What size nonfused, HP rated disconnect is required for a 50 HP, 460 volt, three-phase, Design letter B motor?

71. What size overcurrent protection device (maximum) is required for motor control circuit conductors located in the controller and supplied by a 12 AWG conductor?

72. What size overcurrent protection device (maximum) is required for motor control circuit conductors that are run remote and supplied by a 12 AWG conductor?

73. What size overcurrent protection device is required for motor control circuit conductors that are supplied by a 2400 VA, 480 volt, two-wire control transformer? (Use **Table 450.3(B)**.)

74. What size THWN copper conductors are required to supply a 20 kVA, 208 volt, three-phase capacitor with a 40 HP, 208 volt, three-phase, Design letter B motor?

75. What size FLA rating is required for a 30 HP, 115 volt, three-phase, Design letter B motor using the rule-of-thumb method?

76. What size FLA rating is required for a 30 HP, 220 volt, three-phase, Design letter B motor using the rule-of-thumb method?

77. What size FLA rating is required for a 30 HP, 440 volt, three-phase, Design letter B motor using the rule-of-thumb method?

78. What size FLA rating is required for a 30 HP, 575 volt, three-phase, Design letter B motor using the rule-of-thumb method?

79. What size overcurrent protection device and THWN copper conductors are required for a phase converter with a nameplate rating of 35 amps supplying a piece of equipment classified as a variable load?

80. What size overcurrent protection device and THWN copper conductors are required for a phase converter supplying a 20 HP, 230 volt, three-phase, Design letter B motor classified as a specific load?

81. Markings on controllers shall provide other ______ data for proper application of circuitry.

    (a) needed   (b) necessary
    (c) all of the above   (d) none of the above

82. Where motors are provided with terminal housing, the housings shall be of ———.

    (a) metal   (b) non-metallic
    (c) all of the above   (d) none of the above

83. Intermittent duty operating motors that operate at 5-minute intervals may have conductors sized at _______% of the nameplate amps.

    (a) 75   (b) 80
    (c) 85   (d) 90

84. Conductors for small motors shall not be smaller than _______ AWG unless otherwise permitted.

    (a) 16   (b) 18
    (c) 15   (d) 12

85. Under certain conditions of use, _______ AWG or _______ AWG conductors may be used in a cabinet or enclosure.

    (a) 18   (b) 16
    (c) all of the above   (d) none of the above

86. A class _______ overload relay will provide a longer motor acceleration time than a 10 A.

    (a) 20   (b) 30
    (c) all of the above   (d) none of the above

87. Instantaneous trip circuit breakers are also known as motor-circuit _______.

    (a) fuses   (b) relays
    (c) all of the above   (d) none of the above

88. Per the NEC, _______ fuses intended for the use and protection of electronic devices shall be permitted.

    (a) time-delay   (b) semiconductor
    (c) all of the above   (d) one of the above

89. Motor taps for a motor group installation shall not extend more than _______ ft.

    (a) 10   (b) 25
    (c) 75   (d) 100

90. A disconnecting means for a motor is not required to be installed in a _______ classified area.

    (a) hazardous   (b) motor
    (c) all of the above   (d) none of the above

91. LO/TO procedures for a disconnecting means for a circuit supplying a motor shall comply with Article 120 of NFPA 70_______.

    (a) A   (b) D
    (c) E   (d) F

Section   **Answer**

92. At least _______ of the disconnecting means for a motor shall be readily accessible.

    (a) one   (b) two
    (c) three   (d) all of the above

93. Disconnecting means for a motor shall comply with Sections _______ and _______ in the NEC.

    (a) 109   (b) 110
    (c) all of the above   (d) none of the above

94. The disconnecting means for a motor rated over _______ volts is not required to be located within sight of the motor.

    (a) 208   (b) 480
    (c) 600   (d) 1000

95. A motor rated over _______ HP is not required to have a disconnecting means within sight as outlined in the NEC.

    (a) 25   (b) 50
    (c) 75   (d) 100

96. The disconnecting means for a motor controller rated over 1000 volts shall comply with Section _______ of the NEC.

    (a) 90.2   (b) 100
    (c) 110.25   (d) 240.4(D)

97. A self-protected combination controller shall only be permitted where specifically _______ in the manufacturer's instructions, as outlined in the NEC.

    (a) approved   (b) unlisted
    (c) identified   (d) none of the above

98. A disconnecting means for a controller supplying a 4160 V motor shall be of the _______ type.

    (a) non-lockable   (b) lockable
    (c) all of the above   (d) none of the above

99. High-voltage motor (over 1000 V) shall have the equipment grounding conductor connection comply with the requirements in Part _______ of Article 250.

    (a) I   (b) II
    (c) III   (d) IV

100. Conductors supplying high-voltage motors shall have an _______ not less than the current used to cause the overload protection (selected) to trip as outlined in the NEC.

    (a) ampacity   (b) switch
    (c) all of the above   (d) none of the above

19

Compressor Motors

Article 440 deals with individual or group installations having hermetically sealed motor-compressors. The techniques for designing the proper size conductors, disconnecting means, and controllers are discussed.

The conductors supplying power to heating, air-conditioning, and refrigeration (HACR) equipment are sized from the full-load amp (FLA) ratings of the compressor and condenser motor. These FLA ratings are increased by 125 percent per **440.32** to compensate for the starting periods and overload conditions.

The overcurrent protection devices protecting the branch circuits from short-circuit and ground-fault currents are sized from the provisions listed in **440.22(A)**, which require the FLA ratings to be increased from 175 percent up to 225 percent to allow the HACR equipment to start and run without tripping the overcurrent protection device ahead of the circuit.

Note 1, smaller size devices can be used if they hold during operation.

Note 2, the elements used to supply the branch circuits to HACR equipment may be required to be selected by the branch-circuit selection currents listed on the nameplate of such equipment per **440.4(C)** and **110.3(B)**.

Note 3, refers to **Table 220.3** for a quick reference to size a load in amps for sizing conductors and use **Table 240.4(G)** when the overcurrent protection device is selected greater than 125% of the compressor's FLC in amps.

NAMEPLATE LISTING
440.1

The overcurrent protection devices, running overload protection devices, conductors, disconnecting means, and controllers shall be sized and selected by the information provided on the nameplate listing for air-conditioning and refrigeration equipment. The information on the nameplate is very important to installers and service personnel; therefore, the nameplate shall never be removed from the air-conditioner or refrigeration equipment.

MARKING ON HERMETIC REFRIGERANT MOTOR-COMPRESSORS AND EQUIPMENT
440.4

Hermetic refrigerant motor-compressors shall be provided with a marking on the nameplate giving the manufacturer's name, trademark, or symbol and designating the identification, number of phases, voltage, and frequency. The information provided on the nameplate of the hermetic refrigerant motor-compressor is used to determine the ratings of branch-circuit conductors, ground-fault protection, short circuits, disconnecting means, controllers, and other elements of the electrical system.

MARKING ON CONTROLLERS
440.5

Controllers shall be marked with information that lists the manufacturer's name, trademark or symbol, identifying voltage, phases, full-load current, locked-rotor current rating, or horsepower.

AMPACITY AND RATING
440.6

The full-load current rating listed on the nameplate of the motor-compressor shall be used to determine the branch-circuit conductor rating, short-circuit protection rating, motor overload protection rating, controller rating, or disconnecting means rating. The branch-circuit selection current (if greater) shall be applied if shown instead of the full-load current rating. The full-load current rating, in amps, shall be used to determine the motor's overload protection rating. The full-load current rating listed on the compressor nameplate shall be used when the nameplate for the equipment does not list a full-load current rating based on the branch-circuit selection current. **(See Figure 19-1)**

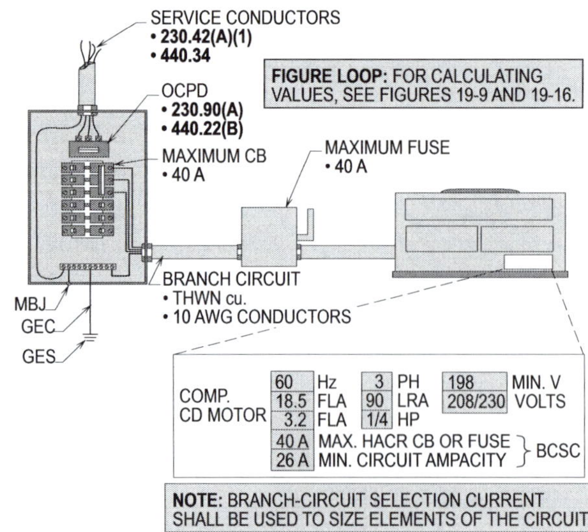

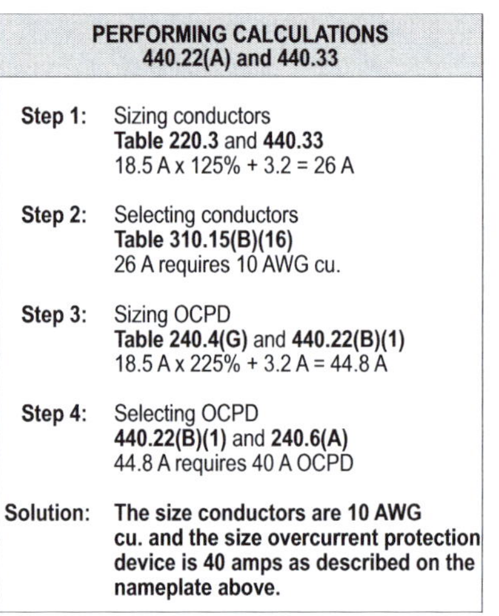

AMPACITY AND RATING
NEC 440.6

Figure 19-1. If the branch-circuit selection current (BCSC) on the nameplate calls for a certain circuit size and overcurrent protection device size, this rating shall be used instead of actually calculating such values and sizes per **440.22(A)** and **440.32**.

HIGHEST RATED (LARGEST) MOTOR
440.7

When sizing the conductors for a feeder supplying air-conditioner units and motors per **430.24**, the full-load current in amps of the largest motor is multiplied by 125 percent. The full-load current ratings of the remaining motors are added to this total to derive the FLA. **See Figures 18-9** and **18-27** for a specific illustration pertaining to this rule.

When sizing the overcurrent protection device for two or motors per **430.62(A)**, the full-load current (in amps) of the largest motor is multiplied by the percentages listed in **Table 430.52**. The full-load current ratings (in amps) of the remaining motors are added to this total to derive the FLA. (Also, see **430.63.**)

The full-load current ratings listed on the nameplate of the motor-compressor shall be used to determine the size conductors and overcurrent protection device using the same procedure. The larger of the two is used.

See Figures 19-2(a) and **(b)** for a feeder supplying motors and air-conditioning units.

Note, the air-conditioning unit is the largest motor and not one of the motors in the group.

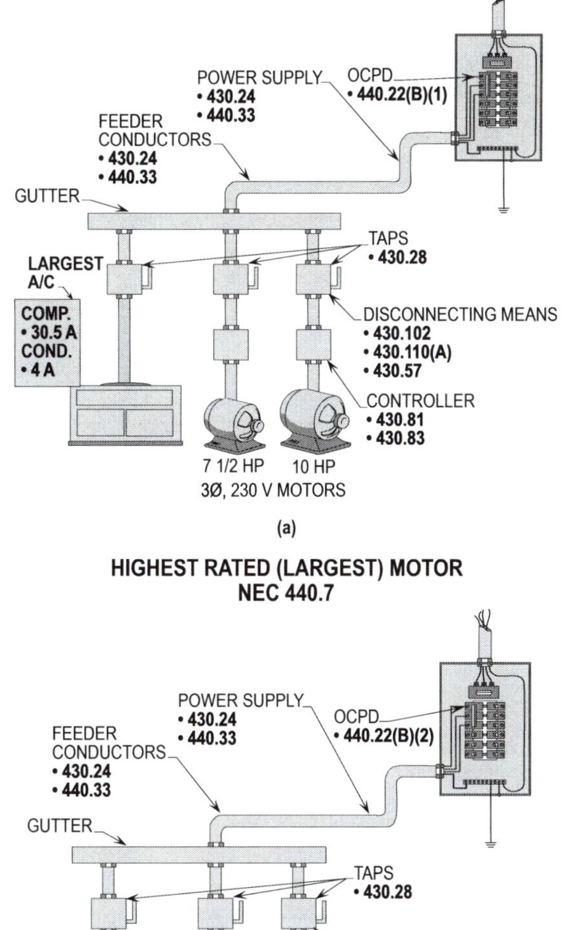

Figure 19-2(a) and (b). The calculation procedure for sizing conductors and overcurrent protection device where the air-conditioning unit or motor is the largest in the group of air-conditioning units and motors.

SINGLE MACHINE
440.8

Each motor controller shall be provided with a disconnecting means. Air-conditioning and through refrigeration systems are considered a single machine even they consist of any number of motors. The number of disconnecting means to be provided is determined by applying **430.87, Ex. 2** and **430.112, Ex.**

DISCONNECTING MEANS
440.11

The full-load current rating of the nameplate or the nameplate branch-circuit selection current of the compressor, whichever is greater, shall be used to size the branch-circuit conductors and the disconnecting means to disconnect air-conditioning and refrigeration equipment.

RATING AND INTERRUPTING CAPACITY
440.12

The full-load current rating of the nameplate or the nameplate branch-circuit selection current of the compressor, whichever is greater, shall be sized at 115 percent to size the disconnecting means. A horsepower rated switch, circuit breaker, or other switches shall be permitted to be used as the disconnecting means per **430.109(A)(1)** and **430.110(A)**. **(See Figure 19-3)**

> **Design Tip:** A minimum load is derived when applying 115 percent for sizing the disconnecting means. Therefore, on larger units the 115 percent may not be of sufficient ampacity for opening the circuit under load.

The horsepower amperage rating shall be selected from **Tables 430.247 through Table 430.250** when corresponding to the nameplate rating or branch-circuit selection current of the motor-compressor or equipment when listed in amperage and not horsepower. The horsepower amperage rating for locked-rotor current shall be selected from **Tables 430.251(A)** and **(B)** when the nameplate fails to list the locked-rotor current.

Note, the disconnecting means shall be sized with enough capacity in horsepower to be capable of disconnecting the total locked-rotor current. **(See Figure 19-4)**

The full-load current rating (in amps) of the nameplate shall be permitted to be used to size a circuit breaker at 115 percent or more to disconnect a hermetically sealed motor from the power circuit. **(See Figure 19-5)**

Design Tip: The circuit breaker shall be sized at 115 percent or more of the branch-circuit selection current if it is greater in rating, so as to be capable of disconnecting the circuit safely.

Two or more hermetic motors or combination loads such as hermetic motor loads, standard motor loads, and other loads shall have their separate values totaled to determine the rating of a single disconnecting means. This total rating shall be sized at 115 percent to determine the size disconnecting means required to disconnect the circuits and elements in a safe and reliable manner. **(See Figure 19-6)**

CORD-CONNECTED EQUIPMENT 440.13

For cord-and-plug connected equipment such as room air conditioners, home refrigerators and freezers, drinking water coolers, and beverage dispensers, a separable connector or an attachment plug and receptacle shall be permitted to be used to serve as a disconnecting means. **(See Figure 19-7)**

Design Tip: In some cases, room air conditioners shall not be permitted to have a cord-and-plug connection to serve as their disconnecting means, as when unit switches for manual control are installed in air conditioners mounted over 6 ft (1.8 m) above finished grade.

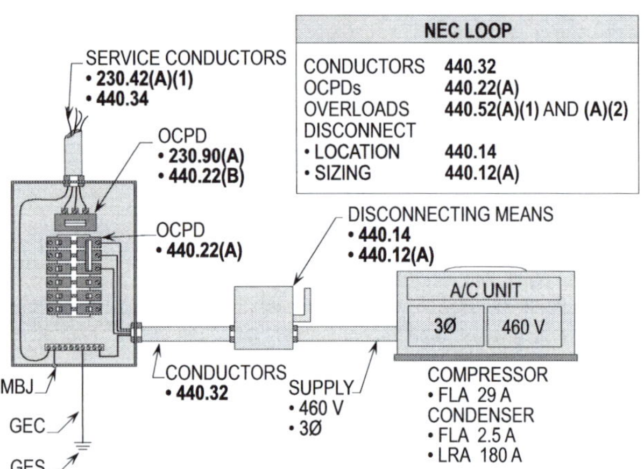

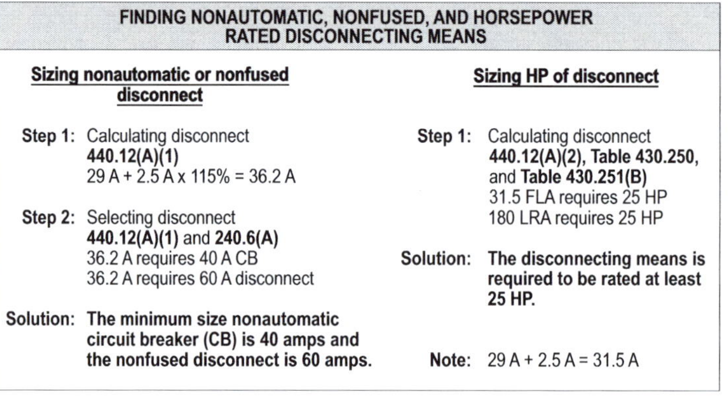

FINDING NONAUTOMATIC, NONFUSED, AND HORSEPOWER RATED DISCONNECTING MEANS

<u>Sizing nonautomatic or nonfused disconnect</u>		<u>Sizing HP of disconnect</u>
Step 1:	Calculating disconnect **440.12(A)(1)** 29 A + 2.5 A x 115% = 36.2 A	**Step 1:** Calculating disconnect **440.12(A)(2), Table 430.250,** and **Table 430.251(B)** 31.5 FLA requires 25 HP 180 LRA requires 25 HP
Step 2:	Selecting disconnect **440.12(A)(1)** and **240.6(A)** 36.2 A requires 40 A CB 36.2 A requires 60 A disconnect	**Solution:** **The disconnecting means is required to be rated at least 25 HP.**
Solution:	**The minimum size nonautomatic circuit breaker (CB) is 40 amps and the nonfused disconnect is 60 amps.**	**Note:** 29 A + 2.5 A = 31.5 A

**RATING AND INTERRUPTING CAPACITY
NEC 440.12(A)**

Figure 19-3. The full-load current rating (in amps) of the nameplate or the nameplate's branch-circuit selection current of the compressor, whichever is greater, shall be sized at 115 percent to size the disconnecting means.

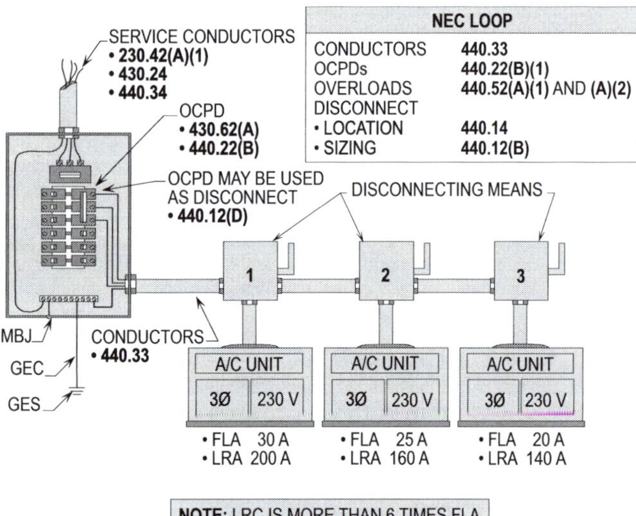

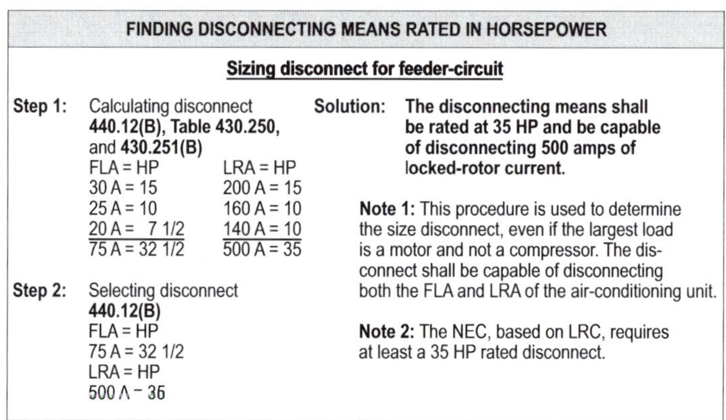

FINDING DISCONNECTING MEANS RATED IN HORSEPOWER

<u>Sizing disconnect for feeder-circuit</u>

Step 1:	Calculating disconnect **440.12(B), Table 430.250,** and **430.251(B)** FLA = HP LRA = HP 30 A = 15 200 A = 15 25 A = 10 160 A = 10 20 A = 7 1/2 140 A = 10 75 A = 32 1/2 500 A = 35	**Solution:** **The disconnecting means shall be rated at 35 HP and be capable of disconnecting 500 amps of locked-rotor current.**
Step 2:	Selecting disconnect **440.12(B)** FLA = HP 75 A = 32 1/2 LRA = HP 500 A = 35	**Note 1:** This procedure is used to determine the size disconnect, even if the largest load is a motor and not a compressor. The disconnect shall be capable of disconnecting both the FLA and LRA of the air-conditioning unit. **Note 2:** The NEC, based on LRC, requires at least a 35 HP rated disconnect.

**RATING AND INTERRUPTING CAPACITY
NEC 440.12(B)**

Figure 19-4. Sizing horsepower rating to select disconnecting means based upon locked-rotor current.

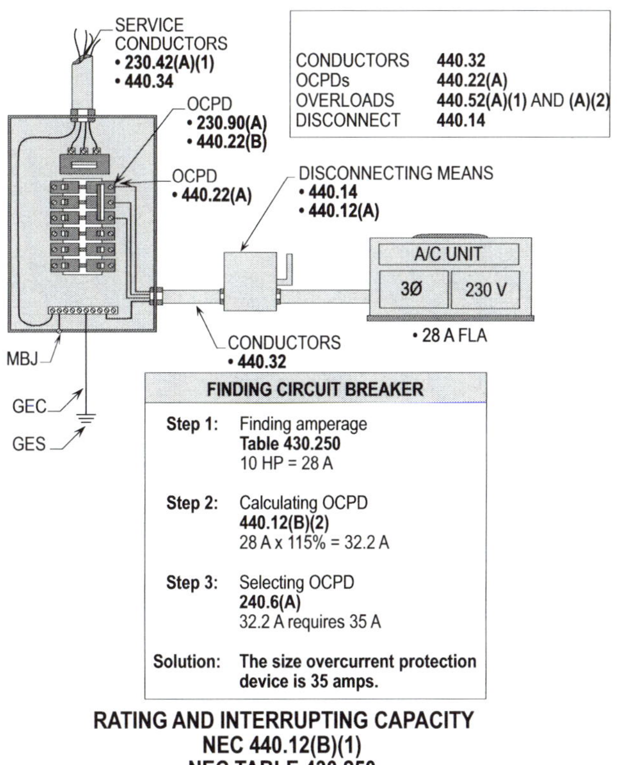

RATING AND INTERRUPTING CAPACITY
NEC 440.12(B)(1)
NEC TABLE 430.250

Figure 19-5. The full-load current rating of the nameplate shall be permitted to be used to size a circuit breaker at 115 percent or more to disconnect a hermetically sealed motor from the power circuit.

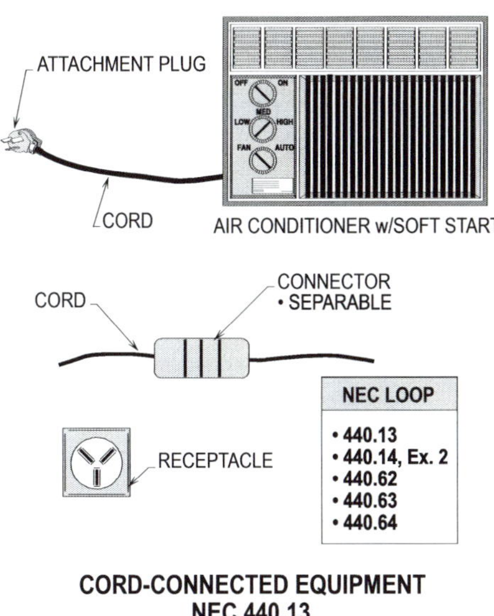

CORD-CONNECTED EQUIPMENT
NEC 440.13

Figure 19-7. Cord-and-plug connected equipment such as room air conditioners, home refrigerators and freezers, drinking water coolers, and beverage dispensers shall be permitted to be disconnected by a cord and receptacle. A separable connector or an attachment plug and receptacle shall be permitted to be used to serve as such disconnecting means.

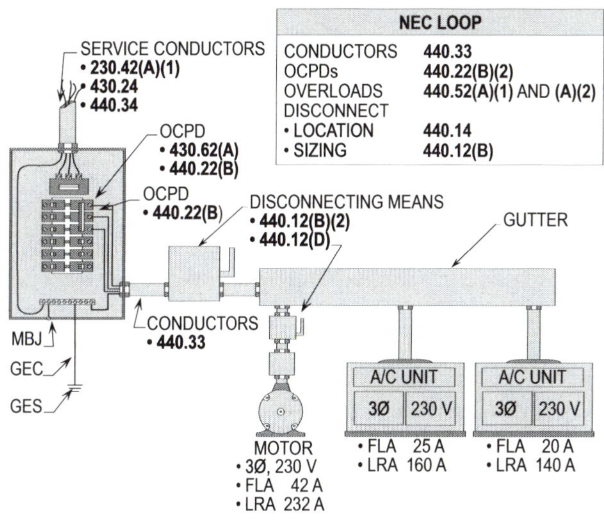

RATING AND INTERRUPTING CAPACITY
NEC 440.12(B)(1) AND (B)(2)

Figure 19-6. Two or more hermetic motors or combination loads, such as hermetic motor loads, standard motor loads, and other loads, shall have their separate values totaled to determine the rating of a single disconnecting means.

LOCATION
440.14

The disconnecting means for air-conditioning or refrigeration equipment shall be located within sight and within 50 ft (15 m) and shall be readily accessible to the user. An additional circuit breaker or disconnecting switch shall be provided at the equipment if the air-conditioning or refrigeration equipment is not within sight or within 50 ft (15 m) per **Article 100**. The disconnecting means shall be permitted to be installed within or on the air-conditioning or refrigeration equipment. For the use of unit switches located in air-conditioning units, review **422.34** per the AHJ. **(See Figure 19-8)**

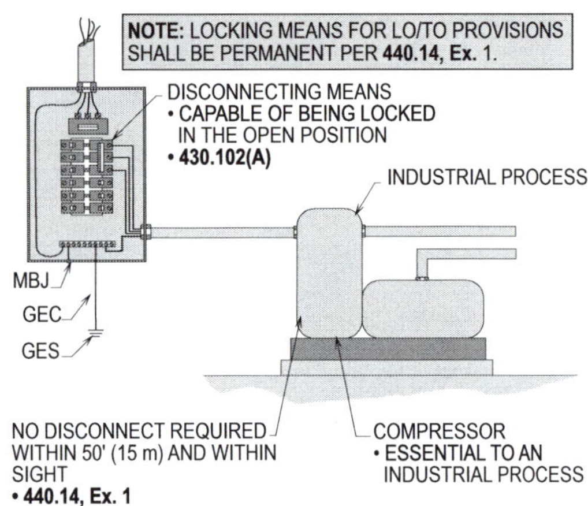

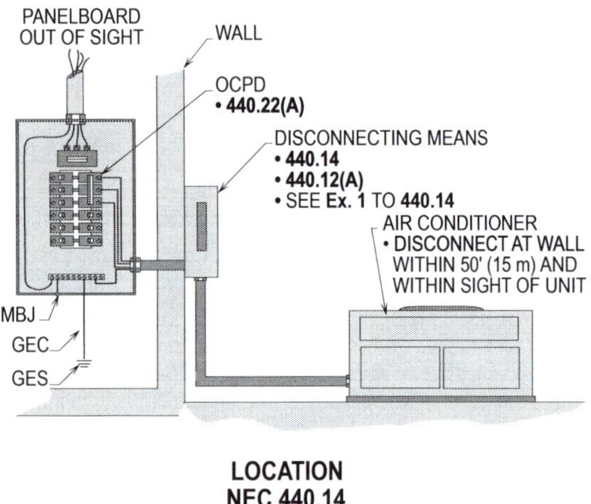

Figure 19-8. The disconnecting means for air-conditioning or refrigeration equipment shall be located within sight and within 50 ft (15 m) per **Article 100** and shall be readily accessible to the user. An additional circuit breaker or disconnecting switch shall be provided at the equipment if the air-conditioning or refrigeration equipment is not within sight or within 50 ft (15 m).

APPLICATION AND SELECTION
440.22

The branch-circuit fuse or circuit breaker ratings for hermetically sealed motors shall be sized with enough capacity to allow the motor to start and develop speed without tripping open the overcurrent protection device due to the momentary inrush current of the compressor and other elements. Maximum protection is always provided by the ratings and settings of the overcurrent protection device being sized with values as low as possible. Hermetic refrigerant motor-compressors shall be protected by properly sizing and selecting the ratings and settings of the overcurrent protection devices to protect the branch-circuit

conductors and other elements in the circuit from short-circuit and ground-fault conditions.

RATING AND SETTING FOR INDIVIDUAL MOTOR-COMPRESSORS
440.22(A)

The overcurrent protection device for hermetic seal compressors shall be selected at 175 percent (for minimum) or 225 percent (for maximum) of the compressor FLA rating or the branch-circuit selection circuit current, whichever is greater. **(See Figure 19-9)**

Overcurrent protection devices for hermetically sealed compressors shall be permitted to be selected up to 225 percent to permit the motor to start if the compressor will not start and develop speed when the rating is 175 percent or less.

Design Tip: A normal circuit breaker shall not be installed when the equipment is marked for a particular fuse size or HACR circuit breaker rating. The branch-circuit conductors shall be protected only by that specified fuse size or HACR circuit breaker rating.

RATING OR SETTING FOR EQUIPMENT
440.22(B)

When sizing the overcurrent protection device, the rating or setting shall be selected and comply with the number of hermetic motors, or combination of hermetic motors, and standard motors installed on a circuit.

SIZING OVERCURRENT PROTECTION DEVICE FOR TWO OR MORE HERMETIC MOTORS
440.22(B)(1)

The overcurrent protection device for a feeder supplying two or more air-conditioning or refrigerating units shall be sized to allow the largest unit to start and allow the other units to start at different intervals of time. The full-load current rating, in amps, of the nameplate or the branch-circuit selection current rating of the largest motor, whichever is greater, shall be sized at 175 percent if there are two or more hermetically sealed motors installed on the same feeder. **(See Figure 19-10)**

Overcurrent protection devices for hermetically sealed motors shall be permitted to be selected up to 225 percent to allow the motor to start if the motor will not start and develop speed when the rating is selected at 175 percent or less. **(See Figure 19-11)**

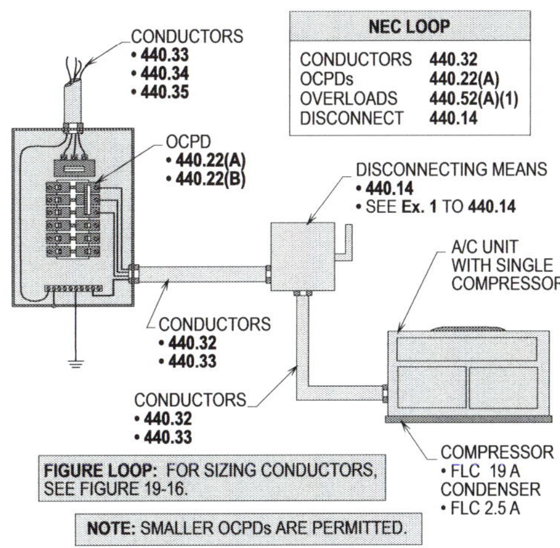

FINDING MINIMUM AND MAXIMUM SIZE OCPD OF THE A/C UNIT

Sizing minimum OCPD	Sizing maximum size OCPD
Step 1: Calculating OCPD **440.22(A)** 19 A x 175% + 2.5 A = 35.75 A	**Step 1:** Calculating OCPD **440.22(A)** 19 A x 225% + 2.5 A = 45.25 A
Step 2: Selecting OCPD **240.4(G)** and **240.6(A)** 35.75 A requires 35 A	**Step 2:** Selecting OCPD **240.4(G)** and **240.6(A)** 45.25 A requires 45 A
Solution: The minimum size overcurrent protection device is 35 amps.	**Solution:** The maximum size overcurrent protection device is 45 amps.

RATING AND SETTING FOR INDIVIDUAL MOTOR-COMPRESSORS NEC 440.22(A)

Figure 19-9. The overcurrent protection device for hermetically sealed compressors shall be selected at 175 percent (for minimum) or 225 percent (for maximum) of the compressor's FLA rating or the branch-circuit selection circuit current, whichever is greater.

Note, a smaller size overcurrent protection device shall be permitted to be used than selected per solution, if the air-conditioning unit will start and run.

SIZING OVERCURRENT PROTECTION DEVICE FOR HERMETIC MOTOR AND OTHER LOADS WHEN A HERMETICALLY SEALED MOTOR IS THE LARGEST 440.22(B)(1)

When installing hermetically sealed motors and other loads such as motors on the same circuit, and the largest motor of the group is hermetic, the same procedure used for two or more hermetic motors on a feeder shall be used to size the overcurrent protection device. The full-load current rating of the nameplate or the branch-circuit selection current rating (in amps) of the largest hermetic motor, whichever is greater, shall be sized at 175 percent, and the sum of the full-load current ratings, in amps, of the other motors added to this largest hermetic motor load.

SIZING OVERCURRENT PROTECTION DEVICE FOR HERMETIC MOTORS AND OTHER LOADS WHEN A MOTOR IS THE LARGEST 440.22(B)(2)

When installing hermetically sealed motors and other loads such as motors on the same circuit, and the largest in the group is a motor, the overcurrent protection device is sized and selected based on the percentages from **Table 430.52**. The maximum branch-circuit overcurrent protection device shall be used when the standard motor is the largest of the group, and the sum of the full-load current ratings of the remaining hermetically sealed motor and other motors of the group added to the largest motor. The next lower standard size overcurrent protection device below this total sum shall be installed per **240.6(A)**. **(See Figure 19-12)**

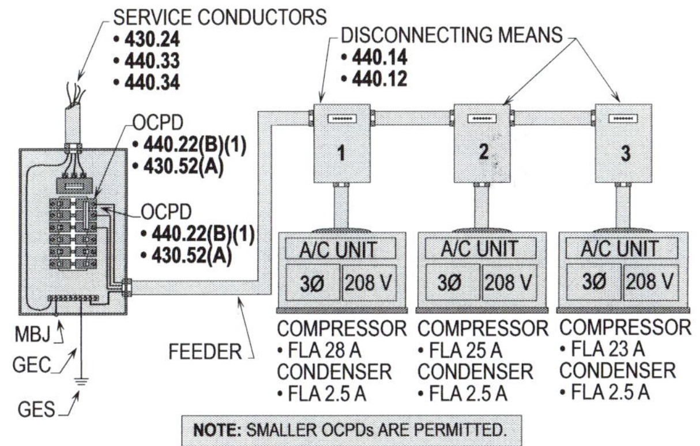

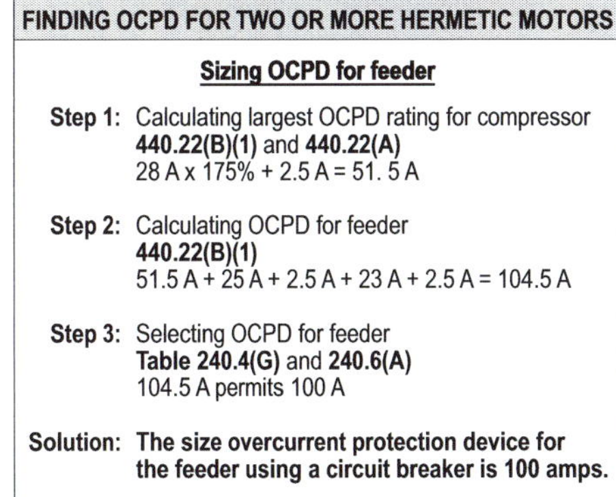

FINDING OCPD FOR TWO OR MORE HERMETIC MOTORS

Sizing OCPD for feeder

Step 1: Calculating largest OCPD rating for compressor **440.22(B)(1)** and **440.22(A)** 28 A x 175% + 2.5 A = 51.5 A

Step 2: Calculating OCPD for feeder **440.22(B)(1)** 51.5 A + 25 A + 2.5 A + 23 A + 2.5 A = 104.5 A

Step 3: Selecting OCPD for feeder **Table 240.4(G)** and **240.6(A)** 104.5 A permits 100 A

Solution: The size overcurrent protection device for the feeder using a circuit breaker is 100 amps.

SIZING OVERCURRENT PROTECTION DEVICE FOR TWO OR MORE HERMETIC MOTORS NEC 440.22(B)(1)

Figure 19-10. The full-load current rating (in amps) of the nameplate or the branch-circuit selection current rating of the largest motor, whichever is greater, shall be sized at 175 percent if there are two or more hermetically sealed motors installed on the same feeder.

Design Tip: The next larger standard size is not permitted to be installed, for there is not an exception to permit the next higher size per **440.22(B)(2)** or **430.62(A)**.

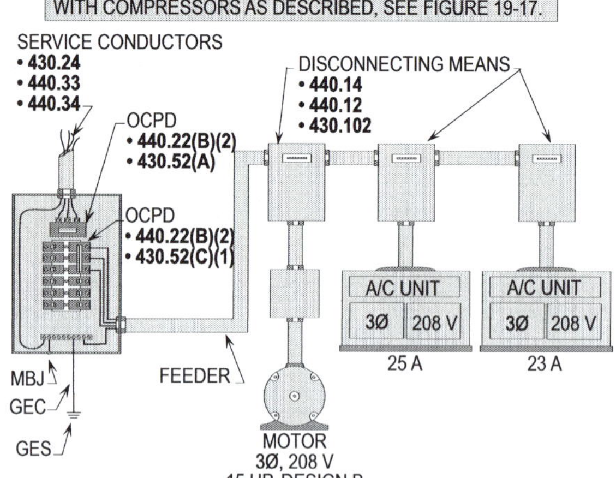

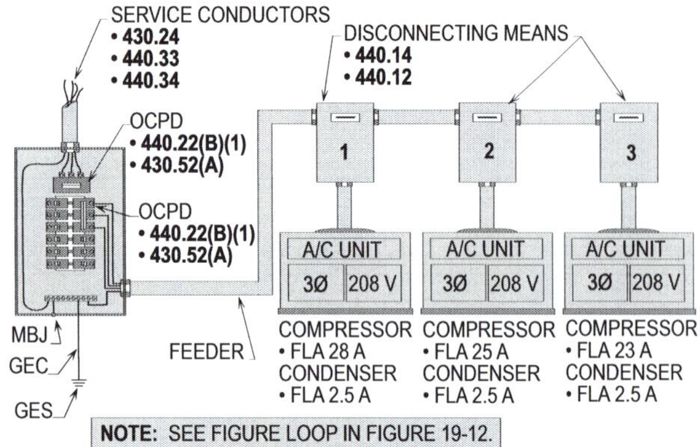

FINDING OCPD FOR TWO OR MORE HERMETIC MOTORS

Sizing OCPD for feeder

Step 1: Calculating largest OCPD rating for compressor
440.22(B)(1) and **440.22(A)**
28 A x 225% + 2.5 A = 65.5 A

Step 2: Calculating OCPD for feeder
440.22(B)(1)
65.5 A + 25 A + 2.5 A + 23 A + 2.5 A = 118.5 A

Step 3: Selecting OCPD for feeder
240.4(G) and **240.6(A)**
118.5 A allows 110 A

Solution: The size overcurrent protection device for the feeder using a circuit breaker is 110 amps.

SIZING OVERCURRENT PROTECTION DEVICE FOR
TWO OR MORE HERMETIC MOTORS
NEC 440.22(B)(1)

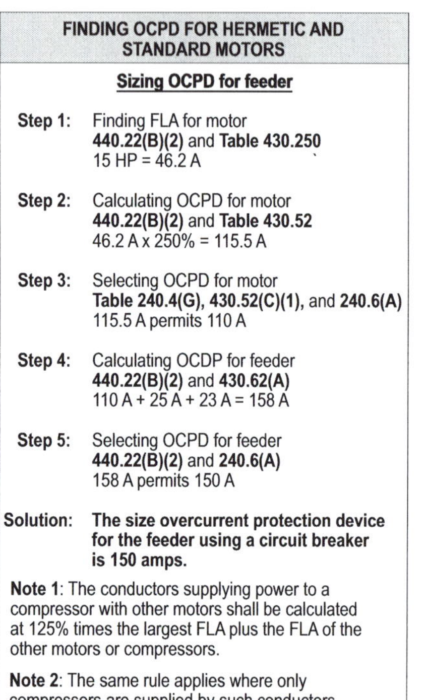

FINDING OCPD FOR HERMETIC AND STANDARD MOTORS

Sizing OCPD for feeder

Step 1: Finding FLA for motor
440.22(B)(2) and **Table 430.250**
15 HP = 46.2 A

Step 2: Calculating OCPD for motor
440.22(B)(2) and **Table 430.52**
46.2 A x 250% = 115.5 A

Step 3: Selecting OCPD for motor
Table 240.4(G), **430.52(C)(1)**, and **240.6(A)**
115.5 A permits 110 A

Step 4: Calculating OCDP for feeder
440.22(B)(2) and **430.62(A)**
110 A + 25 A + 23 A = 158 A

Step 5: Selecting OCPD for feeder
440.22(B)(2) and **240.6(A)**
158 A permits 150 A

Solution: The size overcurrent protection device for the feeder using a circuit breaker is 150 amps.

Note 1: The conductors supplying power to a compressor with other motors shall be calculated at 125% times the largest FLA plus the FLA of the other motors or compressors.

Note 2: The same rule applies where only compressors are supplied by such conductors.

SIZING OVERCURRENT PROTECTION DEVICE FOR
HERMETIC MOTORS AND OTHER LOADS WHEN A
MOTOR IS THE LARGEST
NEC 440.22(B)(2)

Figure 19-11. Overcurrent protection devices for hermetically sealed motors shall be permitted to be selected up to 225 percent to allow the motor to start if the motor will not start and develop speed.

USING A 15 OR 20 AMP OVERCURRENT PROTECTION DEVICE
440.22(B)(2), Ex. 1

Where the equipment will start, run, and operate on a 15 or 20 amp, 120 volt, single-phase branch circuit, or a 15 amp, 208 volt or 240 volt, a single-phase branch circuit, with a 15 or 20 amp overcurrent protection device, such device shall be permitted to be used to protect the branch circuit. However, the values of the overcurrent protection device in the branch circuit shall not exceed the values marked on the nameplate of the equipment. **(See Figure 19-13)**

Figure 19-12. When hermetically sealed motors and other loads, such as motors, are being installed on the same circuit, and the largest in the group is a motor, the overcurrent protection device shall be sized and selected based on the percentages from **Table 430.52**.

USING A CORD-AND-PLUG CONNECTION NOT OVER 250 VOLTS
440.22(B)(2), Ex. 2

The rating of the overcurrent protection device shall be determined by using the rating of the nameplate of the cord-and-plug connected equipment serving single-phase, 250 volts or less, hermetically sealed motors. **(See Figure 19-14)**

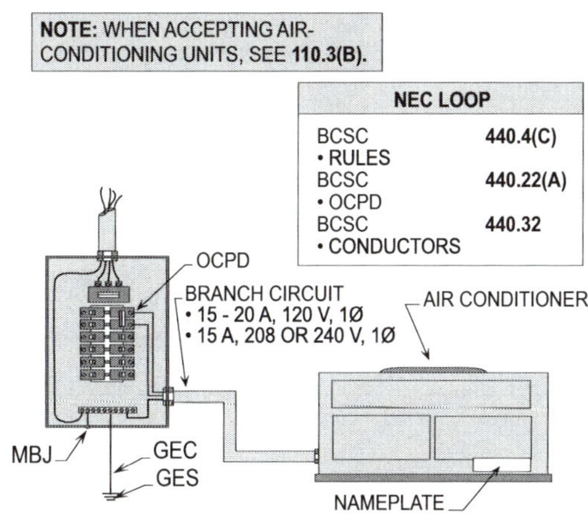

USING A 15 OR 20 AMP OVERCURRENT PROTECTION DEVICE
NEC 440.22(B)(2), Ex. 1

Figure 19-13. Where the equipment will start, run, and operate on a 15 or 20 amp, 120 volt, single-phase branch-circuit, or a 15 amp, 208 volt or 240 volt, a single-phase branch-circuit, a 15 or 20 amp overcurrent protection device shall be permitted to be used to protect the branch circuit.

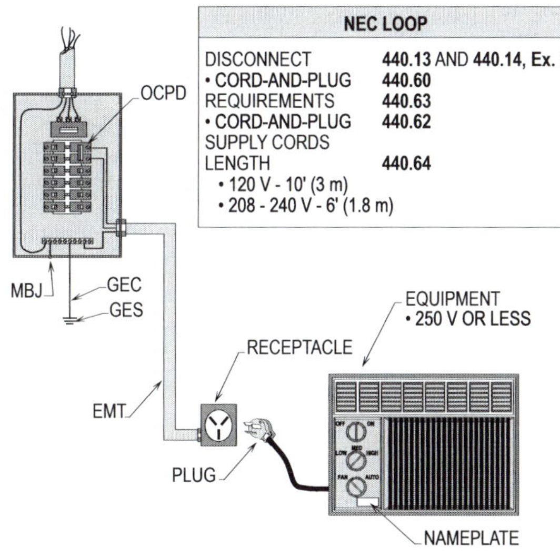

USING A CORD-AND-PLUG CONNECTION NOT OVER 250 VOLTS
NEC 440.22(B)(2), Ex. 2

Figure 19-14. The rating of the overcurrent protection device shall be determined by using the rating of the nameplate of the cord-and-plug connected equipment having single-phase, 250 volt or less, hermetically sealed motors.

PROTECTIVE DEVICE RATING NOT TO EXCEED THE MANUFACTURER'S VALUES
440.22(C)

The manufacturer's values marked on the equipment shall not be exceeded by the overcurrent protection device rating, where the maximum overcurrent protective device ratings on the manufacturer's heater table for use with a motor controller are less than the rating or setting per **440.22(A)** and **(B)**. **(See Figure 19-15)**

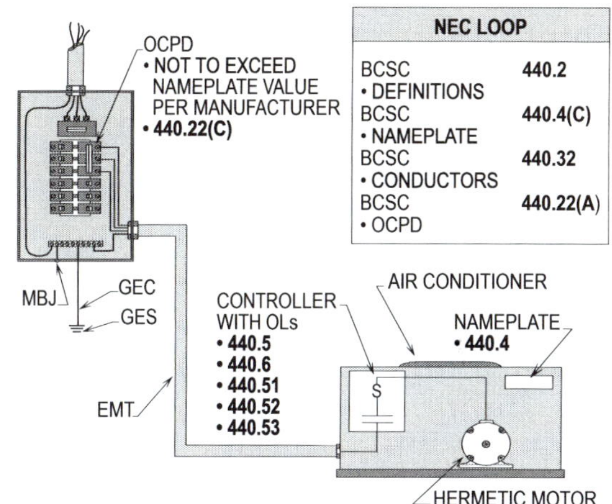

PROTECTIVE DEVICE RATING NOT TO EXCEED THE MANUFACTURER'S VALUES
NEC 440.22(C)

Figure 19-15. The manufacturer's values marked on the equipment shall not be exceeded by the overcurrent protection device rating where the maximum overcurrent protective device ratings on the manufacturer's heater table for use with a motor controller are less than the rating or setting per **440.22(A)** and **(B)**.

BRANCH-CIRCUIT CONDUCTORS
440.31

In general, to prevent conductors and motor elements of the branch circuit from overheating, the conductors shall be sized with enough capacity to allow a hermetic motor to start and run. To ensure adequate sizing, a derating factor of 80 percent shall be applied to the branch-circuit conductors or such conductors shall be sized at 125 percent of the load.

SINGLE MOTOR-COMPRESSORS 440.32

The conductors supplying power to an air-conditioning or refrigerating unit shall be sized to carry the load of the unit plus an overload for a period of time that will not damage the elements. The full-load current rating of the nameplate or branch-circuit selection current, whichever is greater, shall be sized at 125 percent to size and select the conductors supplying hermetically sealed motors. **(See Figure 19-16)**

TWO OR MORE MOTOR-COMPRESSORS 440.33

Two or more compressors plus other motor loads can be connected to a feeder. The largest compressor shall be calculated at 125 percent of its FLA, and the remaining compressor loads are added to this total at 100 percent of their FLA ratings. For units with a branch-circuit selection current, the circuit conductors shall be selected and based on the nameplate values. **(See Figure 19-17)**

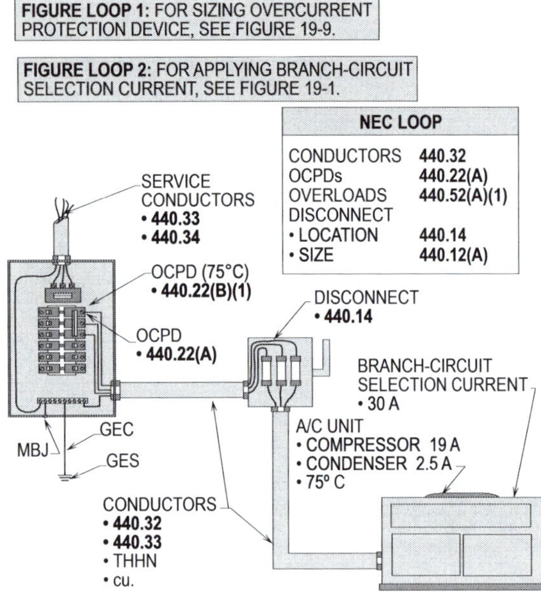

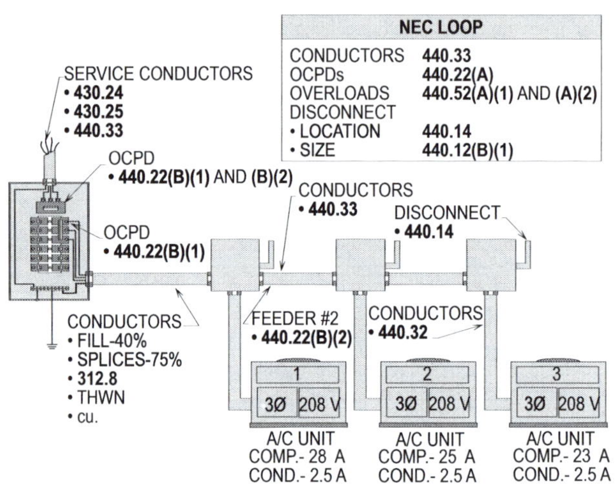

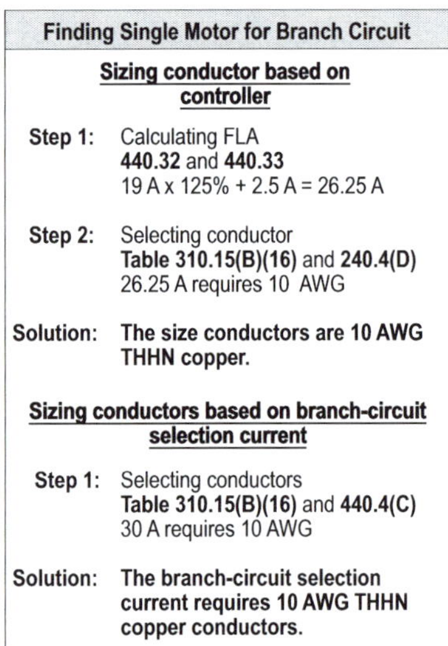

Finding Single Motor for Branch Circuit

Sizing conductor based on controller

Step 1: Calculating FLA
440.32 and **440.33**
19 A x 125% + 2.5 A = 26.25 A

Step 2: Selecting conductor
Table 310.15(B)(16) and **240.4(D)**
26.25 A requires 10 AWG

Solution: **The size conductors are 10 AWG THHN copper.**

Sizing conductors based on branch-circuit selection current

Step 1: Selecting conductors
Table 310.15(B)(16) and **440.4(C)**
30 A requires 10 AWG

Solution: **The branch-circuit selection current requires 10 AWG THHN copper conductors.**

SINGLE MOTOR-COMPRESSORS
NEC 440.32

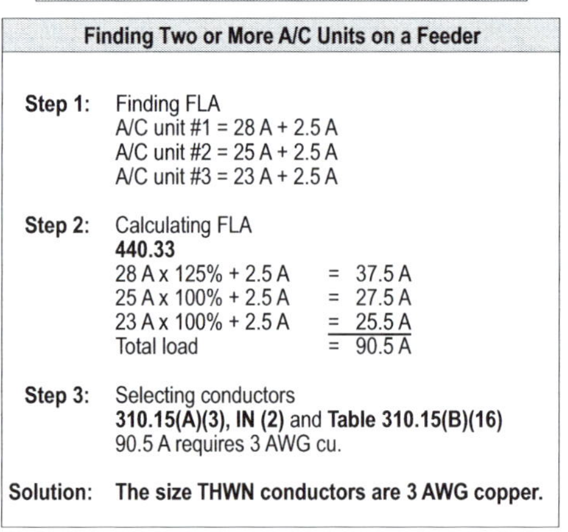

Finding Two or More A/C Units on a Feeder

Step 1: Finding FLA
A/C unit #1 = 28 A + 2.5 A
A/C unit #2 = 25 A + 2.5 A
A/C unit #3 = 23 A + 2.5 A

Step 2: Calculating FLA
440.33
28 A x 125% + 2.5 A   = 37.5 A
25 A x 100% + 2.5 A   = 27.5 A
23 A x 100% + 2.5 A   = 25.5 A
Total load   = 90.5 A

Step 3: Selecting conductors
310.15(A)(3), IN (2) and **Table 310.15(B)(16)**
90.5 A requires 3 AWG cu.

Solution: **The size THWN conductors are 3 AWG copper.**

TWO OR MORE MOTOR-COMPRESSORS
NEC 440.33

Figure 19-16. The full-load current rating of the nameplate or branch-circuit selection current, whichever is greater, shall be sized at 125 percent to size and select the conductors supplying hermetically sealed motors.

Figure 19-17. Two or more compressors plus other motor loads can be connected to a feeder. The largest compressor shall be calculated at 125 percent of its FLA and the remaining compressor loads are added to this total at 100 percent of their FLA ratings.

COMBINATION LOAD
440.34

Two or more motor-compressors with motor loads plus other loads may be connected to a feeder or service conductors. The largest compressor or motor load shall be calculated at 125 percent plus 100 percent of the remaining compressors and motors. The other loads shall be calculated at 125 percent for continuous and 100 percent for noncontinuous operation per **215.2(A)(1)**, and these total values used to select conductors. **(See Figure 19-18)**

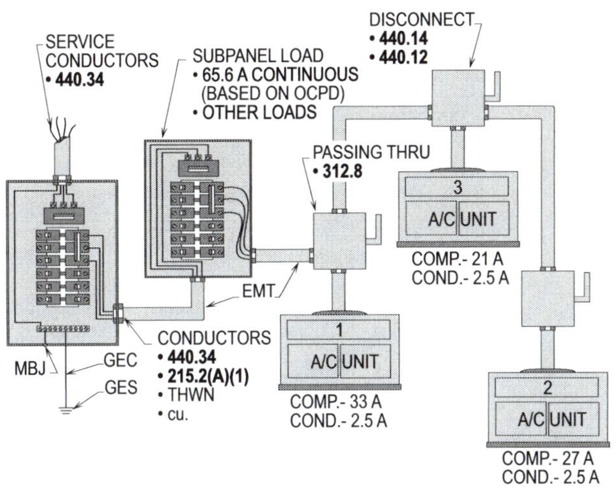

Finding Two or More A/C Units with Other Loads

Step 1: Finding FLA
440.34
A/C unit #1 = 33 A + 2.5 A
A/C unit #2 = 27 A + 2.5 A
A/C unit #3 = 21 A + 2.5 A
Other loads = 65.6 A

Step 2: Calculating FLA
440.34 and **215.2(A)(1)**
33 A x 125% + 2.5 A = 43.75 A
27 A x 100% + 2.5 A = 29.5 A
21 A x 100% + 2.5 A = 23.5 A
65.6 A x 125% = 82 A
Total load = 178.75 A

Step 3: Selecting conductors
310.15(A)(3), IN (2) and **Table 310.15(B)(16)**
178.75 A requires 3/0 AWG cu.

Solution: **The size THWN conductors for the feeder are 3/0 AWG copper.**

Note: The load of 178.75 amps requires the conductors and overcurrent protection device to be rated at 200 amps or per **440.22(B)**.

COMBINATION LOAD
NEC 440.34

Figure 19-18. Two or more motor-compressors with motor loads plus other loads may be connected to a feeder or service conductors. The largest compressor or motor load shall be calculated at 125 percent, plus 100 percent of the remaining compressors and motors, plus the other loads.

MULTIMOTOR AND COMBINATION LOAD EQUIPMENT
440.35

The marking on the nameplate shall be used when sizing the branch-circuit conductors for multimotor and combination load equipment. The conductors shall be installed to have a rating equal to the nameplate rating. Each individual motor or load contained in the unit shall not be required to be calculated individually to size and select the conductors.

CONTROLLERS FOR MOTOR-COMPRESSORS
440.41

When installing the wiring for a motor controller, the circuit supply conductors are run from a motor controller and connected to the terminals of the compressor. The full-load current rating and the locked-rotor current rating of the compressor motor shall be sized for continuous operation.

MOTOR-COMPRESSOR CONTROLLER RATING
440.41(A)

The full-load current rating of the nameplate or the branch-circuit selection current ratings, whichever is greater, shall be used to size and select the motor controller. If necessary, the locked-rotor current rating of the motor shall be permitted to be used to size and select the motor controller. **(See Figure 19-19)**

Design Tip: The motor controller shall be sized and selected using the same procedure as used for the sizing of the disconnecting means.

MOTOR-COMPRESSOR AND BRANCH-CIRCUIT OVERLOAD PROTECTION
440.51

The overload (OL) protection for compressors may be accomplished by using overcurrent protection devices in separate enclosures, separate overload relays, or thermal protectors that are an integral part of the compressor.

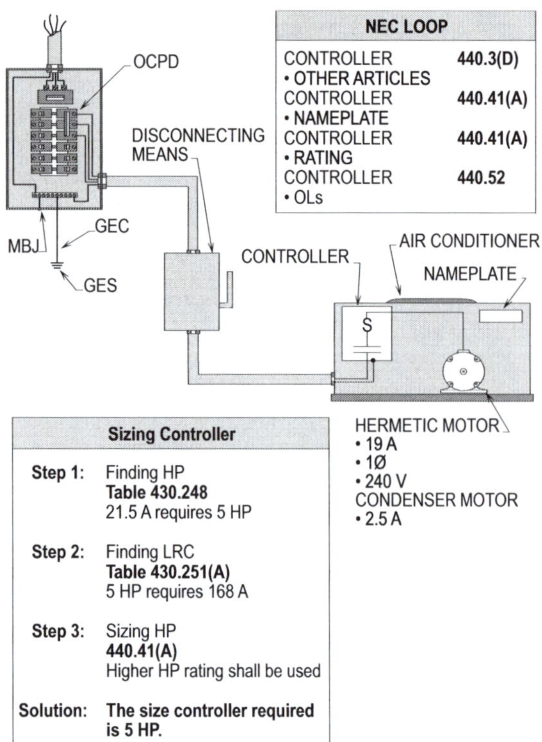

Figure 19-19. The full-load current rating of the nameplate or the branch-circuit selection current ratings, whichever is greater, shall be used to size and select the motor controller.

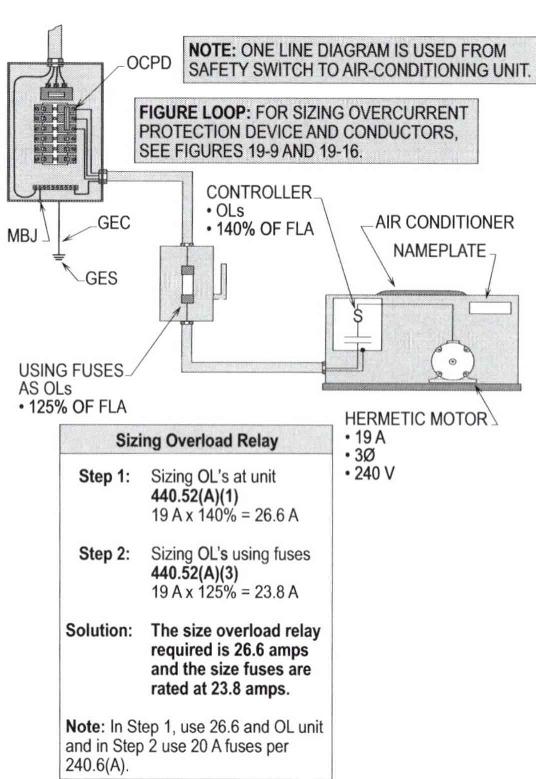

Figure 19-20. The overload relay for the motor-compressor shall trip at not more than 140 percent of the full-load current rating. If a fuse or circuit breaker is used for the protection of the motor-compressor, it shall trip at not more than 125 percent of the full-load current rating.

APPLICATION AND SELECTION
440.52

The overload relay for the motor-compressor shall trip at not more than 140 percent of the full-load current rating. If a fuse or circuit breaker is used for the protection of the motor-compressor, it shall trip at not more than 125 percent of the full-load current rating. **(See Figure 19-20)**

OVERLOAD RELAYS
440.53

Short-circuit and ground-fault protection is not provided by overload relays and thermal protectors. Overload relays and thermal protectors respond to any type of heat buildup and open with a delay action that will not operate instantly, even on short circuits or ground faults. The branch-circuit overcurrent protection device for the circuit shall operate and clear the circuit under short-circuit and ground-fault conditions.

MOTOR-COMPRESSORS AND EQUIPMENT ON A 15 OR 20 AMP BRANCH CIRCUIT NOT CORD-AND-PLUG CONNECTED
440.54

Overload protection shall be provided for direct or fixed-wired motor-compressors and equipment that is connected to 15 or 20 amp, 120 volt, single-phase branch circuits.

Note, 15 amps are used for 240 volt, single-phase branch circuits.

The full-load current rating of the hermetically sealed motor shall be selected at 140 percent when sizing separate overload relays. Hermetic motors shall be provided with fuses or circuit breakers that provide sufficient time delay to allow the motor to come up to running speed without tripping open the circuit due to the high inrush current. **(See Figure 19-21)**

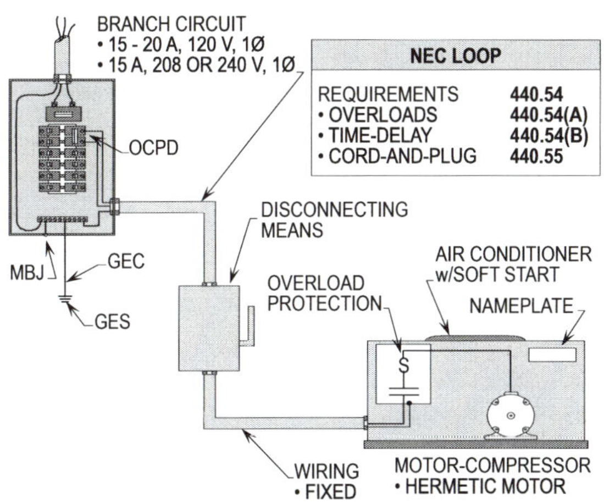

**MOTOR-COMPRESSORS AND EQUIPMENT
ON A 15 OR 20 AMP BRANCH CIRCUIT NOT
CORD-AND-PLUG CONNECTED
NEC 440.54**

Figure 19-21. Overload protection shall be provided for direct or fixed-wired motor-compressors and equipment that is connected to 15 or 20 amp, 120 volt, single-phase branch circuits.

CORD-AND-ATTACHMENT PLUG CONNECTED MOTOR-COMPRESSORS AND EQUIPMENT ON 15 OR 20 AMP BRANCH CIRCUITS 440.55

When attachment plugs and receptacles or cord connectors are used for circuit connection, they shall be rated no higher than 15 or 20 amps for 120 volt, single-phase circuit, or 15 amps, for 208 or 240 volt, single-phase branch circuits. **(See Figure 19-22)**

ROOM AIR-CONDITIONERS 440.60

Room air conditioners are usually cord-and-plug connected when installed on 120/240 volt, single-phase systems. However, they may be hard wired. Air conditioners are always hard-wired when installed on three-phase systems, or on electrical supply systems over 250 volts.

GROUNDING 440.61

The following wiring methods, when utilized to wire in room air conditioners, shall be connected to an equipment grounding conductor:

- Cord-and-plug connected
- Hard wired (if within reach of the ground or grounded object)

- If in contact with metal
- Operating over 150 volts-to-ground
- Wired with metal-clad wiring
- Located in a hazardous location
- Installed in damp location (within reach of the user)

See Figure 19-23 for wiring methods that shall be permitted to be used to ground room air conditioners.

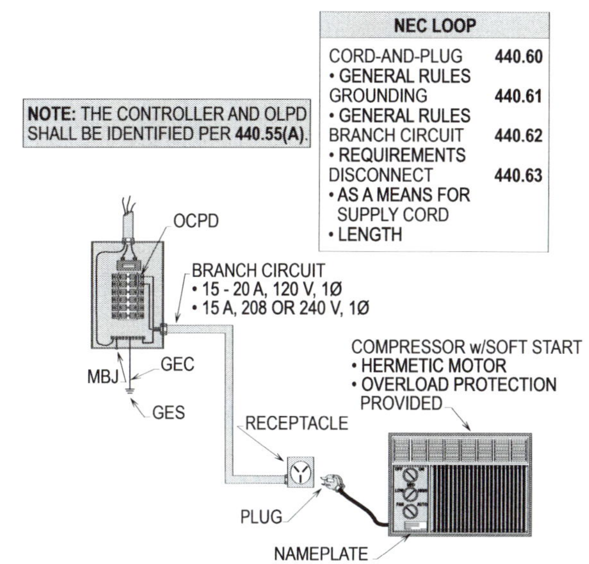

**CORD-AND-ATTACHMENT PLUG CONNECTED
MOTOR-COMPRESSORS AND EQUIPMENT ON
15 OR 20 AMP BRANCH CIRCUITS
NEC 440.55**

Figure 19-22. When attachment plugs and receptacles or cord connectors are used for circuit connection, they shall be rated no higher than 15 or 20 amps, for 120 volt, single-phase circuit, or 15 amps, for 208 or 240 volt, single-phase branch circuits.

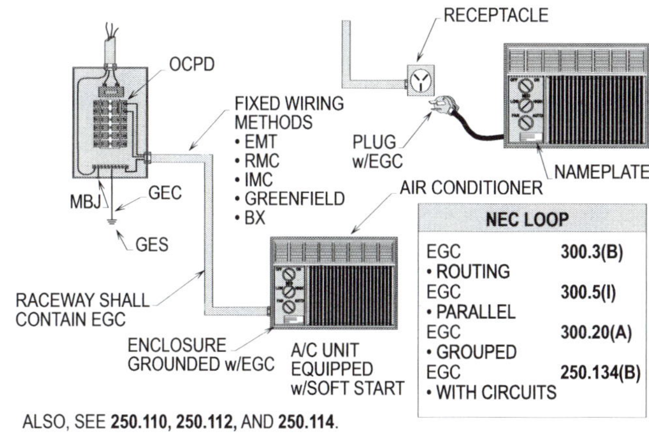

**GROUNDING
NEC 440.61**

Figure 19-23. This illustration shows the wiring methods that shall be permitted to be used to ground room air conditioners.

BRANCH-CIRCUIT REQUIREMENTS
440.62

The full-load current rating of the room air conditioner shall be marked on the nameplate and shall not operate at more than 40 amps on 250 volts. The branch-circuit overcurrent protection device shall be installed with a rating no greater than the circuit conductor's ampacity or the rating of the receptacle serving the unit, whichever is less. The ampacity of a cord-and-plug connected air-conditioning window unit shall not exceed 80 percent of the branch circuit where no other loads are served. If other loads are served by the branch circuit, the cord-and-plug connected air conditioner unit shall not exceed 50 percent of the branch circuit. **[See Figures 19-24(a) and (b)]**

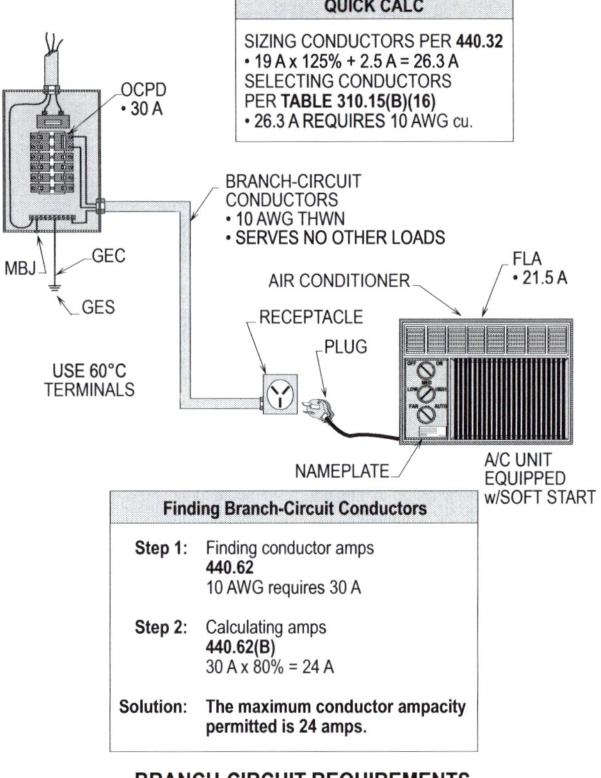

**BRANCH-CIRCUIT REQUIREMENTS
NEC 440.62(B)**

Figure 19-24(a). The ampacity of a cord-and-plug connected air-conditioning window unit shall not exceed 80 percent of the branch circuit where no other loads are served.

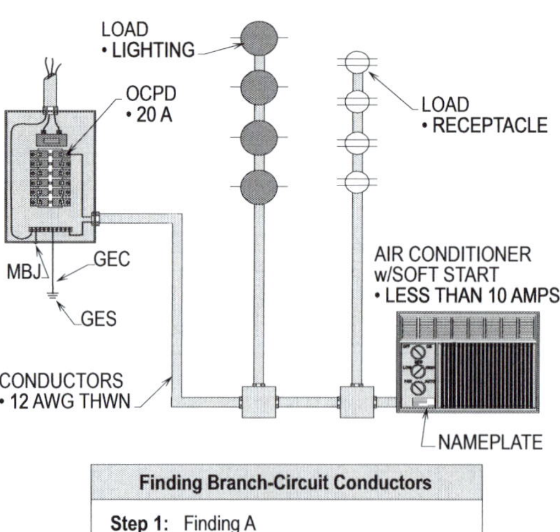

**BRANCH-CIRCUIT REQUIREMENTS
NEC 440.62(C)**

Figure 19-24(b). If other loads are served by the branch-circuit, the cord-and-plug connected air-conditioning unit shall not exceed 50 percent of the branch circuit.

DISCONNECTING MEANS
440.63

A cord-and-plug shall be permitted to serve as the disconnecting means for the room air conditioner if all the following conditions are complied with:

- Operates at 250 volts or less
- Controls are manually operated
- Controls are within 6 ft (1.8 m) of the floor
- Controls are readily accessible to user

A room air conditioner may be hard wired and located within sight of the service equipment, or it may be wired so that it is readily accessible to a disconnecting switch for the user. However, such switch shall be located within sight and within the unit. **[See Figure 19-25(a) and (b)]**

Design Tip: The rules for three-phase room air conditioners shall not be used for these types of units. Three-phase room air conditioners shall be hard wired and shall be installed with a disconnecting means that is readily accessible to the user.

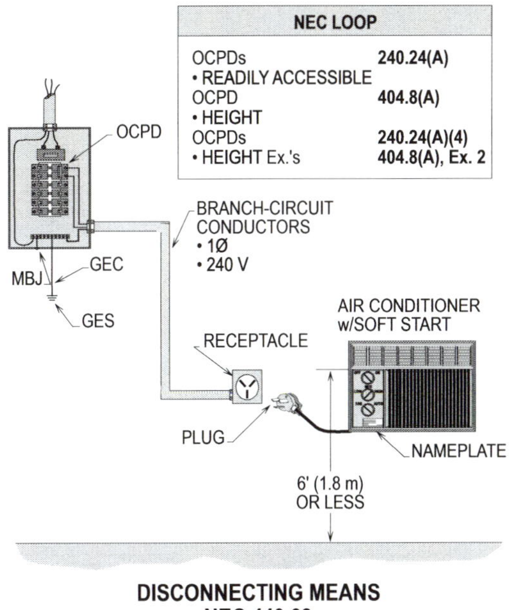

Figure 19-25(a). A cord-and-plug shall be permitted to serve as the disconnecting means for a room air conditioner if it operates at 250 volts or less and its controls are manually operated, within 6 ft (1.8 m) of the floor, and readily accessible to the user.

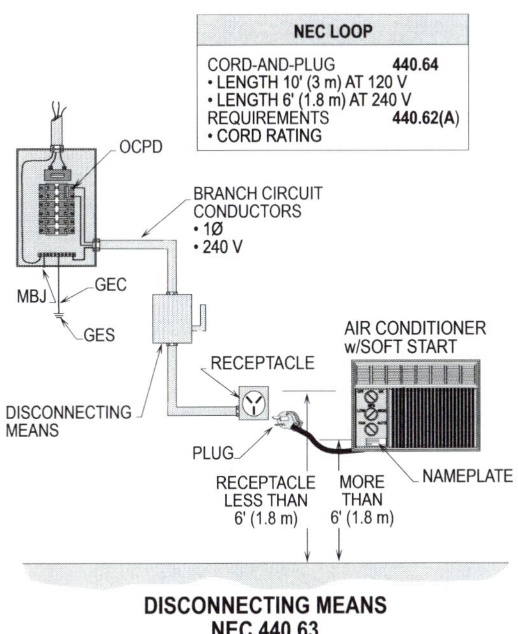

Figure 19-25(b). A cord-and-plug shall be permitted to serve as the disconnecting means even if the room air conditioner's manual controls are located above 6 ft (1.8 m) from the finished grade.

SUPPLY CORDS
440.64

Room air conditioners installed with flexible cords shall be a length that is limited to 10 ft (3 m) for 120 volt circuits and 6 ft (1.8 m) for 208 or 240 volt circuits. Long cords shall not be used because they are dangerous. Long cords can also be a shock or fire hazard. **(See Figure 19-26)**

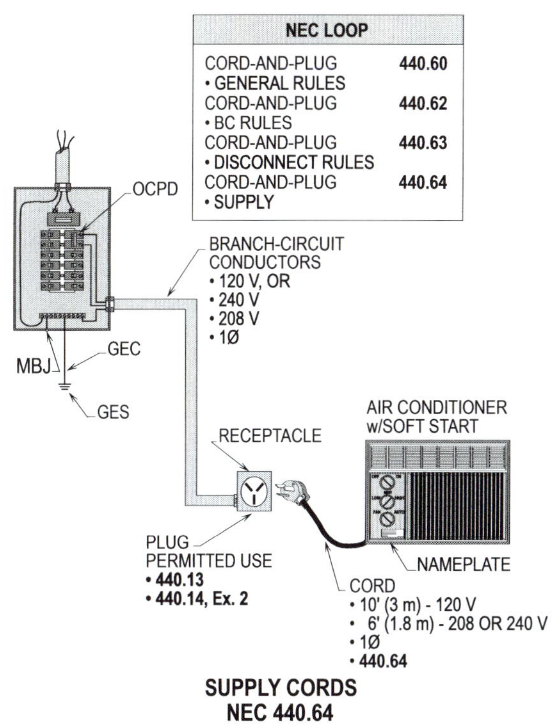

Figure 19-26. Room air conditioners installed with flexible cords shall have a length that is limited to 10 ft (3 m) for 120 volt circuits and 6 ft (1.8 m) for 208 or 240 volt circuits.

LEAKAGE-CURRENT DETECTOR-INTERRUPTER (LCDI) AND ARC-FAULT CIRCUIT INTERRUPTER (AFCI)
440.65

Single-phase cord- and plug-connected room air conditioners shall be provided with factory-installed LCDI or AFCI protection. The LCDI or AFCI protection shall be an integral part of the attachment plug or be located in the power supply cord within 300 mm (12 in.) of the attachment plug. **(See Figure 19-27)**

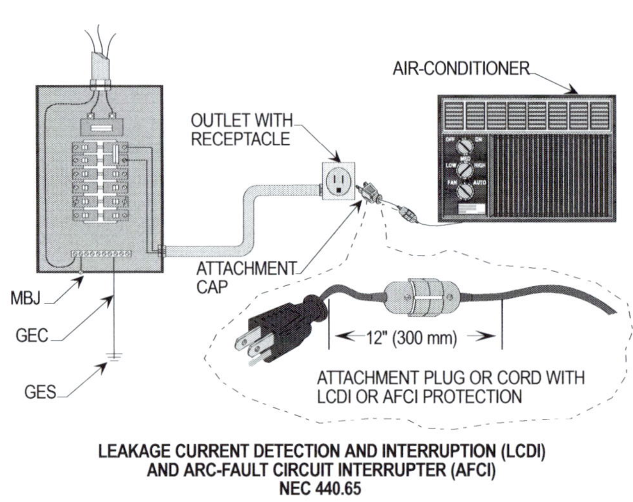

Figure 19-27. This illustration shows guidelines for requiring LCDI or AFCI protection in cord or integral parts of attachment caps.

Chapter 19. Compressor Motors

Section   Answer

1. An additional circuit breaker or disconnecting means shall be provided at the equipment if an A/C unit is not within sight or within _______ ft of the disconnect.

   (a) 25   (b) 40
   (c) 50   (d) 75

2. An overcurrent protection device for hermetic-seal compressors shall be permitted to be selected up to _______ percent of its FLA to allow the motor to start and run.

   (a) 175   (b) 200
   (c) 225   (d) 250

3. If a fuse or circuit breaker is used for the protection of the motor compressor, it shall trip at not more than _______ percent of the full-load current rating.

   (a) 100   (b) 110
   (c) 115   (d) 125

4. The ampacity of a cord-and-plug connected air conditioning (window) unit shall not exceed _______ percent of the branch circuit where no other loads are served.

   (a) 80   (b) 100
   (c) 115   (d) 150

5. Room air conditioners installed with flexible cords shall be of a length that is limited to _______ ft for 120 volt circuits.

   (a) 6   (b) 10
   (c) 12   (d) 15

6. When sizing the conductors for a feeder supplying A/C units and motors, the full-load current in amps of the largest motor (if largest) shall be multiplied by _______ percent.

   (a) 100   (b) 110
   (c) 115   (d) 125

7. The full-load current rating of the nameplate or the nameplate branch-circuit selection current of the compressor, whichever is greater, shall be sized at _______ percent of the disconnecting means.

   (a) 100   (b) 110
   (c) 115   (d) 125

8. The disconnecting means for air conditioning or refrigeration equipment shall be located within sight and within _______ ft and shall be readily accessible to the user.

   (a) 20   (b) 50
   (c) 75   (d) 100

Section   **Answer**

9. The full-load current rating on the nameplate or the branch-circuit selection current rating of the largest motor, whichever is greater, shall be sized at _____ percent if there are two or more hermetically sealed motors installed on the same feeder.

    (a) 125   (b) 135
    (c) 150   (d) 175

10. Two or more motor-compressors plus other motor loads can be connected to a feeder, with the largest (motor) compressor calculated at 125 percent of its FLA and the remaining compressor loads added to this total at _____ percent of their FLA ratings.

    (a) 100   (b) 110
    (c) 115   (d) 125

11. The overload relay for the motor-compressor shall trip at not more than _____ percent of the full-load current rating.

    (a) 110   (b) 115
    (c) 135   (d) 140

12. When attachment plugs and receptacles are used for circuit connection, they shall be rated no higher than _____ amps for 208 or 240 volt, single-phase branch circuits.

    (a) 15   (b) 20
    (c) 30   (d) 50

13. The full-load current rating of the room air conditioner shall be marked on the nameplate and shall not operate at more than _____ amps on 250 volts, single-phase.

    (a) 20   (b) 30
    (c) 40   (d) 60

14. A cord-and-plug shall be permitted to serve as the disconnecting means even if the room air conditioner manual controller is above _____ ft.

    (a) 3   (b) 6
    (c) 10   (d) 12

15. Room air conditioners installed with flexible cord are to be a length that is limited to _____ ft for 208 or 240 volt circuits.

    (a) 3   (b) 5
    (c) 6   (d) 10

16. The overcurrent protection device for a hermetically sealed compressor shall be selected at _____ percent (for minimum) of the compressor's FLA rating or the branch-circuit selection current, whichever is greater.

    (a) 125   (b) 150
    (c) 175   (d) 225

Section   **Answer**

17. The rating of the overcurrent protection device shall be determined by using the rating on the nameplate of the cord-and-plug connected equipment having single-phase, _______ volt or less, hermetically sealed motors.

    (a) 120   (b) 250
    (c) 480   (d) 600

18. Overload protection shall be provided for direct or fixed-wired motor-compressors and equipment that is connected to _______ or _______ amp, 120 volt, single-phase branch circuits.

    (a) 15, 20   (b) 20, 30
    (c) 30, 40   (d) 40, 50

19. Room air conditioners shall be grounded for the protection of _______ .

    (a) equipment   (b) personnel
    (c) all of the above   (d) none of the above

20. A cord-and-plug shall be permitted to serve as the disconnecting means for a room air conditioner if it operates at _______ volts or less.

    (a) 120   (b) 150
    (c) 250   (d) 300

21. What size nonautomatic circuit breaker is required to disconnect an A/C unit with a compressor rated at 29 amps and a condenser rated at 2.5 amps?

22. What size nonfused disconnect is required for an A/C unit with a compressor rated at 29 amps and a condenser rated at 2.5 amps?

23. What size horsepower rated disconnect is required for an A/C unit with a compressor rated at 29 amps and a condenser rated at 2.5 amps with a 180 amp locked-rotor current rating? (Note that the supply is 480 volts, three-phase.)

24. What size horsepower rated disconnect is required for the following loads on a three-phase, 230 volt system?

    • A/C unit with a compressor rated at 29 amps, with a 200 amp locked-rotor current rating
    • A/C unit with a compressor rating 24 amps, with a locked-rotor current of 150 amps
    • A/C unit with a compressor rating of 20 amps, with a locked-rotor current of 140 amps

25. What size circuit breaker is required to disconnect a hermetically sealed motor for an A/C unit rated at 29 amps? (Note that the supply is 208 volts, three-phase.)

26. What size disconnecting means using horsepower is required to disconnect the following loads on a three-phase, 230 volt system?

    • Motor rated at 38 amps, with a 212 amp locked-rotor current rating
    • A/C unit with a compressor rated at 28 amps, with a 160 amp locked-rotor current rating
    • A/C unit with a compressor rated at 24, amps with a 160 amp locked-rotor current rating

Section   **Answer**

27. What is the minimum size overcurrent protection device required for an A/C unit with a compressor rated at 20 amps and a condenser rated at 2.5 amps?

28. What is the maximum size overcurrent protection device required for an A/C unit with a compressor rated at 20 amps and a condenser rated at 2.5 amps?

29. What is the minimum size overcurrent protection device required for a feeder with the following loads on a 230 volt, three-phase system?

   • A/C unit with a compressor rated at 29 amps and a condenser rated at 2.5 amps
   • A/C unit with a compressor rated at 26 amps and a condenser rated at 2.5 amps
   • A/C unit with a compressor rated at 22 amps and a condenser rated at 2.5 amps

30. What is the maximum size overcurrent protection device required for a feeder with the following loads on a 230 volt, three-phase system?

   • A/C unit with a compressor rated at 29 amps and a condenser rated at 2.5 amps
   • A/C unit with a compressor rated at 26 amps and a condenser rated at 2.5 amps
   • A/C unit with a compressor rated at 22 amps and a condenser rated at 2.5 amps

31. What size overcurrent protection device (time delay fuse) is required for a feeder with the following loads on a 230 volt, three-phase system?

   • A/C unit with a compressor rated at 26 amps and a condenser rated at 2.5 amps
   • A/C unit with a compressor rated at 24 amps and a condenser rated at 2.5 amps
   • 10 HP, 230 volt, three-phase, Design letter B motor

32. What size THHN copper conductors are required to supply an A/C unit with a compressor rated at 20 amps and a condenser rated at 2.5 amps?

33. What size THHN copper conductors are required to supply an A/C unit with a branch-circuit selection current of 30 amps?

34. What size THWN copper conductors are required for a feeder with the following loads on a 208 volt, three-phase system?

   • A/C unit with a compressor rated at 30 amps and a condenser rated at 3 amps
   • A/C unit with a compressor rated at 28 amps and a condenser rated at 2.5 amps
   • A/C unit with a compressor rated at 24 amps and a condenser rated at 2.5 amps

35. What size THWN copper conductors are required for a feeder with the following loads on a 208 volt, three-phase system?

   • A/C unit with a compressor rated at 30 amps and a condenser rated at 3 amps
   • A/C unit with a compressor rated at 28 amps and a condenser rated at 2.5 amps
   • A/C unit with a compressor rated at 24 amps and a condenser rated at 2.5 amps
   • Other loads of 80 amps (continuous operation)

36. What size controller is required for an A/C unit with a compressor rated at 20 amps and a condenser rated at 2.5 amps on a 230 volt, single-phase system?

37. What size overload relay and fuses is required for an A/C unit with a compressor rated at 20 amps on a 240 volt, three-phase system?

38. What is the allowable ampacity for a 10 AWG THWN copper conductor supplying an air conditioning window unit?

Section   **Answer**

39. What is the allowable ampacity available for an air conditioning window unit with other loads such as lighting and receptacle loads that are supplied by size 10 AWG THWN copper conductor?

40. Which two Articles shall a compressor installed in a Class I, Division 1 hazardous and classified location comply with?
    (a) 500   (b) 501
    (c) all of the above   (d) none of the above

Transformers

Transformers must be sized with enough capacity to supply power to loads and allow loads with high inrush currents to start and run. In addition, they must be protected by properly sized overcurrent protection devices and be equipped with conductors having allowable ampacity ratings to supply the loads. Overcurrent protection devices and conductors must be designed and installed in such a manner to safely protect the windings of such power sources from dangerous short circuits, ground faults, and overloads.

The overcurrent protection devices and conductors are sometimes required to be adjusted in size in order to protect the transformer windings or the conductors from overload conditions.

Transformers may be utility or customer owned and fall under the rules of the *National Electrical Safety Code*. If customer owned, they are still required to follow the *National Electrical Safety Code* as well as the *National Electrical Code*. And these requirements must be complied with.

Note, When selecting the actual size circuit breaker or fuse for the protection of electrical systems rated over 1000 volts, see one of the *ANSI C Standards*.

> **For example,** for fuses rated at 100 amps or less, see ANSI C 37.46, and for over 100 amps see ANSI 37.46 and ANSI 37.40. When circuit breakers are used to protect high-voltage systems, see ANSI C 37.06. However, there may be protection designs that require reference to other ANSI C standards, and the designer must be prepared to refer to such standards.

SIZING TRANSFORMERS

The total volt-amps of all loads in a building shall be used to size a transformer. Depending on the load requirements of a building, single-phase and three-phase currents may be used to supply the building. The windings are connected in configurations necessary to supply voltage and load requirements of the facility.

WYE-CONNECTED SECONDARIES

The size transformers required to supply a wye-connected secondary system can be found by applying the following:

- Adding the total single-phase and three-phase loads together for an individual transformer

- Dividing the load in VA by 1/3 (.33) to derive three transformers

The kVA rating of three transformers, if they are separately connected together, will add up to one individual transformer. Using this method, a single transformer rating can be sized and selected from the total volt-amps. One transformer with three windings is sized by adding the total VA of all the loads together and selecting the transformer's kVA rating based upon this value. **(See Figure 20-1)**

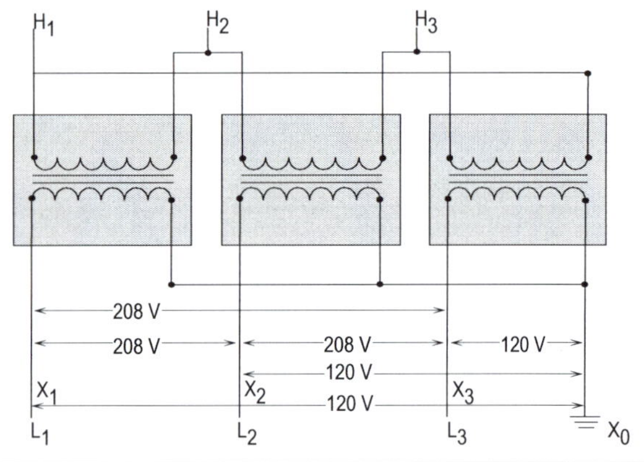

SIZING TRANSFORMERS FOR A BUILDING WITH A TOTAL CONNECTED LOAD OF 20 kVA FOR SINGLE-PHASE LOADS AND 30 kVA FOR THREE-PHASE LOADS

Step 1: Finding kVA load for three transformers
Single-phase: 20 kVA x .33 = 6.6 kVA
Three-phase: 30 kVA x .33 = 9.9 kVA
Total load = 16.5 kVA

Step 2: Sizing individual transformers
Three 20 kVA lighting and power transformers of the same size must be installed (20 kVA x 3 = 60 kVA)

Step 3: Sizing kVA for one transformer
20 kVA + 30 kVA = 50 kVA

Solution: Three transformers of 20 kVA each and one transformer of at least one 60 kVA are recommended.

WYE-CONNECTED SECONDARIES

Figure 20-1. Sizing wye-connected transformers with single-phase and three-phase loads.

CLOSED DELTA-CONNECTED SECONDARIES

The size transformer required to supply a closed delta-connected secondary system can be found by multiplying the following:

- Multiply the single-phase load in VA by 67 percent.

- Multiply the three-phase load in VA by 33 percent.

- Add the kVA load of (1) and (2) together to derive the two lighting and power transformers.

- Multiply the single-phase and three-phase loads in VA by 33 percent.

- Use this total load in kVA to derive the two power transformers.

See Figure 20-2(a) for the rules and regulations for sizing the transformer used in a closed delta-connected system. **Note,** see page 23-9 in this book.

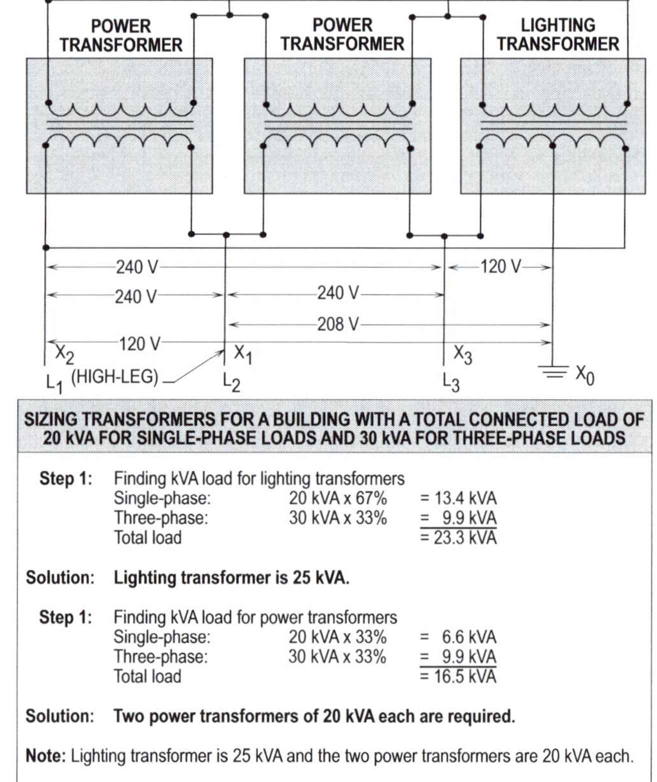

SIZING TRANSFORMERS FOR A BUILDING WITH A TOTAL CONNECTED LOAD OF 20 kVA FOR SINGLE-PHASE LOADS AND 30 kVA FOR THREE-PHASE LOADS

Step 1: Finding kVA load for lighting transformers
Single-phase: 20 kVA x 67% = 13.4 kVA
Three-phase: 30 kVA x 33% = 9.9 kVA
Total load = 23.3 kVA

Solution: Lighting transformer is 25 kVA.

Step 1: Finding kVA load for power transformers
Single-phase: 20 kVA x 33% = 6.6 kVA
Three-phase: 30 kVA x 33% = 9.9 kVA
Total load = 16.5 kVA

Solution: Two power transformers of 20 kVA each are required.

Note: Lighting transformer is 25 kVA and the two power transformers are 20 kVA each.

CLOSED DELTA-CONNECTED SECONDARIES

Figure 20-2(a). Sizing closed delta-connected transformers with single-phase and three-phase loads.

OPEN DELTA-CONNECTED SECONDARIES

Open delta-connected secondary systems can be determined by calculating the single-phase load at 100 percent and the three-phase load at 58 percent and using this total value to size the transformer. By adding these two loads together, the size of a mid-tap transformer can be determined. A power transformer can be sized by calculating the three-phase load at 58 percent, which is the reciprocal of the square root of 3 (1 ÷ 1.732 = 58%). This reduced total is then used to size the power transformer, which will be smaller in rating than the lighting and power transformer. **[See Figure 20-2(b)**and page 23-9**]**

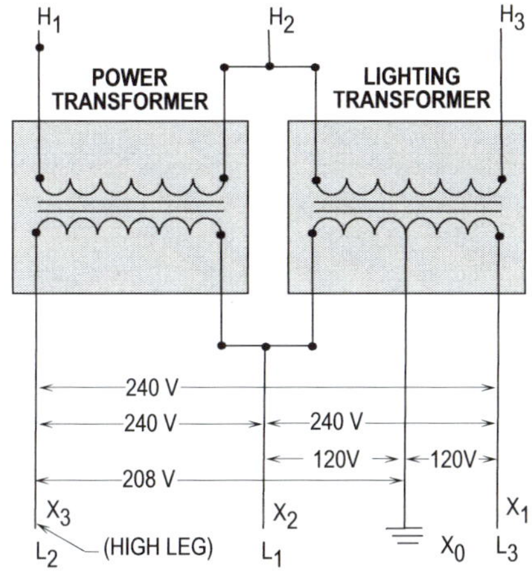

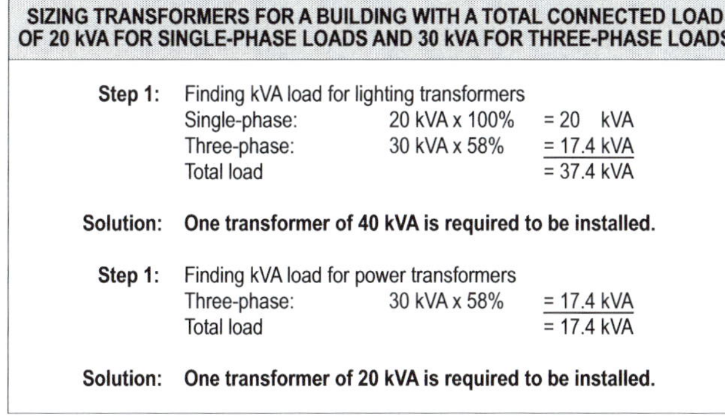

SIZING TRANSFORMERS FOR A BUILDING WITH A TOTAL CONNECTED LOAD OF 20 kVA FOR SINGLE-PHASE LOADS AND 30 kVA FOR THREE-PHASE LOADS

Step 1:	Finding kVA load for lighting transformers			
	Single-phase:	20 kVA x 100%	= 20	kVA
	Three-phase:	30 kVA x 58%	= 17.4 kVA	
	Total load		= 37.4 kVA	
Solution:	One transformer of 40 kVA is required to be installed.			
Step 1:	Finding kVA load for power transformers			
	Three-phase:	30 kVA x 58%	= 17.4 kVA	
	Total load		= 17.4 kVA	
Solution:	One transformer of 20 kVA is required to be installed.			

OPEN DELTA-CONNECTED SECONDARIES

Figure 20-2(b). Sizing open delta-connected transformers with single-phase and three-phase loads.

CALCULATING PRIMARY AND SECONDARY CURRENTS

The transformer's primary amp rating shall be equivalent to the amps of the connected load when installing a feeder to supply the primary of a transformer to step up or step down the voltage. To determine the FLA of a transformer, the kVA of the transformer must be divided by the voltage x 1.732 if the supply is three-phase. **[See Figures 20-3(a) and (b)]**

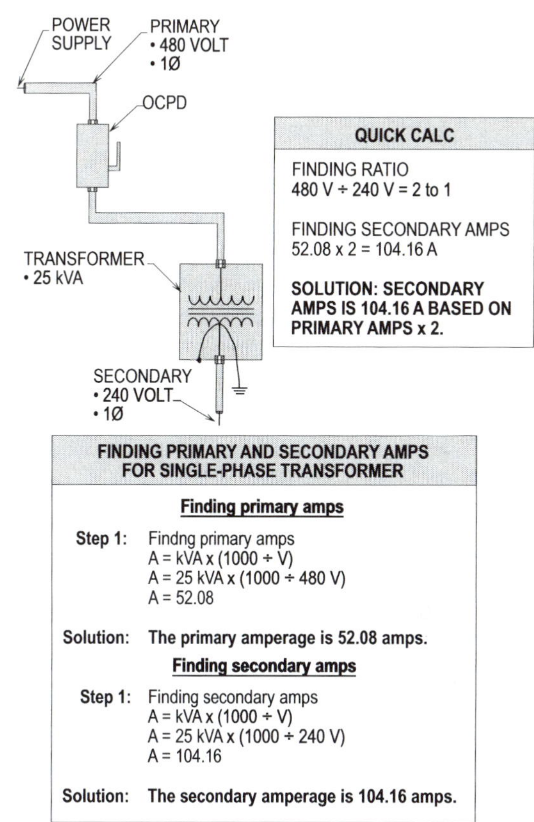

FINDING PRIMARY AND SECONDARY AMPS FOR SINGLE-PHASE TRANSFORMER

	Finding primary amps	
Step 1:	Findng primary amps	
	A = kVA x (1000 ÷ V)	
	A = 25 kVA x (1000 ÷ 480 V)	
	A = 52.08	
Solution:	The primary amperage is 52.08 amps.	
	Finding secondary amps	
Step 1:	Finding secondary amps	
	A = kVA x (1000 ÷ V)	
	A = 25 kVA x (1000 ÷ 240 V)	
	A = 104.16	
Solution:	The secondary amperage is 104.16 amps.	

CALCULATING PRIMARY AND SECONDARY CURRENTS

Figure 20-3(a). Finding amps of a single-phase transformer.

FINDING AMPERAGE

The kVA or amp rating for the primary or secondary of a transformer can be determined for a single-phase system by applying the following formula:

$$kVA = volts \times amps \div 1000$$
$$amps = kVA \times 1000 \div volts$$

The following formula shall be applied to determine the ratio of a transformer having a 480 volt primary and 240 volt secondary:

$$primary \div secondary$$
$$480 V \div 240 V$$
$$2{:}1 \ ratio$$

The amp rating for the primary or secondary can be determined for a three-phase system by applying the following formula:

$$kVA = volts \times 1.732 \times amps \div 1000$$
$$amps = (kVA \times 1000) \div (volts \times 1.732)$$

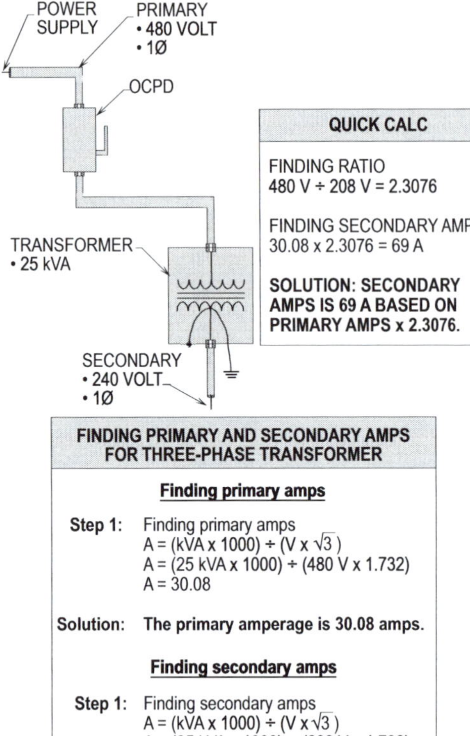

Figure 20-3(b). Sizing amps of a three-phase transformer.

INSTALLING TRANSFORMERS
ARTICLE 450

Transformers shall be installed and protected per **Article 450**. Transformers shall be permitted to be installed inside or outside buildings based upon their design and type.

LOCATION
450.13

Transformers shall be located where readily accessible to qualified personnel for inspection and maintenance. Where it is necessary to use a ladder, lift, or bucket truck to get to a transformer, it shall not be considered readily accessible. See definition of *readily accessible*, in **Article 100**. **(See Figure 20-4)**

There are two exceptions to the general rule to the accessibility rules, and they are explained under the next two headings.

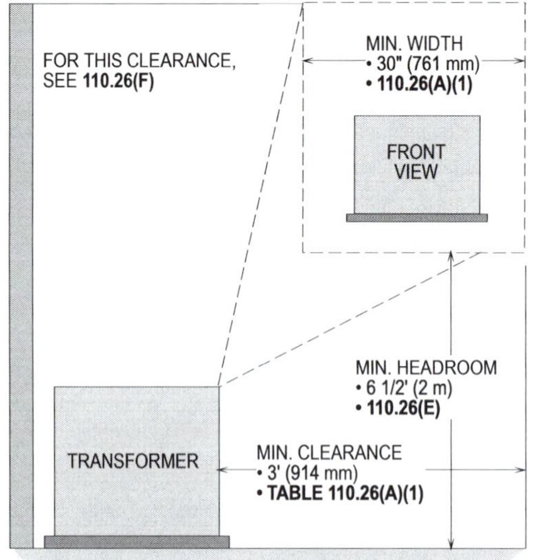

Figure 20-4. The general rule of **450.13** requires transformers to be readily accessible for maintenance, repair, and service. See AHJ for this requirement.

HUNG FROM WALL OR CEILING
450.13(A)

Dry-type transformers not over 1000 volts and located on open walls or steel columns shall not be required to be readily accessible. It is permissible to gain access to this type of installation using a portable ladder or bucket lift. **[See Figure 20-5(a)]**

MOUNTED IN CEILING
450.13(B)

Dry-type transformers not over 1000 volts and 50 kVA shall be permitted to be installed in hollow spaces of buildings. The transformers cannot be permanently closed in and there shall be some access to the transformers, but they do not have to be readily accessible per **Article 100**. It was not clear in the 1993 or previous editions of the NEC whether dry-type transformers not exceeding 600 volts, nominal, and rated 50 kVA or less were permitted to be installed in the space above suspended ceilings with removable panels, even if the transformer was accessible and provided with proper working clearances.

Note, the space where the transformer is installed shall comply with the ventilation requirements of **450.9** and be designed by the rules of **450.21(A)** and **(B)**. If such ceiling space is used as a return air space for air conditioning, **300.22(C)** shall be reviewed and the provisions of this section shall be complied with. **[See Figure 20-5(b)]**

> **Design Tip:** The two exceptions to the general rule are for dry-type transformers. The exceptions do not apply for oil or askarel-filled transformers due to the damage of a possible oil spillage or the threat of fire because of a rupture occurring in the case.

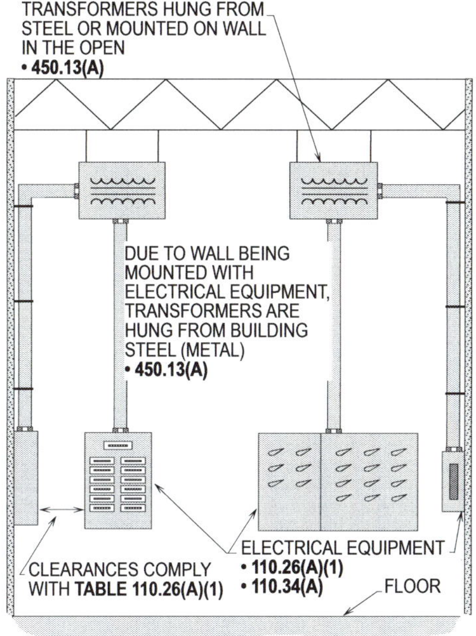

Figure 20-5(a). Transformers hung from the wall or ceiling shall not be required to be readily accessible.

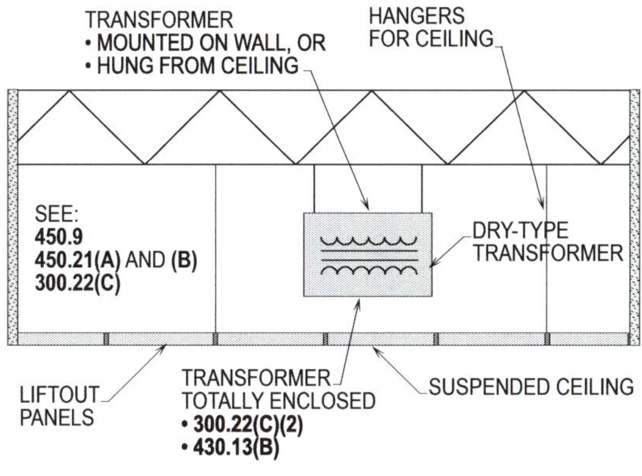

Figure 20-5(b). Transformers mounted in ceiling shall not be required to be readily accessible.

DISCONNECTING MEANS
450.14

A disconnecting means shall be located either in sight or in a remote location for transformers other than Class 2 or Class 3 transformers. The disconnecting means shall be lockable and the location field marked on the transformer where located in a remote location. **(See Figure 20-6)**

OVERCURRENT PROTECTION
450.3(A) AND (B)

There are two sets of rules when providing overcurrent protection of transformers: rules for transformers rated over 1000 volts and transformers of 1000 volts or less. The overcurrent protection device may be placed in the primary only or in the primary and secondary side of the transformer.

PRIMARY ONLY – OVER 1000 VOLTS
450.3(A) AND TABLE 450.3(A)

The term *primary* is often inferred in the field as being the high side, and the term *secondary* as the low side of the transformer. This is really not the proper terminology. The primary is the input side of the transformer and the secondary is the output side. Thus, voltage has nothing to do with "high" or "low."

Each transformer shall be protected by an overcurrent device in the primary side. If the overcurrent protection is fuses, they shall be rated not greater than 250 percent (2.5 times) of the rated primary current of the transformer. When circuit breakers are used, they shall be set not greater than 300 percent (3 times) the rated primary current. **(See Figure 20-7)**

This overcurrent protection device shall be permitted to be mounted in the vault or at the transformer, if approved for such purpose. It shall also be permitted to be mounted in the panelboard and be designed to protect the windings and circuit conductors supplying the transformer.

If not installed in a vault, the overcurrent protection device shall be permitted to be installed outdoors on a pole, with a disconnecting means installed in the vault to disconnect supply conductors.

APPLYING NOTE 1
TABLE 450.3(A), Note 1

Where 250 percent (2.5 times) of the rated primary current of the transformer does not correspond to a standard rating of a fuse, the next higher standard rating shall be permitted, per **240.6(A)**.

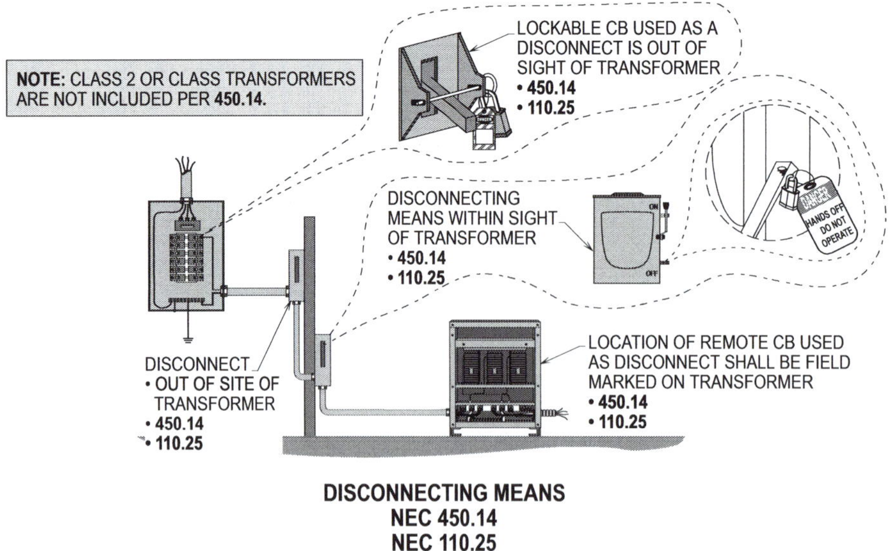

Figure 20-6. This illustration shows the requirements of the disconnecting means for transformers other than Class 2 or Class 3 transformers. Disconnect means shall be lockable type and comply with **110.25** of the NEC.

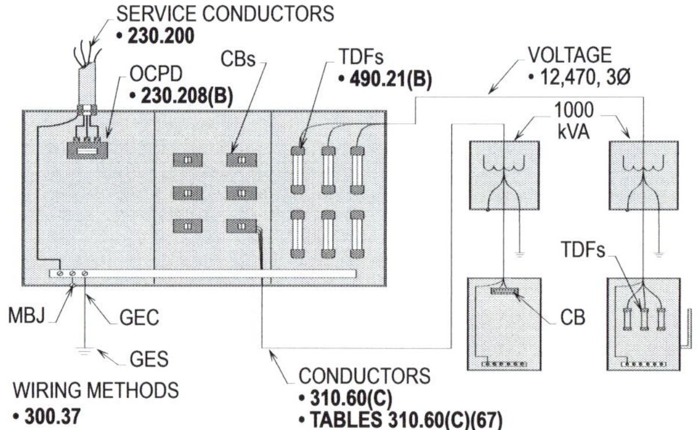

Figure 20-7. If the overcurrent protection is fuses, they shall be rated not greater than 250 percent (2.5 times) of the rated primary current of the transformer. When circuit breakers are used, they shall be set at not greater than 300 percent (3 times) of the rated primary current.

PRIMARY AND SECONDARY OVER 1000 VOLTS
450.3(A) AND TABLE 450.3(A)

A transformer over 1000 volts, nominal, having an overcurrent protection device on the secondary side rated to open not greater than the values listed in **Table 450.3(A),** or a transformer equipped with a coordinated thermal overload protection by the manufacturer, shall not be required to have individual protection in the primary. However, a feeder overcurrent protection device rated or set to open at not greater than the values listed in **Table 450.3(A)** shall be provided.

NONSUPERVISED LOCATIONS
450.3(A) AND TABLE 450.3(A)

Overcurrent protection for a nonsupervised location shall be permitted to be placed in the primary and secondary side of high-voltage transformers if the overcurrent protection devices are designed and installed according to the provisions listed in **Table 450.3(A)**.

If the secondary voltage is 1000 volts or less, the overcurrent protection device and conductors on the secondary side shall be sized at 125 percent of the FLC rating. Overcurrent protection devices sized at 125 percent of the FLC in amps protect the conductors and windings of the transformer from dangerous overload conditions. With higher voltage on the secondary side of the transformer, the percentages for sizing the overcurrent protection devices shall be selected from **Table 450.3(A)** (any location) based on the particular voltage level. **[See Figure 20-8(a)]**

SUPERVISED LOCATIONS
450.3(A) AND TABLE 450.3(A)

Overcurrent protection shall be permitted to be placed in the primary and secondary side of high-voltage transformers if the overcurrent protection devices are designed and installed according to the provisions listed in **Table 450.3(A)**.

Where the facility has trained engineers and maintenance personnel, the overcurrent protection device for the secondary shall be sized at not more than 250 percent of the FLC for voltage 1000 volts or less. With higher voltage on the secondary side of the transformer, the percentages for sizing the overcurrent protection devices shall be selected from **Table 450.3(A)** based on the particular voltage level. **[See Figures 20-8(b) and (c)]**

Note, see Figure 20-9 for certain design conditions that permit the primary overcurrent protection device to be used to protect the primary and secondary sides of two-wire to two-wire connected transformers and three-wire to three-wire delta connected transformers per **240.4(F)** and **240.21(C)(1).**

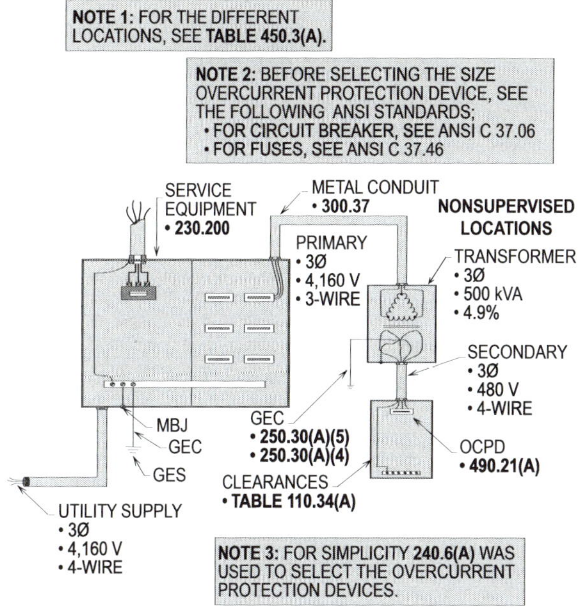

SIZING OCPD FOR PRIMARY SIDE	
Step 1:	Finding FLA of transformer FLA = (kVA x 1000) ÷ (V x $\sqrt{3}$) FLA = (500 x 1000) ÷ (4160 V x 1.732) FLA = 69.4 A
Step 2:	Calculating FLA for OCPD **450.3(A)** and **Table 450.3(A)** FLA = 69.4 A x 600% FLA = 416.4 A
Step 3:	Selecting OCPD **Table 450.3(A), Note 1** and **240.6(A)** 416.4 A permits 450 A
Solution:	**The size overcurrent protection device for primary side is 450 amps.**

Note 1: Higher percentages than 125 percent per **Table 450.3(A)** shall be used to size the overcurrent protection device in the secondary side where the secondary voltage is greater than 1000 volts.

SIZING OCPD FOR SECONDARY SIDE	
Step 1:	Finding FLA of transformer FLA = (kVA x 1000) ÷ (V x $\sqrt{3}$) FLA = (500 x 1000) ÷ (480 V x 1.732) FLA = 601.7 A
Step 2:	Calculating FLA for OCPD **450.3(A)** and **Table 450.3(A)** FLA = 601.7 A x 125% FLA = 752 A
Step 3:	Selecting OCPD **Table 450.3(A), Note 1** 752 A permits 800 A
Solution:	**The size overcurrent protection device for secondary side is 800 amps.**

Note 2: If the secondary voltage is 4160, the overcurrent protection device using a circuit breaker shall be sized at 300 percent and a fuse shall be sized at 250 percent of transformer's FLC.

NONSUPERVISED LOCATIONS (ANY LOCATION)
NEC 450.3(A) AND TABLE 450.3(A)

Figure 20-8(a). Sizing the primary and secondary side of a transformer in a nonsupervised (any) location.

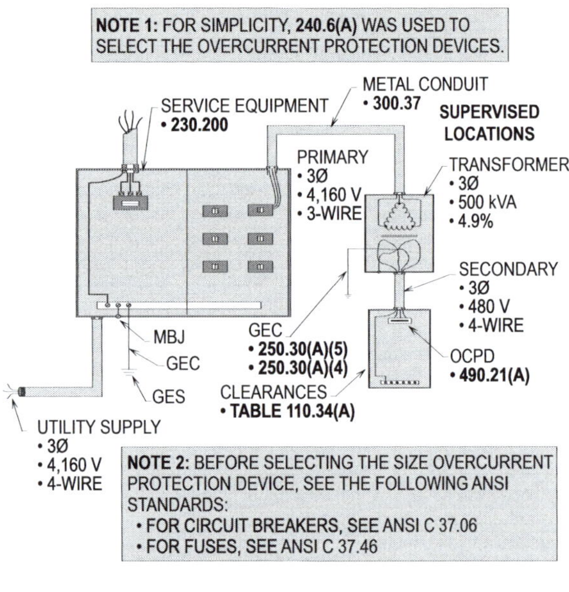

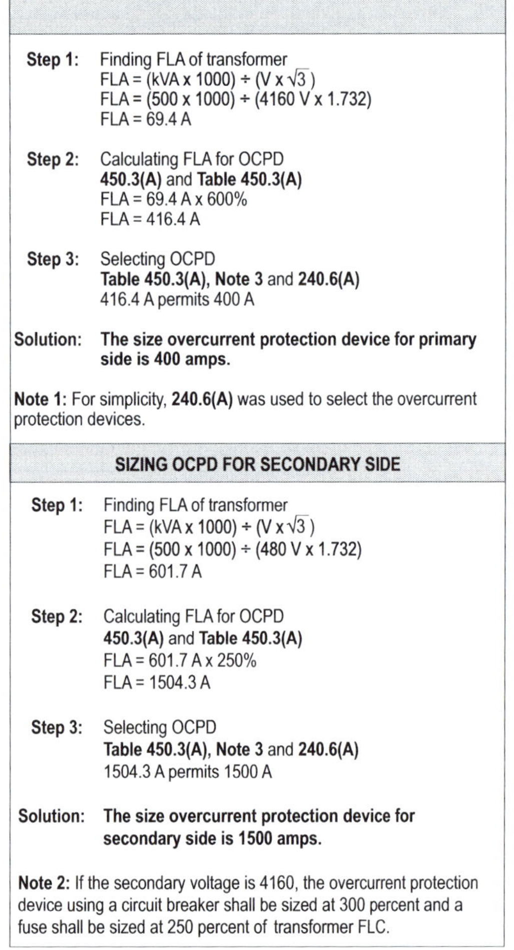

Step 1: Finding FLA of transformer
FLA = (kVA x 1000) ÷ (V x $\sqrt{3}$)
FLA = (500 x 1000) ÷ (4160 V x 1.732)
FLA = 69.4 A

Step 2: Calculating FLA for OCPD
450.3(A) and **Table 450.3(A)**
FLA = 69.4 A x 600%
FLA = 416.4 A

Step 3: Selecting OCPD
Table 450.3(A), Note 3 and **240.6(A)**
416.4 A permits 400 A

Solution: **The size overcurrent protection device for primary side is 400 amps.**

Note 1: For simplicity, **240.6(A)** was used to select the overcurrent protection devices.

SIZING OCPD FOR SECONDARY SIDE

Step 1: Finding FLA of transformer
FLA = (kVA x 1000) ÷ (V x $\sqrt{3}$)
FLA = (500 x 1000) ÷ (480 V x 1.732)
FLA = 601.7 A

Step 2: Calculating FLA for OCPD
450.3(A) and **Table 450.3(A)**
FLA = 601.7 A x 250%
FLA = 1504.3 A

Step 3: Selecting OCPD
Table 450.3(A), Note 3 and **240.6(A)**
1504.3 A permits 1500 A

Solution: **The size overcurrent protection device for secondary side is 1500 amps.**

Note 2: If the secondary voltage is 4160, the overcurrent protection device using a circuit breaker shall be sized at 300 percent and a fuse shall be sized at 250 percent of transformer FLC.

SUPERVISED LOCATIONS
NEC 450.3(A) AND TABLE 450.3(A)

Figure 20-8(b). Sizing the primary and secondary side of a transformer in a supervised location.

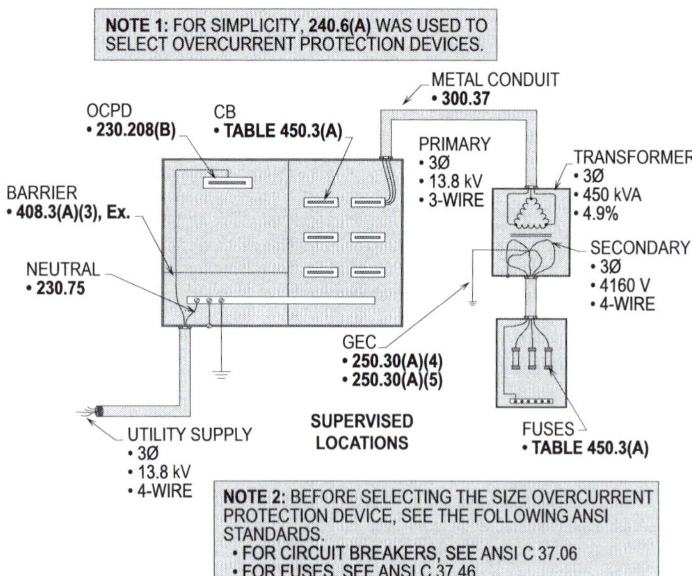

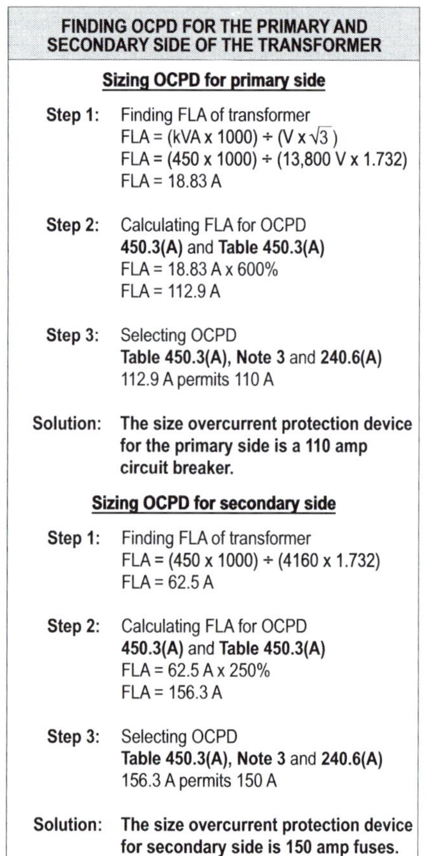

FINDING OCPD FOR THE PRIMARY AND SECONDARY SIDE OF THE TRANSFORMER

Sizing OCPD for primary side

Step 1: Finding FLA of transformer
FLA = (kVA x 1000) ÷ (V x $\sqrt{3}$)
FLA = (450 x 1000) ÷ (13,800 V x 1.732)
FLA = 18.83 A

Step 2: Calculating FLA for OCPD
450.3(A) and **Table 450.3(A)**
FLA = 18.83 A x 600%
FLA = 112.9 A

Step 3: Selecting OCPD
Table 450.3(A), Note 3 and **240.6(A)**
112.9 A permits 110 A

Solution: **The size overcurrent protection device for the primary side is a 110 amp circuit breaker.**

Sizing OCPD for secondary side

Step 1: Finding FLA of transformer
FLA = (450 x 1000) ÷ (4160 x 1.732)
FLA = 62.5 A

Step 2: Calculating FLA for OCPD
450.3(A) and **Table 450.3(A)**
FLA = 62.5 A x 250%
FLA = 156.3 A

Step 3: Selecting OCPD
Table 450.3(A), Note 3 and **240.6(A)**
156.3 A permits 150 A

Solution: **The size overcurrent protection device for secondary side is 150 amp fuses.**

SUPERVISED LOCATIONS
NEC 450.3(A) AND TABLE 450.3(A)

Figure 20-8(c). Sizing the primary and secondary side of a transformer in a supervised location.

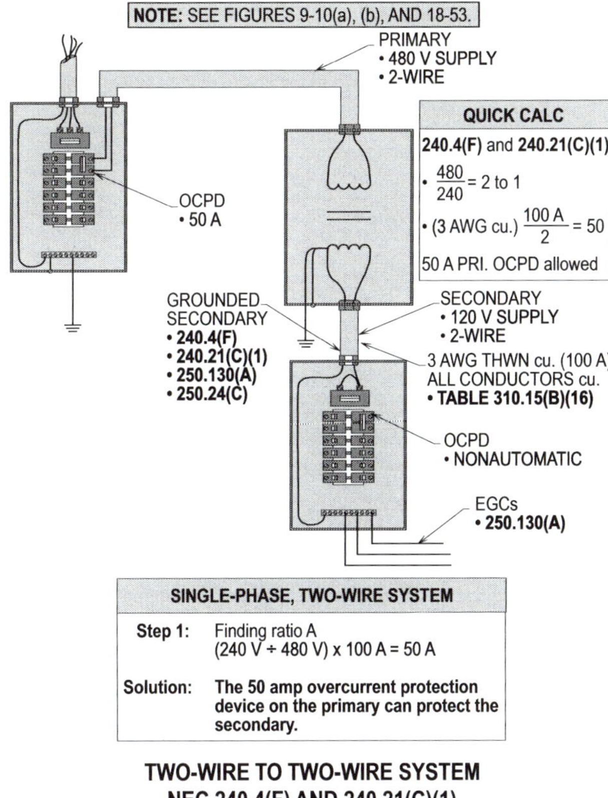

SINGLE-PHASE, TWO-WIRE SYSTEM	
Step 1:	Finding ratio A (240 V ÷ 480 V) x 100 A = 50 A
Solution:	The 50 amp overcurrent protection device on the primary can protect the secondary.

TWO-WIRE TO TWO-WIRE SYSTEM
NEC 240.4(F) AND 240.21(C)(1)

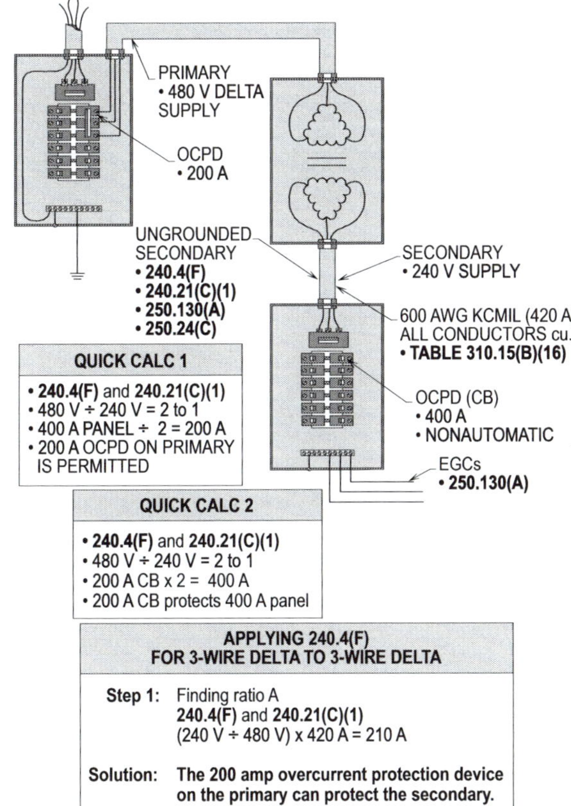

QUICK CALC 1
- 240.4(F) and 240.21(C)(1)
- 480 V ÷ 240 V = 2 to 1
- 400 A PANEL ÷ 2 = 200 A
- 200 A OCPD ON PRIMARY IS PERMITTED

QUICK CALC 2
- 240.4(F) and 240.21(C)(1)
- 480 V ÷ 240 V = 2 to 1
- 200 A CB x 2 = 400 A
- 200 A CB protects 400 A panel

APPLYING 240.4(F) FOR 3-WIRE DELTA TO 3-WIRE DELTA	
Step 1:	Finding ratio A 240.4(F) and 240.21(C)(1) (240 V ÷ 480 V) x 420 A = 210 A
Solution:	The 200 amp overcurrent protection device on the primary can protect the secondary.

THREE-WIRE TO THREE-WIRE SYSTEM
NEC 240.4(F) AND 240.21(C)(1)

Figure 20-9. Sizing the overcurrent protection device for a single-phase, two-wire system and three-phase, three-wire system.

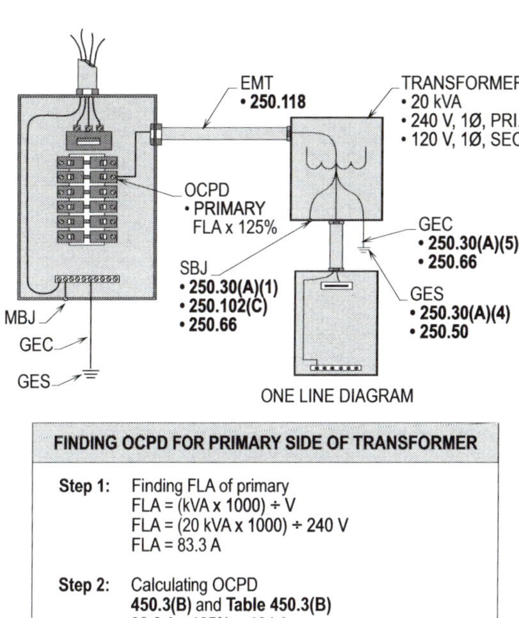

FINDING OCPD FOR PRIMARY SIDE OF TRANSFORMER	
Step 1:	Finding FLA of primary FLA = (kVA x 1000) ÷ V FLA = (20 kVA x 1000) ÷ 240 V FLA = 83.3 A
Step 2:	Calculating OCPD **450.3(B)** and **Table 450.3(B)** 83.3 A x 125% = 104 A
Step 3:	Selecting OCPD **Table 450.3(B)**, **Note 1** and **240.6(A)** 104 A permits 100 A
Solution:	The size overcurrent protection device in the primary side is 100 amps.

PRIMARY ONLY
1000 VOLTS OR LESS
NEC 450.3(B) AND TABLE 450.3(B)

Figure 20-10. A transformer of 1000 volts or less, nominal, having an individual overcurrent protection device on the primary side shall be sized at no more than 125 percent of the transformer's full-load current rating, in amps. **Note,** for other illustrations and similar rules, see **Figures 20-9, 7-18, 9-9(a), and 9-9(b).**

PRIMARY ONLY – 1000 VOLTS OR LESS
450.3(B) AND TABLE 450.3(B)

A transformer 1000 volts or less, nominal, having an individual overcurrent protection device on the primary side shall be sized at no more than 125 percent of the transformer's full-load current rating.

Note, with the overcurrent protection device and conductors sized at 125 percent or less of the transformer's FLC, the supply conductors and transformer windings shall be considered protected from overload conditions. It appears that individual protection in the primary is not recognized per **450.3(B)** and **Table 450.3(B)**. **(See Figure 20-10)**

PRIMARY 9 AMPS OR MORE
450.3(B) AND TABLE 450.3(B)

Where the rated primary current of a transformer is 9 amps or more and 125 percent of this current does not correspond to a standard rating of a fuse or circuit breaker, the next size shall be permitted to be used per **240.6(A)**. Where the rated primary current of a transformer is less than 9 amps but more than 2 amps, an overcurrent device rated or set at no more than 167 percent of primary current shall be used. When the rated primary current of a transformer is less than 2 amps, an overcurrent protection device rated or set at not more than 300 percent shall be used. **[See Figures 20-11(a), (b),** and **(c)]**

PRIMARY AND SECONDARY –
1000 VOLTS OR LESS
450.3(B) AND TABLE 450.3(B)

Combination protection shall be permitted to be provided for both the primary and secondary sides of a transformer. A current value of 250 percent of the rated primary current of the transformer shall be used if 125 percent of the rated primary current of the transformer is not sufficient to allow loads with high inrush currents to start and operate. However, the secondary overcurrent protection device shall be sized at 125 percent of the rated secondary full-load current of the transformer. Where the rated secondary current of a transformer is less than 9 amps, an overcurrent device rated or set at no more than 167 percent of secondary current shall be used. **(See Figure 20-12)**

9 AMPS OR MORE
TABLE 430.3(B), NOTE 1

Where the rated secondary current of a transformer is 9 amps or more and 125 percent of this current does not correspond to a standard rating of a fuse or circuit breaker, the next size shall be permitted to be used per **240.6(A)**.

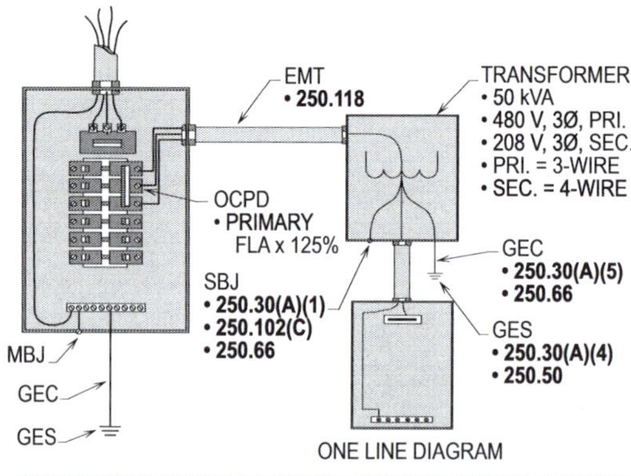

FINDING OCPD FOR PRIMARY SIDE OF TRANSFORMER		
	Sizing primary OCPD (First Level)	
Step 1:	Finding FLA of primary FLA = (kVA x 1000) ÷ (V x √3) FLA = (50 kVA x 1000) ÷ (480 V x 1.732) FLA = 60.2 A	
Step 2:	Calculating OCPD **450.3(B)** and **Table 450.3(B)** 60.2 A x 125% = 75.3 A	
Step 3:	Selecting OCPD **Table 450.3(B), Note 1** and **240.6(A)** 75.3 A permits 80 A	
Solution:	**The size overcurrent protection device in the primary side is 80 amps.**	

PRIMARY 9 AMPS OR MORE
NEC 450.3(B) AND TABLE 450.3(B)

Figure 20-11(a). Where the rated primary current of a transformer is 9 amps or more and 125 percent of this current does not correspond to a standard rating of a fuse or circuit breaker, the next size shall be permitted to be used per **240.6(A)** and **Note 1** to **Table 450.3(B)**.

GROUNDING AUTOTRANSFORMERS
450.5

Autotransformers are connected to three-phase, three-wire ungrounded systems to derive a three-phase, four-wire grounded system. Three autotransformers connected in a star (wye) configuration to the three-phase ungrounded system converts to a three-phase, four-wire grounded system.

Autotransformers are installed today because many electrical systems are not grounded. Existing ungrounded delta systems are grounded with autotransformers to derive a neutral. Three-phase zigzag transformers are generally installed for this purpose.

THREE-WIRE CIRCUIT TO THREE-
PHASE, FOUR-WIRE CIRCUIT
450.5(A)

Grounding autotransformers are connected to derive a neutral from a three-phase, three-wire ungrounded system

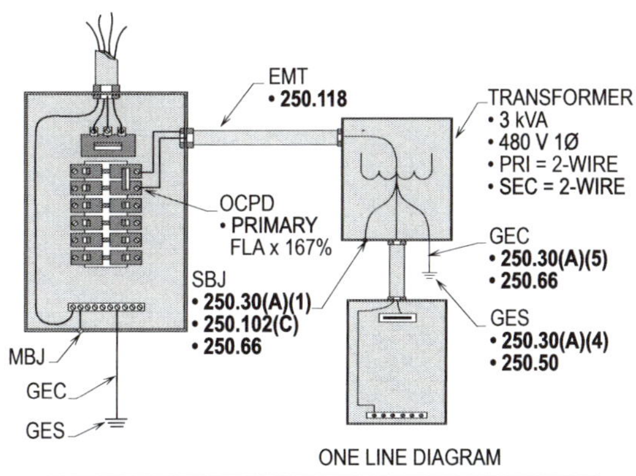

FINDING OCPD FOR PRIMARY SIDE OF TRANSFORMER

Sizing primary OCPD (Second Level)

Step 1: Finding FLA of primary
FLA = kVA x (1000 ÷ V)
FLA = 3 kVA x (1000 ÷ 480 V)
FLA = 6.25 A

Step 2: Calculating OCPD
450.3(B) and **Table 450.3(B)**
6.25 A x 167% = 10.4 A

Step 3: Selecting OCPD
Table 450.3(B) and **240.6(A)**
10.4 A permits 10 A

Solution: The size overcurrent protection device in the primary side is 10 amps.

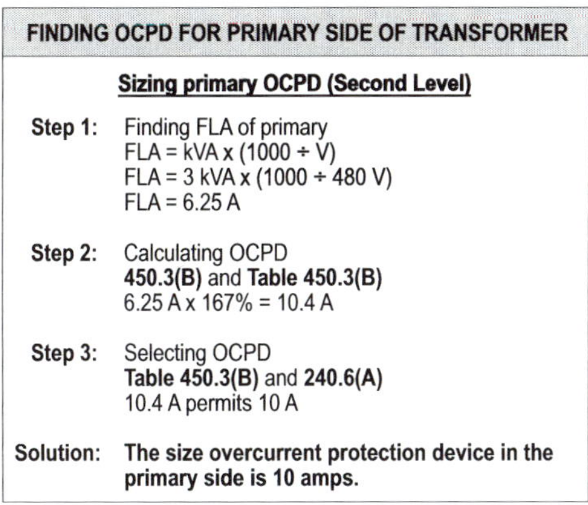

**PRIMARY 2 AMPS OR MORE
BUT LESS THAN 9 AMPS
NEC 450.3(B) AND TABLE 450.3(B)**

Figure 20-11(b). Where the rated primary current of a transformer is less than 9 amps but 2 amps or more, an overcurrent device rated or set at no more than 167 percent of primary current shall be used.

to a three-phase, four-wire grounded system, the following conditions shall apply:

- Proper connections shall be made.
- Overcurrent protection shall be provided.
- Transformer fault sensing shall be installed.
- Rating shall be adequately sized.

CONNECTIONS
450.5(A)(1)

Transformers shall be directly connected to the ungrounded (phase) conductors with no switches or overcurrent protection devices installed between the connection and the autotransformer.

OVERCURRENT PROTECTION
450.5(A)(2)

An overcurrent protection sensing device shall be designed to trip at 125 percent of its continuous current per phase or neutral rating. The next higher standard rating shall be

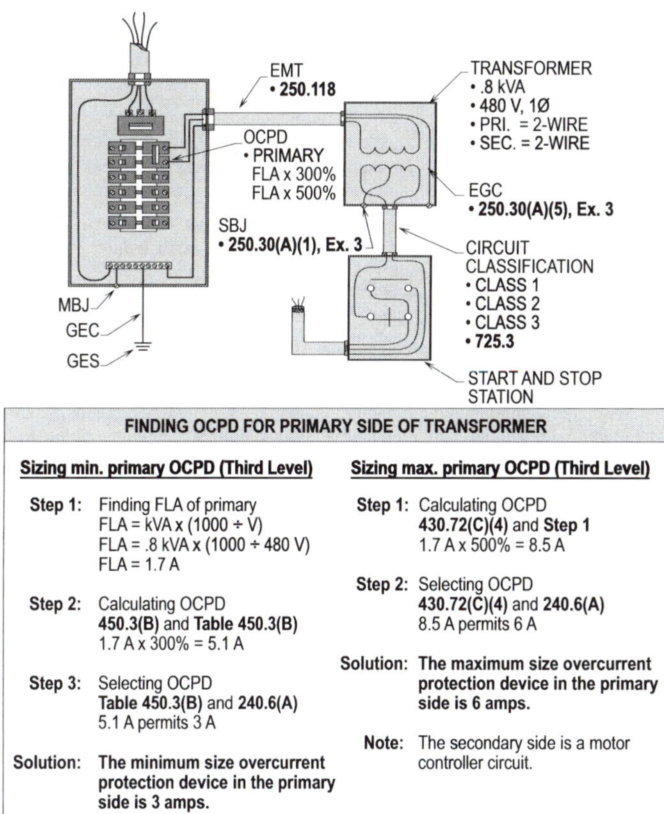

FINDING OCPD FOR PRIMARY SIDE OF TRANSFORMER

Sizing min. primary OCPD (Third Level)	**Sizing max. primary OCPD (Third Level)**
Step 1: Finding FLA of primary FLA = kVA x (1000 ÷ V) FLA = .8 kVA x (1000 ÷ 480 V) FLA = 1.7 A	**Step 1:** Calculating OCPD **430.72(C)(4)** and **Step 1** 1.7 A x 500% = 8.5 A
Step 2: Calculating OCPD **450.3(B)** and **Table 450.3(B)** 1.7 A x 300% = 5.1 A	**Step 2:** Selecting OCPD **430.72(C)(4)** and **240.6(A)** 8.5 A permits 6 A
Step 3: Selecting OCPD **Table 450.3(B)** and **240.6(A)** 5.1 A permits 3 A	**Solution:** The maximum size overcurrent protection device in the primary side is 6 amps.
Solution: The minimum size overcurrent protection device in the primary side is 3 amps.	**Note:** The secondary side is a motor controller circuit.

**PRIMARY LESS THAN 2 AMPS
NEC 450.3(B), NEC 430.72(C)(4), AND TABLE 450.3(B)**

Figure 20-11(c). When the rated primary current of a transformer is less than 2 amps, an overcurrent protection device rated or set at not more than 300 percent shall be used, unless **430.72(C)(4)** is applied.

permitted to be installed where the input current is 9 amps or more and calculated at 125 percent. Input current of 2 amps or less shall not exceed 167 percent. **(See Figure 20-13)**

TRANSFORMER FAULT SENSING
450.5(A)(3)

A main switch or common-trip overcurrent protection device for the three-phase, four-wire system shall be provided with fault sensing systems to guard against single-phasing or internal faults.

RATING
450.5(A)(4)

Autotransformers shall be designed with a continuous neutral current rating sufficient to handle the maximum possible unbalanced neutral load current that could flow in the four-wire system.

DETECTING GROUNDS ON THREE-PHASE, THREE-WIRE SYSTEMS
450.5(B)

The following conditions shall apply when autotransformers are used to detect grounds on three-phase, three-wire systems:

- Proper rating
- Overcurrent protection sized adequately
- Ground reference for damping transitory overvoltages

RATING
450.5(B)(1)

Autotransformers shall have a continuous neutral current rating sufficient for the specified ground fault current that could develop in the system.

OVERCURRENT PROTECTION
450.5(B)(2)

The overcurrent protection device shall open simultaneously with a common trip all ungrounded (phase) conductors and be set to trip at not more than 125 percent of the rated phase current of the transformer.

Note, 42 percent of the overcurrent protection device's rating may be used if connected in the autotransformer's neutral connection. When dealing with high impedance grounded systems per **250.36**, review the **Ex.** to **450.5(B)(2)** and **110.9**. **(See Figure 20-13)**

SECONDARY TIES
450.6

In large industrial plants and facilities, a "network" distribution system is usually utilized for supplying power loads. Three-phase banks of transformers are located at various points throughout the plant or facility. There are normally two high-tension primary circuits feeding such transformers. A double-throw switch that is located at each transformer bank allows either primary circuit to serve any bank of transformers. The primary circuit conductors are sized with enough capacity so that either circuit is capable of carrying the entire load if a fault develops in the other circuit. Secondary voltage is usually three-phase systems rated 1000 volts or less. The transformer secondaries are connected together in a network system, and all transformers are used to feed all the loads involved that can be all at once or as necessary.

Secondary ties shall be protected at both ends, and such protection shall be permitted to be fuses based on the current-carrying capacity of the conductors per **450.6(A)**

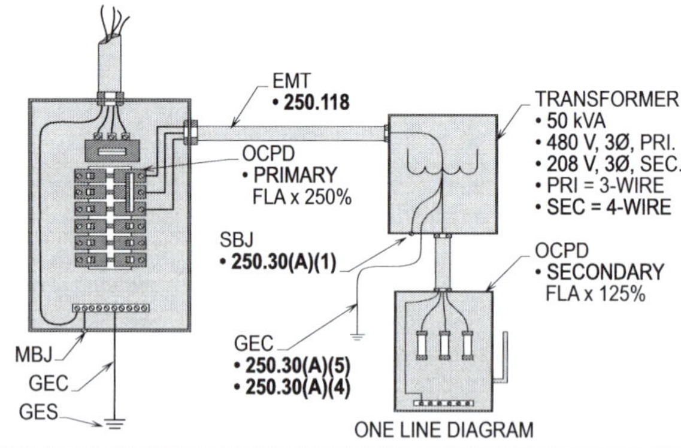

FINDING OCPD FOR PRIMARY AND SECONDARY SIDE OF TRANSFORMER

Sizing OCPD in primary	Sizing OCPD in secondary
Step 1: Finding FLA of primary FLA = (kVA x 1000) ÷ (V x √3) FLA = (50 x 1000) ÷ (480 V x 1.732) FLA = 60.2 A	**Step 1:** Finding FLA of secondary FLA = (kVA x 1000) ÷ (V x √3) FLA = (50 x 1000) ÷ (208 V x 1.732) FLA = 138.9 A
Step 2: Calculating OCPD **450.3(B)** and **Table 450.3(B)** 60.2 A x 250% = 150.5 A	**Step 2:** Calculating OCPD **450.3(B)** and **Table 450.3(B), Note 1** 138.9 A x 125% = 173.6 A
Step 3: Selecting OCPD **Table 450.3(B)** and **240.6(A)** 150.5 A permits 150 A	**Step 3:** Selecting OCPD **Table 450.3(B), Note 1** and **240.6(A)** 173.6 A permits 175 A
Solution: **The minimum size overcurrent protection device in the primary side is 150 amps.**	**Solution:** **The maximum size overcurrent protection device in the secondary side is 175 amps.**
Note: The size of the overcurrent protection device in primary shall not exceed the 250% x FLA of the primary.	**Note:** **Table 450.3(B), Note 1** permits the next higher size overcurrent protection device to be used.

PRIMARY AND SECONDARY
1000 VOLTS OR LESS
NEC 450.3(B) AND TABLE 450.3(B)

Figure 20-12. Sizing overcurrent protection device for the primary and secondary side of a transformer rated 1000 volts or less.

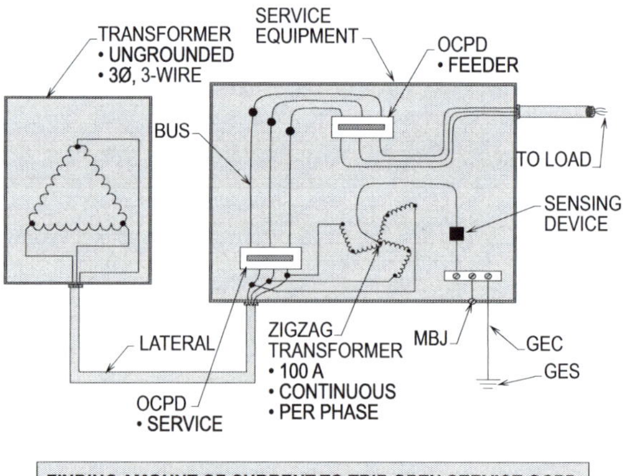

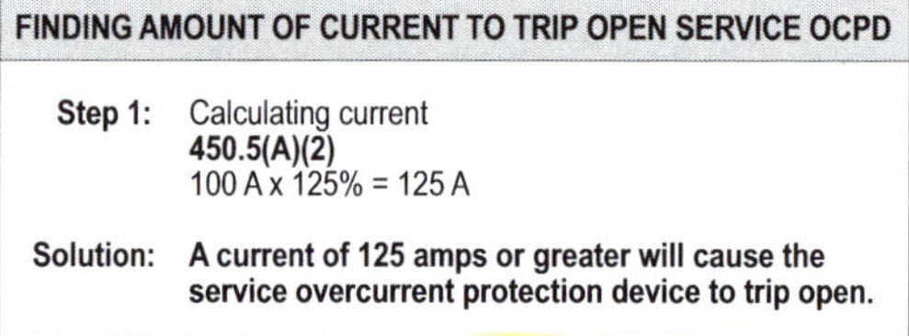

FINDING AMOUNT OF CURRENT TO TRIP OPEN SERVICE OCPD

Step 1:	Calculating current **450.5(A)(2)** 100 A x 125% = 125 A
Solution:	**A current of 125 amps or greater will cause the service overcurrent protection device to trip open.**

OVERCURRENT PROTECTION
NEC 450.5(A)(2)

Figure 20-13. An overcurrent protection sensing device shall be designed to trip at 125 percent of its continuous current per phase or neutral rating.

or the ties protected by a limiter installed at each end per **450.6(A)(3)**. A limiter protects the elements against short circuit; however, it does not provide overload protection. Usually, limiters, rather than fuses, are used for protection of the ties due to the fact they are very current limiting and will protect the circuit elements from damage during short-circuit conditions.

There is normally a load center connected to the tie at the points where a transformer bank connects to the tie. The transformer is protected by a circuit breaker in the secondary leads between the transformer and the load center. Circuit breaker setting shall be permitted to be up to 250 percent (2.5 times) of transformer's secondary current rating per **450.6(B)**. A reverse power relay shall be provided per **450.6(B)** that opens the circuit in case the transformer should fail for any reason. A reverse power relay is provided to prevent current from being fed to an out-of-service transformer from the other transformers of the network. Where the secondary voltage is greater than 150 volts to ground, to ensure adequate protection, ties shall be provided with a switch at each end per **450.6(A)(5)**.

The rules for designing and installing secondary ties can be summed up as follows:

- Where transformers are tied together in parallel and connected by tie conductors that do not have overcurrent protection as per **Article 240**, the ampacity of the ties connecting conductors shall not be less than 67 percent of the rated secondary current of the largest transformer in the tie circuit. **(See Figure 20-15)**

> **Design Tip:** This applies where the loads are at the transformer supply points per **450.6(A)(1)**.

The paralleling of transformers is common, but great care should be exercised to ensure that the transformers are similar in all conditions of use. If they are not, one transformer will try to carry more of the load than the other transformer load. If the transformers are of the same capacity and similar characteristics, they each, in theory, will carry 50 percent of the total load. The 67 percent allows for differences in transformer sizes and thus allows for adjusting solutions.

- Where the load is connected to the tie at any point between the transformer supply points, and overcurrent protection is not provided by the provisions listed in **Article 240**, the rated ampacity of the tie shall not be less than 100 percent of the rated secondary current of the largest transformer connected to the secondary tie system except as provided in **450.6(A)(4)**. **(See Figure 20-15)**

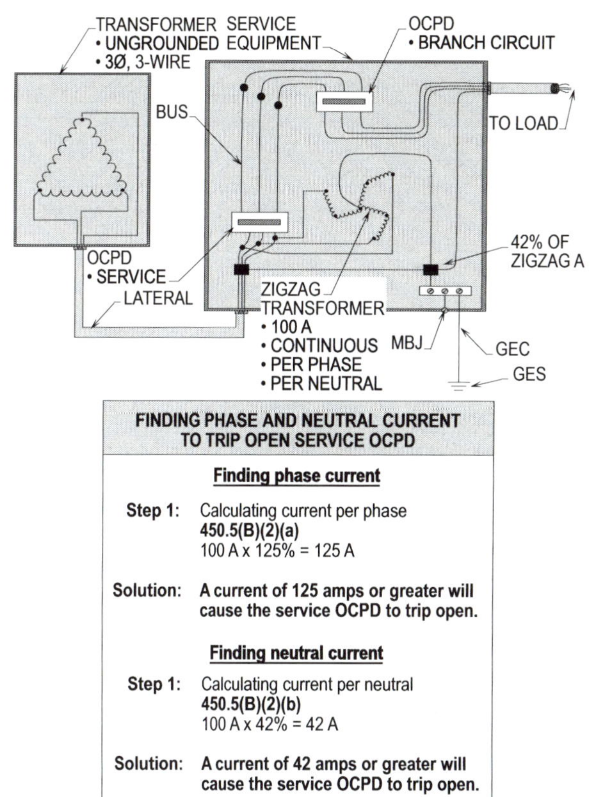

Figure 20-14. The overcurrent protection device shall open simultaneously with a common trip all ungrounded (phase) conductors and be set to trip at not more than 125 percent of the rated phase current of the transformer.

Note, 42 percent of the overcurrent protection device's rating shall be used if connected in the autotransformer's neutral connection. Review Sections **250.24(B), 250.30(A)(1), 250.32(B)(1), Ex**., and **450.5(B)(2)(b)**.

> **Design Tip:** This rule applies mainly where the loads are connected between transformer supply points per **450.6(A)(2)**.

- Sections **450.6(A)(1)** and **(A)(2)** state that both ends of each tie connection shall be provided with a protective device that opens at a certain temperature of the tie conductor. This prevents damage to the tie conductor and its insulation, and such installations shall consist of:

(a) A limiter is a fusible link cable connector. The limiter is selected and designed for the insulation, conductor material, etc. on the tie conductors.

(b) A circuit breaker, actuated by devices having characteristics that are comparable to the above, can be used if designed and sized properly.

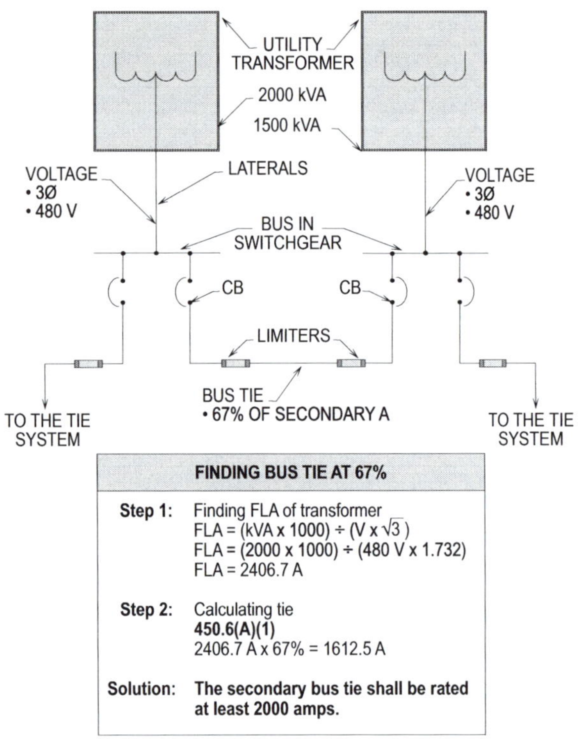

LOADS AT TRANSFORMER SUPPLY POINTS ONLY
NEC 450.6(A)(1)

Figure 20-15. The ampacity of the ties connecting conductors shall not be less than 67 percent of the rated secondary current of the largest transformer in the tie circuit.

Design Tip: The above applies where the tie circuit protection is provided per **450.6(A)(3)**, and the tie conductor shall fully comply with all rules and regulations in such sections.

• Where the tie consists of more than one conductor per phase, the conductors of each phase shall be interconnected in order to create a load supply point. The protection required in **450.6(A)(3)** is to be provided in each tie conductor at this point, except as follows:

Section **450.6(A)(4)(b)** permits the loads to be connected to the individual conductor(s) of each phase and without the protection listed in **450.6(A)(3)** if, at load connection points, the tie conductors of each phase have a combined capacity of not less than 133 percent of the rated secondary current of the largest transformer connected to the secondary tie system. The total load of such taps shall not exceed the rated secondary current of the largest transformer, and the loads shall be equally divided on each phase and on the individual conductors of each phase as closely as possible. **(See Figure 20-17)**

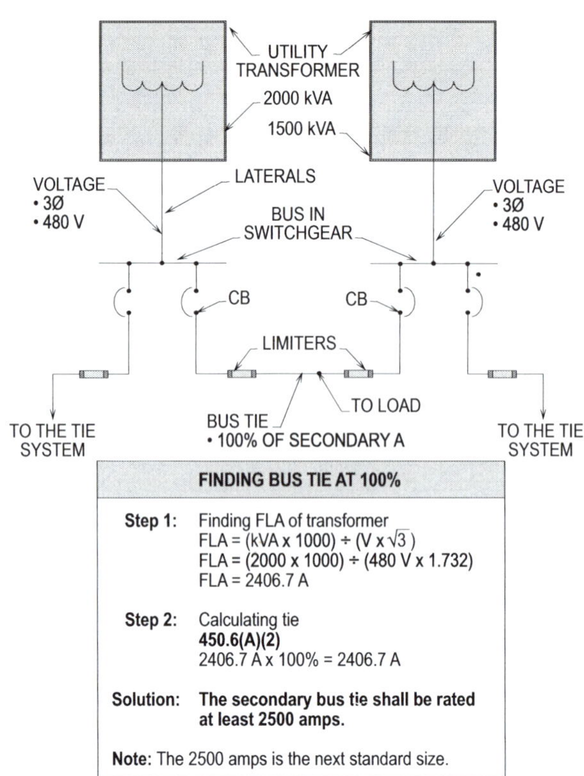

LOADS CONNECTED BETWEEN
TRANSFORMER SUPPLY POINTS
NEC 450.6(A)(2)

Figure 20-16. The rated ampacity of the tie shall not be less than 100 percent of the rated secondary current of the largest transformer connected to the secondary tie system except as provided in **450.6(A)(4)**.

The use of multiple conductors on each phase and the requirement that loads do not have to tap the multiple conductors of the same phase might possibly set up unbalanced current flow in the multiple conductors on the same phase.

The requirement that the combined capacity of the multiple conductors on the same phase be rated at 133 percent of the secondary current of the largest transformer is satisfied. Limiters are necessary at the tap or connections to the transformers that are tied together to properly protect the elements of the circuit.

Design Tip: The above applies where the interconnection of phase conductors between transformers supply points occurs, per **450.6(A)(4)(b)**.

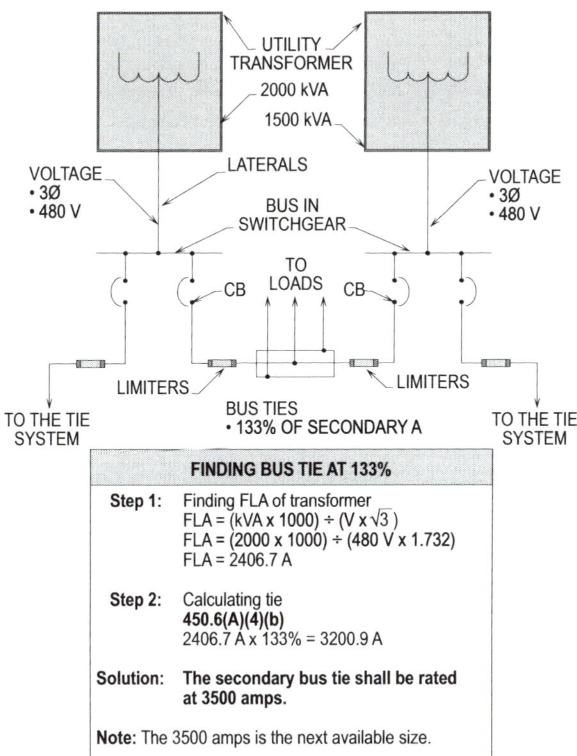

FINDING BUS TIE AT 133%
Step 1: Finding FLA of transformer FLA = (kVA x 1000) ÷ (V x √3) FLA = (2000 x 1000) ÷ (480 V x 1.732) FLA = 2406.7 A
Step 2: Calculating tie **450.6(A)(4)(b)** 2406.7 A x 133% = 3200.9 A
Solution: **The secondary bus tie shall be rated at 3500 amps.**
Note: The 3500 amps is the next available size.

INTERCONNECTION OF PHASE CONDUCTORS BETWEEN TRANSFORMER SUPPLY POINTS NEC 450.6(A)(4)(b)

Figure 20-17. Section **450.6(A)(4)(b)** permits the loads to be connected to the individual conductor(s) of each phase and without the protection listed in **450.6(A)(3)** if, at load connection points, the tie conductors of each phase have a combined capacity of not less than 133 percent of the rated secondary current of the largest transformer connected to the secondary tie system.

- If the operating voltage of secondary ties exceeds 150 volts to ground, there shall be a switch ahead of the limiters and tie conductors that is capable of deenergizing the tie conductors and the limiters. This switch shall comply with the following:

  (a) The current rating of the switch shall not be less than the current rating of the conductors connected to such switch.

  (b) The switch shall be capable of opening its rated current.

  (c) The switch shall not open under the magnetic forces caused by short-circuit currents.

- When secondary ties from transformers are used, an overcurrent device in the secondary of each transformer that is rated or set at not greater than 250 percent (2.5 times) of the rated secondary current of the transformer shall be provided. In addition, there shall be a circuit breaker actuated by a reverse-current relay; the breaker is to be set at not greater than the rated secondary current of the transformer. Such overcurrent protection protects against overloads and short-circuit conditions, and the reverse-current relay and circuit breaker shall be designed to handle any reversal of current flow into the transformer. **(See Figure 20-18)**

PARALLEL OPERATION
450.7

Transformers shall be permitted to be connected in parallel and switched as a unit, provided each transformer has overcurrent protection that is properly sized and complies with **450.3(A)** and **450.3(B)**. **(See Figure 20-19)**

Persons working with paralleled transformers or transformer tie circuits should be extremely careful that there are no feedbacks or other conditions that would affect safety. In order to secure a balance of current between paralleled transformers, all transformers should have characteristics that are very much alike, such as voltage, impedance, and other such pertinent elements.

GUARDING
450.8

Transformers shall be permitted to be isolated in a room or accessible only to qualified personnel to prevent accidental contact with live parts. To safeguard live parts from possible damage, the transformer shall be elevated. The following are acceptable means of safeguarding live parts as required in **110.27(A)** and **110.34(E)**.

- Transformers shall be permitted to be isolated in a room or accessible only to qualified personnel.

- Permanent partitions or screens shall be permitted to be installed.

- Transformers shall be elevated at least 8 ft (2.5 m) above the floor to prevent unauthorized personnel from contact.

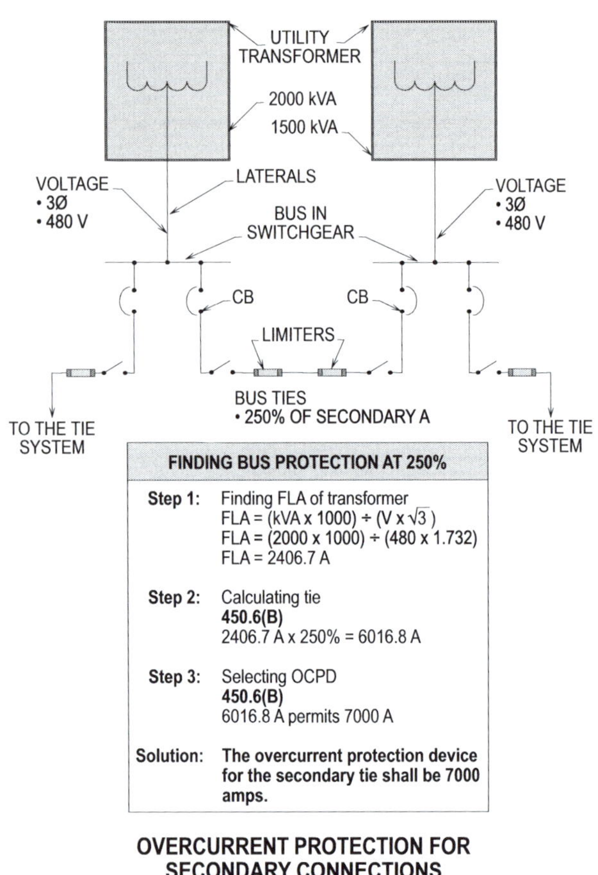

FINDING BUS PROTECTION AT 250%

Step 1: Finding FLA of transformer
FLA = (kVA x 1000) ÷ (V x $\sqrt{3}$)
FLA = (2000 x 1000) ÷ (480 x 1.732)
FLA = 2406.7 A

Step 2: Calculating tie
450.6(B)
2406.7 A x 250% = 6016.8 A

Step 3: Selecting OCPD
450.6(B)
6016.8 A permits 7000 A

Solution: **The overcurrent protection device for the secondary tie shall be 7000 amps.**

**OVERCURRENT PROTECTION FOR
SECONDARY CONNECTIONS
NEC 450.6(B)**

Figure 20-18. When secondary ties from transformers are used, an overcurrent device in the secondary of each transformer that is rated or set at not greater than 250 percent (2.5 times) of the rated secondary current of the transformer shall be provided.

Design Tip: Signs indicating the voltage of live exposed parts of transformers, or other suitable markings, shall be used in areas where transformers are located.

VENTILATION
450.9

Transformers shall be located and installed in rooms or areas that are not subject to exceedingly high temperatures to prevent overheating and possible damage to windings. Transformers with ventilating openings shall be installed so that the ventilating openings are not blocked by walls or other obstructions that could block air flow.

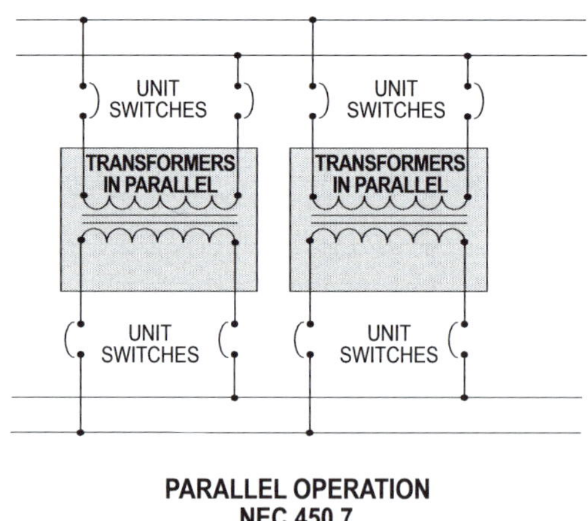

**PARALLEL OPERATION
NEC 450.7**

Figure 20-19. Transformers shall be permitted to be connected in parallel and switched as a unit, provided each transformer has overcurrent protection that is properly sized.

GROUNDING
450.10(A) AND (B)

Transformer cases shall be grounded per **250.110**. Transformers enclosed by fences or guards shall be grounded and bonded. Live parts require a guard such as a fence to prevent unauthorized entry and to protect the general public and unqualified persons from dangerous electrical parts. Such fences shall be grounded and bonded to prevent metal elements from being accidentally energized with voltage. **(See Figure 20-20)**

TYPES OF TRANSFORMERS
PART II TO ARTICLE 450

Transformers are either used indoors or outdoors based upon their type and condition of use. The type of transformer determines where it is permitted to be installed inside or outside of the building. Sometimes it becomes necessary to build rooms of certain fire-rated material or confinement areas to house transformers due to their design and installation.

DRY-TYPE TRANSFORMERS
INSTALLED INDOORS
450.21

The rules for installing dry-type transformers indoors can be summed up as follows:

- Dry-type transformers greater than 112-1/2 kVA, having Class 155 or higher insulation systems, shall have a fire-resistant, heat-insulating barrier placed between transformers and combustible material, or, if no barrier, shall be separated at least 6 ft (1.83 m) horizontally and 12 ft (3.7 m) vertically from the combustible material per **450.21(B), Ex. 1**. **(See Figure 20-21)**

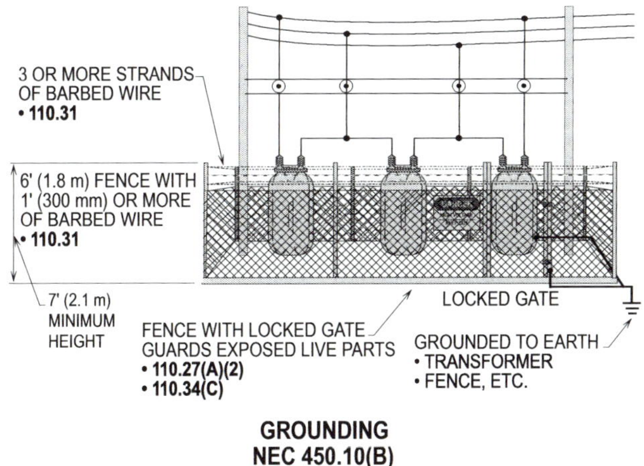

Figure 20-20. Transformers enclosed by fences or guards shall be grounded and bonded. Live parts require a guard such as a fence to prevent unauthorized entry and to protect the general public and unqualified persons from dangerous electrical parts.

- Dry-type transformers greater than 112-1/2 kVA and having Class 155 or higher of insulation systems shall be installed in a fire-resistant transformer room per **450.21(B), Ex. 2**. **(See Figure 20-22)**

- Dry-type transformers rated at 112-1/2 kVA or less and 1000 volts or less shall have a fire-resistant, heat-insulating barrier between transformers and combustible material, or, without a barrier, shall be separated at least 12 in. (300 mm) from the combustible material where the voltage is 1000 volts or less per **450.21(A)**. **(See Figure 20-23)**

- Dry-type transformers rated 112-1/2 kVA or less and 1000 volts or less shall not be required to have a 12 in. (300 mm) separation or barrier if they are completely enclosed, except for vent openings. **(See Figure 20-24)**

- All indoor dry-type transformers of over 35,000 volts shall be installed in a vault. Vault requirements shall fully comply with **Part III** of **Article 450**. **(See Figure 20-25)**

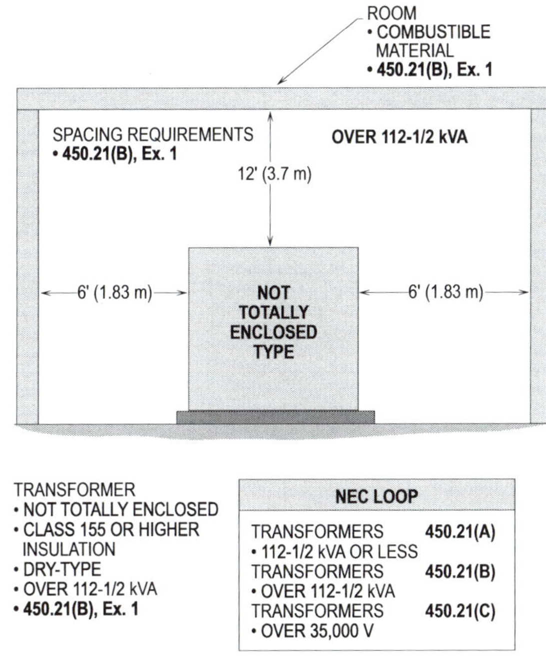

Figure 20-21. Dry-type transformers greater than 112-1/2 kVA and having Class 155 or higher insulation systems shall have a fire-resistant, heat-insulating barrier placed between transformers and combustible material, or, if no barrier, shall be separated at least 6 ft (1.83 m) horizontally and 12 ft (3.7 m) vertically from the combustible material.

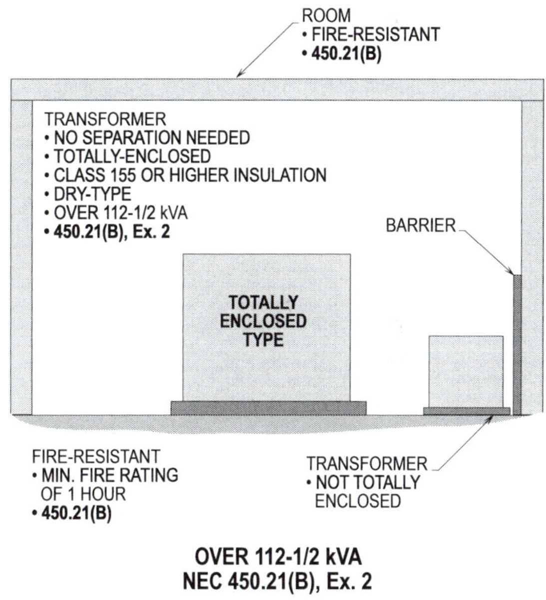

Figure 20-22. Dry-type transformers greater than 112-1/2 kVA and having Class 155 or higher insulation systems shall be installed in a fire-resistant transformer room.

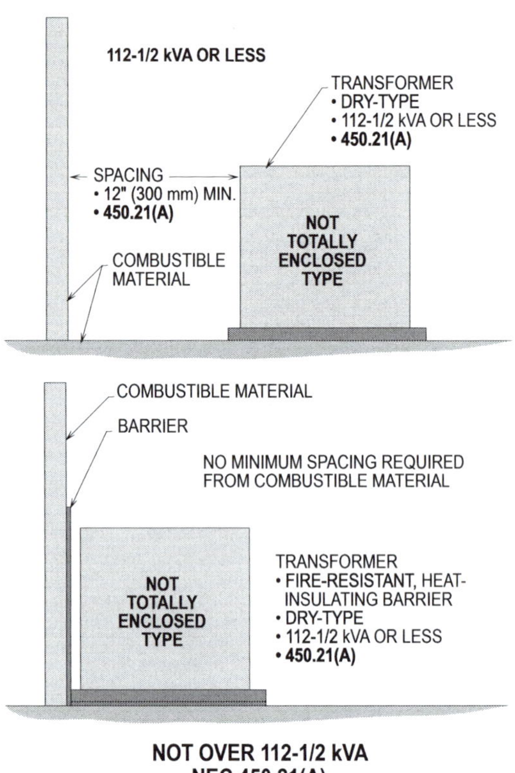

Figure 20-23 Dry-type transformers rated 112-1/2 kVA or less and 1000 volts or less shall have a fire-resistant, heat-insulating barrier between transformers and combustible material, or, without a barrier, shall be separated at least 12 in. (300 mm) from the combustible material where the voltage is over 1000 volts.

DRY-TYPE TRANSFORMERS INSTALLED OUTDOORS
450.22

Dry-type transformers installed outdoors shall have weatherproof enclosures. See the definition in **Article 100** for the difference between "weatherproof" and "watertight."

LESS FLAMMABLE LIQUID-INSULATED TRANSFORMERS
450.23

Transformers using a "listed" high fire point liquid shall be permitted to be installed indoors, but only in "noncombustible" areas of "noncombustible" buildings. The NEC sets the minimum fire point at 300°C (572°F). This is the minimum temperature at which the liquid ignites. Such transformers shall be permitted to be installed indoors, for voltages up to 35,000. Higher voltages require a vault if they are installed indoors. This is due to the safety required because of the higher voltage and associated equipment. **(See Figure 20-26)**

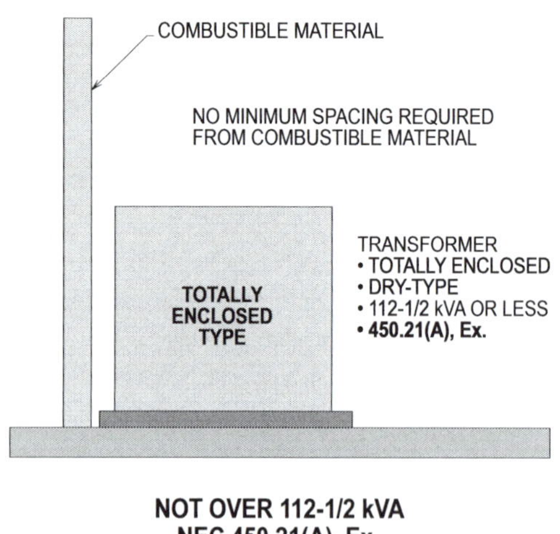

Figure 20-24. Dry-type transformers rated 112-1/2 kVA or less, and 1000 volts or less shall not be required to have a 12 in. (300 mm) separation or barrier if they are completely enclosed except for vent openings.

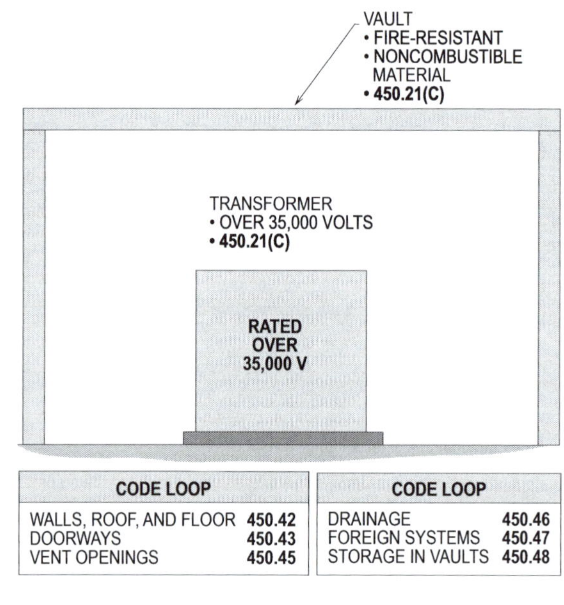

CODE LOOP		CODE LOOP	
WALLS, ROOF, AND FLOOR	450.42	DRAINAGE	450.46
DOORWAYS	450.43	FOREIGN SYSTEMS	450.47
VENT OPENINGS	450.45	STORAGE IN VAULTS	450.48

Figure 20-25. All indoor dry-type transformers of over 35,000 volts shall be installed in a vault.

NONFLAMMABLE FLUID-INSULATED TRANSFORMERS
450.24

Transformers using a "dielectric" nonflammable liquid shall be permitted to be installed indoors in any location, for voltages up to 35,000. Higher voltages require a vault, when installed indoors due to the safety required for the higher voltage and associated equipment.

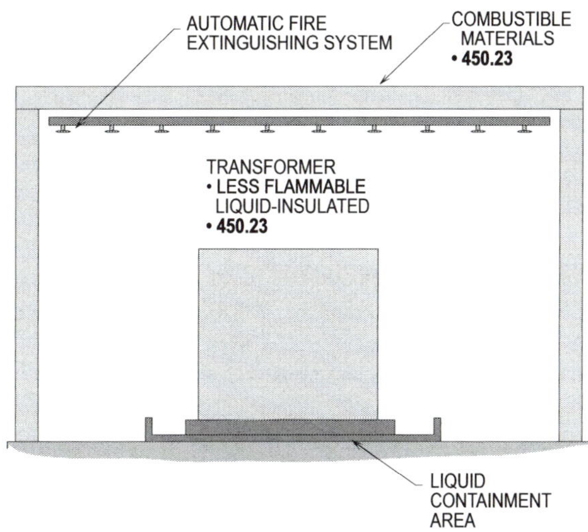

**LESS FLAMMABLE LIQUID-INSULATED TRANSFORMERS
NEC 450.23**

Figure 20-26. Transformers using a "listed" high fire point liquid shall be permitted to be installed indoors, but only in "noncombustible" areas of "noncombustible" buildings. The NEC sets the minimum fire point at 300°C (572°F).

For the purpose of this section, a nonflammable dielectric fluid is one that does not have a flash point or fire point, and is not flammable in air.

ASKAREL-INSULATED TRANSFORMERS INSTALLED INDOORS
450.25

Askarel is a liquid that does not burn; therefore, it is safer than oil for use as a transformer liquid. However, arcing in askarel produces greater gases that are nonexplosive.

Askarel-insulated transformers of over 25 kVA shall be furnished with a relief vent such as a chimney to relieve the pressure built up by gases that may be generated within the transformer.

In rooms that are well ventilated, the vent may be discharged directly to the room. In rooms that are poorly ventilated, the vent shall be piped to a flue or chimney that is capable of carrying the gases out of the room. Or, as an alternative to such ventilating, the transformer can be fitted with a gas absorber placed inside the case. When there is a gas absorber, the vent may also be discharged to the room.

Askarel transformers of more than 35,000 volts shall be installed in a vault because the oil and higher voltage are a hazard to unqualified personnel. **(See Figure 20-27)**

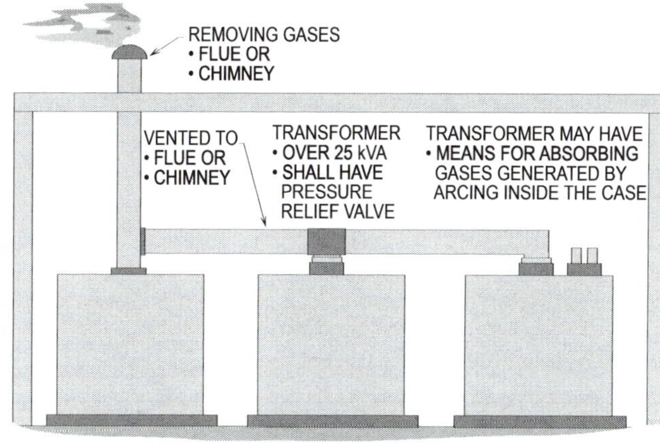

**ASKAREL-INSULATED TRANSFORMERS INSTALLED INDOORS
NEC 450.25**

Figure 20-27. Askarel-insulated transformers of over 25 kVA shall be furnished with a relief vent such as a chimney to relieve the pressure built up by gases that may be generated within the transformer.

OIL-INSULATED TRANSFORMERS INSTALLED INDOORS
450.26

The rules for installing oil-insulated transformers indoors can be summed up as follows:

- Indoor oil-filled transformers greater than 1000 volts shall be installed in a vault, with the following exceptions, where, regardless of voltage, a vault is not required:

    (a) Electric furnace transformers with a total rating of 75 kVA or less shall be permitted to be located in a fire-resistant room.

    (b) Oil-filled transformers may be installed in a building without a vault, provided the building is accessible to qualified personnel only and is used solely for providing electric service to other buildings.

- If suitable provisions are provided to prevent a possible oil fire from igniting other materials, oil-filled transformers of 1000 volts or less shall be permitted to be installed without a vault. When installed without a vault, the total kVA rating of all transformers allowed in a room or section of a building is limited to 10 kVA for nonfire-resistant buildings and to 75 kVA for fire-resistant buildings.

See Figure 20-28 for installing rules when applying the **Ex. 1** to **450.26**.

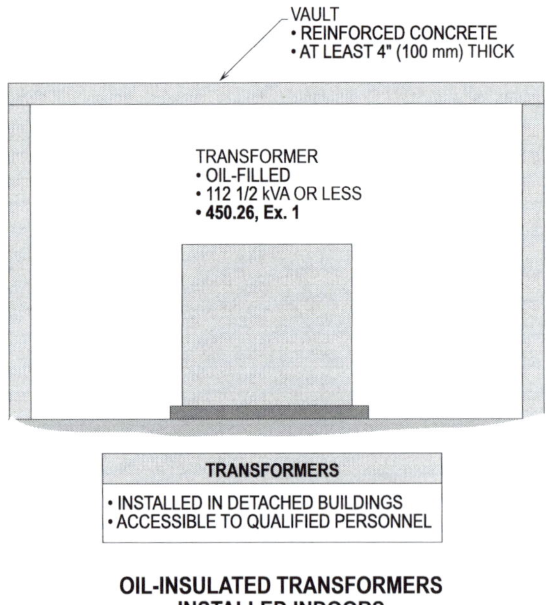

**OIL-INSULATED TRANSFORMERS
INSTALLED INDOORS
NEC 450.26, Ex. 1**

Figure 20-28. Oil-filled transformers rated 112-1/2 kVA or less that are installed in detached buildings and accessible to only qualified personnel shall be installed in a vault with reinforced concrete at least 4 in. (100 mm) thick.

OIL-INSULATED TRANSFORMERS INSTALLED OUTDOORS
450.27

When oil-filled transformers are installed on or adjacent to combustible buildings or material, the building or material shall be safeguarded from possible fire originating in a transformer. Fire-resistant barriers, water-spray systems, and enclosures for the transformers are approved safeguards if, where used, they are installed by the rules of the NEC. **[See Figures 20-29(a) and (b)]**

LOCATION OF TRANSFORMER VAULTS
450.41

Vaults are used to house dry-type transformers that are rated over 35 kV or transformers filled with combustible material used as an aid in cooling their windings.

Vaults shall be designed and built with specific rules and regulations according to **Part III** of **Article 450.**.

Wherever possible, transformer vaults shall be located at an outside wall of the building. This rule is intended to allow ventilation direct to the outside without using ducts, flues, etc. per **450.45**.

WALLS, ROOFS, AND FLOORS
450.42

The rules for construction of vaults are set forth in this section. Floor, walls, and roof shall be of fire-resistant material such as concrete and be capable of withstanding heat from a fire within for at least three hours. A 6 in. (150 mm) thickness is specified for the walls and roof. The floor, when laid and in contact with the earth, shall be at least 4 in. (100 mm) thick. Walls, roof, and floor shall have at least have a 3 hour fire rating. **(See Figure 20-30)**

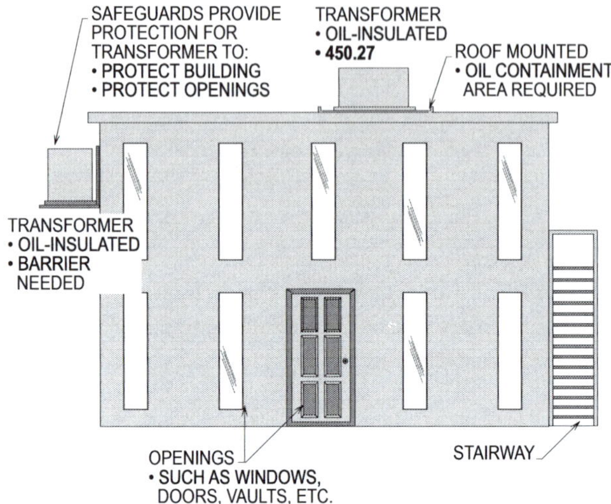

**OIL-INSULATED TRANSFORMERS
INSTALLED OUTDOORS
NEC 450.27**

Figure 20-29(a). When oil-filled transformers are installed on or adjacent to combustible buildings or material, the building or material shall be safeguarded from possible fire originating in a transformer.

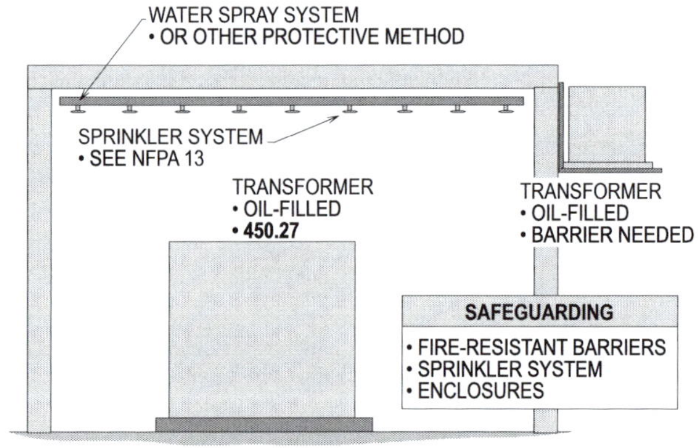

**OIL-INSULATED TRANSFORMER
INSTALLED OUTDOORS
NEC 450.27**

Figure 20-29(b). Fire-resistant barriers, water-spray systems, and enclosures for the transformers are approved safeguards if, where used, they are installed by the rules of the NEC.

DOORWAYS
450.43

The door to a transformer vault shall be built according to the standards of the National Fire Protection Association, which requires a 3 hour fire rating. The door sill shall be at least 4 in. (100 mm) high. This is to prevent any oil that may accumulate on the floor from running out of the transformer room and moving to other areas. Doors shall be kept locked at all times to prevent access of unqualified persons to the vault.

Design Tip: Personnel doors shall swing out and be equipped with listed panic bars, pressure plates, or other devices that open under simple pressure per **450.43(C)**.

VENTILATION OPENINGS
450.45

Where ventilation is direct to the outside, without the use of ducts or flues, the vent opening shall have an area of at least 3 sq. in. (1900 mm²) for each kVA of transformer capacity, but never less than 1 sq. ft (0.1 m²) in area. The vent opening shall be fitted with a screen or grating and an automatic closing damper. If ducts are used in the vent system, the ducts shall have sufficient capacity to maintain a suitable vault temperature. **(See Figure 20-31)**

DRAINAGE
450.46

Drains shall be provided for vaults containing more than 100 kVA transformer capacity to drain off oil that might accumulate on the floor due to a leak in a transformer caused by an accident. This rule is designed to prevent a fire hazard from occurring.

WATER PIPES AND ACCESSORIES
450.47

Piping for fire protection within the vault or piping to water-cooled transformers shall be permitted to be present in a vault. No other piping or duct system shall enter or pass through. Valves or other fittings of a foreign piping or duct system shall not be permitted in a vault containing transformers. **(See Figure 20-32)**

STORAGE IN VAULTS
450.48

No storage of any kind shall be permitted in a vault other than the transformers and equipment necessary for their

operation. This typically means that transformer vaults are not to be used for warehouses or storage areas but to contain transformers and accessories only. The reasons the vault is to be kept clear are the high voltage and safety measures needed for personnel servicing such equipment. Also, consideration shall be given to foreign material being a threat of fire under certain conditions. **(See Figure 20-33)**

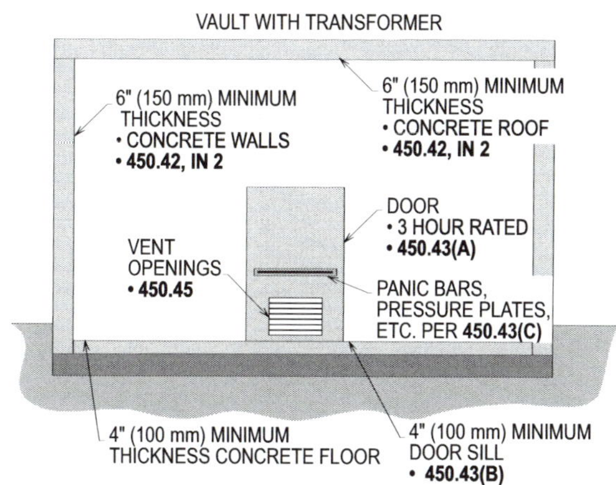

Figure 20-30. Floor, walls, and roof shall be of fire-resistant material such as concrete and be capable of withstanding heat from a fire within for at least three hours. A 6 in. (150 mm) thickness is specified for the walls and roof. The floor, when laid and in contact with the earth, shall be at least 4 in. (100 mm) thick. Also, see **Figure 5-21**.

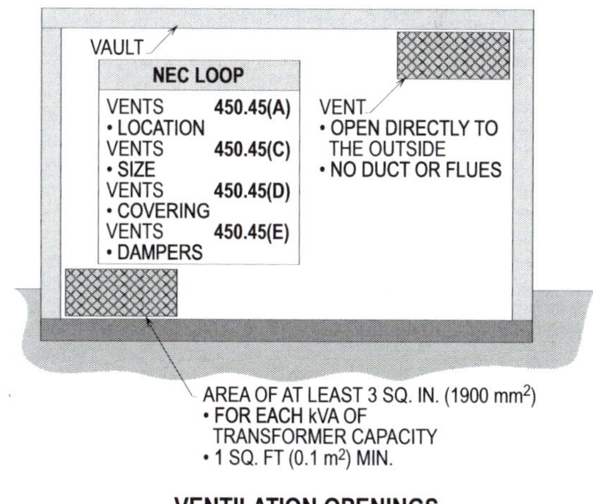

Figure 20-31. Where ventilation is direct to the outside, without the use of ducts or flues, the vent opening shall have an area of at least 3 sq. in. (1900 mm²) for each kVA of transformer capacity, but never less than 1 sq. ft (0.1 m²) in area.

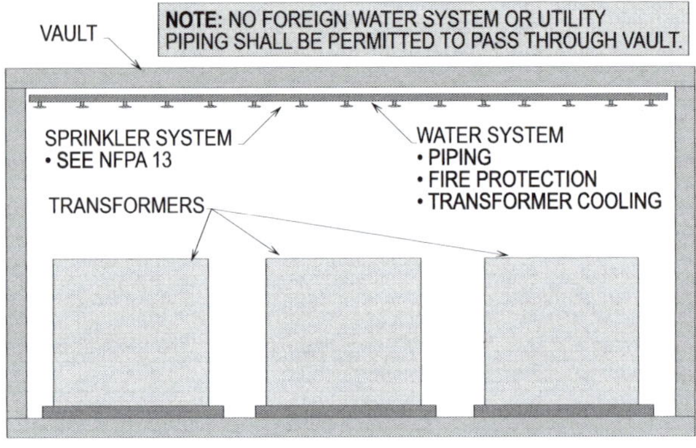

WATER PIPES AND ACCESSORIES
NEC 450.47

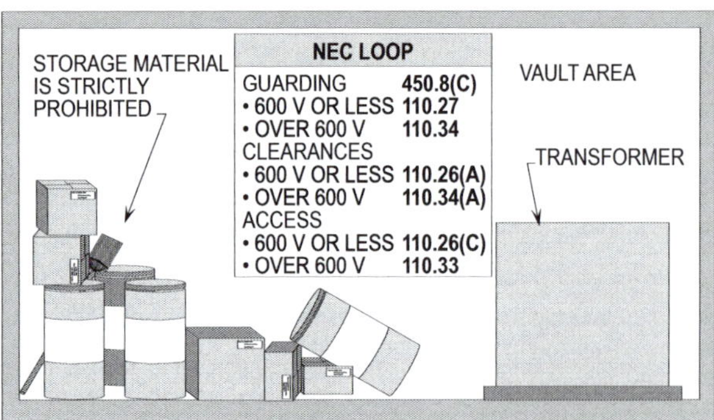

STORAGE IN VAULTS
NEC 450.48

Figure 20-32. Piping for fire protection within the vault or piping to water-cooled transformers shall be permitted to be present in a vault. No other piping or duct system shall enter or pass through.

CONNECTIONS FROM THE SECONDARY OF TRANSFORMERS 240.21(B) AND (C)

Overcurrent protection devices of circuits shall be located at the point where the service to those circuits originates. However, it shall be permitted to make connections from the secondary side of transformers. Such conductors shall be designed and installed by the rules and regulations of **240.21(B)** and **(C)**. Sizing connections, not over 25 ft (7.5 m) long, shall be designed and installed per **240.21(B)(3)** and **(C)(5)**. Transformer secondary conductors of separately derived systems for industrial locations are sized per **240.21(C)(2), (C)(3),** and **(C)(6)**. Outside transformer connections are sized per **240.21(C)(4)**. Overcurrent protection shall be provided by **450.3(B)** and **Table 450.3(B)**. (See **240.92(B)** and **(D)** and **Figure 20-34** for illustrated diagrams.)

NOT OVER 10 FT (3 m) LONG 240.21(C)(2)

Conductors shall be permitted to be connected, without overcurrent protection at the connection, to a feeder or transformer secondary where all the following conditions are met:

- Connecting conductors do not exceed 10 ft (3 m) in length.

- Connecting conductors shall have a current rating not less than the combined calculated loads of the circuits supplied by connecting conductors. Their ampacity shall not be less than the rating of the overcurrent protection device at the termination of the connecting conductors.

Figure 20-33. No storage material of any kind shall be placed in a vault other than the transformers and equipment necessary for their operation.

- The connecting conductors shall not extend beyond the switchboard, panelboard, disconnecting means, or control devices they supply.

- Connecting conductors shall be enclosed in a raceway that will extend from the connection to the enclosure of an enclosed switchboard, panelboard, or control devices, or to the back of an open switchboard.

- The rating of the overcurrent device protecting the primary of the transformer, multiplied by the primary to secondary voltage ratio, shall not exceed 10 times the ampacity of the secondary conductor for field installations where the secondary conductors leave the enclosure or vault.

Overcurrent protection for panelboards shall comply with the provisions outlined in **408.36**, including **Ex. 1, Ex. 2**, and **Ex. 3**, whichever applies. The maximum number of overcurrent devices shall be permitted to be determined per **408.54** and **408.55, Ex. 1**.

See Figure 20-35 for the proper procedure for making a connection using the 10 ft (3 m) rule.

NOT OVER 25 FT (7.5 m) LONG 240.21(B)(3) AND (C)(5)

Conductors supplying a transformer shall be permitted to be tapped, without overcurrent protection at the tap, from a feeder where all the following conditions are met:

- Tapped conductors supplying the primary shall have an ampacity at least 1/3 of the rating of the feeder being tapped.

- Connecting conductors supplying the secondary shall have an ampacity at least 1/3 of the rating of the feeder being connected, based on the primary-to-secondary voltage ratio.

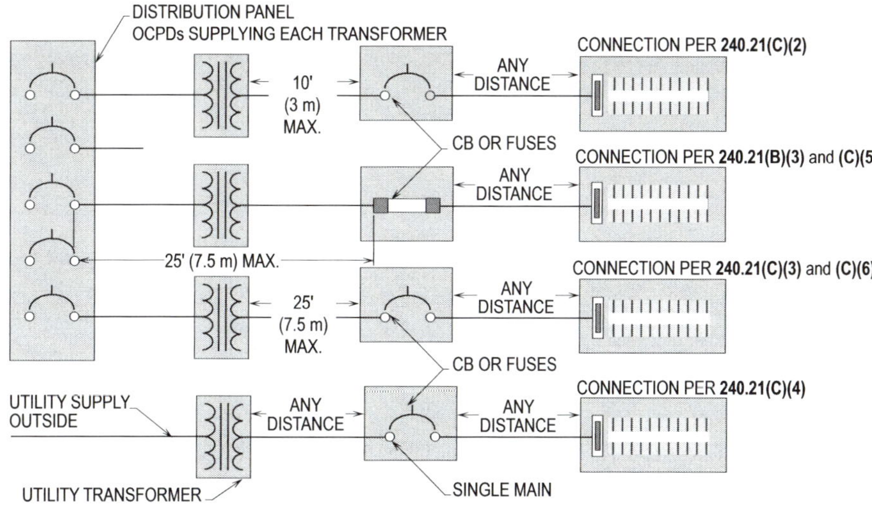

Figure 20-34. This illustration shows the four most used transformer secondary connections that are utilized to supply electrical systems with transformer secondary conductors.

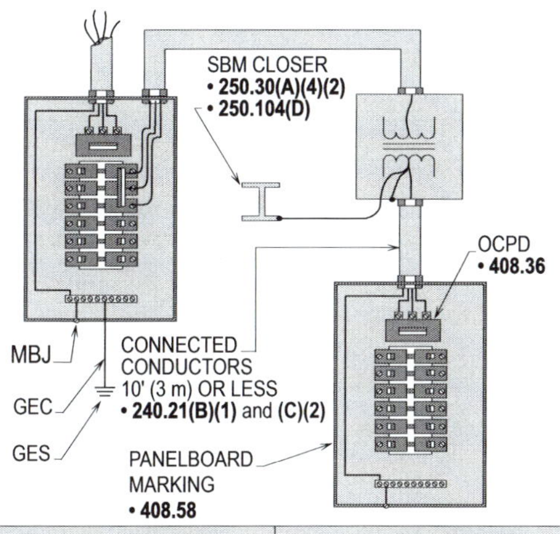

SIZING THWN CU. CONDUCTORS	SIZING OCPD
Step 1: Calculating min. size connection **240.21(C)(2)(1)** Calculated load is 148 A	**Step 1:** Calculating OCPD **240.4(E), 240.21(C)(2)(1), and 240.4(B)** 1/0 AWG cu. = 150 A OCPD rated at 150 A protects conductors from overload
Step 2: Sizing conductors **Table 310.15(B)(16)** 1/0 AWG THWN cu. = 150 A	
Step 3: Verifying size **240.21(C)(2)(1)** 150 A is greater than 148 A	**Solution:** **The size overcurrent protection device is permitted to be 150 amps.**
Solution: **The size THWN copper conductors are 1/0 AWG rated at 150 amps.**	**Note:** See Figure 9-26.

NOT OVER 10 FT (3 m) LONG
NEC 240.21(C)(2)

Figure 20-35. The above illustration shows the procedure for sizing a 10 ft (3 m) connection from the secondary of a transformer.

- The total length of one primary plus one secondary conductor shall not be over 25 ft (7.5 m).

- The primary and secondary conductors shall be protected from physical damage.

- Secondary conductors shall terminate in a single circuit breaker or set of fuses, sized to protect the secondary.

See Figure 20-36 for the proper procedure for making a tap and connection using the 25 ft (7.5 m) rule.

INDUSTRIAL INSTALLATION SECONDARY CONDUCTORS NOT OVER 25 FT (7.5 m) LONG 240.21(C)(3)

Conductors shall be permitted to be connected to a transformer secondary of a separately derived system for industrial locations, without overcurrent protection at the connection, where all the following conditions are met:

- Secondary conductors shall not exceed 25 ft (7.5 m) in length.

- Ampacity of connected conductors shall be equivalent to current rating of the transformer, and the overcurrent protection devices shall not exceed the ampacity of the connected conductors.

- All overcurrent devices are grouped.

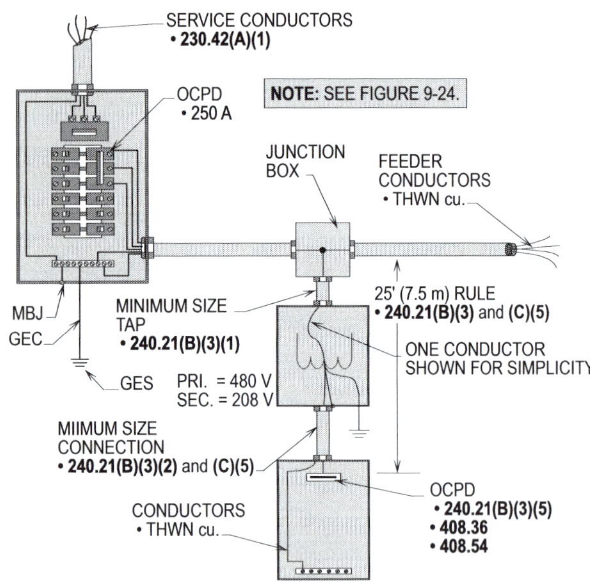

SIZING PRIMARY TAPPED CONDUCTORS

Step 1: Calculating primary tap
240.21(B)(3)(1)
1/3 of 250 A = 83 A

Step 2: Selecting conductors
Table 310.15(B)(16)
83 A requires 4 AWG cu.

Solution: The size THWN copper conductors are 4 AWG.

SIZING SECONDARY CONNECTING CONDUCTORS

Step 1: Calculating secondary connection
240.21(B)(3)(2)
(480 V ÷ 208 V) x (1/3 x 250 A) = 192 A

Step 2: Selecting conductors
Table 310.15(B)(16)
192 A requires 3/0 AWG cu.

Solution: The size THWN copper conductors are 3/0 AWG.

SIZING SECONDARY CONNECTING OCPD

Step 1: Selecting OCPD in secondary
240.4(E), 240.21(B)(3)(2), 240.21(C)(5), and 240.6(A)
200 A (3/0 AWG) requires 200 A

Solution: The size overcurrent protection device is 200 amps.

NOT OVER 25 FT (7.5 m) LONG
NEC 240.21(B)(3) AND (C)(5)

Figure 20-36. The primary tap for this connection rule shall be at least 1/3 of the overcurrent protection device protecting the larger feeder conductors. The secondary connecting conductors shall be at least 1/3 of the overcurrent protection device protecting the feeder conductors based on the primary-secondary transformer ratio.

- Connected conductors shall be protected from physical damage.

See Figure 20-37 for the procedure to be applied when a 25 ft (7.5 m) connection rule is installed from the secondary side of a transformer.

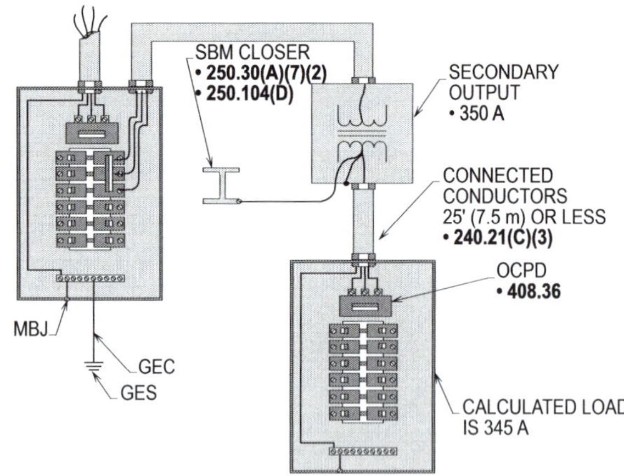

SIZING THWN cu. CONDUCTORS	SIZING OCPD
Step 1: Calculating min. size connection **240.21(C)(3)(2)** Calculated load is 345 A	**Step 1:** Calculating OCPD **240.4(E), 240.21(C)(3)(1), and 240.4(B)** 500 KCMIL cu. = 380 A OCPD rated at 350 A protects conductors from overload
Step 2: Sizing conductors **Table 310.15(B)(16)** 500 THWN cu. = 380 A	**Solution:** The size overcurrent protection device is permitted to be 350 amps.
Step 3: Verifying size **240.21(C)(3)(1)** 380 A is greater than 345 A	**Note 1:** If 6 circuit breakers are used, they must equal to one main.
Solution: The size THWN copper conductors are 500 KCMIL rated at 380 amps.	**Note 2:** Also, see Figure 9-27.

INDUSTRIAL INSTALLATION SECONDARY CONDUCTORS
NOT OVER 25 FT (7.5 m) LONG
NEC 240.21(C)(3)

Figure 20-37. This illustration shows the procedure for sizing a 25 ft (7.5 m) connection from the secondary of a transformer.

OUTSIDE SECONDARY CONDUCTORS 240.21(C)(4)

Outside conductors shall be permitted to be connected to a feeder or be connected at the transformer secondary without overcurrent protection at the connection. However, all of the following conditions shall be complied with:

- The connected conductors are suitably protected from physical damage.

- The conductors terminate at a single circuit breaker or a single set of fuses that will limit the load to the ampacity of the conductors. This single overcurrent protection device can supply any number of additional overcurrent devices of its load side.

- The overcurrent protection device for the conductors is an integral part of a disconnecting means or shall be located immediately adjacent thereto.

- The disconnecting means for the conductors are installed at a readily accessible location either outside of a building or structure or inside, nearest the point of entrance of the conductors.

See **Figure 20-38** for the rule pertaining to outside transformer connections from the secondary side of transformers.

TRANSFORMER SECONDARY CONDUCTORS IN LENGTHS OF 10 FT (3 m) TO 25 FT (7.5 m) 240.21(C)(6)

Conductors over 10 ft (3 m) and up to 25 ft (7.5 m) in length shall be permitted to be connected to the secondary size of a transformer. When applying this section, the 25 ft (7.5 m) secondary connection shall be terminated in a single overcurrent protection device (circuit breaker or fuses) to limit the load and to also comply with the 1/3 rule when multiplied by the secondary-to-primary voltage ratio. The secondary conductors shall be protected from physical damage and abuse. **(See Figure 20-39)**

SUPERVISED INDUSTRIAL INSTALLATIONS – FEEDER AND BRANCH-CIRCUIT CONDUCTORS 240.92(A)

Feeder and branch-circuit conductors shall be protected at the point where the conductors receive their supply. However, this permits a variation of requirements for transformer secondary conductors taken from separately derived systems and outside feeder taps.
(See Figure 20-40)

SUPERVISED INDUSTRIAL INSTALLATIONS AND CONNECTIONS UP TO 100 FT (30 m) 240.92(C)(1)(1) AND (2)

Unprotected lengths of secondary conductors shall be permitted at up to 100 ft (30 m) if the transformer primary overcurrent is sized at a value (reflected to the secondary by the transformer phase voltage ratio) of not more than 150 percent of the secondary conductor ampacity.

Additionally, the conductors shall be protected by a differential relay with a trip setting equal to or less than the conductor ampacity.

Note, a differential relay provides superior short-circuit protection at a trip open value that is almost always well below the conductor ampacity. **(See Figure 20-41)**

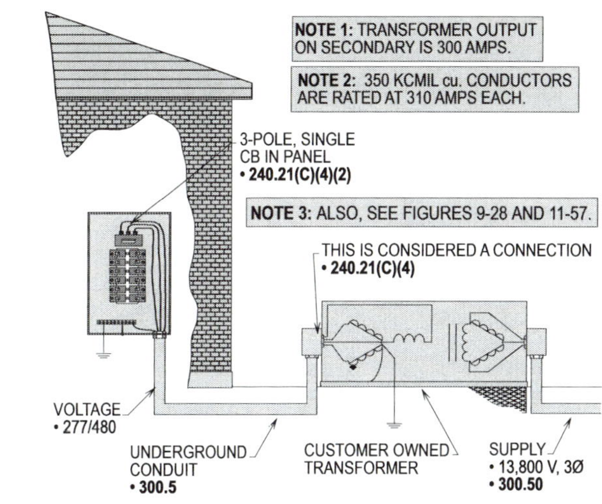

SIZING CONDUCTOR USING THWN cu.		SIZING OCPD BASED UPON SEC. OUTPUT	
Step 1:	Sizing conductors 300 A requires 350 KCMIL	Step 1:	Sizing OCPD 300 A output requires 300 A OCPD
Solution:	The size THWN copper conductors are 350 KCMIL.	Solution:	The size overcurrent protection device required is 300 amps.

OUTSIDE SECONDARY CONDUCTORS
NEC 240.21(C)(4)

Figure 20-38. This illustration shows the rules for sizing the conductors and overcurrent protection device for a feeder connection from a transformer located outside.

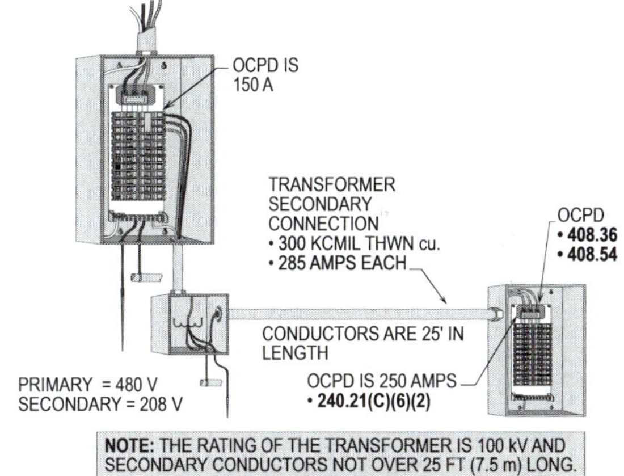

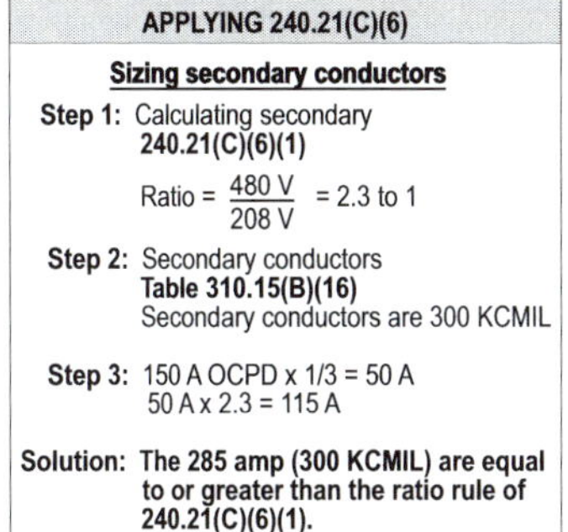

TRANSFORMER SECONDARY CONDUCTORS
IN LENGTHS OF 10 FT (3 m) TO 25 FT (7.5 m)
NEC 240.21(C)(6)

Figure 20-39. This illustration shows the rules for making a 25 ft (7.5 m) secondary conductor connection in other than industrial locations.

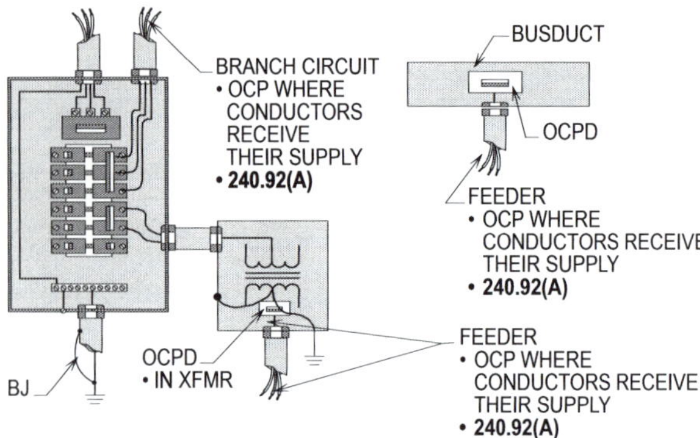

Figure 20-40. This illustration shows feeder and branch-circuit conductors protected at the point where the conductors receive their supply. (Also, see **240.21(C)(4)** and **Figure 9-29** for a similar rule.)

SHORT-CIRCUIT AND GROUND FAULT PROTECTION
240.92(C)(1)(3)

Conductors up to 100 ft (30 m) in length shall be permitted if calculations are made under engineering supervision and it is determined that the secondary conductors will be protected within recognized times versus current limits for all short-circuits and ground fault conditions that could occur. **(See Figure 20-41)**

OVERLOAD PROTECTION
240.92(C)(2)

To provide overload protection, the secondary conductors shall be permitted to be terminated in a single overcurrent protection device or in lugs of the bus, if not more than six overcurrent protection devices with a combined rating are installed that do not exceed the ampacity of the conductors. Another method of protection is to provide overload current relaying with the ability (design into) to trip either the primary overcurrent protection devices or the downstream overcurrent protection devices so that the load current does not exceed the conductor's ampacity. **(See Figure 20-42)**

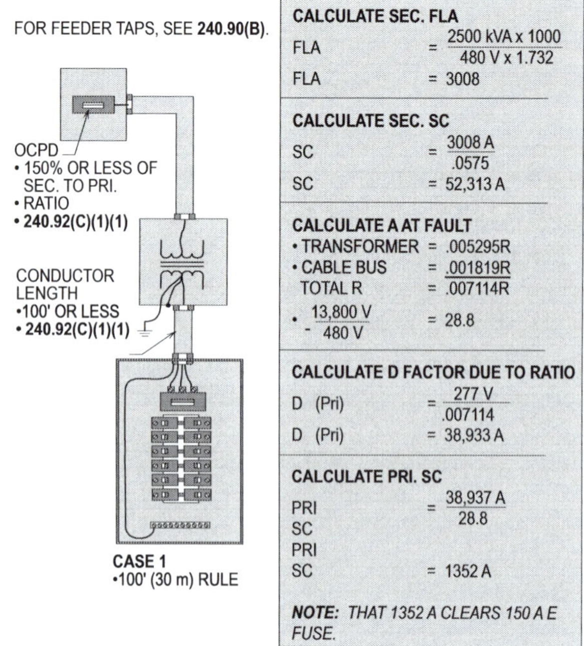

CALCULATE SEC. FLA

$$FLA = \frac{2500 \text{ kVA} \times 1000}{480 \text{ V} \times 1.732}$$

$$FLA = 3008$$

CALCULATE SEC. SC

$$SC = \frac{3008 \text{ A}}{.0575}$$

$$SC = 52{,}313 \text{ A}$$

CALCULATE A AT FAULT
• TRANSFORMER = .005295R
• CABLE BUS = .001819R
TOTAL R = .007114R

$$\frac{13{,}800 \text{ V}}{480 \text{ V}} = 28.8$$

CALCULATE D FACTOR DUE TO RATIO

$$D \text{ (Pri)} = \frac{277 \text{ V}}{.007114}$$

$$D \text{ (Pri)} = 38{,}933 \text{ A}$$

CALCULATE PRI. SC

$$\frac{PRI}{SC} = \frac{38{,}937 \text{ A}}{28.8}$$

$$\frac{PRI}{SC} = 1352 \text{ A}$$

NOTE: THAT 1352 A CLEARS 150 A E FUSE.

SHORT-CIRCUIT AND GROUND FAULT PROTECTION
NEC 240.92(C)(1)(1), (2), AND (3)

Figure 20-41. This illustration shows methods of providing short-circuit and ground fault protection for transformers and conductors. Also, see **Figure 9-33**.

SUPERVISED INDUSTRIAL INSTALLATIONS–OUTSIDE FEEDER TAPS
240.92(D)

Section **240.92(D)** permits alternative means of protecting transformer secondary conductors in supervised industrial installations where the transformer is located outside. The secondary conductors shall be protected against (1) overloads, with the additional stipulation that (2) they are suitably protected against physical damage. **[See Figures 20-43(a) and (b)]**

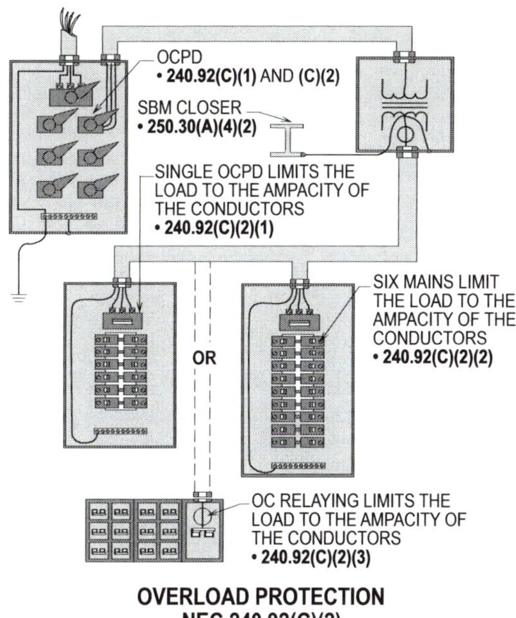

Figure 20-42. The above illustration shows methods of providing overload protection.

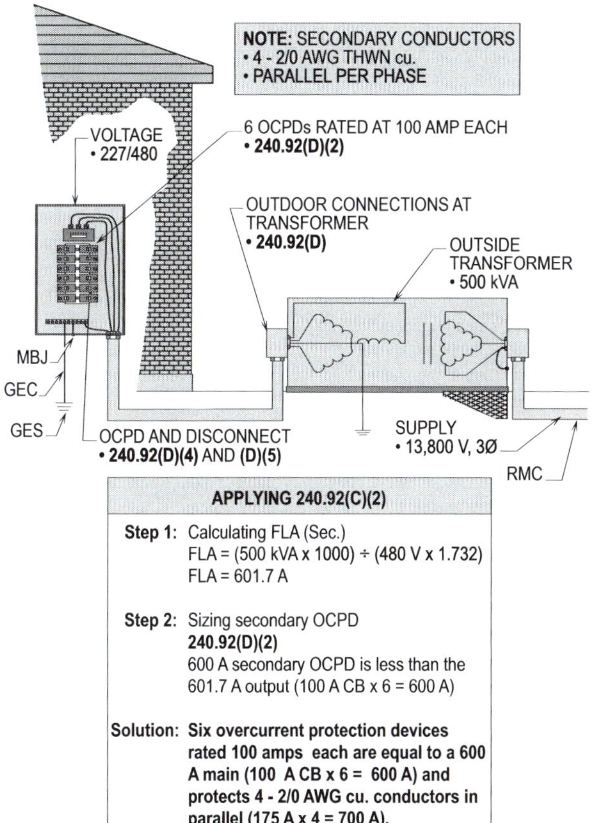

Figure 20-43(a). The above illustration shows alternative means allowed for protecting conductors tapped to a transformer located outside.

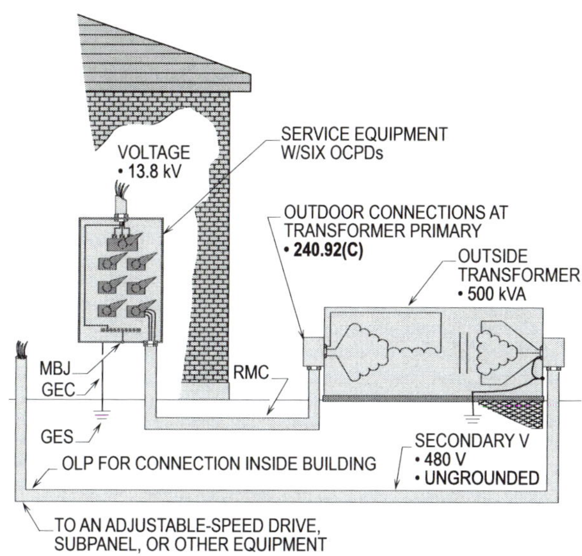

Figure 20-43(b). The above illustration shows alternative means permitted for protecting conductors connected to a transformer located outside.

PROTECTION BY PRIMARY OVERCURRENT DEVICE 240.92(E)

Conductors supplied by the secondary side of a transformer shall be permitted to be protected by overcurrent protection, provided on the primary (supply) side of the transformer, provided the primary device time-current protection characteristic, multiplied by the maximum effective primary-to-secondary transformer voltage ratio, effectively protects the secondary conductors. **(See Figure 20-44)**

Design Tip: This section recognizes overcurrent protection installations where a device in series, with a transformer primary, is used to protect secondary conductors. The ratios given in **240.92(E)** are recognized in numerous industry standards and references, including IEEE Standard C37.91.

EXCEPTION TO 725.3(C)

Type CL2P or CL3P cables and plenum signaling raceways shall be permitted for Class 2 and Class 2 circuits installed in other spaces used for environmental air per **300.22**, if in accordance with **Ex. 2 t**o **725.154.**

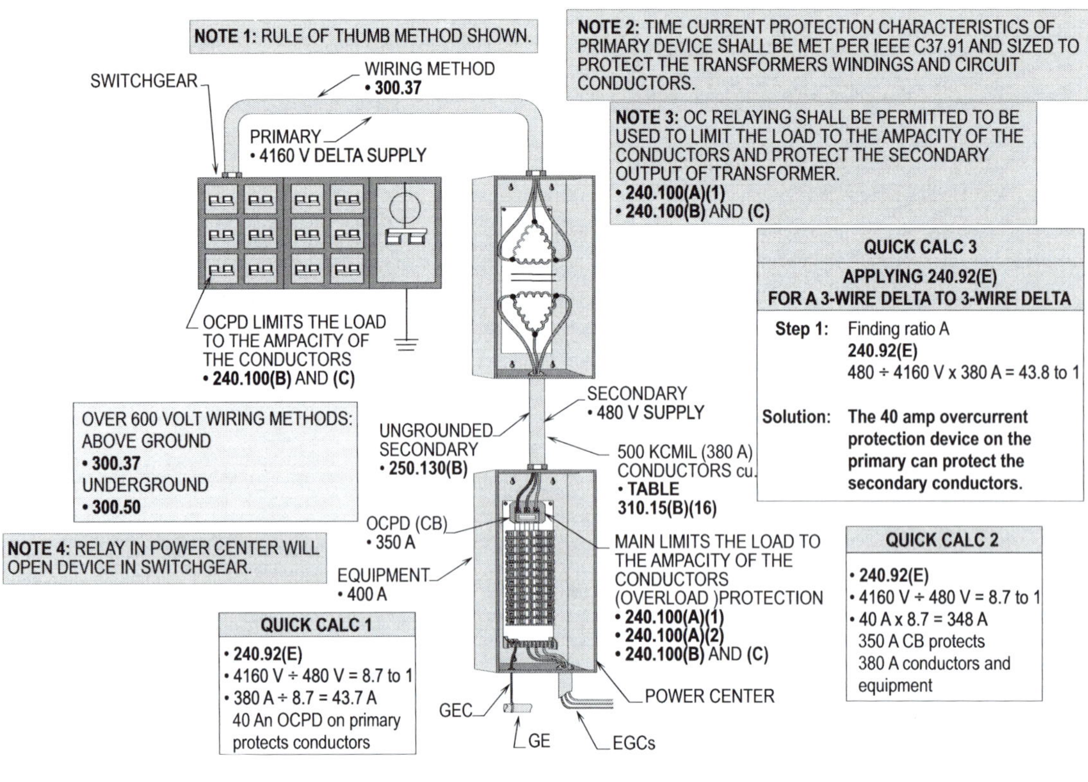

Figure 20-44. The primary protection of a transformer shall be permitted to be used to protect the secondary conductors, provided the primary device time-current protection characteristic, multiplied by the maximum effective primary-to-secondary voltage ratio will effectively protect the secondary conductors.

SOURCE MARKING
450.11(B)

A transformer shall be permitted to be supplied at the marked secondary voltage, provided that the installation is in accordance with the manufacturer's instructions.

Design Tip: Reverse-connecting is the connecting of secondary output windings with the power supply and using the primary input winding to supply the load. Dry-type transformers can be reverse-connected and still supply the same kVA. Single-phase transformers rated at 1 kVA and larger and three-phase transformers rated at 15 kVA and larger can be reverse-connected without losing any kVA capacity. The kVA rating is limited to this value because the turns ratio is the same as the voltage ratio.

Single-phase transformers rated below 1 kVA have a turns ration that compensates for the low voltage winding. The compensation becomes greater as the kVA rating becomes smaller. When the transformer is reverse-connected, the voltage is less at full load than at no load. Before connecting a transformer for a backfed (reverse) operation, always consult with the manufacturer for installation instructions. **(See Figure 20-45)**

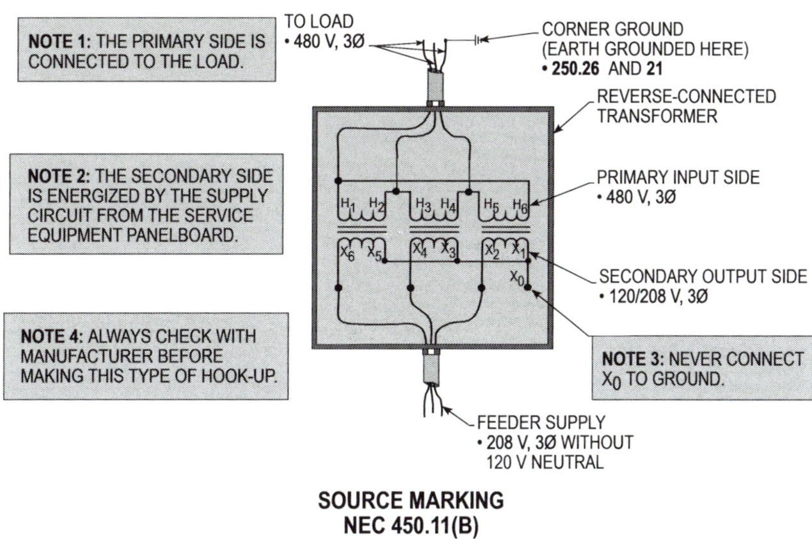

Figure 20-45. This illustration shows the source marking requirements for a transformer.

WIRING AND EQUIPMENT IN SPACES USED FOR ENVIRONMENTAL AIR 300.22(C)(1)

Only wiring methods of a specific type shall be permitted to be installed in ducts used to transport dust, loose stock, or flammable vapors. Wiring methods of any type shall not be permitted to be installed in any duct, or shaft containing only such ducts, used for vapor removal or ventilation of commercial type cooking equipment.

The following wiring methods are only permitted to be installed in ducts or plenums used for environmental air:

- MI cable
- MC cable
- AC cable
- Factory-assembled multiconductor control or power cable specifically listed for the use within an air-handling space
- Listed prefabricated cable assemblies of metallic manufactured wiring systems without nonmetallic sheath
- Electrical metallic tubing
- Flexible metallic tubing
- Intermediate metal conduit
- Rigid metal conduit

Flexible metal conduit and liquidtight flexible metal conduit shall be permitted to be used in lengths not to exceed 4 ft (1.2 m) to connect equipment and devices permitted to be in these ducts and plenum chambers.

Flexible metal conduit and liquidtight flexible metal conduit in single lengths shall be permitted to be used in air-handling ceiling spaces where not exceeding 6 ft (1.8 m). Cables that have a fire-resistant and low-smoke characteristics shall be permitted to be used in air-handling ceiling spaces without conduit per **725.3(C), 760.3(B)** and **800.3(B)**.

See Figure 20-46 for other types of wiring methods permitted in other types of spaces used for environmental air.

Design Tip: Electrical equipment with metal enclosures or nonmetallic enclosures that are listed shall be permitted to be installed in other spaces used for environmental air per **300.22(C)(3)**. A transformer that is totally enclosed may be installed to meet this requirement per **450.13(B)** if approved for such use.

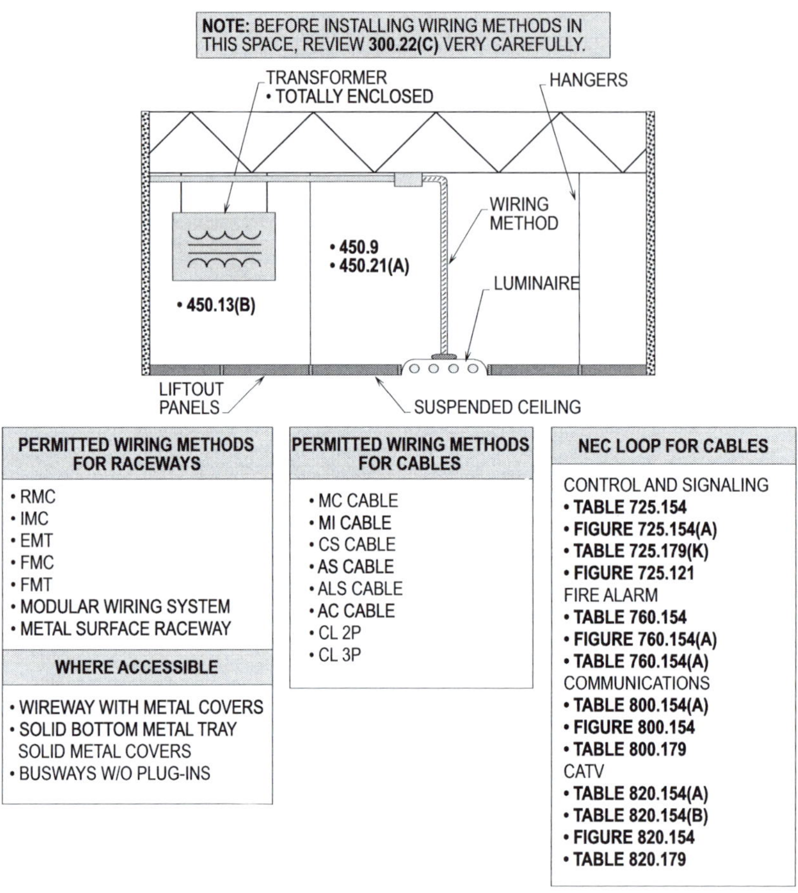

Figure 20-46. The above illustration shows the permitted wiring methods in spaces used for environmental air.

Chapter 20. Transformers

Section   Answer

1. Lighting transformers for a closed delta-connected secondary system can be found by multiplying the three-phase load by _____ percent.

    (a) 33   (b) 67
    (c) 75   (d) 100

2. The lighting transformer for an open delta-connected secondary system can be found by multiplying the three-phase load by _____ percent and adding this value to the single-phase load.

    (a) 33   (b) 58
    (c) 67   (d) 75

3. A transformer 1000 volts or less, nominal, having an individual overcurrent protection device on the primary side shall be sized at not more than _____ percent of the transformer's full-load current rating, in amps. (General rule)

    (a) 100   (b) 110
    (c) 115   (d) 125

4. An overcurrent protection sensing device shall be designed to trip at _____ percent of its continuous current per phase or neutral rating.

    (a) 100   (b) 125
    (c) 150   (d) 250

5. Askarel transformers of more than _____ volts shall be installed in a vault.

    (a) 10,000   (b) 25,000
    (c) 35,000   (d) 50,000

6. Walls, roof, and floor for a transformer vault shall at least have a _____ hour fire resistance rating.

    (a) 1   (b) 2
    (c) 3   (d) 5

7. Flexible metal conduit in single lengths shall be permitted to be used in air-handling spaces where not exceeding _____ ft.

    (a) 3   (b) 4
    (c) 5   (d) 6

8. A closed delta-connected secondary system can be found by multiplying the single-phase load by _____ percent.

    (a) 67   (b) 89
    (c) 100   (d) 125

Section   **Answer**

9. Dry-type transformers not over 1000 volts that are located on open walls or steel columns do not have to be _______ accessible.

   (a) easily   (b) readily
   (c) employee   (d) permanently

10. If installing fuses, the individual overcurrent protection device for the primary side of a transformer rated over 1000 volts shall be rated not greater than _______ percent of the rated primary current of the transformer. (Supervised location)

   (a) 125   (b) 150
   (c) 200   (d) 250

11. For a transformer in a nonsupervised location with a secondary voltage rated 1000 volts or less, the overcurrent protection device and conductors on the secondary side shall be sized at _______ percent of the FLC rating. (Any location)

   (a) 125   (b) 150
   (c) 200   (d) 250

12. For a transformer 1000 volts or less, nominal, where the rated secondary current of a transformer is less than 9 amps but 2 amps or more, an overcurrent protection device rated or set at no more than _______ percent of secondary current shall be permitted to be used.

   (a) 133   (b) 150
   (c) 167   (d) 225

13. Autotransformers shall have a _______ neutral current rating sufficient for the specified ground fault current that could develop in the system.

   (a) noncontinuous   (b) varying
   (c) periodic   (d) continuous

14. Where transformers are tied together in parallel and connected by tie conductors that do not have overcurrent protection, the ampacity of the ties connecting conductors shall not be less than _______ percent of the rated secondary current of the largest transformer in the tie circuit.

   (a) 33   (b) 67
   (c) 85   (d) 100

15. When secondary ties from transformers are used, an overcurrent protection device in the secondary of each transformer that is rated or set at not greater than _______ percent of the rated secondary current of the transformer shall be provided.

   (a) 125   (b) 150
   (c) 200   (d) 250

16. Transformers (1000 volts or less) shall be elevated at least _______ ft above the floor or working space to prevent unauthorized personnel from contact.

   (a) 6   (b) 8
   (c) 10   (d) 15

Section   **Answer**

17. Dry-type transformers greater than 112-1/2 kVA having Class 155 or higher insulation shall be separated at least 6 ft horizontally and ______ ft vertically from the combustible material if no fire-resistant, heat-insulating barrier is provided.

(a) 8   (b) 10
(c) 12   (d) 15

18. All indoor dry-type transformers of over ______ volts shall be installed in a vault.

(a) 15,000   (b) 25,000
(c) 30,000   (d) 35,000

19. Dry-type transformers installed outdoors shall have ______ enclosures.

(a) weatherproof   (b) weathertight
(c) rainproof   (d) raintight

20. The walls and roof for a transformer vault shall have a ______ in. thickness.

(a) 2   (b) 3
(c) 4   (d) 6

21. The door sills for a transformer vault shall be at least ______ in. high.

(a) 2   (b) 3
(c) 4   (d) 6

22. Connecting primary and secondary conductors not over 25 ft long (taps supplying transformer) shall have an ampacity of at least ______ of the rating of the feeder's overcurrent protection device, based on the primary-to-secondary voltage ratio.

(a) 1/4   (b) 1/3
(c) 1/2   (d) 3/4

23. The lighting transformer for an open delta-connected secondary system can be determined by multiplying the single-phase load by ______ percent plus   58 percent of the three-phase load.

(a) 58   (b) 67
(c) 100   (d) 125

24. For a transformer in a supervised location with 6 percent impedance and a secondary voltage rated 1000 volts or less, the overcurrent protection device on the secondary side shall be sized at not more than ______ percent of the FLC rating.

(a) 100   (b) 125
(c) 225   (d) 250

25. Dry-type transformers rated 112-1/2 kVA or less shall be separated at least ______ in. from the combustible material where the voltage is 1000 volts or less.

(a) 6   (b) 12
(c) 18   (d) 24

Section   **Answer**

26. Askarel-insulated transformers of over _______ kVA shall be furnished with a relief vent such as chimney.

    (a) 25   (b) 35
    (c) 50   (d) 75

27. The floor for a transformer vault shall be at least _______ in. thick.

    (a) 2   (b) 4
    (c) 6   (d) 12

28. Dry-type transformers exceeding 112 kVA shall not be located within _______ in. of combustible materials of building, unless the transformer has Class 155 insulation systems or higher and is completely enclosed except for ventilation openings.

    (a) 3   (b) 6
    (c) 10   (d) 12

29. Askarel-insulated transformers installed indoors and rated over _______ VA shall be furnished with a pressure-relief vent.

    (a) 25,000   (b) 30,000
    (c) 35,000   (d) 50,000

30. Where practicable, vaults containing more than _______ kVA transformer capacity shall be provided with a drain or other means.

    (a) 50   (b) 75
    (c) 100   (d) 150

31. With certain conditions of use, a transformer can be _______-connected.

    (a) isolated   (b) bonded
    (c) all of the above   (d) none of the above

32. The terminal bar in a transformer shall be _______ to the enclosure (General Rule)

    (a) reverse   (b) primary
    (c) secondary   (d) all of the above

33. Transformers shall be installed in an area where it can _______ properly

    (a) heat   (b) ventilate
    (c) all of the above   (d) none of the above

34. A vault with a door sill shall be provided with a height of at least _______ in.

    (a) 2   (b) 2-1/2
    (c) 3   (d) 4

35. The walls of a vault (general rule) shall be at least _______ inches thick.

    (a) 3   (b) 4
    (c) all of the above   (d) none of the above

Section   **Answer**

36. The door for a vault shall have a minimum fire rating of ______ hours.

    (a) 2   (b) 3
    (c) all of the above   (d) none of the above

37. Vault ventilation opening shall be located as ______ as possible from combustile material

    (a) close   (b) near
    (c) far   (d) none of the above

38. Under certain conditions of use, transformer secondary conductors can extend up to ______ ft in length.

    (a) 10   (b) 25
    (c) 100   (d) none of the above

39. What is the primary and secondary amperage for a 20 kVA, 480/240 volt, single-phase transformer?

40. What is the primary and secondary amperage for a 20 kVA, 480/240 volt, three-phase transformer?

41. What is the individual overcurrent protection device rating (using circuit breakers and time-delay fuses) for the primary side of a transformer with the following?
- supervised location
- 1500 kVA transformer
- 12,470 volts
- three-phase

42. What is the overcurrent protection device rating for the primary and secondary side of a transformer with the following?
- 400 kVA transformer
- 4160/480 volts
- three-wire to four-wire
- three-phase
- nonsupervised location (any location)

43. What is the overcurrent protection device rating for the primary and secondary side of transformer with the following?
- 400 kVA transformer
- 4160/480 volts
- three-wire to four-wire
- three-phase
- supervised location

44. What is the overcurrent protection device rating for the primary and secondary side of transformer with the following?
- 400 kVA transformer
- 13,800/4160 volts
- three-wire to four-wire
- three-phase
- supervised location

Section   **Answer**

45. What is the individual overcurrent protection device rating for the primary side of a transformer with the following?
  • 25 kVA transformer
  • 240/120 volts
  • single-phase

46. What is the individual overcurrent protection device rating for the primary side of a transformer with the following?
  • 2 kVA transformer
  • 480 volts
  • two-wire to two-wire
  • single-phase

47. What is the minimum and maximum individual overcurrent protection device rating for the primary side of a transformer with the following?
  • .7 kVA transformer
  • 480 volts
  • two-wire to two-wire
  • single-phase

48. What is the overcurrent protection device rating for the primary and secondary side of a transformer with the following?
  • 40 kVA transformer
  • 480/208 volts
  • three-wire to four-wire
  • three-phase

49. What size overcurrent protection device and THWN copper conductors are required for a 10 ft tap with a calculated load of 142 amps?

50. What size overcurrent protection device (secondary) and THWN copper conductors (primary and secondary) are required for a 25 ft tap with the following?
  • 200 amp overcurrent protection device (primary)
  • 480 volt primary
  • 240 volt secondary

21

Hazardous (Classified) Locations

The intent of this chapter is to assist in the classification of areas or locations with respect to hazardous conditions. Such areas or locations are hazardous due to atmospheric concentrations of hazardous gases, vapors, deposits, or accumulations of materials that may be readily ignited.

The requirements are covered for the installation of electrical equipment and wiring in locations that are classified depending on the properties of the flammable vapors, liquids or gases, or combustible dusts that may be present and the likelihood that a flammable or combustible concentration of quantity is present. The hazardous (classified) locations to be covered are assigned following the designations:

(1) Class   I, Division 1
(2) Class   I, Division 2
(3) Class II, Division 1
(4) Class II, Division 2
(5) Class III, Division 1
(6) Class III, Division 2

(For the metric system dimensions, see those listed in the *National Electrical Code*)

GENERAL OVERVIEW

Hazardous areas and locations are classified by group, class, and division. They are determined by the atmospheric mixtures of various gases, vapors, dust, and other materials. The intensity of the explosion that can occur depends upon the concentrations, temperatures, and many other factors, which are listed in the codes from the National Fire Protection Association (NFPA).

Note, all areas designated as hazardous (classified) locations shall be properly documented. Such documentation shall be available to those authorized to design, install, inspect, maintain, or operate electrical equipment in the location involved per **500.4(A)**.

DIVISIONS (GASES)
500.5(B)

Class I locations are identified in the NEC as those in which flammable gases, flammable liquid-produced vapors, or combustible liquid-produced vapors are or may be present in the air in quantities sufficient to produce explosive or ignitible mixtures. The amount of vapor varies all the way from being continuously present to never present at all. Naturally, if vapors are not present, the area is not a classified (hazardous) location. However, where vapors are present, it is very likely that a flammable mixture may or may not be present.

From a designing standpoint, greater care must be exercised if a particular condition is likely to occur, such as the presence of a flammable mixture of vapor and air within the explosive range, than is needed if a flammable mixture within the explosive range is unlikely to occur. Therefore, it is necessary to divide hazardous locations into two divisions.

DIVISION 1 (GASES)
500.5(B)(1)

Division 1 hazardous locations are defined in the NEC as those locations (a) in which ignitible concentrations of flammable gases, flammable liquid-produced vapors, or combustible liquid-produced vapors can exist under normal operating conditions, or (b) in which ignitible concentrations of such flammable gases, flammable liquid-produced vapors, or combustible liquid produced vapors above their flash points may exist frequently because of repair or maintenance operations or because of leakage, or (c) in which breakdown or faulty operation of equipment or processes might release ignitible concentrations of flammable gases, flammable liquid-produced vapors, or combustible liquid-produced vapors and might also cause simultaneous failure of electric equipment in such a way as to directly cause the electrical equipment to become a source of ignition.

Note, in each case, ignitible concentrations are mentioned. Such concentrations fall between the lower and upper flammable or explosive limits.

There are minimum and maximum concentrations of flammable gases and vapors that are above and below the mixture and will not burn or explode. The lower limit is where the substance is too lean to burn or explode. The upper limit is where the mixture has become too rich to burn or explode.

IN 1 to **500.5(B)(1)** describes a number of areas and occupancies that are normally classified as Division 1 locations. Such locations are as follows:

(1) Petroleum refining facilities

(2) Dip tanks containing flammable or combustible liquids

(3) Dry cleaning plants

(4) Plants manufacturing organic coatings

(5) Spray finishing areas (residue must be considered)

(6) Petroleum dispensing areas

(7) Solvent extraction plants

(8) Plants manufacturing or using pyroxylin (nitro cellulose) type and other plastics

(9) Locations where inhalation anesthetics are utilized

(10) Utility gas plants and operations involving storage and handling of liquefied petroleum and natural gas plants

(11) Aircraft hangars and fuel servicing areas

See Figure 21-1 for a detailed illustration of Class I, Division 1 locations.

Design Tip: A flammable liquid is a liquid having a closed-cup flash point below 38°C (100°F), as determined by the test procedures and apparatus set forth in NFPA 30. Flash point is the minimum temperature at which a liquid gives off vapor in sufficient concentration to form an ignitible mixture with air near the surface of the liquid, as specified by test. (See 3.3.6 of NFPA 497 for more details concerning flammable liquids.)

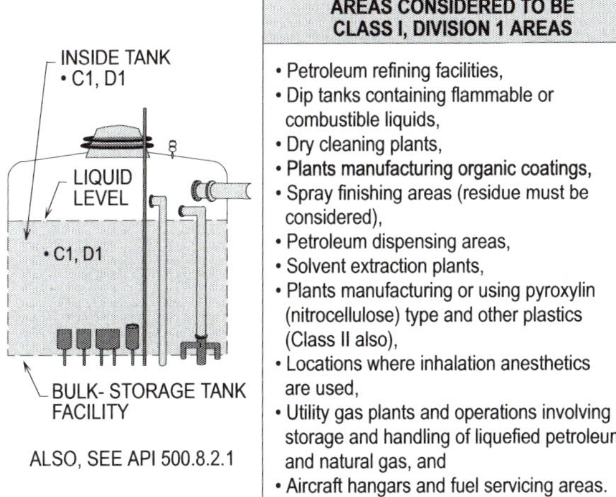

Figure 21-1. The facilities that are listed in this illustration are considered, under certain conditions, to be Class I, Division 1. [Review NFPA 497 – Figure 5.9.4(a)]

DIVISION 2 (GASES) 500.5(B)(2)

The NEC defines Division 2 locations as those locations (a) in which volatile flammable gases, flammable liquid-produced vapors, or combustible liquid-produced vapors are handled, processed, or used, but in which the liquids, vapors, or gases will normally be confined within closed containers or closed systems from which they can escape only in case of accidental rupture or breakdown of such containers or systems or in case of abnormal operation of equipment, or (b) in which ignitible concentrations of flammable gases, flammable liquid-produced vapors, or combustible liquid-produced vapors are normally prevented by positive mechanical ventilation and that might become hazardous through failure or abnormal operation of the ventilating equipment or (c) that are adjacent to a Class I, Division 1 location, and to which ignitible concentrations of flammable gases, flammable liquid-produced vapors, or combustible liquid-produced vapors above their flash points might occasionally be communicated unless such communication is prevented by adequate positive-pressure ventilation from a source of clean air and effective safeguards against ventilation failure are provided.

INs **1** and **2** to **500.5(B)(2)** describe a number of areas and occupancies that are normally classified as Division 2 locations.

For example, piping without valves, checks, meters, and devices does not usually introduce a hazardous condition even though such piping is utilized for flammable liquids. This type of piping is considered a contained system. Therefore, the area around shall be classified as a Division 2 location by the AHJ.

The following areas are considered to be Division 2 locations:

(1) Locations where volatile flammable liquids or flammable gases or vapors are used.

(2) Locations that, in the judgment of the AHJ, would become hazardous only in case of an accident or some unusual operating condition.

(3) Locations where the quantity of flammable material that might escape in case of accident, the adequacy of ventilating equipment, the total area involved, and the record of the industry or business with respect to explosions or fires are all factors that merit consideration in determining the classification and extent of each location.

(4) Locations where piping without valves, checks, meter, and similar devices would not ordinarily introduce a hazardous condition even though used for flammable liquids or gases.

(5) Locations used for the storage of flammable liquids or of liquefied or compressed gases in sealed containers would not normally be considered hazardous unless subject to other hazardous conditions also.

(6) Electrical conduits and their associated enclosures separated from process fluids by a single seal or barrier shall be classified as a Division 2 location if the outside of the conduit and enclosure is an unclassified location.

See Figure 21-2 for an illustration of Class I, Division 2 locations.

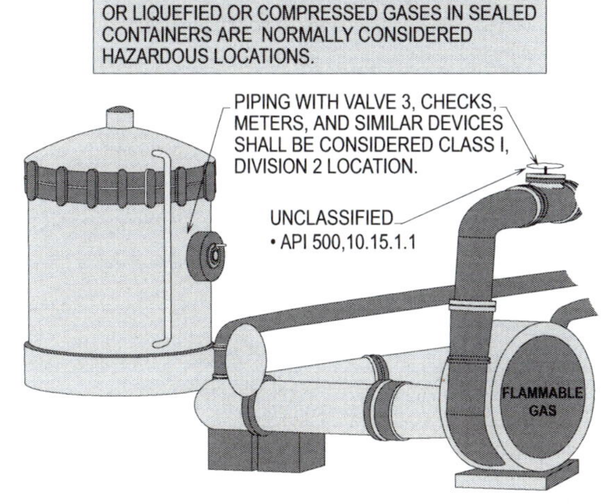

Figure 21-2. Areas in refineries where vessels and pipelines are equipped with valves, meters, and similar devices shall be considered Class I, Division 2 locations.

DIVISION 1 (DUST)
500.5(C)(1)

A Class II, Division 1 location is a location (1) in which combustible dust is in the air under normal operating conditions in quantities sufficient to produce explosive or ignitible mixtures, or (2) where mechanical failure or abnormal operation of machinery or equipment might cause such explosive or ignitible mixtures to be produced, and might also provide a source of ignition through simultaneous failure of electric equipment, through operation of protection devices, or from other causes, or (3) in which Group E combustible dusts may be present in quantities sufficient to be hazardous.

Areas that are considered Class II, Division 1 locations are based upon certain designing techniques and conditions, as follows:

(1) Combustible dusts that are electrically nonconductive include dusts produced in the handling and processing of:

    (a) grain and grain products,

    (b) pulverized sugar and cocoa,

    (c) dried egg and milk powders,

    (d) pulverized spices, starch, and pastes,

    (e) potato and wood flour, oil meal from beans, and

    (f) seed, dried hay, and other organic materials that may produce combustible dusts when processed or handled.

(2) Only Group E dusts are considered to be electrically conductive for classification purposes. Dusts containing magnesium or aluminum are particularly hazardous, and the use of extreme precaution is necessary to avoid ignition and explosion.

See Figure 21-3 for a detailed illustration of Class II, Division 1 locations.

DIVISION 2 (DUST)
500.5(C)(2)

A Class II, Division 2 location is a location (1) in which combustible dust due to abnormal operations may be present in the air in quantities sufficient to produce explosive or ignitible mixtures, or (2) where combustible dust accumulations are normally insufficient to interfere with the normal operation of electrical equipment or other apparatus, but could as a result of infrequent malfunctioning of handling or processing equipment become suspended in the air, or (3) in which combustible dust accumulations on, in, or in the vicinity of the electrical equipment could be sufficient to interfere with the safe dissipation of heat from electrical equipment, or could be ignitible by abnormal operation or failure of electrical equipment.

Areas that are considered Class II, Division 2 locations are based upon certain designing techniques and conditions, as follows:

(1) The quantity of combustible dust that may be present and the adequacy of dust removal systems are factors that merit consideration in determining the classification and may result in an unclassified area.

(2) Where products such as seed are handled in a manner that produces low quantities of dust, the amount of dust deposited may not warrant classification.

See Figure 21-4 for a detailed illustration of Class II, Division 2 locations.

DIVISION 1 (FIBERS/FLYINGS)
500.5(D)(1)

A Class III, Division 1 location is a location in which easily ignitible fibers/flyings are handled, manufactured, or used.

(1) Such locations usually include some parts of:

    (a) rayon, cotton, and other textile mills,

    (b) combustible fiber manufacturing and processing plants,

    (c) cotton gins and cotton-seed mills,

    (d) flax-processing plants,

    (e) clothing manufacturing plants,

    (f) woodworking plants, and

    (g) establishments and industries involving similar hazardous processes or conditions.

(2) Easily ignitible fibers and flyings include:

    (a) rayon,

    (b) cotton (including cotton liners and cotton waste),

    (c) sisal or henequen,

    (d) istle,

    (e) jute, hemp, tow, cocoa fiber, oakum,

    (f) baled waste kapok,

    (g) spanish moss, excelsior, and

    (h) other materials of similar nature.

See Figure 21-5(a) for a detailed illustration of Class III, Division 1 locations.

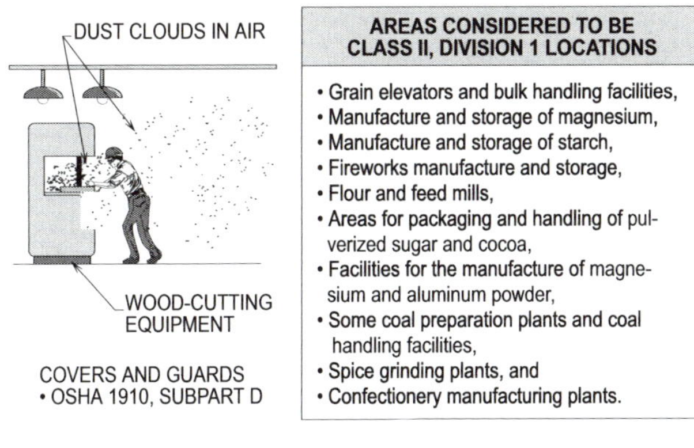

Figure 21-3. These facilities are considered under certain conditions to be Class II, Division 1 locations.

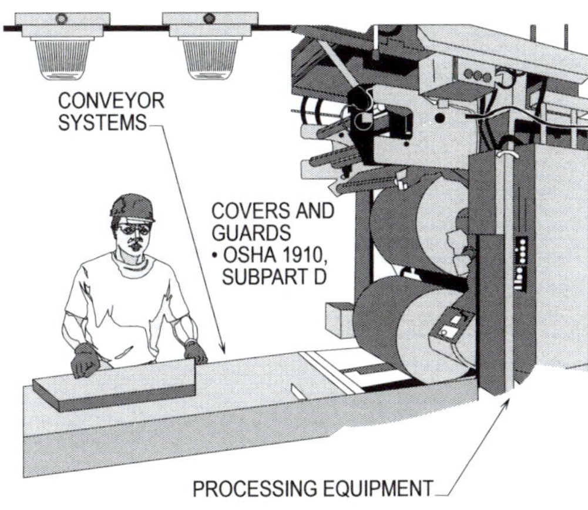

Figure 21-4. These are facilities are considered under certain conditions to be Class II, Division 2 locations.

DIVISION 2 (FIBERS/FLYINGS) 500.5(D)(2)

A Class III, Division 2 location is a location in which easily ignitible fibers/flyings are stored or handled other than in the process of manufacture. **[See Figure 21-5(b)]**

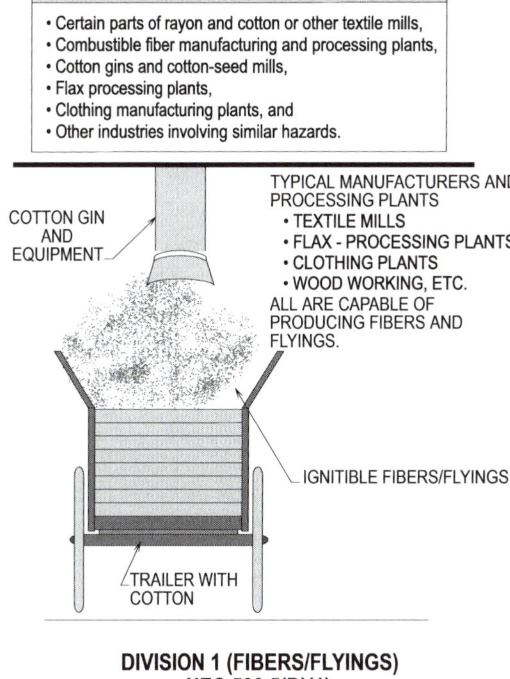

Figure 21-5(a). These facilities are considered, under certain conditions, to be Class III, Division 1 locations.

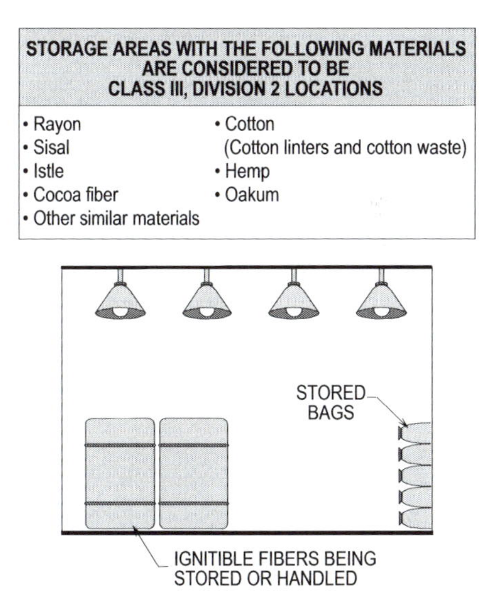

Figure 21-5(b). These facilities are considered under certain conditions to be Class III, Division 2 locations.

MATERIAL GROUPS (CLASS I)
500.6(A)

Until publication of the 1937 edition of the NEC, Class I hazardous locations were not divided into groups. All flammable gases and vapors were classified as a single degree of hazard. It was recognized, however, that the degrees of hazard varied and that equipment suitable only for use where gasoline was handled was not necessarily suitable for use where hydrogen or acetylene was handled.

It was also recognized that manufacturing equipment and enclosures for use in hydrogen atmospheres was very difficult and that the equipment, even if built, was expensive. It was not logical, from a designing standpoint, to require explosion-proof equipment in gasoline filling stations that was also suitable for use in hydrogen atmospheres. Not only would this unnecessarily increase the cost of the electrical installation in one of the most common types of hazardous locations, but it would make some types of equipment unavailable.

By placing flammable materials into groups and classifying them based upon the explosive characteristics of such gases and vapors, electrical equipment and wiring methods could be selected.

GROUP A (GASES)
500.6(A)(1)

As mentioned above, combustible and flammable gases and vapors are divided into four groups; the classification involving determinations of maximum explosion pressures, and maximum safe clearance between parts of a clamped or threaded joint in an enclosure.

Really, there is no consistent relationship between Groups A, B, C, or D classification and flash point/ignition temperature/explosive limits. Instead, the groups are classified by chemical families. Certain chemicals produce higher explosive pressures and heat when ignited. Group A gas produces the greater pressures during an explosion, and therefore is the most difficult to handle and control. Group B is next highest in pressure, then Group C, and lastly Group D.

> **Design Tip:** This is the reason why a Group A or B listing is more difficult to get than a Group C or D listing for electrical equipment. **(See Figure 21-6)**

For example, Group A is an atmosphere containing acetylene, that is capable of producing a very dangerous explosive mixture. **Note,** equipment falling in this group is not available. Therefore, special equipment such as purged and pressurized shall be designed and used.

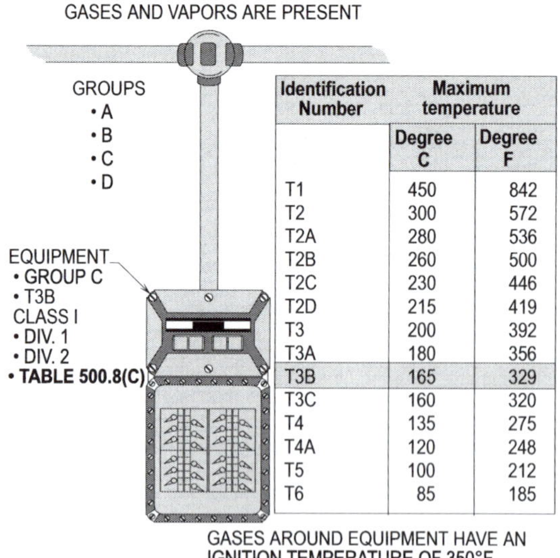

Identification Number	Maximum temperature	
	Degree C	Degree F
T1	450	842
T2	300	572
T2A	280	536
T2B	260	500
T2C	230	446
T2D	215	419
T3	200	392
T3A	180	356
T3B	165	329
T3C	160	320
T4	135	275
T4A	120	248
T5	100	212
T6	85	185

Figure 21-6. This illustration shows equipment is required to have a T3B (T-Code) identification number when installed in a Class I, Division 1 location.

GROUP B (GASES)
500.6(A)(2)

Group B is a flammable gas, flammable liquid-produced vapor, or combustible liquid-produced vapor mixed with air that may burn or explode, having either a maximum experimental safe gap (MESG) value less than or equal to 0.45 mm or a minimum igniting current ratio (MIC ratio) less than or equal to 0.40. (See NFPA 497, 3.3.5.1.2)

Group B is an atmosphere containing hydrogen, fuel, and combustible process gases containing more than 30 percent hydrogen by volume, or it contains gases or vapors of equivalent hazard such as butadiene, ethylene oxide, propylene oxide, and acrolein.

GROUP C (GASES)
500.6(A)(3)

Group C is a flammable gas, flammable liquid-produced vapor, or combustible liquid-produced vapor mixed with air that may burn or explode, having either a maximum environmental safe gas (MESG) value greater than 0.45 mm and less than or equal to 0.75 mm, or a minimum igniting current ratio (MIC ratio) greater than 0.40 mm and less than or equal to 0.80. (See NFPA 497, 3.3.5.1.3)

Group C is an atmosphere such as ethyl ether, ethylene, or gases or vapors of equivalent hazard. Manufacturers make all types of equipment that fall in this group of explosive equipment. [See **500.7(A)**]

GROUP D (GASES)
500.6(A)(4)

Group D is a flammable gas, flammable liquid-produced vapor, or combustible liquid-produced vapor mixed with air that may burn or explode, having either a maximum experimental safe gas (MESG) value greater than 0.75 mm or a minimum igniting current ratio (MIC ratio) greater than 0.80. (See NFPA 497, 3.3.5.1.4)

Group D is an atmosphere such as acetone, ammonia, benzene, butane, cyclopropane, ethanol, gasoline, hexane, methanol, methane, natural gas, naphtha, propane, or gases or vapors of equivalent hazard. There are many types of equipment available in this group.

MATERIAL GROUPS (CLASS II)
500.6(B)

Combustible dusts are divided into three groups; the classification involving the tightness of the joints of assembly and shaft openings to prevent entrance of dust in the dust-ignition proof enclosure, the blanketing effect of layers of dust on the equipment that may cause overheating, and the ignition temperature of the dust are the main concerns.

GROUP E (DUST)
500.6(B)(1)

Group E atmospheres contain combustible metal dusts, including aluminum, magnesium, and their commercial alloys, or other combustible dusts of similar hazard.

Design Tip 1: "Only Group E dusts are considered to be electrically conductive." These dusts are metal dusts, such as aluminum, magnesium, and their commercial alloys or other dusts of small particle size, abrasiveness and/or electrical conductivity that presents a similar hazard. (See NFPA 499 – 3.3.4.1)

Design Tip 2: When the dust is electrically conductive, care must be taken, for these dusts may ignite from bridging the gap between energized terminals, from arcs or from failure of equipment. Where Group E dusts are encountered in hazardous quantities, only Class II, Division 1 electrical equipment can be utilized. There is no such classification as Class II, Group E, Division 2. Either the location has enough electrically conductive dusts to make it a Division 1 location, or there is not enough dust present to even classify it as a hazardous area.

GROUP F (DUST)
500.6(B)(2)

Group F atmospheres contain combustible carbonaceous dusts, including carbon black, charcoal, coal, or coke dusts, that has more than 8 percent total entrapped volatiles or dusts that have been sensitized by other materials.

GROUP G (DUST)
500.6(B)(3)

Group G atmospheres contain combustible dusts not included in Group E or F, including flour, grain, wood, plastic, and chemicals. (See NFPA 499 – 3.3.4.3)

Equipment to be used in these atmospheres shall not only be approved for Class I, II, or III, but also for the specific group [Class I (A, B, C, or D) and II (E, F, or G)].

Design Tip: The explosion characteristics of air mixtures of dust vary with the materials involved. For Class II locations, Groups E, F, and G, the classification involves the tightness of the joints of assembly and shaft openings to prevent the entrance of dust in the dust-ignition proof enclosure. The blanketing effect of layers of dust on the equipment that may cause overheating and the ignition temperature of the dust are also considered. It is necessary, therefore, that equipment be approved not only for the class, but also for the specific group of dust that will be present.

See Figure 21-7 for a detailed illustration of Groups E, F, and G equipment.

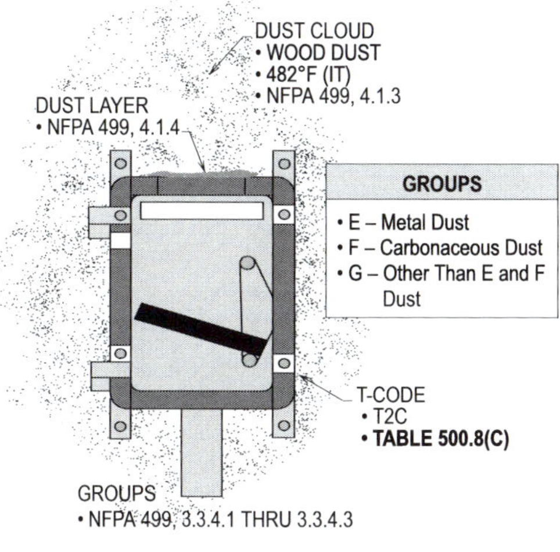

Figure 21-7. This illustration shows equipment is required to have a T2C identification number per **Figure 21-6.**

CLASSES AND DIVISIONS
500.5

Classes are utilized to identify hazardous locations that are subjected to materials that can be explosive if mixed with air to create an ignitible mixture.

Hazardous locations must be well understood by anyone designing, installing, working on, or inspecting electrical equipment and wiring methods located in such areas. These locations are dangerous due to the threat of flammable or combustible gases, vapors, or dusts being present some of the time or all of the time.

CLASS I, DIVISION 1
500.5(B)(1)

A Class I, Division 1 location is where (a) ignitible concentrations of flammable gases, flammable liquid-produced vapors, or combustible liquid-produced vapors can exist under normal operating conditions, or (b) ignitible concentrations of such flammable gases, flammable liquid-produced vapors, or combustible liquids above their flash points may exist frequently because of repair or maintenance operations or because of leakage, or (c) breakdown or faulty operation of equipment or processes might release ignitible concentrations of flammable gases, flammable liquid-produced vapors, or combustible liquid-produced vapors and might also cause simultaneous failure of electrical equipment in such a way as to directly cause the electrical equipment to become a source of ignition. **[See Figure 21-8(a)]**

CLASS I, DIVISION 2
500.5(B)(2)

A Class I, Division 2 location is where (a) volatile flammable gases, flammable liquid-produced vapors, or combustible liquid-produced vapors are handled, processed, or used, but in which the liquids, vapors, or gases will normally be confined within closed containers or closed systems from which they can escape only in case of accidental rupture or breakdown of such containers or systems or in case of abnormal operation of equipment, or (b) where ignitible concentrations of flammable gases, flammable liquid-produced vapors, or combustible liquid-produced vapors are normally prevented by positive mechanical ventilation and that might become hazardous through failure or abnormal operation of the ventilating equipment, or (c) is adjacent to a Class I, Division 1 location and to which ignitible concentrations of flammable gases, flammable liquid-produced vapors, or combustible liquid-produced vapors above their flash points might occasionally be communicated unless such communication is prevented by adequate positive-pressure ventilation from a source of clean air and effective safeguards against ventilation failure are provided. **[See Figure 21-8(b)]**

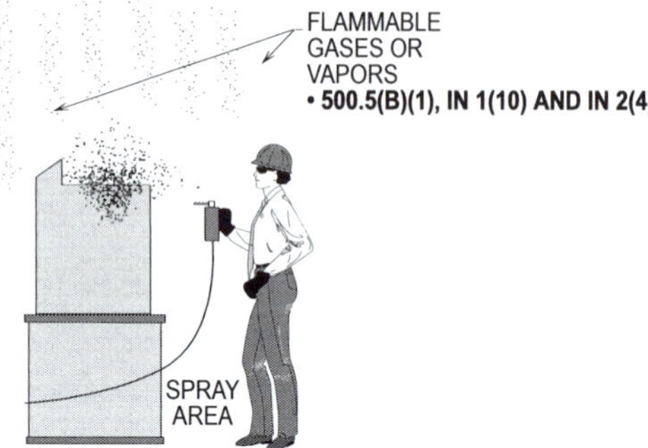

Figure 21-8(a). This illustration is a Class I, Division 1 location, due to the presence of gases or vapors during operation, maintenance, or repair.

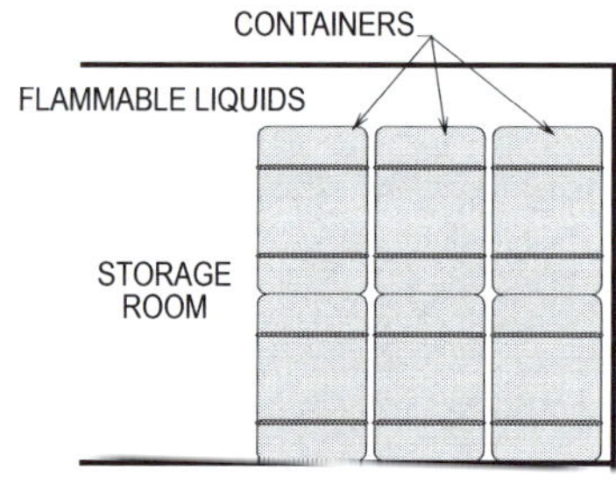

Figure 21-8(b). This illustration shows a Class I, Division 2 location, due to being confined in containers or closed systems.

CLASS II, DIVISION 1
500.5(C)(1)

A Class II, Division 1 location is a location where (a) combustible dust is in the air under normal operating conditions in quantities sufficient to produce explosive or ignitible mixtures, or (b) where mechanical failure or abnormal operation of machinery or equipment might cause such explosive or ignitible mixtures to be produced and might also provide a source of ignition through simultaneous failure of electrical equipment, through operation of protective devices, or from other causes, or (c) where Group E combustible dusts may be present in quantities sufficient to be hazardous. **[See Figure 21-9(a)]**

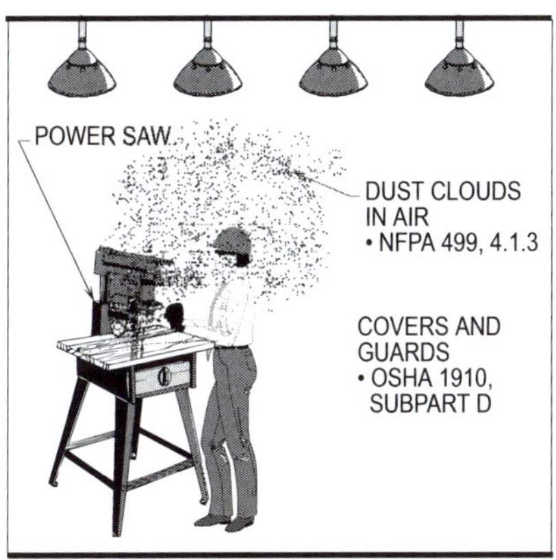

Figure 21-9(a). This illustration shows a Class II, Division 1 location, due to the presence of dust during operation or mechanical failure of equipment.

CLASS II, DIVISION 2
500.5(C)(2)

A Class II, Division 2 location is a location where (a) combustible dust, due to abnormal operations, may be present in the air in quantities sufficient to produce explosive or ignitible mixtures, or (b) dust accumulations are present but are normally insufficient to interfere with the normal operation of electrical equipment or other apparatus but

could as a result of infrequent malfunctioning of handling or processing equipment become suspended in the air, or (c) combustible dust accumulations on, in, or in the vicinity of the electrical equipment could be sufficient to interfere with the safe dissipation of heat from electrical equipment or could be ignitible by abnormal operation or failure of electrical equipment. **[See Figure 21-9(b)]**

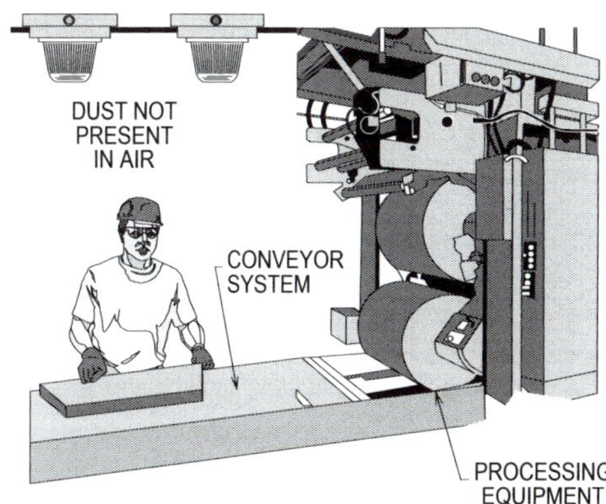

Figure 21-9(b). This illustration shows a Class II, Division 2 location, due to dust being limited during operation of equipment. [For good housekeeping, see NFPA 499 – 6.8.1(9)]

CLASS III, DIVISION 1
500.5(D)(1)

A Class III, Division 1 location is a location in which easily ignitible fibers/flyings are handled, manufactured, or used. **[See Figure 21-10(a)]**

CLASS III, DIVISION 2
500.5(D)(2)

A Class III, Division 2 location is a location in which easily ignitible fibers/flyings are stored or handled other than in the process of manufacture. **[See Figure 21-10(b)]**

Figure 21-10(a). This illustration shows a Class III, Division 1 location, due to the presence of easily ignitible fibers/flyings. [See **Figure 21-5(a)**]

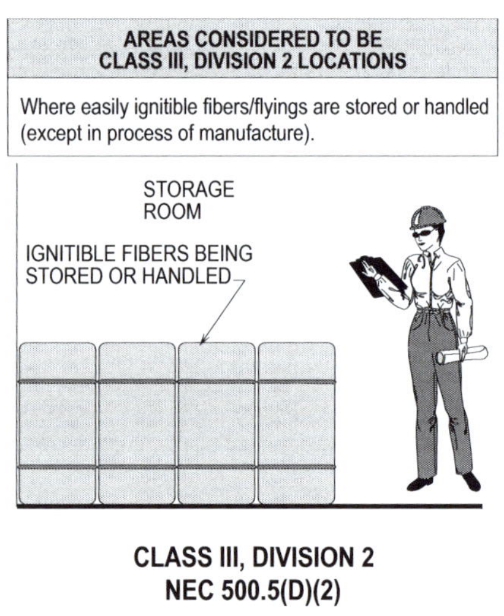

Figure 21-10(b). This illustration shows a Class III, Division 2 location, due to easily ignitible fibers/flyings being stored or handled.

EXPLOSIVE PROPERTIES OF GASES AND VAPORS
NFPA 497 – CHAPTER 3

To select the type of equipment permitted to be installed in Class I, Division 1 and 2 locations, it is necessary to understand the meaning of certain terms and how they are to be applied.

FLASH POINT
NFPA 497, SECTION 3.3.7

Flash point of a liquid is the minimum temperature at which the liquid gives off vapor in sufficient concentration to form an ignitible mixture with the air near the surface of the liquid, as specified by test. An ignitible mixture is within the flammable range (between upper and lower limits) that is capable of propagating flame away from the source of ignition when ignited. Some evaporation takes place below the flash point but not in sufficient quantities to form an ignitible mixture.

Design Tip: The flash point applies mostly to flammable and combustible liquids, although there are certain solids, such as camphor and naphthalene, that slowly evaporate or volatilize at ordinary room temperature, and liquids, such as benzene, that freeze at relatively high temperatures and therefore have flash points while in the solid state. **(See Figure 21-11)**

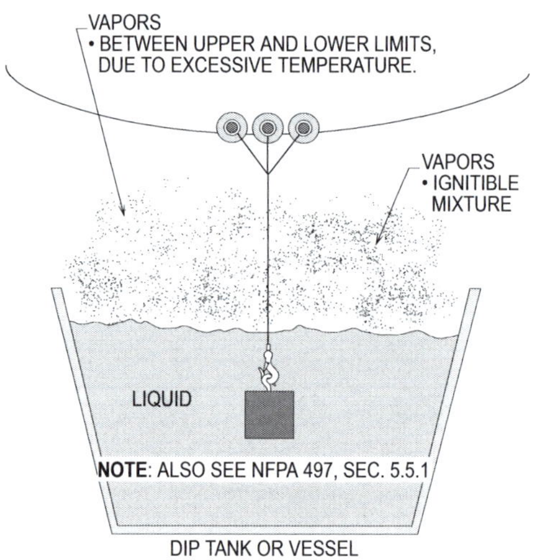

Figure 21-11. This illustration shows a situation where sufficient vapors are driven off by heat due to the surrounding temperature creating an explosive mixture of vapors and air.

IGNITION TEMPERATURE
NFPA 497 – SECTION 3.3.2, 3.3.8, AND 3.3.11

Ignition temperature of a substance, whether solid, liquid, or gaseous, is the minimum temperature required to initiate or cause self-sustained combustion independently of the heating or heated element.

Ignition temperatures observed under one set of conditions may be changed substantially by a change of conditions. For this reason, ignition temperatures should be looked upon only as approximations. Some of the variables known to affect ignition temperatures are the percentage composition of the vapor or gas-air mixture, shape and size of the space where the ignition occurs, rate and duration of heating, kind and temperature of the ignition source, catalytic or other effect of materials that may be present, and oxygen concentration. As there are many differences in ignition temperature test methods, such as size and shape of containers, method of heating and ignition source, ignition temperatures are affected by the test method. **(See Figure 21-12)** Also, see NFPA 497, Table 4.4.2.

> **Design Tip:** Ignition temperature of a substance, whether solid, liquid, or gaseous, is the minimum temperature required to initiate or cause self-sustained combustion in the absence of any source of ignition.

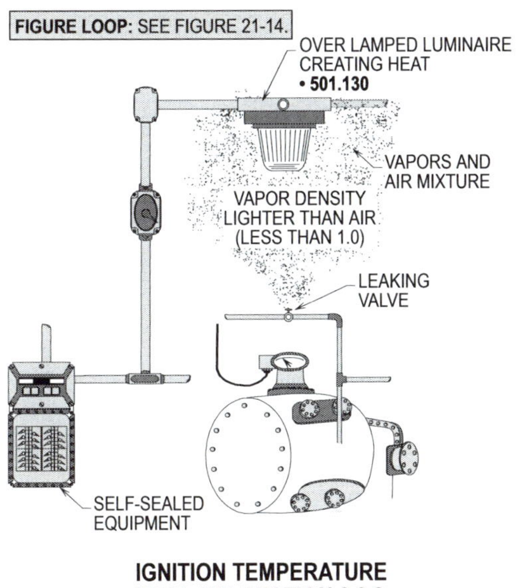

IGNITION TEMPERATURE
NFPA 497, SECTION 3.3.2

Figure 21-12. This illustration shows a mixture of vapors and air that could explode due to the excessive heat from the surface temperature of the luminaire.

FLAMMABLE (EXPLOSIVE) LIMITS
API 500 – SECTION 3.2.21

In the case of gases or vapors that form flammable mixtures with air or oxygen, there is a minimum concentration of vapor in air or oxygen below which propagation of flame does not occur on contact with a source of ignition. There is also a maximum proportion of vapor or gas in the air above in which propagation of flame does not occur. These boundary-line mixtures of vapor or gas with air, which if ignited will just propagate flame, are known as the "lower and upper flammable or explosive limits" and are usually expressed in terms of percentage by volume of gas or vapor in air. **(See Figure 21-13)**

> **Design Tip:** In popular terms, a mixture below the lower flammable limit is too lean to burn or explode and a mixture above the upper flammable limit is too rich to burn or explode.

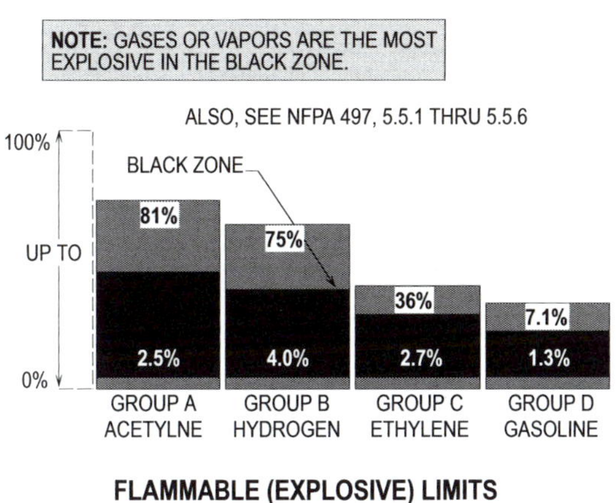

FLAMMABLE (EXPLOSIVE) LIMITS
API 500, SECTION 3.2.21
NFPA 497, TABLE 4.4.2

Figure 21-13. The above shows gases or vapors in their lower and upper limits.

VAPOR DENSITY
NFPA 497– SECTION 4.2.1 AND 4.2.2

Vapor densities are used mainly to determine the settling or rising tendency of a mixture. A figure of less than 1.0 indicates that the vapor is lighter than air and will tend to rise. A figure greater than 1.0 indicates the vapor will settle and move along the grade.

> **Design Tip:** An example of a lighter-than-air gas is methane-natural gas, which has a density of 0.6 and 0.1, respectively. This type of gas in indoor locations will tend to concentrate near the ceiling where luminaires are usually mounted. On the other hand, heavier-than-air mixtures, like ethyl ether vapors, have the ability to travel at low levels for a considerable distance to locations where sources of ignition might be available.

See Figure 21-14 for an illustration showing the different vapor densities of flammable materials.

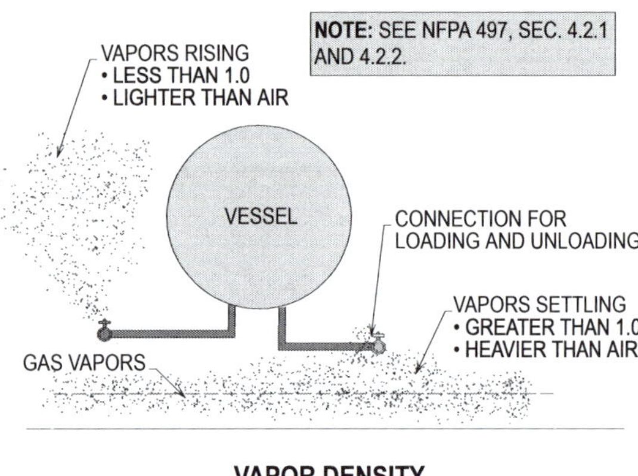

VAPOR DENSITY
NFPA 497, SECTION 4.2.1 AND 4.2.2

Figure 21-14. This illustration shows that vapors lighter than air rise and that vapors heavier than air will settle near the grade.

COMBUSTION PRINCIPLES
NFPA 497 – SECTION 4.2

The following three basic conditions shall be satisfied for a fire or explosion to occur:

(1) A flammable liquid, vapor, or combustible shall be present in sufficient quantity.

(2) The flammable liquid, vapor, or combustible dust shall be mixed with air or oxygen in the proportions required to produce an explosive mixture.

(3) A source of energy shall be applied to the explosive mixture.

In applying these principles, the quantity of the flammable liquid or vapor that may be liberated and its physical characteristics shall be recognized. Vapors from flammable liquids have a natural tendency to disperse into the atmosphere and rapidly become diluted to concentrations below the lower explosion limit, particularly when there is natural or mechanical ventilation. Finally, the possibility that the gas concentration may be above the upper explosion limit does not ensure any degree of safety, as the concentration shall first pass through the explosive range to reach the upper explosion limit. (See NFPA 497, 4.2.6 and 4.2.7)

SOURCES OF IGNITION
NFPA 497 – SECTION 4.3 AND 3.3.2

A source of energy is all that is needed to touch off an explosion where flammable gases or combustible dust are mixed in the proper proportion with air. One prime source of energy is electricity.

Equipment such as switches, circuit breakers, motor starters, push-button stations, or plugs and receptacles can produce arcs or sparks in normal operation when contacts are opened and closed, which could easily cause ignition.

Other hazards are devices that produce heat, such as luminaires and motors. Here, surface temperatures may exceed the safe limits of many flammable atmospheres. Finally, many parts of the electrical system can become potential sources of ignition in the event of insulation failure. This group would include wiring (particularly splices in the wiring), transformers, impedance coils, solenoids, and other low-temperature devices without make-or-break contacts. Nonelectrical hazards such as sparking metal can also easily cause ignition. Thus a hammer, a file, or another tool that is dropped on masonry or on a ferrous surface is a hazard unless the tool is made of non sparking material. For this reason, portable electrical equipment is usually made from aluminum or other material that will not produce sparks if the equipment is dropped. Therefore, electrical safety is of crucial importance.

The electrical installation must prevent accidental ignition of flammable liquids, vapors, and dusts released into the atmosphere. In addition, since much of this equipment is used outdoors or in corrosive atmospheres, the material and finish shall be such that maintenance costs and shutdowns are minimized. **(See Figure 21-15)**

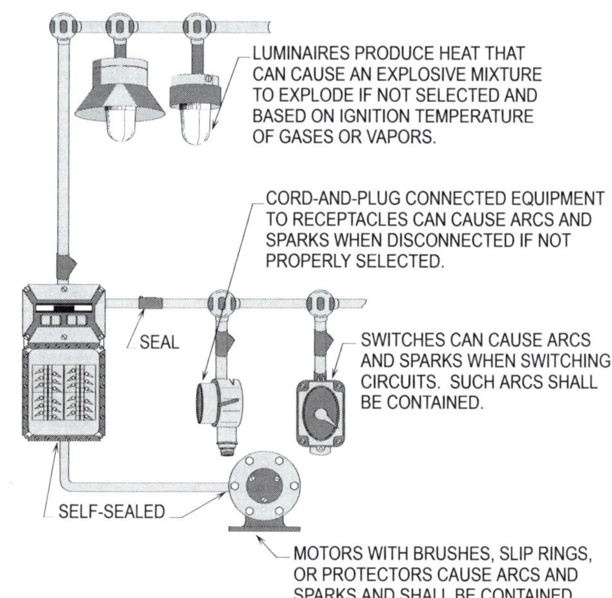

SOURCES OF IGNITION
NFPA 497, SECTION 4.3 AND 3.3.2

Figure 21-15. Ground joint construction type enclosures as shown will withstand an internal explosion and cool the hot escaping gases through the ground surface of the joint.

ENCLOSURES
NEMA 250

Each area that contains gases or dusts that are considered hazardous must be carefully evaluated to make certain the correct electrical equipment is selected. To conform with the NEC, the use of fittings and enclosures that are identified or listed for the specific hazardous gas or dust involved is required.

In Class I, Division 1 and 2 locations, conventional relays, contactors, and switches that have arcing contacts shall be enclosed in explosionproof housings, except for those few cases where general purpose enclosures are permitted by the NEC. By definition, enclosures for these locations shall prevent the ignition of an explosive gas or vapor that may surround it. In other words, an explosion inside the enclosure shall be prevented from starting a larger explosion on the outside. Adequate strength is one requirement for such an enclosure.

For explosionproof equipment, a safety factor of 4 is used. That is, the enclosure shall withstand a hydrostatic pressure test of four times the maximum pressure from an explosion within the enclosure. In addition to being strong, the enclosure shall be flametight. This term does not imply that the enclosure is hermetically sealed but rather that the joints cool the hot gases resulting from an internal explosion so that by the time they reach the outside hazardous atmosphere, they are too cool to effect ignition.

TYPES OF ENCLOSURES
NEMA 250

Type 7 and 10 enclosures, when properly installed and maintained, are designed to contain an internal explosion without causing an external hazard. Type 8 enclosures are designed to prevent combustion through the use of oil-immersed equipment. Type 9 enclosures are designed to prevent the ignition of combustible dust. Descriptions and tests in this standard publication cover equipment that is suitable for installation in locations classified as Division 1 or Division 2. In Division 2 locations, other types of protection and enclosures for nonhazardous locations may be installed if the equipment does not constitute a source of ignition under normal operating conditions.

Intrinsically safe and nonincendive equipment is not capable of releasing sufficient electrical or thermal energy under normal or abnormal conditions to cause ignition of specific hazardous atmospheres and may be installed in any type of enclosure otherwise suitable for the environmental conditions expected.

Equipment installed in enclosures that are suitable for nonhazardous locations, including the hazardous area, may be reduced or eliminated by adequate positive pressure ventilation from a source of clean air in conjunction with effective safeguards against ventilation failure.

TYPE 7 ENCLOSURES
NEMA 250

Type 7 enclosures are for indoor use in locations classified as Class I, Groups A, B, C, or D, as defined in the NEC.

Type 7 enclosures shall be capable of withstanding the pressures resulting from an internal explosion of specified gases and containing such an explosion sufficiently that an explosive gas-air mixture existing in the atmosphere surrounding the enclosure will not be ignited. Enclosed heat-generating devices shall not cause external surfaces to reach temperatures capable of igniting explosive gas-air mixtures in the surrounding atmosphere. Enclosures shall meet explosion, hydrostatic, and temperature design tests.

When Type 7 enclosures are completely and properly installed, they will:

(1) Provide a degree of protection to a hazardous gas environment from an internal explosion or from operation of internal equipment,

(2) Not develop surface temperatures that exceed prescribed limits for the specific gas corresponding to the atmospheres for which the enclosure is intended, when internal equipment is operated at rated load,

(3) Withstand a series of internal explosion design tests that determine:

    (a) The maximum pressure effects of the gas mixture

    (b) Propagation effects of the gas mixtures, and

(4) Withstand, without rupture or permanent distortion, an internal hydrostatic design test based on the maximum internal pressure obtained during explosion tests and on a specified safety factor be marked with the appropriate class and group(s) for which they have been qualified.

TYPE 8 ENCLOSURES
NEMA 250

Type 8 enclosures are for indoor or outdoor use in locations classified as Class I, Groups A, B, C, and D, as defined in the NEC.

Type 8 enclosures and enclosed devices are arranged so that all arcing contacts, connections, and any other parts that could cause arcing are immersed in oil. Arcing is confined under the oil so that it will not ignite an explosive mixture of the specified gases in internal spaces above the oil or in the atmosphere surrounding the enclosure. Enclosed heat generating devices shall not cause external surfaces to reach temperatures capable of igniting explosive gas-air mixtures in the surrounding atmosphere. Enclosures shall meet operation and temperature design tests. Enclosures intended for outdoor use shall also meet the rain test.

When Type 8 enclosures are completely and properly installed, they will:

(1) Provide, by oil immersion, a degree of protection to a hazardous gas environment from operation of internal equipment,

(2) Not develop surface temperatures that exceed prescribed limits for the specific gas corresponding to the atmospheres for which the enclosure is intended when internal equipment is at rated load,

(3) Withstand a series of operation design tests with oil levels arbitrarily reduced and with flammable gas-air mixtures introduced above the oil,

(4) Exclude water when subjected to a water spray design test simulating a beating rain, if installed outdoors, and

(5) Be marked with the appropriate Class and Group(s) for which they have been qualified.

TYPE 9 ENCLOSURES
NEMA 250

Type 9 enclosures are intended for indoor use in locations classified as Class II, Group E or G, as defined in the NEC.

Type 9 enclosures shall be capable of preventing the entrance of dust. Enclosed heat generating devices shall not cause external surfaces to reach temperatures capable of igniting or discoloring dust on the enclosure or igniting dust-air mixtures in the surrounding atmosphere. Enclosures shall meet dust penetration and temperature design tests and prevent aging of gaskets (if used).

When Type 9 enclosures are completely and properly installed, they will:

(1) Provide a degree of protection to a hazardous dust environment from operation of internal equipment,

(2) Not develop surface temperatures that exceed prescribed limits for the Group corresponding to the atmospheres for which the enclosure is intended when internal equipment is operated at rated load,

(3) Withstand a series of operation design tests while exposed to a circulating dust-air mixture to determine that dust does not enter the enclosure and that operation of devices does not cause ignition of surrounding atmosphere, and

(4) Be marked with the appropriate Class and Group(s) for which they have been qualified.

Note, for more information on enclosure types, see www.neca.org.

PREVENTION OF EXTERNAL IGNITION AND EXPLOSION

Explosives are hazardous enough by themselves, but around electricity there are even more hazards present. For this reason, special enclosures are necessary to house electrical elements that are capable of producing arcs and sparks. An arc, spark, or hot surface can easily initiate an explosion. Therefore, these ignition sources shall be contained or the equipment housing such apparatus shall be installed outside the area.

Each area that contains gases or dusts that are considered hazardous must be carefully evaluated to make certain the correct electrical equipment is selected. Many hazardous atmospheres are Class I, Group D, or Class II, Group G. However, certain areas may involve other groups, particularly Class I, Groups B and C. Conformity with the NEC requires the use of fittings and enclosures that are identified or listed for the specific hazardous gas or dust involved. (See NEC **Articles 500** and **501** for more information.)

CLASS I, DIVISION 1 EQUIPMENT
500.2, 500.7, AND 500.8(A)

Class I, Division 1 equipment shall provide a form of construction that will ensure safe performance under conditions of proper use and maintenance and will operate in such a manner to prevent igniting an explosive mixture of gases and air.

Note, Class I, Division 1 equipment shall be permitted to be used in Class II, Division 2 locations. When approving equipment installed in classified areas, see **500.8(A)**. [See **Figure 21-63** in this chapter to illustrate **500.8(A)**.]

EXPLOSIONPROOF EQUIPMENT (CLASS I, DIVISION 1) 500.2 AND 500.7(A)

The enclosure shall withstand an internal explosion of gases or vapors and prevent those gases or vapors from igniting gases and vapors in the surrounding atmosphere outside of the enclosure.

These enclosures are not intended to exclude flammable or combustible gases or vapors, but rather to withstand an internal explosion and prevent the ignition of external gases and vapors. The internal gases are dissipated or cooled before they are released from the enclosure, thereby preventing ignition or an explosion of gases or vapors in the surrounding atmosphere. **(See Figure 21-16)**

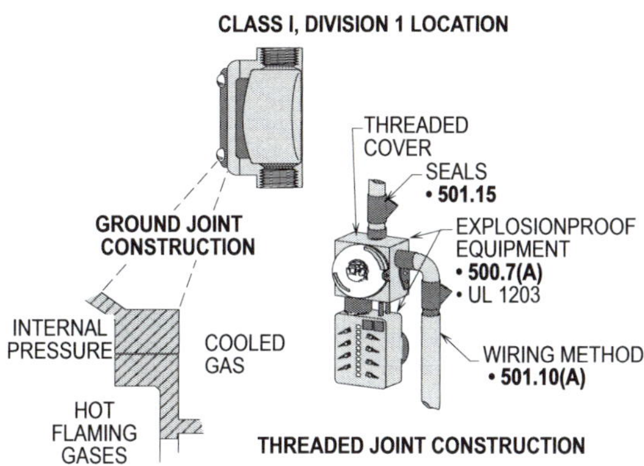

Figure 21-16. This illustration shows an enclosure that is capable of withstanding an internal explosion of gases or vapors and preventing those gases or vapors from igniting gases and vapors in the surrounding atmosphere outside of the enclosure.

PURGED AND PRESSURIZED SYSTEMS (CLASS I, DIVISION 1) 500.2 AND 500.7(D)

Purged and pressurized systems permit the safe operation of electrical equipment under conditions of hazard for which approved equipment may not be commercially available. For instance, most switchgear units and many large-size motors do not come in designs listed for Class I, Groups A and B. Whether cast metal enclosures for hazardous locations or sheet metal enclosures with pressurization should be used is mainly a question of economics if both types are available. As a typical example, if an installation had many electronic instruments that could be enclosed in a single sheet metal enclosure, the installation lends itself to the purging/pressurization system. However, if the instruments, due to their nature, had to be installed in separate enclosures, the cast metal in hazardous location housing would almost invariably prove more economical. Pressurized enclosures require:

(1) A source of clean air or inert gas,

(2) A compressor to maintain the required pressure on the system, and

(3) Pressure control valves, to prevent the power from being applied before the enclosure has been purged and to deenergize the system should pressure fall below a safe value.

In addition, door interlock switches shall prevent access to the equipment while the circuits are energized. It can readily be seen that all of these accessories can add up to a considerable expenditure.

> **Design Tip:** For a detailed description of purged and pressurized systems, see NFPA 496-2008, *Standard for Purged and Pressurized Enclosures for Electrical Equipment.* **(See Figure 21-17)**

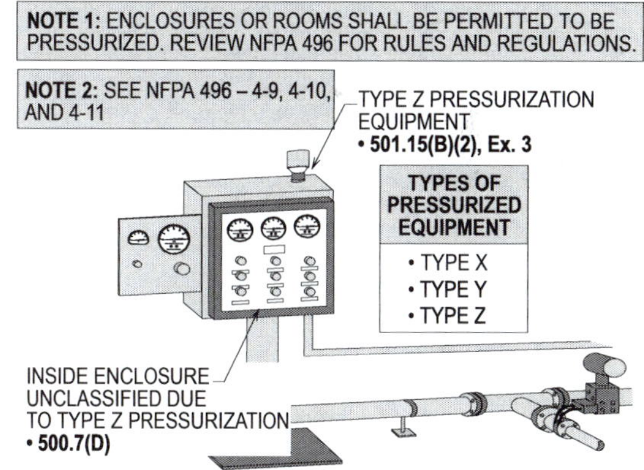

Figure 21-17. This illustration shows the inside of an enclosure being an unclassified area, based upon a Type Z pressurized piece of equipment. Purged or pressurized equipment shall be permitted to be used in Class I, Division 1 or 2 locations.

INTRINSICALLY SAFE EQUIPMENT (CLASS I, DIVISION 1) 504.2 AND 500.7(E)

The use of intrinsically safe equipment is primarily limited to process control instrumentation, since these electrical systems lend themselves to the low energy requirements. ANSI/UL 913-2006 and ANSI/ISA-RP 12.06.01-2003 provide information on the design test and evaluation. The installation rules are covered in **Article 504**. The definition of an intrinsically safe circuit is: "A circuit in which any spark or thermal effect is incapable of causing ignition of a mixture of flammable or combustible material in air under prescribed test conditions." UL and Factory Mutual list several devices in this category.

> **Design Tip:** The equipment and its associated wiring shall be installed so they are positively separated from the nonintrinsically safe circuits. Induced voltages could defeat the concept of intrinsically safe circuits. **(See Figure 21-18)**

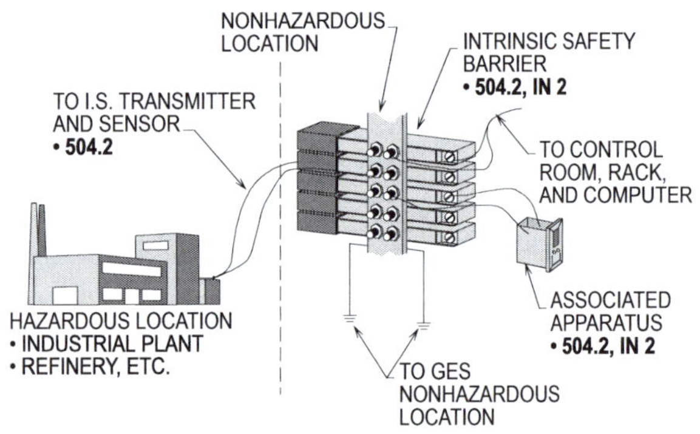

Figure 21-18. Intrinsically safe equipment shall be permitted to be utilized to supply low-voltage instruments, etc. in Class I, Division 1 and 2 locations. See **501.105(B)** and **501.150(B)** and **Figure 4-20** in Chapter 4.

NONINCENDIVE EQUIPMENT (CLASS I, DIVISION 2) 500.2, 500.7(F), (G), AND (H)

Nonincendive equipment is a form of intrinsic safety designed for use in Class I, Division 2 locations. Such equipment is defined as components having contacts that make or break an incendive circuit and elements.

The enclosures in which the contacts are enclosed are so constructed that the components are not capable of igniting the surrounding flammable gases and air mixtures.

General-purpose enclosures shall be permitted to be used to house such circuits and components that under normal operating conditions will not release enough energy to ignite a specific explosive mixture. (See page 4-17)

> **Design Tip:** The housing of nonincendive components is not intended to exclude a flammable atmosphere or contain an explosion. **(See Figure 21-19)**

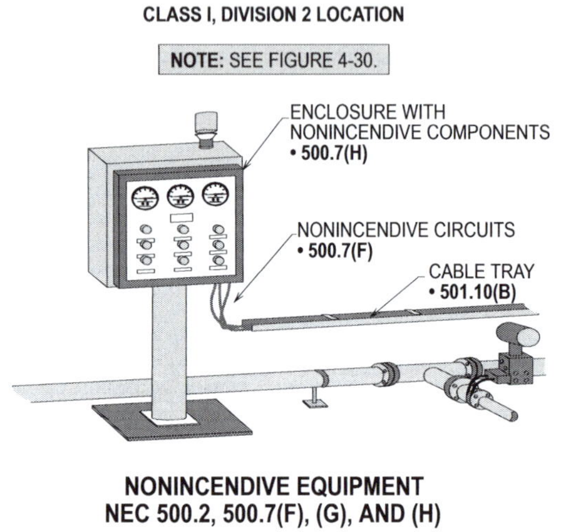

Figure 21-19. This illustration shows nonincendive components and circuits used in Class I, Division 2 locations.

OIL IMMERSION AND HERMETICALLY SEALED CONTACTS 500.2, 500.7(I), AND (J)

The general rule requires switches, circuit breakers, and make-and-break contacts of push buttons, relays, alarm bells, and horns to be installed in enclosures that are identified for Class I, Division 1 locations. However, in Class I, Division 2 locations, general-purpose enclosures shall be permitted to be used if the current-interrupting contacts are:

(1) Immersed in oil or

(2) Enclosed within a chamber hermetically sealed against the entrance of gases or vapors.

See Figure 21-20 for contacts immersed in oil and sealed within an enclosed hermetically sealed chamber.

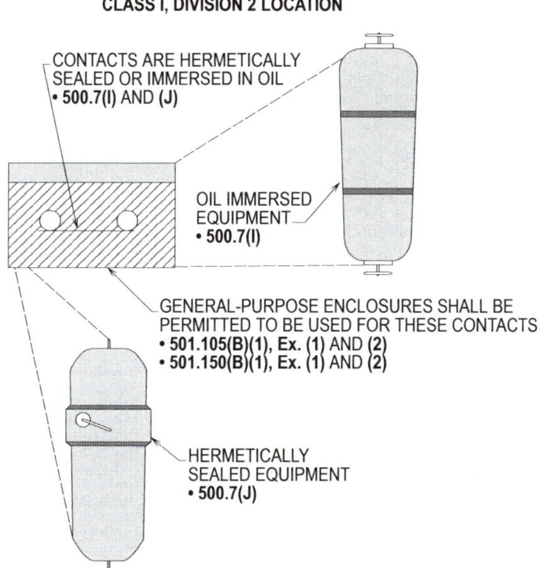

Figure 21-20. This illustration shows contacts installed in general-purpose enclosures that are immersed in oil and hermetically sealed chambers. Such enclosures and controls shall be permitted to be installed in Class I, Division 2 locations.

CLASS I, DIVISION 1 WIRING METHODS 501.10(A)(1)(a) THRU (e)

In Class I, Division 1 locations, threaded rigid metal conduit (RMC), threaded steel intermediate metal conduit (IMC), or Type MI cable with termination fittings that are identified for the location shall be the wiring method employed. All boxes, fittings, and joints shall be threaded for connection to conduit or cable terminations and shall be of explosionproof type per **510.10(A)(3)**. Threaded joints shall be made up with at least five threads fully engaged per **500.8(E)(1)**. Type MI cable shall be installed and supported in such a manner to avoid tensile stress at the termination fittings. Where it is necessary to utilize flexible connections, as at motor terminals, flexible fittings that are listed for Class I locations shall be used per **501.10(A)(2)** and **501.140**.

TYPE PVC OR RTRC (CLASS I, DIVISION 1) 501.10(A)(1)(a), Ex.

The **Ex.** to **501.10(A)(1)(a)** permits Type PVC or RTRC conduit to be installed in Class I, Division 1 areas, if encased in a concrete envelope of at least 2 in. (50 mm) and buried below the surface in not less than 24 in. (600 mm) of earth.

MC/HL CABLE AND ITC/HL CABLE (CLASS I, DIVISION 1) 501.10(A)(1)(c) AND (d)

Section **501.10(A)(1)(c)** and **(d)** permits Type MC/HL and ITC/HL cable that is listed for such use and equipped with a gas/vaportight continuous corrugated aluminum sheath with an overall jacket of suitable polymeric material to be installed in Class I, Division 1 locations. **(See Figure 21-21)**

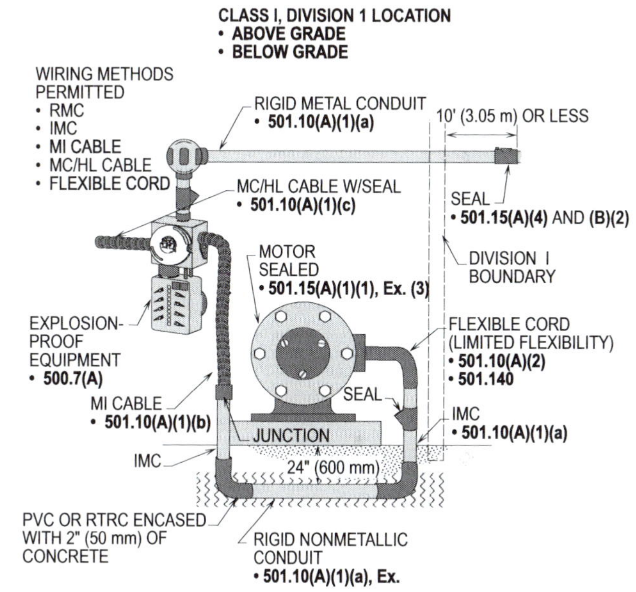

Figure 21-21. As shown, rigid metal conduit, intermediate metal conduit, Type PVC or RTRC, MI and MC/HL cable, and flexible cord under certain conditions of use shall be permitted to be utilized in Class I, Division 1 locations.

WIRING METHODS USED FOR LIMITED FLEXIBILITY (CLASS I, DIVISION 1) 501.10(A)(2)

Flexible fittings that are listed for use in Class I locations are required where it is necessary to employ flexible connections such as at motor terminals, etc.

Section **501.10(A)(2)** refers to **501.140,** which permits flexible cord to be used for that portion of the circuit where the fixed wiring method does not provide the necessary movement for fixed and mobile electrical utilization equipment in an industrial establishment. However, for this rule to be applied, proper maintenance and supervision shall be available. **(See Figure 21-21)**

CLASS I, DIVISION 2 EQUIPMENT
500.2 AND 500.7(A) THRU (L)

Class I, Division 2 equipment shall provide a form of construction that will operate in such a manner as to prevent igniting flammable mixtures of gases and air.

TYPES OF EQUIPMENT
(CLASS I, DIVISION 2)
500.7(A), (D), AND (E)

Equipment installed in Class I, Division 1 areas can be installed in Class I, Division 2 locations. Such equipment is the following:

(1)   Explosionproof

(2)   Purged and pressurized

(3)   Intrinsically safe

> **Design Tip:** See and review the equipment that is either identified or listed and illustrated in this chapter under Class I, Division 1 Equipment.

COMBUSTIBLE GAS DETECTION SYSTEM
500.2 AND 500.7(K)

Under certain conditions of use, a combustible gas detection system shall be permitted to be used.

For example, Class I, Division 2 equipment shall be permitted to be installed in Class I, Division 1 locations and electrical equipment for Class I, Division 2 locations shall be permitted to be installed in unclassified locations.

However, the following requirements shall be complied with when using a combustible gas detection system:

• In a Class I, Division 1 location that is so classified due to inadequate ventilation, electrical equipment

suitable for Class I, Division 2 locations shall be permitted.

• In a building located in, or with an opening into, a Class I, Division 2 location where the interior does not contain a source of flammable gas or vapor, electrical equipment for unclassified locations shall be permitted.

• In the interior of a control panel containing instrumentation utilizing or measuring flammable liquids, gases, or vapors, electrical equipment suitable for Class I, Division 2 locations shall be permitted.

• Gas detection equipment shall be listed for detection of the specific gas or vapor that is to be encountered.

• System shall be installed in industrial establishments, with restricted public access and where the conditions of supervision and maintenance ensure that only qualified persons service the installation.

• The types of detection equipment, installation location(s), alarm and shutdown criteria, and calibration frequency shall be documented when combustible gas detectors are used as a protection technique.

See Figure 21-22 for an illustration of a typical combustible gas detection system.

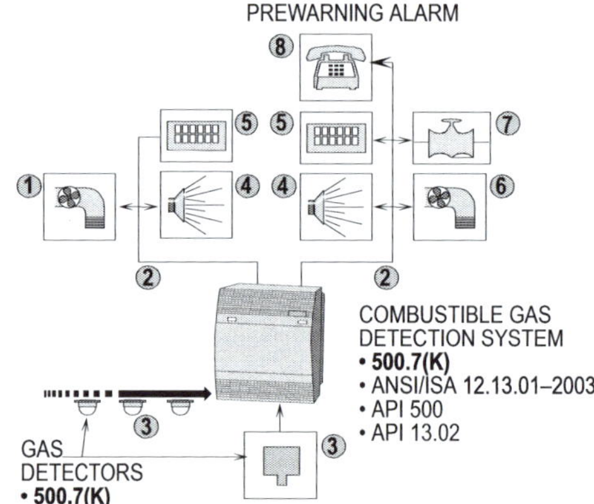

COMBUSTIBLE GAS DETECTION SYSTEM
NEC 500.2 AND 500.7(K)

Figure 21-22. This illustration shows a typical combustible gas detection system.

CLASS I, DIVISION 2 WIRING METHODS 501.10(B)(1)(1) THRU (7)

In Class I, Division 2 locations, threaded rigid metal conduit, threaded intermediate metal conduit, enclosed gasketed busways, enclosed gasketed wireways, or Type PLTC and PLTC-ER cable in accordance with the provisions of **Article 725**, Type MI, MC/HL, ITC/HL, MV, or TC cable with listed termination fittings shall be the wiring method utilized. Type ITC, PLTC-ER, PLTC, MI, MC, MV, or TC cable shall be permitted to be installed in cable tray systems where installed in a manner that avoids tensile stress at the termination fittings.

Design Tip: Boxes, fittings, and joints shall not be required to be explosionproof except when they are used in areas requiring Class I, Division 1 enclosures.

WIRING METHODS USED FOR LIMITED FLEXIBILITY (CLASS I, DIVISION 2) 501.10(B)(2)(1) THRU (7)

If provision must be made for limited flexibility, as at motor terminals, listed flexible metal fittings, flexible metal conduit, liquidtight flexible metal conduit, or liquidtight flexible nonmetallic conduit shall be permitted to be used. [For more wiring methods, review Item **(7)** to **501.10(B)(2)**.]

Design Tip: The above wiring methods shall be provided with listed fittings that provide a proper connection for bonding per **501.30(B)**.

Flexible cord that is listed for extra-hard usage and terminated with listed bushed fittings shall be permitted to be used. However, an additional conductor for equipment grounding conductor shall be included in the flexible cord. **(See Figure 21-23)**

REQUIREMENTS FOR SWITCHES, CIRCUIT BREAKERS, MOTOR CONTROLLERS, AND FUSES 501.115

Enclosures used to house switches, circuit breakers, motor controllers, and fuses shall be rated for either Class I, Division 1 or Division 2. The Division determines the type of enclosure, based on the amount and the time the gas or vapor is present.

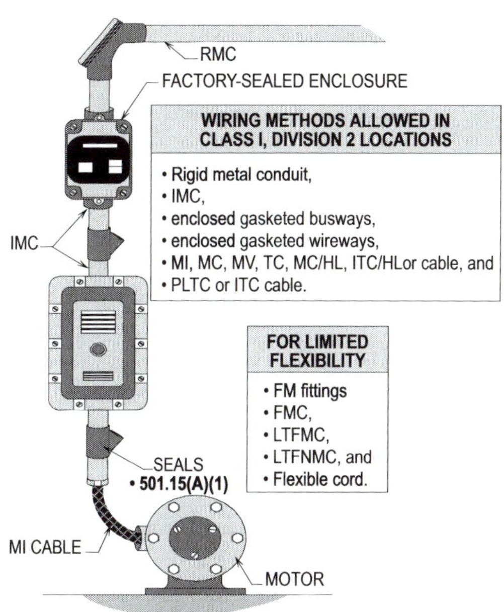

Figure 21-23. As shown above, there are more wiring methods that are permitted in Class I, Division 2 than Class I, Division 1 locations. **See Figure 21-21** for wiring methods permitted in Class I, Division 1 locations.

CLASS I, DIVISION 1 501.115(A)

Identified Class I, Division 1 enclosures shall be used for switches, circuit breakers, motor controllers, and fuses, including push buttons, relays, and similar devices, in order to be installed in Class I, Division 1 locations. **(See Figure 21-24)**

CLASS I, DIVISION 2 501.115(B)

Identified Class I, Division 1 enclosures shall be used for switches, circuit breakers, motor controllers, and fuses, including push buttons, relays, and similar devices, in order to be installed in Class I, Division 2 locations.

However, general-purpose enclosures shall be permitted to be used if the interruption of current occurs in **(1)** a hermetically sealed chamber or **(2)** the current make-and-break contacts are oil-immersed.

The use of general-purpose enclosures shall be permitted if the interruption of current occurs within a factory-sealed explosionproof chamber that is identified for the location. **(See Figure 21-24)**

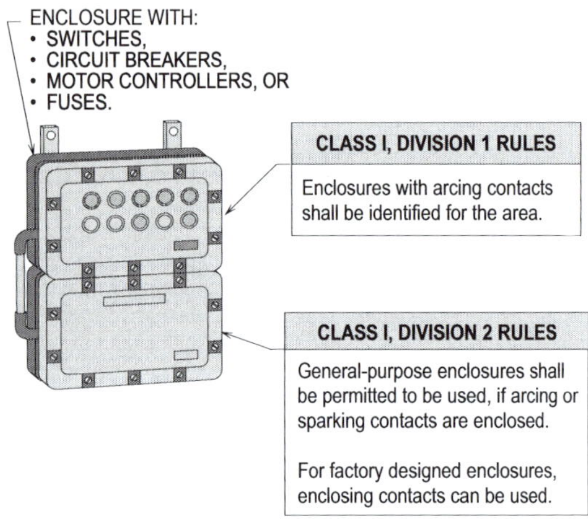

Figure 21-24. Enclosures containing arcing contacts shall be identified for Class I, Division 1 locations. In Class I, Division 2 locations, general-purpose and factory enclosures shall be permitted to be used if the contacts are enclosed in such a manner to handle arcing and sparking conditions.

Design Tip: The use of disconnects and isolating switches in general-purpose enclosures in Class I, Division 2 locations shall be permitted if neither the switch nor fuse operates as a normal current interrupting device. In such cases, fuses can only be used for short-circuit protection.

REQUIREMENTS FOR MOTORS AND GENERATORS
501.125

Electric motors are needed to drive pumps, compressors, fans, blowers, and conveyors, so their presence in hazardous atmospheres is sometimes unavoidable.

The types of hazardous atmospheres and corrosive conditions are major factors in motor selection. The hazardous area dictates the type of motor needed to avoid excessive maintenance and expensive shutdowns. The types available vary all the way from "drip-proof" to "totally enclosed" and "fan cooled" motors.

CLASS I, DIVISION 1
501.125(A)

In Class I, Division 1 locations, only motors that are the explosionproof, totally enclosed, and pressurized with clean air, or totally enclosed inert gas-filled, and special submerged type shall be permitted to be used.

The NEC makes it clear that Class I, Division 1 totally enclosed motors shall have no external surface operating temperature in excess of 80 percent of the ignition temperature of the gas or vapor involved.

Also required are devices to detect and automatically deenergize the motor (or provide an effective alarm) in case of overheating.

In addition, auxiliary equipment shall be of a type that is identified for the location in which it is installed. **(See Figure 21-25)**

CLASS I, DIVISION 2
501.125(B)

Motors for use in Class I, Division 2 locations in which sliding contacts, switching mechanisms, or integral resistance devices are employed shall be explosionproof (Class I, Division 1) or purged and pressurized.

However, open-type motors such as squirrel-cage induction motors without any arcing devices shall be permitted to be used in Class I, Division 2 locations.

Design Tip: UL provides a procedure in which listed explosionproof motors can be repaired. Motor personnel must consult as to which repair shops have been authorized to make such repairs. Unauthorized maintenance of an explosionproof motor can result in voiding the manufacturer's listing.

To enable the AHJ to determine whether or not the maximum temperature exceeds 80 percent of the ignition temperature of the gas or vapor involved, space heaters used in a motor shall have a permanent, visible nameplate marking on the motor, indicating the maximum surface temperature (based on 40°C ambient).

If the temperature of the heater does not exceed 80 percent of the ignition temperature, the motor shall be considered suitable for use in that atmosphere. **(See Figure 21-25)**

REQUIREMENTS FOR LUMINAIRES
501.130(A)

In locations where explosive gases or vapors exist, bare lamps or non-explosionproof enclosed luminaires can create extreme hazards. Bare lamps may be broken, and the arc or spark can cause explosions. For this reason, lamps shall be enclosed in luminaires that are specifically designed for Class I, Divisions 1 or 2 locations, whichever applies.

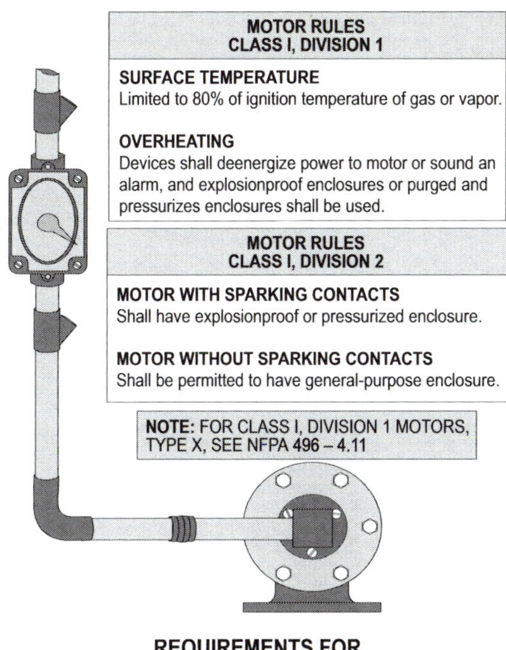

Figure 21-25. The above rules apply when installing motors in Class I, Division 1 and 2 locations.

CLASS I, DIVISION 1
501.130(A)(1)

Surface temperature of Class I, Division 1 luminaires shall not exceed the ignition temperature of the gases or vapors surrounding such luminaires.

Each luminaire shall be identified as a complete assembly for the Class I, Division 1 location. In addition, it shall be clearly marked to indicate the maximum wattage of lamps for which it is identified.

PENDANT LUMINAIRES
501.130(A)(3)

Pendant luminaires for Class I, Division 1 shall be suspended and supplied by threaded metal or intermediate metal conduit stems. Threaded joints of Class I, Division 1 luminaires shall have set-screws to prevent loosening on rigid stems. Where rigid stems (conduit portion from mounting box to luminaire) are longer than 12 in. (300 mm), they shall be braced against movement or provided with flexible fittings. **(See Figure 21-26)**

PORTABLE LIGHTING EQUIPMENT
501.130(A)(1)

Luminaires intended for portable use shall be specifically identified as a complete assembly for that use. Personnel shall not take portable lighting equipment into such classified areas if it is not identified for such area and use. **(See Figure 21-26)**

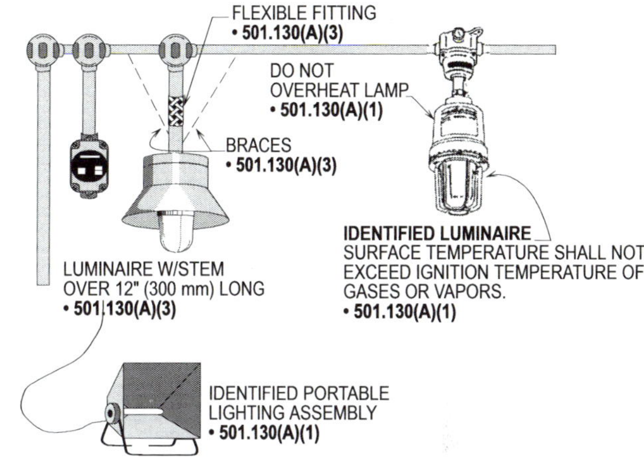

Figure 21-26. This illustration shows the rules and regulations that apply when installing luminaires in Class I, Division 1 locations.

CLASS I, DIVISION 2
501.130(B)(1)

For Class I, Division 2 luminaires, it is the lamp surface temperature, and not the luminaire surface temperature, that shall not exceed the ignition temperature of the gases or vapors present.

Basically, in locations that are classified Class I, Division 2, fixed luminaires that have been tested shall be permitted to operate up to the ignition temperature of the gas or vapor present. However, if the luminaires have not been tested for such use, the maximum temperature shall not exceed 80 percent of the ignition temperature of the gas or vapor present. **(See Figure 21-27)**

PENDANT LUMINAIRES
501.130(B)(3)

In Class I, Division 2 locations, pendant luminaires shall be suspended by flexible hangers unless rigid stems not over 12 in. (300 mm) long are used, or longer stems are permanently braced within 12 in. (300 mm) of the luminaire.

Pendant luminaires shall be suspended and supplied by threaded metal or intermediate metal conduit stems that are screwed into the threaded joints of the luminaires. Set-screws, to prevent loosening on rigid stems, shall also be provided. **See Figure 21-26** for rules pertaining to pendant-hung luminaires.

PORTABLE LIGHTING
501.130(B)(4)

Portable lighting used in Class I, Division 2 locations shall not be required to be identified for Class I, Division 1 if it is mounted on a movable stand and connected by an approved flexible cord. The luminaire only needs to be identified for Class I, Division 2 and be specified as follows:

(1) The luminaire be protected by a suitable guard or location,

(2) The luminaire has a suitable enclosure to prevent sparks or hot metal from a lamp from causing ignition of the surrounding atmosphere, and

(3) The luminaire shall not exceed temperature limitations.

See Figure 21-27 for rules concerning luminaires installed and used in Class I, Division 2 locations.

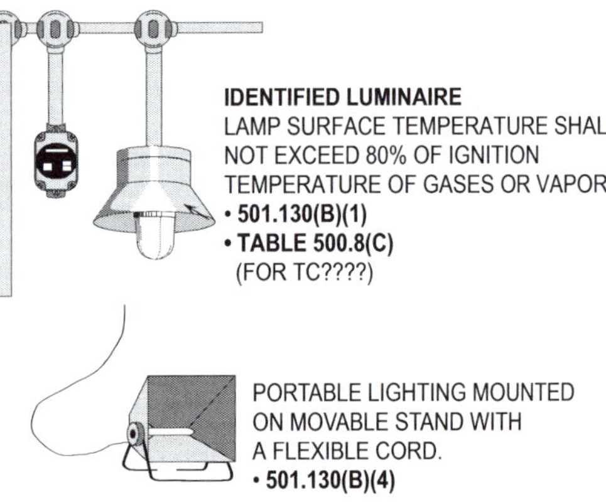

Figure 21-27. This illustration shows that rules and regulations that apply when installing luminaires in Class I, Division 2 locations.

REQUIREMENTS FOR UTILIZATION EQUIPMENT
501.135

Utilization equipment installed in hazardous (classified) areas shall be considered to be appliances specifically designed for such areas.

CLASS I, DIVISION 1
501.135(A)

Utilization equipment, including electrically heated and motor-driven equipment, that is used in Class I, Division 1 locations shall be identified for such location. **(See Figure 21-28)**

CLASS I, DIVISION 2
501.135(B)

Utilization equipment installed in Class I, Division 2 locations shall comply with certain design criteria.

HEATERS
501.135(B)(1)

Heating appliances shall be identified for Class I, Division 1 locations. Heating appliances would include water heaters and room heaters. There are exceptions that permit heaters to be the general-purpose type, and they are as follows:

(1) If the maximum operating temperature of any exposed surface does not exceed 80 percent of the ignition temperature of the gas or vapor surrounding the heater, when operating continuously at 120 percent rated voltage, the heater shall be permitted to be the general-purpose type.

(2) If the maximum operating temperature of any exposed surface does not exceed 80 percent of the ignition temperature of the gas or vapor surrounding the heater, when operating continuously at 100 percent rated voltage, the heater shall be permitted to be the general-purpose type, provided it is supplied with a temperature controller.

To meet the requirements of Class I, Division 1 equipment, operating temperature at rated voltage would have to be no greater than about 55 percent of the ignition temperature of the gas or vapor and all heaters shall be completely enclosed.

See Figure 21-29 for rules for installing heaters in Class I, Division 2 locations.

APPLIANCES WITH MOTORS
501.135(B)(2)

Appliances with motors shall not be required to be identified for the location unless the motor has brushes, a centrifugal switch, or a built-in thermal protector, in which case the appliances shall be identified for Class I, Division 1 locations. [See **501.115(B)(1)** for further information concerning motors.] **(See Figure 21-29)**

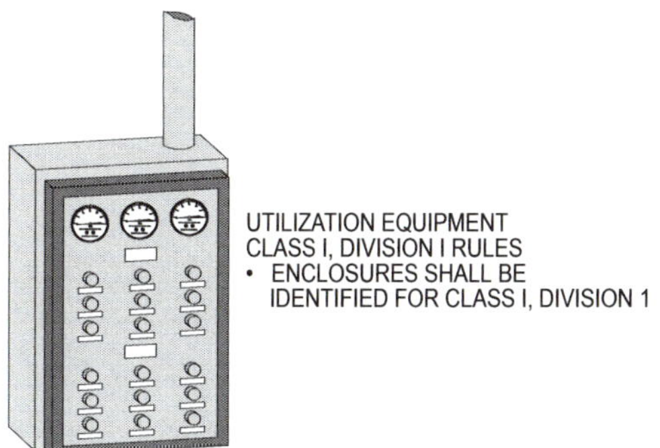

**REQUIREMENTS FOR
UTILIZATION EQUIPMENT
NEC 501.135(A)**

Figure 21-28. Enclosures, used for the components of utilization equipment, shall be identified for Class I, Division 1 locations.

APPLIANCES WITH SWITCHES
501.135(B)(3)

If an appliance has a switch, the switch shall be identified for Class I locations. The rest of the appliance may in some cases have a general-purpose enclosure, but the switch shall always be identified for Class I locations.

> **Design Tip:** Except as required by **501.135(B)(1), (B) (2)**, and **(B)(3)** above, appliances in Class I, Division 2 locations shall be permitted to be the general-purpose type. **(See Figure 21-29)**

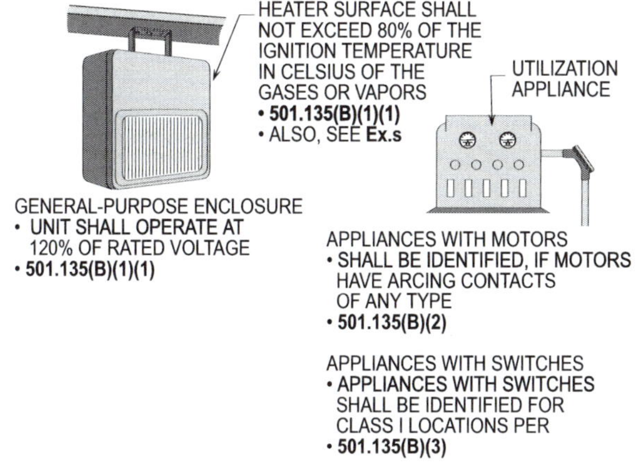

**REQUIREMENTS FOR
UTILIZATION EQUIPMENT
NEC 501.135(B)(1), (B)(2), AND (B)(3)**

Figure 21-29. This illustration shows the rules and regulations that apply when installing utilization equipment (appliances) in Class I, Division 2 locations.

USING FLEXIBLE CORD IN CLASS I, DIVISION 1 AND 2 AREAS
501.140

A flexible cord shall be permitted to be used for connection between a portable lamp or other portable utilization equipment. The fixed portion of its supply circuit and where such connections are used shall:

(1) Be of a type identified for extra-hard usage,

(2) Contain, in addition to the conductors of the circuit, an equipment grounding conductor conforming to **250.118**, that is, of green color and used for no other purpose than for grounding, and

(3) Be supported by clamps or other suitable means in such a manner that there will be no tension on the terminal connections.

(4) In Division 1 or Division 2 locations where the boxes, fittings, or enclosures are required to be explosionproof, the cord shall be terminated with a cord connector or attachment plug listed for the location or a cord connector installed with a seal listed for the location. In Division 2 locations where explosionproof equipment is not required, the cord shall be terminated with a listed cord connector or listed attachment plug per **501.140(B)(4)**, and

(5) Be of continuous length.

In Class I, Division 1 locations, flexible cord shall be permitted to be used for that portion of the circuit where the fixed wiring method of **501.10(A)(1)(a) thru (e)** cannot provide the necessary degree of movement for fixed and mobile electrical utilization equipment. However, proper maintenance and supervision shall be provided, and such equipment shall be located in an industrial establishment.

CORD-AND-PLUG CONNECTED SUBMERSIBLE PUMPS
501.140(A)(3)

Electric submersible pumps with means for removal without entering the wet pit shall be considered portable utilization equipment. The extension of the flexible cord between the wet pit and power source shall be permitted to be enclosed in a suitable raceway.

CORD-AND-PLUG CONNECTED ELECTRIC MIXERS
501.140(A)(4)

Electric mixers traveling in and out of open-type mixing tanks or vats shall be permitted to be classified as portable utilization equipment so that wiring procedures will not have to be too restrictive.

See Figure 21-30 for a detailed illustration of flexible cord being used for such installations.

REQUIREMENTS FOR RECEPTACLES AND ATTACHMENT CAPS
501.145(A) AND (B)

Arcing at exposed contacts shall be prevented in Class I, Division 1 or 2 locations. To accomplish this, receptacles are designed so that plug contacts are safely within an explosionproof enclosure when they are electrically engaged, confining arcing, if any, to the receptacle interior.

RECEPTACLES WITH SWITCHES

501.145 AND UL 498

With this configuration, the plug cannot be inserted unless the switch is in the OFF position and cannot be withdrawn with the receptacle in the ON position. The reason for this is the receptacle contacts are interlocked with a switch located in an explosionproof enclosure. Therefore, arcing does not occur outside the enclosure, due to mated parts being deenergized during plug insertion and removal. **(See Figure 21-31)**

RECEPTACLES WITHOUT SWITCHES
501.145 AND UL 498

Receptacles without switches rely on a mechanical means that provides a delayed action to confine arcing to the receptacle interior during plug insertion and withdrawal. The design used in these receptacles prevents removal of the plug until any flame, spark, or hot metal from an arc has cooled sufficiently to prevent ignition of the surrounding explosive atmosphere. **(See Figure 21-31)**

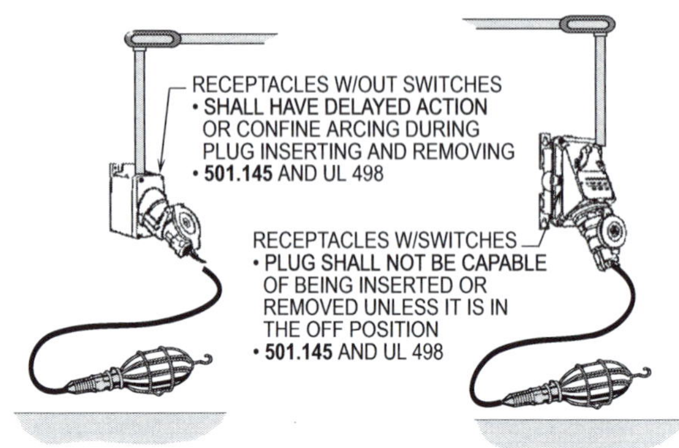

Figure 21-31. This illustration shows the rules and regulations that apply when using cord-and-plug connected equipment in Class I, Division 1 and 2 locations.

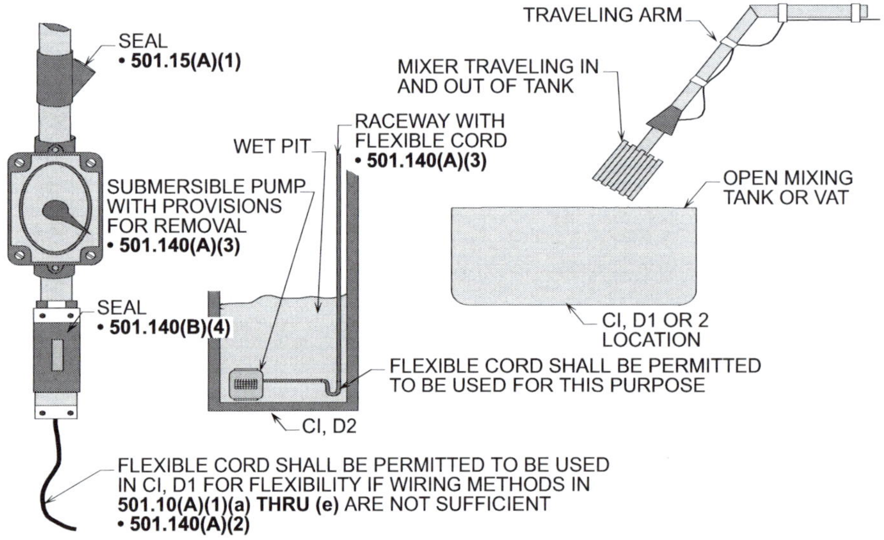

Figure 21-30. This illustration shows the rules and regulations that apply when using flexible cord in Class I, Division 1 and 2 locations.

WIRING METHODS IN CLASS II, DIVISION 1 AND 2 LOCATIONS 502.10(A) OR (B)

In Class II, Division 1 and 2 locations, certain types of wiring methods and enclosures shall be utilized to properly contain and handle dust-related areas.

WIRING METHODS (CLASS II, DIVISION 1) 502.10(A)(1)(1), (A)(2), (A)(3), AND (A)(4)

In Class II, Division 1 locations, the wiring method shall be either metal conduit or Type MI cable (mineral-insulated cable).

Section **502.10(A)(1)(3)** permits Type MC/HL cable, listed for such use and equipped with a gas/vaportight continuous corrugated aluminum sheath with an overall jacket of suitable polymeric material, to be installed in Class II, Division 1 locations. (Review item 4 carefully.)

Design Tip: To utilize this wiring method, a separate equipment grounding conductor, in compliance with **250.122** and with termination fittings listed for the application, shall be used. **(See Figure 21-32)**

FITTINGS AND BOXES (CLASS II, DIVISION 1) 502.10(A)(1)(3)

There are two main parts to this rule that shall be applied, and they are as follows:

(1) For locations where the dusts are hazardous but not of a combustible electrically conductive nature. This includes grain, cocoa, dried egg and milk dust, starch dust, and hay dust locations.

Boxes and fittings that contain splices or taps shall be identified for Class II locations when used in such locations.

Boxes and fittings without splices or taps shall not be required to be identified, but shall have dusttight enclosures with no openings such as screw holes.

(2) For locations where dusts of a combustible electrically conductive nature are present. This includes coal dust, coke, carbon black, charcoal dust, magnesium, and aluminum dust locations.

All fittings and boxes, with or without splices or taps, shall be identified for Class II locations when installed in these locations. **(See Figure 21-32)**

FLEXIBLE CONNECTIONS 502.10(A)(2)

In Class II, Division 1 locations, liquidtight flexible metal conduit and liquidtight flexible nonmetallic conduit with listed fittings or flexible cord, listed for extra-hard usage and terminated with listed dusttight fittings, shall be permitted to be used. Unless other means are provided for grounding, cords shall have an equipment grounding conductor. Where dusts of an electrically conducting nature are present, cords shall have dusttight seals at both ends. **(See Figure 21-32)**

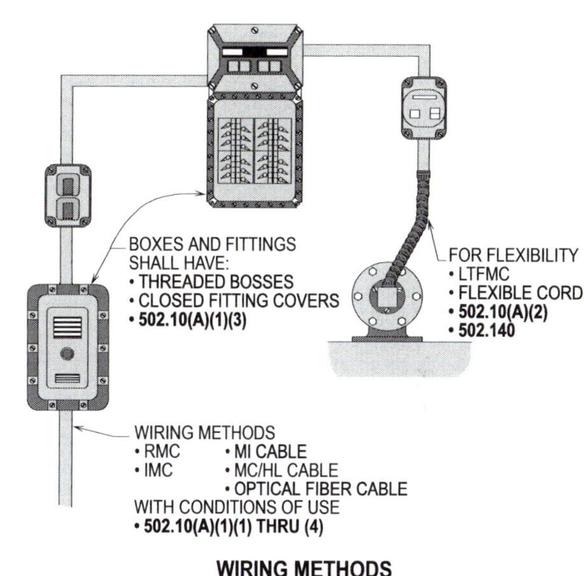

Figure 21-32. This illustration shows the rules and regulations that apply to wiring methods and equipment installed in Class II, Division 1 locations.

WIRING METHODS (CLASS II, DIVISION 2) 502.10(B)(1)(1) THRU (B)(1)(8)

In Class II, Division 2 locations, the following wiring methods shall be permitted:

(1) Rigid metal conduit

(2) Intermediate metal conduit (IMC)

(3) Electrical metallic tubing (EMT)

(4) Dusttight wireways

(5) Type MI cable (mineral-insulated cable)

(6) Type MC cable (metal-clad power cable)

(7) Type PLTC and PLTC-ER in cable trays

(8) Type ITC and ITC-ER in cable trays

(9) Type MC, MI, or TC cable in cable trays

(10) Reinforced thermosetting resin conduit (RTRC) and polyvinyl chloride conduit (PVC) Schedule 80

(11) Nonincendive circuits in any suitable wiring method and optical fiber cables

FLEXIBLE CONNECTIONS
502.10(B)(2)

In Class II, Division 2 locations, liquidtight flexible metal conduit and liquidtight flexible nonmetallic conduit with approved fittings or flexible cord, approved for extra-hard usage and equipped with bushed fittings, shall be permitted to be used. Unless other means are provided for grounding, cords shall have an equipment grounding conductor. Where dusts of an electrically conducting nature are present, cords shall have dusttight seals at both ends. **(See Figure 21-33)**

WIREWAYS, FITTINGS, AND BOXES
502.10(B)(4)

Wireways, fittings, and boxes in Class II, Division 2 locations are not necessarily required to be approved for Class II locations. However, they shall have close-fitting enclosures with no openings, such as screw holes, that might transmit sparks to the outside of the wireway, fitting, or box. Sparking or burning material shall not escape, because it could ignite adjacent combustible material. **(See Figure 21-33)**

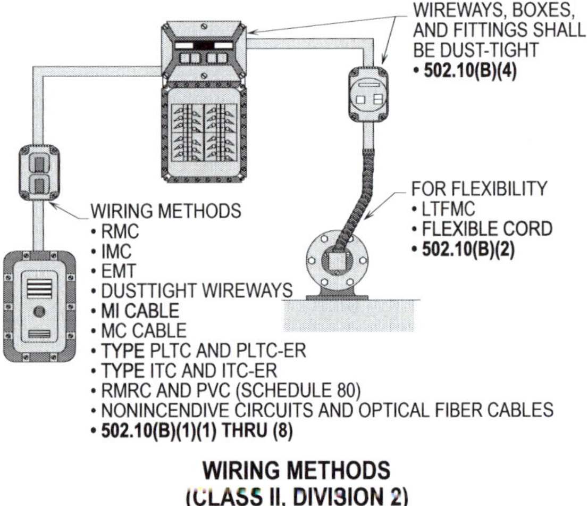

Figure 21-33. This illustration shows the rules and regulations that apply for wiring methods and equipment installed in Class II, Division 2 locations.

REQUIREMENTS FOR SEALS AND DRAINS (CLASS I, DIVISIONS 1 AND 2)
501.15

Seals shall be provided in conduit and cable systems to minimize the passage of gases or vapors from one portion of the system to another portion. Another purpose of the seals is to prevent transmitting an explosion or to keep ignition from traveling between sections of the system.

NEED FOR SEALS
501.15(A)(1) THRU (A)(4)

Seals and drains are recommended to be installed as follows:

(1) To restrict the passage of gases, vapors, or flames from one portion of the electrical installation to another at atmospheric pressure and normal ambient temperatures,

(2) To limit explosions to the sealed-off enclosure and prevent compression or "pressure piling" in conduit systems,

(3) While not a code requirement, many engineers consider it good practice to sectionalize long conduit runs by inserting seals not more than 50 ft (15 m) to 100 ft (30 m) apart, depending on the conduit size, to minimize the effects of "pressure piling." Sealing fittings are required, and

(4) At each entrance to an enclosure housing having an arcing or sparking device and used in Class I, Division 1 and 2 hazardous locations. To be located as close as practical and in no case more than 18 in. (450 mm) from such enclosures. **(See Figure 21-34)**

(5) At each entrance 2 in. (53 mm) size or larger to an enclosure or fitting, housing terminals, splices, or taps when used in Class I, Division 1 location. To be located as close as practical and in no case more than 18 in. (450 mm) from such enclosures. **(See Figure 21-35)**

(6) In conduit systems when leaving a Class I, Division 1 or Division 2 location. **(See Figure 21-36)**, and

(7) In cable systems when the cables either do not have a gas/vaportight continuous sheath or are capable of transmitting gases or vapors through the cable core where these cables leave a Class I, Division 1 or Division 2 location. **(See Figure 21-37)**

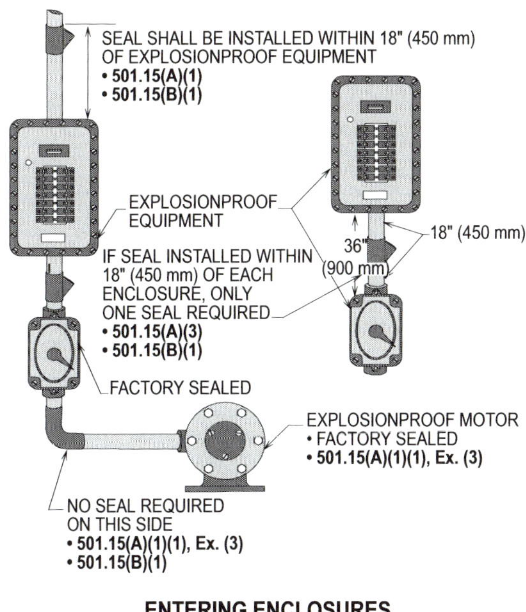

Figure 21-34. Explosionproof equipment or equipment with arcing or sparking devices shall have a seal placed within 18 in. (450 mm) of such equipment.

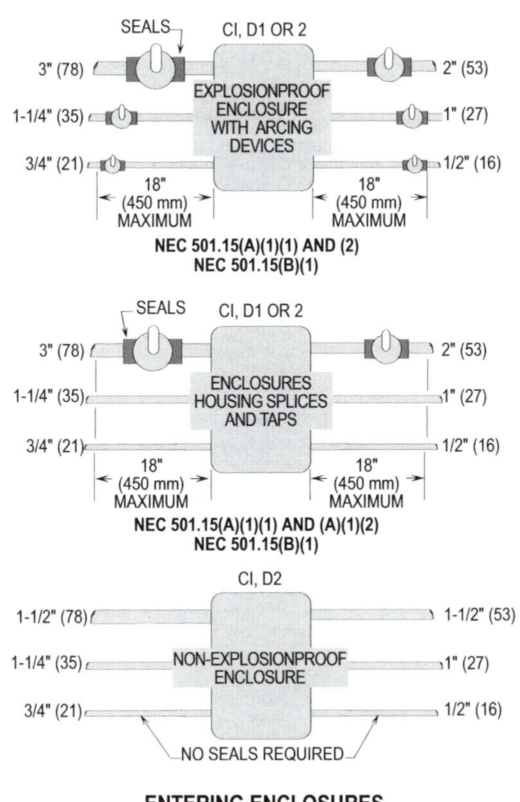

Figure 21-35. This illustration shows the rules that apply to the enclosures of splices, taps, and arcing or sparking devices if they are installed in a Class I, Division 1 or 2 location.

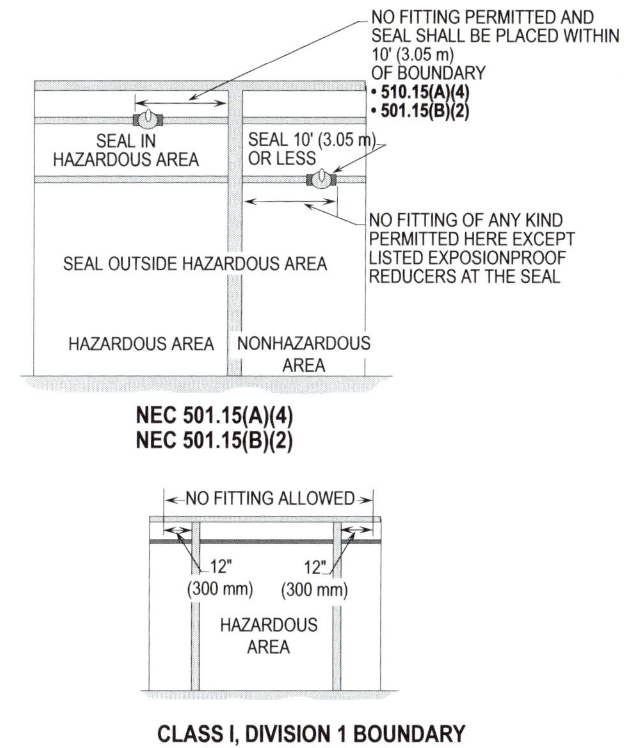

Figure 21-36. This illustration shows the rules that apply when installing seals in conduit runs leaving or passing through a Class I, Divisions 1 or 2 location.

NEED FOR DRAINS
501.15(F)

In humid atmospheres or in wet locations, where it is likely that water can gain entrance to the interiors of enclosures or raceways, the raceways should be inclined so that water will not collect in enclosures or in seals but will be led to low points where it may pass out through ECD drains. Frequently the arrangement of raceway runs makes this method impractical if not impossible. In such instances, Type EZD drain seal fittings shall be used. These fittings prevent accumulations of water above the seal.

In locations that usually are considered dry, surprising amounts of water frequently collect in conduit systems. No conduit system is airtight; therefore, it may breathe. Alternate increases and decreases in temperature and/or barometric pressure due to weather changes or due to the nature of the process carried on in the location where the conduit is installed will cause breathing. Outside air is drawn into the conduit system when it breathes in. If this air carries sufficient moisture, it will be condensed within the system when the temperature decreases and chills this air. Due to the internal conditions being unfavorable to evaporation, the resultant water accumulation will remain and be added to by repetitions of the breathing cycle. In view of this likelihood, it is good practice to ensure against such water accumulations and probable subsequent insulation failures by installing EZD with drain cover or inspection cover even though conditions prevailing at the time of planning or installing may not indicate their need. **(See Figure 21-38)**

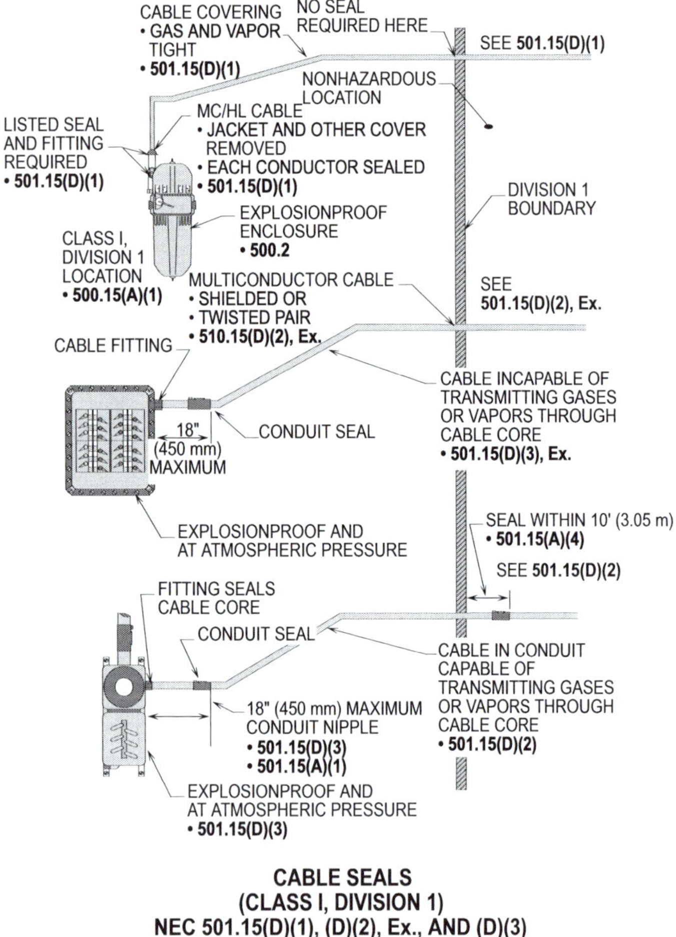

Figure 21-37. This illustration shows the rules that apply when sealing multiconductor cables leaving a Class I, Division 1 location.

SELECTION OF SEALS AND DRAINS

There are different types of seals and drains that are made to be utilized for vertical or horizontal installations and are to be used only for the purpose for which they are designed. Care shall be taken when selecting and installing such fittings.

The following primary considerations shall be used when selecting seals and drains:

(1) Select the proper sealing fitting for the hazardous vapor involved, such as Class I, Groups A, B, C, or D.

(2) Select a sealing fitting for the proper use in

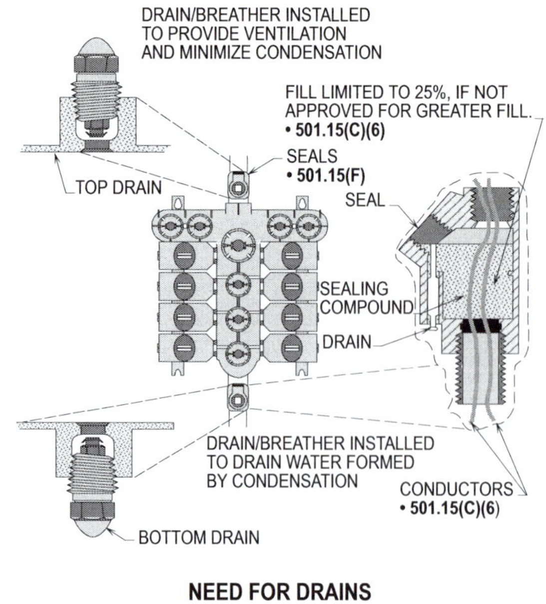

Figure 21-38. Drains and seals installed as shown will minimize water conditions formed by condensation and help prevent mildew from forming.

respect to mounting position. This is particularly critical when the conduit runs between hazardous and nonhazardous areas. Improper positioning of a seal may permit hazardous gases or vapors to enter the system beyond the seal and permit them to escape into another portion of the hazardous area or to enter a nonhazardous area. Some seals are designed to be mounted in any position; others are restricted to horizontal or vertical mounting.

(3) Install the seals on the proper side of the partition or wall as recommended by the manufacturer.

(4) Only trained personnel can install seals, which shall be installed in compliance with the instruction sheets furnished with the seals and sealing compound. Precautionary notes shall be included on installation diagrams to stress the importance of following manufacturers' instructions.

(5) Splices or taps in sealing fittings are strictly prohibited.

(6) Sealing fittings are listed by UL for use in Class I hazardous locations with CHICO A compound only. This compound, when properly mixed and poured, hardens into a dense, strong mass, that is insoluble in water, is not attacked by chemicals, and is not softened by heat. It will withstand ample safety factor pressure of the exploding trapped gases or vapor.

(7) Conductors sealed in the compound shall be permitted to be approved thermoplastic or rubber insulated types. Either may or may not be lead covered (the lead need not be removed).

See Figure 21-39 for installing seals and drains.

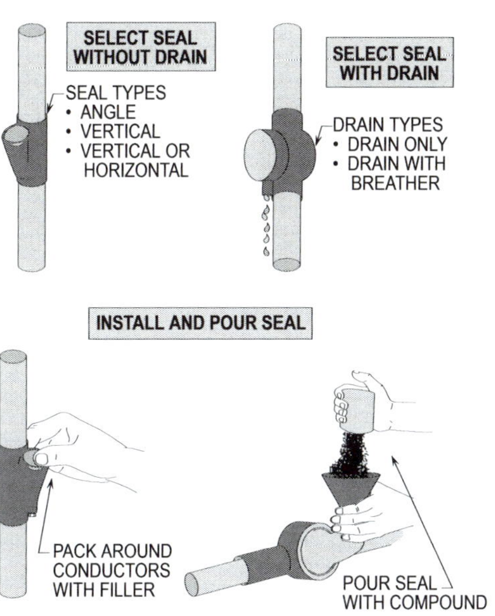

SELECTION OF SEALS AND DRAINS

Figure 21-39. This illustration shows the rules that shall be applied when selecting and installing seals/drains in Class I, Division 1 locations.

TYPES OF SEALING FITTINGS
501.15(C)(1)

The following sealing fittings meet the requirements of the NEC when they are properly installed:

(1) EYS Sealing Fittings—A certain style of EYS sealing fittings are for use with vertical or nearly vertical conduit in sizes from 1/2 (16) through 1 in. (27). Other styles are available in sizes 1/2 (16) through 6 in. (155) for use in vertical or horizontal conduits. In horizontal runs, these are limited to face-up openings. Sizes from 1-1/4 (35) through 6 in. (155) have extra large work openings and separate filling holes, so that CHICO X fiber dams are easy to make. Overall diameter of sizes 1-1/4 (35) through 6 in. (155) is scarcely greater than that of unions of corresponding sizes, permitting close conduit spacings.

Note, check with the manufacturer for the type of compound to be used with a particular seal.

(2) EZS Sealing Fittings—EZS seals are for use with conduit running at any angle, from vertical through horizontal.

See Figure 21-40 for the different types of sealing fittings.

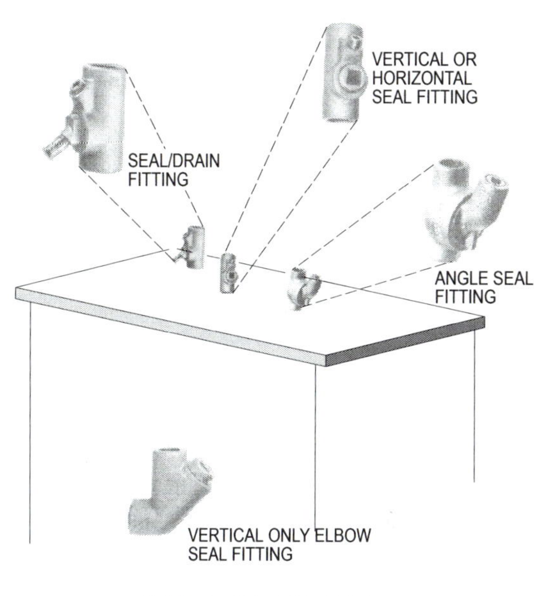

**TYPES OF SEALING FITTINGS
NEC 501.15(C)(1)**

Figure 21-40. As shown, it is most important to select and install the proper seal or seal with drain based on the type of installation.

PROCESS SEALING
501.17

Process sealing applies to process-connected equipment, which includes, but is not limited to canned pumps, submersible pumps, and flow pressure, temperature, or analysis measurement instruments. A process seal is a device to prevent the migration of process fluids from the designed containment into the external electrical system. **(See Figure 21-41)**

An additional means shall be provided to mitigate a single process seal failure where process connected electrical equipment incorporates a single process seal, such as a single compression seal, diaphragm, or tube to prevent flammable or combustible fluids from entering a conduit or cable system capable of transmitting fluids. The additional means may include, but is not limited to the following:

• A suitable barrier meeting the process temperature and pressure conditions that the barrier will be subjected to upon failure of the single process seal.

There shall be a vent or drain between the single process seal and the suitable barrier. Indication of the single process seal failure shall be provided by one of the following:

(1) Visible leakage

(2) An audible whistle

(3) Other means of monitoring

- A listed Type MI cable assembly, rated at not less than 125 percent of the process pressure and not less than 125 percent of the maximum process temperature (in degrees Celsius), installed between the cable or conduit and the single process seal. **(See Figure 21-42)**

- A drain or vent located between the single process seal and a conduit or cable seal. The drain or vent shall be sufficiently sized to prevent overpressuring the conduit or cable seal above 6 in. water column (1493 Pa). Indication of the single process seal failure shall be provided by one of the following:

(1) Visible leakage

(2) An audible whistle

(3) Other means of monitoring

An additional means of sealing shall not be required to be provided for process-connected electrical equipment that does not rely on a single process seal or is listed and marked "single seal" or "dual seal." **(See Figure 21-43)**

REQUIREMENT FOR SEALS (CLASS II, DIVISIONS 1 AND 2) 502.15(1) THRU (4)

When a dust-ignitionproof enclosure and one that is not are installed, there can be communication of dust between the two enclosures under certain conditions of use. The entrance of dust into the dust-ignitionproof enclosure shall be prevented to avoid explosions. This can be accomplished by applying one of the following sealing methods:

(1) By use of a permanent and effective seal, as used in Class I locations,

(2) By connection to a horizontal raceway that is not less than 10 ft (3.05 m) in length, and

(3) By means of a vertical conduit not less than 5 ft (1.5 m) in length, that is installed downward from the dust-ignitionproof enclosure.

(4) Boxes and fittings

Design Tip: Where a conduit provides communication between an enclosure that is required to be dust-ignitionproof and an enclosure in an unclassified location, seals are not required.

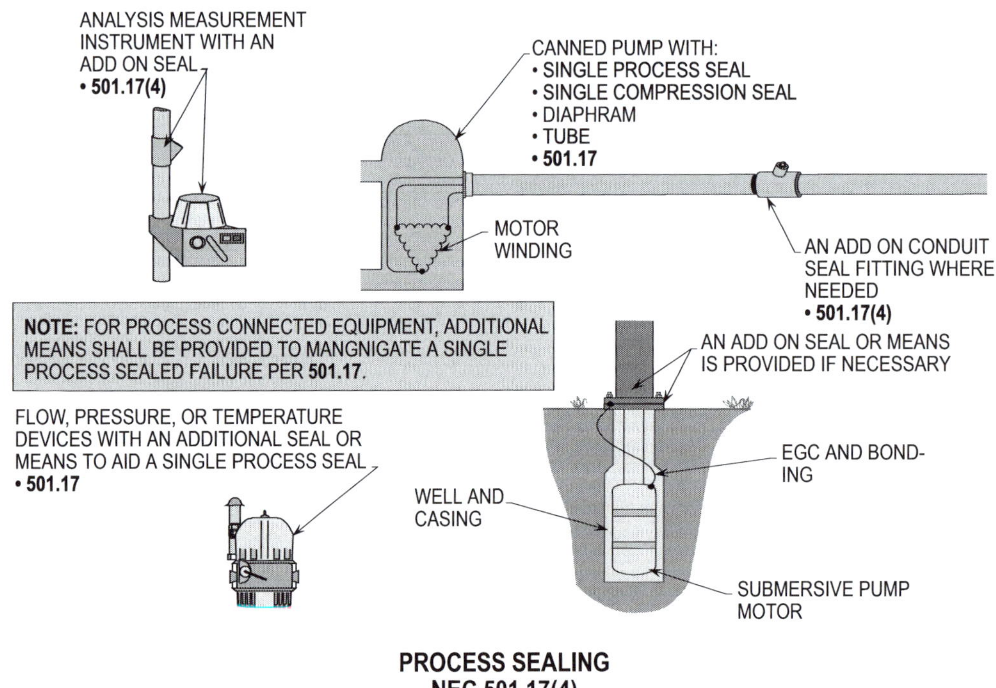

Figure 21-41. This illustration shows the requirements for process sealing in Class I locations.

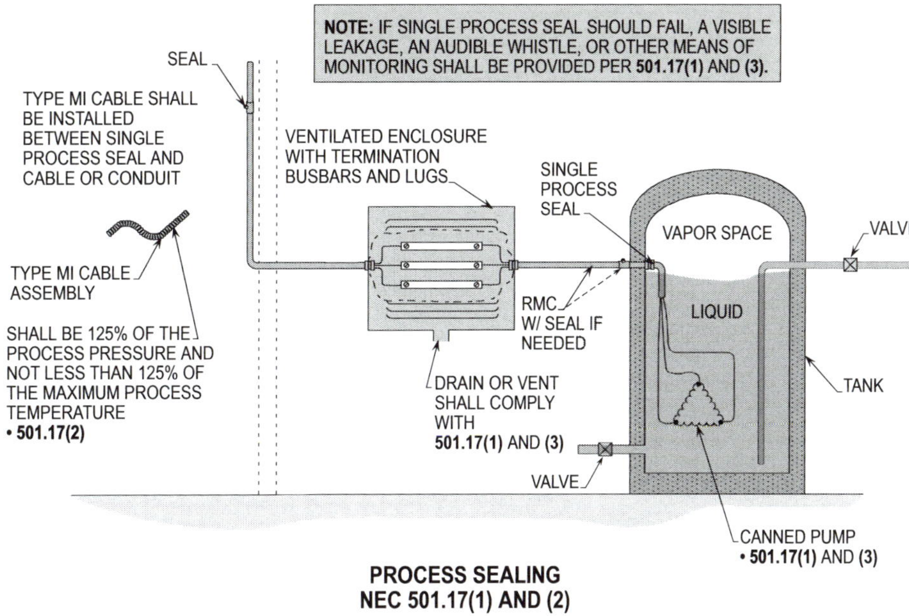

Figure 21-42. This illustration shows the requirements for process sealing in Class I locations.

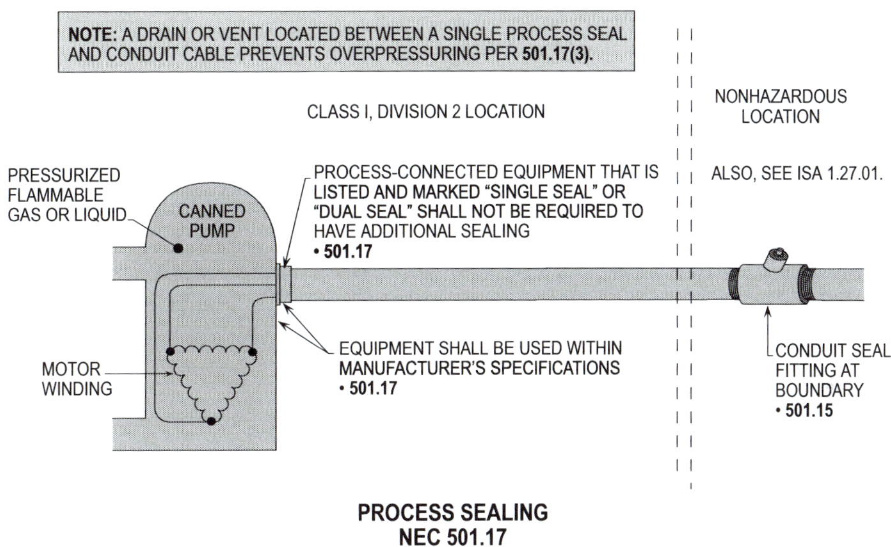

Figure 21-43. This illustration shows a listed and marked "single seal" or "dual seal" that eliminates the requirement for an additional means of sealing.

COMMERCIAL GARAGES, REPAIR, AND STORAGE
ARTICLE 511

Article 511 applies to commercial garages in which repair and service work is done on automobiles, trucks, buses, tractors, etc.

Garages used only for parking or storage are not hazardous areas. The requirements of **Article 511** do not apply to garages in which no maintenance repair or service work is being performed. However, the NEC does require that indoor storage and parking spaces be adequately ventilated to remove exhaust fumes from engines.

EIGHTEEN INCHES ABOVE THE FLOOR AND BELOW CEILING AREA
511.3(C)(1)(b) AND (D)(1)(b)

For each floor, the entire area up to a level of 18 in. (450 mm) above the floor or 18 in. (450 mm) from the ceiling is considered to be a Class I, Division 2 location, except where the AHJ determines that there is sufficient mechanical ventilation to provide a minimum of four air changes per hour. [For air changes, see **502.3(C)(1)(a).**]

ANY PIT OR DEPRESSION BELOW FLOOR LEVEL
511.3(C)(3)(b) AND (D)(3)(b)

Pits or depressions below floor level that extend up to the floor level shall be considered as Class I, Division 1 locations. However, if the pit or depression is ventilated, the AHJ may classify and judge the area to be a Class I, Division 2 or unclassified location.

Design Tip: Any pit or depression in which six air changes per hour are exhausted at the floor level of the pit can be judged by the AHJ to be a Class I, Division 2 location per **511.3(C)(3)(a) and (D)(3)(a).**

ADJACENT AREAS
511.3(E)(1)

Areas adjacent to Class I, Division 2 locations in which there is no likelihood of hazardous vapors being released, such as stock rooms, offices, etc. are still classified as Class I, Division 2 locations. If the floor of the adjacent area is elevated 18 in. (450 mm) above the floor of the hazardous area or a separation between the two areas is provided by either an 18 in. (450 mm) tight curb or partition, the area shall be permitted to be classified as nonhazardous.

Design Tip: Gasoline vapors are heavier than air and settle to and move along the floor area. Since these vapors settle to the floor, they may be transmitted into other rooms that may seem otherwise to be nonhazardous areas. Transmittal of such hazardous vapors can be stopped by an elevated floor, a tight curb, or a properly built partition, each of which shall be at least 18 in. (450 mm) high, between the two rooms.

SPECIAL PERMISSION
ARTICLE 100 AND 511.3(E)(1)

Adjacent areas that by reason of adequate ventilation, air pressure differentials, or physical spacing are such that, in the opinion of the AHJ, no ignition hazardous condition exists, can be classified as nonhazardous.

See Figure 21-44 for rules and regulations pertaining to garages.

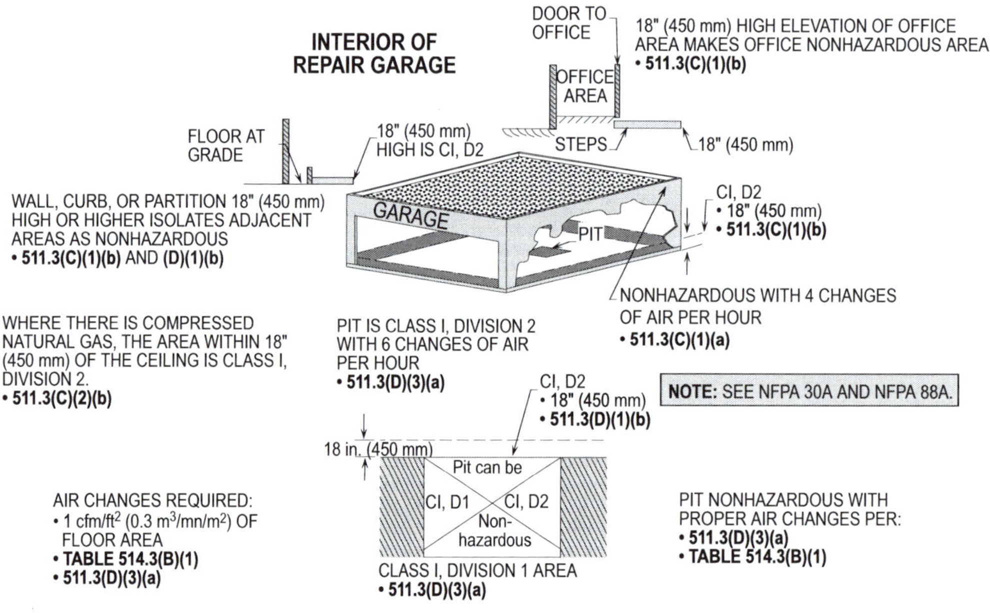

Figure 21-44. In classification of a floor in a garage where vehicles are repaired and volatile flammable fluids are present, the floor area, up to 18 in. (450 mm), is Class I, Division 2. However, if adequate ventilation is present, the 18 in. (450 mm) space above the floor shall be considered to be nonhazardous. Likewise, if the pit is adequately ventilated, it can be judged to be a Class I, Division 2 location or a nonhazardous location.

FUEL-DISPENSING UNITS
511.4(B)(1)

When fuel-dispensing units (other than liquid petroleum gas, which is prohibited), are located within buildings, the requirements of **Article 514** shall be applied.

If adequate mechanical ventilation is provided in the dispensing area, the controls shall be interlocked so that the dispenser cannot operate without ventilation as required by **500.5(B)(2)**.

PORTABLE LIGHTING EQUIPMENT
511.4(B)(2)

If fuel pumps are located inside, the requirements of **Article 514** pertaining to service stations are required to be applied to the pumps and the area around the pumps.

Portable lighting equipment used in garages shall:

(1) Be of hard rubber or other nonmetallic material,

(2) Be equipped with a handle,

(3) Have a guard and hook,

(4) Be the unswitched type, and

(5) Have no plug-in.

> **Design Tip:** If portable lighting equipment is to be used in a hazardous area near the floor, for instance, it shall be a type that is identified for hazardous areas.

If the cord is connected in such a manner that the lamp cannot reach a hazardous level when in use, a portable lamp can be the general-purpose type.

WIRING AND EQUIPMENT IN
CLASS I LOCATIONS
511.4(A) AND 511.3

Hazardous vapors in a garage are concentrated in low areas within a short distance above the floor and within the ceiling area. The code sets the distance as 18 in. (450 mm), and the area below an imaginary plane of 18 in. (450 mm) above the floor is classified as a hazardous area.

Raceways beneath the floor or embedded in a masonry shall be considered to be within the hazardous area if any connections or extensions lead into the hazardous area per **511.3**.

Hazardous vapors seek either a low or high level. Therefore, any ceiling or pit in a garage floor shall be considered to be hazardous down to the bottom of the pit or up to the ceiling area.

All wiring and equipment located in the space below the hazardous level shall be suited for a Division or Zone location if adequate ventilation is not utilized.

> **Design Tip:** If all of the wiring and equipment is routed and installed above the 18 in. (450 mm) height from the floor or below the 18 in. (450 mm) ceiling area, electrical metallic tubing and general-purpose equipment and devices shall be permitted to be used. If the wiring is installed in conduit below the 18 in. (450 mm) boundary in the floor slab, this part of the wiring system shall be a Class I location and the wiring method would have to comply with the rules of this classification. To pass from the hazardous area and be routed into the nonhazardous area, seals would have to be installed at the 18 in. (450 mm) boundary.

SEALING REQUIREMENTS
511.9

Seals shall be provided as follows for wiring methods entering or leaving the Class I, Division 2 area:

(1) If conduit is used, a vertical run, unless unbroken, shall be sealed at the hazardous boundary level, which is 18 in. (450 mm) above the floor.

(2) For a horizontal run, if the run leaves the area at a height below the hazardous boundary level, that is less than 18 in. (450 mm) from the floor, the wiring method shall be sealed at the point where it leaves the hazardous area.

(3) Seals shall be placed in each conduit run entering the enclosures for switches, circuit breakers, fuses, relays, resistors, or any device that produces arcing, sparking, or high temperature, and only if the enclosure is located beneath the hazardous boundary.

(4) In each conduit run of 2 in. (53) or larger, seals shall be installed at junction boxes and fittings if the box or fitting contains splices, taps, or connections and is located beneath the hazardous boundary.

> **Design Tip:** The seal shall be installed within 18 in. (450 mm) of the box or fitting to comply with NEC rules and regulations. [See **501.15** and **501.15(B)(1)**]

WIRING ABOVE CLASS I LOCATIONS
511.7(A)(1)

Above the 18 in. (450 mm) level, the following wiring methods shall be permitted:

(1)   Metal raceways

(2)   Rigid nonmetallic conduit

(3)   Electrical nonmetallic tubing

(4)   EMT

(5)   Intermediate metal-conduit

(6)   Type MC cable (metal clad)

(7)   Type MI cable (mineral-insulated)

(8)   Type TC cable (power and control tray)

(9)   Type PLTC

(10) ITC

(11) Flexible metal conduit

(12) Liquidtight flexible metal conduit

(13) Liquidtight nonmetallic conduit

Design Tip: Cellular metal floor raceways shall be permitted to be used only to supply ceiling outlets or extensions to areas located below the floor. However, outlets shall not be connected above the floor. No electrical conductor shall be permitted to be installed in any cell, header, or duct that contains pipe for any service except electrical or compressed air.

For example, cellular metal floor raceways are a part of the building structure, and if the floor in the garage has cellular metal floor raceways installed, the raceway shall be permitted to be used to supply equipment in the room below the garage. However, it shall not be permitted to be used to supply equipment in the garage. Where the cellular raceway is in the floor above, it shall be permitted to be used for ceiling outlets in the garage.

GROUNDING AND BONDING REQUIREMENTS
511.16

When a circuit that supplies portables or pendants includes an identified grounded conductor (white or gray) as provided in **Article 200**, receptacles, attachment plugs, connectors, and similar devices shall be of the polarized type and the grounded (neutral) conductor of the flexible cord shall be connected to the screw shell of any lampholder or to the grounded terminal of any utilization equipment supplied.

Design Tip: Grounding continuity of the equipment grounding conductor to noncurrent-carrying parts shall be maintained. (Also, see **501.30**)

WIRING AND EQUIPMENT INSTALLED ABOVE CLASS I LOCATIONS
511.7(A) AND (B)

Any equipment that might produce an arc or spark, and that is less than 12 ft (3.7 m) above floor level, shall have a totally enclosed or tight enclosure that will prevent the escape of any arc or spark. Charging panels, motors, generators, and switches, if installed less than 12 ft (3.7 m) above the floor, should be the totally enclosed type, per **511.7(B)(1)(a)**.

Luminaires shall be the totally enclosed type or of a construction that does not allow the escape of arcs or sparks, if located less than 12 ft (3.7 m) above lanes where vehicles are commonly driven or if located where exposed to physical damage, per **511.7(B)(1)(b)**. **(See Figure 21-45)**

Design Tip: Fluorescent and incandescent luminaires in Class I locations shall be fitted with a lens or globe. Exposed tubes and light bulbs shall not be permitted.

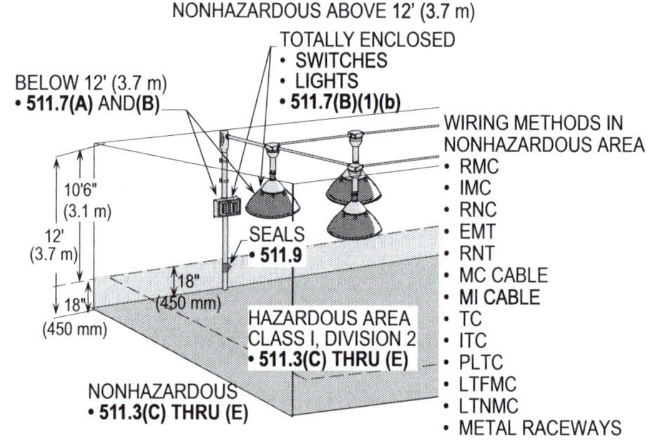

Figure 21-45. This illustration shows the are rules and regulations pertaining to wiring methods and equipment installed in and above the hazardous area in garages.

AIRCRAFT HANGARS
ARTICLE 513

Article 513 applies to hangars that are used for servicing or storing aircraft containing gasoline or other hazardous liquids or gases. Certain areas in aircraft hangars are a Class I location, except as follows:

(1) Locations used exclusively for aircraft that has never contained such volatile flammable gases or liquids.

(2) Aircraft that has been drained or properly purged.

(3) See NFPA 30 and NFPA 409.

CLASSIFICATION OF LOCATIONS
513.3(A) THRU (D)

Pits or depressions located below the hangar floor level shall be considered as Class I, Division 1 or Zone 1 locations, and this classification extends to the floor level per **513.3(A)**.

The entire area of the hangar shall be considered a Class I, Division 2 or Zone 2 location to a height of 18 in. (450 mm) above the floor and includes adjacent areas into which the hazards may be communicated unless suitably cut off from the hangar per **513.3(B)** and **(D)**.

The area immediately adjacent to the aircraft shall be classified as a Class I, Division 2 or Zone 2 location. Such an area is defined as being within 5 ft (1.5 m) horizontally from aircraft power plants, aircraft fuel tanks, or aircraft structures containing fuel. These locations shall extend from the floor level vertically to a level of 5 ft (1.5 m) above the wings and above the engine enclosures per **513.3(C)(1)**.

Aircraft painting hangars shall be classified as Class I, Division 1 or Zone 1 where the area within 10 ft (3 m) horizontally from aircraft surfaces from the floor to 10 ft (3 m) above the aircraft. The area horizontally from aircraft surfaces between 10 ft (3 m) and 30 ft (19 m) from the floor to 30 ft (9 m) above the aircraft surface shall be classified as Class I, Division 2 or Zone 2.

Adjacent areas into which hazardous vapors are likely to be communicated or released, such as stockrooms and electrical control rooms, shall be considered a Class I, Division 2 location up to a height of 18 in. (450 mm). These adjacent areas need not be classified as hazardous if they are effectively cut off from the hangar by walls or partitions and are adequately ventilated per **513.3(D)**. [See **513.3(B)** above] **(See Figure 21-46)**

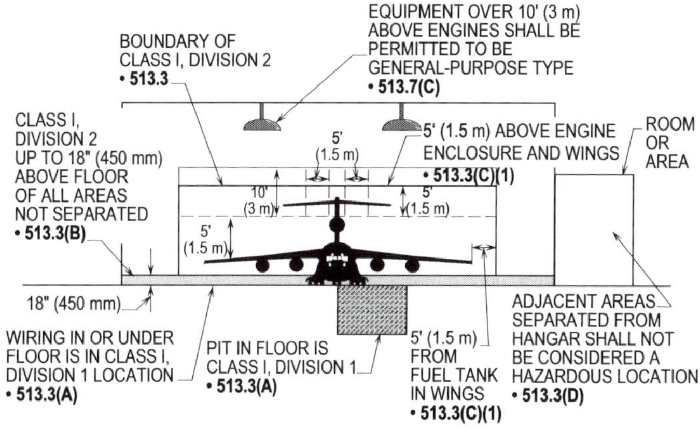

Figure 21-46. This illustration shows the are the rules and regulations for equipment and wiring methods installed in aircraft hangars.

WIRING AND EQUIPMENT IN
CLASS I LOCATIONS
513.4

Section **513.3** presents the classification of areas within a hangar as either a Class I, Division 1 or Zone 1 or Class I, Division 2 or Zone 2 location. All wiring and equipment within a hazardous area in a hangar shall comply with the requirements for either a Class I, Division 1, or Zone 1 or Class I, Division 2 or Zone 2 location, based upon the classification of the area in which the wiring and equipment is installed per **513.4**. Wiring in or under the hangar floor shall be classified as Class I, Division 1 per **513.8**.

Attachment plugs and receptacles in hazardous areas are subject to the approval of the AHJ. Such devices shall be identified for Class I locations or, as an alternative, shall be of a type so designed that they cannot be plugged or unplugged unless the circuit is deenergized.

WIRING NOT INSTALLED IN
CLASS I LOCATIONS
513.7(A)

Wiring that is outside the hazardous areas in a hangar shall be as follows:

(1) Metal raceways,

(2) Type MI cable (mineral-insulated),

(3) Type TC cable (power and control tray cable), and

(4) Type MC cable (metal-clad).

This requirement is for nonhazardous areas in the room where the aircraft is stored, such as areas above the 18 in. (450 mm) level. In adjoining nonhazardous rooms, the wiring method shall be permitted to be any approved type.

GROUNDING AND BONDING REQUIREMENTS 513.16

When circuits supplying portable equipment and pendants include an identified grounded (neutral) conductor (white or gray) per **Article 200**, they shall have the following devices of the polarized type, and the grounded (neutral) conductor of the flexible cord shall be connected to the screw shell of any lampholder or to the identified terminal of utilization of equipment such as:

- **(1)** Receptacles,
- **(2)** Attachment plugs,
- **(3)** Connectors, and
- **(4)** Similar devices.

Grounding continuity shall be provided between fixed raceways and the noncurrent-carrying metal parts of:

- **(1)** Pendant luminaires,
- **(2)** Portable lamps, and
- **(3)** Portable utilization equipment.

This may be accomplished by properly bonding the equipment grounding conductor to the metal raceway system. The insulation of equipment grounding conductors shall be green or green with one or more yellow stripes.

EQUIPMENT NOT INSTALLED IN CLASS I LOCATIONS 513.7(C) AND (D)

In locations other than those described in **513.3**, equipment capable of producing arcs, sparks, or particles of hot metals, such as lamps and lampholders for fixed lighting, cutouts, switches, receptacles, charging panels, generators, motors, or other equipment having make-and-break or sliding contacts, shall be of such a type that the escape of sparks or hot metal particles will be prevented. Equipment of the totally enclosed type, or so constructed as to prevent the escape of sparks or hot metal particles, shall comply with this rule. However, in areas described in **513.3(D)**, equipment shall be permitted to be of the general-purpose type.

> **Design Tip:** Equipment that might produce an arc or spark and that is less than 10 ft (3 m) above wings and engine of aircraft shall have a tight enclosure that will prevent the escape of hot particles from an arc or spark.

STANCHIONS, ROSTRUMS, AND DOCKS 513.7(E)

Where these items are located, or likely to be located within 5 ft (1.5 m) of aircraft fuel tanks or engines outlined as in **513.3(C)(1)**, the entire stanchion, rostrum, or dock shall be considered to be a hazardous location. All wiring and equipment shall comply with the rules and regulations for Class I, Division 2 or Zone 2 locations.

Where they are not located, or not likely to be located, as described in **513.7**, they shall be considered hazardous only up to a height of 18 in. (450 mm) above the floor. Above the 18 in. (450 mm) level, wiring and equipment shall be permitted to be installed by the provision of **513.4(B)**. Wiring and equipment below the 18 in. (450 mm) level shall comply with the requirements for Class I, Division 2 or Zone 2 locations. **(See Figure 21-47)**

> **Design Tip:** Mobile stanchions containing electrical equipment that conforms to **513.3(C)**, **513.7**, and **513.4(B)** shall carry at least one sign, permanently affixed to the stanchion, that must read as follows:
>
> ## WARNING
> ## KEEP 5 FT (1.5 m) CLEAR
> ## OF AIRCRAFT ENGINES
> ## AND FUEL TANK AREAS

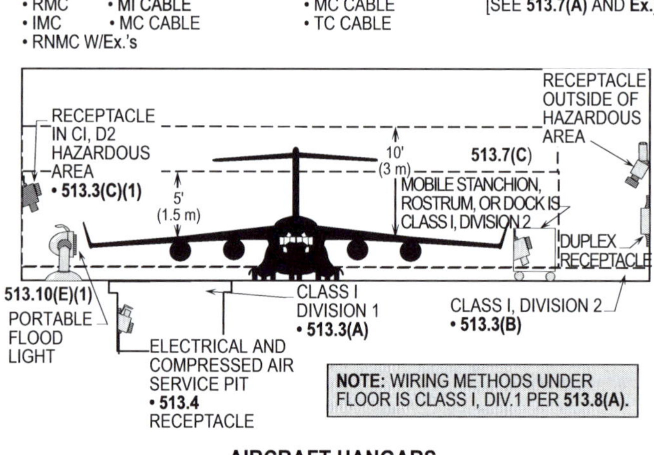

Figure 21-47. This illustration shows wiring methods, equipment, and portable equipment installed in hazardous and nonhazardous areas in aircraft hangars.

SEALING
513.9

A seal shall be provided at every point where a conduit is routed from a hazardous area to a nonhazardous area or from a Division 1 or Zone 1 to a Division 2 or Zone 2 location.

Note, conduits beneath the hangar floor shall be considered to be in a Class I, Division 1 of Zone 1 location per **501.15** and **505.16.**

Conduits that are embedded in or under concrete shall be classified as being in the same hazardous area as that installed above the floor, when any connections lead into or through such areas.

Conduits emerging from such areas shall be considered as passing from a Class I, Division 1 or Zone 1 area to a Class I, Division 2 or Zone 2 area.

> **Design Tip:** Seals shall be provided when connecting conduits to an enclosure where there is a possibility of arcs or sparks or when passing from a hazardous to a nonhazardous area.

SPECIAL EQUIPMENT
513.10(A) THRU (E)

When an aircraft is stored in a hangar, the battery shall be disconnected. It should also be disconnected, if possible, when the aircraft is brought into the hangar for repairs or maintenance.

Aircraft batteries shall not be charged when the aircraft is in a hangar. Such charging shall be done when the aircraft is entirely outside the hangar. Battery chargers should be kept in a separate building when they are not in use.

Electrical equipment on energizers shall be kept at least 5 ft (1.5 m) clear of aircraft engines and fuel tank areas and in addition shall be at least 18 in. (450 mm) above the floor.

> **Design Tip:** Power systems shall have a permanently affixed sign that reads as follows:

WARNING
KEEP 5 FT (1.5 m) CLEAR
OF AIRCRAFT ENGINES
AND FUEL TANK AREAS

MOBILE SERVICING EQUIPMENT WITH ELECTRICAL COMPONENTS
513.10(D)

Mobile servicing equipment that is not suitable for Class I, Division 2 or Zone 2 locations shall be so designed and mounted that all fixed wiring and equipment will be at least 18 in. (450 mm) above the floor. This equipment includes vacuum cleaners, air compressors, air movers, and similar type equipment.

> **Design Tip:** Unless such equipment is approved by the AHJ for Class I, Division 2, or Zone 2 locations, the electrical equipment shall be kept at least 5 ft (1.5 m) clear of aircraft engines and fuel tank areas.

Flexible cords for mobile equipment shall be suitable for the type of service, be listed for extra-hard usage, and include an equipment grounding conductor. Receptacles and attachment plugs shall be suitable for the type of service and approved by the AHJ for the location in which they are installed.

> **Design Tip:** Equipment that is not of a type suitable for Class I, Division 2 or Zone 2 locations shall not be operated in areas where maintenance operations are likely to release hazardous vapors in progress of repair. Such equipment shall carry a warning sign, to read as follows:

WARNING
KEEP 5 FT (1.5 m) CLEAR
OF AIRCRAFT ENGINES
AND FUEL TANK AREAS

GROUNDING AND BONDING REQUIREMENTS
513.16

All metallic raceways and all noncurrent-carrying metallic portions of fixed or portable equipment, regardless of voltage, shall be grounded and bonded according to the provision of **Article 250**. The insulation of the equipment grounding conductors shall be green or green with one or more yellow stripes.

GASOLINE DISPENSING AND SERVICE STATIONS
ARTICLE 514

One of the most common applications of the requirements in **Article 514** would be gasoline service stations. Basically, hazardous locations are areas where fuel (gasoline) is transferred to the fuel tanks of self-propelled vehicles or to auxiliary tanks. **Articles 510** and **511** apply to locations in filling stations such as lubritoriums, service rooms, repair rooms, offices, salesrooms, compressor rooms, storage rooms, and rest rooms, as well as other associated areas.

Gasoline service stations are not the only areas subjected to the requirements of **Article 514**. Any location having a gasoline-dispensing pump, whether in a service station or elsewhere, would fall under the rules of this Article.

CLASS I LOCATIONS
TABLE 514.3(B)(1)

Table 514.3(B)(1) shall be applied where Class I liquids are stored, handled, or dispensed and shall be used to delineate and classify service stations. A Class I location does not extend beyond an unpierced wall, roof, or other solid partition. Locations where the AHJ can satisfactorily determine that flammable liquids such as gasoline having a flash point below 38°C (100°F) will not be present shall be permitted to be classified as nonhazardous. For further information, see NFPA 30A. [See **Table 514.3(B)(1)** for the dimensions that are used in the following text up to **514.4.**]

THE SPACE WITHIN
A GASOLINE PUMP

The space within a gasoline pump shall be classified as a Class I, Division 1 location up to a height of 4 ft (1.2 m) above the base and immediately underneath the base. Normally, the space surrounding a gasoline pump, 18 in. (450 mm) out from the pump and 4 ft (1.2 m) up from its base, is Class I, Division 2. [See ANSI 87 and **Table 514.3(B)(2)** for these dimensions]

OUTSIDE AREA OF PUMP

In addition to the above, the circular outside area of 20 ft (6 m) horizontally surrounding the gasoline pump and out from the 18 in. (450 mm) circle shall be classified as a Class I, Division 2 location up to a height of 18 in. (450 mm) above ground. A building or any part of a building falling within this circle shall be a Class I, Division 2 location, if not suitably cut off by a barrier. In most cases, a solid wall or an 18 in. (450 mm) elevation above grade provides an adequate barrier.

OUTSIDE AREA OF FILL PIPES

The circular outside area surrounding a fill pipe, 10 ft (3 m) out from the pipe, shall be considered a Class I, Division 2 location up to a height of 18 in. (450 mm) above ground. The space within a building that is within the 10 ft (3 m) circle shall be classified as a Class I, Division 2 if not suitably cut off.

> **Design Tip:** A wall or an 18 in. (450 mm) elevation above grade would in most cases provide a suitable barrier.

SUSPENDED PUMP

The area up to 18 in. (450 mm) above grade level within 20 ft (6 m), horizontally measured from a point vertically below the edge of any dispenser enclosure, shall be classified as a Class I, Division 2 location.

SURROUNDING SPACE
FROM DISPENSER

The surrounding space out to a distance of 20 ft (6 m), measured from a point vertically below the edge of the dispenser enclosure, shall be classified as a Class I, Division 2 location up to a height of 18 in. (450 mm) above grade and from pump enclosure. If a building or part of a building is constructed within this space, it is considered nonhazardous if suitably cut off by a ceiling or wall that acts as a barrier.

OUTSIDE AREA OF VENT PIPES

The area 3 ft (900 mm) in all directions from the discharge ends of a vent pipe shall be classified as Class I, Division 1. The space between 3 ft (900 mm) and 5 ft (1.5 m) of open end of vent, extending in all directions shall be classified a Class I, Division 2 location.

AREA AROUND A
LUBRICATION ROOM

A lubrication room shall be classified as a Class I, Division 2 location up to a height of 18 in. (450 mm) above the floor. A pit in a lubrication room shall be classified as a Class I, Division 1 location from the floor down to the bottom of the pit.

See Figure 21-48 for a detailed illustration of classifying area around dispensers and gas stations.

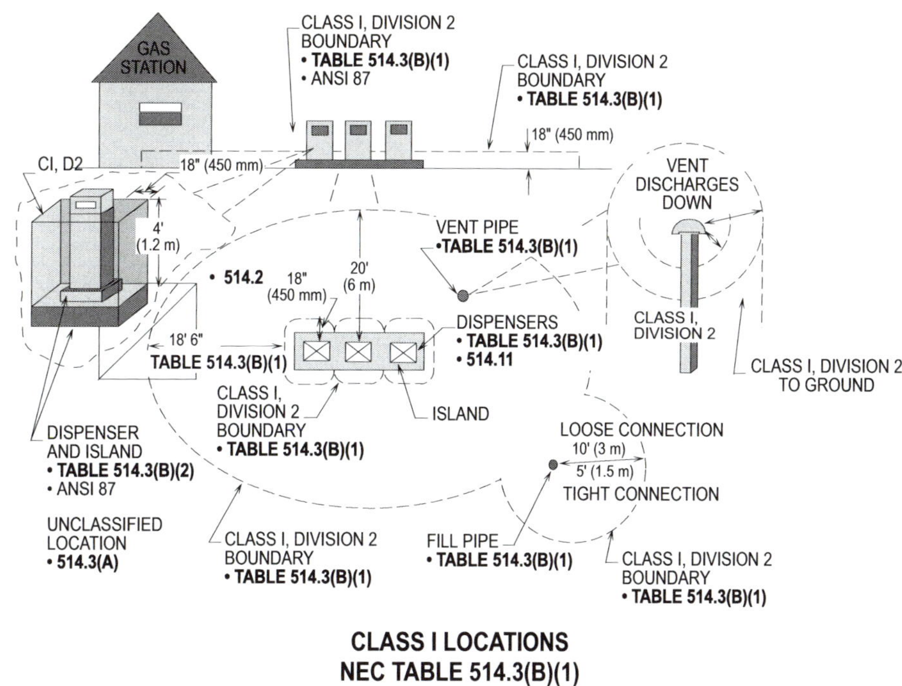

Figure 21-48. This illustration shows the illustrates the classified area around dispensers and gas stations.

WIRING AND EQUIPMENT WITHIN CLASS I LOCATIONS 514.4 AND Ex.

Electrical equipment and wiring installed in the Class I, Division 1 and Class I, Division 2 locations, shall be approved and suitable for such locations by the AHJ. These wiring methods shall be permitted in these areas:

(1) Rigid metal conduit and

(2) Type MI cable.

Note, see **Article 514.3** and **Article 501**.

Design Tip: Underwriters Laboratories has a directory with listings on types of insulations on conductors that are approved for these locations.

WIRING AND EQUIPMENT ABOVE CLASS I LOCATIONS 514.7

The rules for wiring and equipment above hazardous areas [above the 18 in. (450 mm) level] are the same as for commercial garages per **514.3** and **511.7**.

These wiring methods shall be permitted in these locations:

(1) Metal raceways and

(2) Type MI cable.

CIRCUIT DISCONNECTS 514.11 AND 514.13

Each circuit leading to or through a dispensing equipment including all associated power, communications, data, and video circuits, and equipment for remote pumping systems, shall be provided with a switch or other approved means to disconnect simultaneously from the source of supply all conductors of the circuit, including the grounded (neutral) conductors, if used per **514.11** and **514.13**.

The intent of this requirement is to ensure that the supply is disconnected from the source and there are no conductors connected that lead to or through a dispensing pump.

Design Tip: There are special breakers available that have a pigtail that ties to the neutral bus and ensures that the ungrounded (phase) and grounded (neutral) conductor(s) are disconnected when the breaker is in the OFF position.

Therefore, the threat of an arc or spark is limited, should the grounded (neutral) conductor be disconnected with another circuit still energized that is sharing the neutral with other circuits. **(See Figure 21-49)**

> **Design Tip:** Each dispensing device shall be provided with a means to remove all external voltage sources, including feedback, during periods of maintenance and service of the dispensing equipment per **514.13**.

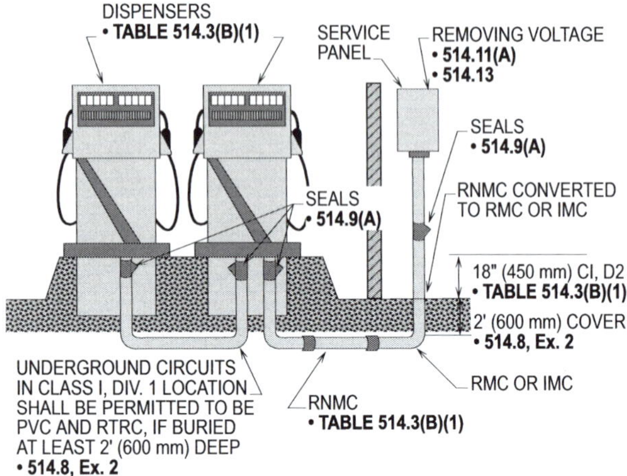

Figure 21-49. This illustration shows the rules and regulations for wiring methods and seals used for dispensers and boundaries to gas stations.

ATTENDED SELF-SERVICE STATIONS 514.11(B)

For attended self-service stations, the emergency controls specified in **514.11(A)** and **(B)** and **514.13** shall be installed at a location acceptable to the AHJ. Such emergency controls shall not be located more than 100 ft (30 m) from the dispensers.

UNATTENDED SELF-SERVICE STATIONS 514.11(C)

For unattended self-service stations, the emergency controls specified in **514.11(A)** and **(C)** shall be installed at a location acceptable to the AHJ. Such emergency controls shall be more than 20 ft (6 m) but less that 100 ft (30 m) from the dispensers.

Additional emergency controls shall be installed on each group of dispensers or the indoor equipment shall be used to control the dispenser.

The main emergency disconnect usually is an across-the-line device. However, a remote control device shall be permitted for the additional controls required, but they shall be capable of being manually reset.

> **Design Tip:** Emergency controls shall shut off all power to all dispensing equipment at the station. Controls shall be manually reset only in a manner approved by the AHJ. (Review **514.11** and **514.13**.)

SEALING AT DISPENSER 514.9(A)

An approved seal shall be provided in each conduit run entering or leaving a dispenser or any cavities or enclosures in direct communications therewith. The sealing fitting shall be the first fitting after the conduit emerges from the earth or concrete.

> **Design Tip:** All seals shall be readily accessible and no seal shall be buried or installed in an inaccessible wall. This rule makes it very clear that no fitting of any kind shall be installed in the conduit between the floor and seal.
>
> **For example,** if a conduit run is below a panelboard and there is a hazardous location below, a seal shall be installed at 18 in. (450 mm) or more above the floor without a fitting between the seal and floor. **(See location of seals in Figure 21-49)**

SEALING AT BOUNDARY 514.9(B)

Additional seals shall be provided as required in **501.15**, **501.15(A)(4)**, and **501.15(B)(2)**. Such sealing rules shall apply to both horizontal and vertical boundaries between the hazardous and nonhazardous areas. **(See Figure 21-50)**

GROUNDING AND BONDING 514.16

Metallic portions of dispensing pumps, metallic raceways, and all noncurrent-carrying metal parts of electric equipment, regardless of voltage, shall be grounded and bonded as required in **Article 250**. Such grounding shall extend back to the service equipment and service ground.

In case of an accidental fault, a poor grounding connection can create an arc and cause an explosion to occur.

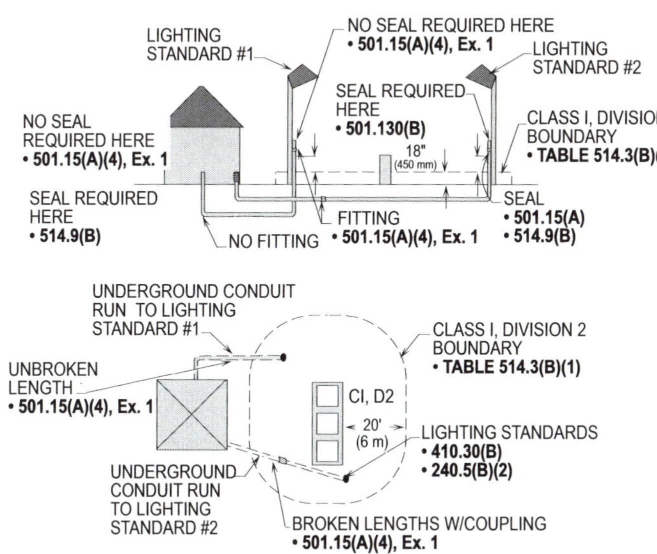

Figure 21-50. This illustration shows additional seals that shall be provided.

UNDERGROUND WIRING
514.8 and Ex. 2

Underground wiring shall be installed in rigid metal conduit or threaded steel intermediate metal conduit, or, where buried under not less than 2 ft (600 mm) of earth, it shall be permitted to be installed in polyvinyl chloride conduit or reinforced thermosetting resin conduit if it complies with **Article 352**. Where polyvinyl chloride conduit or reinforced thermosetting resin conduit is used, threaded rigid metal conduit or threaded steel intermediate metal conduit shall be used for the last 2 ft (600 mm) of the underground run to emergence or to the connection to the aboveground raceway; an equipment grounding conductor shall be included to provide electrical continuity of the raceway system and for grounding noncurrent-carrying metal parts. **(See Figures 21-49 and 50)**

> **Design Tip:** Nonmetallic conduit was added to the NEC to take the place of metallic conduit and ease the problem of corrosion, which might let fumes or gasoline into the conduit system. The use of nonmetallic conduit does not change the rules for sealing. To protect from physical damage, metallic conduit shall be routed up into the dispenser or the nonhazardous location.

BULK STORAGE PLANTS
ARTICLE 515

A bulk storage plant is that portion of a property where flammable liquids are received by tank vessel, pipelines, tank car, or tank vehicle and are stored or blended in bulk for the purpose of distributing such liquids by tank vessel, pipeline, tank car, tank vehicle, portable tank, or container.

For example, such designation includes locations where gasoline or other volatile flammable liquids are stored in tanks having an aggregate capacity of one carload or more and from which these products are distributed normally by tank truck, rail tank, etc.

CLASS I LOCATIONS
515.3 AND TABLE 515.3

Table 515.3 shall be applied where Class I liquids are stored, handled, or dispensed and shall be used to delineate and classify bulk storage plants. The Class I location shall not be required to extend beyond an unpierced wall, roof, or other solid partition.

PUMPS, BLEEDERS, AND WITHDRAWAL FITTINGS LOCATED INDOORS
TABLE 515.3

Such devices, when installed in a gasoline pipeline, can be subject to leakage and therefore present a hazardous condition. Where such devices are located indoors, the hazardous area around the devices extends as follows:

(1) 5 ft (1.5 m) in all directions, to which this boundary includes an imaginary sphere around such device and

(2) 25 ft (7.5 m) out horizontally and 3 ft (900 mm) up from the floor grade, to which this boundary includes an imaginary circular area around such device.

The above areas are considered Class I, Division 2 areas and all wiring and equipment installed in these areas shall comply with the requirements for a Class I, Division 2 location.

PUMPS, BLEEDERS, AND WITHDRAWAL FITTINGS LOCATED OUTDOORS
TABLE 515.3

When such devices are located outdoors, the Class I, Division 2 hazardous area around these devices extends as follows:

(1) 3 ft (900 mm) in all directions, forming an imaginary sphere and

(2) 10 ft (3 m) out along the ground and 18 in. (450 mm) up from the ground, forming an imaginary circular area.

See Figure 21-51 for a detailed illustration of such devices installed outdoors.

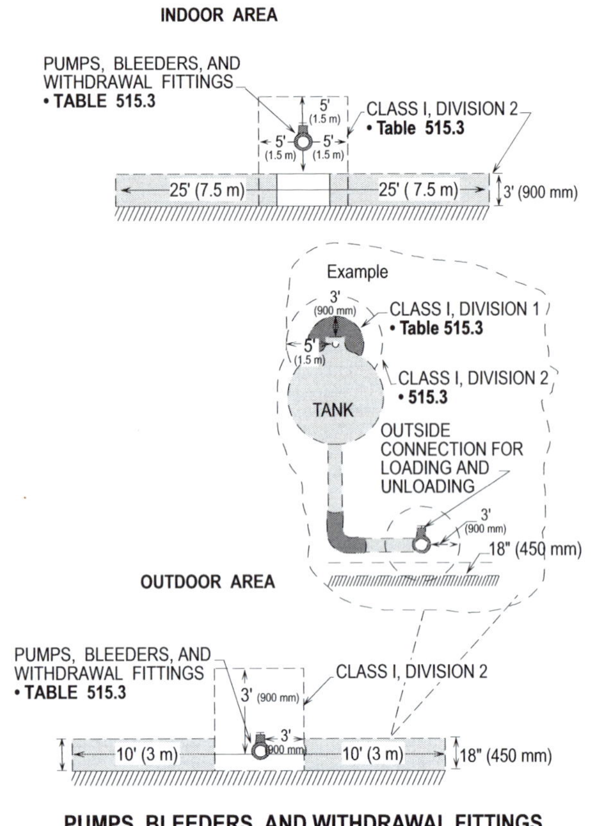

**PUMPS, BLEEDERS, AND WITHDRAWAL FITTINGS
LOCATED INDOORS OR OUTDOORS
NEC 515.3
TABLE 515.3**

Figure 21-51. Classifying the hazardous area around a device or fitting located indoors or outdoors.

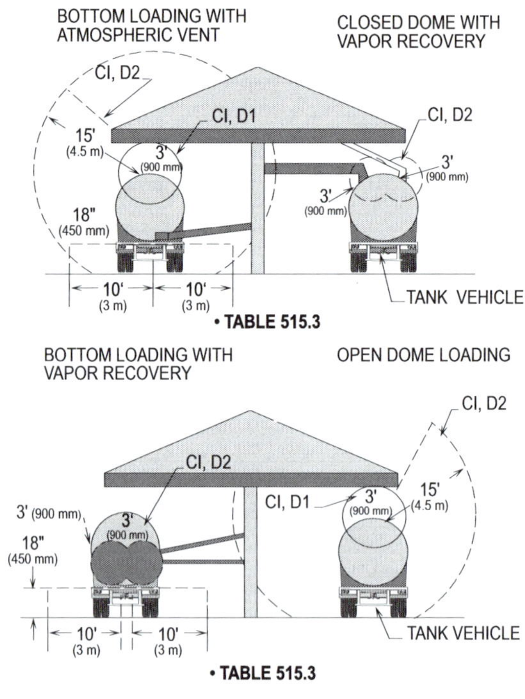

**TANK VEHICLES AND TANK CARS
IN OUTSIDE LOCATIONS
NEC 515.3
TABLE 515.3**

Figure 21-52. This illustration shows the hazardous areas, under certain conditions, around tank and car vehicles, based on top or bottom loading or unloading procedures.

TANK VEHICLES AND TANK CARS IN OUTSIDE LOCATIONS
TABLE 515.3

The hazardous area extends 15 ft (4.5 m) in all directions around an open dome or vent, forming a 15 ft (4.5 m) sphere. The first 3 ft (900 mm) shall be classified as a Class I, Division 1 location, and the remaining 12 ft (3.7 m) shall be classified as a Class I, Division 2 location.

For bottom loading or unloading, the hazardous area extends 3 ft (900 mm) in all directions from the fixed connection and within a 10 ft (3 m) radius and 18 in. (450 mm) up from the ground. These hazardous areas shall be classified as a Class I, Division 2 location, but only during loading and unloading operations. **(See Figure 21-52)**

ABOVEGROUND TANKS
TABLE 515.3

The space above the roof and within the shell of a floating roof type tank shall be classified as a Class I, Division 1 location.

For other tanks of this type, the area within 10 ft (3 m) in all directions shall be classified as a Class I, Division 2 location, except the area within 5 ft (1.5 m) in all directions shall be classified as a Class I, Division 1 location. The area between 5 ft (1.5 m) and 10 ft (3 m) out shall be classified a Class I, Division 2 location. **(See Figure 21-53)**

PITS
TABLE 515.3

A pit that is located in the 10 ft (3 m) or 25 ft (7.5 m) sphere around pumps, bleeders, meters, etc. shall be classified as a Class I, Division 1 location.

A pit located in the 10 ft (3 m) sphere around a fill pipe opening shall be classified a Class I, Division 1 location.

A pit located in a nonhazardous area shall be considered as nonhazardous where there are no piping, valves, or fittings in the pit. If the pit has piping, valves, or fittings, it shall be classified as a Class I, Division 2 area.

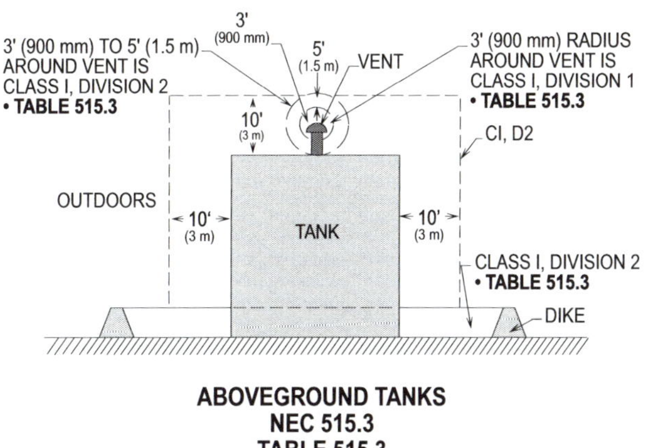

Figure 21-53. This illustration shows the hazardous area around an outdoor bulk storage tank.

GARAGES FOR TANK VEHICLES
TABLE 515.3

Storage and repair garages for tank vehicles shall be classified a Class I, Division 2 location up to a height of 18 in. (450 mm) above the floor and shall be wired with wiring methods and equipment rated for such locations.

ADJACENT LOCATIONS
TABLE 515.3

Office buildings, boiler rooms, etc. shall not be considered hazardous locations if they are not used for handling and storage of gasoline or other flammable material.

WIRING AND EQUIPMENT
WITHIN IN CLASS I LOCATIONS
515.4

All wiring and equipment in a hazardous area shall comply with the requirements of a Class I, Division 1 or 2 location or **Article 505** for the Zones, whichever applies, based on the flammable material.

WIRING AND EQUIPMENT
ABOVE HAZARDOUS LOCATIONS
515.7

The requirements of this Section are basically the same as those for commercial garages. The main concern is sparks, arcs, or hot metal particles that might drop into the hazardous area and create an explosion if there was a proper mixture of gases and air.

Electrical equipment that might produce arcs, sparks, or particles of hot metal, such as lamps and lampholders for fixed lighting, cutouts, switches, receptacles, motors, or other such equipment having make-and-break or sliding contacts, shall be totally enclosed or constructed in such a manner as to prevent the escape of sparks or hot metal particles.

> **Design Tip:** Portable lamps or utilization equipment shall be suitable and shall comply with the provisions of **Article 501** for the hazardous location in which they are to be used.

The wiring methods used above the 3 ft (900 mm) and 18 in. (450 mm) levels to connect the electrical equipment listed above shall be permitted to be one of the following or any combination of such:

(1) Metal raceways,

(2) Type MI cable,

(3) Type TC cable,

(4) Type MC cable,

(5) PVC Schedule 80,

(6) Type PLTC and PLTC-ER, and

(7) Type ITC and ITC-ER

UNDERGROUND WIRING
515.8(A) THRU (C)

For underground wiring routed to and around aboveground storage tanks shall be permitted to be one of the following:

(1) Where buried less than 2 ft (600 mm) in the earth, rigid metal conduit or intermediate metal conduit shall be used.

(2) Where buried 2 ft (600 mm) or more, polyvinyl chloride conduit or rigid thermosetting resin conduit shall be permitted to be used. However, a change shall be made to metal conduit for the last 2 ft (600 mm) before emergence from the ground. Cable requires 2 ft (600 mm) of cover.

(3) Where polyvinyl chloride conduit or rigid thermosetting resin conduit is used, an equipment grounding conductor shall be routed with the circuit conductors to ground all noncurrent-carrying parts.

(4) Where underground cable without a metal sheath is used, the cable shall have an equipment grounding conductor to ensure proper grounding of equipment with metal parts.

(5) Where cable is used, it shall be protected by rigid metal conduit or intermediate metal conduit at points where it emerges from the earth.

(6) Conductor insulation shall be a type approved for the location, to protect from gasoline in case of leakage or an accidental rupture of equipment.

Design Tip: Nonmetallic conduit and cables shall be buried at least 2 ft (600 mm) in the earth or have a 2 ft (600 mm) cover.

SEALING REQUIREMENTS
515.9

Seals shall be provided in accordance with **501.15**. Sealing requirements in **501.15(A)(4)** and **501.15(B)(2)** apply to horizontal as well as to vertical boundaries of the defined Class I locations. Buried raceways under defined hazardous locations shall be considered to be within such locations.

Seals, when required, shall be installed as follows:

(1) Seals shall be placed in each conduit run entering the enclosure for switches, circuit breakers, fuses, relays, resistors, or any other device that is capable of producing arcing, sparking, or high temperature and that is located in a hazardous area. These seals shall be placed no farther than 18 in. (450 mm) from such enclosures.

(2) A seal shall be required at the point where the conduit leaves a hazardous area and passes into a nonhazardous area. The seal shall not be required to be installed at the exact boundary of the hazardous area. It shall be permitted to be installed at a convenient point in the run, on either side of the boundary. However, it is recommended to place the seal as near to the boundary as possible.

A vertical run shall be sealed where it enters or leaves the hazardous level either at 18 in. (450 mm) or 36 in. (900 mm) above the floor or ground. For a horizontal run, if the run leaves the area at a height below the hazardous level, it is mandatory that the conduit be sealed where it leaves the hazardous area.

An exception permits a conduit that passes through a hazardous area, with no fitting within or 12 in. (300 mm) beyond the hazardous boundary, to be installed without seals.

(3) For 2 in. (53) and larger conduit runs, seals shall be required at the entry to an enclosure, if the box or fitting contains a splice, tap, or connection and is located within a hazardous area. Such seals shall be installed within 18 in. (450 mm) of the enclosure.

Design Tip: Conduit installed underneath a hazardous area shall be considered to be in the hazardous area beneath that it is buried and shall be treated as such.

GASOLINE-DISPENSING PUMPS
515.10

When gasoline is dispensed from a bulk storage plant, the rules of **Article 514**, that covers the dispensing of gasoline, shall be applied.

In other words, if there are gasoline pumps on the premises, the pump area shall comply with the rules and regulations for service stations.

GROUNDING AND BONDING
515.16

All metal raceways, metal-jacketed cables, and all non-current-carrying metal parts of fixed or portable electrical equipment, regardless of voltage, shall be grounded and bonded by the provisions in **Article 250**. Grounding in Class I locations shall comply with the rules of **501.30**.

Design Tip: This grounding technique shall be required for all wiring in order to provide proper grounding for raceways and equipment where there is no raceway continuity. (Also, see **505.25**.)

The grounding continuity shall be complete back to the service equipment and the service ground for nonhazardous as well as hazardous areas.

SPRAY APPLICATION, DIPPING, AND COATING PROCESSES
ARTICLE 516

Article 516 applies to locations where paint, lacquer, or powdered finishing materials are frequently applied by brushing, spraying, or dipping. Conditions of process shall always be evaluated based upon use and the effects of the material. (See NFPA 33, 34, and 91.)

For example, the vapors from finishing processes and the storage of paints, lacquers, or other flammable finishes shall be considered.

Another problem is the residue that is the result of the finishing process. Vapors can be easier to control than the residue because residue can be ignited by heat and cause fires to occur. The right mixture of vapors and air can create a dangerous explosion when ignited by an arc or a spark.

> **Design Tip:** NFPA 33 states that water-based paints, when mixed, create no problem. However, when sprayed, a residue condition exists, and this could cause a problem.

CLASS I OR II LOCATIONS 516.3

Classification is in respect to the effects of and exposure to flammable gases and vapors, and in some cases deposits of paint spray.

> **Design Tip:** For deposits and residues requirements, review **516.3(B)** and **(C)** and NFPA 33 – Ch. 6.

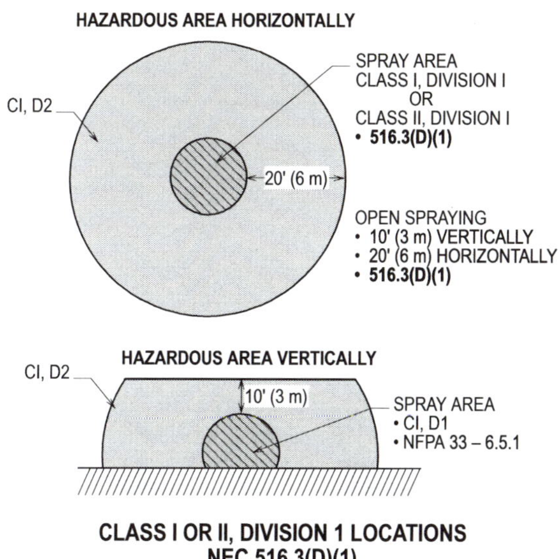

Figure 21-54. This illustration shows the hazardous area for an unenclosed area used for spraying.

CLASS I OR II, DIVISION 1 LOCATIONS 516.3(D)(1)

Where brushing, spraying, or dipping is performed in a spray booth, the hazardous areas are to be considered as follows:

(1) The space around a spraying operation, which contains a dangerous quantity of spray vapor, shall be classified a Class I, Division 1 location. The NEC does not define a definite boundary for such space. The extent of the hazardous boundary is always subject to the judgment of the AHJ.

(2) The space beyond the Class I, Division 1 space shall be classified a Class I, Division 2 location up to 20 ft (6 m) beyond, and up from the floor to a height of 10 ft (3 m) above the spraying area.

(3) For dipping operations, all space within 5 ft (1.5 m) in any direction from the liquid, whether the liquid is in the tank or as a wet coating on the drain board or on the dipped object, shall be classified a Class I, Division 1 location.

> **Design Tip:** Where the brushing, spraying, or dipping is performed in a spray booth, the entire spray booth shall be classified as Class I, Division 1. Exhaust ducts for the spray booth shall also be classified as a Class I, Division 1 location. **(See Figure 21-54)**

CLASS I OR II, DIVISION 2 LOCATIONS 516.3(D)(2)

Where the spray booth is equipped with an open front, the space outside the booth shall be classified as a Class I, Division 2 location and rules are applied as follows:

(1) For spray booths with an interlocked vent system, so designed and arranged that spraying cannot be performed except when the vent system is operating under these conditions, the space outside the booth shall be classified as a Class I, Division 2 location.

(2) For spray booths without an interlocked vent system, the space outside the spray booth shall be classified as a Class I, Division 2 location, due to the possibility of spraying without proper ventilation.

(3) For open-top spray booths, the Class I, Division 2 hazardous area shall be considered to extend to 3 ft (900 mm) above the booth and 3 ft (900 mm) from all openings.

See Figures 21-55(a), (b), and **(c)** for a detailed illustration of hazardous area around spray booths. **Note,** see **NEC Figure 516.3(D)(2)** and NFPA 33 – 6.5.1.

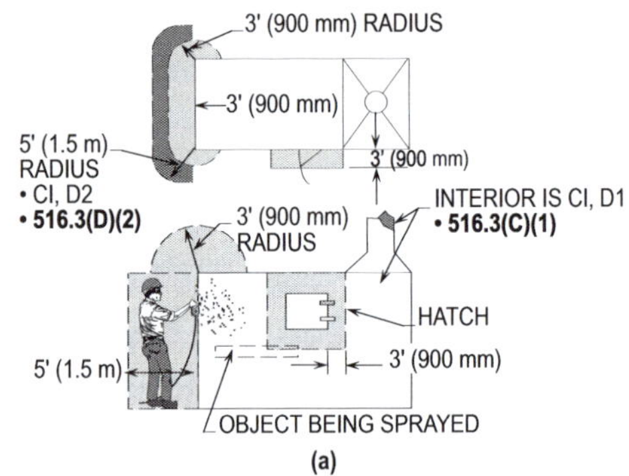

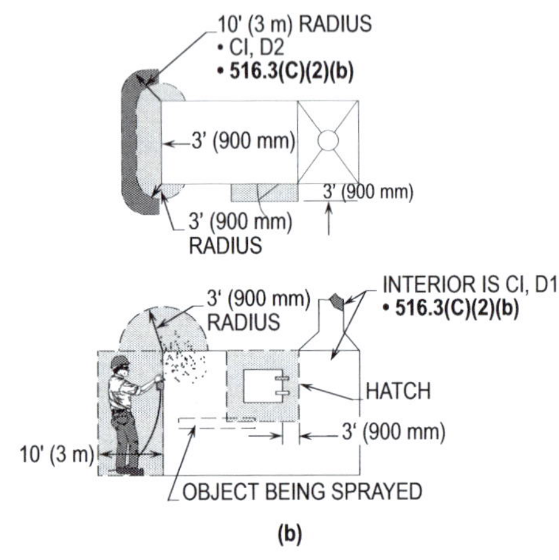

Figure 21-55(a). This illustration shows the hazardous areas around spray booths, based on the ventilation being interlocked or not interlocked with spray operation per NFPA 33 – Figure 6.5.1.

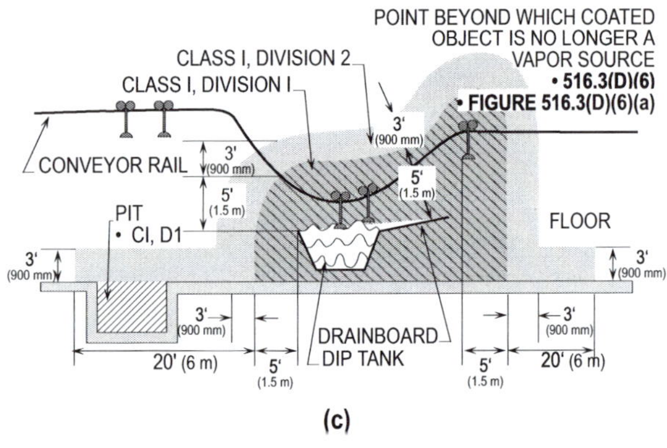

Figure 21-55(c). This illustration shows the hazardous area in and around dip tanks and drain boards.

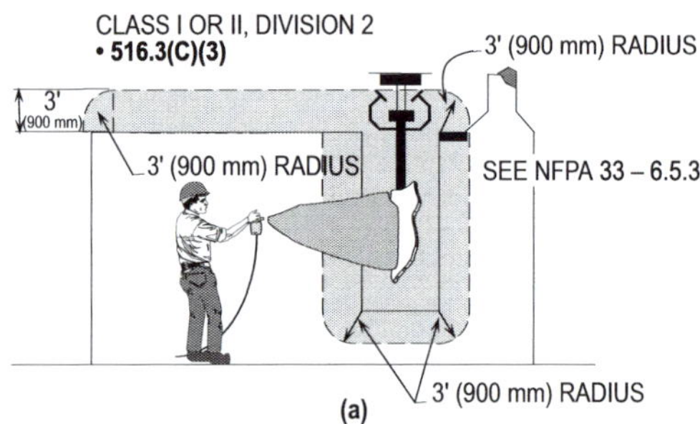

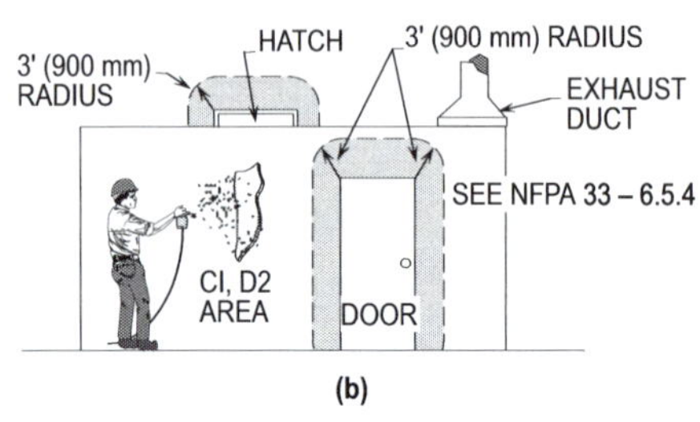

Figure 21-55(b). This illustration shows the hazardous areas in and around open and enclosed spray booths.

WIRING AND EQUIPMENT IN CLASS I LOCATIONS 516.4

All electric wiring and equipment installed within the Class I location containing vapor only and not residue shall comply with the following rules:

(1) All wiring and equipment in the hazardous areas shall comply with the NEC requirements for a Class I, Division 1 or Class I, Division 2 location, whichever applies.

(2) Any equipment installed in a location where paint or lacquer could accumulate on the equipment during operation, to such an extent that a hazard might exist, shall be approved for such condition of use.

(3) Luminaires within a spray booth shall be approved for Class I, Division 1 locations and are usually of an explosionproof type. To avoid use of such expensive luminaires, lighting can be accomplished through glass panels in the wall or ceiling of the spray booth. If the luminaire is installed outside of the Class I, Division 1 location, a less expensive luminaire shall be permitted to be used. **(See Figure 21-56)**

(4) Portable luminaires shall be of a type that are approved for Class I, Division 1 locations. However, portable appliances shall be permitted to be used in a spray booth only when no spraying, brushing, or dipping operation is being performed.

Where deposits of residue present a heating problem, illumination shall be permitted to be provided through panels of glass or other approved transparent or translucent material if the following rules are followed:

- Fixed lighting units are utilized.

- The panel is of a material unlikely to break during conditions of use.

- Panels properly isolate the hazardous location from the area in which the lighting units are installed.

- The accumulation of hazardous residues on the surface of the panel will not rise to a dangerous temperature during spray operations.

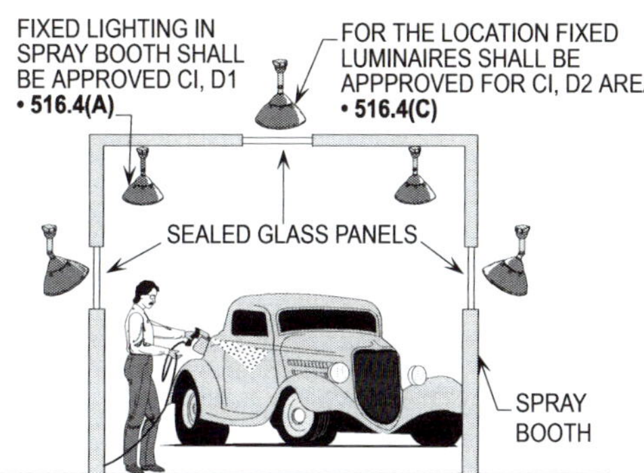

Figure 21-56. This illustration shows the rules for installing luminaires inside or outside of spray booths.

WIRING ABOVE CLASS I LOCATIONS 516.7(A)

Above hazardous areas, the following wiring methods shall be permitted as follows:

(1) Metal raceways,

(2) Polyvinyl chloride conduit

(3) Rigid thermosetting resin conduit

(4) Electrical nonmetallic tubing, and

(5) Type MI cable,

(6) Type TC cable,

(7) Type MC cable,

(8) Rigid nonmetallic conduit

CLASSIFICATION OF AREA

There are basically seven steps to be applied for classifying an area, and they are as follows:

(1) Determining the governing codes, standards, and authorities,

(2) Determining flammable materials,

(3) Determining group,

(4) Determining class,

(5) Determining division,

(6) Determining extent (boundaries) of classified areas, and

(7) Preparing plans and specifications

DETERMINING THE GOVERNING CODES, STANDARDS, AND AUTHORITIES

The first step in area classification consists of establishing the relevant codes, standards, and the authority having jurisdiction (AHJ), and obtaining all permits and other licenses. There are many U.S. companies that have their own operating standards, and these should also be consulted.

The AHJ is the organization, office, or individual responsible for approving equipment, installation, etc. The AHJ can be federal, state, or local, a fire chief or marshal, fire preventive bureau, labor department, a rating bureau, etc. The following are some of the relevant codes, standards, and testing laboratories:

(1) *Underwriters Laboratories* (UL)

(2) *Factory Mutual Research Corporation* (FM)

(3) *Electrical Testing Laboratories* (ETL)

(4) *American Gas Association* (AGA)

(5) *National Electrical Manufacturers Association* (NEMA)

(6) *American Petroleum Institute* (API)

(7) *Occupational Safety and Health Administration* (OSHA)

(8) *Mine Safety and Health Administration* (MSHA)

(9) *United States Coast Guard* (USCG)

(10) *Instrument Society of America* (ISOA)

(11) *Institute of Electrical and Electronic Engineers* (IEEE)

(12) *International Electrotechnical Commission* (IEC)

(13) Local building codes

(14) Manufacturer's data

(15) *National Fire Protection Association* (NFPA)

 • *National Electrical Code* (NEC®)

DETERMINING FLAMMABLE MATERIALS

Flammable liquids (Class I) are defined as being any liquid that has a closed-cup flash point below 100°F (37.8°C) and a Reid vapor pressure not exceeding 40 psia (2068.6 mm Hg) absolute at 100°F (37.8°C). Flammable and combustible liquids are subdivided into Classes I, II, and III. Classes are used to identify flammable and combustible liquids and should not be confused with class as defined in the NEC.

Flammable liquids (Class IA) are those liquids that have flash points below 73°F (22.8°C) and boiling points below 100°F (37.8°C). Class IB liquids are those liquids that have flash points below 73°F (22.8°C) and boiling points at or above 100°F (37.8°C). Class IC liquids are those liquids that have flash point at or above 73°F (22.8°C) and below 100°F (37.8°C).

Combustible liquids (Class II) are those liquids that have flash points at or above 100°F (37.8°C) and below 140°F (60°C). Class III A liquids are those having flash points at or above 140°F (60°C) and below 200°F (93°C). Class IIIB liquids are those having flash points at or above 200°F (93°C).

DETERMINING GROUP

Equipment shall be selected, tested, and approved for the type of flammable material involved. Maximum explosive pressures, MESG, safe operating temperatures (ignition temperature), and ignition energy shall be considered in the design and testing of safe electrical equipment for installation in classified areas. The NEC has a partial list of the most commonly encountered materials that have been tested. They are grouped on the basis of their flammability characteristics:

Group A	acetylene
Group B	hydrogen
Group C	carbon monoxide, ethylene
Group D	gasoline, benzine, propane, ethyl alcohol, methane
Group E–G	dusts

DETERMINING CLASS

The NEC refers to three classes:

Class I	flammable gases and vapors
Class II	combustible dusts
Class III	easily ignitible fibers or flyings

DETERMINING DIVISION

The NEC recognizes two divisions, and they are as follows:

Division 1: A location that is likely to have flammable gases or vapors present under normal conditions.

Division 2: A location that is likely to have flammable gases or vapors present only under abnormal conditions.

DETERMINING EXTENT (BOUNDARIES) OF CLASSIFIED AREAS

It is important to exercise sound engineering experience and judgment in determining the extent (boundaries) of a classified area. Having established the presence of flammable substances and determined the perimeter of the classified area, the class, group, and division is selected. The next step is to select the equipment and installation techniques. The following steps will aid in determining the extent of the boundaries of the classified area:

(1) The flammable materials involved,

(2) The type of installation,

(3) The Class (I, II, or III),

(4) The Group,

(5) The Division (1 or 2),

(6) Flash point of material,

(7) Ignition of sources,

(8) Volume and pressure release,

(9) Ventilation,

(10) Fire walls and barriers, and

(11) Purging and pressurization

PREPARING PLANS AND SPECIFICATIONS

Plans and specifications should be prepared so as to outline the hazardous area and the extent of the classified boundaries. In addition, plans that clearly illustrate the divisions and the extent of the areas should be prepared. Tables should also be developed with properties of the flammable materials and a written description based on the classification that explains the methods and procedures of each area being classified.

QUESTIONS AND ANSWERS FOR CLASSIFYING DIVISIONS

The following questions can be used to determine the Division of a classified location.

ASSIGNMENT OF DIVISION 1 LOCATIONS

(1) Is an ignitible atmospheric mixture likely to exist under "normal" operating conditions?

(2) Is an ignitible atmospheric mixture likely to occur frequently due to repair, maintenance, or leakage?

(3) Would failure of process equipment, piping, or vessels be likely to cause a failure of the electrical system simultaneous with the release of the combustible material?

(4) Is a piping system containing combustible material in an inadequately ventilated space, and is the system likely to leak?

(5) Is the space or area in question below grade level such that heavier-than-air vapors may accumulate there?

(6) Is the space or area in question above grade level such that lighter-than-air vapors may accumulate there?

An answer of yes to any of these questions would require a Division 1 classification.

ASSIGNMENT OF DIVISION 2 LOCATIONS

(1) Is a piping system containing combustible material in an inadequately ventilated space, and is the system not likely to leak?

(2) Is a process equipment system containing a combustible material in an inadequately ventilated area and can the material escape only during abnormal situations such as failure of gaskets or packing?

(3) Is the location adjacent and open to a Division 1 location by trenches, pipes, or ducts?

(4) If mechanical ventilation is used, can failure or abnormal operation of the ventilation equipment permit an ignitible atmospheric mixture?

An answer of yes to any of these questions would require a Division 2 classification.

GENERAL REQUIREMENTS 505.6(A) THRU (C)

Article 505 in Chapter 5 covers the general requirements and how such rules apply to the electrical wiring and equipment installed in locations classified as Class I, Zone 0, Zone 1, or Zone 2. The concept of using Zones, per the IEC, instead of Divisions, per the NEC, has been used internationally for many years. In the past, the International Electrotechnical Commission (IEC) has regulated the requirements for such a system.

The IEC system uses two groups to identify the hazards involved. Group I is used for mining, while Group II is used for surface industries and offshore installations.

Group II consists of three subgroups, A, B, and C. Subgroups A, B, and C are designed to represent categories of flammable gases or vapors that are based upon the minimum ignition energy of the hazard. Subgroup A represents the most difficult flammable gas or vapor to ignite, and Subgroup C is the easiest to ignite. **(See Figure 21-57)**

> **Design Tip:** Check with local NEC and OSHA inspectors to obtain their permission and advice on how to use the Zone concept when designing and installing electrical equipment and wiring methods in hazardous locations.

ZONE CLASSIFICATION 505.5(A) AND (B)

The IEC system uses three Zones to represent the different levels of risk. Zone 0 represents areas in which an explosive gas-air mixture is continuously present or present for long periods of time. Zone 1 represents areas in which an explosive gas-air mixture is likely to occur in normal operation. Zone 2 represents areas in which gas-air mixtures are not likely to occur, and should they occur they exist only for a short period of time. See **500.5(B)(1)** and **(B)(2)** to define Divisions 1 and 2 for similar situations, where gas/air mixtures present risk levels based on conditions. **(See Figure 21-58)**

CLASS I, ZONE 0 LOCATIONS 505.5(B)(1)

A Class I, Zone 0 location is a location in which an explosive gas atmosphere is present continuously or present for long periods of time.

Note, this usually applies to the inside of containers or apparatus such as vaporizers, reactors, storage tanks, etc. Long periods of time could be considered as the time needed for gases and vapors to mix with air and create an explosive mixture. **(See Figure 21-59)**

	NEC GROUP	REPRESENTATIVE GAS	IEC GROUP	
GROUP A AND B ARE MORE IGNITIBLE • 500.6(A)(1); (A)(2)	A	ACETYLENE	IIC	**GROUP IIC IS MORE IGNITIBLE** • 505.6(A), IN
	B	HYDROGEN		
GROUP C • 500.6(A)(3)	C	ETHYLENE	IIB	**GROUP IIB** • 505.6(B), IN
GROUP D • 500.6(A)(4)	D	PROPANE	IIA	**GROUP IIA** • 505.6(C), IN

A COMPARISON OF NEC AND IEC GROUPING
AND CLASSIFICATION SCHEME
NEC 505.6(A) THRU (C)

Figure 21-57. This table above shows a comparison of the NEC and IEC grouping and classification scheme.

TABLE 1	
IEC ZONE CHART	
ZONES	**HAZARDOUS RISK LEVELS**
ZONE 0	IN WHICH AN EXPLOSIVE GAS-AIR MIXTURE IS CONTINUOUSLY PRESENT. • 505.5(B)(1)
ZONE 1	IN WHICH AN EXPLOSIVE GAS-AIR MIXTURE IS LIKELY TO OCCUR IN NORMAL OPERATION. • 505.5(B)(2)
ZONE 2	IN WHICH AN EXPLOSIVE GAS-AIR MIXTURE IS NOT LIKELY TO OCCUR IN NORMAL OPERATION AND IF IT OCCURS WILL ONLY LAST FOR A SHORT PERIOD. • 505.5(B)(3)

TABLE 2		
COMPARISON OF IEC ZONES AND NEC DIVISIONS		
IEC ZONES	0	1	2
NEC DIVISIONS		1	2

ZONE CLASSIFICATION
NEC 505.5(B)(1) THRU (B)(3)

Figure 21-58. This table above can be used to define the different Zones, based upon how often a hazardous gas or vapor is present, using the IEC system concept.

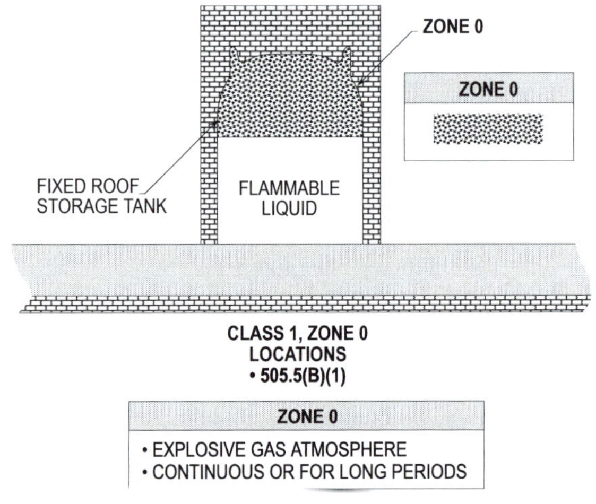

CLASS I, ZONE 0 LOCATIONS
NEC 505.5(B)(1)

Figure 21-59. This illustration shows a Class I, Zone 0 location.

CLASS I, ZONE 1 LOCATIONS
NEC 505.5(B)(2)

A Class I, Zone 1 location is a location:

(1) in which ignitible concentrations of flammable gases or vapors are likely to exist under normal operating conditions,

(2) in which ignitible concentrations of flammable gases or vapors may exist frequently because of repair or maintenance operations or because of leakage,

(3) in which equipment is operated or processes are carried on, of such a nature that equipment breakdown or faulty operations could result in the release of ignitible concentrations of flammable gases or vapors and also cause simultaneous failure of electrical equipment in a mode to cause the electrical equipment to become a source of ignition, and

(4) that is adjacent to a Class I, Zone 0 location from which ignitible concentrations of vapor could be communicated, unless communication is prevented by adequate positive pressure ventilation from a source of clean air and effective safeguards against ventilation failure are provided. **(See Figure 21-60)**

RULE OF THUMB
IEC 70-10 AND API 14F

- Gas or vapor present for 1000 hours or more – Zone 0

- Gas or vapor present for less than 1000 hours but 100 hours or more – Zone 1

- Gas or vapor present for less than 100 hours but 10 hours or more – Zone 2

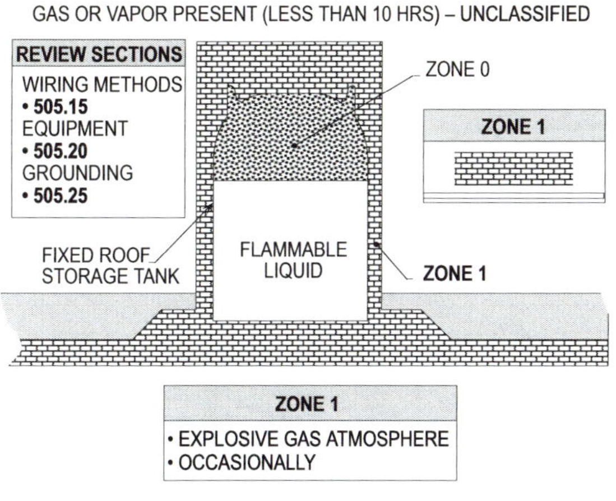

Figure 21-60. This illustration shows a Class I, Zone 1 location.

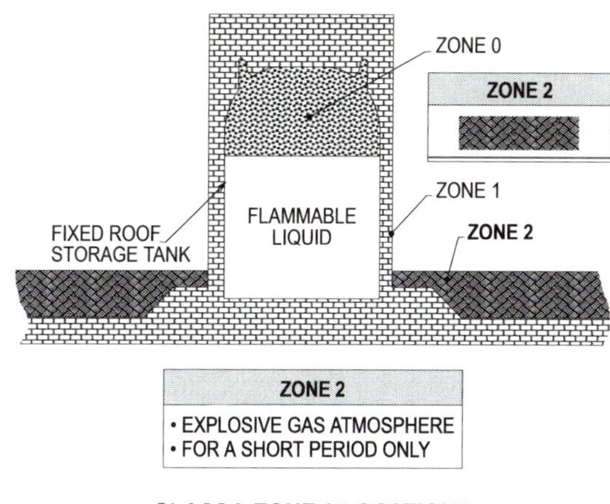

Figure 21-61. This illustration shows a Class I, Zone 2 location.

CLASS I, ZONE 2 LOCATIONS
505.5(B)(3)

A Class I, Zone 2 location is a location:

(1) in which ignitible concentrations of flammable gases or vapors are not likely to occur in normal operation, and if they do occur, will exist only for a short period,

(2) in which volatile flammable liquids, flammable gases, or flammable vapors are handled, processed, or used but in which the liquids, gases, or vapors normally are confined within closed containers of closed systems from which they can escape, only as a result of accidental rupture or breakdown of the containers or system, or as a result of the abnormal operation of the equipment with which the liquids or gases are handled, processed, or used,

(3) in which ignitible concentrations of flammable gases or vapors normally are prevented by positive mechanical ventilation, but may become hazardous as the result of failure or abnormal operation of the ventilation equipment, and

(4) that is adjacent to a Class I, Zone 1 location, from which ignitible concentrations of flammable gases or vapors could be communicated, unless such communication is prevented by adequate positive-pressure ventilation from a source of clean air, and effective safeguards against ventilation failure are provided. **(See Figure 21-61)**

CLASS I, ZONE 0, 1, and 2
EQUIPMENT
505.8(A) THRU (I)

Equipment installed in the zone locations shall be provided in a form of construction that will ensure safe performance under conditions of use. Proper maintenance of the equipment is also necessary to prevent the possible igniting of an explosive mixture of gases and air. **(See Figure 21-62)** Also, see ISA 60079-0.

SUITABILITY OF EQUIPMENT
505.9(A) AND (B)

Suitability of identified equipment shall be determined by one of the following:

(1) Equipment listing or labeling,

(2) Evidence of equipment evaluation from a qualified testing laboratory or inspection agency concerned with product evaluation, or

(3) Evidence acceptable to the AHJ, such as a manufacturer's self-evaluation or an owner's engineering judgment. **(See Figure 21-63)**

LISTING
505.9(B)(1) AND (B)(2)

Section **505.9(B)(1)** permits equipment that is listed for a Zone 0 location to be used in Zone 1 or Zone 2 locations of the same gas group. Likewise, equipment listed or otherwise acceptable for a Zone 1 location shall be permitted to be used in a Zone 2 location of the same gas group. **(See Figure 21-64)**

Equipment shall be permitted to be listed for a specific gas or vapor, specific mixtures of gases or vapors, or any combination of gases or vapors per **505.9(B)(2)**.

> **Design Tip:** One common example is equipment marked for "IIB + H2."

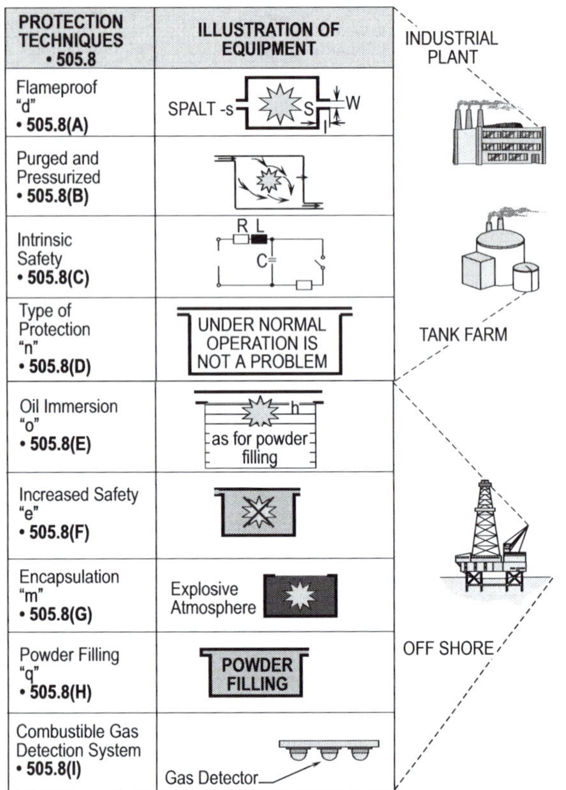

CLASS I, ZONE 0, 1, AND 2 EQUIPMENT
NEC 505.8(A) THRU (I)

Figure 21-62. This illustration shows equipment that is permitted in the zone locations.

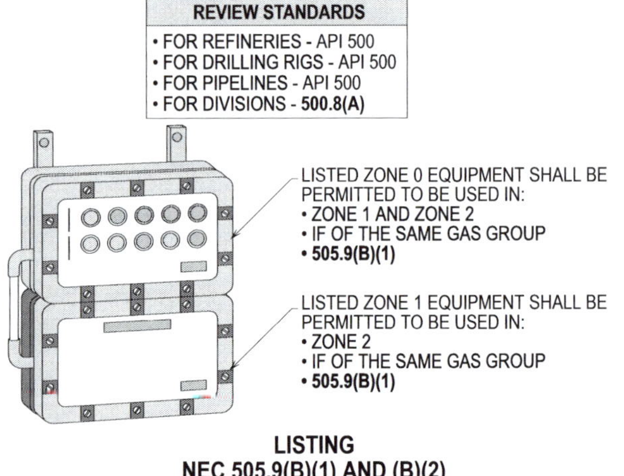

LISTING
NEC 505.9(B)(1) AND (B)(2)

Figure 21-64. Equipment, under certain conditions, shall be permitted to be used from one zone to another.

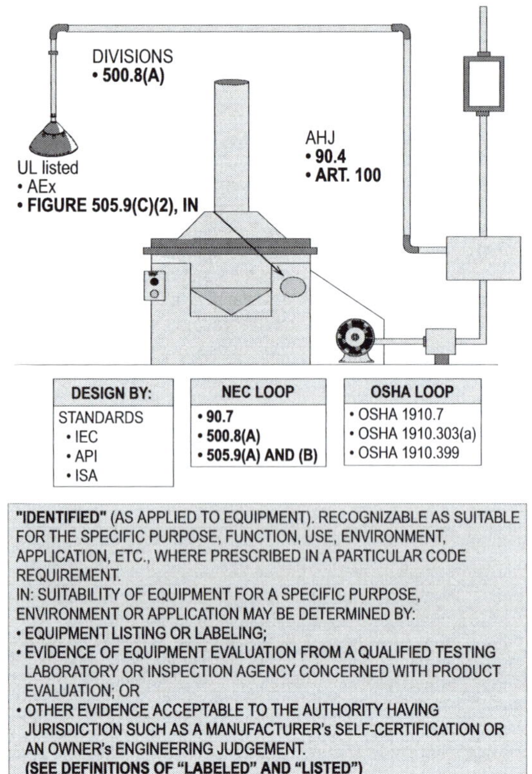

"IDENTIFIED" (AS APPLIED TO EQUIPMENT). RECOGNIZABLE AS SUITABLE FOR THE SPECIFIC PURPOSE, FUNCTION, USE, ENVIRONMENT, APPLICATION, ETC., WHERE PRESCRIBED IN A PARTICULAR CODE REQUIREMENT.
IN: SUITABILITY OF EQUIPMENT FOR A SPECIFIC PURPOSE, ENVIRONMENT OR APPLICATION MAY BE DETERMINED BY:
• EQUIPMENT LISTING OR LABELING;
• EVIDENCE OF EQUIPMENT EVALUATION FROM A QUALIFIED TESTING LABORATORY OR INSPECTION AGENCY CONCERNED WITH PRODUCT EVALUATION; OR
• OTHER EVIDENCE ACCEPTABLE TO THE AUTHORITY HAVING JURISDICTION SUCH AS A MANUFACTURER's SELF-CERTIFICATION OR AN OWNER's ENGINEERING JUDGEMENT.
(SEE DEFINITIONS OF "LABELED" AND "LISTED")

SUITABILITY OF EQUIPMENT
NEC 505.9(A) AND (B)

Figure 21-63 This illustration shows how equipment shall be accepted for Division and Zone locations.

MARKING
505.9(C)

Section **505.9(C)(1)** or **(C)(2)** requires electrical equipment, approved for operation at ambient temperatures exceeding 40°C, to be marked with the maximum ambient temperature for which the equipment is approved and the operating temperature range at that specific ambient temperature.

> **Design Tip:** Electrical equipment shall be selected by a T-code number so that the enclosure will not overheat and cause an explosion to occur. The outer surface shall not exceed the ignition temperature of the specific gas or vapor if the proper T-code number is selected and used. **(See Figure 21-65)**

WIRING METHODS FOR CLASS I, ZONE 0, 1, AND 2 LOCATIONS
505.15(A) THRU (C)

Wiring methods that are permitted to be used in a Class I, Zones 0, 1, or 2 locations are listed in **Figure 21-66** and are based on area classification.

IEC SYSTEM		NEC SYSTEM	
TEMPERATURE CLASS	MAX. SURFACE TEMPERATURE °C	TEMPERATURE IDENTIFICATION NUMBER	IGNITION TEMPERATURE OF GASES OR VAPORS (°C)
T1	450	T1	450
T2	300	T2	300
		> T2A	> 280
		> T2B	> 260
		> T2C	> 230
		> T2D	> 215
T3	200	T3	200
		> T3A	> 180
		> T3B	> 165
		> T3C	> 160
T4	135	T4	135
		> T4A	> 120
T5	100	T5	100
T6	85	T6	85

>: NEC T-CODE NUMBERS FOR TEMPERATURE IDENTIFICATION; THEY ARE NOT LISTED BY THE IEC SYSTEM BUT ARE LISTED IN THE NEC PER TABLE 500.8(C).

WHAT "T" NUMBER IS REQUIRED FOR IGNITION TEMPERATURE OF A GAS RATED AT 300°C?

STEP 1: FINDING T NUMBER
TABLE 505.9(D)(1)
300°C REQUIRES T2

SOLUTION: THE T-CODE NUMBER IS REQUIRED TO BE T2.

MARKING
NEC 505.9(C)

Figure 21-65. This illustration shows the procedure for selecting the temperature identification number for electrical equipment.

WIRING METHODS PERMITTED

ZONE 0

- INTRINSICALLY SAFE WIRING PER **505.15(A)**
- RMC
- IMC
- MI CABLE PER **505.15(B)(1)(c)**
- NONINCENDIVE
- OPTICAL FIBER CABLES

ZONE 1

WIRING METHODS PERMITTED ARE THOSE IN:
- CLASS I, DIVISION 1
- CLASS I, ZONE 0
- PLUS SEALING PER **505.16**
FOR COMPLETE LIST, SEE **505.15(B)(1)(a) THRU (B)(1)(i)**

ZONE 2

WIRING METHODS PERMITTED ARE THOSE IN:
- CLASS I, DIVISION 2
- CLASS I, DIVISION 1
- CLASS I, ZONE 0
- CLASS I, ZONE 1
- **505.15(C)(1)(a) THRU (1)(h)**
- PLUS SEALING PER **505.16**

**WIRING METHODS FOR
CLASS I, ZONE 0, 1, AND 2 LOCATIONS
NEC 505.15(A) THRU (C)**

Figure 21-66. This chart lists the equipment permitted in Class I, Zones 0, 1, and 2 locations.

EQUIPMENT
505.20(A) THRU (E)

Equipment shall be listed and marked specifically for the Zone in which it is going to be installed. **Ex.s** to **505.20(A), (B),** and **(C)** permit equipment, under certain conditions, to be used from one Zone to another Zone.

Design Tip: Electrical equipment installed using the Zone concept shall comply with **Article 505** and be listed for use by a testing laboratory such as UL, utilizing the symbol AEx. **(See Figure 21-67)**

COMPARISON BETWEEN EQUIPMENT USING THE IEC ZONE CONCEPT OR THE 1996 NEC DIVISION CONCEPT			
EQUIPMENT PERMITTED BY THE IEC		EQUIPMENT PERMITTED BY THE NEC	
ZONE 0	ONLY INTRINSICALLY SAFE EQUIPMENT IS PERMITTED	CLASS I, DIVISION 1	THE FOLLOWING EQUIPMENT SHALL BE PERMITTED TO BE USED: • EXPLOSIONPROOF ENCLOSURES • PURGING • INTRINSIC SAFETY
ZONE 1	EQUIPMENT PERMITTED TO BE USED: "d" FLAMEPROOF ENCLOSURE "p" PRESSURIZED APPARATUS "i" INTRINSIC SAFETY "o" OIL IMMERSION "e" INCREASED SAFETY "q" POWDER FILLING		
ZONE 2	ALL EQUIPMENT CERTIFIED FOR ZONE 0 OR 1 REQUIREMENTS SHALL BE PERMITTED TO BE USED IN ZONE 2	CLASS I, DIVISION 2	ALL EQUIPMENT CERTIFIED FOR DIVISION 1 SHALL BE PERMITTED TO BE USED PLUS: • HERMETICALLY SEALED CONTACTS • OIL IMMERSION OF CONTACTS • NONINCENDIVE CIRCUITS

**EQUIPMENT
NEC 505.20(A) THRU (E)
NEC 500.7(A) THRU (L)**

Figure 21-67. This chart lists the equipment permitted in Class I, Zones 0, 1, and 2.

CLASSIFICATION OF AREA

When applying the zone concept, the protection methods required to ensure safety are related to the likelihood of the presence of an explosive gas/air mixture. The higher the probability, the greater the care needed to ensure safety.

Installations where flammable gases, vapors, or liquids are present can be categorized into areas where the probability of the presence of explosive gas/air mixtures is high or low, and the electrical apparatus shall be selected and installed accordingly. It is clear that the overall risk of exposure to an explosive atmosphere is assessed with respect to both the anticipated frequency of release of flammable material and the probable duration of its presence.

See Figure 21-68 for an illustrated comparison between the IEC and NEC classifications, based upon the presence of gas/air mixtures and the conditions of exposure to personnel and equipment.

LISTING, MARKING, AND DOCUMENTATION
505.9(A), (B), (C), AND 505.4(A)

Zone equipment, if used instead of Division equipment, shall be marked with Class, Zone, and the symbol AEx to verify to the user that such equipment complies with American Standards as well as IEC standards. **(See Figures 21-69)**

IEC (Publication 79-10)		NEC [Section **500.5(B)(1)** and **(B)(2)**]	
Zone 0	Area in which an explosive gas-air mixture is continuously present or present for long periods. (**Example:** vapor space of a process vessel or storage tank.)	**Class I, Division 1**	A Class I, Division 1 location • in which ignitible concentrations of flammable gases of vapors exist under normal operating conditions, or • in which ignitible concentrations of such gases or vapors may exist frequently because of repair or maintenance operations or because of leakage, or •in which breakdown or faulty operation of equipment or processes might release ignitible concentrations of flammable gases or vapors, and might also cause simultaneous failure of electric equipment.
Zone 1	Area in which an explosive gas-air mixture is likely to occur in normal operation.		
Zone 2	Area in which an explosive gas-air mixture is not likely to occur, and if it occurs it will only exist for a short time. **NOTE:** ALSO, SEE **505.5(B)(1) THRU (B)(3)**	**Class I, Division 2**	A Class I, Division 2 location •in which volatile flammable liquids or flammable gases are handled, processed or used but in which the liquids, vapors, or gases will normally be confined within closed containers or closed systems from which they can escape only in case of accidental rupture or breakdown of such containers or systems, or in case of abnormal operation of equipment, or •in which ignitible concentrations of gases or vapors are normally prevented by positive mechanical ventilation, and which might become hazardous through failure or abnormal operation of the ventilating equipment, or •that is adjacent to a Class I, Division 1 location, and to which ignitible concentrations of gases or vapors might occasionally be communicated unless such communication is prevented by adequate positive-pressure ventilation from a source of clean air, and effective safeguards against ventilation failure are provided.

CLASSIFICATION OF AREA

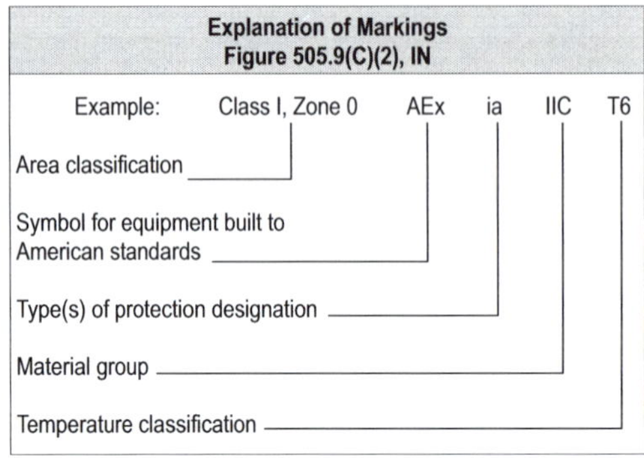

LISTING, MARKING, AND DOCUMENTATION
NEC 505.9(A), (B), (C), AND 505.4(A)

Figure 21-69. This table illustrates an explanation of markings that are used on Zone equipment to identify certain characteristics.

Figure 21-68. The above table illustrates a comparison between IEC and NEC area classifications.

Name ___________________________   Date ___________________________

Section   Answer

1. Class I, Division 2 locations are those locations in which volatile _____ gases are handled,   ________   ______
   processed, or used.

   (a) flammable   (b) non-combustible
   (c) ignitible   (d) explosive

2. Class II, Division 1 locations are those locations in which _____ dust is in the air under normal   ________   ______
   operation conditions in quantities sufficient to produce explosive or ignitable mixtures.

   (a) flammable   (b) combustible
   (c) non-ignitible   (d) non-explosive

3. Class III, Division 2 locations are those locations in which easily _____ fibers/flyings are   ________   ______
   stored or handled except in process of manufacturing.

   (a) non-flammable   (b) non-combustible
   (c) ignitible   (d) non-explosive

4. Equipment used in the Divisions or Zones shall be _____ and suitable for the location.   ________   ______

   (a) marked   (b) unlisted
   (c) labeled   (d) identified

5. Group _____ atmospheres contain combustible metal dusts.   ________   ______

   (a) A   (b) C
   (c) E   (d) G

6. Vapor _____ are used mainly to determine the settling or rising tendency of a mixture.   ________   ______

   (a) percentages   (b) densities
   (c) quantities   (d) temperatures

7. Type _____ enclosures are used only for indoor locations classified as Class I, Groups A, B,   ________   ______
   C, and D.

   (a) 7   (b) 8
   (c) 9   (d) 10

8. Type _____ enclosures are intended for indoor use in locations classified as Class II, Groups   ________   ______
   E or G.

   (a) 7   (b) 8
   (c) 9   (d) 10

Section   **Answer**

9. Flexible cord that is listed for _______ usage and provided with listed bushed fittings shall be permitted to be used in Class I, Division 1 locations.

   (a) hard   (b) dry
   (c) wet   (d) extra-hard

10. Surface temperature of Class I, Division 1 luminaires shall not exceed the _______ temperature of the gases or vapors surrounding such units.

    (a) ignition   (b) flammable
    (c) combustible   (d) normal

11. In commercial garages, EMT shall be permitted to be installed above the _______ in. level.

    (a) 6   (b) 12
    (c) 18   (d) 24

12. A lubrication room (with motor fuel dispensing) shall be considered Class I, Division 2 up to a height of _______ in. above the floor, if ventilation is provided.

    (a) 12   (b) 18
    (c) 24   (d) 30

13. For open-top spray booths, the Class I, Division 2 hazardous area shall be considered to extend to _______ ft above the booth and 3 ft from all openings.

    (a) 3   (b) 4
    (c) 5   (d) 6

14. A Class II, Division 2 location is a location where combustible _______ is not normally in the air in quantities sufficient to produce explosive or ignitible mixtures.

    (a) liquids   (b) dusts
    (c) vapors   (d) fibers/flyings

15. A Class III, Division 1 location is a location in which easily ignitible _______ or materials are handled, manufactured, or used.

    (a) liquids   (b) dusts
    (c) vapors   (d) fibers/flyings

16. Group B is an atmosphere containing flammable gases or _______ liquids.

    (a) flammable   (b) volatile
    (c) combustible   (d) ignitible

17. Group F atmospheres contain combustible _______ dusts.

    (a) flammable   (b) metal
    (c) charcoal   (d) carbonaceous

Section   **Answer**

18. Flash point of a liquid is the minimum _____ at which the liquid gives off sufficient vapor to form an ignitable mixture with the air near the surface of the liquid or within the vessel.

    (a) temperature   (b) ignition
    (c) density   (d) level

19. Explosionproof enclosures will withstand an _____ explosion of gases or vapor and prevent those gases or vapors from igniting gases and vapors in the surrounding atmosphere outside of the enclosure.

    (a) volatile   (b) internal
    (c) external   (d) flammable

20. Threaded joints of rigid metal conduit shall be made up with at least _____ threads fully engaged.

    (a) 3   (b) 4
    (c) 5   (d) 6

21. Rigid nonmetallic conduit shall be permitted to be installed in Class I, Division 1 locations if encased in a concrete envelope of at least 2 in. and buried below the surface in not less than _____ ft of earth.

    (a) 1   (b) 2
    (c) 3   (d) 5

22. In Class I, Division 2 locations, pendant luminaires shall be suspended by a flexible hanger unless rigid stems not over _____ in. long are used.

    (a) 6   (b) 8
    (c) 10   (d) 12

23. Explosionproof equipment or equipment with arcing or sparking devices shall have a seal placed within _____ in. of such equipment.

    (a) 6   (b) 12
    (c) 18   (d) 24

24. In classification of a floor of a garage where vehicles are repaired and volatile flammable fluids are present, the floor area up to _____ in. is Class I, Division 2.

    (a) 12   (b) 18
    (c) 24   (d) 30

25. Any equipment in commercial garages that might produce an arc or spark, and that is less than _____ ft above the floor level, shall have a tight enclosure that will prevent the escape of any arc or spark.

    (a) 12   (b) 15
    (c) 18   (d) 20

Section   **Answer**

26. Any equipment installed in aircraft hangers that is over _______ ft above engines shall be permitted to be the general purpose type.

    (a) 3   (b) 5
    (c) 6   (d) 10

27. The surrounding space out to a distance of _______ ft, measured from a point vertically below the edge of the dispenser enclosure, is Class I, Division 2 up to a height of 18 in. above grade.

    (a) 12   (b) 15
    (c) 18   (d) 20

28. Emergency controls for unattended self-service stations shall be more than 20 ft but less than _______ ft from the dispensers.

    (a) 20   (b) 50
    (c) 75   (d) 100

29. A pit for a bulk-storage tank that is located in the 10 ft or _______ ft sphere (horizontally) around pumps, bleeders, meters, etc. shall be considered as a Class I, Division 1 location.

    (a) 15   (b) 20
    (c) 25   (d) 40

30. Storage and repair garages for tank vehicles shall be considered as Class I, Division 2 up to a height of _______ in. above the floor.

    (a) 18   (b) 24
    (c) 30   (d) 36

31. Underground wiring routed to and around aboveground storage tanks shall be permitted to be installed with rigid metal conduit where buried less than _______ ft in the earth.

    (a) 2   (b) 3
    (c) 5   (d) 6

32. Portable lamps within a spray booth shall be of a type that are _______ for Class I, Division 1 locations.

    (a) listed   (b) identified
    (c) labeled   (d) approved

33. Receptacles used to cord-and-plug connect equipment in Class I, Division 1 or 2 locations shall be _______ for such use.

    (a) listed   (b) labeled
    (c) identified   (d) approved

Section   Answer

34. Group _______ is an atmosphere such as ethyl ether, ethylene, or gases or vapors of equivalent hazard.

    (a) A   (b) B
    (c) C   (d) D

35. Group _______ is an atmosphere that contains combustible dusts such as flour, grain, wood, plastic, and chemicals.

    (a) D   (b) E
    (c) F   (d) G

36. A single barrier seal (process sealing) requires an add-on secondary _______ to be installed.

    (a) seal   (b) bushing
    (c) connector   (d) coupling

37. Hermetically sealed contacts can be installed in a Class I, Division 2 location in _______-purpose enclosures when used for instruction purposes.
    (a) normal   (b) general
    (c) all of the above   (d) none of the above

38. In Zone 2, flexible cord can be used for _______ connections.

    (a) motor   (b) instruction
    (c) all of the above   (d) none of the above

39. In Zone locations, grounding and bonding shall comply with Article 250 as well as the requirements in Sections _______ and _______.

    (a) 505.25(A)   (b) 505.25(B)
    (c) all of the above   (d) none of the above

40. Process-connected electrical equipment in the Zones with a dual seal shall not be required to be provided with an add-on _______ seal.

    (a) primary   (b) secondary
    (c) all of the above   (d) none of the above

Residential Calculations

Residential calculations are the most difficult to perform because the rules and regulations of the *National Electrical Code* are more restrictive than those for commercial and industrial facilities. The standard or optional calculation shall be permitted to be used to calculate the loads to size and select the elements for the feeder or service. The optional calculation seems to be the favorite method used by designers and electricians. This is true because once loads are calculated, it produces smaller VA or amps than the more complicated standard calculation. Therefore, smaller components are required in the electrical system and greater savings in wiring methods are achieved. The procedure for laying out residential calculations will be different in some ways from those used for commercial and industrial.

APPLYING THE STANDARD CALCULATION
ARTICLE 220, PARTS II AND III

Residential occupancies are known in the industry as dwelling units or single-family dwellings. This chapter mainly deals with one- and two-family dwelling units.

When using the standard calculation for calculating loads for a residential occupancy, all loads are divided into three groups and four columns. The groups are as follows:

Group 1
General lighting and receptacle loads
Group 2
Small-appliance loads
Group 3
Special-appliance loads

See Figure 22-1 for a detailed illustration of the three groups of loads.

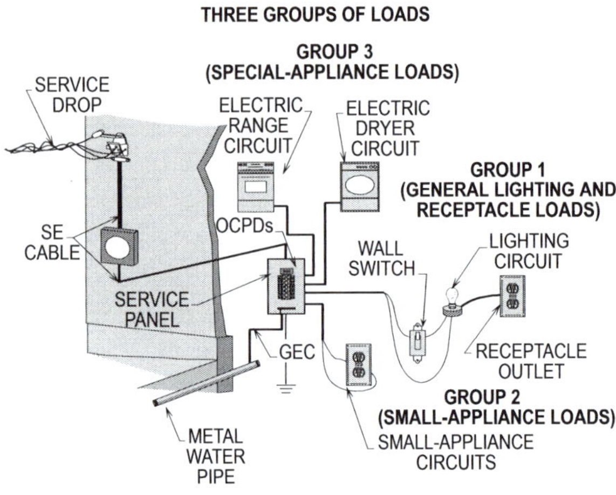

For example: Calculate the general lighting and receptacle load for a 60 ft x 55 ft dwelling unit.

Step 1: Calculating the load in VA
220.12
60' x 55' = 3300 sq. ft

Step 2: Calculating VA
Table 220.12
3300 sq. ft x 3 VA = 9900 VA

Solution: **Table 220.12 requires 9900 VA for the general lighting and receptacle loads.**

Figure 22-1. The loads in a dwelling unit are divided into three groups and four columns in which demand factors shall be permitted to be applied. The demand factors reduce the loads by a percentage based on the NEC.

GENERAL LIGHTING LOAD
220.12 AND TABLE 220.12

The general lighting load for a dwelling unit shall be determined by multiplying the square footage by 3 VA per sq. ft per **Table 220.12**. The required square footage per unit load VA (volt-amps) is found in **Table 220.12**. All lighting loads and general-purpose receptacle loads in a dwelling shall be determined by the general lighting load. All lighting loads per **210.70(A)**, and general-purpose receptacle loads per **Article 100** and **210.52(A) through (I),** shall be calculated per **Table 220.12**. The locations in which general-purpose receptacle outlets are installed are bedrooms, bathrooms, dens, living rooms, halls, garages, and outside areas.

See Figure 22-2 for calculating the general-purpose lighting and receptacle loads in a dwelling unit.

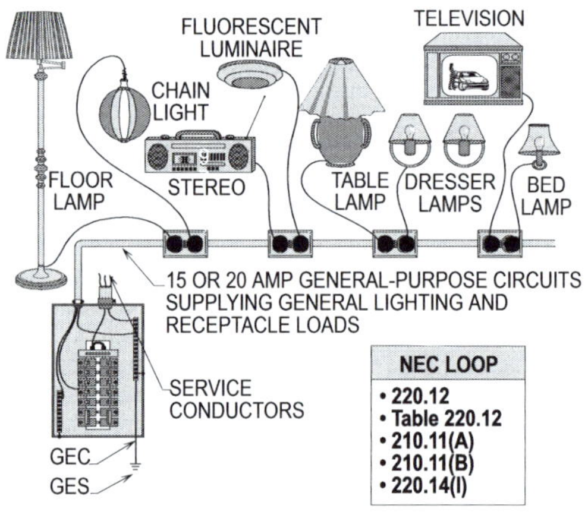

Calculate the general lighting and receptacle load for a 60 ft x 60 ft dwelling unit?

Step 1: Calculating the VA
220.12
60' x 60' = 3600 sq. ft

Step 2: Table 220.12
3600 sq. ft x 3 VA = 10,800 VA

Solution: The lighting load is 10,800 VA.

GENERAL LIGHTING LOAD
NEC 220.12

For example: Calculate the general lighting and receptacle load for a 2400 sq. ft dwelling unit.

Step 1: Calculating the load in VA
Table 220.12
2400 sq. ft x 3 VA = 7200 VA

Solution: **Table 220.12 requires 7200 VA for the general lighting and receptacle loads.**

Figure 22-2. The general lighting load for a dwelling unit shall be calculated by multiplying the square footage by 3 VA per sq. ft per **Table 220.12**. All lighting loads and general-purpose receptacle loads in a dwelling shall be calculated by the general lighting load calculation. See the asterisk by the dwelling units in **Table 310.15(B)(16)** and the **Note** below the table. **(See Figure 14-1)**

SMALL-APPLIANCE AND LAUNDRY LOADS
220.52(A) AND (B)

All small-appliance circuits shall be located in a dwelling unit per **210.52(B)(1)** and **210.11(C)(1)** and **(C)(2)**. At least two small-appliance circuits shall be required to supply receptacle outlets located in the kitchen, breakfast room, pantry, and dining room per **220.52(A)**. A laundry room receptacle outlet shall be required per **220.52(B)**. All small-appliance and laundry loads shall be calculated at 1500 VA to determine the size feeder conductors and elements to size the service.

See Figure 22-3 for calculating the small-appliance and laundry loads in a dwelling unit.

For example: Calculate the minimum VA rating for small-appliance and laundry loads required in a dwelling unit.

> **Step 1:** Calculating the load in VA
> **220.52(A)**
> 1500 VA x 2 = 3000 VA
>
> **Step 2:** Calculating the load in VA
> **220.52(B)**
> 1500 VA x 1 = 1500 VA
>
> **Solution:** Sections 220.52(A) and (B) require 4500 VA for the small-appliance and laundry circuits.

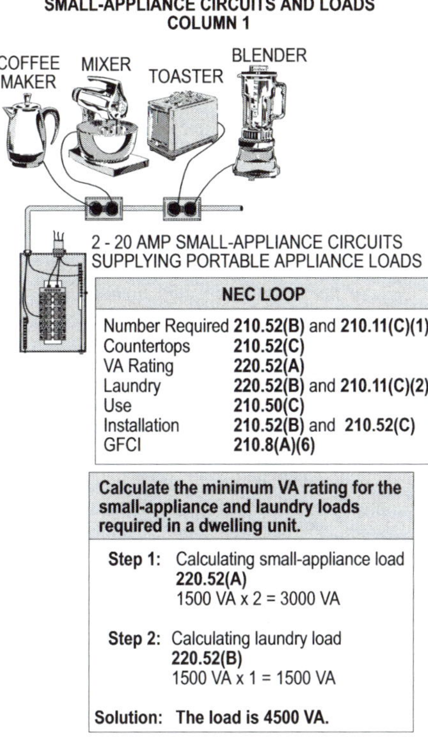

SMALL-APPLIANCE AND LAUNDRY LOADS
NEC 220.52(A) AND (B)

Figure 22-3. All small-appliance and laundry loads shall be calculated at 1500 VA to determine the feeder conductors and elements to size the service. At least three small appliance circuits shall be required. However, more circuits are permitted. **Note,** for commercial and industrial locations, see **Figure 23-3**.

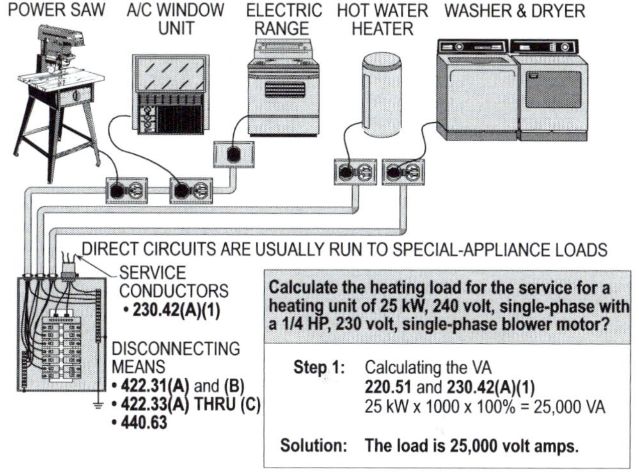

SPECIAL- APPLIANCE LOADS
NEC 220.14(A) AND 230.42(A) AND (B)

Figure 22-4. All direct circuit loads shall not be permitted to be connected to the general lighting load. The kilowatt rating listed on the nameplate for special-appliance loads shall be calculated at 125 percent for continuous operation and 100 percent for noncontinuous operation.

SPECIAL-APPLIANCE LOADS
220.14(A) THRU (C), 230.42(A), AND (B)

Special-appliance loads are usually supplied by direct circuits. These loads are water heaters, heating units, ranges, air conditioners, dishwashers, motors, etc. Direct circuit loads shall not be connected to the general lighting load. The VA rating for the overcurrent protection device for special-appliance loads shall be calculated at 125 percent for continuous operation and 100 percent for noncontinuous operation, with demand loads being determined by the kilowatt rating listed on the nameplate times a percentage.

See Figure 22-4 for calculating the special-appliance loads.

For example: Calculating the special-appliance load for a 8 kW water heater.

Step 1: Calculating the VA
210.19(A)(1)(a), 230.42(A)(1), and **422.13**
8 kW water heater = 8000 watts (volt-amps)

Solution: Sections 230.42(A)(1), 210.19(A)(1)(a), and 220.14(A) require 8000 VA for the water heater load.

For example: Calculate the heating load for the service and branch-circuit load for a heating unit of 20 kW, 240 volt, single-phase with a 1/4 HP, 230 volt, single-phase blower motor.

Step 1: Calculating the VA
220.51
20 kW x 1000 x 100% = 20,000 VA

Solution: Section 220.51 requires 20,000 VA for the service load.

Step 1: Calculating the branch-`circuit load
424.3(A); (B) and **Table 430.248**
Heating load = 20,000 VA
Motor load (2.9 A x 240 V) = 696 VA
Total load = 20,696 VA

Step 2: Calculating the total VA
424.3(A) and **(B)**
20,696 VA x 125% = 25,870 VA

Solution: Section 424.3(A) and (B) requires 25,870 VA for the branch-circuit load.

Design Tip: Some designers and inspectors include the blower motor load with the kW rating of heating unit. Verify with local codes for interpretation.

DEMAND FACTORS
ARTICLE 220, PART III

The following four loads are separated into two columns of loads and demand factors are applied:

Column 1:
General lighting and receptacle loads
and small-appliance loads   **Table 220.42**

Column 2:
Cooking equipment loads   **220.55** and **Table 220.55**
Fixed-appliance loads   **220.53**
Dryer loads   **220.54** and **Table 220.54**

General lighting and receptacle loads and the small-appliance circuits plus laundry circuit shall be permitted to have demand factors applied.

The total number of fixed-appliance loads shall be permitted to have demand factors applied. The total number of ranges and dryers in a dwelling unit shall be permitted to be reduced by a percentage.

See Figure 22-5 for the four loads that shall be permitted to have demand factors applied.

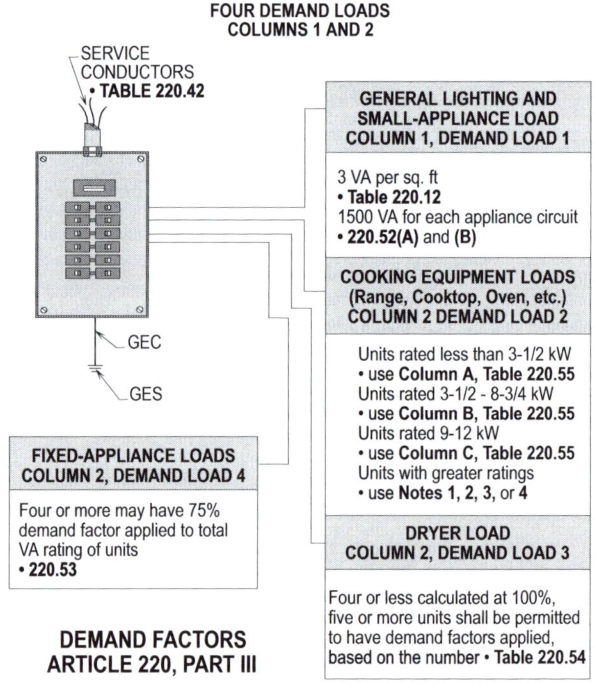

Figure 22-5. General lighting and receptacle loads and small-appliance loads, cooking equipment loads, fixed-appliance loads, and dryer loads are four loads in Columns 1 and 2 to which demand factors shall be permitted to be applied.

GENERAL LIGHTING AND RECEPTACLE LOADS AND SMALL-APPLIANCE AND LAUNDRY LOADS
COLUMN 1 – TABLE 220.42 AND 220.52(A) AND (B)

The general lighting load for a dwelling unit shall be calculated by multiplying the square footage by 3 VA per sq. ft per **Table 220.12**. The required square footage per unit load (volt-amps) is found in **Table 220.12**. All small-appliance and laundry loads shall be calculated at 1500 VA per **220.52(A)** and **(B)**. A demand factor shall be permitted per **Table 220.42**. The demand factors for the general lighting and receptacle loads per **Table 220.42** for dwelling units are as follows:

             Volt-amps
    0 -   3000 at 100%
    3001 - 120,000 at   35%
    120,001 and up at   25%

See Figure 22-6 for calculating the general-purpose lighting and receptacle loads, including the small-appliance and laundry loads. **Note,** for the laundry circuits see **Figure 14-3**.

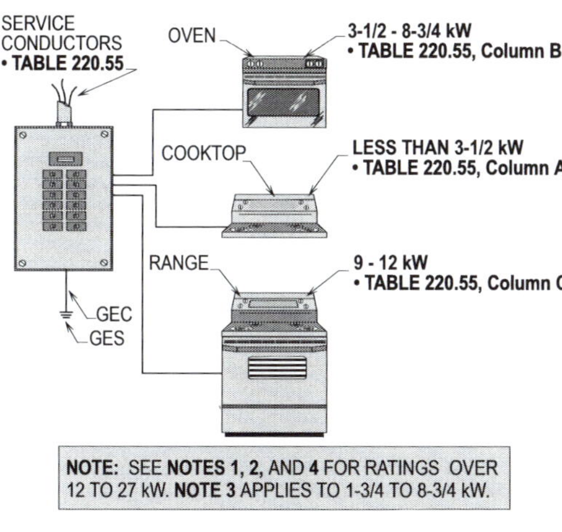

COOKING EQUIPMENT LOADS
NEC 220.55

Figure 22-7. The demand factors listed in **Table 220.55** shall be used to apply the demand loads for cooking equipment. The demand factors of **Table 220.55, Columns A, B,** or **C** are based on the kW rating of the cooking equipment. If the kW rating is greater than the kW rating of the equipment listed in **Columns A, B,** or **C**, **Notes 1, 2, 3, 4** or **5** to **Table 220.55** shall be applied.

For example: Calculate the demand load for the general lighting load for a 2800 sq. ft dwelling unit.

Column 1 and Demand load 1

Step 1: General lighting load
Table 220.12
2800 sq. ft x 3 VA   = 8400 VA

Step 2: Small-appliance load
220.52(A)
1500 VA x 2   = 3000 VA

Step 3: Laundry load
220.52(B)
1500 VA x 1   = 1500 VA

Step 4: Total load
General lighting load = 8,400 VA
Small -appliance load = 3,000 VA
Laundry load   = 1,500 VA
Total load   = 12,900 VA

Step 5: Applying demand factors
Table 220.42
First 3000 VA x 100% = 3000 VA
Next 9900 VA x 35% = 3465 VA
Total load   = 6465 VA

Solution: Demand load 1 requires 6465 VA for the general lighting and receptacle loads, including the small-appliance and laundry loads.

COOKING EQUIPMENT LOADS
COLUMN 2 – 220.55 AND TABLE 220.55

The cooking equipment loads and Demand load 2 are separated from Group 3 and placed in Column 2, and demand factors applied accordingly.

The demand factors listed in **Table 220.55** apply to the demand loads for cooking equipment. The **Footnotes** are based on the kW rating and number of units. Ranges, wall-mounted ovens, and counter-mounted cooktops are units of cooking equipment per **Table 220.55**.

See Figure 22-7 for the demand factors listed in **Table 220.55, Columns A, B,** or **C**.

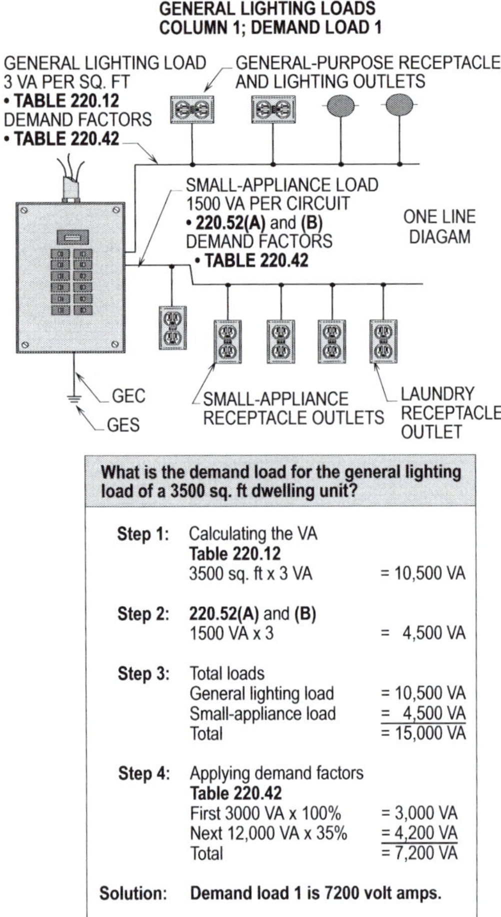

What is the demand load for the general lighting load of a 3500 sq. ft dwelling unit?

Step 1:	Calculating the VA **Table 220.12** 3500 sq. ft x 3 VA	= 10,500 VA
Step 2:	**220.52(A) and (B)** 1500 VA x 3	= 4,500 VA
Step 3:	Total loads General lighting load Small-appliance load Total	= 10,500 VA = 4,500 VA = 15,000 VA
Step 4:	Applying demand factors **Table 220.42** First 3000 VA x 100% Next 12,000 VA x 35% Total	= 3,000 VA = 4,200 VA = 7,200 VA
Solution:	**Demand load 1 is 7200 volt amps.**	

**GENERAL LIGHTING AND RECEPTACLE
LOADS AND SMALL-APPLIANCE AND LAUNDRY LOADS
TABLE 220.12 AND TABLE 220.42
NEC 220.52(A) AND (B)**

Figure 22-6. The general lighting and receptacle loads, including the small-appliance loads, are calculated in VA when determining the size service-entrance equipment and conductors. This is Demand load 1 in the standard calculation.

DEMAND LOAD 2
TABLE 220.55, COLUMN C

The demand load of cooking equipment is calculated in kW. The maximum demand for the size and number of ranges is already calculated for selecting the elements of the feeder or service. Therefore, cooking equipment does not need to be multiplied by the kW rating of the unit by a percentage until **Columns A** or **B** are utilized.

See Figure 22-8 for demand loads that shall be permitted to be applied in **Table 220.55, Column C**. Also, see **Figures 14-4 thru 14-11.**

For example: Calculating the demand load for a 11.5 kW range.

Step 1:	Calculating the load in VA **Table 220.55, Column C** 11.5 kW = 8 kVA
Solution:	**Column C to Table 220.55 permits 8 kVA for the range.**

For example: Calculating the demand load for a 12 kW and 10 kW cooking unit.

Step 1:	Calculating VA **Table 220.55, Column C** 12 kW and 10 kW = 11 kVA
Solution:	**Column C to Table 220.55 permits 11 kVA for the two cooking units.**

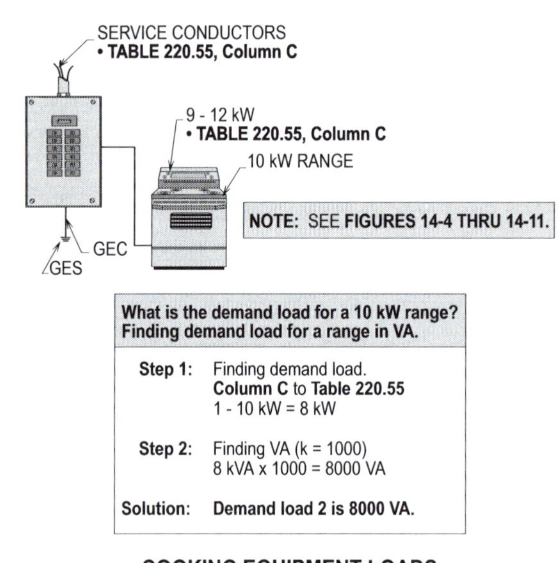

**What is the demand load for a 10 kW range?
Finding demand load for a range in VA.**

Step 1:	Finding demand load. **Column C to Table 220.55** 1 - 10 kW = 8 kW	
Step 2:	Finding VA (k = 1000) 8 kVA x 1000 = 8000 VA	
Solution:	**Demand load 2 is 8000 VA.**	

**COOKING EQUIPMENT LOADS
TABLE 220.55, Col. C**

Figure 22-8. The demand load in kW for cooking equipment in **Column C** is already calculated per **Table 220.55**.

DEMAND LOAD 2
TABLE 220.55, COLUMN A

The nameplate (kW) wattage rating of a range shall be calculated by the number of cooking units times the percentage factor found in **Table 220.55**. This calculation is used to obtain the maximum demand load.

See **Figure 22-9** for demand loads to be applied in **Table 220.55, Column A**.

For example, what is the percentage permitted for three cooking units rated at 3 kW, 2-1/2 kW, and 2 kW respectively? The first step is to select the percentage to be applied, based on the number of cooking units. Three cooking units permit a demand factor of 70 percent per **Table 220.55, Column A**.

For example: Calculating the demand load for a piece of cooking equipment with a 2.5 kW rating.

    Step 1:   Calculating the VA
                    Table 220.55, Column A
                    2.5 kW x 80% = 2 kVA

    Solution: Column A to Table 220.55 permits 2 kVA for the cooking equipment.

DEMAND LOAD 2
TABLE 220.55, COLUMN B

The nameplate (kW) wattage rating of a range shall be calculated by the number of cooking units times the percentage factor applied in **Table 220.55**. This calculation derives the maximum demand load.

See **Figure 22-10** for demand loads to be applied from **Table 220.55, Column B**.

For example: Calculating the demand load for a piece of cooking equipment with a 8.5 kW rating.

    Step 1:   Calculating the VA
                    Table 220.55, Column B
                    8.5 kW x 80% = 6.8 kVA

    Solution: Column B to Table 220.55 permits 6.8 kVA for the cooking equipment.

DEMAND LOAD 2
TABLE 220.55, NOTE 1

For cooking equipment rated over 12 kW to 27 kW in **Column C**, each kW over 12 kW shall be increased 5 percent to calculate the demand load per **Note 1**.

See **Figure 22-11** for demand factors to be applied from **Table 220.55, Column C, Note 1**.

For example: Calculating the demand load for a range with a 25 kW rating.

    Step 1:   Calculating the percentage
                    Table 220.55, Note 1
                    25 kW - 12 kW = 13 kW
                    13 kW x 5% = 65%

    Step 2:   Calculating the VA
                    Table 220.55, Column C
                    8 kW x 165% = 13.2 kVA

    Solution: Note 1 to Table 220.55 permits 13.2 kVA for the range.

DEMAND LOAD 2
TABLE 220.55, NOTE 2

Cooking equipment of unequal values rated over 12 kW to 27 kW in **Column C, Note 2** shall be calculated by adding the kW ratings of all units and dividing by the number of units; all ranges below 12 kW shall be calculated at 12 kW. When an average rating is found, the number of units shall be increased by 5 percent for each kW exceeding 12 kW, to derive the allowable kW.

See **Figure 22-12** for demand factors that are applied per **Table 220.55, Column C, Note 2**.

Note, the demand factor selected from **Table 220.55, Column C** shall be based on the number of units.

For example: Determine the demand load for three pieces of cooking equipment with a 12 kW, 14 kW, and 20 kW rating respectively.

    Step 1:   Calculating the percentage
                    Table 220.55, Note 2
                    Total kW rating
                    12 kW + 14 kW + 20 kW = 46 kW
                    Average rating
                    46 kW ÷ 3 = 15.3 (round up)
                    16 - 12 = (4 x 5%) = 20%

    Step 2:   Calculating the VA
                    Table 220.55, Column C
                    14 kW x 120% = 16.8 kVA

    Solution: Note 2 to Table 220.55 permits 16.8 kVA demand load for three pieces of cooking equipment.

Design Tip: It is permissible per **Note 3** to **Table 220.55** to add all pieces of cooking equipment with ratings over 1-3/4 kW through 8-3/4 kW together and multiply by the percentage of **Columns A** or **B**, whichever produces the smaller kW rating. This calculation shall be permitted to be applied if it provides the smaller kW rating of all the methods available in **Table 220.55** and **Notes**.

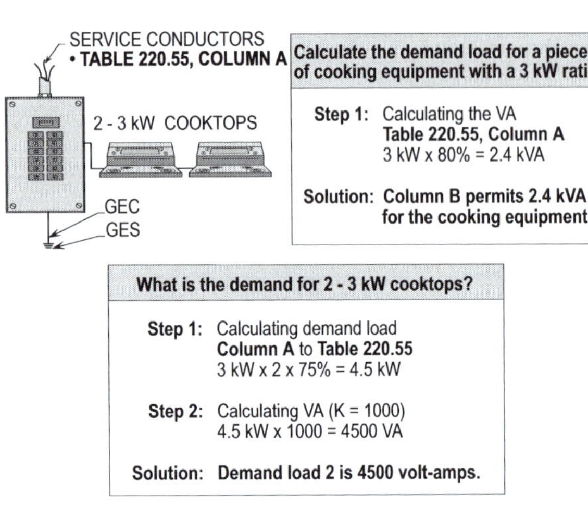

COOKING EQUIPMENT LOADS
TABLE 220.55, COLUMN A

Figure 22-9. The maximum demand load shall be calculated by the number of cooking units times the percentage factor from **Table 220.55, Column A**. For more information, see **Figure 14-4** and **14-11**.

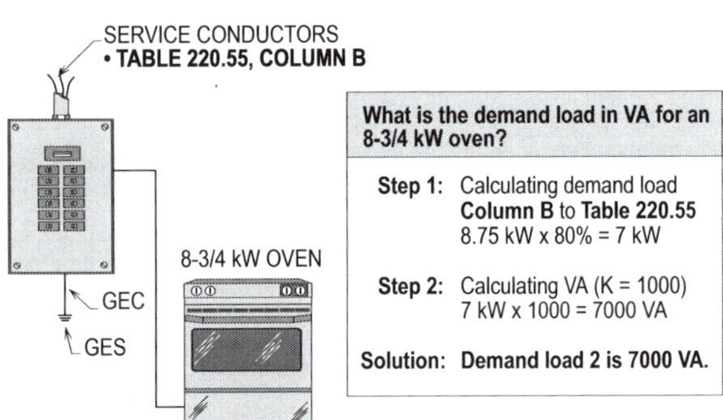

COOKING EQUIPMENT LOADS
TABLE 220.55, COLUMN B

Figure 22-10. The maximum demand load shall be calculated by the number of cooking units times the percentage factors from **Table 220.55, Column B**. This calculation produces smaller volt-amp ratings and allows smaller elements.

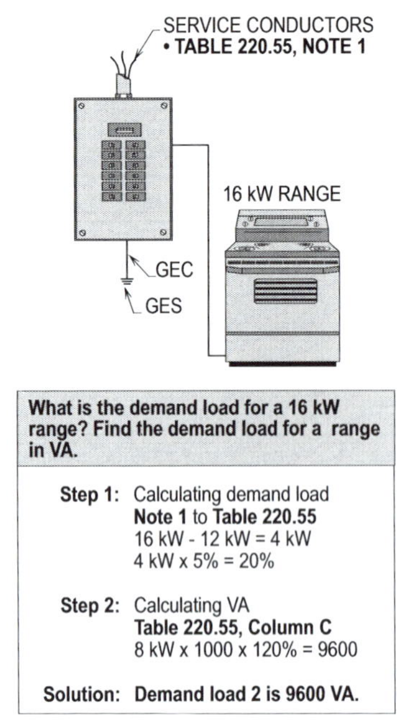

COOKING EQUIPMENT LOADS
TABLE 220.55, NOTE 1

Figure 22-11. For cooking equipment rated over 12 kW to 27 kW in **Column C**, each kW over 12 kW shall be increased 5 percent to calculate the demand load per **Note 1**. This percentage times 8 kW will calculate the demand load to be used to size the elements. For more information, see **Figure 14-4** and **14-11**.

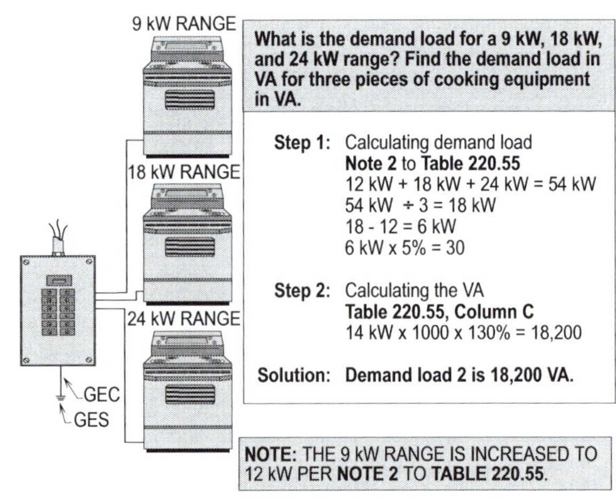

COOKING EQUIPMENT LOADS
TABLE 220.55, NOTE 2

Figure 22-12. For cooking equipment of unequal values rated over 12 kW to 27 kW in **Column C, Note 2** shall be calculated by adding the kW ratings of all units and dividing by the number of units; all ranges below 12 kW shall be calculated at 12 kW. When an average rating is determined, the number of units shall be increased 5 percent for each kW exceeding 12 kW.

DEMAND LOAD 2
TABLE 220.55, NOTE 4

The demand load for a cooktop and two or less wall-mounted ovens shall be calculated by finding the average rating of each unit in kW. Each kilowatt that exceeds 12 kW shall be increased by 5 percent. The nameplate rating of the appliance shall be calculated per **Table 220.55, Column C**. Sections **240.21(A)** and **210.19(A)(3), Ex. 1** list requirements for each piece of cooking equipment to be supplied by a tap. Each piece of cooking equipment shall be installed in the same room in order to comply with **Note 4** to **Table 220.55**. The demand load for each kW exceeding 12 kW is found by multiplying the kW rating by 5 percent to determine the average rating per **Table 220.55, Column C**.

See Figure 22-13 for demand factors to be applied from **Table 220.55, Column C, Note 1** and **4**.

For example: Calculating the demand load for a 12 kW cooktop and 2 - 6 kW ovens for a dwelling unit.

Step 1:	Calculating the percentage **Table 220.55, Note 4** Total kW rating 12 kW + 6 kW + 6 kW = 24 kW 24 kW - 12 kW = 12 kW 12 kW x 5% = 60%
Step 2:	Calculating the VA **Table 220.55, Column C** 8 kW x 160% = 12.8 kVA
Solution:	**Note 4 to Table 220.55 permits 12.8 kVA demand load for one cooktop and two ovens.**

What is the demand load for an 8 kW, 10 kW, and 12 kW oven in VA?

Step 1: Calculating demand load
Note 4 to 220.55
Total kW rating - 8 kW + 10 kW + 12 kW = 30 kW
30 kW - 12 kW = 18 kW
18 kW x 5% = 90%

Step 2: Calculating the VA
Table 220.55, Column C
8 kW x 1000 x 190% = 15,200

Solution: Demand load 2 is 15,200 VA.

COOKING EQUIPMENT LOADS
TABLE 220.55, NOTE 4

See Figure 22-13. The demand load for a cooktop and two or less wall-mounted ovens shall be calculated by finding the amperage rating of each unit in kW. Each kilowatt that exceeds 12 kW shall be increased by 5 percent to obtain the multiplier. The multiplier times the demand for one unit in **Column C** to **Table 220.55** derives the demand load for the elements of the circuit. (Also, see **Figure 23-13.**)

FIXED-APPLIANCE LOAD
COLUMN 2 – 220.53

The fixed-appliance load for cooking equipment loads, dryer equipment loads, air-conditioning loads, and heating equipment loads for three or less fixed appliances is determined by adding wattage (volt-amps) values by the nameplate ratings for each appliance. A 75 percent demand factor shall not be applied for these loads per **220.53**. However, these fixed-appliance loads shall be permitted to have demand factors applied if there are four or more. All other fixed appliances of four or more grouped into a special-appliance load shall be found by adding wattage ratings from appliance nameplates and multiplying the total wattage (volt-amps) by 75 percent to obtain demand load.

See Figure 22-14 for demand factors to be applied per **220.53**. **Note,** this is demand load 4.

Three or less fixed-appliance loads shall be calculated at 100 percent. The 75 percent per **220.53** shall not be applied unless there are four or more present.

Fixed-appliance loads include dishwashers, compactors, disposals, water heaters, attic fans, water circulating pumps, etc. It shall be permitted to apply a demand factor to these loads to calculate the elements of the service or feeder equipment. However, the branch-circuit elements shall be calculated and sized according to other Sections in the NEC.

For example, the elements of a water heater shall be calculated at 125 percent times the amperage of the total elements load per **422.13**. A dishwasher shall be calculated at 100 percent of its nameplate rating per **422.10(A)** and **422.62**.

An attic fan shall be calculated per **430.22** based on the FLA selected from **Table 430.248** for single-phase motors used for such purposes.

> **Design Tip:** The elements for branch circuits shall be calculated at 125 percent for continuous operation and 100 percent for noncontinuous operation. This includes the conductors and overcurrent protection devices feeding and protecting branch circuits.

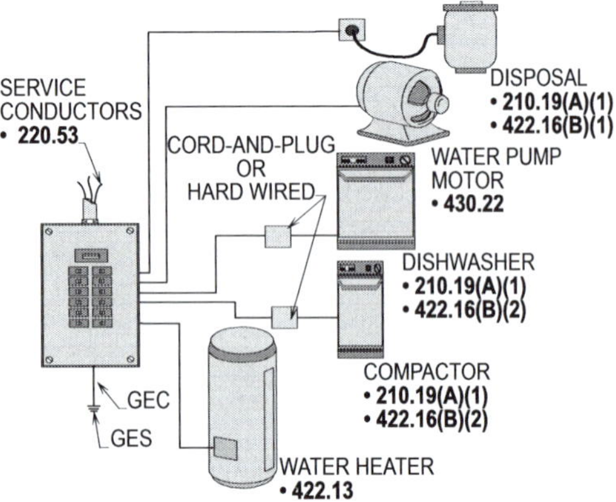

What is the demand load for the fixed-appliance load in VA?

5000 VA A/C	240 V, single-phase
15,000 VA heating unit	240 V, single-phase
6000 VA water heater	240 V, single-phase
9000 VA oven	240 V, single-phase
7500 VA cooktop	240 V, single-phase
1600 VA water pump	240 V, single-phase
900 VA disposal	120 V, single-phase
1200 VA compactor	120 V, single-phase
1000 VA microwave	120 V, single-phase
5000 VA dryer	240 V, single-phase
700 VA blower motor	240 V, single-phase

Step 1: Finding the demand load
220.53
Remove the following fixed appliances

Heating load	15,000 VA heating unit
Air-conditioning load	5000 VA A/C unit
Dryer load	5000 VA dryer
Cooking equipment load	9000 VA oven and 7500 VA cooktop

Step 2: Calculate the VA
220.53

water heater load	6,000 VA
water pump load	1,600 VA
disposal load	900 VA
compactor load	1,200 VA
microwave load	1,000 VA
blower motor load	700 VA
Total load	11,400 VA

Step 3: Applying demand factors
220.53
11,400 VA x 75% = 8550 VA

Solution: Demand load 4 is 8550 VA.

FIXED-APPLIANCE LOAD
NEC 220.53

Figure 22-14. All fixed appliances of four or more grouped in a special-appliance load shall be found by adding wattage ratings from appliance nameplates and multiplying the total wattage (volt-amps) by 75 percent. Calculation derives demand load.

For example: Calculating the demand load for the following fixed appliances.

6000 VA A/C	240 V, single-phase
10,000 VA heating unit	240 V, single-phase
5000 VA water heater	240 V, single-phase
8000 VA oven	240 V, single-phase
8500 VA cooktop	240 V, single-phase
2600 VA water pump	240 V, single-phase
1000 VA disposal	120 V, single-phase
1200 VA compactor	120 V, single-phase
1600 VA dishwasher	120 V, single-phase
1000 VA microwave	120 V, single-phase
5000 VA dryer	240 V, single-phase
800 VA blower motor	240 V, single-phase

Step 1: Special appliance loads, removing the following loads:
220.53
Heating load
• 10,000 VA heating unit
Air-conditioning load
• 6000 VA A/C unit
Dryer load
• 5000 VA dryer
Cooking equipment load
• 8000 VA oven
• 8500 VA cooktop

Step 2: Calculate the VA
220.53

Water heater load	=	5,000 VA
Water pump load	=	2,600 VA
Disposal load	=	1,000 VA
Compactor load	=	1,200 VA
Dishwasher load	=	1,600 VA
Microwave load	=	1,000 VA
Blower motor load	=	800 VA
Total load	=	13,200 VA

Step 3: Applying demand factors
220.53
13,200 VA x 75% = 9900 VA

Solution: Section 220.53 allows 9900 VA demand load for the fixed appliance.

> **Design Tip:** After the heating load, air-conditioning load, cooking equipment load, and dryer load have been removed from the fixed-appliance load, all other appliances shall be considered fixed appliances per **220.53**.

DRYER LOAD
COLUMN 2 – 220.54 AND TABLE 220.54

The demand load for household dryers shall be calculated at 5 kVA or the nameplate rating, whichever is greater. Dryer equipment of four or fewer dryers shall be calculated at 100 percent of the nameplate rating. Dryer equipment of five or more dryers shall be permitted to have a percentage applied based on the number of units per **Table 220.54**.

See Figure 22-15 for demand factors to be applied in **220.54** and **Table 220.54**.

For example: Calculate the demand load for a 4 kW dryer.

> **Step 1:** Calculating the kW
> **220.54**
> 4 kW = 5 kW
>
> **Step 2:** Applying demand factors
> **Table 220.54**
> Four or fewer dryers = 100%
> 5 kW x 100% = 5 kVA
>
> **Solution: Table 220.54 permits 5 kVA demand load for the dryer.**

For example: Calculate the demand load for 5 dryers rated at 8000 VA each.

> **Step 1:** Selecting percentage
> **220.54** and **Table 220.54**
> 5 dryers = 85%
>
> **Step 2:** Applying demand factors
> **Table 220.54**
> 8000 VA x 5 x 85% = 34,000 VA
>
> **Solution: Table 220.54 permits 34,000 VA demand load for 5 dryers.**

Note, a dryer rated at 4500 VA shall be calculated per **220.54** at 5000 VA for determining the components for sizing a branch circuit, feeder, or service. Where applying the optional calculation, the volt-amp rating shall be calculated at the nameplate values only.

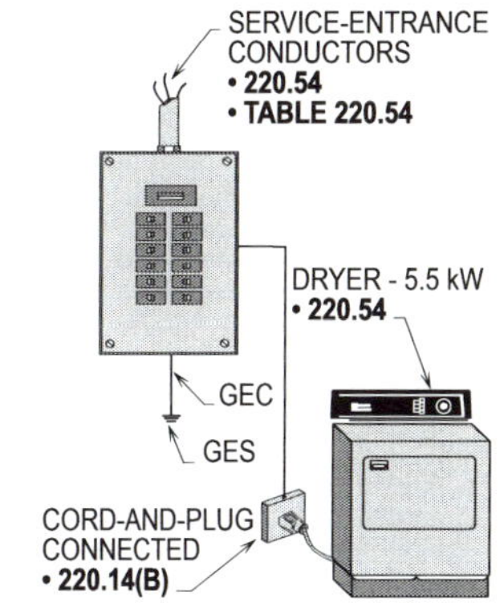

Figure 22-15. The demand load for household dryers shall be calculated at 5 kVA or the nameplate rating, whichever produces the greater rating. Four or fewer dryers shall be calculated at 100 percent of the nameplate rating. Five or more dryers shall be permitted to have a percentage applied based on the number of units per **Table 220.54**. The Table is based on five dryers being used at different times, and the load is limited to about 85 percent of total. **Table 220.54** is used for dwelling units in apartment complexes.

LARGEST LOAD BETWEEN HEATING AND AIR CONDITIONING
COLUMN 3 – 220.60

Section **220.60** shall be applied when determining the largest load between heating and air conditioning. The heating and air-conditioning loads shall be calculated at 100 percent, and the smaller of the two loads is dropped.

See Figure 22-16 for demand factors to be applied per **220.60**.

Design Tip: Some designers recognize the air-conditioning unit as still being eligible for the largest motor per **220.50**, even if it has been dropped per **220.60**.

For example: Calculating the load for a 10 kW heating unit and a 5.5 kW air-conditioning unit load in a dwelling unit.

Step 1:   Calculating the VA
          220.60
          Heating load
          10 kW x 100% = 10 kVA
          A/C load
          5.5 kW x 100% = 5.5 kVA

Solution: **Section 220.60 requires 10 kVA load for the largest load between the heating and air-conditioning load.**

For example: Calculating the VA load for a 3 HP, 230 volt, single-phase motor, which is to be used for the largest load.

Step 1:   Finding FLA
          Table 430.248
          3 HP = 17 A

Step 2:   Calculating amps
          220.50, 430.22, and **430.24**
          17 A x 25% = 4.25 A

Step 3:   Calculating VA
          Text
          4.25 A x 240 V = 1020 VA

Solution: **Section 220.50 requires 1020 VA load to supply the largest motor load.**

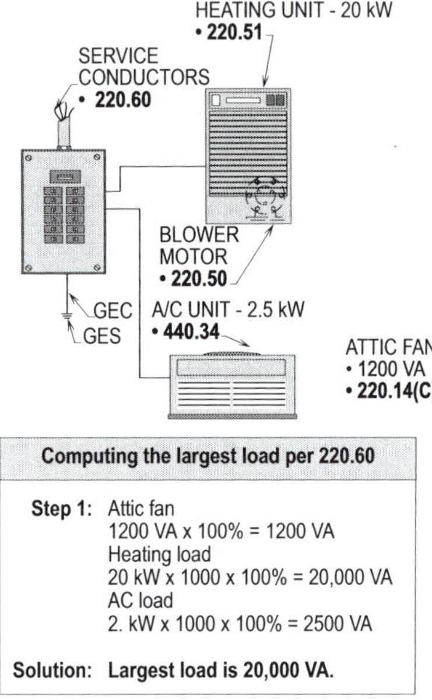

Computing the largest load per 220.60

Step 1: Attic fan
         1200 VA x 100% = 1200 VA
         Heating load
         20 kW x 1000 x 100% = 20,000 VA
         AC load
         2. kW x 1000 x 100% = 2500 VA

Solution: Largest load is 20,000 VA.

**LARGEST BETWEEN HEATING AND AIR CONDITIONING
NEC 220.60**

Figure 22-16. The heating, air-conditioning, and attic fan loads shall be calculated at 100 percent and the smaller of the two dropped and not used again until the branch circuit for each is calculated. **Note,** heat pumps are usually calculated with the heating load. (Their total VA ratings are combined.)

LARGEST MOTOR LOAD
COLUMN 4 – 220.50

The motor's total full-load current rating, in amps, shall be calculated at 25 percent per **220.50**, which is required per **430.24** and **430.25** for calculating the load of one or more motors with other loads.

See Figure 22-17 for demand factors to be applied in **220.50**.

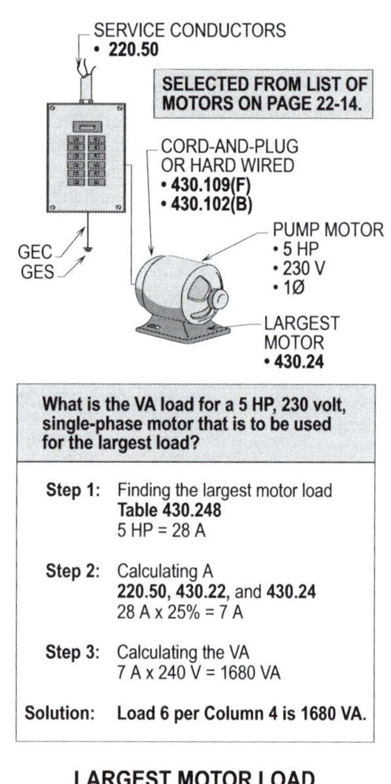

What is the VA load for a 5 HP, 230 volt, single-phase motor that is to be used for the largest load?

Step 1:   Finding the largest motor load
          Table 430.248
          5 HP = 28 A

Step 2:   Calculating A
          220.50, 430.22, and **430.24**
          28 A x 25% = 7 A

Step 3:   Calculating the VA
          7 A x 240 V = 1680 VA

Solution: Load 6 per Column 4 is 1680 VA.

**LARGEST MOTOR LOAD
COLUMN 4
NEC 220.50**

Figure 22-17. The motor's total full-load current rating, in amps, shall be calculated at 25 or 125 percent per **220.50**, which refers to **430.24** for calculating the load of one or more motors with other loads.

For example: Calculating the load for a 7.5 HP, 230 volt, single-phase motor with 1400 VA of other loads.

Step 1:	Finding FLA	
	430.6(A)(1) and **Table 430.248**	
	Motor load	
	7.5 HP = 40 A	
	40 A x 240 V	= 9,600 VA
	Other loads	
	1400 VA	= 1,400 VA
	Total loads	= 11,000 VA
Step 2:	Calculating the VA	
	220.50, 430.24, and **430.22**	
	Total loads	= 11,000 VA
	Largest motor load	
	9600 VA x 25%	= 2,400 VA
	Total load	= 13,400 VA
Solution:	**Section 220.50 requires 13,400 VA demand load to supply the largest motor load.**	

Select largest motor from fixed-appliance load

20 kW heating unit	240 V, single-phase
5.5 kW A/C unit	240 V, single-phase
6 kW water heater	240 V, single-phase
1.2 kW compactor	120 V, single-phase
1.8 kW dishwasher	120 V, single-phase
1.7 kW disposal	120 V, single-phase
1.6 kW attic fan	120 V, single-phase
1.3 kW microwave	120 V, single-phase
5 HP pump motor	240 V, single-phase
12 kW range	240 V, single-phase

The first step is to select the largest motor from the list of loads that are eligible to be considered the largest motor. The 20 kW heating unit is larger than the 5.5 kW air-conditioning unit, which eliminates the air-conditioning unit per **220.60**. After scanning the other motors to find the largest, the **5 HP motor** becomes the largest per **220.50**.

The largest motor load shall always be added into the calculation, and it really does not matter what size the largest motor is. The NEC does not distinguish between the size of the motor, but requires one to be selected and calculated based on HP and voltage. **(See Design Tip on Page 22-10) Note,** the largest motor load is calculated at 25 or 125 percent of the load that is considered the largest motor.

ONE-FAMILY DWELLING
STANDARD CALCULATION

For example, calculate the following loads of a 2800 sq. ft dwelling unit and size the service-entrance conductors required for Phases A and B and the neutral.

Loads grouped

Group 1:
General lighting and receptacle load
Group 2:
Small-appliance and laundry load
Group 3:
Special-appliance load

6000 VA A/C	240 V, single-phase
10,000 VA heating unit	240 V, single-phase
5000 VA water heater	240 V, single-phase
8000 VA oven	240 V, single-phase
8500 VA cooktop	240 V, single-phase
2600 VA water pump	120 V, single-phase
1000 VA disposal	120 V, single-phase
1200 VA compactor	120 V, single-phase
1600 VA dishwasher	120 V, single-phase
1000 VA microwave	120 V, single-phase
5000 VA dryer	240 V, single-phase
800 VA blower motor	240 V, single-phase

Column 1
General lighting and receptacle load

Table 220.12
2800 sq. ft x 3 VA   = 8,400 VA

Small-appliance and laundry loads
220.52(A) and **(B)**
1500 VA x 2   = 3,000 VA
1500 VA x 1   = 1,500 VA
Total load   = 4,500 VA

Applying demand factors for demand load 1
Table 220.42
General lighting load   = 8,400 VA
Small-appliance and
laundry load   = 4,500 VA
Total load   = 12,900 VA

First 300 VA x 100%   = 3,000 VA
Next 9900 VA x 35%   = 3,465 VA
Total load   = **6,465 VA** • √

Column 2
Special appliance loads

Cooking equipment loads and demand load 2
Table 220.55, Column B
Total kW rating
8 kW + 8.5 kW   = 16.5 kW
16.5 kW x 65%   = 10.725 kVA •
10.725 kVA x 100% x 1000   = **10,725 kVA** •

Fixed-appliance load and demand load 3
220.53
Water heater   = 5,000 VA
Water pump   = 2,600 VA √
Disposal   = 1,000 VA √
Compactor   = 1,200 VA √
Dishwasher   = 1,600 VA √
Microwave   = 1,000 VA √
Blower motor   = 800 VA
Total load   = 13,200 VA
13,200 VA x 75%   = **9,900 VA** •

Dryer load and demand load 4
220.54 and **Table 220.54**
5000 VA x 100%   = **5,000 VA** •

Column 3
Largest between heating or A/C load

220.60
Heating load
10,000 VA x 100%   = **10,000 VA** •

Column 4
Largest motor load

220.50
Water pump
2600 VA x 25%   = **650 VA** •

Finding total VA for Phases A and B

General lighting load   = 6,465 VA •
Cooking equipment   = 10,725 VA •
Fixed-appliance load   = 9,900 VA •
Dryer load   = 5,000 VA •
Heating load   = 10,000 VA •
Largest motor load   = 650 VA •
Total load   = 42,740 VA

Finding amps for Phases A and B
220.5(B)

I = VA ÷ V
I = 42,740 VA ÷ 240 V
I = 178 A

Total VA loads (Neutral)

Column 1
General lighting load and demand load 1

220.61(A)
6465 VA   =   **6,465 VA** √

Column 2
Cooking equipment load and demand load 2

(Use 70% of cooking load)
220.61(B) and **(1)**
10,725 VA x 70%   =   **7,508 VA** √

Column 2 - Use 120 V loads (√)
Fixed-appliance load and demand load 3

(Use 75% of 120 V load)
7400 VA x 75% = 5550 VA
220.53
5550 VA   =   **5,550 VA** √

Column 2
Dryer load and demand load 4

(Use 70% of dryer load)
220.61(B) and **(1)**
5000 VA x 70%   =   **3,500 VA** √

Column 4
Largest motor load

(Use 25% of largest motor load)
2600 VA x 25%   =   **650 VA** √

Finding total VA for neutral

General lighting load	= 6,465 VA √
Cooking equipment	= 7,508 VA √
Dryer load	= 3,500 VA √
Fixed-appliance load	= 5,550 VA √
Largest motor load	= 650 VA √
Total load	= 23,673 VA

Finding amps for neutral
$I = VA \div V$
$I = 23,673 \div 240$
$I = 99\ A$

Table 310.15(B)(16) and **Table 310.15(B)(7)**
Phases A and B

Table 310.15(B)(16) permits
3/0 AWG THWN cu. conductors

Table 310.15(B)(7) permits
2/0 AWG THWN cu. conductors

Neutral is 3 AWG THWN cu. conductor

See Design Problem 22-1 on page 22-19 for a detailed illustration of calculating the loads for a dwelling unit using the standard calculation.

APPLYING THE OPTIONAL CALCULATION
220.82

The optional calculation for dwelling units provides an easier method for calculating the load per **220.82(B)** and **(C)**. The loads are separated into two columns. The first column of loads consist of all loads except heating and air-conditioning loads, which are described as general loads. Heating and air-conditioning loads are the second column of loads. The elements of the service shall be determined by using the total loads of these two columns.

The optional calculation has percentages applied that are derived from the demand factors. The total kVA of a dwelling unit shall be used in determining the demand factors to be applied. The percentages in **220.82(B)** and **(C)** shall be used to calculate the load in dwelling units. Separate units located in a multifamily dwelling shall be permitted to have the optional calculation applied per **220.82(B)** and **(C)**. The optional calculation method shall only be applied when an ampacity of at least 100 amps is applied to the service conductors. This method shall be permitted to be applied to newly constructed or older existing dwelling units. **(See Design Problem 22-2 on page 22-20)**

GENERAL LOADS
220.82(B)

General loads are the first columns of loads to be calculated. General lighting and general-purpose receptacle loads shall be calculated at 3 VA per sq. ft per **220.82(B)(1)**. Small-appliance and laundry loads shall be calculated at 1500 VA per **220.82(B)(2)**, as covered in **210.11(C)(1)** and **(C)(2)**. These loads are then applied to the other loads in the column. Heating and air-conditioning loads shall not be applied to the other loads in the column. Heating and air-conditioning loads shall not be applied to other loads per **220.82(B)(3)**. Special-appliance loads shall be added to general loads per **220.82(B)(3)**. Section **220.82(B)(4)** includes motor loads in the general loads column. Section **220.50** shall not require the largest motor load at 25 percent to be added to general loads. The nameplate ratings in the general columns of loads shall be calculated at 100 percent. The first 10,000 VA of the general loads shall be calculated at 100 percent of the demand factor, and the remaining VA shall be calculated at 40 percent of the demand factor permitted per **220.82(B)**.

HEATING OR AIR-CONDITIONING LOADS
220.82(C)(1) THRU (C)(6)

The second column of loads consists of heating, air conditioning, or heating or heat pumps. The loads shall be determined by the following steps:

- Three or fewer units shall be calculated at 65 percent of the total kW rating of the heating load.

- Four or more units shall be calculated at 40 percent of the total kW rating of the heating load.

- The air-conditioning load shall be calculated at 100 percent of its kVA rating.

- The total load VA rating of the heating unit shall be compared to the air-conditioning load, and the smaller load is dropped per **220.82(C)**.

- Heat pumps that operate with the heating unit shall be calculated at 100 percent and added to the heating load. **(See Design Problem 22-3 on page 22-21)**

APPLYING THE OPTIONAL CALCULATION FOR EXISTING UNITS
220.83

Existing dwelling units per **220.83** shall be permitted to use the optional calculation to size the components for the service equipment to determine if additional loads can be added to the service. A 120/240 or 120/208 volt, three-wire, single-phase system shall be required to supply the service. Two columns are used in separating the loads in the dwelling unit. General lighting and general-purpose receptacle loads shall be calculated at 3 VA per sq. ft per **220.82(A) (1)**. All other loads shall be calculated at 100 percent of their nameplate ratings. Heating and air-conditioning loads shall be calculated at 100 percent, and the smaller load is dropped per **220.83(B)**.

OTHER LOADS
220.83

Existing loads are the first column to be selected. This column shall consist of adding 3 VA per sq. ft to the small-appliance loads plus the nameplate ratings of each special-appliance load to determine the existing load in a dwelling unit. The demand factors in **220.83** shall be used in reducing the VA rating to the existing load, and this value is then added to the second column, which contains the appliance load to be added.

ADDED APPLIANCE LOAD
220.83

Added appliance loads are the second column to be applied. This column shall be determined by adding the total VA rating of the load at 100 percent. The existing loads shall be added to the added loads to determine the total VA rating of the dwelling unit. The added load usually consists of a heating unit, air conditioner, dryer, or some other type of special-appliance load.

From the following loads in an existing dwelling unit, it will be determined if a 5040 VA air-conditioning unit load can be added to the service conductors. (Service is rated 100 amps.)

- 1800 sq. ft dwelling unit
- 2 small-appliance circuits
- 1 laundry circuit

• 12 kW range	240 V, single-phase
• 5 kW dryer	240 V, single-phase
• 1000 VA compactor	120 V, single-phase
• 900 VA disposal	120 V, single-phase
• 1200 VA dishwasher	120 V, single-phase

See Design Problem 22-4 on page 22-22 to verify if the air-conditioning load can be added without upgrading the size of the service conductors.

It is a different story if a heat pump is involved with the heating unit load. There are two methods in which a heat pump shall be calculated in relation to the heating unit. The first method is where the heat pump operates independently and does not operate with the heating unit. In this case, it is not added to the heating unit load at 100 percent to derive the total load. If it does operate with the heating load, it is added to the heating load at 100 percent to derive the total load.

Heat pumps are usually not effective when the temperature is below freezing. Heating elements are normally installed to melt the frozen ice from the coil. Section **220.82(B)(3)** addresses the supplemental heating required to provide this service. However, the supplementary heating elements performing this duty shall be permitted to be disconnected when the temperature reaches a certain temperature and the heating unit can operate independently.

ONE-FAMILY DWELLING OPTIONAL CALCULATION

For example, calculating the following loads of a 2800 sq. ft dwelling unit and size the service-entrance conductors required for Phases A and B and the neutral.

Loads grouped

Group 1:
- General lighting and receptacle loads
- Small-appliance and laundry loads
- Special-appliance loads

5000 VA water heater	240 V, single-phase
8000 VA oven	240 V, single-phase
8500 VA cooktop	240 V, single-phase
2600 VA water pump	120 V, single-phase
1000 VA disposal	120 V, single-phase
1200 VA compactor	120 V, single-phase
1600 VA dishwasher	120 V, single-phase
1000 VA microwave	120 V, single-phase
5000 VA dryer	240 V, single-phase
800 VA blower motor	240 V, single-phase

Group 2:

6000 VA A/C	240 V, single-phase
10,000 VA heating unit	240 V, single-phase

Column 1
General (other) loads

General lighting and receptacle load
220.82(B)(1) and **Table 220.12**
2800 sq. ft x 3 VA = 8,400 VA •

Small-appliance and laundry loads
220.82(B)(2), 210.11(C)(1), and **(C)(2)**
1500 VA x 2 = 3,000 VA •
1500 VA x 1 = 1,500 VA •

Special-appliance loads
220.82(B)(3) and **(B)(4)**

Oven	=	8,000 VA •
Cooktop	=	8,500 VA •
Water heater	=	5,000 VA •
Water pump	=	2,600 VA •
Disposal	=	1,000 VA •
Compactor	=	1,200 VA •
Dishwasher	=	1,600 VA •
Microwave	=	1,000 VA •
Dryer	=	5,000 VA •
Blower motor	=	800 VA •
Total load	=	47,600 VA

Column 2
Largest load between heating and A/C load

220.82(C)(1), (C)(2), and **(C)(4)**

A/C unit (6000 VA x 100%)	=	6,000 VA
Heating unit (10,000 VA x 65%)	=	6,500 VA
Total load (heating selected)	=	6,500 VA

Calculating general loads and largest load per 220.82(B)

First 10,000 VA x 100%	=	10,000 VA
Next 37,600 VA x 40%	=	15,040 VA
Largest load (Between heat and A/C)	=	6,500 VA

Calculating the VA

General loads	=	10,000 VA
	=	15,040 VA
Largest load (Between heating and A/C)	=	6,500 VA
Total load	=	31,540 VA

Calculating the amps

$$I = VA \div V$$
$$I = 31,540 \text{ VA} \div 240 \text{ V}$$
$$I = 131 \text{ A}$$

Applying demand factors
310.15(B)(7)
131 A x 83% = 108.73 amps

Table 310.15(B)(16) and **310.15(B)(7)**
Phases A and B

Table 310.15(B)(16) permits
1/0 AWG THWN cu. conductors

310.15(B)(7) permits
2 AWG THWN cu. conductors

Neutral is 3 AWG THWN cu. conductor
per **310.15(B)(7), 22061, 215.2,** and **230.42**

Note, see the calculation for the neutral in the previous explanation of the standard calculation on **pages 22-14** and **15**.

MULTIFAMILY STANDARD CALCULATION
PARTS III AND IV TO ARTICLE 220

When applying the standard calculation for multifamily dwelling units, the loads shall be calculated the same as using the standard calculation for one-family dwellings. The only difference is to calculate the loads of each unit and multiply the total number of dwelling units and pieces of electrical equipment together to derive the total VA or amps to size the elements of the service or feeder. **(See Design Problem 22-5 on page 22-23)**

MULTIFAMILY OPTIONAL CALCULATION
PARTS III AND IV TO ARTICLE 220

When applying the optional calculation for multifamily dwelling units, the loads shall be calculated the same as using the optional calculation for one-family dwellings. The only difference is to calculate the total number of dwelling units and pieces of electrical equipment together and apply a percentage based on the number to derive the total VA or amps to size the elements of the service or feeder. **(See Design Problem 22-6 on page 22-24)**

FEEDER TO MOBILE HOME STANDARD CALCULATION
550.18

Service calculations for mobile homes are performed at the factory. However, it is the responsibility of the designer or electrician to size and select the proper size feeder to supply power to the mobile home using the standard calculation. Such feeder shall be a four-wire circuit with all conductors insulated. The size of the conductors shall be permitted to be selected from **Table 310.15(B)(16)** or **310.15(B)(7)**. The service equipment on a pole or pedestal shall be rated at least 100 amps. **(See Design Problem 22-7 on page 22-25)**

MOBILE HOME PARK SERVICE AND FEEDERS - OPTIONAL CALCULATION
550.31

The elements of the service shall be permitted to be calculated using the optional calculation. All loads are added together based on the total number of mobile homes and multiplied by a percentage to derive the total load. Use 16,000 VA for each mobile home if the calculated load per **550.31** produces a lower VA rating. **(See Design Problem 22-8 on page 22-26)**

CALCULATION PROBLEMS
PARTS III AND IV TO ARTICLE 220

The elements of electrical systems shall be permitted to be calculated by using the standard or optional calculation. The size of these elements are determined by whichever method the designer chooses to calculate these loads.

The following calculations are typical examples of how these loads are calculated, sized, and selected. The step-by-step procedures are easy to follow and have condensed the more complicated rules pertaining to calculating loads into a compact listing, that provides easier understanding of how to perform calculations according to the provisions of the NEC.

A broad assortment of basic NEC calculations have been selected to represent the main principles of designing and installing electrical systems in residential occupancies.

MINIMUM RATING OF SERVICE EQUIPMENT FOR A MOBILE HOME
550.32(A)

Generally, the mobile home service equipment shall be located adjacent to the mobile home and not mounted in or on the mobile home. The service equipment shall be located in sight from and not more than 30 ft (9 m) from the exterior wall of the mobile home it serves. Mobile home service equipment shall be rated at not less than 100 amps at 120/240 volts, and provisions shall be made for connecting a mobile home feeder assembly by a permanent wiring method.

Note, a 50 amp power outlets shall also be permitted to be used as service equipment.

DESIGN PROBLEM 22-1: What is the load in VA and amps for a residential dwelling unit with the following loads?

General lighting and receptacle load

- 2500 sq. ft dwelling unit
- 2 small-appliance circuits
- 1 laundry circuit

120 V, single-phase loads

- 2600 VA water pump
- 1000 VA disposal
- 1200 VA compactor
- 1600 VA dishwasher

240 V, single-phase loads

- 5000 VA dryer
- 6000 VA A/C unit
- 20,000 VA heating unit
- 6000 VA water heater
- 10,000 VA oven
- 9000 VA cooktop
- 800 VA blower motor
- 1000 VA pool pump

Sizing phases = •
Sizing neutral = √

COLUMN 1
CALCULATING GENERAL LIGHTING AND RECEPTACLE LOAD

Step 1: General lighting and receptacle load
Table 220.12
2500 sq. ft x 3 VA = 7,500 VA

Step 2: Small appliance and laundry load
220.52(A) and **(B)**
1500 VA x 2 = 3,000 VA
1500 VA x 1 = 1,500 VA
Total load = 12,000 VA

Step 3: Applying demand factors
Demand load 1; **Table 220.42**
First 3000 VA x 100% = 3,000 VA
Next 9000 VA x 35% = 3,150 VA
Total load = 6,150 VA • √

COLUMN 2
CALCULATING COOKING EQUIPMENT LOAD

Step 1: Applying demand factors for phases A and B
Demand load 2; **Table 220.55, Column C**
9 kW and 10 kW **= 11,000 VA •**

Step 2: Applying demand factors for neutral
220.61(B)(1)
11,000 VA x 70% **= 7,700 VA √**

COLUMN 2
CALCULATING DRYER LOAD

Step 1: Applying demand factors for phases A and B
Demand load 3; **Table 220.54**
5000 VA x 100% **= 5,000 VA •**

Step 2: Applying demand factors for neutral
220.61(B)(1)
5000 VA x 70% **= 3,500 VA • √**

COLUMN 2
CALCULATING FIXED-APPLIANCE LOAD

Step 1: Applying demand factors for phases A and B
Demand load 4; **220.53**
2600 VA x 75% = 1,950 VA √
1000 VA x 75% = 750 VA √
1200 VA x 75% = 900 VA √
1600 VA x 75% = 1,200 VA √
800 VA x 75% = 600 VA
1000 VA x 75% = 750 VA
6000 VA x 75% = 4,500 VA
Total load = 10,650 VA •

Step 2: Applying demand factors for neutral
Demand load 4; **220.53** and **220.61(A)**
2600 VA x 75% = 1,950 VA
1000 VA x 75% = 750 VA
1200 VA x 75% = 900 VA
1600 VA x 75% = 1,200 VA
Total load = 4,800 VA √

COLUMN 3
LARGEST LOAD BETWEEN HEATING AND A/C LOAD

Step 1: Selecting largest load
Demand load 5; **220.51** and **220.60**
Heating unit
20,000 VA x 100% **= 20,000 VA •**

COLUMN 4
CALCULATING LARGEST MOTOR LOAD

Step 1: Selecting largest motor load for phases A and B
220.50 and **430.24**
2600 VA x 25% **= 650 VA •**

Step 2: Selecting largest motor load for neutral
220.50 and **430.24**
2600 VA x 25% **= 650 VA √**

CALCULATING PHASES (ADD ALL •)

- General lighting load = 6,150 VA •
- Cooking load = 11,000 VA •
- Dryer load = 5,000 VA •
- Appliance load = 10,650 VA •
- Heating load = 20,000 VA •
- Largest motor load = 650 VA •
Total load = 53,450 VA

CALCULATING NEUTRAL (ADD ALL √)

- General lighting load = 6,150 VA √
- Cooking load = 7,700 VA √
- Dryer load = 3,500 VA √
- Appliance load = 4,800 VA √
- Largest motor load = 650 VA √
Total load = 22,800 VA

FINDING AMPS FOR PHASES A AND B

I = VA ÷ V
I = 53,450 VA ÷ 240 V
I = 223 A

FINDING AMPS FOR NEUTRAL

I = VA ÷ V
I = 22,800 VA ÷ 240 V
I = 95 A

DESIGN PROBLEM 22-2: What is the load in VA and amps for a residential dwelling unit with the following loads? (See standard calculation in Design Problem 22-1 for sizing the neutral.)

General lighting and receptacle load	120 V, single-phase loads	240 V, single-phase loads	Sizing phases = •
• 2500 sq. ft dwelling unit	• 2600 VA water pump	• 5000 VA dryer	
• 2 small-appliance circuits	• 1000 VA disposal	• 6000 VA A/C unit	
• 1 laundry circuit	• 1200 VA compactor	• 20,000 VA heating unit	
	• 1600 VA dishwasher	• 6000 VA water heater	
		• 10,000 VA oven	
		• 9000 VA cooktop	
		• 800 VA blower motor	
		• 1000 VA pool pump	

COLUMN 1
GENERAL LOAD

Step 1: General lighting load
220.82(B)(1)
2500 sq. ft x 3 VA = 7,500 VA

Step 2: Small-appliance and laundry load
220.82(B)(2), 210.11(C)(1), and (C)(2)
1500 VA x 2 = 3,000 VA
1500 VA x 1 = 1,500 VA

Step 3: Appliance load
220.82(B)(3) and (B)(4)

Cooktop load	=	9,000 VA
Oven load	=	10,000 VA
Dryer load	=	5,000 VA
Water heater load	=	6,000 VA
Disposal load	=	1,000 VA
Compactor load	=	1,200 VA
Dishwasher load	=	1,600 VA
Pool pump load	=	1,000 VA
Blower motor load	=	800 VA
Water pump load	=	2,600 VA
Total load	=	50,200 VA

Step 4: Applying demand load
220.82(B)
First 10,000 VA x 100% = 10,000 VA
Next 40,200 VA x 40% = 16,080 VA
Total load = 26,080 VA •

COLUMN 2
LARGEST LOAD BETWEEN HEATING AND A/C LOAD

Step 5: Selecting largest load
220.82(C)(1), (C)(2), and (C)(4)
Heating load
20,000 VA x 1 x 65% = 13,000 VA •
A/C load
6000 VA x 1 x 100% =   6,000 VA
Total load **= 13,000 VA •**

TOTALING COLUMNS 1 AND 2
220.82(B) AND (C)

Column 1 load = 26,080 VA •
Column 2 load = 13,000 VA •
Total load   **= 39,080 VA**

FINDING AMPS FOR PHASES A AND B

I = VA ÷ V
I = 39,080 VA ÷ 240 V
I = 163 A

FINDING AMPS FOR NEUTRAL

I = VA ÷ V
I = 22,800 VA ÷ 240 V
I = 95 A

Note, see "Calculating neutral" and "Finding amps for neutral" in Design Problem 22-1 on page 22-19.

DESIGN PROBLEM 22-3: What is the load in VA and amps for a residential dwelling unit with the following loads? (See standard calculation in Design Problem 22-1 for sizing the neutral.)

General lighting and receptacle load

- 2500 sq. ft dwelling unit
- 2 small-appliance circuits
- 1 laundry circuit

120 V, single-phase loads

- 2600 VA water pump
- 1000 VA disposal
- 1200 VA compactor
- 1600 VA dishwasher

240 V, single-phase loads

- 5000 VA dryer
- 6000 VA heat pump
- 20,000 VA heating unit
- 6000 VA water heater
- 10,000 VA oven
- 9000 VA cooktop
- 800 VA blower motor
- 1000 VA pool pump

Sizing phases = •

Note: Heat pump may be used with heating unit.

COLUMN 1
GENERAL LOADS

Step 1:   General lighting load
220.82(B)(1)
2500 sq. ft x 3 VA   = 7,500 VA

Step 2:   Small-appliance and laundry load
220.82(B)(2), 210.11(C)(1), and (C)(2)
1500 VA x 2   = 3,000 VA
1500 VA x 1   = 1,500 VA

Step 3:   Appliance load
220.82(B)(3) and (B)(4)

Cooktop load	= 9,000 VA
Oven load	= 10,000 VA
Dryer load	= 5,000 VA
Water heater load	= 6,000 VA
Disposal load	= 1,000 VA
Compactor load	= 1,200 VA
Dishwasher load	= 1,600 VA
Pool pump load	= 1,000 VA
Blower motor load	= 800 VA
Water pump load	= 2,600 VA
Total load	= 50,200 VA

Step 4:   Applying demand load
220.82(B)
First 10,000 VA x 100%   = 10,000 VA
Next 40,200 VA x 40%   = 16,080 VA
Total load   **= 26,080 VA** •

COLUMN 2
LARGEST LOAD BETWEEN HEATING AND A/C LOAD

Step 5:   Selecting largest load
220.82(C)(1), (C)(2), and (C)(4)
Heating load
20,000 VA x 1 x 65%   = 13,000 VA
Heat pump
6000 VA x 1 x 100%   = 6,000 VA
Total load   **= 19,000 VA** •

TOTALING COLUMNS 1 AND 2
220.82(B) AND (C)

Column 1 load = 26,080 VA •
Column 2 load = 19,000 VA •
Total load   **= 45,080 VA**

FINDING AMPS FOR PHASES A AND B

I = VA ÷ V
I = 45,080 VA ÷ 240 V
I = 188 A

FINDING AMPS FOR NEUTRAL

I = VA ÷ V
I = 22,800 VA ÷ 240 V
I = 95 A

Note, the neutral load in VA and amps is calculated as shown in Design Problem 22-1 on page 22-19. See "Calculating neutral" and "Finding amps for neutral."

DESIGN PROBLEM 22-4: Can a 5040 VA combination air-conditioning unit heat pump be added to the existing dwelling unit without upgrading the service elements? (Service is rated 100 amps)

General lighting and receptacle load

• 1800 sq. ft dwelling unit
• 2 small-appliance circuits
• 1 laundry circuit

120 V, single-phase loads

•   900 VA disposal
• 1000 VA compactor
• 1200 VA dishwasher

240 V, single-phase loads

•   5000 VA dryer
• 12,000 VA range
•   5040 VA A/C unit and heat pump to be added

COLUMN 1
CALCULATING EXISTING LOADS

Step 1:   General lighting load
220.83(B)(1)
1800 sq. ft x 3 VA   = 5,400 VA

Step 2:   Small-appliance and laundry load
220.83(B)(2), 210.11(C)(1), and (C)(2)
1500 VA 2   = 3,000 VA
1500 VA x 1   = 1,500 VA

Step 3:   Existing load
220.83(B)(3)
Range load   = 12,000 VA
Dryer load   = 5,000 VA
Disposal load   =   900 VA
Compactor load   = 1,000 VA
Dishwasher load   = 1,200 VA
Total load   = **30,000 VA**

Step 4:   Applying demand load
220.83(B)
First   8000 VA x 100%   = 8,000 VA
Next 22,000 VA x 40%   = 8,800 VA
Total load   = **16,800 VA** •

COLUMN 2
ADDED LOAD

Step 5:   Calculating added load
220.83(B)
Fixed-appliance load
5040 VA x 100%   = 5,040 VA •

TOTALING COLUMNS 1 AND 2
220.83(B)(1) THRU (B)(3)

Column 1 load = 16,800 VA •
Column 2 load = 5,040 VA •
Total load   = **21,840 VA**

FINDING AMPS FOR PHASES A AND B

I = VA ÷ V
I = 21,840 VA ÷ 240 V
I = 91 A
Existing service   = 100 A
New calculated   = **91 A**

Note, if calculated load is less than service load, the new load can be added. Since 91 amps is less than the 100 amp service listed in Design Problem 22-4, the air-conditioning unit heat pump load of 5040 VA may be added to the existing service.

DESIGN PROBLEM 22-5: What is the load in VA and amps for 25 multifamily dwelling units with the following loads? **Note,** parallel service conductors, 6 times per phase.

General lighting and receptacle load
- 25 - 1000 sq. ft dwelling unit
- 2 small-appliance circuits per unit
- 1 laundry circuit per unit

120 V, single-phase loads
- 25 - 1000 VA dishwashers
- 25 - 1200 VA disposals

240 V, single-phase loads
- 25 - 12,000 VA ranges
- 25 -   6000 VA water heaters
- 25 - 20,000 VA heating units

Sizing phases = •
Sizing neutral = √

COLUMN 1
CALCULATING GENERAL LIGHTING AND RECEPTACLE LOAD

Step 1: General lighting and receptacle load
Table 220.12

1000 sq. ft x 3 VA x 25	= 75,000 VA

Step 2: Small-appliance and laundry load
220.52(A) and **(B)**

1500 VA x 2 x 25	= 75,000 VA
1500 VA x 1 x 25	= 37,500 VA
Total load	= 187,500 VA

Step 3: Applying demand factors
Demand load 1; **Table 220.42**

First 3000 VA x 100%	= 3,000 VA
Next 117,000 VA x 35%	= 40,950 VA
Remaining 67,500 VA x 25%	= 16,875 VA
Total load	= **60,825 VA** • √

COLUMN 2
CALCULATING COOKING EQUIPMENT LOAD

Step 1: Applying demand factors for phases A and B
Demand load 2; **Table 220.55, Column C**

25 - 12,000 VA ranges	= **40,000 VA** •

Step 2: Applying demand factors for neutral
220.61(B)(1)

40,000 VA x 70%	= **28,000 VA** √

COLUMN 2
CALCULATING FIXED APPLIANCE LOAD

Step 1: Applying demand factors for phases A and B
Demand load 4; **220.53**

1000 VA x 25 x 75%	= 18,750 VA
1200 VA x 25 x 75%	= 22,500 VA
6000 VA x 25 x 75%	= 112,500 VA
Total load	= **153,750 VA** •

Step 2: Applying demand factors for neutral
Demand load 4; **220.61(A)**

1000 VA x 25 x 75%	= 18,750 VA
1200 VA x 25 x 75%	= 22,500 VA
Total load	= **41,250 VA** √

COLUMN 3
LARGEST LOAD BETWEEN HEATING AND A/C LOAD

Step 1: Selecting largest load
Demand load 5; **220.60**
Heating unit

20,000 VA x 25 x 100%	= **500,000 VA** •

COLUMN 4
CALCULATING LARGEST MOTOR LOAD

Step 1: Selecting largest motor load for phases A and B
220.50 and **430.24**

1200 VA x 25%	= **300 VA** •

Step 2: Selecting largest motor load for neutral
220.50 and **430.24**

1200 VA x 25%	= **300 VA** √

CALCULATING PHASES A AND B (add all •)

• General lighting load	= 60,825 VA •
• Cooking load	= 40,000 VA •
• Appliance load	= 153,750 VA •
• Heating load	= 500,000 VA •
• Largest motor load	= 300 VA
Total load	= **754,875 VA**

CALCULATING NEUTRAL (add all √)

• General lighting load	= 60,825 VA √
• Cooking load	= 28,000 VA √
• Appliance load	= 41,250 VA √
• Largest motor load	= 300 VA √
Total load	= **130,375 VA**

FINDING AMPS FOR PHASES A AND B

I = VA ÷ V
I = 754,875 VA ÷ 240 V
I = 3145 A

FINDING AMPS FOR NEUTRAL

I = VA ÷ V
I = 130,375 VA ÷ 240 V
I = 543 A

FINDING SIZE CONDUCTORS IN PARALLEL FOR PHASES A AND B

Phases A and B
310.10(H)
I = 3145 ÷ 6 (No. runs per phase)
I = 524 A

Neutral (applying demand factors)
220.61(B)(2)

543 A
First 200 A x 100% = 200 A
Next 343 A x 70%   = 240 A
Total load   = **440 A**
310.10(H) and **250.24(C)(2)**

I = 440 A ÷ 6 (No. runs per phase)
I = 73 A

Table 310.15(B)(16)

Phases A and B
6 - 1000 KCMIL THWN copper conductors per phase
Neutral
6 - 1/0 AWG THWN copper conductors per phase

Note, the neutral conductor shall be 2/0 AWG per **250.24(C)(2).**
Column 1.

DESIGN PROBLEM 22-6: What is the load in VA and amps for 25 multifamily dwelling units with the following loads? (See standard calculation in Design Problem 22-5 for sizing the neutral.) **Note,** parallel service conductors, 6 times per phase.

General lighting and receptacle load

• 25 - 1000 sq. ft dwelling unit
• 2 small-appliance circuits per unit
• 1 laundry circuit per unit

120 V, single-phase loads

• 25 - 1000 VA dishwashers
• 25 - 1200 VA disposals

240 V, single-phase loads

• 25 - 12,000 VA ranges
• 25 - 6000 VA water heaters
• 25 - 20,000 VA heating units

Sizing phases = •

COLUMN 1
CALCULATING GENERAL LIGHTING AND RECEPTACLE LOAD

Step 1: General lighting and receptacle load
220.84(C)(1)
1000 sq. ft x 3 VA x 25 = 75,000 VA

Step 2: Small-appliance and laundry load
220.84(C)(2)
1500 VA x 2 x 25 = 75,000 VA
1500 VA x 1 x 25 = 37,500 VA
Total load = **187,500 VA** •

COLUMN 2
CALCULATING COOKING EQUIPMENT LOAD

Step 1: Applying demand factors for phases A and B
Demand load 2; **220.82(C)(3)**
12,000 VA x 25 = **300,000 VA** •

COLUMN 2
CALCULATING FIXED-APPLIANCE LOAD

Step 1: Applying demand factors for phases A and B
Demand load 4; **220.82(C)(3)**
1000 VA x 25 = 25,000 VA
1200 VA x 25 = 30,000 VA
6000 VA x 25 = 150,000 VA
Total load = **205,000 VA** •

COLUMN 3
LARGEST LOAD BETWEEN HEATING AND A/C LOAD

Step 1: Selecting largest load
Demand load 5; **220.82(C)(5)**
Heating unit
20,000 VA x 25 x 100% = **500,000 VA** •

CALCULATING PHASES

• General lighting load = 187,500 VA •
• Cooking load = 300,000 VA •
• Appliance load = 205,000 VA •
• Heating load = 500,000 VA •
Total load = **1,192,500 VA**

APPLYING DEMAND FACTORS
TABLE 220.84

$I = VA \div V$
$I = 1,192,500 \text{ VA} \div 240$
I = 4969

FINDING AMPS FOR PHASES A AND B
TABLE 220.84

$I = A \times \%$
$I = 4969 \times 35\%$
I = 1739

FINDING SIZE CONDUCTORS FOR PHASES A AND B

Phases A and B
310.10(H)
$I = 1739 \div 6$ (No. runs per phase)
I = 290 A

Table 310.15(B)(16)
Phases A and B
6 - 350 KCMIL THWN copper conductors

Note, the neutral in VA and amps is calculated as shown in Design Problem 22-5 on page 22-23. See "Calculating neutral," "Finding amps for neutral," .

DESIGN PROBLEM 22-7: What is the load in VA and amps for a mobile home with the following loads?

General lighting and receptacle load

Sizing phases = •
Sizing neutral = √

• 800 sq. ft dwelling unit
• 2 small-appliance circuits
• 1 laundry circuit
• 8500 VA range
• 6000 VA water heater
• 540 VA disposal
• 800 VA dishwasher
• 5500 VA heating

CALCULATING GENERAL LIGHTING AND RECEPTACLE LOAD

Step 1: General lighting and receptacle load
550.18(A)(1)
800 sq. ft x 3 VA = 2,400 VA

Step 2: Small-appliance and laundry load
550.18(A)(2) and (A)(3)
1500 VA x 2 = 3,000 VA
1500 VA x 1 = 1,500 VA
Total load = 6,900 VA

Step 3: Applying demand factor
550.18(A)(5)
First 3000 VA x 100% = 3,000 VA
Next 3900 VA x 35% = 1,365 VA
Total load = **4,365 VA** • √

CALCULATING SPECIAL-APPLIANCE LOAD

Step 1: Applying demand factors for phases A and B
550.18(B)(2), (B)(3), and (B)(4)
Water heater = 6,000 VA
Dishwasher = 800 VA √
Disposal = 540 VA √
Heating = 5,500 VA
Total load = **12,840 VA** •

CALCULATING RANGE LOAD

Step 1: Applying demand factor for phases A and B
550.18(B)(5)
8500 VA x 80% = **6,800 VA** •
6800 VA x 70% = **4,760 VA** √

CALCULATING LARGEST MOTOR LOAD

Step 1: Selecting largest motor load for phases A and B
550.18(B)(3)
540 VA x 25% = **135 VA** • √

CALCULATING LOAD FOR PHASES A AND B (add all •)

• General lighting load = 4,365 VA •
• Special-appliance load = 12,840 VA •
• Range load = 6,800 VA •
• Largest motor load = 135 VA •
Total load = **24,140 VA**

FINDING AMPS FOR PHASES A AND B

$I = VA \div V$
$I = 24{,}140 \text{ VA} \div 240 \text{ V}$
I = 101 A

CALCULATING NEUTRAL LOAD (add all √)

• General lighting load = 4,365 VA √
• Dishwasher load = 800 VA √
• Disposal load = 540 VA √
• Range = 4,760 VA √
• Largest motor = 135 VA √
Total load = **10,600 VA**

FINDING AMPS FOR NEUTRAL

$I = VA \div V$
$I = 10{,}600 \text{ VA} \div 240 \text{ V}$
I = 44 A

Finding size conductors for phases A and B
Table 310.15(B)(16)
Phases A and B
101 A requires 2 AWG THWN cu.
Neutral
44 A requires 8 AWG THWN cu.

310.15(B)(7)
Phases A and B
101 A requires 3 AWG THWN cu.
Neutral
44 A requires 8 AWG THWN cu.

DESIGN PROBLEM 22-8: What is the load in VA and amps for 28 mobile homes with the following loads?

Mobile homes

• 28 units
• 17,000 VA each based on calculated load

FINDING TOTAL VA LOAD

Step 1: Finding VA load
550.31
Mobile home = 17,000 VA

Step 2: Calculating VA load
550.31(2) and **Table 550.31**
17,000 VA x 28 x 24% **= 114,240 VA**

SIZING CONDUCTORS

Step 1: Finding VA for phases A and B
550.31
Total VA = 114,240 VA

Step 2: Calculating A for phases A and B
550.31
A = 114,240 VA ÷ 240 V
A = 476

Step 3: Selecting size conductors for phases A and B
Table 310.15(B)(16) and **310.10(H)**
Phases A and B (Parallel)
A = 476 ÷ 3 (No. runs per phase)
A = 158.7 (round up)
159 A requires 2/0 AWG THWN cu.

SIZING NEUTRAL BASED UPON CALCULATED LOAD

Step 1: Finding VA for neutral
550.31
Total VA = 114,240 VA

Step 2: Calculating A for neutral
550.31
A = 114,240 VA ÷ 240 V
A = 476

Step 3: Applying demand factors
220.61(B)
First 200 A x 100% = 200 A
Next 276 A x 70% = 193 A
Total load = 393 A

Step 4: Selecting conductors for phases A and B and neutral
Table 310.15(B)(16) and **310.10(H)**
Neutral (parallel)
A = 393 A ÷ 3 (No. runs per phase)
A = 131
131 A requires 1/0 AWG THWN cu.

SIZING ELEMENTS
DESIGN PROBLEM 22-1

Using the service amps of Design Problem 22-1 on page 22-19, size the elements of the following:

- Size THWN copper conductors per **Table 310.15(B)(16)**
- Size overcurrent protection device
- Size panelboard
- Size conduit using rigid metal conduit
- Size grounding electrode conductor (copper)
- Size supplementary ground
- Size grounded (neutral) conductor

SIZING THE CONDUCTORS FOR THE SERVICE PER TABLE 310.15(B)(16) AND 310.15(B)(7)

Step 1: Calculated loads
Phases = 223 A x 83% = 185 A
Neutral = 95 A

Step 2: Selecting conductors
Table 310.15(B)(16)
Phases = 223 A requires 4/0 AWG THWN cu.
Neutral = 95 A requires 3 AWG THWN cu.

Step 3: Applying **310.15(B)(7)**
Phases = 185 A requires 2/0 AWG THWN cu.
Neutral = 95 A requires 3 AWG THWN cu.

Solution: The ungrounded (phase) conductors are 2/0 AWG THWN copper conductors and the grounded (neutral) conductor is a 2 AWG copper conductor, per 250.24(C)(1).

Note, 4/0 AWG THWN copper conductors were selected based on Step 2 above and not Step 3.

SIZING THE OVERCURRENT PROTECTION DEVICE FOR THE SERVICE CONDUCTORS PER TABLE 310.15(B)(16) AND 110.14(C)(1) AND (C)(2)

Step 1: Amperage of load or conductor
240.4(A) thru (G) and **240.6(A)**
223 A requires 225 A OCPD

Solution: The size overcurrent protection device required is 225 amps.

SIZING THE PANELBOARD FOR SERVICE PER 240.4(A) THRU (G) AND 408.36

Step 1: Amperage of load or conductor
240.4(A) thru (G) and **240.6(A)**
185 A requires 200 A panelboard

Solution: The size panelboard required is 200 amps.

SIZING THE CONDUIT FOR THE SERVICE CONDUCTORS USING RIGID METAL CONDUIT PER TABLES 5 AND 4 TO CHAPTER 9

Step 1: Different size conductors (maximum size)
Table 5 and Table 4 to Chapter 9
3/0 AWG THWN
.2679 sq. in. x 2 = .5358
2 AWG THWN
.1158 sq. in. x 1 = .1158
Total sq. in. area = .6516

Step 2: Selecting size
Table 4 to **Chapter 9**
.6516 sq. in requires 1-1/2" (41) conduit

Solution: The size rigid metal conduit required is 1-1/2 in. (41).

SIZING THE GEC TO GROUND THE SERVICE TO A METAL WATER PIPE PER 250.6, TABLE 250.66, AND 250.102(C)(1)

Step 1: Size of ungrounded (phase) conductors (maximum size)
250.66 and **Table 250.66**
4/0 AWG THWN requires 2 AWG cu.

Solution: The size grounding electrode conductor required is 2 AWG cu.

SIZING THE GEC REQUIRED TO GROUND THE SERVICE TO A DRIVEN ROD TO SUPPLEMENT THE METAL WATER PIPE PER 250.53(D)(2), 250.104(A), AND 250.52(A)(1)

Step 1: Size of ungrounded (phase) conductors (maximum size)
250.66(A)
4/0 AWG THWN requires 6 AWG cu.

Solution: The size of the grounding electrode conductor is 6 AWG cu.

SIZING THE GROUNDED (NEUTRAL) CONDUC-TOR REQUIRED TO CLEAR A GROUND FAULT PER 220.61 AND 250.24(C)(1)

Step 1: Size of ungrounded (phase) conductors
250.24(C)(1), 220.61(B)(2), and **Table 250.102(C)(1)**
4/0 AWG requires 2 AWG cu.

Solution: The size grounded service conductor is required to be 2 AWG copper.

Note 1, the calculated grounded (neutral) per **220.61(B)(2),** under condition of use, many times produces the smaller grounded (neutral) conductor. However, such grounded (neutral) conductors shall be sized per **Table 250.102(C) (1)**, because it is used as a grounded (neutral) conductor and also as an effective path for fault current to travel over. See the neutral calculation of Design Problem 22-1 on Page 22-19.

Note 2, for selecting the proper size grounded (neutral) conductor to carry the amount of fault current that it might be called on to carry, see pages 11-15 through 11-18 of Chapter 11.

Note 3, for information on application of **310.15(B)(7),** see Figure 6-47 in this book.

Chapter 22. Residential Calculations

Section   Answer

1. The general lighting load for a dwelling unit shall be determined by multiplying the square footage by _______ VA.

   (a) 1   (b) 2
   (c) 3   (d) 3 1/2

2. All small appliance and laundry loads shall be calculated at _______ VA to determine the size feeder conductors and elements to size the service.

   (a) 1000   (b) 1500
   (c) 1800   (d) 2000

3. The VA rating for the overcurrent protection device for special appliance loads shall be calculated at 100 percent for noncontinuous duty and _______ percent for continuous duty, with demand loads determined by the kilowatt rating listed on the nameplate times a percentage.

   (a) 100   (b) 110
   (c) 115   (d) 125

4. For four or more fixed appliances that are grouped into a special appliance load can be found by adding wattage ratings from appliance nameplates and multiplying the total wattage (volt-amps) by _______ percent to obtain the demand load.

   (a) 75   (b) 80
   (c) 100   (d) 125

5. The demand load for household dryers shall be calculated at _______ kVA or the nameplate rating, whichever is greater.

   (a) 2   (b) 3
   (c) 4   (d) 5

6. The heating and A/C loads shall be calculated at _______ percent and the smaller of the two is dropped.

   (a) 75   (b) 100
   (c) 115   (d) 125

7. The optional calculation method shall only be permitted to be applied when an ampacity of at least _______ amps is applied to the service conductors.

   (a) 50   (b) 75
   (c) 100   (d) 175

8. When adding appliance loads for the optional calculation method, the total VA rating of the load shall be determined at _______ percent.

   (a) 50   (b) 70
   (c) 80   (d) 100

Section   **Answer**

9. The VA rating for the overcurrent protection device for special appliance loads shall be calculated at 125 percent for continuous duty and ______ percent for noncontinuous duty, if a demand factor shall not be applied based on a number.

(a) 100   (b) 115
(c) 125   (d) 150

10. The fixed appliance load for three or less fixed appliances shall be determined by adding wattage (volt-amps) values by ______ percent.

(a) 75   (b) 100
(c) 125   (d) 150

11. Dryer equipment of four or fewer units shall be calculated at ______ percent of the nameplate rating or 5000 VA, whichever is greater.

(a) 70   (b) 75
(c) 80   (d) 100

12. The largest motor load shall be calculated at ______ percent, for calculating the load of one or more motors with other loads.

(a) 50   (b) 100
(c) 125   (d) 150

13. The general lighting load for a dwelling unit shall be determined by multiplying the square footage by ______ VA.

(a) 1   (b) 2
(c) 3   (d) 4

14. At least two small appliance circuits shall be required to supply receptacle outlets located in the:

(a) kitchen   (b) pantry
(c) dining room   (d) all of the above

15. The demand load for four or more fixed appliances grouped into a special appliance load is found by adding wattage ratings from the appliance nameplates and multiplying the total wattage (volt-amps) by:

(a) 65 percent   (b) 75 percent
(c) 80 percent   (d) 100 percent

16. The demand load for a household dryer shall be calculated by the nameplate rating or ______ kVA, whichever is greater.

(a) 2   (b) 3
(c) 4   (d) 5

17. The heating and A/C load shall be calculated at ______ percent and the smaller of the two dropped.

(a) 80   (b) 100
(c) 125   (d) 150

Section   **Answer**

18. Dryer equipment shall be permitted to have a demand factor of ______ percent for 8 dryers.

    (a) 60   (b) 65
    (c) 70   (d) 75

19. A service supplying cooking equipment shall be permitted to have an additional demand factor of ______ percent.

    (a) 60   (b) 65
    (c) 70   (d) 75

20. Fixed electric space-heating loads shall be calculated at ______ percent of the total connected load.

    (a) 70   (b) 100
    (c) 115   (d) 125

21. All 120-volt, single-phase, 15 and 20 amp branch circuits supplying ______ and ______ installed in dwelling unit laundry areas shall be AFCI protected.

    (a) outlets   (b) devices
    (c) all of the above   (d) none of the above

22. The branch circuit wiring from a listed OCB type arc-fault circuit interrupter to the first outlet is ______ ft for a 12 AWG conductor.

    (a) 6   (b) 10
    (c) 25   (d) 70

23. All 120-volt, single-phase, 15 and 20 amp branch circuits supplying ______ and ______ installed in dwelling unit laundry areas shall be AFCI protected

    (a) outlets   (b) devices
    (c) all of the above   (d) none of the above

24. There is no longer a ______-derate required when sizing conductors involving continuous loads, adjustment, and correction factors.

    (a) triple   (b) 250%
    (c) all of the above   (d) none of the above

25. In no case shall the ______ of a branch circuit exceed the branch-circuit ampere rating.

    (a) voltage   (b) load
    (c) all of the above   (d) none of the above

26. At lease one 120-volt, single-phase, 15 or 20 amp rated receptacle outlet shall be installed within ______ ft of the service equipment for a commercial building.

    (a) 50   (b) 75
    (c) 100   (d) none of the above

Section   **Answer**

27. The positive polarity of a DC feeder conductor shall be identified by using the color _____.

    (a) white   (b) gray
    (c) black   (d) red

28. Where the building is designed and constructed to comply with a _____ code adopted by the AHJ, the lighting shall be permitted to be calculated per such code.

    (a) IEC   (b) energy
    (c) NEMA   (d) NECA

29. What is the general lighting and receptacle load in VA for a 50 ft x 50 ft dwelling unit?

30. What is the small appliance load in VA for 2 small appliance circuits and 1 laundry circuit?

31. What is the largest load between the heating and A/C load in VA of a 20 kW heating unit and a 6000 VA A/C unit?

32. What is the demand load in VA for a 9 kW range?

33. What is the demand load in VA for a 3-1/2 kW cooktop?

34. What is the demand load in VA for two 3-1/2 kW cooktops?

35. What is the demand load in VA for a 8-3/4 kW oven?

36. What is the demand load in VA for a 18 kW range? (Use **Note 1** to **Table 220.19**)

37. What is the demand load in VA for a 8 kW, 16 kW, and 24 kW range? (Use **Note 2** to **Table 220.19**)

38. What is the demand load in VA for a 8 kW and 10 kW oven and a 10 kW cooktop? (Use **Note 4** to **Table 220.19**)

39. What is the demand load for the fixed (special) appliance load in VA for a 6000 VA A/C unit, 20,000 VA heating unit, 5000 VA water heater, 10,000 VA oven, 8000 VA range, 1400 VA water pump, 1000 VA compactor, 800 VA blower motor, 1200 VA microwave, 900 VA disposal, and a 4500 VA dryer?

40. What is the demand load in VA for a 4500 VA dryer?

41. What is the demand load in VA for a 5500 VA dryer?

42. What is the demand load in VA for 6 dryers rated at 6000 VA?

43. What is the largest motor load in VA for a 5 HP, 230 volt, single-phase motor?

Section   Answer

44. What is the amp load for a 3000 sq. ft dwelling unit with a 240 volt, single-phase service with the following loads? (use the standard calculation)

- 2 small appliance circuits
- 1 laundry circuit
- 6,000 VA A/C unit   240 volt, single-phase
- 35,000 VA heating unit   240 volt, single-phase
- 5000 VA water heater   240 volt, single-phase
- 12,000 VA oven   240 volt, single-phase
- 9000 VA cooktop   240 volt, single-phase
- 5000 VA dryer   240 volt, single-phase
- 2400 VA sump pump   240 volt, single-phase
- 1000 VA pool pump   240 volt, single-phase
- 900 VA microwave   120 volt, single-phase
- 1600 VA dishwasher   120 volt, single-phase
- 1050 VA disposal   120 volt, single-phase
- 900 VA compactor   120 volt, single-phase

(a) What size (minimum and maximum) THWN copper conductors are required.

(b) What size overcurrent protection device based on calculated load is required.

(c) What size panelboard is required.

(d) What size RMC conduit is required.

(e) What size cu. grounding electrode conductor is required.

45. What is the amp load for a 3000 sq. ft dwelling unit with a 240 volt, single-phase service with the following loads? (use the optional calculation)

- 2 small appliance circuits
- 1 laundry circuit
- 6 000 VA A/C unit   240 volt, single-phase
- 35,000 VA heating unit   240 volt, single-phase
- 5000 VA water heater   240 volt, single-phase
- 12,000 VA oven   240 volt, single-phase
- 9000 VA cooktop   240 volt, single-phase
- 5000 VA dryer   240 volt, single-phase
- 2400 VA sump pump   240 volt, single-phase
- 1000 VA pool pump   240 volt, single-phase
- 900 VA microwave   120 volt, single-phase
- 1600 VA dishwasher   120 volt, single-phase
- 1050 VA disposal   120 volt, single-phase
- 900 VA compactor   120 volt, single-phase

(a) What size (max.) THWN copper conductors are required?

(b) What size overcurrent protection device based on calculated load is required?

(c) What size panelboard is required?

(d) What size RMC conduit is required?

(e) What size cu. grounding electrode conductor is required?

Note: Use the standard calculation to size the grounded (neutral) conductor. (See problem 36)

Section   **Answer**

_______________ _____________

46. From the following loads in an existing dwelling unit, determine if a 25 amp,   A/C unit load (calculated load) can be added to the service conductors. The existing service conductors are 3 AWG THWN copper conductors. (use the existing optional calculation)

- 2000 sq. ft dwelling unit
- 2 small appliance circuits
- 1 laundry circuit
- 11,000 VA range   240 volt, single-phase
-   5000 VA dryer   240 volt, single-phase
-   1200 VA compactor   120 volt, single-phase
-    800 VA disposal   120 volt, single-phase
-   1400 VA dishwasher 120 volt, single-phase

_______________ _____________

47. What is the amp load for 20-1000 sq. ft multifamily dwelling units with   a 240 volt, single-phase service with the following loads? (Use the standard calculation – parallel service conductors, six times per phase)

- 2 small appliance circuits
- 1 laundry circuit
- 20 - 11,000 VA ranges   240 volt, single-phase
- 20 -   5000 VA water heaters 240 volt, single-phase
- 20 - 25,000 VA heating units 240 volt, single-phase
- 20 -   1000 VA dishwashers 120 volt, single-phase
- 20 -   1200 VA disposals 120 volt, single-phase

_______________ _____________

48. What is the amp load for 20-1000 sq. ft multifamily dwelling units with a 240 volt, single-phase service with the following loads? (Use the optional calculation – parallel service conductors, six times per phase)

- 2 small appliance circuits
- 1 laundry circuit
- 20 - 11,000 VA ranges   240 volt, single-phase
- 20 -   5000 VA water heaters 240 volt, single-phase
- 20 - 25,000 VA heating units 240 volt, single-phase
- 20 -   1000 VA dishwashers 120 volt, single-phase
- 20 -   1200 VA disposals 120 volt, single-phase

_______________ _____________

49. What is the amp load for a 1000 sq. ft mobile home with a 240 volt, single-phase service with the following loads?

- 2 small appliance circuits
- 1 laundry circuit
- 8500 VA range   240 volt, single-phase
- 5500 VA water heater 240 volt, single-phase
-   600 VA disposal   120 volt, single-phase
-   800 VA dishwasher 120 volt, single-phase
- 6000 VA heating unit   240 volt, single-phase

_______________ _____________

50. What is the amp load for 26 mobile homes with following loads?
- 26 units
- 15,000 VA each based on calculated load
- Per **550.18** in the NEC

23

Commercial Calculations

Commercial facilities such as offices, banks, stores, and restaurants have diverse loads. These loads are classified as continuous or noncontinuous, or such loads may cycle on and off, allowing demand factors to be applied.

The procedure and manner in which the lighting, receptacle, and equipment loads are used in the electrical system determines how they are classified.

Loads shall be calculated based on the type of occupancy and the requirements of the equipment supplied. Either the standard or optional calculation is utilized to calculate the loads in volt-amps or amps to size the service equipment and associated elements.

APPLYING THE STANDARD CALCULATION
ARTICLE 220, PART III

The standard calculation may be used to calculate the VA or amp rating in order to size and select the elements of the service equipment and associated components. The selection of loads for applying the standard calculation is arranged in a different manner for commercial loads than it is for loads used in residential occupancies. There are seven loads utilized to determine the service load. Based upon conditions of use, demand factors shall be permitted to be applied to certain loads, which reduces the VA or amps.

The loads are grouped into seven individual loads, and the proper *National Electrical Code* rule is applied to each of these loads based on use. The loads are grouped and classified as follows:

(1) Lighting loads
- General lighting load per **220.12**
- Show window load per **220.43(A)**
- Track lighting load per **220.43(B)**
- Low-voltage lighting load per **Article 411**
- Outside lighting load per **230.42(A)(1)** and **(A)(2)**
- Outside sign lighting load per **220.14(F)**

(2) Receptacle loads
- General-purpose receptacle load [Noncontinuous per **220.14(I)**, **Table 220.44**, and **230.42(A)(1)** and **(A)(2)**]
- General-purpose receptacle load [Calculated per **220.14(I)**, **230.42(A)(1)**, **(A)(2)**, and **Table 220.44**]
- Multioutlet assembly load [Used simultaneously per **220.14(H)(2)**] [Not used simultaneously per **220.14(H)(1)**]

(3) Special-appliance loads
- Noncontinuous load per **230.42(A)(1)** and **220.14(A)**
- Continuous load per **230.42(A)(1)**
- Demand factor per various Sections of the NEC

(4) Compressor loads
- Refrigeration per **440.34** and **230.42(A)(1)**
- Cooling per **440.34** and **230.42(A)(1)**

(5) Motor loads
- Single-phase per **430.25**
- Three-phase per **430.25**

(6) Heat or air-conditioning loads
- Heating per **220.51**
- Air conditioning per **440.34**
- Heat pump per **440.34**

(7) Largest motor loads
- Taken from loads (4), (5), or (6) per **220.50**

The seven loads shall be calculated at continuous operation or noncontinuous operation. Demand factors shall be applied to the noncontinuous operated loads by specific Sections of the NEC.

Generally, no demand factors shall be permitted to be applied to the loads for commercial occupancies, as the loads are usually used at continuous operation. However, **Table 220.42** permits the general lighting loads in hospitals, hotels, motels, and warehouses to have demand factors applied because of load diversity.

LIGHTING LOADS
ARTICLES 220, 410, AND 411

Lighting loads are the first of the loads to be calculated. Six lighting loads shall be calculated to derive the total lighting load in commercial facilities. These six loads are as follows:

- General lighting loads per **Table 220.12**
- Show window loads per **220.43(A)**
- Lighting track loads per **220.43(B)**
- Low-voltage lighting per **Article 411**
- Outside lighting load per **230.42(A)(1)** and **(A)(2)**
- Sign lighting load per **220.14(F)**

Each lighting load shall be calculated by the operation in which it is used. Loads shall be calculated at continuous or noncontinuous operation, and other lighting loads shall be permitted to have demand factors applied, where permitted by the NEC. Also, see IC 90.1 – Energy Code.

GENERAL LIGHTING LOADS
220.12, TABLE 220.12, AND IC 90.1

General lighting loads consist of lighting units installed inside the facility. This load shall be calculated by the VA rating times sq. ft from **Table 220.12** based on the type of commercial occupancy.

The general lighting load found in listed occupancies is calculated according to the number of VA per sq. ft and not based on the number of outlets served. When fluorescent lighting is used, either the area load of VA per sq. ft of the facility or the total connected load of each ballast is used, whichever is greater in rating.

For lighting loads, either the VA per sq. ft or individual units shall be calculated at 100 percent for noncontinuous operation or at 125 percent for continuous operation.

For example: A noncontinuous lighting load of 60 amps and a continuous load of 100 amps is calculated as follows:

Step 1: Calculating load
230.42(A)(1)
60 A x 100% = 60 A
100 A x 125% = 125 A
Total load   = 185 A

Solution: The calculated load for the lighting is 185 amps.

NONCONTINUOUS AND CONTINUOUS OPERATION
230.208(B), 230.42(A)(1), AND (A)(2)

The requirements for derating the overcurrent protection device by 80 percent for continuous operation is no longer found in 384-16(d), as it was in the 1999 NEC. For overcurrent protection devices rated over 1000 volts, the rules are listed in **230.208(B)**, and under certain conditions the 80 percent derating rule does not apply. For feeders rated over 1000 volts, see **215.2(B)**.

To apply the 80 percent derating rule for loads rated at 600 volts or less, **230.42(A)(1)** requires such loads to be calculated at 125 percent (1 ÷ 80% = 1.25) if they operate for three hours or more. Loads operating for a period of less than three hours shall be calculated at 100 percent per **230.42(A)(1)**. The ampacity of the conductors as well as the overcurrent protection device shall be calculated and sized at 125 percent and 100 percent or a combination of both based on the operation of such loads. [For feeders, see **215.2(A)(1)(a)** and **(b)**.]

Section **230.90(A)** with **Ex.s** refers to various Sections of the NEC to calculate the size of overcurrent protection devices. Loads that are not motor related shall be calculated based upon their operation procedures, which are listed in **230.42(A)(1)** and **(A)(2)**. **(See Figure 23-1)**

LISTED OCCUPANCIES
220.12 AND TABLE 220.12

Table 220.12 is used to select the VA rating for listed occupancies.

> **For example,** a store building shall be calculated at 3 VA per sq. ft and an office building shall be calculated at 3.5 VA per sq. ft. Other types of occupancies have different VA ratings per sq. ft based on the type of occupancy involved.

For example: What is the load in VA for the general-purpose lighting load in an 8000 sq. ft office per **Table 220.12**?

    Step 1: Calculating load
    Table 220.12
    8000 sq. ft x 3.5 = 28,000 VA

    Solution: The general-purpose lighting load is 28,000 VA. Note, if the number of receptacle outlets is not known, an extra 1 VA per sq. ft shall be added to the above.

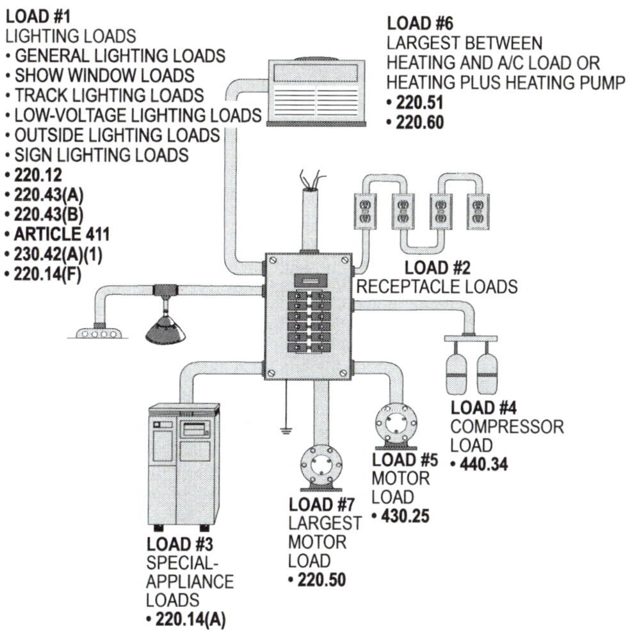

Figure 23-1. As outlined, there are seven loads to be calculated when applying the standard calculation to determine the service load in VA or amps. (For the Energy Code requirements, see the **Ex.** to **220.12**.)

See Figure 23-2 for a detailed illustration of calculating the lighting load for a listed occupancy.

UNLISTED OCCUPANCY
220.18, 220.14(D), AND (L)

If an occupancy is not listed in **Table 220.12**, the general-purpose lighting load shall be calculated in the following manner.

- Lamps for incandescent lighting per **220.14(L)**
- Lamps for recessed luminaires per **220.14(D)**
- Ballasts for electric discharge lighting per **220.18(B)**
- Show lighting units per **220.43(A)**
- Track lighting unit per **220.43(B)**
- Low-voltage systems per **Article 411**
- Energy Code IC 90.1 per **220.12, Ex.**

An unlisted VA rating shall be calculated at 125 percent for sizing the overcurrent protection device and conductors for continuous operation and at 100 percent for noncontinuous operated loads per **230.42(A)(1)**.

For example: What is the load in VA for 60, 120 volt, lighting ballasts rated at 1.5 amps each and used for 12 hours a day?

Step 1: Calculating load in A
220.18(B)
60 x 1.5 A = 90 A

Step 2: Calculating continuous load
230.42(A)(1)
90 A x 125% = 112.5 A

Step 3: Calculated VA
112.5 A x 120 V = 13,500 VA

Solution: The lighting load for the unlisted occupancy is 13,500 VA.

See **Figure 23-3** for a detailed illustration of calculating the lighting load for an unlisted occupancy.

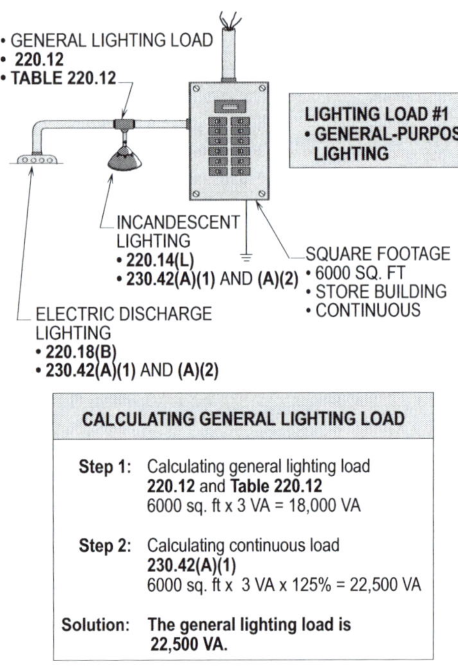

Figure 23-2. The general lighting load (listed occupancy) shall be calculated by multiplying the sq. ft of the facility by the VA per sq. ft times 125% (if continuous) per **Table 220.12** and **230.42(A)(1)**.

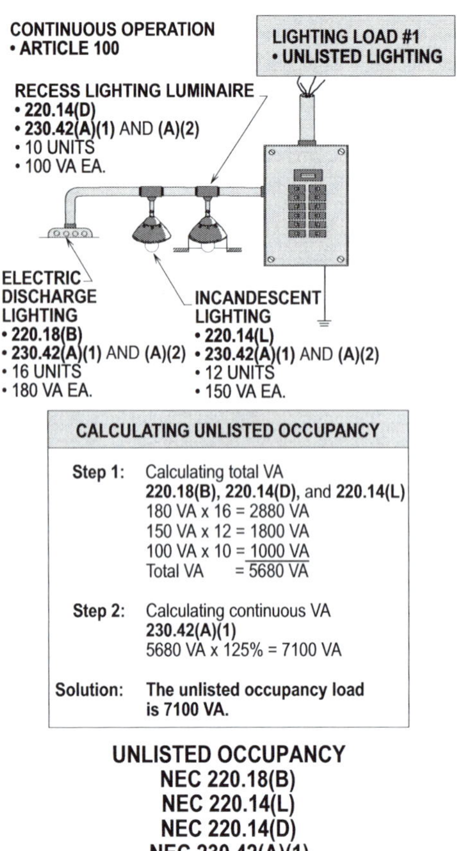

Figure 23-3. The unlisted lighting load shall be permitted to be calculated by multiplying the VA of each lighting load by the number and increasing this value by 125 percent if used for three hours or more.

SHOW WINDOW LIGHTING LOAD 220.43(A)

The lighting load in VA for the show window shall be calculated by multiplying the linear feet of the show window by 200 VA per foot. Such lighting load shall be calculated at 100 percent for noncontinuous operation and at 125 percent for continuous operation per **230.42(A)(1)**. Conductors and overcurrent protection devices shall be increased to comply with **240.3** and **240.4**.

Note 1: Raceways supplying lighting outlets, units, receptacle outlets, multicount assemblies, etc. are EMT runs.

Note 2: For application of the energy code, see NEC **220.12, Ex.** and IC 90.1 (See Figure 23-21)

For example: What is the lighting load in VA for a 80 ft show window used at noncontinuous or continuous operation?

Step 1: Calculating noncontinuous load
220.43(A) and **230.42(A)(1)**
80' x 200 VA x 100% = 16,000 VA

Step 2: Calculating continuous load
220.43(A) and **230.42(A)(1)**
80' x 200 VA x 125% = 20,000 VA

Solution: The noncontinuous load is 16,000 VA and the continuous load is 20,000 VA.

If the number of lighting outlets is known, the VA rating of each luminaire shall be multiplied by 125 percent for sizing the show window load. If the VA is not known, each outlet shall be calculated at 180 VA times 125 percent to obtain the lighting load in VA for the show window.

Note, the greater of either the 200 VA per linear foot or each individual unit calculation shall be used.

See Figure 23-4 for a detailed illustration of calculating the show window lighting load.

TRACK LIGHTING LOAD
220.43(B)

The lighting load in VA for track lighting shall be calculated by multiplying the track lighting by 150 VA and dividing by 2. Such VA rating shall be multiplied by 100 percent or 125 percent based on noncontinuous or continuous operation.

For example: What is the load in VA for 80 ft of lighting track used at noncontinuous or continuous operation?

Step 1: Calculating noncontinuous load
220.43(B) and **230.42(A)(1)**
80' ÷ 2' x 150 VA x 100% = 6000 VA

Step 2: Calculating continuous load
220.43(B) and **230.42(A)(1)**
80' ÷ 2' x 150 VA x 125% = 7500 VA

Solution: The noncontinuous load is 6000 VA and the continuous load is 7500 VA.

See Figure 23-5 for a detailed illustration of calculating the track lighting load.

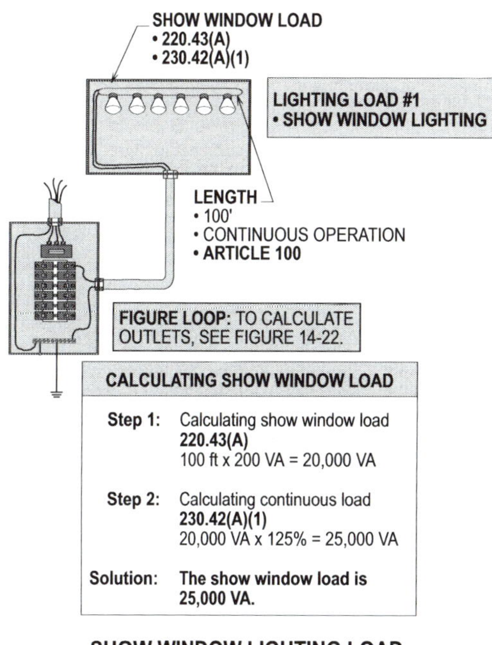

Figure 23-4. The show window load shall be calculated by multiplying the linear feet by 200 VA. This value shall be increased by 125 percent since such load is continuous.

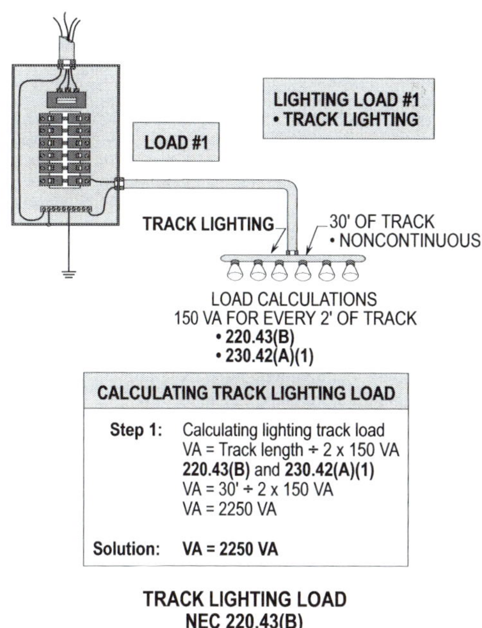

Figure 23-5. The track lighting load shall be calculated by dividing the length of the track by 2 and multiplying by 150 VA. This value shall be increased by 125 percent if it is used for three hours or more.

LOW-VOLTAGE LIGHTING LOAD
ARTICLE 411, 230.42(A)(1), AND (A)(2)

The lighting load in VA for low-voltage lighting systems shall be calculated by multiplying the FLA of the isolation transformer by 100 percent for noncontinuous operation and by 125 percent for continuous operation.

For example: What is the load in VA for a low-voltage lighting system supplied by an isolation transformer with a FLA of 50 amps used at noncontinuous or continuous operation?

Step 1: Calculating noncontinuous load
Article 411 and **230.42(A)(1)**
50 A x 100% = 50 A

Step 2: Calculating continuous load
Article 411 and **230.42(A)(1)**
50 A x 125% = 62.5 A

Solution: The noncontinuous load is 50 amps and the continuous load is 62.5 amps.

See Figure 23-6 for a detailed illustration of calculating the low-voltage lighting load.

OUTSIDE LIGHTING LOAD
220.18(B), 230.42(A)(1), AND (A)(2)

The lighting load in VA for outside lighting loads shall be calculated by multiplying the VA rating of each lighting unit by 100 percent for noncontinuous operation and by 125 percent for continuous operation.

For example: What is the lighting load in VA for 30 continuously operated luminaires with a 75 VA ballast in each unit and for 10 noncontinuously operated luminaires with each ballast having a rating of 75 VA?

Step 1: Calculating load
220.18(B) and **230.42(A)(1)**
75 x 30 x 125%   = 2812.5 VA
75 x 10 x 100%   =   750   VA
Total load   = 3562.5 VA

Solution: The total outside lighting load is 3562.5 VA.

See Figure 23-7 for a detailed illustration for calculating the outside lighting load at continuous operation.

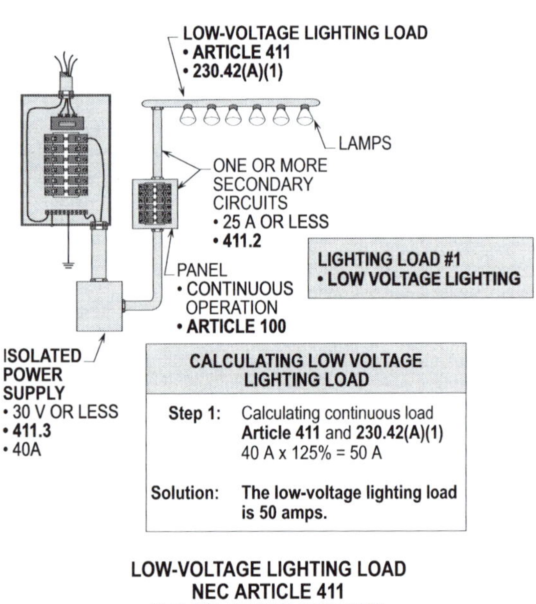

Figure 23-6. The low-voltage lighting load shall be calculated by multiplying the FLA of the isolation transformer by 125 percent if used for three hours or more.

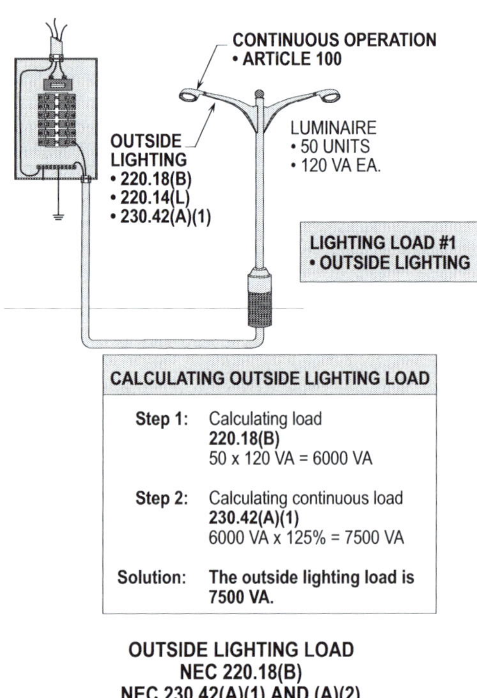

Figure 23-7. The outside lighting load shall be calculated by multiplying the number of ballasts by 125 percent if the load operates for three hours or more.

OUTSIDE SIGN LIGHTING LOAD
220.14(F), 230.42(A)(1), AND (A)(2)

The lighting loads for signs shall be calculated according to the ground floor footage accessible to pedestrians in a commercial occupancy or facility. Occupancies with grade level access for pedestrians shall have a minimum of 1200 VA provided for a sign lighting load. This VA rating shall be multiplied by 125 percent for signs operating for three hours or more and by 100 percent for those operating less than three hours.

See Figure 23-8 for a detailed illustration for calculating the outside sign lighting load.

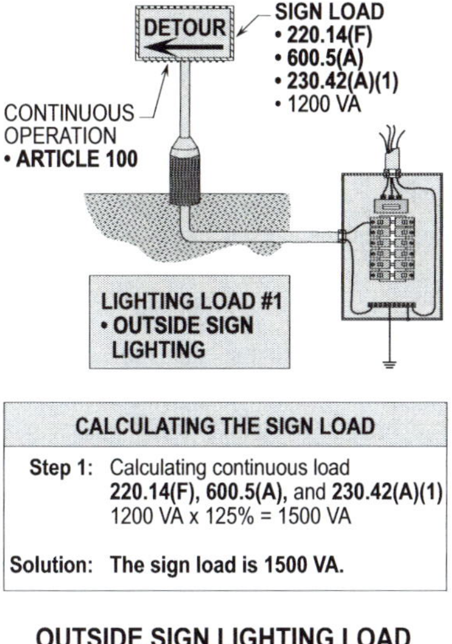

Figure 23-8. The outside sign lighting load shall be calculated by multiplying the VA of the sum by 125 percent if it operates for three hours or more.

RECEPTACLE LOADS
220.14(I) AND TABLE 220.44

Receptacle loads are the second group of loads to be calculated. Such loads are divided into two subgroups as follows:

- General-purpose receptacle outlets
- Multioutlet assemblies

Each load in the subgroup shall be calculated differently to derive total VA. The load in VA for the general-purpose receptacle load shall be calculated by multiplying the number of outlets times 180 VA each, times 100 percent for noncontinuous operation, and times 125 percent for continuous operation.

For example: What is the load in VA for 48 general-purpose receptacles used to serve noncontinuous and continuous related loads?

Step 1: Calculating noncontinuous load
220.14(I) and **230.42(A)(1)**
180 VA x 48 x 100% = 8640 VA

Step 2: Calculating continuous load
220.14(I) and **230.42(A)(1)**
180 VA x 48 x 125% = 10,800 VA

Solution: **The noncontinuous load is 8640 VA and the continuous load is 10,800 VA.**

See Figure 23-9 for a detailed illustration for calculating the general-purpose receptacle load.

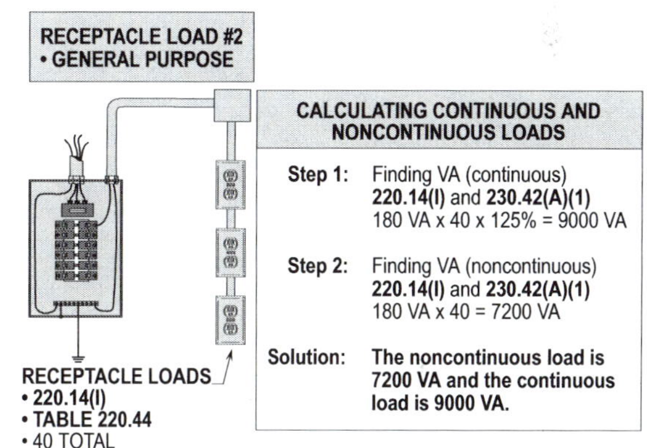

Figure 23-9. The general-purpose receptacle load shall be calculated by multiplying the VA rating of each receptacle by the number and increasing this value by 125 percent if used for three hours or more.

APPLYING DEMAND FACTORS
220.14(I) AND TABLE 220.44

General-purpose receptacle outlets for cord-and-plug connected loads used at noncontinuous operation are calculated per **220.14(I)** and **Table 220.44**. Noncontinuous operated receptacles with a VA rating of 10,000 VA or less shall be calculated at 100 percent. If the VA rating of the receptacle load exceeds 10,000 VA, a demand factor of 50 percent shall be permitted to be applied to all VA exceeding 10,000 VA per **Table 220.44**.

For example: What is the VA rating for 125 general-purpose receptacle outlets to cord-and-plug connect loads used at noncontinuous operation?

Step 1: Calculating load
220.14(I) and **230.42(A)(1)**
125 x 180 VA = 22,500 VA

Step 2: Applying demand factors
Table 220.44
First 10,000 VA x 100%   = 10,000 VA
Next 12,500 VA x 50%   =   6,250 VA
Total load   = 16,250 VA

Solution: The demand load is 16,250 VA.

See **Figure 23-10(a)** for a detailed illustration for calculating the (noncontinuous) receptacle demand load.

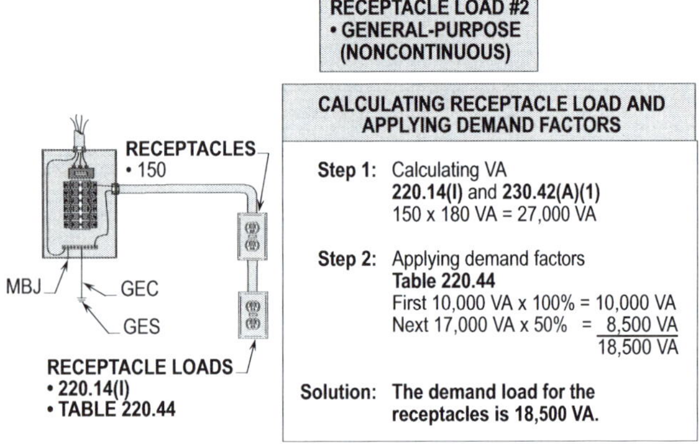

Figure 23-10(a). The demand load for general-purpose receptacles (noncontinuous) shall be calculated by taking the first 10,000 VA at 100 percent and all remaining VA above 10,000 VA at 50 percent.

MULTIOUTLET ASSEMBLIES
220.14(H)(1) AND (H)(2)

For connected loads not operating simultaneously, the VA rating shall be calculated by dividing the length of the assembly by 5 ft and multiplying by 180 VA. For connected loads operating simultaneously, each foot of multioutlet assembly is multiplied by 180 VA. The fixed multioutlet assembly load shall be permitted to be added to the noncontinuous receptacle load and demand factors applied per **Table 220.44**.

For example: What is the load in VA for 100 ft of multioutlet assembly used to cord-and-plug connect loads that are not used simultaneously and used simultaneously? [**220.14(H)(1)**]

Step 1: Connecting load for
nonsimultaneous use
220.14(A)(1)
VA = length ÷ 5' x 180 VA
VA = 100' ÷ 5' x 180 VA
VA = 3600

Step 2: Calculating load for simultaneous
use
220.14(A)(2)
VA = length x 1' x 180 VA
VA = 100' x 1' x 180 VA
VA = 18,000

**Solution: The load in VA for the
nonsimultaneous load is
3600 VA and for the simultaneous
load is 18,000 VA.**

See **Figures 23-10(b)** and **(c)** for detailed illustrations for calculating the multioutlet assembly load.

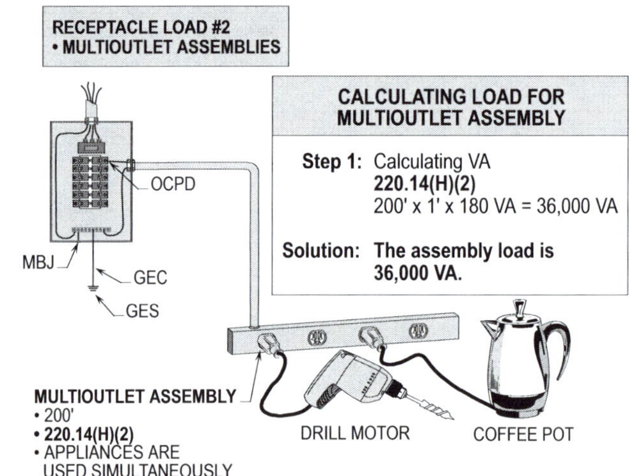

Figure 23-10(b). The multioutlet assembly load shall be calculated by multiplying the total length of the assembly (each 1 ft) by 180 VA where appliances are likely to be used simultaneously.

SPECIAL-APPLIANCE LOADS
220.14(A), 230.42(A)(1), AND (A)(2)

Special-appliance loads are the third group of loads to be calculated. These loads, which include calculators, processing machines, etc., are usually served by individual circuits.

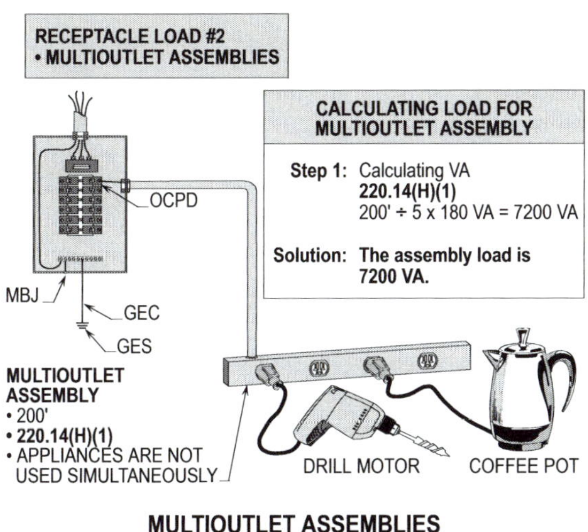

MULTIOUTLET ASSEMBLIES
NEC 220.14(H)(1)

Figure 23-10(c). The multioutlet assembly load shall be calculated by multiplying the total length of the assembly by 180 VA and dividing by 5 where appliances are not likely to be used simultaneously.

CONTINUOUS AND NONCONTINUOUS OPERATION
230.42(A)(1) AND (A)(2)

The load in VA for special-appliance loads shall be calculated by multiplying the VA rating of each load by 100 percent for noncontinuous operation and by 125 percent for continuous operation. To determine classification, special-appliance loads operating for less than three hours shall be classified as a noncontinuous operated load. However, a special -appliance load operating for three hours or more shall be classified as continuous operated load.

For example: What is the VA rating for a 208 volt, three-phase, 65 amp special-appliance load operating for 10 hours and supplied by an individual branch circuit?

Step 1: Calculating VA
220.5(A)
VA = V x 1.732 (360 V) x I
VA = (208 V x 1.732) x 65
VA = 23,400

Step 2: Calculating continuous load
230.42(A)(1)
23,400 VA x 125% = 29,250 VA

Solution: The load at continuous operation is 29,250 VA.

For example: Consider and calculate the VA rating for a special-appliance load of 52 amps operating at 480 volts, three-phase, for a period of 2-1/2 hours every four hours.

Step 1: Calculating VA
220.5(A)
VA = V x 1.732 (831 V) x I
VA = (480 V x 1.732) x 52 A
VA = 43,212

Step 2: Calculating noncontinuous load
230.42(A)(1)
43,212 VA x 100% = 43,212 VA

Solution: The load in VA for the noncontinuous load is 43,212 VA.

See Figure 23-11 for a detailed illustration for calculating the VA of a continuous special-appliance load.

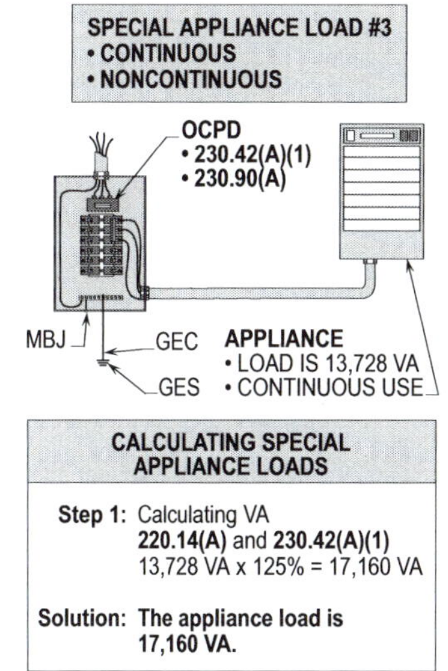

CONTINUOUS AND NONCONTINUOUS OPERATION
NEC 230.42(A)(1) AND (A)(2)

Figure 23-11. The appliance load shall be calculated by multiplying the VA of the appliance by 125 percent if used for three hours or more.

APPLYING DEMAND FACTORS
TABLE 220.56

Demand factors shall be permitted to be applied to cooking equipment in restaurants with three or more cooking units. The load in VA for cooking equipment shall be permitted to be calculated by applying the optional calculation listed in **Table 220.56**.

For example: What is the demand load in amps for 10 - 208 volt, three-phase cooking units rated 8 kW each?

Step 1: Calculating VA
220.56
8 kW x 10 = 80 kW

Step 2: Calculating amps
220.5(A)
I = (kW x 1000) ÷ (V x 1.732)
I = (80 kW x 1000) ÷ (208 V x 1.732)
I = 222 A

Step 3: Applying demand factors
Table 220.56
222 A x 65% = 144.3 A

Solution: The demand load is 144.3 A.

See Figure 23-12 for a detailed illustration for calculating demand loads for certain types of equipment.

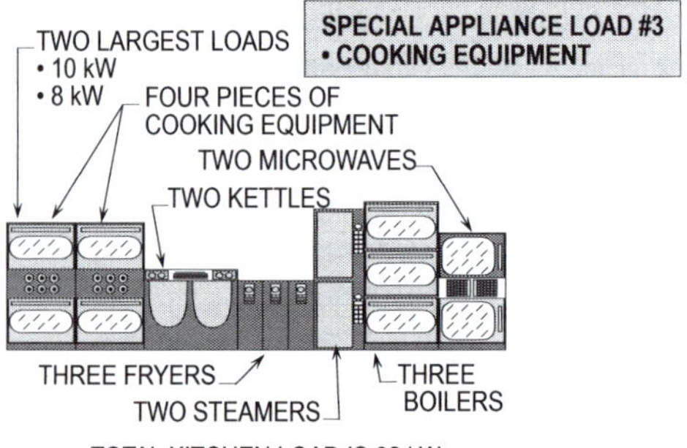

CALCULATING LOAD FOR COOKING EQUIPMENT

Step 1: Calculating percentage
Table 220.56
16 pieces allowed 65%

Step 2: Applying demand factors
Table 220.56 and 220.56
82 kW x 65% = 53.3 kVA

Solution: The demand load of 53.3 kVA is greater than the two largest loads of 18 kVA.

APPLYING DEMAND FACTORS
NEC 220.56
NEC TABLE 220.56

Figure 23-12. The demand load shall be calculated based on the number and the percentage per **Table 220.56**.

COMPRESSOR LOADS
440.34

Compressor loads are the fourth group of loads to be calculated. Special considerations shall be applied when calculating loads for hermetically sealed compressors supplying refrigerant and cooling related equipment.

CONTINUOUS OR NONCONTINUOUS OPERATION
440.34, 230.42(A)(1), AND 215.2(A)(1)(a)

Compressor-related equipment shall be calculated at 100 percent of their VA or amps. If one of such is the largest motor per load #7, it is added to the total calculation of all loads at 125 percent of its FLA rating.

For example: What is the load in VA for 5 compressors rated at 26.5 amps each and supplied by a 480 volt, three-phase supply?

Step 1: Calculating VA
220.5(A) and **440.34**
26.5 A x 480 V x 1.732 = 22,031 VA
22,031 VA x 5 = 110,155 VA

Step 2: Calculating continuous load
230.42(A)(1), 215.2(A)(1)(a) and **440.34**
Largest motor
26.5 A x 480 V x 1.732 = 22,031 VA
22,031 VA x 25% = 5508 VA
22,031 + 5508 VA = 27,539 VA

Solution: The continuous load rating is 27,539 VA.

See Figure 23-13 for a detailed illustration for calculating compressor related loads.

MOTOR LOADS
220.50 AND 430.24

Motor loads are the fifth group of loads to be calculated. The VA rating of motors is converted from FLA to VA by multiplying the FLA from **Table 430.248** for single-phase or **Table 430.250** for three-phase by the supply voltage.

Design Tip: Motors can be used as a single unit to drive a piece of equipment. Motors used in an approved assembly such as a processing machine are not usually considered individual motor loads.

For example: What is the VA rating for a group of 480 volt, three-phase motors rated at 30 HP, 20 HP, and 15 HP, respectively?

Step 1: Finding FLA
Table 430.250
30 HP = 40 A
20 HP = 27 A
15 HP = 21 A

Step 2: Calculating total VA (using 831 V)
220.5(A)
VA = (V x 1.732) x I
30 HP
(480 V x 1.732) x 40 A = 33,240 VA
20 HP
(480 V x 1.732) x 27 A = 22,437 VA
15 HP
(480 V x 1.732) x 21 A = 17,451 VA
Total VA   = 73,128 VA

Solution: The total load for the motors is 73,128 VA.

See **Figure 23-14** for a detailed illustration for calculating individual motor loads.

HEATING OR AIR-CONDITIONING LOADS 220.60

Heating or air-conditioning loads are the sixth group of loads to be calculated. The largest VA rating between the heating or air-conditioning load shall be selected, and the smaller of the two loads is dropped. To determine the largest of the two loads, the VA rating of each load shall be calculated at 100 percent and the largest load of the two is selected. The load dropped is not used again in the calculation. **(See Figure 23-15)**

Design Tip: There is no need to calculate both loads to select the elements of the service equipment, for the loads are never used simultaneously in the electrical system.

Note 1: For one and two family dwellings, see **Figure 22-16.**

Note 2: An attic fan or any dissimilar load can be dropped in the calculation.

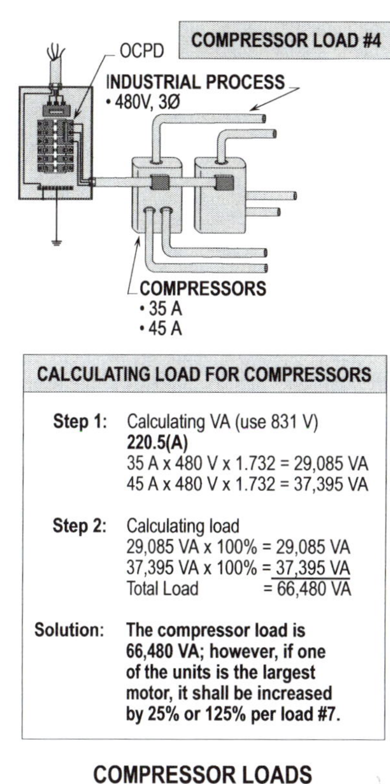

Figure 23-13. The compressor load shall be calculated at 100 percent for each compressor, and if one of such is the largest motor, it shall be increased by 25 percent (or 125 percent) and added to the other loads.

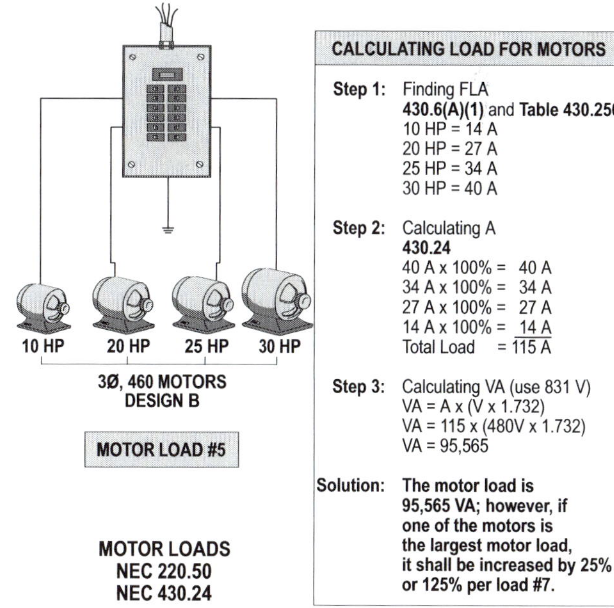

Figure 23-14. The motor load shall be calculated at 100 percent for each motor, and if one of such is the largest motor load, it shall be increased by 25 percent (or 125 percent) and added to the other loads.

For example: What is the largest load between a 30 kW heating unit and a 32.5 amp air-conditioning unit? The voltage is supplied by a 208 volt, three-phase system.

Step 1: Selecting largest load (using 360 V)
220.60
Heating load
30 kW x 1000 x 100% = **30,000 VA**
A/C load
(208 V x 1.732) x 32.5 A = **11,700 VA**

Solution: The 30,000 VA heating unit is the largest load.

See **Figure 23-15** for a detailed illustration for calculating the largest VA rating between the heating and air-conditioning load.

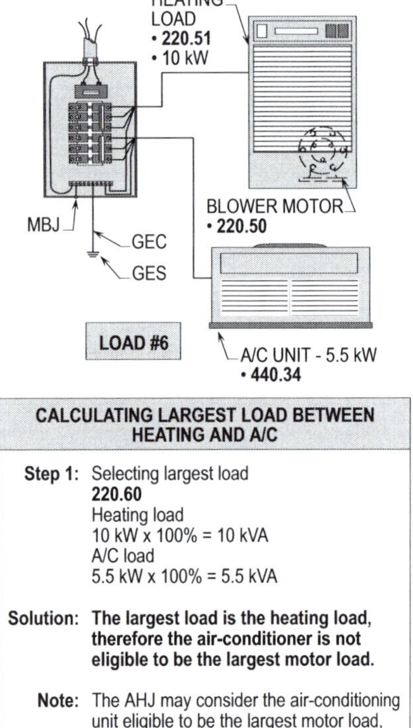

Figure 23-15. The largest load between the heating and air-conditioning unit in VA shall be selected, and the smaller load dropped. (For dwellings units, see **Figure 22-16**.)

LARGEST MOTOR LOAD
220.50 AND 430.24

The largest motor load in VA is the seventh of the loads to be calculated. The largest motor load shall be selected from one of the motor related loads listed in the fourth, fifth, or sixth loads. The VA rating of the largest motor shall be calculated by multiplying the amperage of the unit by the voltage times 25 percent or 125% per **430.24**.

For example: What is the largest motor from the following loads?
Fourth load = compressor of 35 A
Fifth load   = motor of **40 A**
Sixth load   = A/C unit   = 30 A
(larger than the gas heating)

Step 1: Selecting largest load
220.50, 440.34, and **430.24**
The motor load of 40 A is the largest load

Solution: The largest motor load is 40 amps.

See **Figure 23-16** for a detailed illustration of calculating the largest motor load in amps.

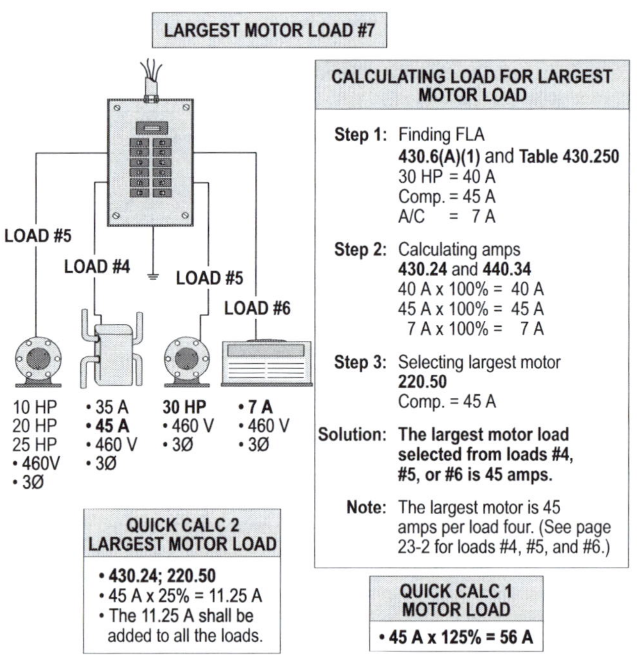

Figure 23-16. The largest motor load is the largest between the compressor loads, air-conditioning unit loads, where eligible, or the motor loads, whichever is greater.

APPLYING THE OPTIONAL CALCULATION
ARTICLE 220, PART IV

The load in VA and amps may be calculated by the optional calculation instead of the standard calculation. The optional calculation is based upon specific use of the electrical system or type of occupancy and its use and operation.

KITCHEN EQUIPMENT
220.56 AND TABLE 220.56

Table 220.56 shall be permitted to be used for load calculation for commercial electrical cooking equipment, such as dishwashers, booster heaters, water heaters, and other kitchen equipment. The demand factors shown in the Table are applicable to all equipment that is thermostatically controlled or is only intermittently used as part of the kitchen equipment. In no way do the demand factors apply to the electric heating, ventilating, or air-conditioning equipment. In calculating the demand, the demand load shall not be permitted to be less than the sum of the two largest kitchen equipment loads. **(See Figure 23-12)**

SCHOOLS
220.86 AND TABLE 220.86

Table 220.86 shall be permitted to be used to calculate the service or feeder loads for schools if they are equipped with electric space heating, air conditioning, or both. The demand factors in **Table 220.86** apply to both interior and exterior lighting, power, water heating, cooking, or other loads, and the larger of the space-heating load or the air-conditioning load.

When using this optional calculation, the grounded (neutral) conductor of the service or feeder loads shall be permitted to be calculated as required in **220.61**. Feeders within the building or structure where the load is calculated by this optional method may use the reduced ampacity as connected, but the ampacity of any feeder need not be larger than the individual ampacity for the entire building. Portable classrooms or buildings are not included in this Section. **(See Figure 23-17)**

NEW RESTAURANTS
220.88 AND TABLE 220.88

When calculating the service or feeder load for a new restaurant, and the feeder carries the entire load, **Table 220.88** shall be permitted to be used to size the elements necessary to supply the load. Overload protection shall be in accordance with **230.90, 215.3,** and **240.4**. Also, feeder or subfeeder conductors do not have to be larger than service conductors, regardless of calculations. **(See Figure 23-18)**

Figure 23-17. This illustration calculation shows the optional calculation being applied for a school.

OPTIONAL CALCULATIONS FOR ADDITIONAL LOADS TO EXISTING INSTALLATIONS
220.87

When additional loads are added to existing facilities having feeders and service as originally calculated, the maximum kVA calculations in determining the load on the existing feeders and service shall be permitted to be used if the following conditions are complied with:

- If the maximum data of the demand in kVA is available for a minimum of one year, such as demand meter ratings.

- If the demand ratings for that period of one year at 125 percent and the addition of the new load do not exceed the rating of the service. Where demand meters are used, in most cases the load as calculated will probably be less than the demand meter indications.

- If the overcurrent protection meets **230.90, 215.3,** and **240.4** for the feeder or service.

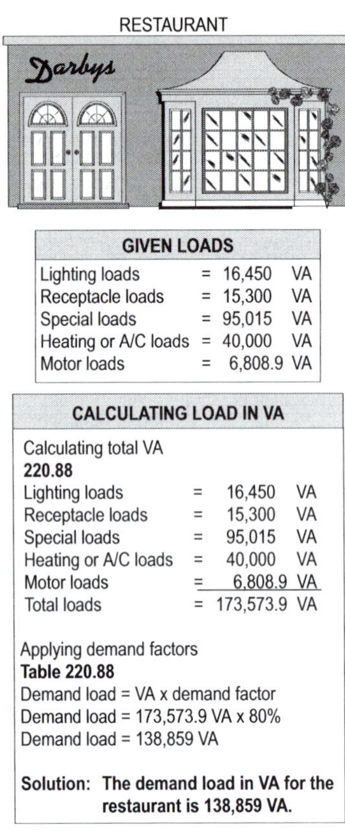

Figure 23-18. This illustration shows the optional calculation being applied for a restaurant.

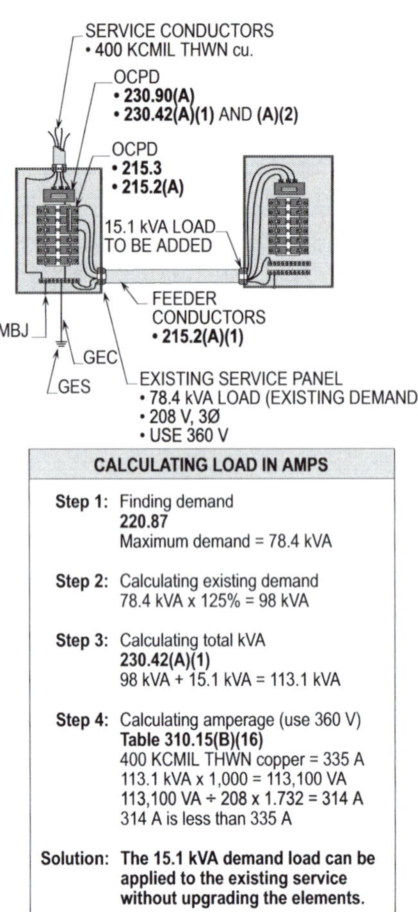

Figure 23-19. This illustration is the calculation for a service or feeder.

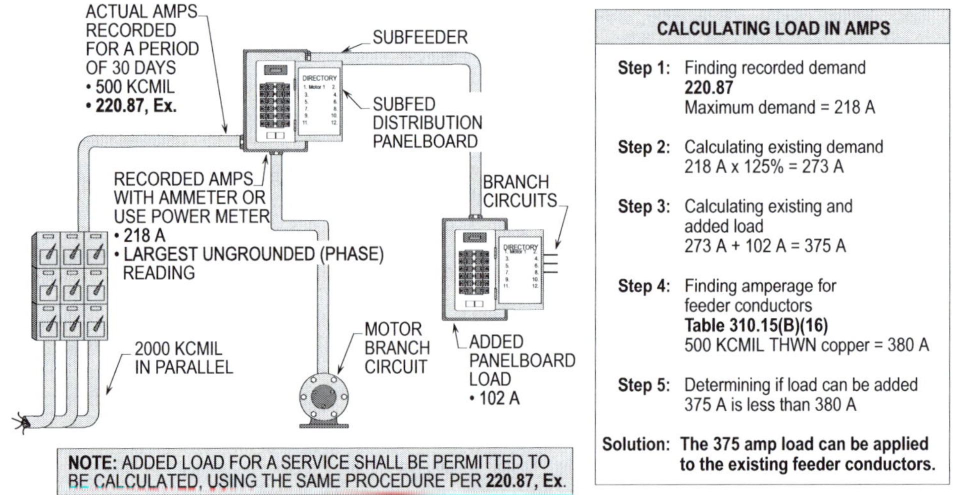

Figure 23-20. This illustration shows the optional calculation being applied for adding a load to an existing feeder.

APPLYING Ex. TO 220.87
220.87, Ex.

If the maximum demand data for a one year period is not available, the calculated load shall be permitted to be based on the maximum demand (measure of average power demand over a 15-minute period) continuously recorded over a minimum 30 day period using a recording ammeter or power meter connected to the highest loaded ungrounded (phase) of the feeder or service, based on the initial loading at the start of the recording. **(See Figure 23-19)**

Design Tip: By measurement or calculation, the larger of the heating or cooling equipment load shall be included in the load to be added. **(See Figure 23-20)**

CALCULATING THE GROUNDED (NEUTRAL) CONDUCTOR
220.61 AND 310.15(B)(5)(c)

For a service or feeder, the maximum unbalanced load controls the ampacity selected for the grounded (neutral) conductor. Grounded (neutral) feeder load shall be considered wherever a grounded (neutral) conductor is used in conjunction with one or more ungrounded (phase) conductors. On a single-phase feeder using one ungrounded (phase) conductor and a grounded (neutral) conductor, the grounded (neutral) conductor will carry the same amount of current as the ungrounded (phase) conductor. A two-wire feeder is seldom used, so in considering the grounded (neutral) feeder current, always assume that there is a grounded (neutral) conductor and two or more ungrounded (phase) conductors. If there are two ungrounded (phase) conductors that are connected to the same phase, and a grounded (neutral) conductor, the grounded (neutral) conductor would be required to carry the total current from both ungrounded (phase) conductors, which would not be an accepted practice.

For three-wire DC or single-phase AC; four-wire, three-phase; three-wire, two-phase; and five-wire, two-phase systems, a further demand factor of 70 percent shall be permitted to be applied to that portion of the unbalanced load in excess of 200 amperes. There shall be no reduction of the grounded (neutral) conductor capacity for that portion of the load that consists of electric-discharge lighting, electronic calculator/data processing, or similar equipment, when supplied by four-wire, wye-connected, three-phase systems. **(See Figure 23-21)**

For example, on a four-wire, three-phase wye circuit where the major portion (over 50 percent) of the load consists of nonlinear loads, there are harmonic currents present in the grounded (neutral) conductor, and the grounded (neutral) conductor shall be considered to be a current-carrying conductor. In other words, the ampacity of the conductor shall be derated per **310.15(B)(3)(a)**. [See **400.5(A)**]

Review the rules and examples of Chapters 14 and 15 for the sizing and use of the grounded (neutral) conductor in service, feeders, and branch circuit installations.

As an example, the grounded (neutral) conductor served by a 277/480 volt supply would be calculated per **Figure 23-21,** where there is electrical discharge lighting (inductive), incandescent lighting (resistive), and other resistive related loads.

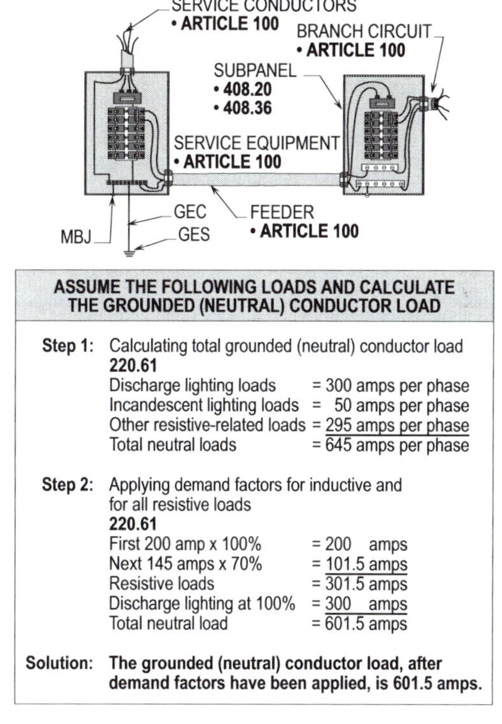

Figure 23-21. This calculation shows the procedure for calculating the grounded (neutral) conductor for a service or feeder and applying demand factors, where permitted.

Lighting Load for Specified Occupancies
220.12

A unit load of not less than that specified in **Table 220.12** for occupancies specified therein shall constitute the minimum lighting load. The floor area for each floor shall be calculated from the outside dimension of the building, dwelling unit, or other area involved. For dwelling units, the calculated floor area shall not include open porches, garages, or unused or unfinished spaces not adaptable for future use.

Exception: Where the building is designed and constructed to comply with an energy code adopted by the local authority, the lighting load shall be permitted to be calculated at the values specified in the energy code where the following conditions are met:

(1) A power monitoring system is installed that will provide continuous information regarding the total general lighting load of the building.

(2) The power monitoring system will be set with alarm values alert the building owner or manager if the lighting load exceeds the values set by the energy code.

(3) The demand factors specified in **220.42** are not applied to the general lighting load.
(See Figure 23-21)

CALCULATION PROBLEMS
ARTICLE 220, PARTS III AND IV

The elements of electrical systems shall be permitted to be calculated by using the standard or optional calculation. The size of these elements are determined by which method the designer chooses to calculate these loads. The following calculations are typical examples of how these loads are calculated, sized, and selected. The step-by-step procedures are easy to follow and have condensed the more complicated rules pertaining to calculating loads into a compact listing, that provides easier understanding of how to perform calculations according to the provisions of the NEC. A broad assortment of basic code calculations have been selected to represent the main principles of designing and installing electrical systems per NEC rules.

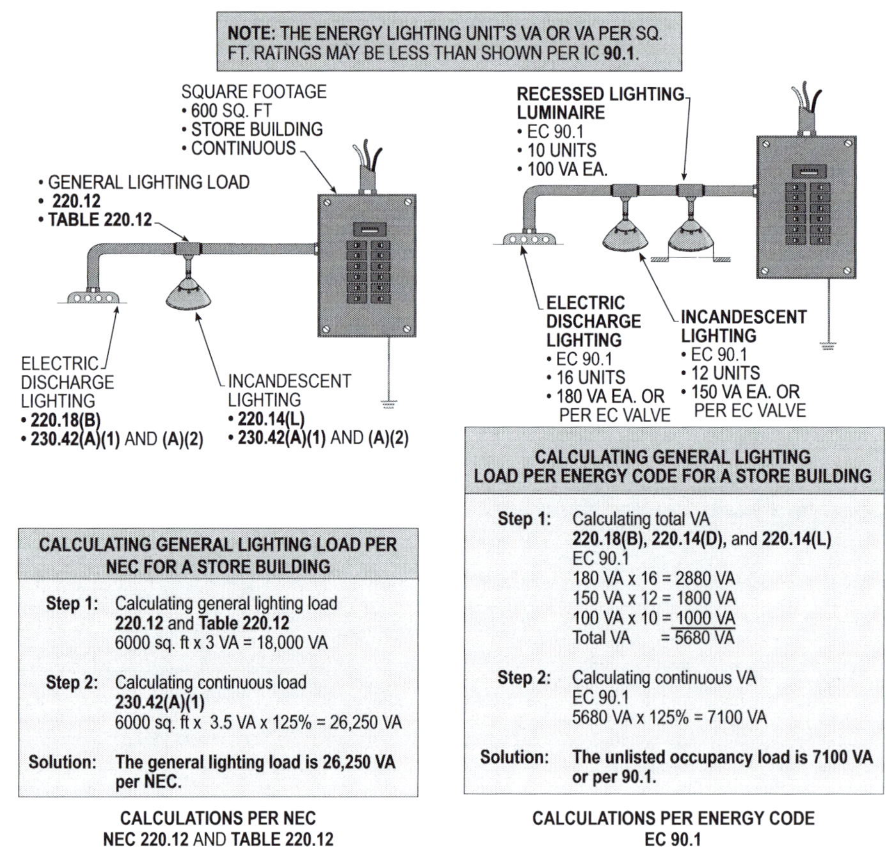

Figure 23-21. This illustration shows the lighting load calculated at the values specified in the energy code where certain conditions are complied with.

PROCEDURE FOR CALCULATING THE LOADS IN VA AND AMPS ARTICLE 220, PARTS III AND IV

Commercial loads shall be calculated by applying the following steps:

- The first step is to calculate the general-purpose lighting load by the VA per sq. ft according to the provisions of **Table 220.12** and **230.42(A)(1)** and **(A)(2)** if the occupancy is listed or use IC 90.1.

- The second step is to calculate the general-purpose receptacle load by multiplying the total number by 180 VA by the provisions of **220.14(I)** and **230.42(A) (1)** and **(A)(2)**. If the total exceeds 10 kVA, a demand factor of 50 percent shall be permitted to be applied to all VA ratings exceeding 10 kVA. **Tables 220.42 and 220.44** permit the reduction of such loads.

- The third step is to calculate the total load for all special appliances available in the facility. These appliances shall be calculated at nameplate rating based on noncontinuous and continuous use or a combination of both.

- The fourth step is to calculate the compressor load at noncontinuous use and set aside as the largest in case it is the largest motor load.

- The fifth step is to calculate the motor loads. Each motor in VA or amps shall be added together at 100 percent value to obtain the total and set aside as the largest in case it is the largest motor load.

- The sixth step is to calculate the largest of the A/C unit or electric heating load, including any other dissimilar loads and drop the smaller loads.

- The seventh step is to calculate the largest motor load by 25 percent (or 125 percent) and add to the other loads in the steps above. The largest motor load is selected from one of the loads in steps four, five, and six, respectively. (Apply 25 percent rule.)

The final step is to total the calculated loads in all the steps and divide by the voltage if in VA and to size the electrical elements for a service or feeder. **(See Problem 23-1)**

STORE BUILDING SUPPLIED BY 120/240 VOLT POWER SOURCE TABLE 220.12 – (LISTED OCCUPANCY)

It is the loads in a facility that determines the voltage for designing and sizing the service or feeder elements.

> **For example,** 120/240 volt supply is usually used to supply a facility having an equal number of 240 volt loads and 120 volt related loads.

The disadvantage of using a 120/240 volt supply is it produces larger ratings for selecting the elements for service equipment and feeders. **(See Design Problem 23-1)**

STORE BUILDING SUPPLIED BY 120/208 VOLT POWER SOURCE TABLE 220.12 – (LISTED OCCUPANCY)

A facility equipped with a large number of 120 volt and 208 volt three-phase loads is normally supplied by a four-wire, three-phase wye-connected system.

On a three-phase wye-connected system, three 120 volt ungrounded (phase) conductors are obtained from ground; therefore, three ungrounded (phase) conductors may be routed with each grounded (neutral) conductor. This type of installation requires fewer grounded (neutral) conductors and therefore saves on the amount of copper or aluminum that would otherwise be needed if one grounded (neutral) conductor were pulled with each ungrounded (phase) conductor.

See Design Problem 23-2 for calculating the total load for sizing the elements to be used with 120/208 volt, three-phase, four-wire systems.

STORE BUILDING SUPPLIED BY 277/480 VOLT POWER SOURCE TABLE 220.12 – (LISTED OCCUPANCY)

Smaller store buildings are usually supplied by 120/208 volt power systems. Loads such as lighting, receptacles, and other related loads are served by the lower voltage of 120 volts. Equipment is normally served by the higher voltage rated at 208 volts phase-to-phase.

Larger office buildings utilize 277/480 volt, three-phase, four-wire systems. The higher 480 volt, three-phase voltage supplies the heavier equipment, and the 277 volts, single-phase voltages supplies lighting. Transformers are used to step down the 480 volts to 120/208 volts or 120/240 volts to supply the lower voltage loads and equipment. **(See Design Problem 23-3)**

STORE BUILDING SUPPLIED BY 120/240 VOLT, THREE-PHASE POWER SOURCE TABLE 220.12 – (LISTED OCCUPANCY)

Store buildings with a greater number of three-phase loads than single-phase loads may be supplied by a three-phase, four-wire, 120/240 volt service. The 120 volts may be obtained from two of the ungrounded (phase) conductors to ground. This phase-to-ground voltage is taken from the lighting and power transformer.

Transformers on a delta-connected system are connected in an open or closed delta configuration.

Closed delta systems require three transformers, while open delta systems require only two transformers. One of the advantages of closed delta systems is that if one transformer fails, the remaining two may be connected in an open delta configuration and continue to supply the load until a replacement transformer is purchased and installed. **(See Design Problem 23-4)**

OFFICE BUILDING SUPPLIED BY 277/480 VOLT POWER SOURCE TABLE 220.12 – (LISTED OCCUPANCY)

Office buildings consist mostly of lighting loads and receptacle loads supplying small sensitive electronic machines used for office-related work. Heavier loads such as equipment, heating, air-conditioning, and other three-phase loads are supplied by the higher voltage.

The advantage of 277/480 volt systems is that they permit overcurrent protection devices, conductors, and other electrical elements to be smaller in size. Naturally, these smaller elements reduce the cost of installation. **(See Design Problem 23-5)**

SCHOOL BUILDING SUPPLIED BY 277/480 VOLT POWER SOURCE TABLE 220.12 – (LISTED OCCUPANCY)

School buildings supplied by 277/480 volt services are calculated with the basic steps used to calculate the load for any other commercial occupancy. **(See Design Problem 23-6)**

RESTAURANT SUPPLIED BY 120/208 VOLT POWER SOURCE TABLE 220.12 – (LISTED OCCUPANCY)

Small restaurants consist of lighting and receptacle loads, with the larger loads being the cooking equipment and other such pertinent apparatus.

Based on the number of cooking units, demand factors shall be permitted to be applied to the total load per **220.56** and **Table 220.56**. Larger restaurants are supplied with 277/480 volt services, with step-down transformers being utilized to serve smaller 120 volt loads. **(See Design Problem 23-7)**

HOSPITAL BUILDING SUPPLIED BY 277/480 VOLT POWER SOURCE TABLE 220.12 – (LISTED OCCUPANCY)

The loads in hospitals are calculated by their conditions of use. They are either calculated at continuous operation or noncontinuous operation, or demand factors shall be permitted to be applied for certain loads. The service voltage is determined by the size of the facility and related equipment. The procedure for calculating the load is to use the seven steps listed in this chapter for calculating the total load for a premises. **(See Design Problem 23-8)**

WELDING SHOPS SUPPLIED BY 120/208 VOLT POWER SOURCE ARTICLE 220, PARTS II AND III – (UNLISTED OCCUPANCY)

Unlisted occupancies are those not appearing in **Table 220.12;** therefore, their VA ratings shall be calculated from other sections than those listed in **Table 220.12**. The load for unlisted occupancies shall be calculated by applying the same step procedure listed in this chapter. The only difference is that the lighting is not obtained per **Table 220.12**. **(See Design Problem 23-9)**

SIZING ELEMENTS

Design problems 23-1 through 23-9 cover specific questions on problems pertaining to sizing elements that are found in commercial facilities. Questions are based on the calculations of **Design Problems 23-1 through 23-9**. Elements such as overcurrent protection devices, conductors, conduits, etc. are determined using step-by-step procedures.

SIZING ELEMENTS
DESIGN PROBLEM 23-1

(1) What size THWN copper conductors are required for the service when they are paralleled 5 times per phase?

Step 1: Paralleling conductors
310.10(H)
Amps of conductors = service A ÷ No. in parallel
A = 1274 A ÷ 5
A = 254.8

Step 2: Selecting conductors size
Table 310.15(B)(16) and **220.5(B)**
254.8 A requires 250 KCMIL
250 KCMIL = 255 A

Solution: It takes 5 - 250 KCMIL THWN copper conductors to supply a load of 1274 amps (255 A x 5 = 1275 A).

(2) What size overcurrent protection device is required for the service based on the ampacity of the conductors?

Step 1: Sizing OCPD
230.90(A), 240.4(C), and **240.6(A)**
1274 A requires 1250 A

Solution: The size overcurrent protection device based on ampacity of conductors is 1250 amps.

(3) What size grounded (neutral) conductor is required for the service when they are paralleled 5 times per phase?

Step 1: Selecting conductor size
310.10(H)
Amps of conductors = service A ÷ No. in parallel
A = 759 A ÷ 5
A = 151.8

Step 2: Selecting conductor size
Table 310.15(B)(16) and **220.5(B)**
152 A requires 2/0 AWG cu.
2/0 AWG cu. = 175 A

Solution: It takes 5 - 2/0 AWG THWN copper conductors to supply a load of 759 amps (175 A x 5 = 875 A).

(4) What size rigid metal conduit is required to enclose the conductors for each run?

Step 1: Sizing sq. in. area
Table 5, Ch. 9
250 KCMIL cu.   = 0.397
2/0 AWG THWN cu. = 0.2223

Step 2: Calculating total sq. in. area
Table 5, Ch. 9
0.3970 x 2   = .794 sq. in.
0.2223 x 1   = .2223 sq. in.
Total sq. in. = 1.0163 sq. in.

Step 3: Selecting RMC
Table 4, Ch. 9
1.0163 sq. in. = 2" (53)

Solution: The size rigid metal conduit for each is 2 in. (53).

SIZING ELEMENTS
DESIGN PROBLEM 23-2

(1) What size THWN copper conductors are required for the service when they are paralleled 5 times per phase?

> **Step 1:** Paralleling conductors
> **310.10(H)**
> Amps of conductors = service A ÷ No. in parallel
> A = 850 A ÷ 5
> A = 170
>
> **Step 2:** Selecting conductors size
> **Table 310.15(B)(16)**
> 170 A requires 2/0 AWG cu.
> 2/0 AWG cu. = 175 A
>
> **Solution: It takes 5 - 2/0 AWG THWN copper conductors to supply a load of 850 amps (175 A x 5 = 875 A).**

(2) What size overcurrent protection device is required for the service based on the calculated load?

> **Step 1:** Sizing OCPD
> **230.90(A), 240.4(C),** and **240.6(A)**
> 850 A requires 800 A
>
> **Solution: The size overcurrent protection device based on calculated load is 800 or 850 amps, if listed.**

(3) What size grounded (neutral) conductor is required for the service when they are paralleled 5 times per phase?

> **Step 1:** Selecting conductor size
> **310.10(H)**
> Amps of conductors = service A ÷ No. in parallel
> A = 506 A ÷ 5
> A = 101
>
> **Step 2:** Selecting conductor size
> **310.10(H), Table 310.15(B)(16),**
> **220.5(B),** and **250.24(C)(2)**
> 101 A requires 1/0 AWG cu.
> 1/0 AWG cu. = 150 A
>
> **Solution: It takes 5 - 1/0 AWG THWN copper conductors to supply a load of 506 amps (150 A x 5 = 750 A).**

(4) What size rigid metal conduit is required to enclose the conductors for each run?

> **Step 1:** Sizing sq. in. area
> **Table 5, Ch. 9**
> 2/0 AWG THWN = 0.2223
> 1/0 AWG THWN = 0.1855
>
> **Step 2:** Calculating total sq. in. area
> **Table 5, Ch. 9**
> 0.2223 x 3 = .6669 sq. in.
> 0.1855 x 1 = .1885 sq. in.
> Total sq. in. = .8554 sq. in.
>
> **Step 3:** Selecting RMC
> **Table 4, Ch. 9**
> .8554 sq. in. = 2" (53)
>
> **Solution: The size rigid metal conduit for each run is 2 in. (53).**

(5) What size copper grounding electrode conductor is required to ground the service to building structural steel?

> **Step 1:** Sizing GEC
> **Table 8, Ch. 9**
> 2/0 AWG cu. = 133,100 CM
> CM = CM x No. of conductors
> CM = 133,100 CM x 5
> CM = 665,500 CM
> KCMIL = CM ÷ 1,000
> KCMIL = 665,500 CM ÷ 1000
> KCMIL = 665.5
>
> **Step 2:** Selecting GEC
> **Table 250.66**
> 665.5 KCMIL = 2/0 AWG cu.
>
> **Solution: The size of the grounding electrode conductor required to ground to building structural steel is 2/0 AWG copper.**

SIZING ELEMENTS
DESIGN PROBLEM 23-3

(1) What size THWN copper conductors are required for the service when they are paralleled 2 times per phase?

Step 1: Paralleling conductors
310.10(H)
Amps of conductors = service A ÷ No. in parallel
A = 369 A ÷ 2
A = 184.5

Step 2: Selecting conductors size
Table 310.15(B)(16) and **220.5(B)**
185 A requires 3/0 AWG THWN cu.
3/0 AWG THWN cu. = 200 A

Solution: It takes 2 - 3/0 AWG THWN copper conductors to supply a load of 369 amps (200 A x 2 = 400 A).

(2) What size overcurrent protection device is required for the service based on the ampacity of conductors?

Step 1: Sizing OCPD
230.90(A), 240.4(B), and **240.6(A)**
369 A requires 400 A

Solution: The size overcurrent protection device based on the ampacity of the conductors is 400 amps.

(3) What size grounded (neutral) conductor is required for the service when they are paralleled 5 times per phase?

Step 1: Selecting conductor size
310.10(H)
Amps of conductors = service A ÷ No. in parallel
A = 150 A ÷ 2
A = 75

Step 2: Selecting conductor size
310.10(H), Table 310.15(B)(16), and **250.24(C)(2)**
75 A requires 1/0 AWG cu.
1/0 AWG cu. = 150 A

Solution: It takes 2 - 1/0 AWG THWN copper conductors to supply a load of 150 amps (150 A x 2 = 300 A).

(4) What size rigid metal conduit is required for each run?

Step 1: Sizing sq. in. area
Table 5, Ch. 9
3/0 AWG THWN = 0.2679
1/0 AWG THWN = 0.1855

Step 2: Calculating total sq. in. area
Table 5, Ch. 9
0.2679 x 3 = .8037 sq. in.
0.1855 x 1 = .1855 sq. in.
Total sq. in. = .9892 sq. in.

Step 3: Selecting RMC
Table 4, Ch. 9
.9892 sq. in. = 2" (53)

Solution: The size rigid metal conduit for each run is 2 in. (53).

(5) Will the 3/0 AWG THHN copper conductors supply the service load of 356 amps if four conductors in each rigid metal conduit run are current-carrying?

Step 1: Applying derating factors
Table 310.15(B)(3)(a) and **110.14(C)**
3/0 AWG THWN cu. = 225 A
225 A x 80% = 180 A

Step 2: Checking amps
310.10(H)
180 A x 2 = 360 A

Solution: Yes, the derating of 360 amps will supply a load of 356 amps.

SIZING ELEMENTS
DESIGN PROBLEM 23-4

(1) What size THWN copper conductors are required to supply Phases A and C when they are paralleled 4 times per phase?

Step 1: Paralleling conductors
310.10(H)
Amps of conductors = service A ÷ No. in parallel
A = 1119 A ÷ 4
A = 279.75

Step 2: Selecting conductors
Table 310.15(B)(16) and **220.5(B)**
280 A requires 300 KCMIL
300 KCMIL THWN cu. = 285 A

Solution: It takes 4 - 300 KCMIL THWN copper conductors to supply a load of 1119 amps (285 A x 4 = 1140 A).

(2) What size THWN copper conductors are required to supply the high leg, which is Phase B? (Phase B is also paralleled 4 times per phase.)

Step 1: Paralleling conductors
310.10(H) and **220.5(B)**
No. of conductors = 215 A ÷ 4 = 54 A

Solution: Section 310.10(H) requires at least 1/0 AWG conductors to be connected in parallel. Therefore, Phase B requires 1/0 THWN copper conductors per phase.

(3) What size THWN copper conductors are required to supply the grounded (neutral) load?

Step 1: Paralleling conductors
310.10(H) and **220.5(B)**
Amps of conductors = service A ÷ No. in parallel
A = 759 A ÷ 4
A = 189.8 (round up to 190 A)

Step 2: Selecting conductors
Table 310.15(B)(16) and **250.24(C)(2)**
190 A requires 3/0 AWG cu.
3/0 AWG cu. THWN = 200 A

Solution: It takes 4 - 3/0 AWG THWN copper conductors to supply a load of 759 amps (200 A x 4 = 800 A).

(4) What color is the high leg?

Step 1: Determining color code
110.15, 230.56, and **408.3(F)(1)**
Orange shall be used

Solution: Orange, per code, is the color required for the high leg when used in an open or closed delta-connected system.

SIZING ELEMENTS
DESIGN PROBLEM 23-5

(1) What size grounding electrode conductor is required per **Table 250.66** when the service conductors are paralleled 6 times per phase?

    Step 1: Sizing conductors in parallel
        310.10(H), Table 310.15(B)(16), and
        220.5(B)
        A of conductors ÷ No. in parallel
        A = 1042 A ÷ 6
        A = 174 A
        2/0 AWG THWN cu. = 175 A
        175 A supplies 174 A

    Step 2: Calculating KCMIL
        Table 8, Ch. 9
        2/0 AWG cu. = 133,100 CM
        CM = 133,100 CM x 6
        CM = 798,600
        KCMIL = 798,600 ÷ 1000
        KCMIL = 798.6

    Step 3: Selecting GEC
        Table 250.66
        798.6 KCMIL requires 2/0 AWG cu.

    Solution: The size grounding electrode conductor is 2/0 AWG copper.

(2) What size copper supply-side bonding jumper is required to bond all of the rigid metal conduits to the grounded busbar?

    Step 1: Selecting S-SBJ
        250.102(C)(2) and **Table 250.102(C)(1)**
        798.6 KCMIL requires 2/0 AWG cu.

    Solution: The size supply-side bonding jumper is 2/0 AWG copper.

(3) What size THWN copper grounded (neutral) conductors are required per phase?

    Step 1: Selecting grounded (neutral) conductor
        250.24(C)(2) and **Table 250.102(C)(1)**
        798.6 KCMIL requires 2/0 AWG cu.

    Step 2: Calculating amps
        310.10(H) and **220.5(B)**
        Amps of conductors ÷ No. in parallel
        A = 634 A ÷ 6
        A = 106 A
        106 A requires 2/0 AWG cu. per
        250.24(C)(2)

    Solution: The size grounded (neutral) conductor per phase is 2/0 AWG THWN copper, which is the correct size per 250.24(C)(2).

SIZING ELEMENTS
DESIGN PROBLEM 23-6

(1) What is the allowable ampacity for 400 KCMIL THHN copper current-carrying conductors routed through an ambient temperature of 120°F?

    Step 1: Selecting ungrounded (phase) conductors
        310.15(A)(3), IN (2) and
        Table 310.15(B)(16)
        335 A requires 400 KCMIL cu.

    Step 2: Applying adjustment factors
        Table 310.15(B)(3)(a)
        380 A x 80% = 304 A

    Step 3: Applying correction factors
        Table 310.15(B)(16) and **220.5(B)**
        304 A x 82% = 249 A

    Step 4: Applying adjustment and correction factors (large enough)
        Table 310.15(B)(16) and
        Table 310.15(B)(3)(a)
        700 KCMIL cu. = 520 A
        520 A x 80% x 82% = 341 A

    Solution: The size THHN copper conductors are 700 KCMIL. Note, it would be more logical to parallel the number of conductors necessary to supply the load.

SIZING ELEMENTS
DESIGN PROBLEM 23-7

(1) What size kVA transformer is required to supply the calculated load? (Based on calculated load)

Step 1: Calculating the load in VA
Load = 137,185 VA

Step 2: Sizing transformer
page 23-32
kVA = VA ÷ 1000
kVA = 137,185 VA ÷ 1000
kVA = 137.185

Step 3: Selecting transformer
Chart (inside back cover of book)
137.185 kVA requires 150 kVA

Solution: The size transformer to supply the load is 150 kVA.

---

(2) What size panelboard is required to supply the calculated load?

Step 1: Calculating the load in amps
220.5(A)
$I = VA \div (V \times \sqrt{3})$
$I = 137,185 \text{ VA} \div (208 \text{ V} \times 1.732)$
$I = 381 \text{ A}$

Step 2: Selecting panelboard
408.36, 240.4(B), and **220.5(B)**
Chart (inside back cover of book)
381 A requires 400 A

Solution: The size panelboard to handle the calculated load is 400 amps.

SIZING ELEMENTS
DESIGN PROBLEM 23-8

(1) What size busway is required to supply the calculated load?

Step 1: Calculating the load in amps
Chart
$I = VA \div (V \times \sqrt{3})$
$I = 1,142,563 \text{ VA} \div (480 \text{ V} \times 1.732)$
$I = 1375 \text{ VA}$

Step 2: Selecting busway
Chart (inside back cover of book)
1375 A requires 1600 A

Solution: The size busway required to supply the calculated load is 1600 amps. Note, if available by the manufacturer, a 1500 amp busway shall be permitted to be used.

---

(2) What size disconnect switch is required ahead of the distribution panelboard?

Step 1: Sizing fuses
240.6(A)
Chart (inside back cover of book)
1375 A requires 1400 A

Solution: The size disconnect switch required to hold the fuses is 1600 amps. Note, 240.6(A) permits a listed manufacturer fuse of 1400 amps to be used.

SIZING ELEMENTS
DESIGN PROBLEM 23-9

(1) What is the load, in amps, for Phases A, B, and C when adding the amps of each individual load?

> **Step 1:** Calculating amps
> **220.5(A)**
> General lighting load (•)
>
> $I = VA \div (V \times \sqrt{3})$
> $I = 13,800 \text{ VA} \div (208 \text{ V} \times 1.732)\ 360$
> $I = \textbf{38.33 A}$
>
> Receptacle loads (•)
>
> $I = 13,500 \text{ VA} \div 360 \text{ V}$
> $I = \textbf{37.5 A}$
>
> Special loads (•)
>
> $I = 56,468 \text{ VA} \div 360 \text{ V}$
> $I = \textbf{156.86 A}$
>
> Compressor and motor loads (•)
>
> $I = 13,464 \text{ VA} \div 360 \text{ V}$
> $I = \textbf{37.4 A}$
>
> Heating load (•)
>
> $I = 20,000 \text{ VA} \div 360 \text{ V}$
> $I = \textbf{55.55 A}$
>
> Largest motor load (•)
>
> $I = 2178 \text{ VA} \div 360 \text{ V}$
> $I = \textbf{6.05 A}$
> Total load = **331.69 A**

Solution: **Round up to 332 amps per Tables, Ch. 9 and 220.5(B).**

(2) Does the added amps per phase for each load equal the calculated amps in Design Problem 23-9 on page 23-34?

> **Step 1:** Calculating amps
> Added amps per phase equals
> calculated amps per phase

Solution: **Yes, the amps per phase are equal.**

DESIGN PROBLEM 23-1: What is the load in VA and amps to calculate and size the elements for 120/240 volt, single-phase service supplying a 40,000 sq. ft store with 20,000 sq. ft of warehouse space?

120 V, single-phase loads

- 80 linear ft of show window (noncontinuous operation)
- 120 ft of lighting track
- 30 - 180 VA ballasts outside lighting (continuous operation)
- 3600 VA sign lighting (continuous operation)
- 65 receptacles (noncontinuous operation)
- 28 receptacles (continuous operation)
- 80 ft multioutlet assembly (heavy duty)

240 V, single-phase loads

- 7380 VA freezer
- 5580 VA ice cream boxes
- 1 - 1/2 HP exhaust fan
- 10,000 VA water heater
- 9540 VA walk-in cooler
- 50,000 VA heating unit
- 23,320 VA A/C unit
- 1 - 2 HP water pump

Sizing phases = •
Sizing neutral = √
Sizing total load = *

Note 1: For sizing elements, see page 23-18 of this chapter.

Note 2: Add asterisks and checks to obtain total load.

CALCULATING LIGHTING LOAD

Step 1: General lighting load
Table 220.12 and **230.42(A)(1)**

40,000 sq. ft x 3 VA	= 120,000 VA √
120,000 VA x 125%	= 150,000 VA *
20,000 sq. ft x 1/4 VA	= 5,000 VA √
5,000 VA x 125%	= 6,250 VA *

Step 2: Show window load
220.43(A)
80 ft x 200 = 16,000 VA * √

Step 3: Track lighting load
220.43(B)
120 ft ÷ 2 x 150 VA = 9,000 VA * √

Step 4: Outside lighting load
230.42(A)(1)
30 x 180 VA = 5,400 VA √
5400 VA x 125% = 6,750 VA *

Step 5: Sign lighting load
220.14(F) and **230.42(A)(1)**
3600 VA x 100% = 3,600 VA √
3600 VA x 125% = 4,500 VA *
Total load = 192,500 VA •

CALCULATING RECEPTACLE LOAD

Step 1: Noncontinuous operation
220.14(H)(2), 220.14(I), and **230.42(A)(1)**
65 x 180 VA = 11,700 VA
80' x 180 VA = 14,400 VA
Total Load = 26,100 VA
Table 220.44
First 10,000 VA x 100% = 10,000 VA
Next 16,100 VA x 50% = 8,050 VA
Total load = 18,050 VA * √

Step 2: Continuous operation
220.14(I) and **230.42(A)(1)**
28 x 180 VA = 5,040 VA √
5040 VA x 125% = 6,300 VA *
Total load = 24,350 VA •

CALCULATING SPECIAL LOAD

Step 1: Water heater load
10,000 VA x 100% = **10,000 VA * •**

CALCULATING COMPRESSOR LOAD

Step 1: Freezer load
230.42(A)(1) and **440.34**
7380 VA x 100% = 7,380 VA *

Step 2: Ice cream boxes
5580 VA x 100% = 5,580 VA *

Step 3: Walk-in cooler
9540 VA x 100% = 9,540 VA *
Total load = **22,500 VA •**

CALCULATING MOTOR LOADS

Step 1: Water pump load
430.24 and **Table 430.248**
12 A x 240 V x 100% = 2,880 VA *

Step 2: Exhaust fan load
4.9 A x 240 V x 100% = 1,176 VA *
Total load = **4,056 VA •**

CALCULATING HEATING OR A/C LOAD

Step 1: Heating load selected
220.60
50,000 VA x 100% = **50,000 VA * •**
23,320 VA x 100% = **23,320 VA**

CALCULATING LARGEST MOTOR LOAD

Step 1: Walk-in cooler
220.50, 430.24, and **440.34**
9540 VA x 25% = **2,385 VA * •**

CALCULATING FOR PHASES A AND B (ADD ALL •)

Lighting loads	= 192,500 VA •
Receptacle loads	= 24,350 VA •
Special loads	= 10,000 VA •
Compressor loads	= 22,500 VA •
Motor loads	= 4,056 VA •
Heating load	= 50,000 VA •
Largest motor load	= 2,385 VA •
Total load for facility	= **305,791 VA**

FINDING AMPS FOR PHASES A AND B

I = VA ÷ V
I = 305,791 VA ÷ 240 V
I = 1274 A

CALCULATING NEUTRAL (ADD ALL √)

Lighting load	= 159,000 VA √
Receptacle load	= 23,090 VA √
Total load	= **182,090 VA**

FINDING AMPS FOR NEUTRAL (CALCULATED AT 100% OF VA)

I = VA ÷ V
I = 182,090 VA ÷ 240 V
I = 759 A

See **220.5(B), 220.61** and Design Tip No. 5 on page 23-29.

DESIGN PROBLEM 23-2: What is the load in VA and amps to calculate and size the elements for 120/208 volt, three-phase, four-wire service supplying a 40,000 sq. ft store with 20,000 sq. ft of warehouse space?

120 V, single-phase loads

• 80 linear ft of show window (noncontinuous operation)
• 120 ft of lighting track
• 30 - 180 VA ballasts outside lighting (continuous operation)
• 3,600 VA sign lighting (continuous operation)
• 65 receptacles (noncontinuous operation)
• 28 receptacles (continuous operation)
• 80 ft multioutlet assembly (heavy duty)

208 V, three-phase loads

• 7,380 VA freezer
• 5,580 VA ice cream boxes
• 1 - 1 HP exhaust fan
• 10,000 VA water heater
• 9,540 VA walk-in cooler
• 50,000 VA heating unit
• 23,320 VA A/C unit
• 1 - 2 HP water pump

Sizing phases = •
Sizing neutral = √
Sizing total load = *

Note 1: For sizing elements, see page 23-19 of this chapter.

Note 2: Add asterisks and checks to obtain total load.

CALCULATING LIGHTING LOAD

Step 1: General lighting load
Table 220.12 and **230.42(A)(1)**
40,000 sq. ft x 3 VA = 120,000 VA √
120,000 VA x 125% = 150,000 VA *
20,000 sq. ft x 1/4 VA = 5,000 VA √
5000 VA x 125% = 6,250 VA *

Step 2: Show window load
220.43(A)
80 ft x 200 = 16,000 VA * √

Step 3: Track lighting load
220.43(B)
120 ft ÷ 2 x 150 VA = 9,000 VA * √

Step 4: Outside lighting load
230.42(A)(1)
30 x 180 VA = 5,400 VA √
5400 VA x 125% = 6,750 VA *

Step 5: Sign lighting load
220.14(F) and **230.42(A)(1)**
3600 VA x 100% = 3,600 VA √
3600 VA x 125% = 4,500 VA *
Total load = 192,500 VA •

CALCULATING RECEPTACLE LOAD

Step 1: Noncontinuous operation
220.14(H)(2), 220.14(I), and **230.42(A)(1)**
65 x 180 VA = 11,700 VA
80' x 180 VA = 14,400 VA
Total Load = 26,100 VA
Table 220.44
First 10,000 VA x 100% = 10,000 VA
Next 16,100 VA x 50% = 8,050 VA
Total load = 18,050 VA * √

Step 2: Continuous operation
220.14(H) and **230.42(A)(1)**
28 x 180 VA = 5,040 VA √
5040 VA x 125% = 6,300 VA *
Total load = 24,350 VA •

CALCULATING SPECIAL LOAD

Step 1: Water heater load
10,000 VA x 100% = 10,000 VA * •

CALCULATING COMPRESSOR LOAD

Step 1: Freezer load
230.42(A)(1) and **440.34**
7380 VA x 100% = 7380 VA *

Step 2: Ice cream boxes
5580 VA x 100% = 5,580 VA *

Step 3: Walk-in cooler
9540 VA x 100% = 9,540 VA *
Total load = 22,500 VA •

CALCULATING MOTOR LOADS

Step 1: Water pump load
430.24 and **Table 430.250**
7.5 A x 360 V x 100% = 2,700 VA *

Step 2: Exhaust fan load
4.6 A x 360 V x 100% = 1,656 VA *
Total load = 4,356 VA •

CALCULATING HEATING OR A/C LOAD

Step 1: Heating load selected
220.60
50,000 VA x 100% = 50,000 VA * •
23,320 VA x 100% = 23,320 VA

CALCULATING LARGEST MOTOR LOAD

Step 1: Walk-in cooler
220.50, 430.24, and **440.34**
9540 VA x 25% = 2,385 VA * •

CALCULATING FOR PHASES A, B, AND C (ADD ALL •)

Lighting loads = 192,500 VA •
Receptacle loads = 24,350 VA •
Special loads = 10,000 VA •
Compressor loads = 22,500 VA •
Motor loads = 4,356 VA •
Heating load = 50,000 VA •
Largest motor load = 2,385 VA •
Total load for facility = 306,091 VA

FINDING AMPS FOR PHASES A, B, AND C

I = VA ÷ V
I = 306,091 VA ÷ (208 V x 1.732) 360 V
I = 850 A

CALCULATING NEUTRAL (ADD ALL √)

Lighting load = 159,000 VA √
Receptacle load = 23,090 VA √
Total load = 182,090 VA

FINDING AMPS FOR NEUTRAL

I = VA ÷ V
I = 182,090 VA ÷ (208 V x 1.732) 360 V
I = 506 A

See Design Tip 5 on page 23-29.

DESIGN PROBLEM 23-3: What is the load in VA and amps to calculate and size the elements for 277/480 volt, three-phase, four-wire service supplying a 40,000 sq. ft store with 20,000 sq. ft of warehouse space with 277 volt lighting?

120 V, single-phase loads

- 80 linear ft of show window (noncontinuous operation)
- 120 ft of lighting track
- 30 - 180 VA ballasts outside lighting (continuous operation)
- 3,600 VA sign lighting (continuous operation)
- 65 receptacles (noncontinuous operation)
- 28 receptacles (continuous operation)
- 80 ft multioutlet assembly (heavy duty)

480 V, three-phase loads

- 7,380 VA freezer
- 5,580 VA ice cream boxes
- 1 - 1 HP exhaust fan
- 10,000 VA water heater
- 9,540 VA walk-in cooler
- 50,000 VA heating unit
- 23,320 VA A/C unit
- 1 - 2 HP water pump

Sizing phases = •
Sizing neutral = √
Sizing total load = *

Note 1: For sizing elements, see page 23-20 of this chapter.

Note 2: Add asterisks and checks to obtain total load.

CALCULATING LIGHTING LOAD

Step 1: General lighting load
Table 220.12 and **230.42(A)(1)**
40,000 sq. ft x 3 VA = 120,000 VA √
120,000 VA x 125% = 150,000 VA *
20,000 sq. ft x 1/4 VA = 5,000 VA √
5000 VA x 125% = 6,250 VA *

Step 2: Show window load
220.43(A)
80 ft x 200 = 16,000 VA *

Step 3: Track lighting load
220.43(B)
120 ft ÷ 2 x 150 VA = 9,000 VA *

Step 4: Outside lighting load
230.42(A)(1)
30 x 180 VA = 5,400 VA
5400 VA x 125% = 6,750 VA *

Step 5: Sign lighting load
220.14(F) and **230.42(A)(1)**
3600 VA x 100% = 3,600 VA
3600 VA x 125% = 4,500 VA *
Total load = 192,500 VA •

CALCULATING RECEPTACLE LOAD

Step 1: Noncontinuous operation
220.14(H)(2), 220.14(I), and **230.42(A)(1)**
65 x 180 VA = 11,700 VA
80' x 180 VA = 14,400 VA
Total load = 26,100 VA
Table 220.44
First 10,000 VA x 100% = 10,000 VA
Next 16,100 VA x 50% = 8,050 VA
Total load = 18,050 VA *

Step 2: Continuous operation
220.14(I) and **230.42(A)(1)**
28 x 180 VA = 5,040 VA
5040 VA x 125% = 6,300 VA *
Total load = 24,350 VA •

CALCULATING SPECIAL LOAD

Step 1: Water heater load
10,000 VA x 100% = 10,000 VA * •

CALCULATING COMPRESSOR LOAD

Step 1: Freezer load
230.42(A)(1) and **440.34**
7380 VA x 100% = 7,380 VA *

Step 2: Ice cream boxes
5580 VA x 100% = 5,580 VA *

Step 3: Walk-in cooler
9540 VA x 100% = 9,540 VA *
Total load = 22,500 VA •

CALCULATING MOTOR LOAD

Step 1: Water pump load
430.24 and **Table 430.250**
3.4 A x 831 V x 100 = 2,825 VA *

Step 2: Exhaust fan load
2.1 A x 831 V x 100 = 1,745 VA *
Total load = 4,570 VA •

CALCULATING HEATING OR A/C LOAD

Step 1: Heating load selected
220.60
50,000 VA x 100% = 50,000 VA * •
23,320 VA x 100% = 23,320 VA

CALCULATING LARGEST MOTOR LOAD

Step 1: Walk-in cooler
220.50 and **430.24**
9540 VA x 25% = 2,385 VA * •

CALCULATING FOR PHASES A, B, AND C (ADD ALL •)

Lighting loads = 192,500 VA•
Receptacle loads = 24,350 VA•
Special loads = 10,000 VA•
Compressor loads = 22,500 VA•
Motor loads = 4,570 VA•
Heating load = 50,000 VA•
Largest motor load = 2,385 VA•
Total load for facility = 306,305 VA

FINDING AMPS FOR PHASES A, B, AND C

I = VA ÷ V
I = 306,305 VA ÷ (480 V x 1.732) 831 V
I = 369 A

CALCULATING NEUTRAL (ADD ALL √)

Lighting load = 125,000 VA √
Total load = 125,000 VA

FINDING AMPS FOR NEUTRAL

I = VA ÷ V
I = 125,000 VA ÷ (480 V x 1.732) 831 V
I = 150 A

DESIGN PROBLEM 23-4: What is the load in VA and amps to calculate and size the elements for 120/240 volt, three-phase, four-wire service supplying a 40,000 sq. ft store with 20,000 sq. ft of warehouse space?

120 V, single-phase loads

• 80 linear ft of show window (noncontinuous operation)
• 120 ft of lighting track
• 30 - 180 VA ballasts outside lighting (continuous operation)
• 3,600 VA sign lighting (continuous operation)
• 65 receptacles (noncontinuous operation)
• 28 receptacles (continuous operation)
• 80 ft multioutlet assembly (heavy duty)

240 V, three-phase loads

• 7,380 VA freezer
• 5,580 VA ice cream boxes
• 1 - 1 HP exhaust fan
• 10,000 VA water heater
• 9,540 VA walk-in cooler
• 50,000 VA heating unit
• 23,320 VA A/C unit
• 1 - 2 HP water pump

Sizing phases = •
Sizing neutral = √
Sizing total load = *

Note 1: For sizing elements, see page 23-21 of this chapter.

Note 2: Add asterisks and checks to obtain total load.

CALCULATING LIGHTING LOAD

Step 1: General lighting load
Table 220.12 and **230.42(A)(1)**
40,000 sq. ft x 3 VA	= 120,000 VA √
120,000 VA x 125%	= 150,000 VA *
20,000 sq. ft x 1/4 VA	= 5,000 VA √
5,000 VA x 125%	= 6,250 VA *

Step 2: Show window load
220.43(A)
80 ft x 200 = 16,000 VA * √

Step 3: Track lighting load
220.43(B)
120 ft ÷ 2 x 150 VA = 9,000 VA * √

Step 4: Outside lighting load
230.42(A)(1)
30 x 180 VA	= 5,400 VA √
5400 VA x 125%	= 6,750 VA *

Step 5: Sign lighting load
220.14(F) and **230.42(A)(1)**
3600 VA x 100%	= 3,600 VA √
3600 VA x 125%	= 4,500 VA *
Total load	**= 192,500 VA •**

CALCULATING RECEPTACLE LOAD

Step 1: Noncontinuous operation
220.14(H)(2), 220.14(I), and **230.42(A)(1)**
65 x 180 VA	= 11,700 VA
80' x 180 VA	= 14,400 VA
Total load	= 26,100 VA

Table 220.44
First 10,000 VA x 100%	= 10,000 VA
Next 16,100 VA x 50%	= 8,050 VA
Total load	= 18,050 VA * √

Step 2: Continuous operation
220.14(I) and **230.42(A)(1)**
28 x 180 VA	= 5,040 VA √
5040 VA x 125%	= 6,300 VA *
Total load	**= 24,350 VA •**

CALCULATING SPECIAL LOAD

Step 1: Water heater load
10,000 VA x 100% = 10,000 VA * •

CALCULATING COMPRESSOR LOAD

Step 1: Freezer load
230.42(A)(1) and **440.34**
7380 VA x 100% = 7,380 VA *

Step 2: Ice cream boxes
5580 VA x 100% = 5,580 VA

Step 3: Walk-in cooler
9540 VA x 100%	= 9,540 VA *
Total load	**= 22,500 VA •**

CALCULATING MOTOR LOAD

Step 1: Water pump load
430.24 and **Table 430.250**
6.8 A x 416 V x 100% = 2,829 VA *

Step 2: Exhaust fan load
4.2 A x 416 V x 1.732 x 100%	= 1,747 VA *
Total load	**= 4,576 VA •**

CALCULATING HEATING OR A/C LOAD

Step 1: Heating load selected
220.60
50,000 VA x 100%	= 50,000 VA * •
23,320 VA x 100%	= 23,320 VA

CALCULATING LARGEST MOTOR LOAD

Step 1: Walk-in cooler
220.50 and **430.24**
9540 VA x 25% = 2,385 VA * •

SINGLE-PHASE LOAD

Lighting loads	= 192,500 VA •
Receptacle loads	= 24,350 VA •
Total load	**= 216,850 VA**

THREE-PHASE LOAD (SPECIAL LOAD)

Water heater load	= 10,000 VA •
Compressor load	= 22,500 VA •
Motor load	= 4,576 VA •
Heating load	= 50,000 VA •
Largest motor load	= 2,385 VA •
Total load	**= 89,461 VA**

SINGLE-PHASE NEUTRAL LOAD

Lighting loads	= 159,000 VA √
Receptacle loads	= 23,090 VA √
Total load	**= 182,090 VA**

CALCULATING SINGLE-PHASE LOAD

I = 216,850 VA ÷ 240 V
I = 904 A

CALCULATING THREE-PHASE LOAD (HIGH LEG)

I = 89,461 VA ÷ (240 V x 1.732) 416 V
I = 215 A

CALCULATING NEUTRAL LOAD

I = 182,090 VA ÷ 240 V
I = 759 A

CALCULATING PHASES A AND C

Single-phase load	= 904 A
Three-phase load	= 215 A
Total load	**= 1,119 A**

CALCULATING PHASE B (HIGH LEG)

Three-phase load	**= 215 A**

---

(1)
Design Tip (OPEN DELTA SYSTEM): The power and lighting transformer will consist of 120/240 volt single-phase loads plus the three-phase loads at 240 volts, respectively. The power transformer will consist of the three-phase loads only. **[See Figure 20-2(b)]**

Note, there will be one larger transformer (power plus lighting loads) and one smaller transformer (power three-phase loads only).

(2)
Design Tip (ADDING LOADS TOGETHER ON AN OPEN DELTA SYSTEM): The larger transformer is determined by adding the single-phase and three-phase loads together. The smaller transformer is determined by adding the three-phase loads together, which will not include the single-phase loads. **[See Figure 20-21(a)]**

(3)
Design Tip (CLOSED DELTA SYSTEM): There will be three transformers on a closed delta system that are connected at each corner of the windings to form a closed delta system. A closed delta-connected system should be used when the greater of the loads are three-phase motors, compressors, etc.

(4)
Design Tip (ADDING LOADS TOGETHER ON A CLOSED DELTA SYSTEM): The two larger transformers supplying power to the single-phase and three-phase loads is determined by adding the single-phase and three-phase loads together.

The smaller transformer(s) is determined by adding the three-phase loads together. However, in some installations, it is possible to add the 240 volt single-phase loads of phases A and C to phase B, which is the high leg. When this is done, the high leg load will be greater in size. Note that phases A and C in a delta system will usually always have a greater calculated load than phase B.

(5)
Design Tip [CALCULATING LOAD FOR THE GROUNDED (NEUTRAL) CONDUCTOR]: There is really no reason for calculating the load in VA or amps at 125 percent to size the grounded (neutral) conductor. Remember that the grounded (neutral) conductor connects to the lugs of the busbar and not to the terminals of an overcurrent protection device. However, there are designers who will calculate such load at 125 percent. It is your choice whether to calculate the grounded (neutral) conductor at 125 percent or not. The grounded (neutral) conductor in this book is calculated at 100 percent of the VA or amps. Section **366.23(A)** in the NEC does not require a busbar (bare copper) to be derated 80 percent of its rating. Therefore, the 125 percent rule in **210.19(A)(1) (a)** and **210.20** or **215.2(A)(1)(a)** and **215.3** as well as **230.42(A) (1)** and **230.90** does not necessarily have to be applied.

DESIGN PROBLEM 23-5: What is the load in VA and amps to calculate and size the elements for 277/480 volt, three-phase, four-wire service supplying a 150,000 sq. ft office facility with 3000 sq. ft hall area equipped with 277 volt lighting units?

120 V, single-phase loads

- 60 ft of lighting track
- 20 - 180 VA ballasts outside lighting (continuous operation)
- 4800 VA sign lighting (continuous operation)
- 182 receptacles (noncontinuous operation)
- 121 receptacles (continuous operation)
- 6000 VA isolation transformer for LVLS continuous operation

Sizing phases = •
Sizing neutral = √
Sizing total load = *

208 V, three-phase loads

- 200 ft multioutlet assembly (heavy duty)
- 5 - 1450 VA copying machines
- 8500 VA water heater
- 25 - 225 VA data processors
- 10 - 175 VA word processors
- 4 - 1200 VA printers

480 V, three-phase loads

- 40 HP elevator (15 minute intermittent duty)
- 40 kW heating unit
- 12,000 VA A/C unit

Note 1: For sizing elements, see page 23-22 of this chapter.

Note 2: Add asterisks and checks to obtain total load.

CALCULATING LIGHTING LOAD

Step 1: General lighting load
Table 220.12 and **230.42(A)(1)**
150,000 sq. ft x 3.5 VA   = 525,000 VA √
525,000 VA x 125%   = 656,250 VA *
3,000 sq. ft x 1/2 VA   = 1,500 VA √
1,500 VA x 125%   = 1,875 VA *

Step 2: Track lighting load
220.43(B)
60 ft ÷ 2 x 150 VA   = 4,500 VA *

Step 3: Low-voltage lighting load
Art. 411 and **230.42(A)(1)**
6000 VA x 100%   = 6,000 VA
6000 VA x 125%   = 7,500 VA *

Step 4: Outside lighting load
230.42(A)(1)
20 x 180 VA   = 3,600 VA
3600 VA x 125%   = 4,500 VA *

Step 5: Sign lighting load
220.14(F) and **230.42(A)(1)**
4800 VA x 100%   = 4,800 VA
4800 VA x 125%   = 6,000 VA *
Total load   = 680,625 VA •

CALCULATING RECEPTACLE LOAD

Step 1: Noncontinuous operation
220.14(I) and **230.42(A)(1)**
182 x 180 VA   = 32,760 VA
200' x 180 VA   = 36,000 VA
Total load   = 68,760 VA
Table 220.44
First 10,000 VA x 100%   = 10,000 VA
Next 58,760 VA x 50%   = 29,380 VA
Total load   = 39,380 VA *

Step 2: Continuous operation
220.14(I) and **230.42(A)(1)**
121 x 180 VA   = 21,780 VA
21,780 VA x 125%   = 27,225 VA *
Total load   = 66,605 VA •

CALCULATING SPECIAL LOAD

Step 1: Copying machine load
230.42(A)(1)
1450 VA x 5   = 7,250 VA
7250 VA x 125%   = 9,063 VA *

Step 2: Water heater load
422.13 and **230.42(A)(1)**
8500 VA x 100%   = 8,500 VA *

Step 3: Data processor load
225 VA x 25   = 5,625 VA
5625 VA x 125%   = 7,031 VA *

Step 4: Word processor load
230.42(A)(1)
175 VA x 10   = 1,750 VA
1750 VA x 125%   = 2,188 VA *

Step 5: Printer load
230.42(A)(1)
1200 VA x 4   = 4,800 VA
4800 VA x 125%   = 6,000 VA *
Total load   = 32,782 VA •

CALCULATING MOTOR LOAD

Step 1: 40 HP elevator (using 831 V)
430.24;, 430.22(E), and **Table 430.22(E)**
52 A x (480 V x 1.732) x 85%   = 36,730 VA * •

CALCULATING HEATING OR A/C LOAD

Step 1: Heating load selected
220.60 and **220.51**
40,000 VA x 100%   = 40,000 VA * •

CALCULATING LARGEST MOTOR LOAD

Step 1: 40 HP elevator
220.50 and **430.24**
36,730 VA x 25%   = 9,183 VA *•
Total load for facility   = 865,925 VA

FINDING AMPS FOR PHASES A, B AND C

$I = VA ÷ (V \times \sqrt{3})$
I = 865,925 VA ÷ (480 V x 1.732) 831 V
I = 1,042 A

CALCULATING NEUTRAL (ADD ALL √)

General lighting load
(office building)   = 525,000 VA √
(halls)   = 1,500 VA √
Total load   = 526,500 VA

FINDING AMPS FOR NEUTRAL

$I = VA ÷ (V \times \sqrt{3})$
I = 526,500 VA ÷ (480 V x 1.732) 831 V
I = 634 A

DESIGN PROBLEM 23-6: What is the load in VA and amps to calculate and size the elements for 277/480 volt, three-phase, four-wire service supplying a 30,000 sq. ft classroom area, 5000 sq. ft auditorium area, and 1000 sq. ft assembly hall area? (School building general lighting load is supplied by 277 volt luminaires.)

120 V, single-phase loads

- 200 receptacles (noncontinuous duty)
- 50 receptacles (continuous duty)
- 200 ft multioutlet assembly (heavy duty)

Single-phase and three-phase motor loads

- 4 - 1 HP hood fans
    208 V, single-phase
- 3 - 3/4 HP grill vent fans
    208 V, single-phase
- 20 - 3/4 HP exhaust fans
    480 V, three-phase

Cooking equipment

- 2 - 1 kW toasters
  120 V, single-phase
- 4 - 1.5 kW refrigerators
  120 V, single-phase
- 3 - 1.5 kW freezers
  120 V, single-phase

- 4 - 12 kW ranges
  208 V, single-phase
- 3 - 9 kW ovens
  208 V, single-phase
- 4 - 4 kW fryers
  208 V, single-phase

Note: All loads are continuous

Sizing phases = •
Sizing neutral = √
Sizing total load = *

Note 1: For sizing elements, see page 23-22 of this chapter.

Note 2: Add asterisks and checks to obtain total load.

CALCULATING LIGHTING LOAD

Step 1: General lighting load
Table 220.12 and **230.42(A)(1)**

30,000 sq. ft x 3 VA	= 90,000 VA √
90,000 VA x 125%	= 112,500 VA *
5,000 sq. ft x 1	= 5,000 VA √
5,000 VA x 125%	= 6,250 VA *
1,000 sq. ft x 1	= 1,000 VA √
1,000 VA x 125%	= 1,250 VA *
Total load	**= 120,000 VA •**

CALCULATING RECEPTACLE LOAD

Step 1: Noncontinuous operation
220.14(I) and **230.42(A)(1)**

200 x 180 VA	= 36,000 VA
200 ft x 180 VA	= 36,000 VA
Total load	= 72,000 VA
Table 220.44	
First 10,000 VA x 100%	= 10,000 VA
Next 62,000 VA x 50%	= 31,000 VA
Total load	= 41,000 VA *

Step 2: Continuous operation
220.14(I) and **230.42(A)(1)**

50 x 180 VA	= 9,000 VA
9000 VA x 125%	= 11,250 VA *
Total load	**= 52,250 VA •**

CALCULATING SPECIAL LOAD

Step 1: Kitchen equipment
220.56

Toasters	
2 x 1 kW x 1000	= 2,000 VA
Refrigerators	
4 x 1.5 kW x 1000	= 6,000 VA
Freezers	
3 x 1.5 kW x 1000	= 4,500 VA
Ranges	
4 x 12 kW x 1000	= 48,000 VA
Ovens	
3 x 9 kW x 1000	= 27,000 VA
Fryers	
4 x 4 kW x 1000	= 16,000 VA
Total load	= 103,500 VA

Step 2: Applying demand factors

103,500 VA x 65%	**= 67,275 VA * •**

CALCULATING MOTOR LOAD
TABLES 430.248 AND 430.250

Step 1: Exhaust fans

32 A x 100% x 480 V	= 15,360 VA
15,360 VA x 1.732	= 26,604 VA *
(1.6 A x 20 = 32 A)	

Step 2: Hood fans

35.2 A x 100% x 208 V	= 7,322 VA *
(8.8 A x 4 = 35.2 A)	

Step 3: Grill vent fans

22.8 A x 100% x 208 V	= 4,742 VA *
(7.6 A x 3 = 22.8)	
Total load	**= 38,668 VA •**

CALCULATING LARGEST MOTOR LOAD

Step 1: Hood fan

8.8 A x 100% x 208 V	= 1,830 VA
1830 VA x 25%	= 458 VA * •
Total load for facility	**= 278,651 VA**

FINDING AMPS FOR PHASES A, B, AND C

$I = VA \div (V \times \sqrt{3})$
$I = 278,651 \text{ VA} \div (480 \text{ V} \times 1.732)$ 831 V
$I = 335 \text{ A}$

CALCULATING NEUTRAL (ADD ALL √)

General lighting load	= 96,000 VA √
Largest motor load	= 375 VA √
Total load	**= 96,375 VA**

FINDING AMPS FOR NEUTRAL

$I = VA \div (V \times \sqrt{3})$
$I = 96,375 \text{ VA} \div (480 \text{ V} \times 1.732)$ 831 V
I = 116 A

Note: Largest 120 volt motor is calculated by taking 1.5 kW x 1000 x .25% = 375 VA.

DESIGN PROBLEM 23-7: What is the load in VA and amps to calculate and size the elements for 120/208 volt, three-phase, four-wire service supplying a restaurant with an area of 5600 sq. ft?

120 V, single-phase loads

Lighting load

30 ft lighting track (continuous)
10 - 180 VA outside lighting (continuous)
1200 VA sign lighting (continuous)

Receptacle load

35 receptacles (noncontinuous)
25 receptacles (continuous)
20 ft multioutlet assembly (heavy duty)

208 V, three-phase loads

Special loads

2 - 20 kW heating units
208 V, three-phase
2 - 8650 VA A/C units
208 V, three-phase

Motor loads

7322 VA hood fans
208 V, single-phase
4742 VA grill vent fans
208 V, single-phase

208 V, three-phase loads

Kitchen equipment

3800 VA boiler
2 - 2700 deep fat fryers
20 A walk-in cooler
6000 VA water heater

208 V, single-phase loads

13 A freezer
11,000 VA cooktop
2 - 9000 VA ovens
12,000 VA range
14 A refrigerator
3650 VA ice cream box

Note 1: For sizing elements, see page 23-23 of this chapter.

Note 2: Add asterisks and checks to obtain total load.

CALCULATING LIGHTING LOAD

Step 1: General lighting load
Table 220.12 and **230.42(A)(1)**
5600 sq. ft x 2 VA = 11,200 VA √
11,200 VA x 125% = 14,000 VA *

Step 2: Track lighting load
220.43(B) and **230.42(A)(1)**
30 ft ÷ 2 x 150 VA = 2,250 VA √
2250 VA x 125% = 2,813 VA *

Step 3: Outside lighting load
220.14(L) and **230.42(A)(1)**
180 VA x 10 = 1,800 VA √
1800 VA x 125% = 2,250 VA *

Step 4: Sign lighting load
220.14(F), 230.42(A)(1), and **(A)(2)**
1200 VA x 100% = 1,200 VA √
1200 VA x 125% = 1,500 VA *
Total load = **20,563 VA** •

CALCULATING RECEPTACLE LOAD

Step 1: Receptacle load (noncontinuous)
220.14(I) and **230.42(A)(2)**
35 x 180 VA = 6,300 VA * √

Step 2: Receptacle load (continuous)
220.14(I) and **230.42(A)(1)**
25 x 180 VA = 4,500 VA √
4500 VA x 125% = 5,625 VA *

Step 3: Multioutlet assembly
220.14(H)(2) and **230.42(A)(1)**
20 ft x 180 VA = 3,600 VA * √
Total load = **15,525 VA** •

CALCULATING SPECIAL LOAD

Step 1: Kitchen equipment
220.56
Boiler = 3,800 VA
Deep fat fryer = 5,400 VA
Walk-in cooler = 7,200 VA
Water heater = 6,000 VA
Ice cream box = 3,650 VA
Freezer = 2,704 VA
Cooktop = 11,000 VA
Ovens = 18,000 VA
Range = 12,000 VA
Refrigerator = 2,912 VA
Total load = 72,666 VA

Applying demand factor
Table 220.56
72,666 VA x 65% = **47,233 VA** * •

CALCULATING MOTOR LOAD

Step 1: Hood fans
430.22(A), 430.24, and **430.25**
7322 VA x 100% = 7,322 VA *

Step 2: Grill vent fans
4742 VA x 100% = 4,742 VA *
Total load = **12,064 VA** •

CALCULATING HEATING OR A/C LOAD

Step 1: Heating load
220.60
20 kW x 2 x 1000 = **40,000 VA** * •

CALCULATING LARGEST MOTOR LOAD

Step 1: Walk-in cooler (using 360 V)
220.50, 430.22, and **440.34**
20 A x 100% x (208 V x 1.732) = 7,200 VA
7200 VA x 25% = 1,800 VA * •
Total load = **137,185 VA**

CALCULATING VA LOAD (NEUTRAL)
220.61, 230.42(A)(1), AND (A)(2)

Lighting load = 16,450 VA √
Receptacle load = 14,400 VA √
Total load = **30,850 VA**

FINDING AMPS FOR PHASES A, B, AND C

$I = VA \div (V \times \sqrt{3})$
$I = 137,185 \text{ VA} \div (208 \text{ V} \times 1.732)\ 360 \text{ V}$
I = 381 A

FINDING AMPS FOR NEUTRAL

$I = VA \div (V \times \sqrt{3})$
$I = 30,850 \text{ VA} \div (208 \text{ V} \times 1.732)\ 360 \text{ V}$
I = 86 A

DESIGN PROBLEM 23-8: What is the load in VA and amps to calculate and size the elements for 277/480 volt, three-phase service supplying a hospital with an office area of 150,000 sq. ft illuminated by 277 volt lighting units?

277 V, single-phase loads

• 150,000 sq. ft office
• 3000 sq. ft halls
• 800 sq. ft of closets
• 1000 sq. ft of hallways
• 4000 sq. ft of storage space

Note 1: For sizing elements, see page 23-23 of this chapter.

Note 2: Add asterisks and checks to obtain total load.

480 V, three-phase motor loads

• 6 - 40 HP elevators (15 minute intermittent duty)
• 12,000 VA A/C unit

480 V, three-phase loads

Emergency system loads

• 40 kW heating unit
• 60,000 VA life safety branch
• 35,000 VA critical branch
• 30,000 VA life support equipment
• 45,000 VA essential system loads
(All loads continuous)

Sizing phases = •
Sizing neutral = √
Sizing total load = *

CALCULATING LIGHTING LOAD

Step 1:	General lighting load			
	Table 220.12 and **230.42(A)(1)**			
	(office)			
	150,000 sq. ft x 3.5 VA	=	525,000 VA √
	525,000 VA x 125%	=	656,250 VA *
	(halls)			
	3000 sq. ft x 1/2 VA	=	1,500 VA √
	1500 VA x 125%	=	1,875 VA *
	(closets)			
	800 sq. ft x 1/2 VA	=	400 VA √
	400 VA x 125%	=	500 VA *
	(stairways)			
	1000 VA x 1/2 VA	=	500 VA √
	500 VA x 125%	=	625 VA *
	(storage space)			
	4000 VA x 1/4 VA	=	1,000 VA √
	1000 VA x 125%	=	1,250 VA *
	Total load	=	**660,500 VA •**

CALCULATING SPECIAL LOAD

Step 1:	Emergency system loads			
	230.42(A)(1)			
	(Life safety branch)			
	60,000 VA x 125%	=	75,000 VA *
	(Critical branch)			
	35,000 VA x 125%	=	43,750 VA *
	(Life support equipment)			
	30,000 VA x 125%	=	37,500 VA *
	(Essential system)			
	45,000 VA x 125%	=	56,250 VA *
	Total load	=	**212,500 VA •**

CALCULATING MOTOR LOAD

Step 1:	40 HP elevators (using 831 V)			
	430.24, 430.22(E), and **Table 430.22(E)**			
	52 A x (480 V x 1.732) x 85%	=	36,730 VA
	36,730 VA x 6	=	**220,380 VA * •**

CALCULATING HEATING OR A/C LOAD

Step 1:	Heating load			
	220.60 and **220.51**			
	40,000 VA x 100%	=	**40,000 VA * •**

CALCULATING LARGEST MOTOR LOAD

Step 1:	40 HP elevator			
	220.50 and **430.24**			
	36,730 VA x 25%	=	**9,183 VA * •**

CALCULATING FOR PHASES A, B AND C

General lighting load	=	660,500 VA •
Special loads	=	212,500 VA •
Motor loads	=	220,380 VA •
Heating loads	=	40,000 VA •
Largest motor load	=	9,183 VA •
Total load	=	**1,142,563 VA**

CALCULATING NEUTRAL (ADD ALL √)

General lighting load		
(Office)	=	525,000 VA √
(Halls)	=	1,500 VA √
(Closets)	=	400 VA √
(Stairways)	=	500 VA √
(Storage)	=	1,000 VA √
Total load	=	**528,400 VA**

FINDING AMPS FOR PHASES A, B, AND C

$I = VA \div (V \times \sqrt{3})$
$I = 1,142,563 \text{ VA} \div (480 \text{ V} \times 1.732)\ 831$
I = 1375 A

FINDING AMPS FOR NEUTRAL

$I = VA \div (V \times \sqrt{3})$
$I = 528,400 \text{ VA} \div (480 \text{ V} \times 1.732)\ 831$
I = 636 A

DESIGN PROBLEM 23-9: What is the load in VA and amps to calculate and size the elements for 120/208 volt, three-phase service supplying a welding shop?

120 V, single-phase loads

• 9000 VA inside lighting loads (continuous operation)
• 6 - 180 VA outside lighting loads (continuous operation)
• 1200 VA sign lighting loads (noncontinuous operation)
• 60 receptacles (continuous operation)

Sizing phase = •
Sizing neutral = √
Sizing total load = 13,800 VA
Sizing total load = *

Note 1: A welding shop is not a listed occupancy per **Table 220.12**.
Note 2: For sizing elements, see page 23-24 of this chapter.
Note 3: Add asterisks and checks to obtain total load.

208 V, three-phase loads

• 2 - 10 kW heating units
• 5400 VA A/C units
• 7.5 HP air compressor
• 2 - 1 1/2 HP grinders
• Welders - resistance (50% duty cycle)
• 12 kW
• 8 kW
• Welders - motor-generator arc (90% duty cycle)
• 14 kW
• 12 kW
• Welders - nonmotor-generator arc (80% duty cycle)
• 13 kW
• 9 kW

CALCULATING LIGHTING LOAD

Step 1: Inside lighting load
230.42(A)(1)

9000 VA x 100%	=	9,000 VA √
9000 VA x 125%	=	11,250 VA *

Step 2: Outside lighting load
230.42(A)(1)

6 x 180 VA	=	1,080 VA √
1080 VA x 125%	=	1,350 VA *

Step 3: Sign lighting load
220.14(F) and **230.42(A)(1)**

1200 VA x 100%	=	1,200 VA * √
Total load	**=**	**13,800 VA •**

CALCULATING RECEPTACLE LOAD

Step 1: Continuous duty
220.14(I) and **230.42(A)(1)**

60 x 180 VA	=	10,800 VA √
10,800 VA x 125%	=	13,500 VA * •

CALCULATING SPECIAL LOAD

Step 1: Welders - resistance
630.31(A) and **(B)**

12,000 VA x 71%	=	8,520 VA *
8000 VA x 71% x 60%	=	3,408 VA *

Step 2: Welders - motor-generator arc
630.11(A) and **(B)**

14,000 VA x 96%	=	13,440 VA *
12,000 VA x 96%	=	11,520 VA *

Step 3: Welders - nonmotor-generator arc
630.11(A) and **(B)**

13,000 VA x 89%	=	11,570 VA *
9000 VA x 89%	=	8,010 VA *
Total load	**=**	**56,468 VA •**

CALCULATING MOTOR LOAD

Step 1: Air compressor (using 360 V)
430.24, 430.22(E), and **Table 430.22(E)**

24.2 A x 100% x (208 V x 1.732)	=	8,712 VA *

Step 2: Grinders

(6.6 A x 2) x 100% x (208 V x 1.732)	=	4,752 VA *
Total load	**=**	**13,464 VA •**

CALCULATING HEATING OR A/C LOAD

Step 1: Heating load
220.60 and **220.51**

20,000 VA x 100%	=	**20,000 VA * •**

CALCULATING LARGEST MOTOR LOAD

Step 1: Air compressor (using 360 V)

24.2 A x (208 V x 1.732) x 25%	=	**2,178 VA * •**

CALCULATING TOTAL LOAD

Lighting loads	=	13,800 VA •
Receptacle loads	=	13,500 VA •
Special loads	=	56,468 VA
Compressor and motor load	=	13,464 VA •
Heating loads	=	20,000 VA •
Largest motor load	=	2,178 VA •
Total load	**=**	**119,410 VA**

FINDING AMPS FOR PHASES A, B, AND C

$I = VA \div (V \times \sqrt{3})$
$I = 119{,}410 \text{ VA} \div (208 \text{ V} \times 1.732)\ 360 \text{ V}$
I = 332 A

CALCULATING NEUTRAL (ADD ALL √)

220.61

Lighting loads (9000 + 1080 + 1200 VA)	=	11,280 VA √
Receptacle loads	=	10,800 VA √
Total load	**=**	**22,080 VA**

FINDING AMPS FOR NEUTRAL

$I = VA \div (V \times \sqrt{3})$
$I = 22{,}080 \text{ VA} \div (208 \text{ V} \times 1.732)\ 360 \text{ V}$
I = 61 A

Chapter 23. Commercial Calculations

Section   Answer

1. The lighting load in VA for lighting track shall be calculated by multiplying the lighting track by _______ VA and dividing by 2.

   (a) 100   (b) 150
   (c) 180   (d) 200

2. Occupancies with grade level access for pedestrians shall have a minimum of ______ VA provided for a sign lighting load.

   (a) 1200   (b) 1500
   (c) 1800   (d) 2400

3. There are ______ loads to be calculated when using the standard calculation to determine the load in VA or amps for the receptacle load.

   (a) 2   (b) 3
   (c) 4   (d) 5

4. Multioutlet assemblies with cord-and-plug connected appliances that operate simultaneously shall be calculated at ______ VA per foot.

   (a) 120   (b) 150
   (c) 180   (d) 200

5. In a commercial building, receptacles shall be calculated at ______ VA for each outlet. (General rule)

   (a) 150   (b) 180
   (c) 200   (d) 225

6. The total VA rating for a 8000 sq. ft office is ______ per **Table 220.12**.

   (a) 16,000   (b) 20,000
   (c) 24,000   (d) 28,000

7. The total rating for 60 ft of show window area is ______ VA if used noncontinuous.

   (a) 9000   (b) 10,800
   (c) 12,000   (d) 15,000

8. The total rating for 70 ft of multioutlet assembly having connected loads that are not simultaneously is ______ VA.

   (a) 2520   (b) 2530
   (c) 2560   (d) 2620

Section   **Answer**

__________ __________

9. The total VA rating for 40 ft of lighting track is _____VA when used at continuous operation.

   (a) 2000   (b) 2500
   (c) 3000   (d) 3750

10. The demand load for 130 general purpose receptacles that are used noncontinuous in an office is _____ VA.

   (a) 16,600   (b) 16,650
   (c) 16,700   (d) 23,400

11. The total load for 130 receptacles used at continuous operation in a bank is _____ VA.

   (a) 16,000   (b) 16,700
   (c) 23,400   (d) 29,250

12. If a 460 volt, three-phase compressor (largest motor load) is rated at 42 amps, the total rating for the largest motor load is _____ VA.

   (a) 8640   (b) 8726
   (c) 34,680   (d) 34,902

13. The total rating for a continuous 120 volt, single-phase, low voltage isolation transformer with a nameplate rating of 20 amps is _____ VA.

   (a) 2200   (b) 2400
   (c) 2500   (d) 3000

14. The total rating for a service load having a three-phase 35,000 VA heating unit and a three-phase 8280 VA heat pump is _____ amps. (277 / 480 volts)
   Note, the units can operate together.

   (a) 10   (b) 42
   (c) 52   (d) 65

15. The total rating for 50 ft of lighting track operating for 15 hours a day is _____ VA.

   (a) 3550.5   (b) 3660.8
   (c) 3750   (d) 4687.5

16. The demand for one of the following receptacle load is _____ VA.
   • 150 ft of multioutlet assembly appliances used simultaneously
   • 100 ft of multioutlet assembly appliances not used simultaneously
   • 70 general purpose receptacles operated at noncontinuous use

   (a) 1300   (b) 26,600
   (c) 39,600

17. The total rating for 45 receptacles used at continuous operation in a bank is _____ VA.

   (a) 8000   (b) 8100
   (c) 10,125

Section   Answer

18. The total rating for the largest motor load based on the following motors is _____
amps. (Apply 25 percent rule)
- 20 HP, three-phase, 460 volt motor
- 15 HP, three-phase, 208 volt motor
- 10 HP, three-phase, 230 volt motor

    (a) 6.75   (b) 7
    (c) 11.5

19. The total rating for the above motor loads is _____ amps for a 480 volt, three-phase
supply. (Round up amps.)

    (a) 35   (b) 61
    (c) 68

20. The total load for a 40 ft x 200 ft bank with 60 general purpose receptacles is _____
VA. (Calculate VA without applying 125 percent rule.)

    (a) 35,600   (b) 38,400
    (c) 38,800

21. The total load for a 10,000 sq. ft office with 50 general purpose receptacles is
_____ VA. (Calculate VA without applying 125 percent rule.)

    (a) 44,000   (b) 52,750
    (c) 55,000

22. The total load for a 400 ft hallway, 600 ft of stairway areas, and 200 ft of storage
space is _____ VA. (Calculate VA without applying 125 percent rule.)

    (a) 550   (b) 600
    (c) 750

23. The total load for 2000 sq. ft church with an 8000 sq. ft auditorium is _____ VA.
(Calculate for continuous load)

    (a) 9500   (b) 10,000
    (c) 12,500

24. The total load for 40 ballasts rated at .86 amp each and used for ten hours a day
is _____ amps. (Calculated applying 125 percent rule)

    (a) 33   (b) 34
    (c) 43

25. The total load for a small 20,000 sq. ft school with 2400 sq. ft of assembly hall area
is _____ VA. (Calculate VA without applying 125 percent rule.)

    (a) 62,400   (b) 75,000
    (c) 76,200

26. The Annex J outlines recommended information to be used regarding _____
accessibility design.

    (a) ABC   (b) ADD
    (c) ACC   (d) ADA

Section   **Answer**

27. Outlets installed for the purpose of charging electric vehicles shall be supplied by a ______ branch circuit.

   (a) combination   (b) parallel
   (c) AC/DC   (d) separate

28. Where there are no adjustment or correction factors involved in a branch circuit supplying a load, the ______ percent rule is the procedure used for continuous loads.

   (a) 100   (b) 110
   (c) 115   (d) 125

29. When calculating the load in VA per sq. ft. for a facility, Table ______ can be used. (Listed Occupancy)

   (a) 220.3   (b) 220.12
   (c) 250.66   (d) 250.122

30. Each noncontinuous duty receptacle outlet shall be calculated at ______ VA (general rule).

   (a) 125   (b)180
   (c) 175   (d) 225

31. Inductive and LED lighting loads shall be determined by calculating the load based on the unit's ______ rating.

   (a) amp   (b) VA
   (c) all of the above   (d) none of the above

32. What is the amp load for a 50,000 sq. ft store including a 30,000 sq. ft warehouse space with a 120/240 volt, single-phase service with the following loads:

   120 V, single-phase loads
   - 100 linear feet of show window (noncontinuous operation)
   - 120 ft of lighting track (noncontinuous operation)
   - 40 - 180 VA ballasts outside lighting (continuous operation)
   - 4200 VA sign lighting (continuous operation)
   - 74 receptacles (noncontinuous duty)
   - 24 receptacles (continuous duty)
   - 100 ft multioutlet assembly (simultaneously operated)

   240 V, single-phase loads
   - 12,000 VA water heater
   - 60,000 VA heating unit
   - 24,800 VA A/C unit
   - 7240 VA freezer
   - 6480 VA ice cream box
   - 9560 VA walk-in cooler
   - 1 - 1/2 HP exhaust fan
   - 1 - 2 HP water pump

Section   **Answer**

33. What is the amp load for a 50,000 sq. ft store including a 30,000 sq. ft warehouse
space with a 120/208 volt, three-phase service with the following loads:

120 V, single-phase loads
- 100 linear feet of show window (noncontinuous operation)
- 120 ft of lighting track
- 40 - 180 VA ballasts outside lighting (continuous operation)
- 4200 VA sign lighting (continuous operation)
- 74 receptacles (noncontinuous duty)
- 24 receptacles (continuous duty)
- 100 ft multioutlet assembly (simultaneously operated)

208 V, three-phase loads (Use 208 V x 1.732 = 360 V)
- 12,000 VA water heater
- 60,000 VA heating unit
- 24,800 VA A/C unit
- 7240 VA freezer
- 6480 VA ice cream box
- 9560 VA walk-in cooler
- 1 - 1/2 HP exhaust fan
- 1 - 2 HP water pump

34. What is the amp load for a 50,000 sq. ft store including a 30,000 sq. ft warehouse
space with a 277 volt lighting system and a 277/480 volt, three-phase
service with the following loads:

120 V, single-phase loads
- 100 linear feet of show window (noncontinuous operation)
- 120 ft of lighting track
- 40 - 180 VA ballasts outside lighting (continuous operation)
- 4200 VA sign lighting (continuous operation)
- 74 receptacles (noncontinuous duty)
- 24 receptacles (continuous duty)
- 100 ft multioutlet assembly (simultaneously operated)

480 V, three-phase loads (Use 480 V x 1.732 = 831 V)
- 12,000 VA water heater
- 60,000 VA heating unit
- 24,800 VA A/C unit
- 7240 VA freezer
- 6480 VA ice cream box
- 9560 VA walk-in cooler
- 1 - 1/2 HP exhaust fan
- 1 - 2 HP water pump

Section   **Answer**

____________ ___________

35. What is the amp load for a 50,000 sq. ft store including a 30,000 sq. ft warehouse space with a 120/240 volt, three-phase service with the following loads:

120 V, single-phase loads
- 100 linear feet of show window (noncontinuous operation)
- 120 ft of lighting track
- 40 - 180 VA ballasts outside lighting (continuous operation)
- 4200 VA sign lighting (continuous operation)
- 74 receptacles (noncontinuous duty)
- 24 receptacles (continuous duty)
- 100 ft multioutlet assembly (simultaneously operated)

240 V, three-phase loads (Use 240 V x 1.732 = 416 V)
- 12,000 VA water heater
- 60,000 VA heating unit
- 24,800 VA A/C unit
- 7240 VA freezer
- 6480 VA ice cream box
- 9560 VA walk-in cooler
- 1 - 1/2 HP exhaust fan
- 1 - 2 HP water pump

____________ ___________

36. What is the amp load for a 150,000 sq. ft office facility with a 2500 sq. ft of halls, equipped with a 277 volt lighting system supplied with a 277/480 volt, three-phase service with the following loads:

120 V, single-phase loads
- 50 ft of lighting track (noncontinuous operation)
- 20 - 180 VA ballasts outside lighting (continuous operation)
- 4200 VA sign lighting (continuous operation)
- 174 receptacles (noncontinuous duty)
- 114 receptacles (continuous duty)
- 6000 VA isolation transformer for LVLS (continuous operation)
- 160 ft multioutlet assembly (simultaneously operated)

208 V, three-phase loads
- 4 - 1275 VA copying machines (noncontinuous load)
- 1 - 8000 VA water heater (noncontinuous load)
- 22 - 225 VA data processors (continuous load)
- 8 - 175 VA work processors (continuous load)
- 2 - 1000 VA printers (continuous load)

480 V, three-phase loads
- 40 HP elevator (15 minute intermittent duty)
- 40 kW heating unit

Section   Answer

37. What is the amp load for a 20,000 sq. ft classroom area, a 4000 sq. ft auditorium area, and 1000 sq. ft assembly hall area with a 277/480 volt, three-phase service with the following loads: (lighting supplied by 277 volts)

120 V, single-phase loads
- 170 receptacles (noncontinuous duty)
- 40 receptacles (continuous duty)
- 160 ft multioutlet assembly (simultaneously operated)

120 V, single-phase cooking equipment
- 2 - 1   kW toasters
- 4 - 1.5 kW refrigerators
- 2 - 1.5 kW freezers

208 V, single-phase cooking equipment
- 4 -   9 kW ranges
- 3 - 10 kW ovens
- 4 -   3 kW fryers

208 V, single-phase motor loads
- 3 -   1 HP vent-hood fans
- 3 - 3/4 HP grill-vent fans

480 V, three-phase motor loads
- 18 - 3/4 HP exhaust fans

38. What is the amp load for a 6000 sq. ft restaurant with a 120/208 volt (use 360 volt), three-phase service that is equipped with the following loads:

120 V, single-phase loads
- 35 ft of lighting track (continuous duty)
- 10 - 180 VA outside lighting (continuous duty)
- 1200 VA sign lighting (continuous duty)
- 35 receptacles (noncontinuous duty)
- 30 receptacles (continuous duty)
- 20 ft multioutlet assembly (simultaneously operated)

208 V, single-phase loads
- 6950 VA vent-hood fans
- 4758 VA grill-vent fans
- 13 A   freezer
- 8000 VA cooktop
- 2 - 10,000 VA range
- 11,000 VA range
- 14 A refrigerator
- 3750 VA ice cream box

208 V, three-phase loads
- 2 - 25 kW heating units
- 2 - 7850 VA A/C units
- 3600 VA boiler
- 2 - 2600 VA deep fat fryers
- 20 A walk-in cooler
- 6500 VA water heater

Section   **Answer**

_____________ _____________   **39.** What is the amp load for a hospital having an office area of 150,000 sq. ft that is illuminated by a 277 volt lighting system with a 277/480 volt (use 831 volt), three-phase service with the following loads:

277 V, single-phase loads
- 150,000 sq. ft office space
- 2500 sq. ft hall space
- 600 sq. ft closet space
- 1200 sq. ft hallway
- 3800 sq. ft of storage space

480 V, three-phase motor loads
- 4 - 40 HP elevators (15 minute intermittent duty)
- 11,000 VA A/C unit

480 V, three-phase loads (emergency system loads)
- 50 kW heating unit (continuous duty)
- 50,000 VA life safety branch (continuous duty)
- 35,000 VA critical branch (continuous duty)
- 40,000 VA life support equipment (continuous duty)
- 40,000 VA essential system load (continuous duty)

_____________ _____________   **40.** What is the amp load for a welding shop with a 120/208 volt, three-phase service with the following loads:

120 V, single-phase loads
- 8500 VA inside lighting loads (continuous duty)
- 6 - 180 VA outside lighting loads (continuous duty)
- 1200 VA sign lighting load (noncontinuous duty)
- 50 receptacles (continuous duty)

208 V, three-phase loads
- 2 - 12 kW heating units
- 6,000 VA A/C unit
- 7.5 HP air-compressor
- 2 - 1 1/2 HP grinders
- 2 - welders - resistance (30% duty cycle)
  - 11 kW
  - 9 kW
- 2 - welders - motor generator arc (80% duty cycle)
  - 12 kW
  - 10 kW
- 2 - welders - nonmotor-generator arc (90% duty cycle)
  - 12 kW
  - 9 kW

Industrial Calculations

The *National Electrical Code* recognizes certain rules for calculating loads for sizing and selecting elements of electrical systems used to supply power to industrial occupancies. According to NEC requirements, each service and feeder shall be calculated and sized with enough capacity to carry a load current that is not less than the sum of all branch circuits it supplies in the electrical system. These calculations vary, depending on the type of facility, and the size and nature of the total load served.

In any electrical system, the distribution system consists of the equipment and wiring methods used to carry power from the supply transformer to the service equipment's overcurrent devices.

Distribution systems are used to carry power to lighting panelboards, power panelboards, switchboards, and motor control centers that house feeders and branch-circuit protective devices for supplying individual and multiple power loads. Adequate calculations will ensure that the elements of the system will provide the right amount of power at the right voltage to each distribution point.

LAYING OUT THE LOADS
ARTICLE 220, PART III

Since many industrial occupancies are not a listed occupancy, lighting loads shall be calculated without the use of **Table 220.12**. However, the other loads shall be calculated in the same manner as commercial facilities. They are laid out using the standard calculation as follows:

- Lighting loads
- Receptacle loads
- Special loads
- Compressor loads
- Motor loads
- Largest between heat and A/C or other loads
- The largest motor load

Note, see Chapter 23 for a detailed description of these loads and the number and types of loads that are associated with each specific load.

UNLISTED OCCUPANCY
220.14(A) THRU (L)

If an occupancy is not listed in **Table 220.12**, the general-purpose lighting load shall be calculated in the following manner per **220.14**.

- Lamps for incandescent lighting per **220.14(L)**
- Lamps for recessed lighting per **220.14(D)**
- Ballasts for electric discharge lighting per **220.18(B)**
- Show windows per **220.43(A)**
- Track lighting units per **220.43(B)**
- Low-voltage systems per **Article 411**

An unlisted VA rating shall be calculated at 125 percent for sizing the overcurrent protection device and conductors for continuous operation and at 100 percent for noncontinuous operated loads per **215.2(A)(1)(a)** and **230.42(A)(1)**. **(See Figure 23-3)**

Note, for high-voltage calculations, see **220.50** and **215.2(B) (1) through (B)(3).** For overcurrent protection device selection and settings, see **240.11 and 240.101.**

For example: What is the load in VA for 160, 120 volt, lighting ballasts rated at 1.5 amps each and used for 12 hours a day?

Step 1: Calculating load in amps
220.18(B)
160 x 1.5 A = 240 A

Step 2: Calculating continuous load
215.2(A)(1)(a) and **230.42(A)(1)**
240 A x 125% = 300 A

Step 3: Calculated VA
300 A x 120 V = 36,000 VA

Solution: The lighting load for the unlisted occupancy is 36,000 VA.

SHOW WINDOW LIGHTING LOAD
220.43(A)

The lighting load in VA for a show window shall be calculated by multiplying the linear feet of the show window by 200 VA per foot. Such lighting load shall be calculated at 100 percent for noncontinuous operation and at 125 percent for continuous operation per **215.2(A)(1)(a)** and **230.42(A) (1)**. Conductors and overcurrent protection devices shall be increased to comply with **240.3** and **240.4**.

For example: What is the lighting load in VA for a 40 ft show window used at noncontinuous or continuous operation?

Step 1: Calculating noncontinuous load
220.43(A), 215.2(A)(1)(a), and
230.42(A)(1)
40' x 200 VA x 100% = 8000 VA

Step 2: Calculating continuous load
220.43(A), 215.2(A)(1)(a), and
230.42(A)(1)
40' x 200 VA x 125% = 10,000 VA

Solution: The noncontinuous load is 8000 VA and the continuous load is 10,000 VA.

If the number of lighting outlets is known, the VA rating of each luminaire shall be multiplied by 125 percent for sizing the show window load. If the VA is not known, each outlet shall be calculated at 180 VA times 125 percent to obtain the lighting load in VA for the show window.

Note, the greater of either the 200 VA per linear foot or each individual calculation shall be used.

See Figure 23-4 for a detailed illustration of calculating the show window lighting load.

TRACK LIGHTING LOAD
220.43(B)

The lighting load in VA for lighting track shall be calculated by multiplying the lighting track by 150 VA and dividing by 2. Such VA rating shall be multiplied by 100 percent or by 125 percent based on noncontinuous or continuous operation per **90.7** and **110.3(B)**. **(See Figure 23-5)**

For example: What is the load in VA for 180 ft of lighting track used at noncontinuous or continuous operation?

Step 1: Calculating noncontinuous load
220.43(B), 215.2(A)(1)(a), and
230.42(A)(1)
180' ÷ 2' x 150 VA x 100% = 13,500 VA

Step 2: Calculating continuous load
220.43(B), 215.2(A)(1)(a), and
230.42(A)(1)
180' ÷ 2' x 150 VA x 125% = 16,875 VA

Solution: The noncontinuous load is 13,500 VA and the continuous load is 16,875 VA.

LOW-VOLTAGE LIGHTING LOAD
ARTICLE 411, 215.2(A)(1)(a), AND 230.42(A)(1)

The lighting load in VA for low-voltage lighting systems shall be calculated by multiplying the full-load amps of the isolation transformer by 100 percent for noncontinuous operation and by 125 percent for continuous operation.

For example: What is the load in VA for a low-voltage lighting system supplied by an isolation transformer with a FLA of 150 amps used at noncontinuous or continuous operation?

Step 1: Calculating noncontinuous load
Article 411, 215.2(A)(1)(a), and
230.42(A)(1)
150 A x 100% = 150 A

Step 2: Calculating continuous load
Article 411, 215.2(A)(1)(a), and
230.42(A)(1)
150 A x 125% = 187.5 A

Solution: The noncontinuous load is 150 amps and the continuous load is 187.5 amps.

OUTSIDE LIGHTING LOAD
220.18(B), 215.2(A)(1)(a), AND 230.42(A)(1)

The lighting load in VA for outside lighting loads shall be calculated by multiplying the VA rating of each lighting unit by 100 percent for noncontinuous operation and by 125 percent for continuous operation. **(See Figure 23-7)**

For example: What is the lighting load in VA for 130 continuously operated luminaires with a 175 VA ballast in each unit and 110 noncontinuously operated units with each ballast having a rating of 175 VA?

Step 1: Calculating load
220.18(B), 215.2(A)(1)(a), and
230.42(A)(1)
175 x 130 x 125% = 28,437.5 VA
175 x 110 x 100% = 19,250   VA
Total load = 47,687.5 VA

Solution: The total outside lighting load is 47,687.5 VA.

OUTSIDE SIGN LIGHTING LOAD
220.14(F), 215.2(A)(1)(a), AND 230.42(A)(1)

The lighting loads for signs shall be calculated based on the commercial occupancy or facility having ground floor footage accessible to pedestrians. Occupancies with grade-level access for pedestrians shall have a minimum of 1200 VA provided for a sign lighting load. This VA rating is multiplied by 125 percent for signs operating for three hours or more and by 100 percent for those operating less than three hours. **(See Figure 23-8)**

RECEPTACLE LOADS
220.14(I) AND TABLE 220.44

Receptacle loads are the second group of loads to be calculated. Such loads are divided into two subgroups as follows:

- General-purpose receptacle outlets
- Multioutlet assemblies

Each load in the subgroup shall be calculated differently to derive total VA.

GENERAL-PURPOSE RECEPTACLE LOADS
220.14(I), 215.2(A)(1)(a), AND 230.42(A)(1)

The load in VA for the general-purpose receptacle load shall be calculated by multiplying the number of outlets times 180 VA each, times 100 percent for noncontinuous operation, and 125 percent for continuous operation. **(See Figure 23-9)**

For example: What is the load in VA for 55 general-purpose receptacles used to serve noncontinuous and continuous related loads?

Step 1: Calculating noncontinuous load
220.14(I), 215.2(A)(1)(a), and
230.42(A)(1)
180 VA x 55 x 100% = 9900 VA

Step 2: Calculating continuous load
220.14(I), 215.2(A)(1)(a), and
230.42(A)(1)
180 VA x 55 x 125% = 12,375 VA

Solution: The noncontinuous load is 9900 VA and the continuous load is 12,375 VA.

Note, a demand factor as listed in **Table 220.44** shall not be permitted to be applied to the continuous load of 12,375 VA even if this value exceeds 10,000 VA.

APPLYING DEMAND FACTORS
220.14(I) AND TABLE 220.44

General-purpose receptacle outlets for cord-and-plug connected loads used at noncontinuous operation shall be calculated per **220.14(I)** and **Table 220.44**. Noncontinuous operated receptacles with a VA rating of 10,000 VA or less shall be calculated at 100 percent. If the VA rating of the receptacle load exceeds 10,000 VA, a demand factor of 50 percent shall be permitted to be applied to all VA exceeding 10,000 VA per **Table 220.44**. **[See Figure 23-10(a)]**

For example: What is the VA rating for 225 general-purpose receptacle outlets to cord-and-plug connect loads used at noncontinuous operation?

Step 1: Calculating load
220.14(I)
225 x 180 VA = 40,500 VA

Step 2: Applying demand factors
Table 220.44
First 10,000 VA x 100% = 10,000 VA •
Next 30,500 VA x 50% = 15,250 VA •
Total load   = 25,250 VA

Solution: The demand load is 25,250 VA.

MULTIOUTLET ASSEMBLIES
220.14(H)(1) AND (H)(2)

For connected loads not operating simultaneously, the VA rating shall be calculated by dividing the length of the assembly by 5 ft and multiplying by 180 VA. For connected loads operating simultaneously, each foot of multioutlet assembly shall be multiplied by 180 VA. The fixed multioutlet assembly load shall be permitted to be added to the noncontinuous receptacle load and a demand factor applied per **Table 220.44**. **[See Figures 23-10(b) and (c)]**

For example: What is the load in VA for 200 ft of multioutlet assembly used to cord-and-plug connect loads that are not used simultaneously and used simultaneously? **[220.14(A)(1)]**

Step 1: Calculating load for
nonsimultaneous use
VA = length ÷ 5 ft x 180 VA
VA = 200 ft ÷ 5 ft x 180 VA
VA = 7200

Step 2: Calculating load for simultaneous use
VA = length x 180 VA
VA = 200 ft x 180 VA
VA = 36,000

**Solution: The load in VA for the
nonsimultaneous load is 7200 VA
and for the simultaneous load is
36,000 VA.**

SPECIAL LOADS
215.2(A)(1)(a) AND (b) AND 230.42(A)(1)

Special-appliance loads are the third group of loads to be calculated. These loads, which include computers, processing machines, etc., are usually served by individual circuits.

CONTINUOUS AND NONCONTINUOUS OPERATION
215.2(A)(1)(a) AND 230.42(A)(1)

The load in VA for special-appliance loads shall be calculated by multiplying the VA rating of each load by 100 percent for noncontinuous operation and by 125 percent for continuous operation. To determine the classification, special-appliance loads operating for less than three hours shall be classified as a noncontinuous operated load. However, a special-appliance load operating for three hours or more shall be classified as a continuous operated load. **(See Figure 23-11)**

For example: What is the VA rating for a 208 volt, three-phase, 165 amp special-appliance load operating for 10 hours and supplied by an individual branch circuit? [Use 360 V (208 x 1.732)]

Step 1: Calculating VA (using 360 V)
220.5(A)
VA = (V x 1.732) x I
VA = (208 x 1.732) x 165
VA = 59,400

Step 2: Calculating continuous load
215.2(A)(1)(a) and 230.42(A)(1)
59,400 VA x 125% = 74,250 VA

**Solution: The load at continuous operation
is 74,250 VA.**

For example: Consider and calculate the VA rating for a special-appliance load of 82 amps operating at 480 volts, three-phase, for a period of 2-1/2 hours every four hours. [Use 831 V (480 V x 1.732)]

Step 1: Calculating VA (using 831 V)
220.5(A)
VA = (V x 1.732) x I
VA = (480 V x 1.732) x 82 A
VA = 68,142

Step 2: Calculating noncontinuous load
215.2(A)(1)(a) and 230.42(A)(1)
68,142 VA x 100% = 68,142 VA

**Solution: The load in VA for the
noncontinuous load is 68,142 VA.**

COMPRESSOR LOADS
440.34

Compressor loads are the fourth group of loads to be calculated. Special considerations shall be applied when calculating loads for hermetically sealed compressors supplying refrigerant and cooling related equipment.

CONTINUOUS OR NONCONTINUOUS OPERATION
440.34, 215.2(A)(1)(a), AND 230.42(A)(1)

Compressor-related equipment shall be calculated at 100 percent of it's VA or amps. If one of such is the largest motor per load #7, it is added to the total calculation of all loads at 125 percent of its nameplate rating. **(See Figure 23-13)**

For example: What is the load in VA for 6 compressors rated at 42 amps each and supplied by a 480 volt, three-phase supply? (All used in one process at the same time)

> **Step 1:** Calculating VA (using 831 V)
> **220.5(A)**
> (42 A x 6) x (480 V x 1.732) =
> 209,412 VA
>
> **Step 2:** Calculating continuous load
> **440.34, 215.2(A)(1)(a),** and **230.42(A)(1)**
> 209,412 VA x 125% = 261,765 VA
>
> **Solution: The load in VA for the 6 compressors used in an industrial process at the same time is 261,765 VA.**

MOTOR LOADS
220.50 AND 430.24

Motor loads are the fifth group of loads to be calculated. The VA rating of motors is converted from amperage to VA by multiplying the amperage from **Table 430.248** for single-phase, or **Table 430.250** for three-phase, by the supply voltage. **(See Figure 23-14)**

For example: What is the VA rating for a group of 480 volt, three-phase motors rated at 125 HP, 40 HP and 30 HP?

> **Step 1:** Finding FLA
> **Table 430.250**
> 125 HP   = 156 A
> 40 HP   = 52 A
> 30 HP   = 40 A
>
> **Step 2:** Calculating total VA (using 831 V)
> **220.5(A)**
> VA = (V x 1.732) x I
> 125 HP
> (480 V x 1.732) x 156 A = 129,636 VA •
> 40 HP
> (480 V x 1.732) x 52 A = 43,212 VA •
> 30 HP
> (480 V x 1.732) x 40 A = 33,240 VA •
> Total VA   = 206,088 VA
>
> **Solution: The total load for the motors is 206,088 VA.**

Design Tip: Motors can be used as a single unit to drive a piece of equipment. Motors used in an approved assembly such as a processing machine are not usually considered individual motor loads.

HEATING OR AIR-CONDITIONING LOADS
220.60

Heating or air-conditioning loads are the sixth group of loads to be calculated. The largest VA rating between the heating or air-conditioning load is selected, and the smaller of the two loads is dropped. To determine the largest of the two loads, the VA rating of each load shall be calculated at 100 percent and the largest load of the two is selected. The load dropped is not used again in the calculation. **(See Figure 23-15)**

Design Tip: There is no need to calculate both loads (or any load) to select the elements of the service equipment, for the loads are never used simultaneously in the electrical system. For heat pump rules, **see Figure 23-16**.

For example: What is the largest load between a 240 kW heating unit and a 97 amp air-conditioning unit? The voltage is supplied by 480 volts, three-phase system.

> **Step 1:** Selecting largest load (using 831 V)
> **220.60**
> Heating load
> 240 kW x 1000 x 100% = 240,000 VA
> A/C load
> 97 A x (480 V x 1.732) = 80,607 VA
>
> **Solution: The 240,000 VA heating unit is the largest load.**

LARGEST MOTOR LOAD
220.50 AND 430.24

The largest motor load in VA is the seventh of the loads to be calculated. The largest motor load is selected from one of the motor related loads listed in the fourth, fifth, or sixth loads. The VA rating of the largest motor shall be calculated by multiplying the amperage of the unit by the voltage, times 25 percent. **(See Figure 23-16)**

For example: What is the largest motor from the following loads?

> Fourth load = compressor of 52 A
> Fifth load = motor of 65 A
> Sixth load = A/C unit = 23 A
>
> **Step 1:** Selecting largest load
> **220.50, 440.34,** and **430.24**
> The motor load of 65 A is the largest load
>
> **Solution: The largest motor load is 65 amps.**

OPTIONAL CALCULATIONS FOR ADDITIONAL LOADS TO EXISTING INSTALLATIONS
220.87

When additional loads are added to existing facilities having feeders and service as originally calculated, the maximum kVA calculations in determining the load on the existing feeders and service shall be permitted to be used if the following conditions are complied with:

- If the maximum data of the demand in kVA is available for a minimum of one year, such as demand meter ratings.

- If the demand ratings for that period of one year at 125 percent and the addition of the new load does not exceed the rating of the service. Where demand meters are used, in most cases the load as calculated will probably be less than the demand meter indications.

- If the overcurrent protection device meets **230.90, 215.3,** and **240.4** for feeders or a service. **(See Figure 23-19)**

APPLYING Ex. TO 220.87
220.87, Ex.

If the maximum demand data for a one year period is not available, the calculated load shall be based on the maximum demand (measure of average power demand over a 15 minute period) continuously recorded over a minimum 30 day period using a recording ammeter or power meter connected to the highest loaded phase of the feeder or service, based on the initial loading at the start of the recording. **(See Figure 23-20)**

Design Tip: By measurement or calculation, the larger of the heating or cooling equipment load shall be included if it is not in the demand data.

CALCULATING THE NEUTRAL
220.61 AND 310.15(B)(5)(c) TO TABLE 310.15(B)(16)

For a service or feeder, the maximum unbalanced load controls the ampacity of the grounded (neutral) conductor. The grounded (neutral) conductor feeder load shall be considered wherever a grounded (neutral) conductor is used in conjunction with one or more ungrounded (phase) conductors. On a single-phase feeder using one ungrounded (phase) conductor and a grounded (neutral) conductor, the grounded (neutral) conductor will carry the same amount of current as the ungrounded (phase) conductor. A two-wire feeder is seldom used, so in considering the grounded (neutral) conductor feeder current, always assume that there is a grounded (neutral) conductor and two or more ungrounded (phase) conductors. If there are two ungrounded (phase) conductors that are connected to the same phase and a neutral, the grounded (neutral) conductor would be required to carry the total current from both ungrounded (phase) conductors, which would not be an accepted practice.

For three-wire DC or single-phase AC; four-wire, three-phase; three-wire, two-phase; and five-wire, two-phase systems, a further demand factor of 70 percent shall be permitted to be applied to that portion of the unbalanced load in excess of 200 amperes. There shall be no reduction of the grounded (neutral) conductor capacity for that portion of the load that consists of electric-discharge lighting, electronic computer/data processing, or similar equipment, when supplied by four-wire, wye-connected, three-phase systems.

For example, on a four-wire, three-phase wye circuit where the major portion (over 50 percent) of the load consists of nonlinear loads, there are harmonic currents present in the grounded (neutral) conductor, and the grounded (neutral) conductor is considered to be a current-carrying conductor. In other words, the ampacity of the conductor shall be derated per **310.15(B)(3)(a)** and **Table 310.15(B)((3)(a)**.

Review the rules and examples of Chapters 6, 14 and 15 for the sizing and use of the grounded (neutral) conductor in service, feeder, and branch-circuit installations.

USING A ONE-LINE DIAGRAM
90.8 AND 490.48(C)

When calculating the load for an existing electrical system or to design an entirely new system, an important tool is a good, up-to-date line diagram of the system. It indicates by single lines and standard symbols the routed course and component parts of an electric circuit or system of circuits.

A schedule of loads and values shall be developed, and such load values calculated to size and select components and wiring methods. **(See Figure 24-1)**

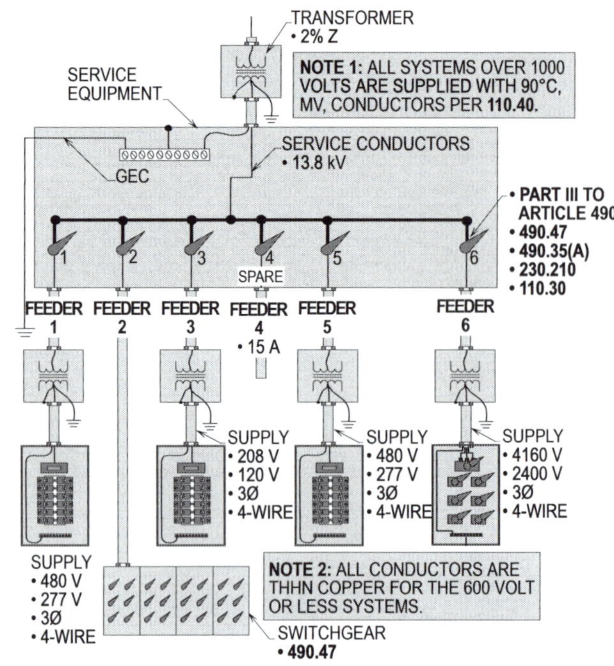

Figure 24-1. This one-line diagram depicts the electrical equipment in an industrial plant.

HIGH-VOLTAGE REVIEW SECTIONS

- Calculating Loads – **215.2(B)(1) THRU (B)(3)**
- Terminal Rating – **110.40**
- Conductor Sizes – **310.60(C)(4) THRU 310.60(C)(86)**
- Duct Runs – **Figure 310.60**
- Shields – **310.40, 310.19(E)** and **(F), 250.190(C)(2)**
- Circuit Breakers – **490.21(A)**
- Fuses – **490.21(B)**
- Isolating Means – **490.22, 490.21(B)(4) THRU (B)(7)**
- Warning – **110.21(B)**
- Live Parts – **490.35(A)**
- Visual Inspections – **490.40**
- Switchgear used as Service Equipment – **490.47**
- Substations – **490.48**

Note, refer to **225.50, 210.19(B), 215.2(B), 230.200, 230.202(A) and (B)** as well as **240.100** and **240.101, when performing calculations and then selecting and sizing overcurrent protection devices.**

CALCULATING FEEDER NO. 1

(1) Lighting loads

Number	Type load	Phases	Volts	Amps
• 60	2 ballast	1Ø	277 V	.38 A ea.
• 42	HID 1000 W	1Ø	480 V	.86 A ea.
• 6	Large equip.	3Ø	480 V	21 A ea.
• 10	process units	3Ø	480 V	34 A ea.

Note: All loads are used at continuous operation.

(2) Calculating total amps for feeder No. 1
    220.18(B), 215.2(A)(1)(a), and **440.34**
       (2 ballast at .38 A ea.)
          • 60 x 2 x .38 x 125% = 57 A •
       (HID 1000 W at .86 A ea.)
          • 42 x .86 A x 125% = 45.15 A •
          • 6 x 21 A x 125% = 157.5 A •
          • 10 x 34 A x 125% = 425 A •
          Total load = 684.65 A

Rounded up to 685 amps per **220.5(B)**

(3) Sizing conductors for feeder No. 1
    Table 310.15(B)(16)

    Step 1: Paralleling three per phase
          310.10(H)
          A of conductors = A ÷ No. of conductors
          A = 685 A ÷ 3
          A = 228

    Step 2: Selecting conductors for feeder No. 1
          Table 310.15(B)(16)
          229 A requires 4/0 AWG cu.
          4/0 AWG THHN cu. = 230 A

    Step 3: Total amps of conductors
          310.10(H)
          4/0 AWG cu. = 230 A x 3 = 690 A
          690 A supplies 685 A

    Solution: The size THHN copper conductors are
           4/0 AWG paralleled 3 times per phase.

(4) Sizing overcurrent protection device based on load
    240.4(B) and **240.6(A)**

685 A or 690 A requires 700 A OCPD

    Solution: The size overcurrent protection device
           for 3 - 4/0 paralleled THHN copper
           conductors is 700 amps.

CALCULATING FEEDER NO. 2

(1) What size 90ºC, MV, copper conductors and overcurrent protection device is required to supply power to the switchgear based on the following loads per **Part III** to **Article 220**?

Number	Type load	Phases	Volts	Amps
• 2	Heavy equip.	3Ø	13.8 kV	2 A ea.
• 2	Large motors	3Ø	13.8 kV	1.5 ea.
• 1	Distribution center	3Ø	13.8 kV	15 A

Note: all loads are used at continuous operation.

(2) Calculating total amps for feeder No. 2
    230.202, 230.208(B), (simultaneously) **215.2(B)(1) thru (3),** and **430.24**
       (2 heavy equipment at 2 A ea.)
          • 2 x 2 A x 125% = 5 A
       (2 large motors at 1.5 ea.)
          • 2 x 1.5 A x 125% = 3.75 A
       (1 distribution center at 15 A)
          • 1 x 15 A x 125% = 18.75 A
       (largest motor load)
          • 1.5 A x 25% = .375 A
          Total loads = 27.875 A

(2) What size 90°C, MV copper conductors are required for an underground run in conduit to supply the distribution equipment?

Number	Type load	Phases	Volts	Loads
• 1	distribution run	3Ø	13.8 kV	27.875 A

(3) Calculating load for underground feeder
    Figure 310.60, Detail 1; Table 310.60(C)(77)

       27.875 A requires 6 AWG cu.

    Solution: The size 90°C, MV conductors for the
           underground run is 6 AWG copper.

(4) How many mains are allowed for disconnecting the feeder if it were run to a separate building?

    Step 1: Finding number of mains
          225.33(A), 225.34(A), and **225.52**
          The number of mains is 6

    Solution: Six mains are allowed to disconnect the
           feeder.

Note: In most designs, the loads supplied are multiplied by 125% per **225.50,** but high-voltage overcurrent protection devices can be supplied at 100% of the loads per **230.208(B).** Consult with the AHJ for the procedure to be used.

CALCULATING FEEDER NO. 3
PART II TO ARTICLE 220

Number	Type load	Phases	Volts	Amps
• 150	4 - 34 W fluorescent	1Ø	120 V	.86 A ea.
• 50	recessed luminaires	1Ø	120 V	1.25 A ea.
• 40	150 W bulbs	1Ø	120 V	1.25 A ea.
• 200	receptacles (180 W ea.)	1Ø	120 V	1.5 A ea.
• 10	100 ft multi-outlet assembly	1Ø	120 V	
• 10	isolation receptacles	1Ø	120 V	1.5 A ea.

Note: all the loads except the receptacles and bullet four are used at continuous operation.

(1) Calculating total amps for feeder No. 3
220.14(I), 220.14(H)(2), 215.2(A)(1)(a), and **Table 220.44**
(150 fluorescent at .86 A ea.)
 • 150 x .86 A x 125%   = 161.25 A
(50 recessed luminaires at 1.25 A ea.)
 • 50 x 1.25 A x 125%   = 78.125 A
(40 - 150 W bulbs at 1.25 A ea.)
 • 40 x 1.25 A x 125%   = 62.5   A
(200 receptacle at 1.5 A ea.)
 • 200 x 180 W   = 36,000 W
 First 10,000 W x 100% = 10,000 VA
 • 10 x 180 VA   = 1,800 VA
 Total load   = 37,800 VA
 Next 27,800 W x 50%   = 13,900 VA
 Total load   = 23,900 VA

 I = 23,900 VA ÷ (208 x 1.732) = 66.38 A
(10 isolation receptacles at 1.5 A ea.)
 • 10 x 1.5 x 125%   = 18.75 A
 Total load (TD)   = 387.005 A

(2) What is the minimum size overcurrent protection device required on the primary side of the transformer for feeder No. 3?

 Step 1: Sizing the transformer based on secondary
 GE manual (based on 125% of TD.)
 kVA = I x (V x $\sqrt{3}$) ÷ 1000
 kVA =
 387.005 A x (208 V x 1.732) ÷ 1000
 kVA = 139.322

 Step 2: Selecting size of the transformer
 ACME chart (based on 125% of LD.)
 139.322 kVA requires 225 kVA

 Solution: The size transformer to supply the load is 225 kVA per ACME XFMR chart.

 Step 3: Finding FLA of transformer
 I = (kVA x 1000) ÷ (V x $\sqrt{3}$)
 I = (225 kVA x 1000) ÷ (13,800 V x 1.732)
 I = 9.4 A

 Step 4: Finding size of OCPD for primary
 Table 450.3(A) and **240.6(A)**
 9.4 A x 600% = 56.4 A
 56.4 A requires 50 A

 Solution: Under certain conditions, 230.208(B) permits the load for over 600 volt systems to be calculated at 100 percent. Size overcurrent protection device is 50 amp.

(3) What size 90°C, MV copper conductors, based on the overcurrent protection device, are required to supply the primary of the transformer for Feeder No. 3?

 Step 1: Selecting conductors based on OCPD
 Table 310.60(C)(77) and **110.40**
 50 A OCPD requires 6 AWG cu.

 Solution: The size of the conductors for feeder No. 3 are 6 AWG copper based on the overcurrent protection device.

Note 1: Where applicable, the energy code, IC 90.1, can be used per **Ex.** to **220.12.**

Note 2: For selecting the size of transformer, see chart of transformer's manufacturer (XFMR).

Note 3: The primary voltage of the transformer is tree-wire, three phase, 13,800 volts and the secondary voltage is four-wire, three phase, 120/208 volts.

CALCULATING FEEDER NO. 4
PART II TO ARTICLE 220

Number	Type load	Phases	Volts	Amps
• 1	Spare	3Ø	13.8 kVA	15 A √

(1) Providing load capacity for Feeder No. 4

A load capacity of 15 amps is provided for future use.

CALCULATING FEEDER NO. 5
PART III TO ARTICLE 220

Number	Type load	Phases	Volts	Amps
• 10	10 HP motors	3Ø	460 V	14 A ea.
• 12	15 HP motors	3Ø	460 V	21 A ea.
• 15	5 HP motors	3Ø	460 V	7.6 A ea.
• 16	3 HP motors	3Ø	460 V	4.8 A ea.

(1) What size conductors using the 10 ft (3 m) connection rule are required to supply the motors on the secondary side of the transformer?

Step 1: Calculating motor load
430.24

10 x 14 A	= 140 A
12 x 21 A	= 252 A
15 x 7.6 A	= 114 A
16 x 4.8 A	= 76.8 A
21 A x 25%	= 5.3 A
Total load	= 588.1 A

(2) Using the 10 ft (3 m) connection rule, per **240.21(C)(2),** how many 3/0 AWG, THHN copper conductors are required for a parallel hook-up between the transformer and panel?

Step 1: Calculating the number of conductors
310.10(H) and **Table 310.15(B)(16)**
(3/0 AWG = 200 A)
No. of conductors = total A ÷ A of conductors
No. of conductors = 588.1 A ÷ 200 A
No. of conductors = 2.94 A

Step 2: Finding the number of conductors
310.10(H) and **Table 310.15(B)(16)**
2.94 requires 3

Solution: **The parallel hook-up requires 3 - 3/0 AWG per phase.**

(3) What size overcurrent protection device (CB) is required for the connected secondary conductors?

Step 1: Sizing OCPD for largest motor load
430.62(A), 430.52(C)(1), and **Table 430.52**
21 A x 250% = 52.5 A

Step 2: Selecting size OCPD
430.52(C)(1) and **Table 430.52**
52.5 A requires 50 A (rounding down)

Step 3: Sizing OCPD for tapped conductors
430.28(1) and **430.62(A)**

Largest OCPD	= 50 A
(See steps (2) to (3)	
Other motors	= 140 A
(252 A - 21 A = 231 A)	= 231 A
[See step 1 to (1)]	= 114 A
	= 76.8 A
Total load	= 611.8 A

Step 4: Selecting OCPD for the secondary conductors
430.62(A) and **240.6(A)**
611.8 A requires 600 A

Solution: **The size overcurrent protection device for the feeder using a circuit breaker is 600 amps. Note, there is no Ex. to 430.62(A) that will permit the next size overcurrent protection device above 611.8 amps to be used.**

(4) What size copper grounding electrode conductor, supply-side bonding jumper (S-SBJ), and grounded (neutral) conductor are required to ground the secondary to building steel?

Step 1: Sizing the GEC
250.30(A)(5), Table 250.66, and **Table 8, Ch. 9**
3/0 AWG = 167,800 CM x 3 in parallel = 503,400 CM
KCMIL = 503,400 CM ÷ 1000 = 503.4 KCMIL
503.4 KCMIL requires 1/0 AWG cu.

Solution: **The size of the grounding electrode is 1/0 AWG copper.**

Step 1: Sizing the S-SBJ
250.30(A)(1), 250.102(C)(1), and **Table 250.102(C)(1)**
503.4 KCMIL requires 1/0 AWG cu.

Solution: **The size of the supply-side bonding jumper shall be at least 1/0 AWG copper.**

Step 1: Sizing the grounded (neutral) conductor
250.24(C)(2), Table 250.1-2(C)(1), and **310.10(H)**
503.4 KCMIL requires 1/0 AWG copper

Solution: **The size of the grounded (neutral) conductor shall be 1/0 AWG copper in each conduit run.**

CALCULATING ELEMENTS FOR FEEDER NO. 6

Number	Type load	Phases	Volts	Amps
2	Heavy load (machine)	3Ø	4160 V	12 A
4	Large motors (in a process)	3Ø	4160 V	
1	motor			20 A
1	motor			26 A
1	motor			15 A
1	motor			25 A
3	motors			50 A
1	distribution panel	3Ø	4160 V	50 A
1 motor control center				
	• 1 - 200 HP	3Ø	4160 V	27.9 A
	• 1 - 150 HP	3Ø	4160 V	20.9 A
	• 1 - 125 HP	3Ø	4160 V	18.5 A
	• 2 - 50 HP	3Ø	4160 V	7.6 A

(1) What is the total load for Feeder No. 6?

Step 1: Calculating total load
215.2(B)(1) thru (3), 230.200, 430.24, and **430.25**
(2 heavy loads)

2 x 12 A	=	24	A

(7 large motors)

1 x 20 A	=	20	A
1 x 26 A	=	26	A
1 x 15 A	=	15	A
1 x 25 A	=	25	A
3 x 50 A	=	150	A

(1 distribution panel at 50 A)

1 x 50 A	=	50	A

(motor control center - 5 motors)

1 x 27.9 A	=	27.9 A
1 x 20.9 A	=	20.9 A
1 x 18.5 A	=	18.5 A
2 x 7.6 A	=	15.2 A

(largest motor load)

50 A x 25%	=	12.5 A
Total load	=	405 A √

CALCULATING THE SERVICE LOAD IN AMPS FOR EACH VOLTAGE
230.42(A)(1), 430.24, and **440.34**

Step 1: Calculating amps of each feeder
220.5(A)

Feeder No. 1 (277 ÷ 480 V)	=	684.65 A√
Feeder No. 2 (13.8 kV)	=	27.875 A√
Feeder No. 3 (120 ÷ 208 V)	=	387.005 A√
Feeder No. 4 (277 / 480 V)	=	15 A√
Feeder No. 5 (13.8 kV)	=	588.1 A√
Feeder No. 6	=	405 A√
Total load		= 2,107.63 A

Step 2: Calculating kVA of feeders 1, 3, 5, and 6 based on supply voltage and load
220.5(A)
Feeder No. 1 on page 24-9:
kVA = 684.65 A x 480 V x 1.732 ÷ 1000
kVA = 569.19
Feeder No. 3 on page 24-10:
kVA = 387.005 A x 208 V x 1.732 ÷ 1000
kVA = 139.42
Feeder No. 5 on page 24-11:
kVA = 588.1 x 480 V x 1.732 ÷ 1000
kVA = 488.92
Feeder No. 6 on page 24-12:
kVA = 405 x 4160 V x 1.732 ÷ 1000
kVA = 2918.07

Step 3: Calculating amps of each feeder based on supply voltage and load
220.5(A)
Feeder No. 1 on page 24-9:
I = (kVA x 1000) ÷ (V x $\sqrt{3}$)
I = (569.19 x 1000) ÷ (13,800 x 1.732)
I = 23.81 A√
Feeder No. 2 on page 24-9:
Amps at 13,800 V = 27.85 A√
Feeder No. 3:
I = (kVA x 1000) ÷ (V x $\sqrt{3}$)
I = (139.42 x 1000) ÷ (13,800 x 1.732)
I = 5.83 A√
Feeder No. 4 on page 24-10:
Amps at 13,800 V = 15 A√
Feeder No. 5:
I = (kVA x 1000) ÷ (V x $\sqrt{3}$)
I = (488.92 x 1000) ÷ (13,800 x 1.732)
I = 20.46 A√
Feeder No. 6:
I = (kVA x 1000) ÷ (V x $\sqrt{3}$)
I = (2918.07 x 1000) ÷ (13,800 x 1.732)
I = 122.08 A√
Total amps = 215.03 A

Solution: **The service load in amps to size the elements of the service is 215.03 amps.**

Step 4: Calculating the 90°C, MV, conductors of the service
Table 310.60(C)(77), Column 4
215.03 A at 13.8 kV requires 4/0 AWG

Solution: **The size conductors for the service are 2/0 AWG copper.**

WHAT SIZE TRANSFORMER IS REQUIRED TO SUPPLY THE SERVICE EQUIPMENT LOADS?
220.5(A) AND PAGE 24-10

Step 1: $kVA = I \times (V \times \sqrt{3})$
$kVA = 215.03\ A \times (13,800\ V \times 1.732)$
$kVA = 5139.56$

Step 2: Selecting transformers
ACME chart
Use a transformer bank

Solution: Use a transformer bank that can handle 5139.56 kVA at 13,800 volts.

WHAT IS THE FLC IN AMPS OF THE TRANSFORMER?

Step 1: $FLC = (kVA \times 1000) \div (V \times \sqrt{3})$
$FLC = (5139.56\ kVA \times 1000) \div (13,800\ V \times 1.732)$
$FLC = 215.03\ A$

Solution: The FLC of the transformer is 215.03 amps.

WHAT IS THE AVAILABLE FAULT CURRENT AT THE TERMINALS OF THE TRANSFORMER?

Step 1: $AFC = FLA\ of\ transformer \div Z$
$AFC = 215.03\ A \div .02$
$AFC = 10,752\ A$

Solution: The AFC at the terminals of the transformer is 10,752 amps (rounded up).

SEE FIGURE 24-2 FOR THE SIZE ELEMENTS OF EACH FEEDER
220.3

Note 1: Figure 24-2 has the size elements of each feeder shown for easy identification after such elements have been calculated and selected.

Note 2: Figure 24-2 has a summary of the elements in Figure 24-1 after they were sized from the load calculations.

Note 3: The NEC defines low-voltage systems as 1000 volts or less, and high-voltage systems are those operating over 1000 volts.

Note 4: IEEE-141 normally defines low-voltage systems as those that are 1000 volts or less and medium voltage as systems over 1000 volts up to 69,000 volts. High-voltage systems are greater than 69,000 volts.

Feeder No. 1 on page 24-9

Size OCPD for the panelboard
• 700 A
Size conductors for panelboard
• 3 - 4/0 AWG THWN cu. conductors per phase

Feeder No. 2 on page 24-9

Size OCPD for the switchgear
• 30 A or 50 A based on conductors
Size conductors for the switchgear
• 6 MV cu. conductors

Feeder No. 3 on page 24-10

Size OCPD for the primary of transformer
• 50 A
Size conductors for the primary of transformer
• 6 MV cu. conductors

Feeder No. 4 on page 24-10

Size OCPD for the future load
• 15 A
Size conductors for the future load
• 6 MV cu. based on NEC

Feeder No. 5 on page 24-11

Size OCPD for the connection
• 600 A
Size conductors for the connection
• 3 - 3/0 THWN cu. conductors per phase

Feeder No. 6 on page 24-12

Total load for feeder in amps
• 405 A √

Service elements on pages 24-12 and 13

Size conductor for the service
• 2/0 MV cu. conductors per phase
Size transformer for the service
• transformer bank

Note: Use Detail 1 to **Table 310.60(C)(77).**

Note: The NEC is equipped with demand factors (less than 1). Diversity factors (more than 1) can be found in the McGray-Hill Electrical Engineering Handbook.

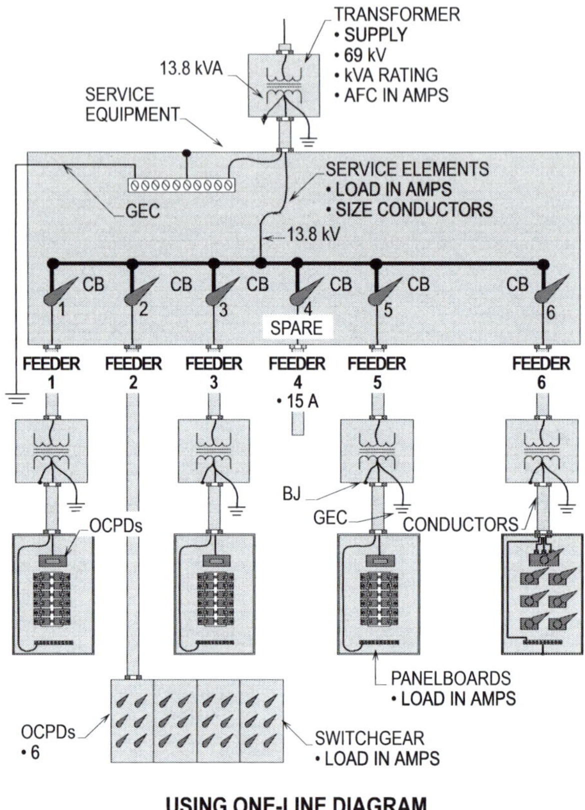

Figure 24-2. One-line diagram showing electrical equipment and wiring methods, with the size of individual elements of service and feeders after they were sized from load calculations. For calculation procedure for each element, refer to the page number listed below the sizes shown.

Chapter 24. Industrial Calculations

Section   Answer

1. What is the load in VA for an unlisted occupancy feeder having 140 - 120 volt lighting ballasts rated at 1.5 amps each and used for 6 hours a day?

    (a) 25,200 VA   (b) 30,000 VA
    (c) 31,500 VA   (d) 33,500 VA

2. What is the lighting load in VA for an unlisted occupancy feeder having 50 ft show window used at continuous operation?

    (a) 9,000 VA   (b) 10,000 VA
    (c) 10,500 VA   (d) 12,500 VA

3. What is the load in VA for 200 ft of lighting track on a service used at noncontinuous operation?

    (a) 15,000 VA   (b) 18,000 VA
    (c) 18,750 VA   (d) 22,500 VA

4. What is the load in VA for 50 general purpose receptacles on a service used to serve continuous related loads?

    (a) 9,000 VA   (b) 10,000 VA
    (c) 11,250 VA   (d) 12,500 VA

5. What is the load in VA for 200 general purpose receptacle outlets to cord-and-plug connect loads used at noncontinuous operation?

    (a) 23,000 VA   (b) 28,750 VA
    (c) 36,000 VA   (d) 45,000 VA

6. What is the load in VA for 150 ft of multioutlet assembly used to cord-and-plug connect loads that are used simultaneously?

    (a) 18,000 VA   (b) 27,000 VA
    (c) 30,000 VA   (d) 33,750 VA

7. What is the VA rating for a 208 volt, three-phase, 155 amp special appliance load operating for eight hours and supplied by an individual branch circuit?

    (a) 55,800 VA   (b) 64,480 VA
    (c) 69,750 VA   (d) 80,600 VA

8. What is the VA rating for a 208 volt, three-phase, 155 amp special appliance load operating for two hours and supplied by an individual branch circuit?

    (a) 32,240 VA   (b) 40,300 VA
    (c) 55,000 VA   (d) 69,750 VA

Section   **Answer**

_______ _______ **9.** What is the load in amps for 4 compressors rated at 38 amps each and supplied by a 480 volt, three-phase supply? (All used in one process at the same time)

      (a) 152   (b) 162
      (c) 168   (d) 174

_______ _______ **10.** What is the VA rating for a group of 480 volt, three-phase motors rated at 100 HP, 50 HP, and 25 HP? (Calculate for a feeder.)

      (a) 213   (b) 254
      (c) 262   (d) 266

Annex

TABLE A					
SIZE AWG/ KCMIL	OHMS TO NEUTRAL PER 1000 FEET				
	AC Resistance for Uncoated Copper Wires			AC Resistance for Aluminum Wires		
	PVC Conduit	Alu. Conduit	Steel Conduit	PVC Conduit	Alu. Conduit	Steel Conduit
14	3.1	3.1	3.1	-----	-----	-----
12	2.0	2.0	2.0	3.2	3.2	3.2
10	1.2	1.2	1.2	2.0	2.0	2.0
8	0.78	0.78	0.78	1.3	1.3	1.3
6	0.49	0.49	0.49	0.81	0.81	0.81
4	0.31	0.31	0.31	0.51	0.51	0.51
3	0.25	0.25	0.25	0.40	0.41	0.40
2	0.19	0.20	0.20	0.32	0.32	0.32
1	0.15	0.16	0.16	0.25	0.26	0.25
1/0	0.12	0.13	0.12	0.20	0.21	0.20
2/0	0.10	0.10	0.10	0.16	0.16	0.16
3/0	0.077	0.082	0.079	0.13	0.13	0.13
4/0	0.062	0.067	0.063	0.10	0.11	0.10
250	0.052	0.057	0.054	0.085	0.090	0.086
300	0.044	0.049	0.045	0.071	0.076	0.072
350	0.038	0.043	0.039	0.061	0.066	0.063
400	0.033	0.038	0.035	0.054	0.059	0.055
500	0.027	0.032	0.029	0.043	0.048	0.045
600	0.023	0.028	0.025	0.036	0.041	0.038
750	0.019	0.024	0.021	0.029	0.034	0.031
1000	0.015	0.019	0.018	0.023	0.027	0.025
Note, see **Table 9, Ch. 9** of the NEC.					

Note, for a detailed illustration using **Table A**, see **Method 2** in **Figure 6-34**.

TABLE B					
(THREE SINGLE CONDUCTORS) **"C" VALUE FOR CONDUCTORS AND BUSWAYS**					
Copper **AWG** **or** **KCMIL**	**Three Single Conductors** **Conduit** **Steel**				
	600 V	**5 kV**	**15 kV**	**600 V**	**5 kV**	**15 kV**
14	389	389	389	389	389	389
12	617	617	617	617	617	617
10	981	981	981	981	981	981
8	1557	1551	1557	1558	1555	1558
6	2425	2406	2389	2430	2417	2406
4	3806	3750	3695	3825	3789	3752
3	4760	4760	4760	4802	4802	4802
2	5906	5736	5574	6044	5926	5809
1	7292	7029	6758	7493	7306	7108
1/0	8924	8543	7973	9317	9033	8590
2/0	10755	10061	9389	11423	10877	10318
3/0	12843	11804	11021	13923	13048	12360
4/0	15082	13605	12542	16673	15351	14347
250	**16483**	14924	13643	18593	17120	15865
300	18176	16292	14768	20867	18975	17408
350	19703	17385	15678	22736	20526	18672
400	20565	18235	16365	24296	21786	19731
500	22185	19172	17492	26706	23277	21329
600	22965	20567	17962	28033	25430	22690
750	24136	21386	18888	28303	25430	22690
1000	25278	22539	19923	31490	28083	24887
Aluminum						
14	236	236	236	236	236	236
12	375	375	375	375	375	375
10	598	598	598	598	598	598
8	950	950	951	951	950	951
6	1480	1476	1472	1481	1478	1476
4	2345	2332	2319	2350	2341	2333
3	2948	2948	2948	2958	2958	2958
2	3713	3669	3626	3729	3701	3672
1	4645	4574	4497	4678	4631	4580
1/0	5777	5669	5493	5838	5766	5645
2/0	7186	6968	6733	7301	7152	6986
3/0	8826	8466	8163	9110	8851	8627
4/0	10740	10167	9700	11174	10749	10386
250	12122	11460	10848	12862	12343	11847
300	13909	13009	12192	14922	14182	13491
350	15484	14280	13288	16812	15857	14954
400	16670	15355	14188	18505	17321	16233
500	18755	16827	15657	21390	19503	18314
600	20093	18427	16484	23451	21718	19635
750	21766	19685	17686	23491	21769	19976
1000	23477	21235	19005	28778	26109	23482

Note, for a detailed illustration using **Table B**, see **Method 1** in **Figure 6-34**.

TABLE B					
(THREE CONDUCTOR CABLE) "C" VALUE FOR CONDUCTORS AND BUSWAYS					
Copper AWG or KCMIL	Three Single Conductors Conduit Steel			Nonmagnetic		
	600 V	5 kV	15 kV	600 V	5 kV	15 kV
14	389	389	389	389	389	389
12	617	617	617	617	617	617
10	981	981	981	981	981	981
8	1559	1557	1559	1559	1558	1559
6	2431	2424	2414	2433	2428	2420
4	3830	3811	3778	3837	3823	3798
3	4760	4790	4760	4802	4802	4802
2	5989	5729	5827	6087	6022	5957
1	7454	7364	7188	7579	7507	7364
1/0	9209	9086	8707	9472	9372	9052
2/0	11244	11045	10500	11703	11528	11052
3/0	13656	13333	12613	14410	14118	13461
4/0	16391	15890	14813	17482	17019	16012
250	18310	17850	16465	19779	19352	18001
300	20617	20051	18318	22524	11938	20163
350	22646	21914	19821	24904	24126	21982
400	24253	23371	21042	26915	26044	23517
500	26980	25449	23125	30028	28712	25916
600	28752	27974	24896	32236	31258	27766
750	31050	20024	26932	32404	31338	28303
1000	33864	32688	29320	37197	35748	31959
Aluminum						
14	236	236	236	236	236	236
12	375	375	375	375	375	375
10	598	598	598	598	598	598
8	951	951	951	951	951	951
6	1481	1480	1478	1482	1481	1479
4	2351	2347	2339	2353	2349	2344
3	2948	2956	2948	2958	2958	2958
2	3733	3719	3693	3739	3724	3709
1	4686	4663	4617	4699	4681	4646
1/0	5852	5820	5717	5875	5851	5771
2/0	7327	6968	6733	7301	7152	6986
3/0	9077	8980	8750	9242	9164	8977
4/0	11184	10121	10642	11408	11277	10968
250	12796	12636	12115	13236	13105	12661
300	14916	14698	13973	15494	15299	14658
350	15413	16490	15540	17635	17351	16500
400	18461	18063	16921	19587	17321	16233
500	18755	16827	15657	21390	19243	18154
600	23633	23195	21348	25750	25243	23294
750	26431	25789	23750	25682	25141	23491
1000	29864	29049	26608	32938	31919	29135

Note, these values are equal to one over the impedance per foot for impedences found in IEEE. Std. 241-1990, *IEEE Recommended Practice for Commercial Building Power System.*

TABLE B						
AWG or MCM	Copper Three Single-Conductors				Copper Three-Conductor Cable	
	Steel-Conduit		Nonmagnetic Conduit		Steel Conduit	Nonmagnetic Conduit
	600 V and 5 kV Nonshielded	5 kV Shielded and 15 kV	600 V and 5 kV Nonshielded	5kV Shielded and 15 kV	600 V and 5 kV Nonshielded	600 V and 5 kV Nonshielded
12	588		588			
10	909		1449			
8	1429	1230	1449	1230	1230	1230
6	2222	1940	2273	1940	1950	1950
4	3333	3040	3448	3070	3080	3090
3	4167	3830	4348	3870	3880	3900
2	5000	4670	5263	4780	4830	4850
1	6250	5750	6250	5920	6020	6100
1/0	7692	6990	7692	7250	7410	7580
2/0	9091	8260	9091	8770	9090	9350
3/0	10638	9900	11364	10700	11100	11900
4/0	12500	10800	13514	12600	13400	14000
250	13699	12500	17857	14000	14900	15800
300	15385	13600	16949	15500	16700	17900
350	16667	14700	18868	17000	18600	20300
400	17857	15200	20408	17900	19500	21100
500	20000	16500	23256	19700	21900	24000
600	21277	17200	25000	20900	23300	25700
750	23256	18300	27778	22500	25600	28200
1000	25000		31250			

Note, these tables were used for fault calculations before Tables B on pages III and IV were available.

AWG or MCM	Aluminum Three Single Conductors or Three-Conductor Cables	
	Steel Conduit	Nonmagnetic Conduit
	600 V and 5 kV Nonshielded	600 V and 5 kV Nonshielded
12	357	357
10	555	556
8	909	909
6	1388	1408
4	2173	2173
3	2702	2702
2	3333	3333
1	4000	4166
1/0	5000	5000
2/0	6250	6250
3/0	7142	7692
4/0	9090	9090
250	10000	10638
300	11363	12195
350	12500	13698
400	13698	15384
500	15625	17543
600	17241	19607
750	19230	22222
1000	21739	25641

TABLE C								
		Conductors				DC Resistance at 75ºC (167ºF)		
Size AWG/KCMIL	Area Cir. Mils	Stranding		Overall		Copper		Aluminum
		Quantity	Diam. In.	Diam. In.	Area Sq. In.²	Uncoated ohm/kFT	Coated ohm/kFT	ohm/kFT
18	1620	1	——	0.040	0.001	7.77	8.08	12.8
18	1620	7	0.015	0.046	0.002	7.95	8.45	13.1
16	2580	1	——	0.051	0.002	4.89	5.08	8.05
16	2580	7	0.019	0.058	0.003	4.99	5.29	8.21
14	4110	1	——	0.064	0.003	3.07	3.19	5.06
14	4110	7	0.024	0.073	0.004	3.14	3.26	5.17
12	6530	1	——	0.081	0.005	1.93	2.01	3.18
12	6530	7	0.030	0.092	0.006	1.98	2.05	3.25
10	10380	1	——	0.102	0.008	1.21	1.26	2.00
10	10380	7	0.038	0.116	0.011	1.24	1.29	2.04
8	16510	1	——	0.128	0.013	0.764	0.786	1.26
8	16510	7	0.049	0.146	0.017	0.778	0.809	1.28
6	26240	7	0.061	0.184	0.027	0.491	0.510	0.808
4	41740	7	0.077	0.232	0.042	0.308	0.321	0.508
3	52620	7	0.087	0.260	0.053	0.245	0.254	0.403
2	66360	7	0.097	0.292	0.067	0.194	0.201	0.319
1	83690	19	0.066	0.332	0.087	0.154	0.160	0.253
1/0	105600	19	0.074	0.373	0.109	0.122	0.127	0.201
2/0	133100	19	0.084	0.419	0.138	0.0967	0.101	0.159
3/0	167800	19	0.094	0.470	0.173	0.0766	0.0797	0.126
4/0	211600	19	0.106	0.528	0.219	0.0608	0.0626	0.100
250	——	37	0.082	0.575	0.260	0.0515	0.0535	0.0847
300	——	37	0.090	0.630	0.312	0.0429	0.0446	0.0707
350	——	37	0.097	0.681	0.364	0.0367	0.0382	0.0605
400	——	37	0.104	0.728	0.416	0.0321	0.0331	0.0529
500	——	37	0.116	0.813	0.519	0.0258	0.0265	0.0424
600	——	61	0.099	0.893	0.626	0.0214	0.0223	0.0353
700	——	61	0.107	0.964	0.730	0.0184	0.0189	0.0303
750	——	61	0.111	0.998	0.782	0.0171	0.0176	0.0282
800	——	61	0.114	1.03	0.834	0.0161	0.0166	0.0265
900	——	61	0.122	1.09	0.940	0.0143	0.0147	0.0235
1000	——	61	0.128	1.15	1.04	0.0129	0.0132	0.0212
1250	——	91	0.117	1.29	1.30	0.0103	0.0106	0.0169
1500	——	91	0.128	1.41	1.57	0.00858	0.00883	0.0141
1750	——	127	0.117	1.52	1.83	0.00735	0.00756	0.0121
2000	——	127	0.126	1.63	2.09	0.00643	0.00662	0.0106

Note, See **Table 8, Ch. 9** of the NEC.

CONNECTION OF STARTING ON A WYE AND RUNNING ON A DELTA

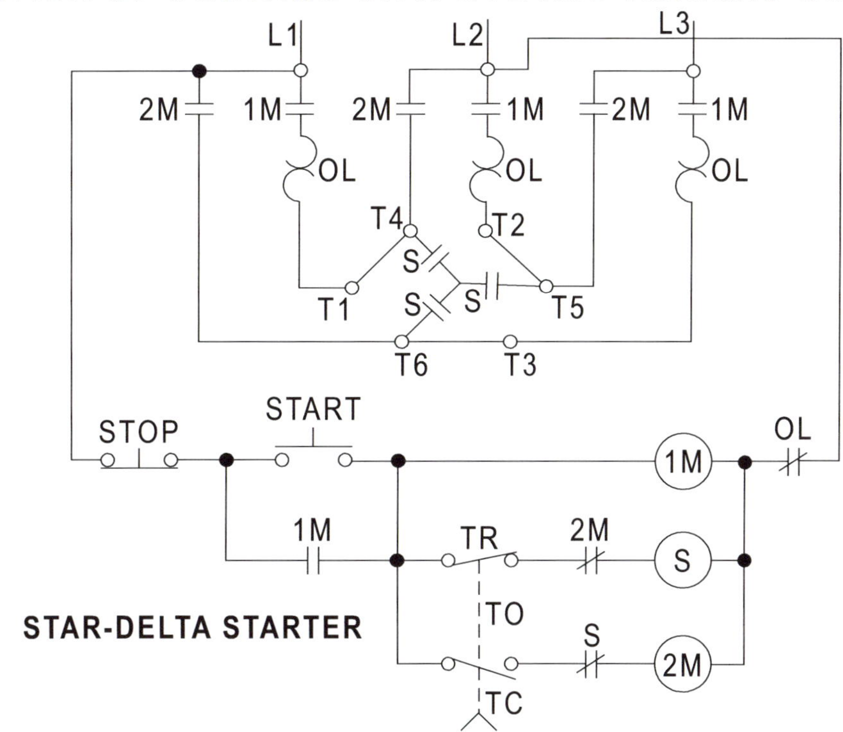

STAR-DELTA STARTER

CONNECTION OF PART-WINDING MOTORS

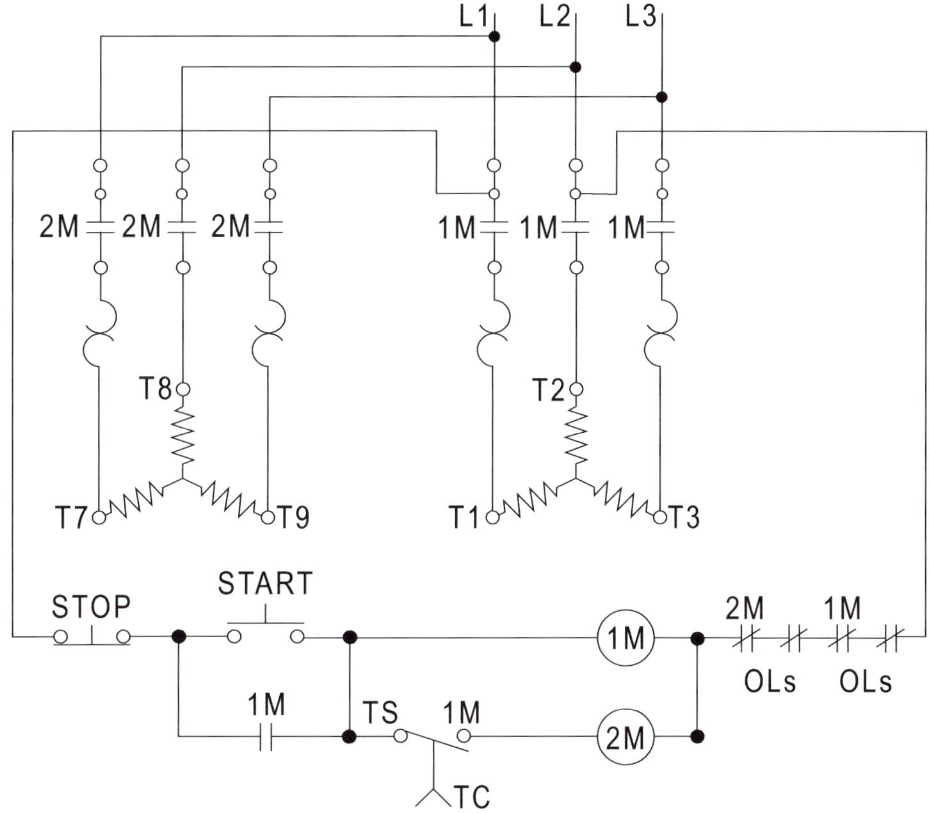

PART-WINDING STARTER

TABLE D

Abbreviations

A

A - amps
AC - alternating current
A/C - air conditioning
AEGCP - assured equipment grounding conductor program
AHJ - authority having jurisdiction
Alu. - aluminum
ASCC - available short-circuit current
AWG - American Wire Gauge

B

BC - branch circuit
BCSC - branch-circuit selection current
BJ - bonding jumper
BK - black
BL - blue
BR - brown

C

°C - Celsius
CB - circuit breaker
CEE - concrete-encased electrode
CL - code letter
CM - circular mils
CMP - code-making panel
Comp. - compressor
Cond. - condenser
Cont. - continuous
cu. - copper
cu. in. - cubic inches

D

DC - direct current
dia. - diameter
DPCB - double-pole circuit breaker

E

EBJ - equipment bonding jumper
EExde - increase safety
Eexe - flameproof/increased safety components
Eff. - efficiency
EGB - equipment grounding bar

EGC - equipment grounding conductor
EMT - electrical metallic tubing
ENT or ENMT - electrical nonmetallic tubing
Epf - explosionproof
Ex. - Exception

F

°F - Fahrenheit
FLA - full-load amperage
FLC - full-load current
FMC - flexible metal conduit
FPN - fine print note
ft - foot

G

G - ground
GE - grounding electrode
GEC - grounding electrode conductor
GES - grounding electrode system
GFCI - ground-fault circuit interrupter
GFL - ground-fault limiter
GFPE - ground-fault protection of equipment
GR - green
GRY - gray
GSC - grounded service conductor

H

H - hot conductor
HACR - heating, air conditioning, cooling, and refrigeration
HP - horsepower
Htg. - heating
Hz - hertz

I

I - amperage or current
IEC - International Electrotechnical Commission
IG - isolated ground
in. - inches
IN - informal note
INST. CB - instantaneous trip circuit breaker
INVT - inverse-time circuit breaker
IRA - inrush amps
ITSC - intrinsically safe circuits

K

kFT - 1000 ft
kV - kilovolts
kVA - kilovolt-amps
kW - kilowatts
kWH - kilowatt-hour

L

L - length of conductor
Ld. - load
LFMC - liquidtight flexible metal conduit
LFNC - liquidtight flexible nonmetallic conduit
LPB - lighting panelboard

LRA - locked-rotor amps
LRC - locked-rotor current
LTR - long-time rated

M

MA - milliamps
max. - maximum
MEL - maximum energy level
mf - microfarads
MGFA - maximum ground fault available
min. - minimum
min. - minute
MR - momentary rated
Mt. - motor

N

N - neutral
NACB - nonautomatic circuit breaker
NB - neutral bar
NEC - *National Electrical Code*
NEMA - National Electrical Manufacturers Association
NFD - nonfused disconnect
NFPA - National Fire Protection Association
NLTFMC - nonmetallic liquidtight flexible metal conduit
NPC - nameplate current of motor
NTDF - nontime-delay fuse

O

OCP - overcurrent protection
OCPD - overcurrent protection device
OL - overload
OLP - overload protection
OLs - overloads
OR - orange
OSHA - Occupational Safety and Health Administration

P

PF - power factor
Ph. - phases
pri. - primary
PSA - power supply assembly
PU - purple

R

R - ohms or resistance
RD - red
RMC - rigid metal conduit

S

SBS - structural building steel
SCC - short-circuit current
SDS - separately derived system
sec. - secondary
SF - service factor
SIA - seal-in amps
SP - single-pole
SPCB - single-pole circuit breaker
sq. ft - square foot (feet)
sq. in. - square inches

STR - short-time rated
SWD - switched disconnect
SWG - switchgear

T

TDC - time-delay cycle
TDF - time-delay fuse
TDL - time-delay limiter
TP - thermal protector
TR - temperature rise
TS - trip setting
TV - touch voltage

U

UF - underground feeder

V

V - volts
VA - volt-amps
VD - voltage drop

W

W - watts
WT - white
WP - weatherproof

X

XFMR - transformer

Y

YEL - yellow

Glossary

A

Across-the-line starter is a device consisting of contactor and overload relay that is used to start an electric motor by connecting it directly to the supply line.

Active power is the true electrical power or real power supplying the load.

Air gap is the air space between two electrically related parts, such as the space between poles of a magnet or poles in an electric motor.

Alternating current (AC) is the current in an electrical circuit that alternates in flowing first with a positive polarity and then with a negative polarity.

Alternator is a rotating machine whose output is AC.

Ambient conditions are the conditions of the atmosphere adjacent to electrical equipment.

Ambient temperature is the temperature of the surrounding atmosphere cooling medium, which comes into contact with the heated parts of equipment.

Ambient temperature compensated is a device, such as an overload relay, that is not affected by the temperature surrounding it.

Ampacity is the maximum current, in amperes, that a conductor can carry continuously under the conditions of use without exceeding its temperature rating.

Ampere is a unit of intensity of electrical current produced in a conductor by an applied voltage.

Apparatus is a set of control devices used to help perform the intended control functions.

Apparent power is the sum of active power and reactive power. It is determined by multiplying voltage times current.

Arc-chute is a cover around contacts, designed to protect surrounding parts from arcing effects.

Armature is a specially designed rotor.

Armature reaction is the reaction of the magnetic field produced by the current on the magnetic lines of force, which are produced by the field coil of an electric motor or generator.

Automatic is performing a function without the necessity of human intervention.

Automatic controller is a motor or other that mechanism which uses automatic pilot devices as activating devices. These devices may be pressure switches, level switches, or thermostats.

Autotransformer starter is equipped with an autotransformer that is designed to reduce the voltage to the motor terminals and reduce the starting current, and still start the motor, etc.

Auxiliary contacts are contacts in addition to the main circuit contacts, and function with the movement of the latter.

Auxiliary device is any device other than a motor or motor starter necessary to fully operate the machine or equipment.

Auxiliary interlock:

• Mechanical - A physical device or arm so arranged that it cannot close both starter circuits at the same time.

• Electrical - An additional contact mounted on the side of a magnetic starter.

B

Bearings are devices used to support the motor shaft and allow it to rotate smoothly.

Bimetallic disc is a disc made up of two strips of dissimilar metals combined to form a single strip.

Branch circuit is the circuit conductors between the final overcurrent device protecting the circuit and the outlet(s).

Breakdown torque is the maximum torque that a motor develops under increasing load conditions at rated voltage and frequency, without a sudden drop in rotating speed.

Brushes are sliding contacts, usually made of carbon, which are located between a commutator and the outside circuit in a generator or motor.

C

Capacitance is the ability to store electricity in an electrostatic field.

Capacitor is a device that is designed to introduce capacitance into an electric circuit.

Capacitor-start motor is an AC split-phase induction motor that has a capacitor connected in series with an auxiliary winding, which provides a way for it to start. This auxiliary circuit is designed to disconnect to the motor when it reaches its speed.

Circuit is an electrical network of conductors that provides one or more paths for current.

Circuit breaker is a device designed to open and close a circuit by a nonautomatic means and to open the circuit automatically on a predetermined overcurrent, without damage to itself, when properly applied within its rating.

Combination starter is a magnetic starter having a manually operated disconnecting means built into the enclosure that houses the magnetic contactor or starter.

Commutator is a device that reverses the connections to the revolving loops on the armature.

Compensating windings are the windings embedded in the main pole pieces of a compound DC motor.

Component is the smallest element of a circuit.

Contactor is an electro mechanical device for connecting and disconnecting an electric power circuit.

Contacts are connecting parts which co-act with other parts to connect or disconnect a circuit.

Control is a device or group of devices that is used in some predetermined manner to govern the electric power delivered to an apparatus.

Control, three-wire is a control function that utilizes a momentary contact pilot device and a holding circuit contact to provide voltage to the coil of a controller. The holding circuit maintains the control circuit voltage.

Control, two-wire is a control function which utilizes a maintained contact-type pilot device to provide undervoltage release.

Control circuit is the control apparatus that carries the signals directing the performance of the controller.

Control circuit transformer is utilized to supply a reduced voltage suitable for the operation of control devices.

Control circuit voltage is the voltage providing the operation to the coils of magnetic devices.

Controller is a device or group of devices that serves to govern, in some predetermined manner, the electric power delivered to the apparatus to which it is connected.

Copper loss is the electrical power lost through the resistance of the coils due to the current flowing through the wire of the coils.

Core is the magnetic path through the center of coil or transformer.

Core losses are the loss of power in the coil (core) due to eddy currents and hysteresis.

Core transformer is an electrical transformer which has the core inside of the coils.

Counter torque is a repulsion force between two magnetic fields.

Counterelectromotive force is the voltage induced in the armature coil of an electric motor.

D

Delta-delta connected is a coil connection in which the primary and secondary coils are delta connected.

Delta-wye connected is a connection in which the primary winding is delta connected while the secondary windings are wye connected.

Diagram is a connection diagram showing the electrical connection between the parts of the control and the external connections.

Direct current (DC) is a current that always flows in only one direction.

Disconnecting means is a device or group of devices, or other means by which the conductors of a circuit can be disconnected from their source of supply.

E

Eddy currents are the electrical currents circulating in the core of a transformer as the result of induction.

Efficiency is the ratio of output power (watts) to input power (watts).

Electric motor is a machine that converts electrical energy to mechanical energy.

Electricity is electrical charges in motion. Such movement is called current and is measured in amps.

Electrolytic capacitor is a capacitor that uses a liquid or paste as one of its electrical storage plates.

Electromagnet is a magnet comprised of a coil of wire wound around a soft iron core. When current is passed through the wire, a magnetic field is produced.

Electromagnetism is a magnetic field that exists around a wire or other conductor if a current is passing through it.

Electromechanical is a device that uses electrical energy to create mechanical motion of force.

Electromotive force is a voltage or force which causes free electrons to move in a conductor.

Electron is a negative electric charge.

Electron flow is the flow of electrons from a negative point to a positive point in a conductor.

Electrostatic charge is the electrical charge stored by a capacitor.

Electrostatic field is the stored electrical charges on the surface of an insulator.

Excitation is creating a magnetic field to be used to create electromagnetics when an electric current is passed through a coil.

F

Feeders are all circuit conductors between the service equipment, the source of a separately derived system, or other power supply source and the final branch-circuit overcurrent device.

Float switch is a switch that is operated by a float and is responsive to the level of liquid.

Foot switch is a switch that is suitable for operation by an operator's foot.

Frequency is the rate at which AC changes its direction of flow; it is normally expressed in terms of hertz (cycles) per second.

Fuse is an overcurrent protection device with a circuit opening fuseable member that opens when overheated by current passing through it.

G

Gate is one of the leads on a thyristor. This lead is the one that normally controls output when it is correctly biased.

Generator is a rotating machine that changes mechanical energy into DC.

Generator action is inducing voltage into a wire that is cutting a magnetic field.

Ground is the earth.

Guarded is covered, shielded, fenced, enclosed, or otherwise protected by means of suitable covers or casings, barriers, rails or screens, mats, or platforms to remove the likelihood of dangerous contact or approach by persons or objects to a point of danger.

H

Hermetic refrigerant motor-compressor is a combination consisting of a compressor and motor, both of which are enclosed in the same housing, with no external shaft or shaft seals, and the motor operating in the refrigerant.

Hertz is a measurement of frequency; it actually means "cycles per second" of AC.

High side is a transformer marking that indicates the high-voltage winding.

Horsepower is a unit of measure for power that represents the force times distance times time. For example, one horsepower (HP) equals 746 watts, or 33,000 ft lb. per minute, or 550 ft lb. per second.

Hysteresis is the property of a magnetic substance that causes the magnetization to lag behind the magnetizing force.

I

Impedance is the total opposition to current flow in a circuit and is measured in ohms.

Induced current is the current that flows in a conductor because of a changing magnetic field.

Inductance is electromotive force resulting from a change in magnetic flux surrounding a circuit or conductor.

Induction is the generation of electricity by magnetism.

Inductive reactance is the opposition in ohms to an AC as a result of induction. This is voltage resulting from cutting lines of magnetic force.

Interlock is an electrical or mechanical device actuated by the operation of a different device to which it is directly related.

Intermittent duty is a requirement or service that demands operations for alternate intervals of (1) load and no load; (2) load and rest; or (3) load, no load, and rest, such alternate intervals being definitely specified.

Isolating transformer is transformer used to electrically isolate one circuit from another.

Inverter is a circuit capable of receiving a positive signal and sending out a negative one, or vice versa. It is a device which changes AC to DC or vice versa.

J

Jogging is the rapid and repeated opening and closing of the circuit to start a motor from rest for the purpose of creating small movements of the motor or driven load.

K

kVA is the term used to rate transformers.

KVAR is the reactive power in a circuit.

kW is used to rate the load of certain types of equipment, etc.

L

Lamination consists of sheet material that is sandwiched together to construct a stator or rotor of a rotating machine.

Limit switch is a switch that is operated by a part or motion of a power-driven piece of equipment. Such operation alters the electric or electronic circuits related to the equipment.

Locked-rotor current of a motor is the current taken from the line when the motor starts or the rotor becomes locked in place.

Low side is a transformer marking that indicates which is the low voltage winding.

M

Magnetic starter is a starter that is actuated by an electro-magnetic means.

Manual controller is a device that manually closed or opened .

Manual reset is a device which requires manual action to re-engage the contacts after an overload.

Magnetic drive (magnetic clutch) is an electromagnetic device that is connected between a three-phase motor and its load. Its main purpose is regulating the speed at load rotated speed.

Magnetic field is the invisible lines of force found between the north and south poles of a magnet.

Magnetic lines of force in a magnetic field are imaginary lines which show the direction of the magnetic flux.

Maintained contacts close the circuit when the push button is pressed and will open the circuit when the push button is pressed again.

Megaohm is one million ohms.

Motor action is the mechanical force that exists between magnets. Two magnets approaching each other will either pull toward or push away from the other. In other words, there is a pull-and-push action between the rotor and field poles of the motor.

Multi speed motor is a motor that is capable of operating at two or more fixed speeds.

N

NEMA (National Electrical Manufacturers Association) is an organization which establishes certain voluntary standards relating to motors such as operating characteristics, terminology, basic dimensions, ratings, and testing.

No-load speed is the speed reached by the rotor or armature when it rotates.

Nonautomatic is requiring human intervention to perform a function.

Nonreversing is a control function that provides for operation in one direction only.

Normally open and normally closed is a term that when applied to a magnetically operated switching device signifies the position that the contacts are in.

Normally closed contacts are motor control contacts (set) that are open when the push button is depressed.

Normally open contacts are contacts (set) which are closed when the push button is depressed.

O

Ohm is a unit of electrical resistance of a conductor.

Out-of-phase is a condition where two or more phases of AC are changing direction at different intervals of time.

Overcurrent protection device (OCPD) is a device that operates on excessive current, which causes the interruption of power to the circuit if necessary.

Over excited is a condition where a synchronous motor is equipped with a DC field that supplies more magnetization than is needed.

Overload protector is a device affected by an abnormal operating condition, which causes the interruption of current flow to the device governed.

Overload relay is a device that provides overload protection for conductors and electrical equipment.

P

Parallel circuit is a circuit in which all positive terminals are connected at a common point and all negative terminals are connected at another point.

Periodic duty is a type of intermittent duty in which the load conditions are regularly recurrent.

Permanent-capacitor motor is a single-phase electric motor which uses a phase winding and capacitor in conjunction with the main winding. The phase winding is controlled by the capacitor, which remains in the circuit at all times.

Permanent magnetism is a condition in which a magnet keeps its magnetic properties indefinitely.

Permeability is a condition in which domains in a magnetic core can be made to line up to create magnetism.

Phase is the relationship of two wave forms to have the same frequency.

Phase angle is the difference in angle between two sine wave vectors.

Phase shift is the creation of a lag or advance in voltage or current in relation to another voltage or current in the same electrical circuit.

Phase voltage is the voltage across a coil.

Polarity is a condition where a magnet has north and south poles are positive and negative charge.

Polyphase is more than one phase, usually three-phase, that when related to generators, transformers, and motors.

Pounds force is an English unit of conventional measurement for force.

Power factor is the figure that indicates what portion of the current delivered to the motor is used to do work.

Primary coil is one of two coils in a transformer.

Prime mover is the primary power source that can be used to drive a generator.

Pull-in to torque is the maximum torque at which an induction motor will pull into step.

Pull-out torque is the maximum torque developed by a motor for one minute before it pulls out of step due to an overload.

Pull-up torque is the minimum torque developed by an induction motor during the period of acceleration from rest to full speed.

Push button control is the control and operation of equipment through push buttons used to activate relays.

Push button switch is a switch utilizing a button for activating a coil and contact to open or close a circuit.

R

Rainproof is an enclosure constructed, protected, or treated so as to prevent rain from interfering with the successful operation of the apparatus under specified test conditions.

Raintight is an enclosure constructed or protected so that exposure to a beating rain will not result in the entrance of water under specified test conditions.

Rated-load current is the current for a hermetic refrigerant motor-compressor is the current resulting when the motor-compressor is operated at the rated load, rated voltage, and rated frequency of the equipment it serves.

Rating is a designated limit of operating characteristics based on conditions of use such as load, voltage, frequency, etc.

Rating, continuous is the rating which defines the substantially constant load that can be carried for an indefinitely long time.

Reactive power is the reactive voltage times the current, or voltage times the reactive current, in an AC circuit.

Rectifier is an electrical device which converts AC to DC by allowing the current to move in only one direction.

Relay is a device that operates by a variation of a condition that affects the operation of other devices in an electric circuit.

Relay contacts are the contacts that are closed or opened by movement of a relay armature.

Reluctance is the ratio between the magnetomotive force and the resulting flux.

Reset is to restore a mechanism or device to a prescribed state.

Reset, automatic is a function that operates automatically to re-establish certain circuit conditions.

Reset, manual is a function that requires a manual operation to re-establish certain circuit conditions.

Residual magnetism is the magnetism remaining in the core of a coil or an electromagnet after the current flow has been removed.

Resistance is a property of conductors that makes them resist the movement of current flow.

Resistance starting is a reduced-voltage starting method employing resistances are short-circuited in one or more steps to complete the starting cycle of a motor, etc.

Resistors are electrical-electronic devices that are attached to a circuit to produce resistance to current flow.

Rheostat is a variable resistor with a fixed terminal and a movable contact.

Rotor is the rotating section that rotates within the stator of a motor.

Rotor impedance is the phasor sum of resistance and inductive reactance.

RPM is the number of revolutions per minute.

Running torque is the torque or turning effort determined by the horsepower and speed of a motor at any given point of operation.

S

Saturated is the point at which an electrical or magnetic component cannot receive any more electrical current or magnetism.

Saturation is a point at which a magnet will receive any more flux density.

Sealing, voltage or current is the voltage or current required to seat the armature of a magnetic circuit closing device to the make position.

Secondary coil is the coil that is connected to the load in the electrical circuit.

Self-excitation is a condition of supplying excitation voltages by a device on the generator rather than from an outside source.

Self-induction is a counterelectromotive force produced in a conductor when the magnetic field produced by the conductor collapses or expands after a change in current flow.

Separate excitation is a condition of producing generator field current from an independent source.

Series circuit is a circuit in which all resistances and other components are connected so that the same current flows from point to point.

Series field is the total magnetic flux caused by the action of the series winding in a rotating piece of machine.

Series motor is a motor in which the field and armature circuits are connected in series.

Service factor is the number by which the horsepower rating is multiplied to determine the maximum safe load that a motor can carry continuously at its rated voltage and frequency.

Shaded-pole motor is a single-phase squirrel cage induction motor with stator poles slotted and used to create two sections in each pole.

Shading coil is a copper ring or coil that is set into a section of the pole piece; its function is to produce the lagging part of a rotating magnetic field for starting torque.

Short is any two points of a motor where there is zero, or extremely low, resistance between them or between two motor components.

Short-time rating is referring to the motor load that can be carried for a short and definitely specified time.

Shunt field is a type of field coil designed for a DC motor that is connected in parallel with the armature.

Silicon controlled rectifier (SCR) is a semiconductor device that has the ability to block a voltage that is applied in either direction. On a signal applied to its gate, it is capable of conducting current even when the signal has been removed.

Single-phase is having only one AC or voltage in a circuit.

Slip is the difference between the synchronous speed of a motor and the speed at which it operates.

Slip ring motor is a motor that has a rotor with the same number of magnetic poles at the stator.

Slip rings are equipped with circular bands on a rotor, which are used to transmit current from rotor coils to brushes.

Slip speed is the difference between the rotor speed and synchronous speed in an induction motor.

Soft neutral position is a condition where the brushes of a repulsion electric motor are aligned with the stator field.

Solid-state controls are devices that control current to motors through semiconductors.

Solid-state devices contain circuits and components using semiconductors.

Solid-state relay is a relay that uses semiconductor devices.

Split-phase (resistance-start) motor is a single-phase induction motor equipped with an auxiliary winding that is connected in parallel with the main winding.

Squirrel-cage rotor is designed with a rotor which is made up of metal bars that are short-circuited at each end.

Stall torque is the amount of torque that the rotor of an energized motor produces when the rotor is not rotating.

Starter is a controller for accelerating a motor from rest to its running speed.

Starter, automatic is a starter that automatically controls the starting of a motor.

Starter, autotransformer is a starter that is provided with an autotransformer that provides a reduced voltage for starting.

Starter, part-winding is a starter that provides applied voltage to partial sections of the primary winding of an AC motor.

Starter, reactor is a starter that includes a resistor connected in series with the primary winding of an induction motor to provide reduced voltage for starting.

Starter, wye-delta is a starter that connects the motor leads in a wye configuration for reduced voltage in starting and reconnects the leads in a delta configuration for the run position.

Starting torque is the amount of torque produced by a motor as it breaks the motor shaft from standstill and accelerates to its running speed.

Static electricity is electricity at rest. It is also known in the industry as a static charge.

Stator is the portion of motor that contains the stationary parts of the magnetic circuit with their associated windings.

Stator field contains a magnetic field that is set up in the electric motor when the motor is energized and electric current is flowing.

Stator poles are the shoes on an electric motor stator that hold the windings and the magnetic poles of the stator.

Switch is a device for making, breaking, or changing the connections in an electric circuit.

Switch, float is a switch that is responsive to the level of a liquid.

Switch, foot is a switch that is operated by an operator's foot.

Switch, general-use is a switch intended for use in general distribution and branch circuits. It is rated in amperes, and it is capable of interrupting the rated current at the rated voltage.

Switch, limit is operated by some part or motion that alters the electrical circuit associated with the equipment.

Switch, master controls the operation of contactors, relays, or other similar operated devices.

Switch, motor circuit is rated in horsepower that is capable of interrupting the maximum operating overload current of the motor of the same horsepower rating as the switch at the rated voltage.

Switch, pressure is operated by fluid pressure, etc.

Switch, selector is a manually operated multiposition switch that is used for selecting an alternative control circuit.

Synchronous is a condition where the currents and voltages are in-step or in-phase.

Synchronous motor is an induction motor that runs at synchronous speed.

Synchronous speed is the constant speed to which an AC motor adjusts itself, depending on the frequency of the power source and the number of poles in the motor.

T

Tachometer is a device that is capable of measuring the rotational speed of rotating machines.

Tap changer is a mechanical device that has the ability to change the voltage output of a transformer.

Taps are fixed electrical connections that are located at specific positions on a transformer's coil.

Temperature, ambient is the temperature of the medium, such as air, oil, etc., into which the heat of the equipment is dissipated.

Terminal is a point at which an electrical element may be connected to another electrical element.

Terminal board is an insulating base equipped with one or more terminal connectors used for making electrical connections.

Thermal, cutout is an overcurrent protection device that has a heater element that affects a fusible member that opens the circuits due to an overload.

Thermal protector is a protective device for assembly as an integral part of the motor or motor-compressor that, when properly applied, protects the motor against dangerous overheating due to overload and failure to start.

Thermocouple is a device that consists of two unlike metals that are joined together; when heat is applied, a current will flow.

Thermostat is an instrument that responds to changes in temperature to affect control over an operating condition.

Three-phase alternator is a rotating machine that generates three separate phases of AC.

Three-phase electric motor is a motor that operates from a three-phase power supply.

Timer is a device that is designed to delay the closing or opening of a circuit for a specific period of time.

Torque is a force that produces a rotating or twisting action.

Torque, breakdown is the maximum torque that a motor develops with rated voltage when applied at rated frequency.

Torque, locked rotor is the minimum torque that a motor develops at standstill when rated voltage is applied at rated frequency.

Transformer is a device designed to change the voltage in an AC electrical circuit. Step-up transformers increase the voltage and lower the current. Step-down transformers decrease the voltage and raise the current.

Transformer efficiency is the ratio of input power to output power.

Turns ratio is the ratio of the number of turns in the primary winding of a transformer to the number of turns in the secondary winding of a transformer.

Two-capacitor motor is an induction motor which uses one capacitor for starting and one for running.

U

Under-excited is a term used to describe the magnetizing power of a synchronous motor.

Undervoltage protection is a device that operates on the reduction or failure of voltage and has the ability to maintain the interruption of power.

Undervoltage release is a device that operates on the reduction or failure of voltage and has the ability to interrupt the power, but not to prevent the re-establishment of the circuit.

Unity power factor is a power factor of 1; this is the best PF that can be obtained in an electrical system.

V

Vector is an in-phasor diagram having lines with a specific length and direction.

Voltage is a force that, when applied to a conductor, produces a current in the conductor.

W

Watt is a unit of electrical power; it is the product of voltage and amperage.

Wattmeter is an instrument used for measuring electrical power.

Wye or star connection is an electrical connection in that all terminals are joined at the neutral junction, resembling a wye connection.

Wye-wye connection is the coil arrangement in which both the primary and the secondary coils are wye-connected.